Impact Fees

Principles and Practice of Proportionate-Share Development Fees

Arthur C. Nelson, FAICP
James C. Nicholas
Julian C. Juergensmeyer

American Planning Association
Planners Press

Making Great Communities Happen

Chicago | Washington, D.C.

Copyright 2009 by the American Planning Association
122 S. Michigan Ave., Suite 1600, Chicago, IL 60603
1776 Massachusetts Ave., NW, Suite 400, Washington, DC 20036
www.planning.org/plannerspress

ISBN (paperback edition): 1-932364-54-4 and 978-1-932364-54-5
ISBN (hardbound edition): 1-932364-55-2 and 978-1-932364-55-2
Library of Congress Control Number 2009923823
All rights reserved
Printed in the United States of America

Copyediting by Joanne Shwed, Backspace Ink.

We dedicate this book to the true pioneers of impact
fees—locally elected officials and their professional staffs,
consultants, and citizen leaders who advance proportionate-
share fiscal impact accountability—and to

Dwight H. Merriam, FAICP

Contents

List of Tables...ix

List of Figures xiii

List of Acronyms xiv

Acknowledgments... xv

Prologue: Reflections on Impact Fees xvii

Part 1: Foundations 1

Chapter 1: The Progression of Impact Fees... 3
    The Evolutionary Process 3
    Impact Fees of the Future 10

Chapter 2: National Impact Fee Survey 15
    What Qualifies as an Impact Fee? 15
    Some Caveats 16
    Fee Incidence by State 17
    Average Fees by Facility Type 17
    Average Fees by Land Use 17
    Average Fees by State 17
    Fee Increases, 2004–2008 19
    Fee Increases, 2007–2008 22
    Summary 23

Chapter 3: Legal Principles of Impact Fees 93
    Introduction 93
    Evolution of Impact Fees... 94
    Constitutionality of Impact Fees 95
    Land-Use Regulation or Taxation? 95
    Tests for Impact Fee Validity.. 96
    Equal Protection Issues 98
    The Taking Issue: The Rational Nexus Test Revisited?... 99

The Relationship of Impact Fees to the Comprehensive Plan 102
State Authorizing Legislation 103
Drafting Impact Fees to Pass Judicial Scrutiny 103
Impact Fee Uses 105
Extending the Applicability of Impact Fees Across the Development Spectrum 106
Making Impact Fees More Sensitive to Affordable Housing and Other Societal Needs 106
Conclusion 107

Chapter 4: State Impact Fee Enabling Acts **113**
Distribution of Enabling Acts 113
Eligible Facilities 116
Planning and Analysis Requirements 118
Substantive Requirements 121
Procedural Requirements 122
Recent Developments 123
A Cautionary Tale 124
To the Future 124

Part 2: Context **127**

Chapter 5: Proportionate-Share Basics **129**
Overview of Impact Fee Analysis 130
Policy Framework 132
Level-of-Service Standards 133
Service Areas 135
Procedural Issues 136
Summary 139

Chapter 6: Credits **141**
Introduction 141
Overview of Forms of Credit and Their Applications 143
Principles for Estimating Credit With Applications 145
Development Credits 151
Summary Observations 153

Chapter 7: Impact Fees and the Planning Connection **155**
Impact Fees and Exactions 157
Capital Improvements Element 158
Levels of Service 159
Service Areas 159
Projections of Facility Needs 160
Schedule of Improvements 161
Description of Funding Sources 162
Recoupment 163
Relation of Impact Fees to Community Planning Goals 163
Summary Comment 164
Appendix 7A: Sample Capital Improvements Element 165

Chapter 8: Uniform Measures of Impact... 171
Common Measures of Impact 171
Measures of Impact and Planning.. 172
The Need for Common Measures of Impact 172
Fire and Police Demand Multipliers: Calls for Service Versus Functional Population 173
Extensions of Functional Population: Toward Truly Uniform Impact Assessments 176
Appendix 8A: Review of Consulting Studies 179

Chapter 9: Variations of Proportionate-Share Fee Design 181
General Calculation Approaches.. 181
Review of Impact Fee Programs Selected Nationally... 188
Florida Impact Fee Survey Findings 194

Part 3: Applications 207

Chapter 10: Proportionate-Share Fees for Physical Infrastructure.............................. 209
Are Impact Fees Needed? 209
Impact Fees for Public Facilities... 209

Chapter 11: Proportionate-Share Fees for Social Infrastructure 257
Proportionate-Share Principles to Provide Workforce Housing from Commercial Development 257
Proportionate-Share Principles to Provide Workforce Housing from Residential Development 263
Proportionate-Share Development Fees for Other Social Infrastructure............................. 283
Concluding Observations 284
Appendix 11A: Workforce Housing Linkage Programs in California 286
Appendix 11B: Sample Workforce Housing Mitigation Impact Fee Ordinance 291

Chapter 12: Proportionate-Share Environmental Mitigation Fees for Green Infrastructure 305
Legal and Economic Foundations 305
Case Study Application... 317
Appendix 12A: Environmental Lands Impact Fee Draft Ordinance 324

Chapter 13: Proportionate-Share Fees for Operations and Maintenance 333
Introduction 333
Transit Impact Development Fee... 333
Transportation Utility Fees 334
Case Study: Aventura, Florida Transportation Operations and Maintenance Mitigation Fee 337
Summary Observations... 342
Appendix 13A: Sample Ordinance Implementing Operations and Maintenance
Proportionate Share Fees... 343

Part 4: Implementation 347

Chapter 14: Model Proportionate-Share Development Fee Ordinance............................. 349
Principles of Ordinance Design and Drafting 349
Appendix 14A: Model Ordinance 355
Appendix 14B: City of Canton, Georgia, Road Impact Fee Ordinance 361

Chapter 15: Development Impact Fee Administrative Code 367
    Appendix 15A: Sample Impact Fee Administrative Code 369

Epilogue 387
    Impact Fees in the Future 388
    Unification of Developer Funding Requirements 388
    Expanding the Base and Scope of Infrastructure Funding Requirements 389
    Innovative Funding Programs 389
    State and Regional Impact Fees 390
    State and Federal Funding to Cure Infrastructure Deficiencies 390
    Conclusion 391

References and Selected Bibliography 393

Index 399

About the Authors 412

List of Tables

Table 1-1 Metropolitan and Incorporated Population Trends, 1980–2006 4
Table 1-2 Governmental Units in the United States, 1972–2002 7
Table 1-3 Special Service Districts by Function, 1992–2002 8
Table 1-4 National Average Impact Fees, 2006 9
Table 1-5 Reported Impact Fee Revenue by Government Type in Florida, 1993–2004 9
Table 1-6 Number of Governmental Entities Reporting Impact Fee Revenues,
      Fiscal Years 1993–2004 10
Table 1-7 Reported Impact Fee Revenues by Fee Category, Fiscal Years 1993–2004 11
Table 1-8 Number of Governmental Entities Reporting Impact Fee Revenues by Fee Category,
      Fiscal Years 1993–2004 12
Table 2-1 Average Impact Fees by Type and Land Use, 2008 18
Table 2-2 Total Nonutility Single-Family Impact Fees by Selected State, 2004–2008 20
Table 2-3 Jurisdictions Charging Impact Fees by Facility Type, 2004–2008 21
Table 2-4 Average Impact Fees by Facility Type, Single-Family Unit, 2004–2008 22
Table 2-5 Average Impact Fees by Type, Single-Family Unit, 2007–2008 23
Table 2-6 National Survey Appendix 25
Table 4-1 State Impact Fee Enabling Acts 114
Table 4-2 Basic State Enabling Act Standards 116
Table 4-3 Facilities Eligible for Impact Fees by State 117
Table 4-4 State Enabling Act Planning Requirements 119
Table 4-5 State Enabling Act Substantive Provisions 120
Table 4-6 State Enabling Act Procedural Provisions 122
Table 5-1 Level-of-Service Standard 133
Table 5-2 Service Area Criteria for Atlanta, Georgia 135
Table 6-1 Examples of Fund Sources for Capital Facilities 146
Table 6-2 Revenue Credit for Motor Fuel Taxes, Average Single-Family Home 147
Table 6-3 General Road Impact Fee Calculation Model 147
Table 6-4 Law Enforcement Facility Gross Impact Cost Per Functional Resident 148
Table 6-5 Simple Future Revenue Credit and Net Impact Cost 149
Table 6-6 Annual Future Revenue Credit 149
Table 6-7 Cash Flow Future Revenue Credit and Net Impact Cost 150
Table 7-1 Level-of-Service Standards 159
Table 7-2 Service Area Delineation 160
Table 7A-1 Inventory of Parks and Recreational Facilities 165
Table 7A-2 Existing Parks and Recreation Level of Service 166
Table 7A-3 Projection of Parks and Recreational Facility Needs, 2005–2030,
       Unincorporated DeKalb County 166
Table 7A-4 Summary Schedule of Parks and Recreational Facility Improvements 168
Table 7A-4a Schedule of Parks and Recreational Facility Improvements
       Impact Fee-Eligible Projects, North Benefit District 168
Table 7A-4b Schedule of Parks and Recreational Facility Improvements
       Impact Fee-Eligible Projects, South Benefit District 169

Table 7A-4c   Schedule of Parks and Recreational Facility Improvements Impact
Fee-Eligible Projects, East Benefit District. 170
Table 8-1   Facilities Applicable to Standards-Based Level-of-Service Standards 172
Table 8-2   Facilities Applicable to Plan-Based Level-of-Service Standards 172
Table 8-3   Nonresidential Functional Population. 174
Table 8-4   Summary of Fire Calls (Equivalent Dwelling Units). 175
Table 8-5   Summary of Police Calls (Equivalent Dwelling Units). 175
Table 8-6   Functional Population Equivalent Dwelling Units by Various Assumptions 176
Table 8-7   Functional Population Applied to Schools, Park and Recreational Facilities,
and Libraries (Illustrative Only). 177
Table 8A-1   Equivalent Dwelling Units Based on Fire Calls 179
Table 8A-2   Equivalent Dwelling Units Based on Police Calls 180
Table 9-1   Alternative Wastewater System Development Charge Methods Basic Assumptions 184
Table 9-2   Growth-Related Cost Allocation Method 185
Table 9-3   Recoupment Value Method. 185
Table 9-4   Replacement Cost Method. 186
Table 9-5   Marginal Cost Method 186
Table 9-6   Average Cost Method. 187
Table 9-7   Total Cost Attribution Method 187
Table 9-8   Summary of Methods. 188
Table 9-9   Jurisdictions Selected for Content Analysis of Impact Fee Studies. 188
Table 10-1   Functional Population 215
Table 10-2   Functional Population by Type of Development Based on Population 24 Hours
Per Day, Seven Days Per Week 215
Table 10-3   Level of Service for Fire and Emergency Protection 216
Table 10-4   Needed Fire and Emergency Capital Improvements 216
Table 10-5   Cost Per Capita and Per Unit Fire and Emergency Protection. 216
Table 10-6   Park and Recreation and Open Space Trail Level of Service by Service Area 217
Table 10-7   Population and Housing 2004 to 2025 by Cash in Lieu and Service Area
Within Current City Limits 218
Table 10-8   Dwelling Unit Occupancies. 218
Table 10-9   Existing Level of Service, 2004 219
Table 10-10   Existing Provision of Recreational Facilities, 2004. 219
Table 10-11   Local Park Need and Availability. 220
Table 10-12   Cash in Lieu Balances and Land Acquisition Cost, 2004. 221
Table 10-13   Gross Costs Per Capita. 222
Table 10-14   Historic and Anticipated Funding 222
Table 10-15   Park, Recreation, Trail, and Open Space Impact Costs by Service Areas 223
Table 10-16   Park, Recreation, Trail, and Open Space Credits and Deficiencies by Service Area 224
Table 10-17   Park, Trail, and Open Space Impact Fees Per Dwelling Unit and Per Square Foot
of Floor Area 225
Table 10-18   Impact Fee Per Dwelling by Size of Dwelling Example 225
Table 10-19   Parks and Recreation Impact Fee Schedule, Northside Service Area 225
Table 10-20   Land-Use Assumptions, Canton, Georgia. 226
Table 10-21   Park, Recreation, and Open Space Improvement Program, City of Canton, 2002–2006 227
Table 10-22   Park, Recreation, and Open Space, Capital Revenues, City of Canton, 2002–2006. 228
Table 10-23   Level of Service for City of Canton 228
Table 10-24   Development in Canton, 2002 and 2015 228
Table 10-25   Projected Tax Base, City of Canton, 1996–2025. 229
Table 10-26   Bond Issue Debt Service, City of Canton, 2002–2021. 229
Table 10-27   Parks Bond Parameters 230
Table 10-28   Growth Costs. 230
Table 10-29   Library Facilities and Materials 231
Table 10-30   Library Facility Costs 232
Table 10-31   Net Library Materials Impact Cost. 232
Table 10-32   Net Library Facility Impact Cost 232
Table 10-33   Net Impact Cost Schedule 233

Table 10-34   General Government Building Inventory, 2003 and 2017 ... 233
Table 10-35   Baseline Population and Employment Data ... 234
Table 10-36   Functional Population Coefficients ... 235
Table 10-37   Functional Population, 2003 and 2017 ... 236
Table 10-38   Observed and Projected General Government Building Level of Service, 2003 and 2017 ... 236
Table 10-39   General Government Facilities Impact Cost Per Functional Resident ... 236
Table 10-40   New Development Share of Total Development ... 237
Table 10-41   Assessed Property Value, 2003 ... 238
Table 10-42   Impact Cost Per Functional Resident ... 238
Table 10-43   Relationship Between House Size and Occupancy Level Status (Nation, Urban, Suburban, and South), 2001 ... 238
Table 10-44   Net Impact Fee Schedule ... 240
Table 10-45   Funding for Recent Drainage Projects ... 242
Table 10-46   City of Albuquerque, Planned Growth Strategy Implementation, Proposed Drainage Impact Fees ... 243
Table 10-47   Road Facility Capacity and Cost Analysis ... 245
Table 10-48   Road Facility Local Impact Cost ... 246
Table 10-49   Gasoline Tax Credit Amount Per Gallon, Estimation of Revenues Per Penny of Gasoline Tax ... 246
Table 10-50   Estimation of Gasoline Tax Used for New or Expanded Facilities ... 247
Table 10-51   Impact Cost Calculation ... 248
Table 10-52   Net Impact Cost Calculation ... 249
Table 10-53   Estimated Cost Per Lane-Mile by Service Area Within the City of Albuquerque, 2002–2025 ... 251
Table 10-54   Equivalent Pennies of Gas Tax Proxy Revenue ... 251
Table 10-55   Growth Rates and Revenue Generation Factors by Service Area, 2004–2025 ... 251
Table 10-56   Vehicle-Miles of Capacity, Vehicle-Miles Traveled, and Population Change by Service Area, 2000–2025 ... 251
Table 10-57   Estimated Capacity Added Per Lane-Mile and Cost Per Vehicle-Mile of Capacity Added by Service Area, 2002–2025 ... 252
Table 10-58   City of Albuquerque—Net Impact Cost Schedule ... 253
Table 11-1   Home Price Trends, 1993–2006 ... 258
Table 11-2   Income, Housing Starts, Resale Prices, and Employment and Population Change by State ... 259
Table 11-3   Housing Mitigation Requirements, Households Required ... 261
Table 11-4   Definition of Income Category for Subsidy Calculations ... 262
Table 11-5   Distribution of New Households by Income Category ... 262
Table 11-6   Cost to Produce Additional Households—For Sale ... 262
Table 11-7   Subsidy Required—For Sale Housing, With Linkage Fee Estimate ... 263
Table 11-8   Cost to Produce Additional Households—Rental ... 263
Table 11-9   Subsidy Required—Rental Housing With Linkage Fee Estimate ... 264
Table 11-10   Linkage Program Variables ... 264
Table 11-11   Linkage Programs Around the Country ... 265
Table 11-12   Median Resale Price of a Single-Family Home ... 266
Table 11-13   Collier County and Florida Housing Resales by Month, 2003–2006 ... 267
Table 11-14   Median Household Income, Resale Prices, and Affordability Limits, Collier County ... 268
Table 11-15   Annual Earnings by Industry, Collier County ... 271
Table 11-16   Employment and Household Earnings by Industry, Collier County, 2006 ... 272
Table 11-17   Employees Per Household, Collier County ... 272
Table 11-18   Entry-Level Workforce Housing, Collier County ... 273
Table 11-19   Income Needed to Afford Housing ... 273
Table 11-20   Employment Assignable to Residences ... 274
Table 11-21   Residential Operations and Maintenance, Employee Earnings ... 275
Table 11-22   Residential Operations and Maintenance, Employee Assistance ... 276
Table 11-23   Operations and Maintenance Employees, by Type and Size of Residence ... 276
Table 11-24   Residential Employees by Size of Residence ... 276
Table 11-25   Critical Employees—School Teachers ... 277

Table 11-26   Critical Employees—Fire and Rescue 277
Table 11-27   Critical Employees—Fire and Rescue Wages 278
Table 11-28   Critical Employees—Law Enforcement. 278
Table 11-29   Critical Employees—Law Enforcement Wages 278
Table 11-30   Residential Employees by Size of Residence 279
Table 11-31   Employment in Collier County, 2001–2005 279
Table 11-32   New Jobs in Collier County, 2001–2005 280
Table 11-33   Distribution of Employees to Land Uses. 281
Table 11-34   Floor Area Per Employee, Collier County. 282
Table 11-35   Earned Household Income by Land Use, Collier County 282
Table 11-36   Employment Per 1,000 Sq. Ft. Survey Results and Estimate 283
Table 11-37   Nonresidential Housing Affordability Gap by Land Use, Collier County. 284
Table 11-38   Affordable Units, Density, and Profit. 284
Table 11A-1   Jobs-Housing Balance Linkage Programs for High-Fee Cities, California. 286
Table 11A-2   Jobs-Housing Balance Linkage Programs for Medium-Fee Cities, California. 287
Table 11A-3   Jobs-Housing Balance Linkage Programs for Low-Fee Cities, California 288
Table 11B-1   Residential Units for Non-Full-Time Residents 296
Table 11B-2   Residential Units for Full-Time Residents. 296
Table 11B-3   Attainable Units Per Square Feet of Floor Area 296
Table 12-1   Environmentally Significant Lands Program, St. Lucie County 318
Table 12-2   Historic and Projected Population, St. Lucie County 320
Table 12-3   Population and Conservation Lands, St. Lucie County 320
Table 12-4   Environmental Lands Level of Service 321
Table 12-5   Needed Environmental Lands, St. Lucie County. 321
Table 12-6   Dwelling Occupancy Characteristics, St. Lucie County, 2000 321
Table 12-7   Environmental Land Cost Per Unit 321
Table 12A-1   Environmental Lands Impact Fee Countywide Assessment 325
Table 13-1   Original San Francisco Transit Operations Linkage Fee 334
Table 13-2   Orlando Transportation Utility Fee Proposal 335
Table 13-3   Street Maintenance Fee, Lake Oswego, Oregon. 336
Table 13-4   Fort Collins, Colorado, Stormwater Runoff Coefficient Categories 337
Table 13-5   Transportation Mitigation Per Unit, City of Aventura, Florida 338
Table 13-6   Circulator Service, City of Aventura 340
Table 13-7   Service Area Population, City of Aventura 340
Table 13-8   Functional Population City of Aventura 341
Table 13-9   Functional Population Per Unit, City of Aventura. 341
Table 13-10   Circulator Cost Per Seat, City of Aventura 341
Table 13-11   Circulator Level of Service, City of Aventura 341
Table 13-12   Circulator Cost Per Capita, City of Aventura 342
Table 13-13   Transportation Mitigation Fee Per Unit, City of Aventura 342
Table 14B-1   City of Canton, Georgia Development Impact Fee Schedule. 362

List of Figures

Figure 1-1   Rate of Inflation, 1970–2008 6
Figure 1-2   Hypothetical Projection of Impact Fees Compounded Over Time 11
Figure 2-1   Survey Jurisdictions by State, 2008 17
Figure 2-2   National Average Fees Per Single-Family Unit, 2008 18
Figure 2-3   Average Fees by Land Use, 2008 19
Figure 2-4   Average Nonutility Fees Per Single-Family Unit by State, 2008 19
Figure 2-5   Number of Jurisdictions by State, 2004–2008 Constant Sample 20
Figure 2-6   Total Nonutility Single-Family Fees, 2004–2008 21
Figure 2-7   Percent of Jurisdictions Charging Fees, 2004–2008 22
Figure 2-8   Increase in Single-Family Fees by Type, 2004–2008 23
Figure 4-1   States With Enabling Acts 113
Figure 5-1   Basic Impact Fee Calculation Steps 130
Figure 6-1   Relationship of Credits to Impact Fees 142
Figure 6-2   Past and Future Credits in Relation to Impact Fees 151
Figure 7-1   Impact Fees and the Planning Process 156
Figure 7A-1   Unincorporated DeKalb County Parks and Recreation Service Area 165
Figure 7A-2   Benefit Districts Within DeKalb County Parks and Recreation Service Area 166
Figure 10-1   Decision Chart for Public Safety Facilities 210
Figure 10-2   Decision Chart for Water-Based Utilities 211
Figure 10-3   Decision Chart for Public Amenity Facilities 212
Figure 10-4   Decision Chart for Transportation Facilities 213
Figure 10-5   Public Safety Service Areas, City of Albuquerque, New Mexico 214
Figure 10-6   Service Areas for Parks and Recreation Impact Fees, City of Albuquerque, New Mexico 217
Figure 10-7   Albuquerque Drainage Service Areas 239
Figure 10-8   Transportation Impact Fee Service Areas, City of Albuquerque 246
Figure 10-9   Ratio of Existing to Growth Revenues, 2004–2025 247
Figure 11-1   Median House Price: Collier, Florida, and U.S. 266
Figure 11-2   Collier Monthly Sales 269
Figure 11-3   Median Price of Existing Homes 269
Figure 11-4   Existing Home Prices and Median Income, Collier County 270
Figure 11-5   Collier County Housing Affordability 270

List of Acronyms

AMAFCA	Albuquerque Metropolitan Arroyo Flood Control Agency
BART	Bay Area Rapid Transit
CDD	community development district
CIE	capital improvements element
CIP	capital improvements program (or capital improvements plan)
CMSA	combined metropolitan statistical area
CPI	Consumer Price Index
CWA	Clean Water Act
EDU	equivalent dwelling unit
EMS	emergency medical service
EPA	Environmental Protection Agency
ERU	equivalent residential unit
FIRE	finance, insurance, and real estate
GO	general obligation [bond]
HOST	Homestead Option Sales Tax
HUD	[U.S. Department of] Housing and Urban Development
ITE	Institute of Transportation Engineers
IUG	Integrated Utilities Group, Inc.
LCIR	[Florida] Legislative Committee on Intergovernmental Relations
LOS	level of service
MSA	metropolitan statistical area
NAA	National Apartment Association
NAICS	North American Industrial Classification System
NEPA	National Environmental Policy Act
O & M	operations and maintenance
PGS	Planned Growth Strategy
RECLAIM	[California's] Regional Clean Air Incentives Market
SCAQMD	South Coast Air Quality Management District
SDC	systems development charge
SFE	single-family equivalent
sfgla	square feet gross leasable area
SUF	stormwater utility fee
TCEA	Transportation Concurrency Exception Area
TCU	transportation, communications, and utilities
TIDF	transit impact development fee
TIF	tax increment financing
TOD	transit-oriented development
TTU	trade, transportation, and utilities
TUF	transportation utility fee
VMC	vehicle-mile of capacity
VMT	vehicle-mile traveled

Acknowledgments

It is with gratitude and enormous respect that we acknowledge collectively the thousands of people each of us has worked with and learned from over more than four decades. These professional planners, engineers, consultants, attorneys, elected officials, and citizen leaders have helped shape our thinking about exactions generally and impact fees in particular. Their collective wisdom is reflected in this volume. We acknowledge the staff of the American Planning Association who have helped us prepare this and numerous other writings on impact fees. We acknowledge especially Joanne Shwed of Backspace Ink for her editing.

We thank the faculty, staff, and students who have helped us shape our impact fee thinking spanning nearly half a century during our individual service at Florida Atlantic University, Georgia Institute of Technology, Georgia State University, University of Florida, University of New Orleans, University of Utah, and Virginia Tech.

We offer special thanks to Liza Bowles of Newport Partners, LLC, and Jinna Song at the University of Utah for generating numerous graphics used in the book.

For Chapter 12, we gratefully acknowledge permission from the University of New Mexico College of Law for allowing us to include passages from and adaptations of the article "Market Based Approaches to Environmental Preservation: To Environmental Mitigation Fees and Beyond" (Nicholas and Juergensmeyer (2003)).

For the Epilogue, we gratefully acknowledge permission from Florida State University College of Law for allowing us to include passages from and adaptations of the article "Infrastructure and the Law: Florida's Past, Present and Future" (Juergensmeyer (2008)).

We owe a special debt to Clancy Mullen. Not only did he contribute significantly to several chapters, but his discerning questions along with a close eye on earlier drafts improved this book immeasurably.

Prologue:
Reflections on Impact Fees

These newcomers arrive in our community seeking opportunity. They come seeking a new beginning, a new start with hope, or a final fulfillment of life's just reward.

They come for the same reasons that we came. They stay for the same reasons that we stay in this community and state we all love.

These newcomers bring with them all their fondest dreams of the future. They bring dreams that are the same as ours—dreams of a better life and a better future.

What they don't bring with them are the roads, the bridges, the schools, the hospitals, the libraries, the parks, the utilities, the sewers, the waterlines, and all the vast and varied human services that will be needed to realize our dreams (adapted from Florida State Comprehensive Plan Committee (1987), 6).

These words, written a generation ago, still capture the angst that local governments face in meeting the challenges of new development while also assuring a desired quality of life. Various "tax revolts," federal and state unfunded mandates, court cases mandating higher quality facilities, and increasing demand by citizens for facilities and services of high quality put locally elected officials into a corner. They often cannot raise taxes because voters won't let them; they cannot raise new revenues through exotic or risky ventures because of statutory limitations; they cannot borrow their communities out of short-term facility deficits because of underwriting limitations—yet they want to leave behind a community in which they are proud to have served. For better or worse, impact fees have become a significant element of doing just that.

Local governments throughout the United States have learned that the cost of providing a residential dwelling unit with new or expanded public facilities—including water, sewer, drainage, police, fire, library, school, park, recreational, and other public facilities—for new development is considerable, ranging routinely from \$20,000 to \$100,000 or more per new home. As we show in Chapter 1, this cost has been rising at a pace that exceeds local government revenue generating capability. The increasing cost of maintenance of existing infrastructure, combined with the decline of public support for taxation alternatives, has forced local jurisdictions to seek alternatives. Impact fees have become one such alternative.

Development impact fees are scheduled charges applied to new development to generate revenue for the construction or expansion of capital facilities, known as "system improvements," benefiting it. A generation ago, they generally were not used legally for operation, maintenance, repair, alteration, or replacement of capital facilities; for social purposes such as affordable housing and day care; or for "green" purposes such as habitat preservation. As will be seen in this book, these limitations are eroding.

It is very difficult to estimate the number of communities that assess impact fees. One of the complications is the lack of standard terminology. In some communities, these developer charges are called "impact fees"; in others, they may be called "benefit assessments" or "connection charges." Developers tend to call them "exactions" or "extractions." To local governments, they are seen as "mitigation" of the facility impacts associated with new development. Earlier studies indicated that impact fees were relatively common in California, Florida, Oregon, and growth spots of other states including Colorado and Texas. More recent studies show that impact fees in some form are probably assessed in every state, with the number of communities assessing them ranging well into the thousands. In very large measure, impact fees have become institutionalized as a common source of revenue.

Impact fees are generally imposed as a condition for approved projects to proceed with development. They fall within the general system of land development regulation as contrasted with revenue raising (taxation) programs. The objective of impact fees is not to raise money but rather to ensure that adequate capital facilities are available commensurate with the impact of new development.

The adequacy of capital facilities is critically important to the entire system of land development regulation. Where capital facilities are not adequate, permitting development is contrary to the responsibility of a local government to protect public health, safety, and welfare. Therefore, a requirement that development proceed only when such adequacy is either attained or ensured is an act protecting the public from the harm that would occur in the absence of these facilities.

Protecting the public from harm is an exercise of a local government's police powers, granted by the states solely to authorize such protection. Though such grants of authority to local jurisdictions will vary in nature and extent from state to state, all local governments are legislatively authorized to protect the public from harm. Building codes, subdivision regulations, speed limits, gun controls, and impact fees are generally permissible to the extent that they prevent public harm. Before it establishes regulations to protect against harm, however, government must define the harm and its source.

No one would assert an owner's right to harm others in the use of their land. The specifics of what constitutes "harm" are a matter of contention. While most would agree that inadequate (off-site) roads provide a reasonable basis for denying an owner a proposed land use, some find it unreasonable to impose a charge on that owner to provide those necessary roads. Who should be financially responsible for such adequacy?

Three possible candidates for fiscal responsibility are the local government, the property owner, or "someone else." The latter category would include entities such as state and federal governments. In general, local governments and property owners can readily agree that "someone else" should bear the cost of roads or other capital facilities, but their agreement has not, however, resulted in funding. Moreover, it flies in the face of modern fiscal reality. The federal government is not going to provide increased funding for local infrastructure; on the contrary, federal support has been declining. The states have generally not filled the vacuum created by the federal withdrawal. The simple reality is that the community and the property owner are the only available candidates to bear the financial burden. Which of these should bear this burden and how should the burden be borne?

On the one hand, it may be argued that the community should be financially responsible for needed facilities because that community benefits. Land development is part of the creation of socially and economically beneficial products (e.g., new housing, factories, and stores), which satisfy needs within the community where it takes place. Land development creates jobs and enhances the tax base. Moreover, it may be argued that impact fees are fundamentally unfair because they shift to new development costs that were formerly borne by the community.

On the other hand, it may be argued that imposing such costs upon an unwilling community is harmful. It is harmful in the higher taxes and user fees charged to individuals who had no part in the decision to develop the property and who may receive no benefits from the development. This argument has been going on for a number of years and will undoubtedly continue. Clearly, a community may pay for needed facilities, but must it? Increasingly, the answer is that a community need not absorb all costs but may impose a proportionate—or fair—share of such costs upon new development. This is a permissive rule, and certainly individual communities may elect not to follow it.

The impact fee presupposes that new development should pay a proportionate share of facility costs. "Proportionate share," in the impact fee context, would generally be no more than the total cost but more than nothing. This book establishes bases on which to determine proportionate share. Its method is twofold:

1. It draws upon the experience of various communities that have defined and measured proportionate share; and
2. It draws upon case law and judicial rationale.

A word of caution is in order. This book addresses a dynamic issue, one in the very process of evolving. Relying upon actual experience, as it does, it necessarily draws examples only from states where impact fees are in use and have been found to be an acceptable form of land development regulation. Both case law and local authority with respect to development regulation vary tremendously across states. This book will not discuss the jurisdictional variation in regulatory or home rule powers, but they are critical to the outcome of an impact fee program. In attempting to develop and implement impact fees, one must note the nature of local regulatory powers.

Impact fees practiced today are a response to meeting the development needs of the past generation. Over the next generation, America will add about 100 million people and about 60 million jobs. The supply of homes will need to increase by more than 40 million and nonresidential space by more than 30 billion square feet. Private development will top $30 trillion, but public investment in facilities will top $6 trillion. Raising a substantial share of those funds through higher taxes is possible but is not likely to pay all the bills. For better or worse, impact fees have become a necessary component of local governments' toolkit to accommodate new development with public facilities of reasonable quality. That said, impact fee practice has evolved considerably over the past generation and will evolve even more during the next.

This book is organized into four parts. The first part lays the foundations that have shaped current impact fee practice. It includes four chapters that provide a historical perspective (Chapter 1), summarize the current extent of impact fees (Chapter 2), offer perspectives on evolving legal considerations (Chapter 3), and review impact fee enabling statutes (Chapter 4). The second part provides the context for modern impact fees and is composed of five chapters. It starts with a review of proportionate-share basics (Chapter 5), continues by exploring the issue of credits (Chapter 6), then discusses the role of impact fees in the broader planning context (Chapter 7), proceeds to present various ways in which to measure development impact (Chapter 8), and presents perspectives on the variations in impact fee calculation, concluding that "one size does not fit all." The third part consists of four chapters that present, in detail, many current and evolving applications of proportionate-share development fees. The leading chapter reviews impact fee design

for numerous communities throughout the nation for such standard facility types as utilities, roads, schools, public safety, and parks and recreational facilities (Chapter 10). The proportionate-share logic is then extended to "social infrastructure" such as affordable housing, day care centers, public art, and other socially beneficial investments (Chapter 11). The proportionate-share logic is extended further in a chapter dedicated to "green infrastructure" (Chapter 12). The final chapter in this suite applies proportionate-share principles to operations and maintenance (O & M) (Chapter 13). The last part is composed of two chapters, the first offering a model proportionate-share development fee ordinance (Chapter 14) and the second a model proportionate-share development fee administrative code (Chapter 15). As we started this book with a prologue, we end it with an epilogue.

Our hope is that, over the next generation, we go beyond impact fees in the narrowly defined and applied sense to *proportionate-share development fees* broadly applied to publicly provided facilities and services and their operations. This is a book about the transition from one generation to the next. Our generation pioneered the principles of proportionality through development and regulatory impact fees. Our work and the work of many, many others has gone all the way to the U.S. Supreme Court, more than once, and to several state supreme courts. Together with our professional and academic colleagues, we believe the major debates on the efficacy of development and regulatory impact fees have been settled. We must now move on, applying the lessons of the past and recognizing the needs of the future. This book is not so much the last word on impact fees but, we hope, the first word on the broader, new, and exciting area we call *proportionate-share development fees*. The next generation is invited to perfect and expand on the principles we offer here.

Arthur C. Nelson, FAICP (Salt Lake City, Utah)
James C. Nicholas (Gainesville, Florida)
Julian C. Juergensmeyer (Atlanta, Georgia)
April 2009

1

Foundations

Part 1 provides the **Foundations** that shape the evolving discussions of proportionate-share development fees from impact fees to new and evolving applications. *Chapter 1* provides the background on impact fees and how they have evolved over time. It includes data on how impact fees are being assessed today with tables summarizing national data and several useful local examples illustrating specific impact fee structures. *Chapter 2* summarizes the results of a detailed survey of impact fees that individual jurisdictions across the country are charging. The results of the survey reveal where impact fees are most common, how much jurisdictions in various states are charging, and the types of facilities for which fees are being charged. The chapter provides an opportunity to observe changes over time in the types and amounts of impact fees charged in different parts of the country. *Chapter 3* provides perspectives on the evolving legal principles surrounding impact fees. It includes important historical contexts, identifies some debates that courts have essentially settled— namely the big ones relating to authority and general mitigation guidance, and emerging legal discussions. A review of state impact fee enabling acts is presented in *Chapter 4*, focusing on several areas of commonality among the states and commenting on nuances in some states.

1

The Progression
of Impact Fees

Impact fees result from several factors but the chief one is obviously that, in many communities, traditional sources of revenue—principally local taxes—have proven to be insufficient to finance new or expanded facilities to meet the needs of growth. In addition, the public's expectations for the quantity and quality of facilities increase and, along with it, costs rise. This chapter reviews the principal epochs of development exactions associated with impact fees, summarizes the current state of affairs in meeting the needs of new development within the context of a public finance system in the United States that is changing fundamentally, introduces the experience of Florida with impact fees—an experience that is instructive nationally—and outlines new directions in impact fee designs.

Let us first put the discussion into the context of growth patterns. In 1900, the Census Bureau classified 60 percent of the U.S. population as rural but, by 2006, more than 93 percent was considered metropolitan. A century ago, most people did not use automobiles, most of the nation's population did not have public water or wastewater service, fire protection was spotty, libraries were limited mostly to larger cities, and generally the public did not receive modern public services perhaps

because they were either considered unneeded or unaffordable, or both.

What a difference a century makes! Between 1900 and 2006, the United States evolved from a mostly rural country to a nearly completely metropolitan one. Indeed, growth in metropolitan areas and cities appears to be increasing, as shown in Table 1-1. Between 1980 and 2006, for instance, metropolitan areas accounted for practically all the nation's growth. Incorporated places accounted for nearly two-thirds of all metropolitan growth. It is unlikely that these trends will reverse themselves. It is more likely that, as more people are added to metropolitan areas, local governments may be increasingly stressed to accommodate their facility demands. As the next section shows, local government has been struggling for decades trying to find ways in which to meet this challenge, with limited success overall.

THE EVOLUTIONARY PROCESS

Development impact fees are a product of evolution in public policy toward land use and provision of public facilities. Before the U.S. Commerce Department's model planning and zoning enabling acts of the 1920s, most growing communities had no effective land-use controls. It was not uncommon to find

Table 1-1
Metropolitan and Incorporated Population Trends, 1980–2006

Population Size	1980	2006	Numerical Growth	Percent Growth	Growth Share
U.S. population	226,546	299,398	72,852	32.2%	
Metropolitan population	209,075	279,892	70,817	33.9%	97.2%
Nonmetropolitan population	18,150	19,506	1,356	7.5%	1.9%
Total incorporated	140,300	186,100	45,800	32.6%	62.9%
1,000,000 or more	17,500	23,800	6,300	36.0%	8.6%
500,000 to 999,999	10,900	15,400	4,500	41.3%	6.2%
250,000 to 499,999	11,800	12,900	1,100	9.3%	1.5%
100,000 to 249,999	16,600	28,800	12,200	73.5%	16.7%
50,000 to 99,999	17,600	29,200	11,600	65.9%	15.9%
25,000 to 49,999	18,400	23,700	5,300	28.8%	7.3%
10,000 to 24,999	19,800	23,700	3,900	19.7%	5.4%
Under 10,000	28,000	28,700	700	2.5%	1.0%

Source: U.S. Census Bureau, Statistical Abstract of the United States, *2001 and 2006. Figures in thousands. Sums may not add due to rounding.*

speculators, for example, subdividing vast tracts of land considerable distances from cities in anticipation that purchasers and home builders would eventually receive city services (Nelson (1988a)). There were no land-use regulations controlling the location, timing, or dimensions of those developments, nor were public facility extension policies linked to land-use regulation. The model acts are the genesis of modern land-use regulation. They were adopted by most states, many verbatim. Today a person can travel to virtually any state and find commonalities in land-use regulation process and substance that are rooted in the model acts.

An immediate outcome of the model acts were regulations requiring developers to provide necessary facilities on-site. Prior to the model acts, developers often demanded and received street, water, sewer, and drainage facilities to each part of their development. The model acts gave public officials legal rationale for requiring developers to internalize that cost.

It must always be remembered that development impact fees are land development regulations and have evolved just as the regulation of land development has evolved. The object of development regulations is to protect the public. In certain circumstances, protecting the public has required the prohibition of certain types of developments in certain locations.

Requiring developers to provide adequate facilities is common. In fact, subdivision regulations typically mandate that the subdivider must provide a number of public facilities as a condition of development approval. Initially, required dedications were confined to improvements on-site (i.e., within the bounds of the property to be subdivided).

Concern about the adequacy of public facilities extends beyond the limits of the subdivided property. As zoning and other land-use regulatory forms evolved, so did required improvements, or exactions. Developers are now required to provide property or improvements that were external (i.e., outside of the subdivision). Such requirements are found to be within the authority of a local jurisdiction if there was a valid public purpose and the result was reasonable.

FIRST ERA: MANDATORY LAND DEDICATION AND IN-LIEU FEES

The four decades following the 1920s saw public officials wrestle with providing facilities outside the boundaries of the development. For example, local officials discovered that fiscal resources could not satisfy the appetite generated by new development for new parks and schools. The initial resolution of this problem was to require developers of residential subdivisions to dedicate land for park and school use, which is usually facilitated by state enabling legislation.

Sometimes land dedicated by development was in the wrong place, was too small, or for other reasons could not be reasonably used to satisfy community demand for parks and schools. As an adjunct to subdivision dedications, therefore, a system of payment in lieu of dedication came into use. Payment in lieu is employed when actual dedication or provision of land or improvements is not practical or feasible. For example, under a requirement to set aside 5 percent of a development's land area as open space, a five-acre subdivision would reserve one-quarter acre. Such a site might prove to be totally impractical for both the subdivision and the community. The alternatives were either to exempt smaller subdivisions from such requirements or to allow a payment to be made in lieu of dedication. This resulted in local governments requiring money in lieu of land dedication. The money exacted was to equal the value of the land that would have been dedicated.

By the 1940s, local government's power to demand land or money for facilities located off-site was firmly established, but mandatory dedication and in-lieu laws did not necessarily enable modern impact fees. This is because in-lieu fees are related to mandatory land dedication. There is usually no mandatory land dedication for water, sewer, drainage, roads, and many other facilities. The need for these facilities and services would have to be satisfied on a different, but related, basis.

SECOND ERA: RECONSIDERING THE GROWTH ETHIC

Until the 1960s and 1970s, most communities believed that growth and new development were fundamentally good. This is because it brought an improved tax base that could be used to build better facilities that all community residents enjoyed. Growth meant improving services at declining average cost to taxpayers. Challenges to the growth ethic emerged in the 1960s, however, as residents of desirable, rapidly growing communities discovered that unbridled growth caused pollution, congestion of streets, overuse of other facilities, and a general lowering of the quality of life. Furthermore, cost-revenue studies showed that, in many cases, new development placed new demands for community facilities that actually increased average tax burdens for existing taxpayers. Citizens concluded that growth was inimical to their reasons for choosing to live in their communities. A new land-use regulation ethic emerged calling for new development to

internalize all the costs it imposes on existing residents. Regulations based on such logic have been found to be within the power of local jurisdictions provided that there is a clear public purpose and that the regulations are reasonable. Protecting the public also commonly requires that certain types of developments be denied because the necessary supporting facilities are lacking. The development would become acceptable once the needed facilities were provided.

THIRD AND CONTINUING ERA: LOCAL GOVERNMENT FISCAL STRESS

A number of changes in the attitude toward financing public facilities emerged in the 1970s and continues to the present. The fiscal revolt of the 1970s and 1980s was at the forefront of these changes. Other factors included inflation, rising facility standards, and rising expectations of existing residents on the preferred range of public services.

The fiscal revolt manifested itself in rejection of new general obligation (GO) and revenue bonds for capital improvements needed to accommodate new development. It also manifested itself in electorates imposing on local government severe restrictions in the taxation of real property, the most regressive of the major taxes. Propositions 13 in California and 2½ in Massachusetts are only two of the more visible outcomes of this revolt.

The fiscal revolt extended to state and federal levels as well. When combined with inflation, dramatically declining public fiscal support for public facilities resulted. As a further result, government capital financing has not kept pace with either inflation or population growth since about 1965. Government capital financing was 3.4 percent of the gross national product in 1965, for example; however, by 2006, it had fallen to just 1.5 percent.

While capital spending at all levels of government rose from $20 billion in 1965 to about $200 billion in 2006, construction price inflated outlays in constant 2004 dollars per capita fell from about $800 to $600.[1] Coupled with the fiscal revolt are rising facility standards and rising expectations for facilities by existing residents. Improved water and wastewater treatment, and larger and better designed highways, are not so much demanded by the public as they are required by state and federal regulatory agencies.

New arts centers, public day care centers, and expanded parks facilities, however, are examples of the rising public appetite for new or expanded infrastructure. The bottom line is that local governments are forced to consider all possible revenue enhancing sources. These include new or higher user fees, privatization of some services, negotiated exactions of new development requiring planning approval, and development impact fees.

FUNDAMENTAL CHANGES IN AMERICAN PUBLIC FINANCE

Urbanization brings with it certain economic efficiencies that increase incomes. As incomes rise, so do expectations, especially of the quality and quantity of local government facilities and services. The vacant lot that served as a neighborhood ballfield is now a multipurpose athletic field replete with grandstands and rest rooms. The volunteer fire department is now a professional operation that includes emergency medical services (EMSs). Schools have progressed from providing classrooms to offering multimedia experiences, science labs, and libraries unimaginable just a generation ago. As long as incomes rose and local tax systems kept pace, the costs of rising expectations could probably be financed.

However, in recent decades, costs have risen faster than incomes. Figure 1-1 shows annual rates of inflation from 1970 to 2008. During the time period, the average was 6.37 percent per year, approximately twice the long-term rate of inflation. Annual inflation during 1980 was 13.5 percent and the year-over-year rate peaked during 1980 at over 17 percent. Such a rate of inflation meant that the purchasing power of fixed-base taxes, such as the motor fuel tax, declined proportionately. At the same time, however, inflation can and often does increase the price of real estate, the tax on which is the principal source of revenue for most local governments nationally.[2]

In theory, as prices increase so do the property taxes needed to pay the costs; however, this assumes that incomes also rise. This is often not the case. During the 1970s, property taxes indeed rose faster than incomes because property values also rose faster than incomes. The squeeze put on voters, especially those owning homes, led to California's Proposition 13, enacted in 1978. Proposition 13 rolled back property taxable values to 1975 levels and capped their rate of increase.[3] Massachusetts soon followed with Proposition 2½ in 1980, which is named for the annual limit on property taxes being no more than 2.5 percent of taxable value.[4] Since then, all states have limited property tax increases to some extent.[5]

The tax revolt of the 1970s and 1980s fundamentally changed the philosophy of taxation between the "Ability to Pay" and the "Benefit" principles (see Musgrave and Musgrave (1989)). General taxes are based usually on one's "Ability to Pay," resulting in situations where affluent people may pay proportionately more in taxes than lower income people even though both may receive roughly the same benefits. The "Benefit" principle holds that one's payment to government, regardless of form, should be accompanied by a roughly comparable benefit in return. Caught with declining tax revenues associated with the tax revolt, inflation, and rising expectations, locally elected officials had to choose from among championing higher taxes regardless of the political risks, reducing facility quality and even quantity, or finding an alternative source of revenue.

It did not help matters that federal mandates required local governments to make sizable infrastructure investments. For example, local governments were compelled by the federal government to make massive investments in water pollution control facilities.[6] Initially, the federal government funded these investments up to 85 percent of the cost, but they are now funded by federal loans amounting to just 45 percent. Similar trends in federal support for local infrastructure exist in other areas. For their part, states have elected not to make up for declining federal support of local infrastructure because of cost combined with revenue limits. The principal responsibility for these and other major public investments has thus fallen to local jurisdictions by default.

Figure 1-1
Rate of Inflation, 1970–2008

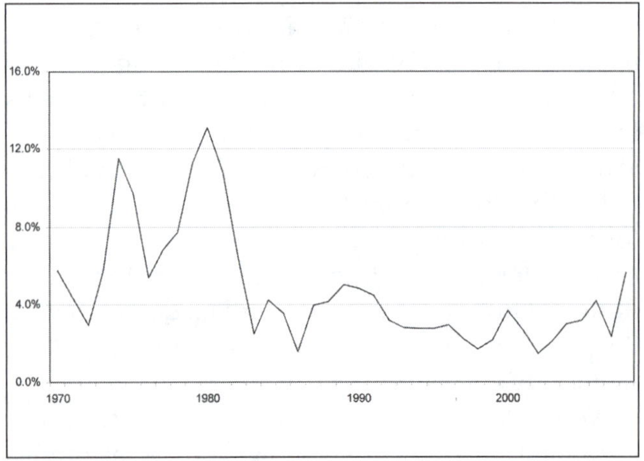

For their part, although local governments have considerable discretion in choosing how to protect the public's health, safety, and welfare, they have little discretion in their power to tax. Local governments found that growth and development meant more traffic, wastewater, and school children that had to be accommodated. Growth and development came to be viewed not as detrimental.[7] The detrimental aspects of growth provided the legal basis to use the police powers function of local government to protect the public against the loss of the "quality of life" that further growth would impose.

It is against this backdrop that impact fees arose. They were not based on any great thought or plan, but simply from desperation resulting from conflicting demands placed on local officials. Citizens demanded quality public services but also lower taxes. Builders demanded the ability to market their products. Local governments were often successful in showing they had the authority to impose impact fees on new developments to provide facilities proportionate to the fees paid and consistent with their responsibility to protect the public's health, safety, and welfare. The impact fee satisfied many demands.

The rise of impact fees is symptomatic of the fundamental major restructuring of the public finance system in the United States. One indicator of this is the rise of special service districts. While the total number of states, counties, and cities has remained essentially constant for the past several decades, there has been a proliferation of special service districts, as illustrated in Table 1-2. Indeed, between 1972 and 2002, special districts grew about 50 percent to more than 35,000.

Why the rapid growth in local governments, especially special districts? There are two principle answers. First, people want more things from government than ever before. Second, state and federal governments often find that it is in the broad public interest for government to address certain issues—such as water quality, education, and health care—but require implementation by local governments. Consider the expansion of special service districts by function over the 10-year period 1992 to 2002 (Table 1-3). Total special districts increased by 11 percent or just about the decadal growth rate of 13 percent during the 1990s. In contrast, the number of municipalities and counties remained essentially unchanged.

What is happening? The principal phenomenon is that local governance is being restructured. Instead of a city or county managing its park system, a special district may be formed to provide that function, and does so with a dedicated tax base that voters approve. However, there is an even more interesting aspect. Increasingly, local governments see new development—especially large-scale, master planned developments—as more capable than smaller ones of internalizing public facility costs. For example, it is quite common for cities and counties in California, Florida, Texas, and other states to condition approval of large-scale developments on the formation of a special assessment district that

Table 1-2
Governmental Units in the United States, 1972–2002

Governmental Unit	1972	1982	1992	2002	Total Change 1972–2002
Total units	78,269	81,831	85,006	87,504	9,235
U.S. government	1	1	1	1	0
State government	50	50	50	50	0
Local governments	78,218	81,780	84,955	87,525	9,307
County	3,044	3,041	3,043	3,034	(10)
Municipal	18,517	19,076	19,279	19,429	912
Township and town	16,991	16,734	16,656	16,504	(487)
School district	15,781	14,851	14,422	13,506	(2,275)
Special district	23,885	28,078	31,555	35,052	11,167

Source: U.S. Census Bureau, 2002 Census of Governments, Preliminary Report No. 1, *Series GC02-1(P).*

Table 1-3
Special Service Districts by Function, 1992–2002

Function	1992	2002	Change	Percent Change
Education	757	518	(239)	-31.6%
Libraries	1,043	1,580	537	51.5%
Hospitals	737	711	(26)	-3.5%
Health	584	753	169	28.9%
Highways	636	743	107	16.8%
Airports	435	510	75	17.2%
Other transportation	235	205	(30)	-12.8%
Fire protection	5,260	5,725	465	8.8%
Drainage and flood control	2,709	3,247	538	19.9%
Soil and water conservation	2,428	2,506	78	3.2%
Other natural resources	1,091	1,226	135	12.4%
Parks and recreation	1,156	1,287	131	11.3%
Housing and community development	3,470	3,399	(71)	-2.0%
Sewerage	1,710	2,004	294	17.2%
Solid waste management	395	455	60	15.2%
Water supply	3,302	3,406	104	3.1%
Other utilities	461	485	24	5.2%
Cemeteries	1,628	1,666	38	2.3%
Industrial development and mortgage credit	155	234	79	51.0%
Other single-function districts	844	1,161	317	37.6%
Total single-function districts	29,036	31,821	2,785	9.6%
Total multifunction districts	2,519	3,175	656	26.0%
Total special service districts	31,555	34,996	3,441	10.9%

Source: U.S. Census Bureau, 1992 Census of Governments, Government Organization, *Table 14, and* 2002 Census of Governments, Government Organization, *Table 9.*

not only pays for the capital costs of infrastructure but maintains it as well. The special districts may also be managed by the local government to assure adequate maintenance and operations of the local facilities.

The upshot of America's public finance restructuring is that the cost of infrastructure, and often its O & M, is being shifted from the public generally to the individual development and often to large-scale new developments. Impact fees are only symptomatic of this effort to essentially privatize the provision of public facilities.

IMPACT FEE REVENUES

Just how much revenue do impact fees generate? Average 2006 impact fees are shown in Table 1-4. These data are averages of fees in a number of states and thus are not representative of any individual state or locality. Nonetheless, these data do provide a context for the discussion of the evolving role of impact fees in local government finance.

The fees per unit of new development are collected and aggregated into total receipts. Only the State of Florida has aggregated total impact fee receipts and thus only for Florida can the role of impact fees be measured.

Florida's Legislative Committee on Intergovernmental Relations (LCIR) compiles data concerning impact fee revenues reported annually by counties, municipalities, independent special districts, and school districts. In 1993, reported impact fee revenues in Florida totaled $177 million. Eleven years later, in 2004, impact fee revenues totaled $1.07 billion statewide. This growth in impact fee revenues

Table 1-4
National Average Impact Fees, 2006

Land-use Type	Roads	Parks	Schools	Total Nonutility	Utility	Total
Single-family (unit)	$2,326	$2,112	$4,138	$6,506	$5,320	$8,979
Multifamily (unit)	$1,580	$1,615	$2,427	$4,375	$2,912	$5,622
Retail (1,000 sq. ft.)	$4,589	$820	$333	$5,626	$1,220	$5,544
Office (1,000 sq. ft.)	$2,665	$838	$333	$3,548	$1,126	$3,670
Industrial (1,000 sq. ft.)	$1,595	$696	$333	$2,383	$1,155	$2,578

Source: Chapter 2.

represents a 505 percent increase with much of the accelerated growth since the late 1990s. This is an annual rate of increase of 17.8 percent per year. Cumulatively, from 1993 through 2004, reported impact fee revenues totaled nearly $5.3 billion. This represents approximately 23 percent of all local government infrastructure spending in the State of Florida.[8]

Impact fee revenue collections vary by type of governmental entity. Between 1993 and 2004, counties accounted for the largest amount of impact fee revenue collections at $3.5 billion. Municipalities follow with $1.2 billion in impact fee revenue collections. Prior to 2002, school districts reported very few impact fee revenue collections. Since 2002, however, school districts have become a major beneficiary of impact fees with $500 million in impact fee collections, and that amount is expected to grow

substantially in the future. This increase in impact fee revenues is a result of Florida's rapid population growth, the growing number of local governments imposing impact fees, and the rising cost of land and building infrastructure (see Table 1-5).

The LCIR also reported impact fee revenues by fee category (e.g., transportation, physical environment, and public safety) during the same time period of 1993 to 2004. As a percentage of total cumulative revenues, transportation impact fees represented the largest impact fee category, totaling $2.2 billion or 38 percent of the total. Physical environment impact fees represented the second largest category, totaling $1.3 billion or 24 percent of the total.

When looking at the number of governmental entities reporting impact fee revenues by fee category,

Table 1-5
Reported Impact Fee Revenue by Government Type in Florida, 1993–2004

Year	Counties	Municipalities	Independent Special Districts	School Districts	Annual Totals	Percent Change
1993	$107,959,016	$65,159,178	$3,748,855	$51,082	$176,918,131	
1994	$142,835,074	$70,215,815	$5,761,159	$91,919	$218,903,967	24%
1995	$157,598,994	$46,722,317	$4,589,574	$1,126,903	$210,037,788	-4%
1996	$160,396,998	$41,189,959	$4,687,187	$1,275,037	$207,549,181	-1%
1997	$196,634,639	$57,600,001	$9,014,576	$2,198,842	$265,448,058	28%
1998	$214,357,753	$73,655,715	$8,685,871	$2,295,472	$298,994,811	13%
1999	$262,544,090	$102,323,355	$9,616,597		$374,484,042	25%
2000	$324,233,477	$83,707,192	$15,675,246	$3,429,300	$427,045,215	14%
2001	$385,440,874	$119,024,491	$17,651,599	$3,505,450	$525,622,414	23%
2002	$466,571,715	$132,851,319	$18,033,558	$124,451,364	$741,907,956	41%
2003	$479,479,595	$180,966,895	$21,711,285	$117,672,871	$799,830,646	8%
2004	$560,496,789	$230,918,802	$20,501,638	$258,581,444	$1,070,498,673	34%
Total	$3,458,549,014	$1,204,335,039	$139,677,155	$514,677,684	$5,317,240,881	

Source: Counties, municipalities, and independent special districts: Florida Department of Financial Services. School districts: Florida Department of Education, Office of Funding and Financial Reporting. Compiled by LCIR staff (Jan. 20, 2006).

more governmental entities reported public safety impact fees than any other category, followed by the number of jurisdictions imposing physical environment, cultural and recreational, and transportation impact fees. Note may be taken of the fact that Florida has a total of 477 units of general purpose local government (67 counties and 410 municipalities). Therefore, 54 percent of Florida local governments imposed impact fees in 2004. Furthermore, a review of the data illustrates that a relatively small number of governmental entities accounts for the majority of impact fee revenues reported in Florida (see Tables 1-6, 1-7, and 1-8).

IMPACT FEES OF THE FUTURE

Although more will be said about how impact fees of the future may be shaped to improve local government fiscal decision making, in this section we summarize historical perspectives, emerging practices, and lingering realities.

Impact fees began as minor supplements to traditional sources of capital improvements financing. The water and sewer impact fees that were at issue in the 1975 case of *Contractors and Builders Assn. of Pinellas County v. City of Dunedin*[9] were $325 for water and $475 for sewer.[10] These 1975 amounts are substantially below the $4,320 of today.[11] Similarly, the "transportation" fee litigated in *Broward County v. Janis Development Corp.*[12] was $100, which is very much less than the average road impact fee of $2,326, even after considering inflation.[13] The amounts of impact fees thus began small and became much larger. The role of impact fees began as supplemental and is now primary, but the impact fee debate continues. That debate has evolved, however, from *whether* impact fees should be assessed at all to *how* they are assessed.

Between 2003 and 2007, the average nonutility impact fee assessed on a single-family home grew by 77 percent (see Chapter 2), an annual rate of growth of 15.4 percent. Scaling back the rate of increase to 12 percent means that the average 2007 impact fee of $9,362 including utilities assessed on a single-family home would grow to $16,499 in five years, $29,077 in 10 years, and $80,633 in 20 years, as shown in Figure 1-2. While this amount of money would yield substantial revenues to local governments, certain consequences with respect to housing costs would be expected to follow. However, the trends observed today suggest that impact fees will continue to rise at rapid rates until market forces or legislative restrictions rein them in.

Such levels of impact fees elicit concerns about societal matters, especially the goal of home ownership and matters of equity. Impact fees are here to stay, so doing away with impact fees in the name of home ownership or equity is not an option. However, the manner and form of impact fees can be structured in order to have very different consequences on home ownership and equity. While these concepts of equity are important, the focus of

Table 1-6
Number of Governmental Entities Reporting Impact Fee Revenues, Fiscal Years 1993–2004

Year	Counties	Municipalities	Independent Special Districts	School Districts	Annual Totals
1993	28	100	32	2	162
1994	26	108	32	1	167
1995	34	108	30	3	175
1996	34	125	32	2	193
1997	34	118	35	1	188
1998	35	134	33	3	205
1999	36	139	31	0	206
2000	34	148	37	1	220
2001	37	150	36	1	224
2002	40	155	44	15	254
2003	39	150	46	14	249
2004	39	154	46	19	258

Sources: Counties, municipalities, and independent special districts (Florida Department of Financial Services); school districts (Florida Department of Education, Office of Funding and Financial Reporting).

Figure 1-2
Hypothetical Projection of Impact Fees Compounded Over Time

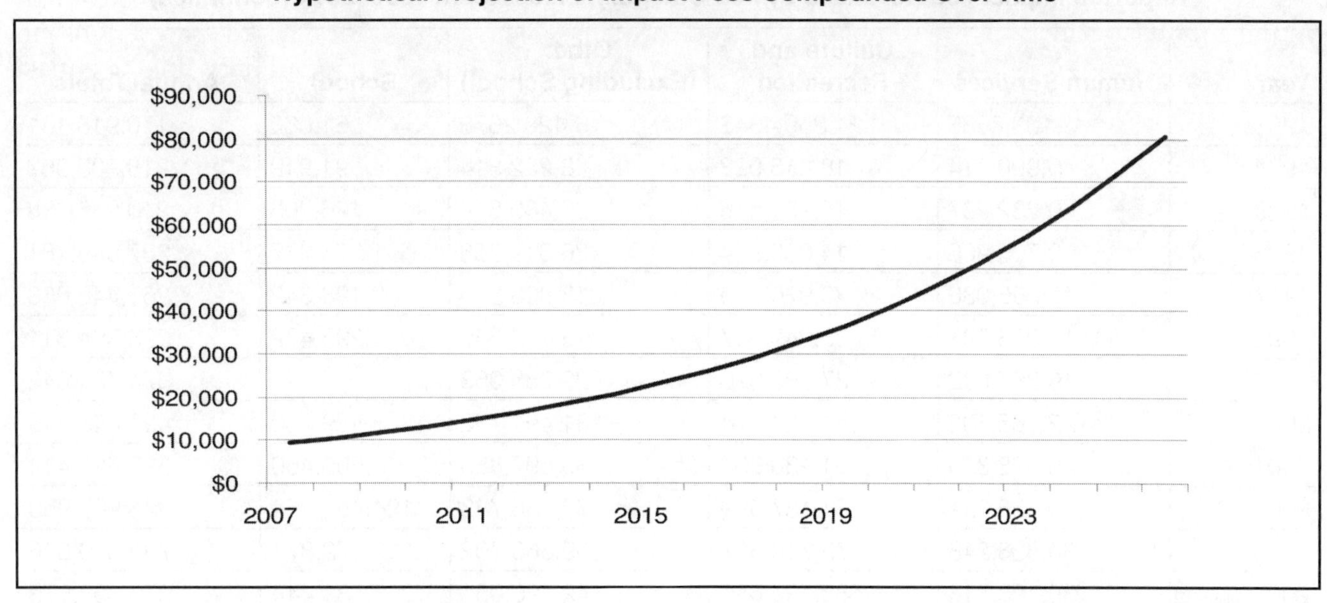

this book is how to address proportionate equity (i.e., the extent to which an impact fee reflects the actual impact different housing units have on community facilities).

A critical aspect of proportionality is the extent to which impact fees are based on the impact of new development on facilities. Many impact fee programs assume that each residential unit has the same impact on facilities regardless of size, type, density, location, or other factors. Hence, the impact fee for a large, single-family detached home is the same as for a small efficiency apartment, despite the fact that census figures clearly show substantial differences in occupancy rates. These impact fees are described as "flat rate" fees and are inherently unfair. The result is that flat rate impact fees thus designed have a "regressive" effect (i.e., they fall disproportionately on those with lower incomes than on those with higher ones). We thus find increasing interest in crafting impact fees that take account of these more refined elements. After all, if impact fees rise anywhere near the level illustrated in Figure 1-2 the public will likely demand more careful analysis.

Table 1-7
Reported Impact Fee Revenues by Fee Category, Fiscal Years 1993–2004

Year	Public Safety	Physical Environment	Transportation	Economic Environment
1993	13,359,098$	47,064,732$	84,796,721$	257,129$
1994	17,961,508	76,250,262	91,299,136	363,686
1995	13,516,287	52,446,808	91,767,344	295,065
1996	12,084,897	53,459,818	91,114,607	492,017
1997	26,749,870	44,193,293	137,230,917	245,818
1998	28,283,164	71,480,495	133,889,335	302,177
1999	31,269,609	95,142,652	163,351,985	5,284,835
2000	36,281,163	86,834,615	194,806,718	312,071
2001	51,230,054	161,538,461	194,779,870	761,684
2002	49,208,473	197,441,075	204,438,019	1,268,562
2003	61,765,409	173,228,181	281,112,115	2,132,563
2004	76,675,162	210,580,467	352,460,793	2,321,554
Cum. totals	418,384,694$	1,269,660,859$	2,021,047,560$	14,037,161$

Table 1-7
Reported Impact Fee Revenues by Fee Category, Fiscal Years 1993–2004 *(continued)*

Year	Human Services	Culture and Recreation	Other (Excluding School)	School	Annual Totals
1993	3,103,668$	21,859,434$	6,426,267$	51,082	176,918,131
1994	5,900,114	18,815,028	8,222,314	91,919	218,903,967
1995	9,232,987	15,251,576	26,400,818	1,126,903	210,037,788
1996	8,705,905	14,096,944	26,319,956	1,275,037	207,549,181
1997	10,055,086	30,970,673	13,803,559	2,198,842	265,448,058
1998	11,373,691	33,247,837	18,122,640	2,295,472	298,994,811
1999	19,887,082	37,292,826	22,255,053	—	374,484,042
2000	22,165,102	51,724,474	31,491,772	3,429,300	427,045,215
2001	26,578,310	51,130,696	36,097,889	3,505,450	525,622,414
2002	30,156,321	61,187,399	73,756,743	124,451,364	741,907,956
2003	30,836,248	73,716,557	59,366,702	117,672,871	799,830,646
2004	39,183,513	88,199,689	42,496,051	258,581,444	1,070,498,673
Cum. totals	217,178,027$	497,493,133$	364,759,764$	514,679,683	5,317,240,881

Table 1-8
Number of Governmental Entities Reporting Impact Fee Revenues by Fee Category, Fiscal Years 1993–2004

Year	Public Safety	Physical Environment	Trans-portation	Economic Environ-ment	Human Services	Culture and Rec-reation	Other (Excluding School)	School	Annual Totals
1993	79	54	55	1	3	48	27	2	269
1994	77	63	55	4	2	51	30	1	283
1995	87	57	58	3	2	67	31	3	308
1996	89	62	70	2	2	70	36	2	333
1997	97	59	70	1	2	72	35	1	337
1998	110	64	71	2	3	83	38	3	374
1999	106	68	80	5	3	84	35	0	381
2000	112	75	82	5	2	89	42	1	408
2001	108	95	85	4	3	90	43	1	429
2002	115	97	87	3	3	87	55	15	462
2003	123	96	90	4	3	91	53	14	474
2004	128	111	83	4	2	97	48	19	492

In summary, impact fees are here to stay, but the role and scope of impact fees will continue to evolve. The task is to develop new methodologies that enable local government to finance an ever-increasing share of their capital costs while also addressing equity implications of impact fees. That is what this book hopes to accomplish.

NOTES

1. *Engineering News-Record*, "Construction Cost Index" (August 2003 to August 2007).
2. Between 1980 and 2000, all prices rose at 3.8 percent per year while shelter costs rose at 4.4 percent. See *Statistical Abstract of the U.S.* (Washington, D.C.: U.S. Department of Commerce, Census Bureau, 2001), at 454. The median sales price of a new single-family home grew by 4.9 percent per year. See *ibid*. at 598. The median price of existing home sales rose by 4.1 percent per year.
3. See John Kirlin, *The Political Economy of Fiscal Limits* (Lexington, Mass.: Lexington Books, 1982).
4. *Ibid*.
5. Therese J. McGuire, "Proposition 13 and Its Offspring: For Good or Evil?" 52 *National Tax Journal* (1999): 129–38.
6. The Water Pollution Control (Clean Water) Act, 33 U.S.C. Sections 1251 et seq. (1994).
7. See William K. Reiley, *The Use of Land* (New York: Crowell, 1972).
8. See J. Nicholas et al., "Impact Fees in Florida: Their Evolution, Methodology, Current Issues and Comparisons with Other States," prepared for the Florida Impact Fee Task Force, Tallahassee (September 2005), citing data from the 2003 Census of Government.
9. 329 So.2d 314 (Fla.1976), on remand 330 So.2d 744 (Fla.App.1976).
10. *Ibid*. at 315. These fees are for a single-family detached unit.
11. The 1975 water fee of $325 would be $1,265 after adjustment for changes in the Consumer Price Index and the $475 sewer fee would amount to $1,603. These indicate that the relative amount of Dunedin's fees has remained about the same.
12. 311 So.2d 371 (Fla. 4th DCA 1975).
13. Adjusting the $200 from 1974 to 2002 by the Consumer Price Index yields a 2002 value of $683.

2

National Impact Fee Survey

With Clancy Mullen

This chapter summarizes the results of a detailed survey of impact fees that individual jurisdictions across the country are charging. Unlike in-kind developer exactions, impact fees are expressed in dollars and have published fee schedules, making it easy to compare fees charged by different jurisdictions. The results of the survey reveal where impact fees are most common, how much jurisdictions in various states are charging, and the types of facilities for which fees are being charged. Comparisons with survey results from previous years also show how fees have been changing over time.

WHAT QUALIFIES AS AN IMPACT FEE?

The multitude of names used to refer to impact fees is one obstacle to developing an accurate survey of such fees. Common terms used to refer to impact fees include "capacity fees," "facility fees," "system development charges," and "capital recovery fees." Their common characteristics are that:

1. They are charged only to new development;
2. They are standardized fees as opposed to ad hoc, negotiated payments; and

3. They are designed and used to fund capital improvements needed to serve growth.

UTILITY CONNECTION FEES

Water and wastewater connection fees that are used to fund growth-related capital improvements should be classified as impact fees. However, connection fees often mix impact fee components with service fees that cover other types of costs, such as the purchase of a water meter, the inspection of the connection, or the administrative cost of establishing a new customer account. This presents the researcher with a problem. Counting only clearly labeled water and wastewater impact fees is likely to underrepresent them, but seldom are there sufficient resources to interview local officials to determine what portion of a connection fee is actually an impact fee. As a general rule, a single-family connection fee in excess of $1,000 for either water or wastewater is likely to be an impact fee in whole or in part. In addition, because water and wastewater fees preceded other kinds of impact fees, they are often less controversial than other types of impact fees. For these reasons, it is often useful to look at "nonutility" impact fees separately from total impact fees.

IN-LIEU FEES

Fees charged in lieu of land dedication for parks and schools are conceptually very similar to impact fees, and should also be counted in an impact fee survey. Essentially, they function much like an impact fee for the land component of the facility. Indeed, some communities use an impact fee for the construction cost component, and combine that with a land dedication/fee-in-lieu requirement for the land component. In California, park fees in lieu of land dedication are known as "Quimby fees," after the name of the 1966 state act authorizing such fees. Because they are not labeled as impact fees, land dedication in-lieu fees are often overlooked in impact fee surveys.

DEVELOPMENT TAXES

Another class of fee that is functionally very similar to an impact fee is the development tax, which is sometimes referred to as a "development excise tax," "privilege tax," or "facilities tax." This is a tax that only applies to new development, often on a per-square-foot basis, and is earmarked for capital improvements. For example, Boulder, Colorado, hired consultants to conduct a nexus study and adopted an ordinance that had all of the trappings of an impact fee ordinance, including earmarking of funds for specific types of capital facilities and providing credit against the charges for developer-constructed improvements. However, instead of adopting them as impact fees, they adopted them as development taxes. This survey includes development taxes.

SOME CAVEATS

The results of impact fee surveys can be misinterpreted. This can be avoided if the reader keeps the following caveats in mind.

NOT EXHAUSTIVE SAMPLES

Like most impact fee surveys, this survey only includes communities that charge some impact fees and excludes those that do not. Thus, an "average impact fee" must be understood as an average fee for those communities that charge impact fees, not as an average for all communities. Although, in California, state limits on local taxing authority and relatively liberal impact fee enabling legislation have combined to make impact fees virtually universal, in most other parts of the country, communities that have impact fees (other than the ubiquitous water and wastewater connection fees) still tend to be in the minority.

NOT RANDOM SAMPLES

Impact fee surveys tend to be opportunistic. For the most part, the inclusion of a community is determined by the availability of the information. Communities that post their fee schedules on the Internet are more likely to be included in a survey than communities that do not. Consultants who compile surveys are more likely to include communities that have been clients or that are in the same region with former clients. For example, Duncan Associates compiled extensive surveys of impact fees in Arizona and Florida for client communities in those states. For these reasons, the fact that a state is not well represented in a national survey does not necessarily mean that the state does not have many impact fees (although that may be true).

AVERAGE TOTAL FEE OR SUM OF AVERAGE FEES

In this chapter, average fees are presented for a variety of capital facilities. These averages exclude communities that are represented in the survey but do not charge impact fees for the particular facility type. One could sum these average fees by facility type, but this "sum of the average fees" does not represent the average fee for communities that charge impact fees. A more meaningful statistic, and the one reported here, is the "average of the total impact fees" charged by all communities represented in the survey.

ONLY PUBLISHED FEES

The fact that a community does not charge a particular impact fee does not mean that developers make no contributions to that type of capital facility. This is particularly true in the case of roads because many communities without road impact fees require developers to dedicate rights-of-way and often to make substantial improvements to abutting roadways as a condition of development approval. In communities with road impact fees, developers who are required to make in-kind contributions receive credit against their impact fees for the value of those contributions. Thus, developers may contribute more on average to the cost of major road improvements in communities without road impact fees than in communities with modest road impact fees.

FEE INCIDENCE BY STATE

This survey is opportunistic, so the number of jurisdictions represented in the survey is not proportional to the actual incidence of impact fees. Nevertheless, the survey jurisdictions do provide some indication of the states where impact fees are most common. Not surprisingly, impact fees are most common in the South and West, especially Washington, Oregon, California, Arizona, Colorado, and Florida (see Figure 2-1). On the other hand, impact fees are relatively rare in the Northeast and Midwest.

AVERAGE FEES BY FACILITY TYPE

Average impact fees per single-family detached dwelling by type of facility are graphically illustrated in Figure 2-2. The total amount of impact fees charged by jurisdictions surveyed averages 11,239. Excluding utility fees, the average total fee is $8,093. School impact fees, although not charged in many states, are the highest, followed by water, wastewater, road, and park impact fees. Police, fire, and library fees, on the other hand, tend to be relatively low. General government facility impact fees and stormwater drainage impact fees are relatively

uncommonly charged (general government fees are not authorized in most states, and drainage fees are difficult to implement because they generally must be based on a comprehensive drainage master plan).

AVERAGE FEES BY LAND USE

Average impact fees by land-use type are presented in Table 2-1 and illustrated in Figure 2-3. Except in the few states where school fees are charged,[1] road, park, and utility fees are the primary components of total fees for residential land uses. Other types of fees tend to be small (e.g., fire, police, library) or infrequently charged (e.g., general government or drainage). For nonresidential land uses, the dominant component of the total fee is for roads. For nonresidential land uses, park fees are seldom charged, and road and utility fees are the dominant components of the total fee.

AVERAGE FEES BY STATE

Average single-family impact fees, excluding water and wastewater utility fees, are illustrated in Figure 2-4 for states with at least four jurisdictions included in the 2008 survey. Total fees for the majority of states start at less than $1,000 in Arkansas and, with the exception of three states, peak at under $7,000. It is not a coincidence that the three states with the highest fees—California, Florida, and Maryland—are all

Figure 2-1
Survey Jurisdictions by State, 2008

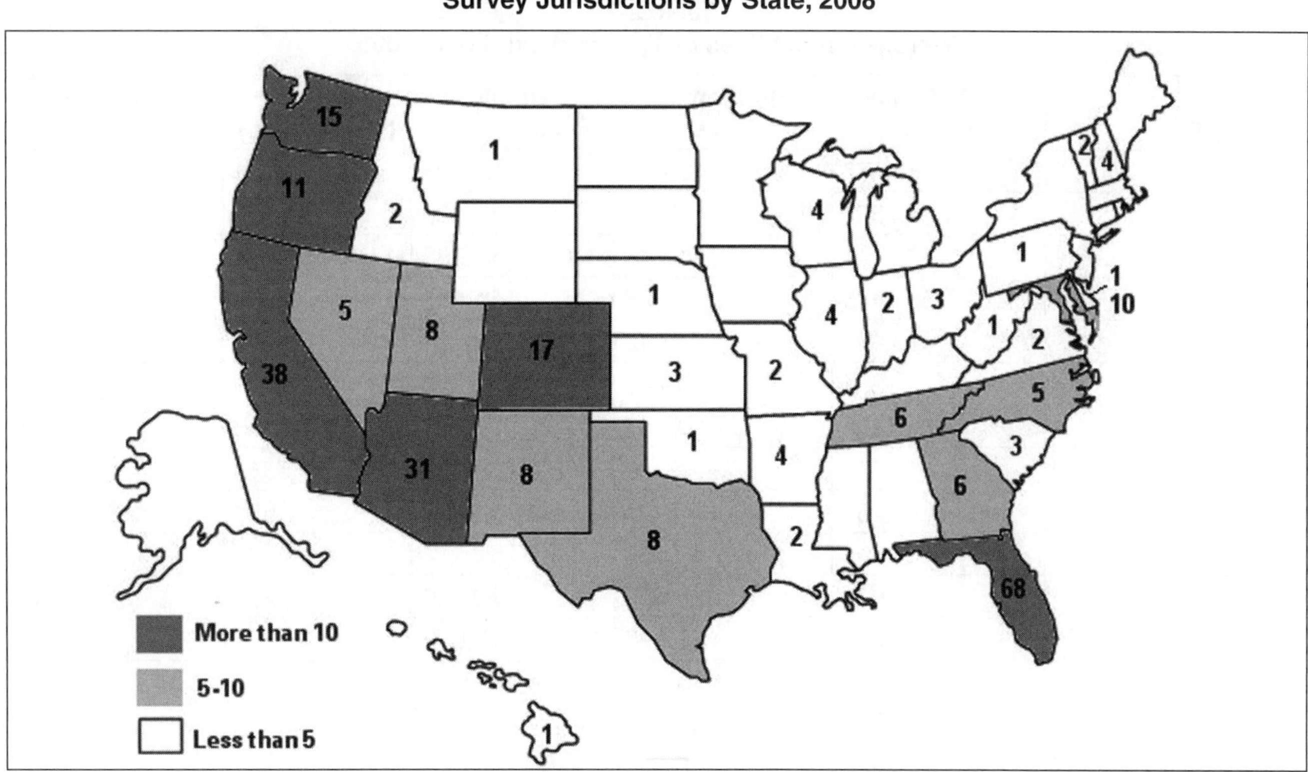

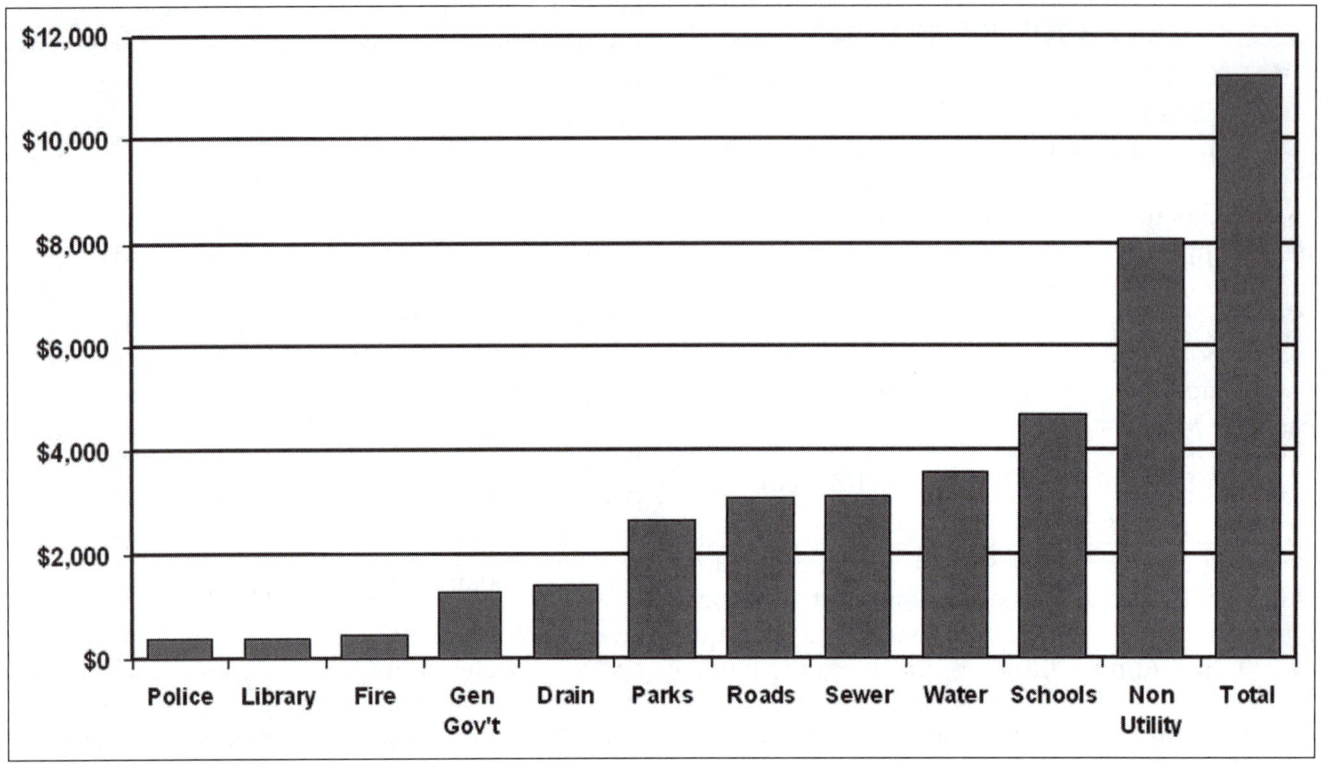

Table 2-1
Average Impact Fees by Type and Land Use, 2008

Facility Type	Single-Family (Unit)	Multifamily (Unit)	Retail (1,000 sq. ft.)	Office (1,000 sq. ft.)	Industrial (1,000 sq. ft.)
Roads	$3,077	$2,095	$5,327	$3,381	$2,067
Water	$3,584	$1,706	$1,130	$1,108	$1,108
Wastewater	$3,141	$1,746	$1,683	$1,648	$1,678
Drainage	$1,415	$868	$1,081	$868	$1,055
Parks	$2,667	$2,042	**	**	**
Library	$394	$296	**	**	**
Fire	$452	$347	$397	$338	$243
Police	$377	$289	$487	$313	$201
General government	$1,257	$994	$625	$587	$597
Schools	$4,693	$2,562	**	**	**
Total nonutility*	$8,093	$5,569	$6,180	$4,294	$2,918
Total*	$11,239	$7,092	$7,022	$5,257	$3,955

* Totals do not represent sum of average fees, since not all jurisdictions charge all types of fees.
** Rarely charged to nonresidential land uses, with the exception of school fees in California.

Source: Duncan Associates, 2008 survey of 280 jurisdictions.

Figure 2-3
Average Fees by Land Use, 2008

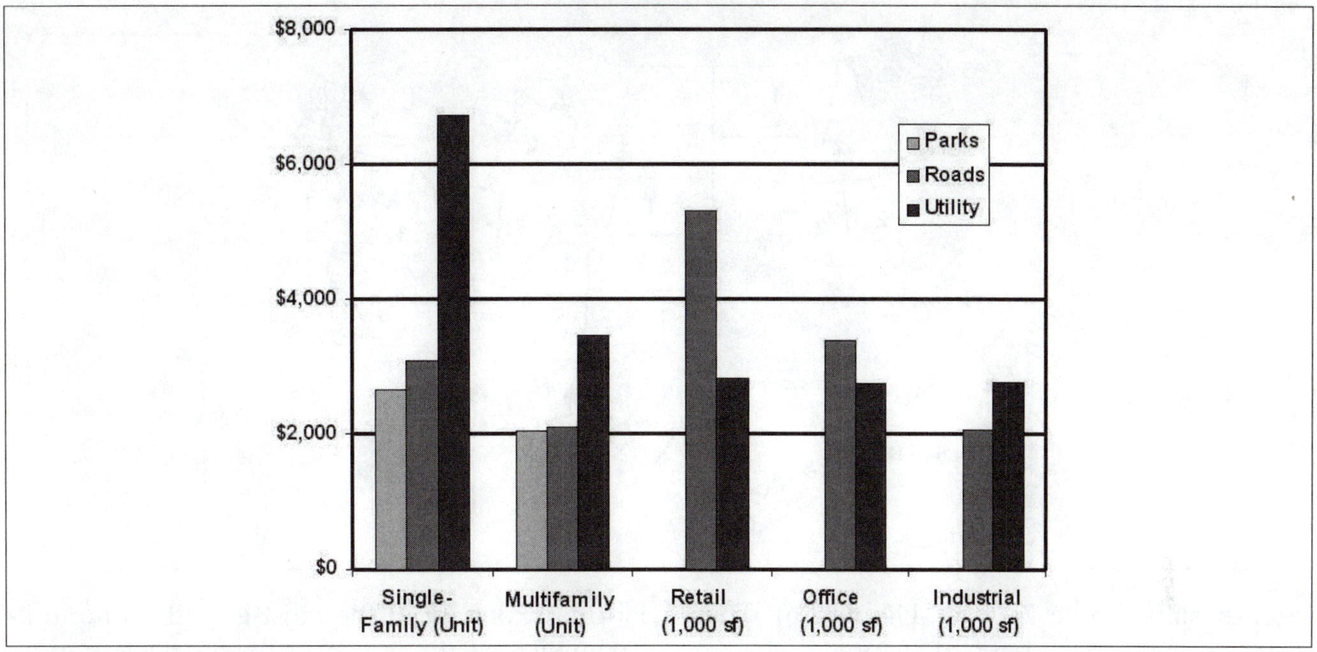

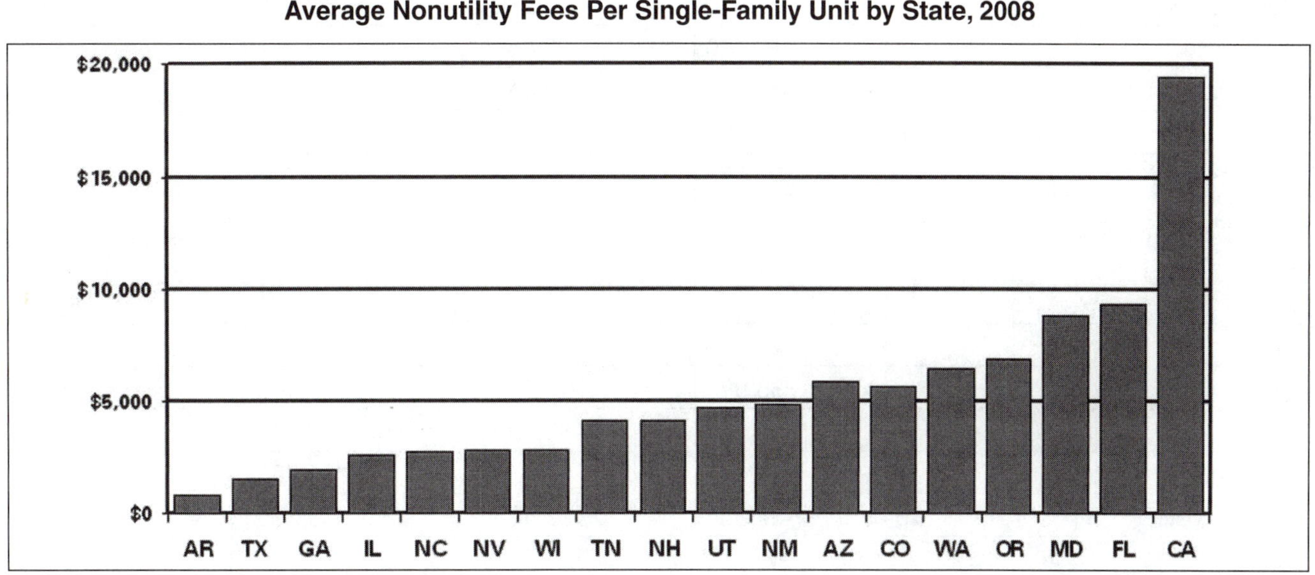

states with large numbers of school impact fees, which, as seen earlier, are the highest facility fee per single-family unit. The average total fee in California ($19,506) more than doubles the fee in the second highest state of Florida ($9,320). It is not a coincidence that the states with the most jurisdictions charging fees are also the states with the highest fees.

FEE INCREASES, 2004–2008

Impact fee amounts have increased significantly since this survey was published in 2004. At that time, the survey had 197 jurisdictions (compared to 280 jurisdictions currently). Comparing average fees from the 2004 and 2008 surveys could be misleading since we could have added some jurisdictions that already had high fees in 2004 but were not included in the original survey. In order to avoid this effect, average fees are compared for the 185 jurisdictions included in both surveys. While California is unfortunately underrepresented, the 2004–2008 constant sample is otherwise fairly robust and representative of the incidence of impact fees around the country (see Figure 2-5).

First, let's look at increases in total nonutility fees charged by our constant sample jurisdictions

Figure 2-4
Average Nonutility Fees Per Single-Family Unit by State, 2008

Figure 2-5
Number of Jurisdictions by State, 2004–2008 Constant Sample

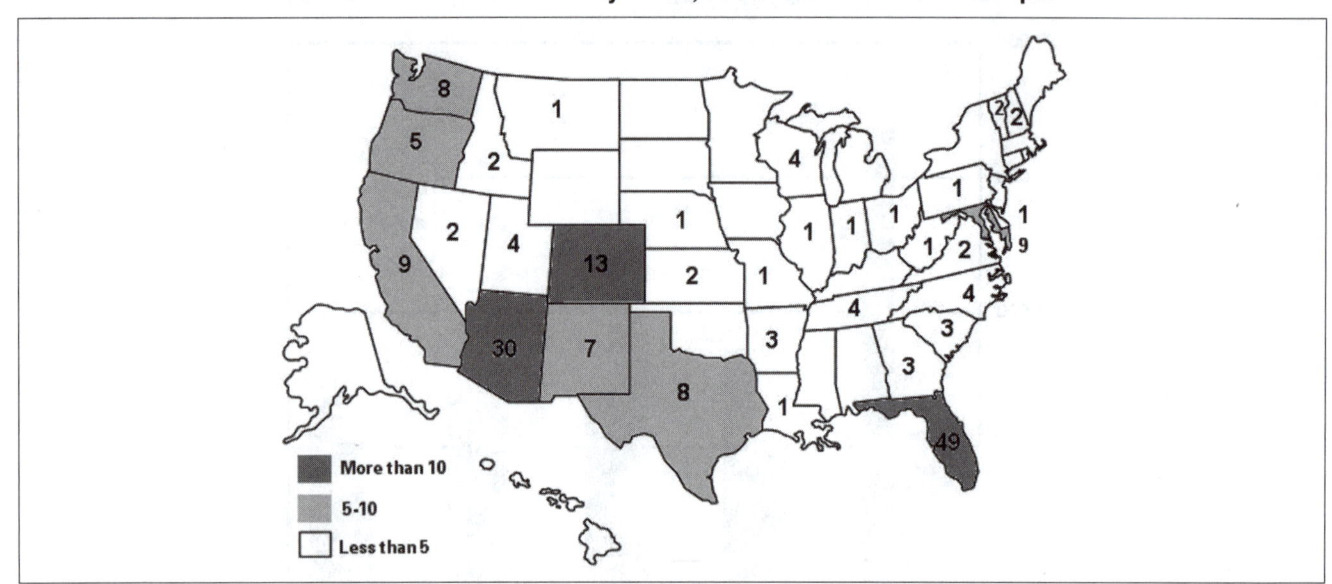

in each state (Table 2-2 and Figure 2-6). These increases are the result of two factors:

1. Jurisdictions raising fees that they already charged in 2004; and
2. Jurisdictions adopting new impact fees.

Our observations are restricted to the 13 states with at least four jurisdictions in the constant sample. Nationally, the total nonutility fee per single-family unit increased 76 percent over the four-year period, from $4,236 to $7,455. This represents an annual average increase of about 15.2 percent.

Florida experienced the most growth in nonutility impact fee amounts over the four-year period, in both absolute and percentage terms, more than doubling the average fee per single-family unit from $4,752 to $10,846 per unit. Florida went from the fifth highest to the second highest average total nonutility impact fee in the nation, after California.

Within our constant sample of 185 jurisdictions, an increase in the average total fee charged can be the result of two different trends: adopting new

Table 2-2
Total Nonutility Single-Family Impact Fees by Selected State, 2004–2008

State	Sample Size	2004	2008	Increase	Percent Increase
Texas	8	$1,160	$1,520	$360	31%
New Mexico	7	$1,314	$4,276	$2,962	225%
Wisconsin	4	$2,180	$2,887	$707	32%
North Carolina	4	$2,304	$2,830	$526	23%
Utah	4	$2,334	$4,324	$1,990	85%
Tennessee	4	$2,878	$3,644	$766	27%
Arizona	30	$3,127	$5,929	$2,802	90%
Washington	8	$3,482	$5,682	$2,200	63%
Florida	49	$4,752	$10,846	$6,094	128%
Colorado	13	$5,373	$6,568	$1,195	22%
Oregon	5	$5,969	$6,458	$489	8%
Maryland	9	$6,144	$8,856	$2,712	44%
California	9	$14,178	$19,536	$5,358	38%
Total survey	185	$4,236	$7,455	$3,219	76%

Source: Duncan Associates, constant sample survey of 185 jurisdictions.

Figure 2-6
Total Nonutility Single-Family Fees, 2004–2008

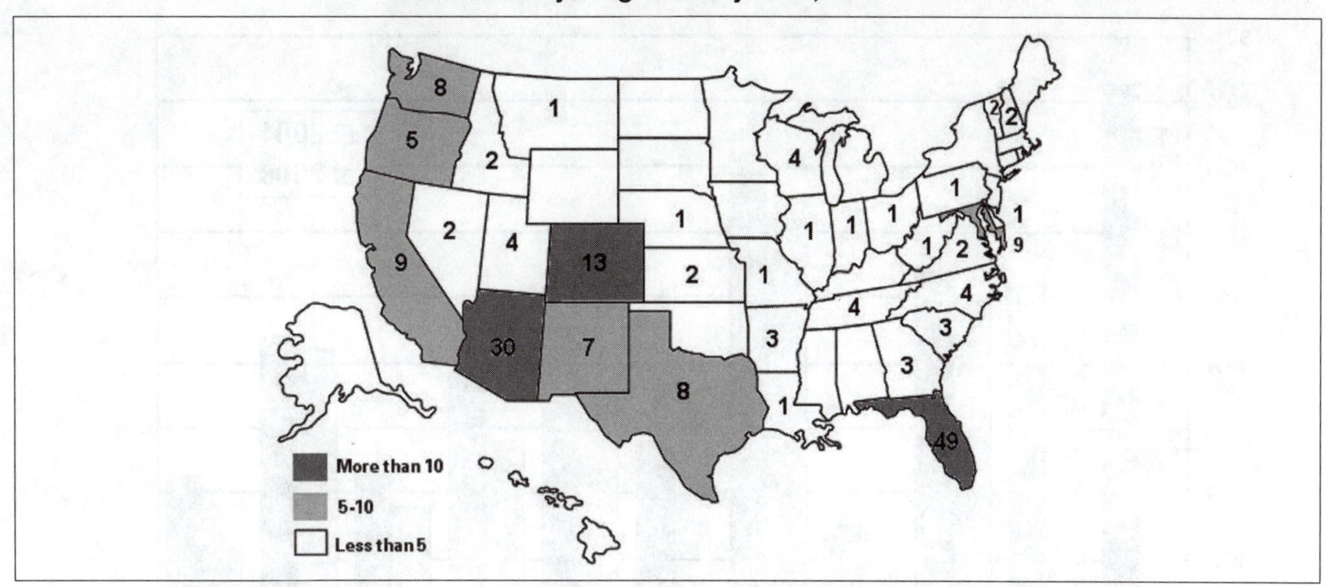

fees and raising existing fees. Many new fees were adopted over the four-year period (shown in Table 2-3 and Figure 2-7). On average, another 6 percent of the jurisdictions was charging each type of impact fee at the end of the four years. The increase was greatest for fire, police, and park fees, and lowest for drainage and school fees.

In addition to adopting new fees, jurisdictions are also raising existing fees for individual types of facilities (or adopting new fees at levels higher than the average) (see Table 2-4 and Figure 2-8). Only small increases were seen in water and wastewater utility impact fees, which are the oldest types of impact fees. Instead, the increases have been seen primarily in the nonutility fees. In dollar terms, the biggest increases have been in road and school fees. The school fee increases have been occurring primarily in Florida (school impact fees are only allowed in a few states and, in California, they are capped and can increase only with the cost of living). With the exception of drainage impact fees, which are the least common type, all of the other

Table 2-3
Jurisdictions Charging Impact Fees by Facility Type, 2004–2008

Type of Fee	Number of Jurisdictions			Percent of Jurisdictions		
	2004	2008	New	2004	2008	New
Roads	141	153	12	76%	83%	6%
Water	90	97	7	49%	52%	4%
Wastewater	92	100	8	50%	54%	4%
Drainage	24	28	4	13%	15%	2%
Parks	115	134	19	62%	72%	10%
Library	42	52	10	23%	28%	5%
Fire	69	96	27	37%	52%	15%
Police	52	73	21	28%	39%	11%
General government	33	43	10	18%	23%	5%
Schools	78	82	4	42%	44%	2%
Other	30	42	12	16%	23%	6%

Source: Duncan Associates, constant sample survey of 185 jurisdictions

Figure 2-7
Percent of Jurisdictions Charging Fees, 2004–2008

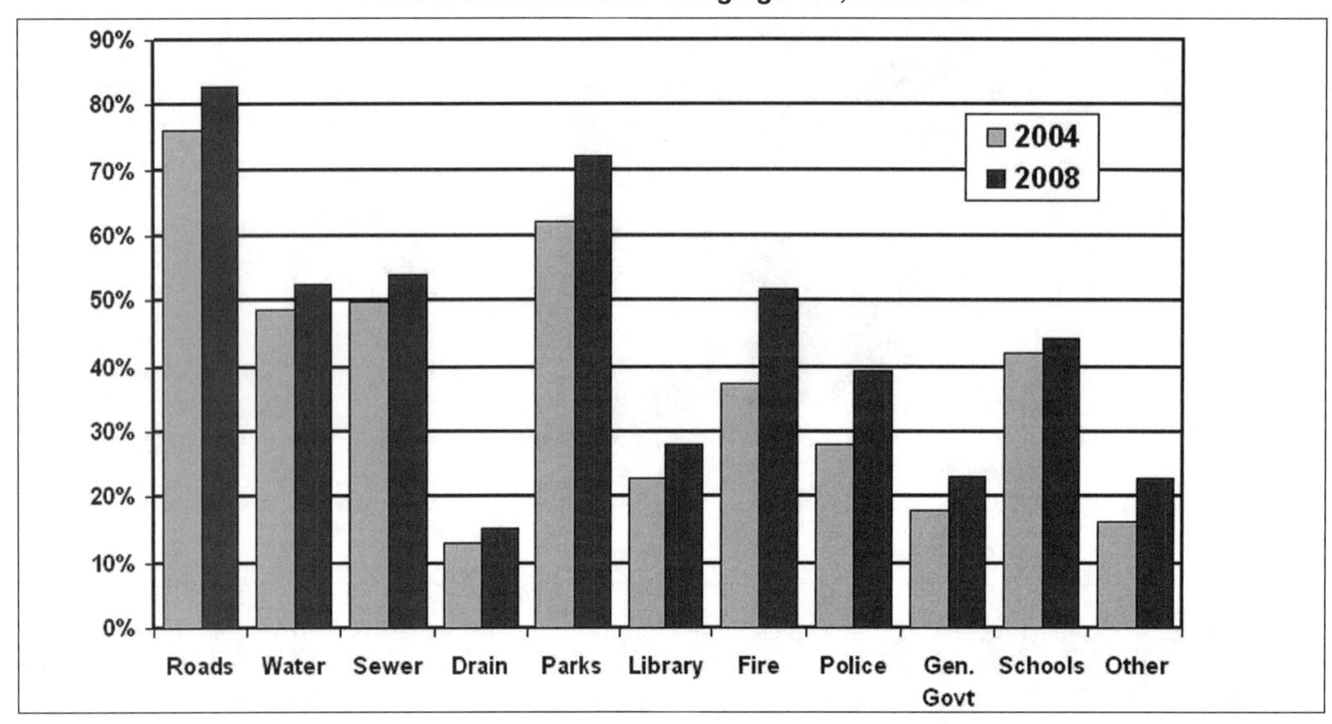

nonutility fees increased by significantly more than construction costs, which increased 18.9 percent from 2003 to 2007.[2]

FEE INCREASES, 2007–2008

More recent trends can be observed by comparing the last two surveys. The 2007 and 2008 surveys are almost identical in terms of the jurisdictions included. The only differences are that one Florida county was added, and four Florida cities were dropped because of the difficulty of getting information for them. The 279 jurisdictions included in both surveys increased their impact fees on average by about 9 percent over the last year (see Table 2-5).

The slowdown in the growth of nonutility impact fees, from an average rate of 15.2 percent over the last four years to 8.8 percent this last year, may be attributable to the housing downturn. A

Table 2-4
Average Impact Fees by Facility Type, Single-Family Unit, 2004–2008

Type of Fee	2004	2008	Increase	Percent Increase
Police	$216	$314	$98	45%
Fire	$281	$445	$164	58%
Library	$331	$383	$52	16%
General government	$425	$1,055	$630	148%
Drainage	$1,124	$1,295	$171	15%
Parks	$1,272	$1,822	$550	43%
Roads	$1,798	$3,039	$1,241	69%
Wastewater	$2,141	$2,769	$628	29%
Water	$2,187	$2,995	$808	37%
Schools	$2,837	$5,107	$2,270	80%
Total nonutility*	$4,236	$7,455	$3,219	76%
Total*	$6,090	$10,264	$4,174	69%

* Totals do not represent sum of average fees, since not all jurisdictions charge all types of fees.

Source: Duncan Associates, constant sample survey of 185 jurisdictions.

Table 2-5
Average Impact Fees by Type, Single-Family Unit, 2007–2008

Type of Fee	2007	2008	Percent Increase
Police	$359	$376	4.7%
Library	$378	$397	5.0%
Fire	$421	$455	8.1%
General government	$1,150	$1,266	10.1%
Stormwater drainage	$1,360	$1,415	4.0%
Parks	$2,484	$2,679	7.9%
Roads	$2,886	$3,088	7.0%
Sewer	$2,938	$3,141	6.9%
Water	$3,333	$3,584	7.5%
Schools	$4,382	$4,723	7.8%
Total nonutility*	$7,455	$8,108	8.8%
Total, all fee types*	$10,387	$11,276	8.6%

* Totals do not represent sum of average fees.

Source: Duncan Associates, constant sample survey of 279 jurisdictions.

few jurisdictions in hard-hit Florida, for example, lowered their fees in a vain attempt to reverse the effects of the housing crisis by stimulating residential construction.

SUMMARY

Impact fees and similar development charges are not universal; they are found primarily in the South and West, and are relatively rare in the Northeast and Midwest. Total impact fees charged in 2008 average $11,276 per single-family unit, and are significantly higher in California than in the rest of the country. School impact fees are the highest single fee for residential development, and total single-family fees are highest in three states (California, Florida, and Maryland) where school impact fees are authorized by statute and regularly imposed. The biggest fees are for roads, parks, schools, and

Figure 2-8
Increase in Single-Family Fees by Type, 2004–2008

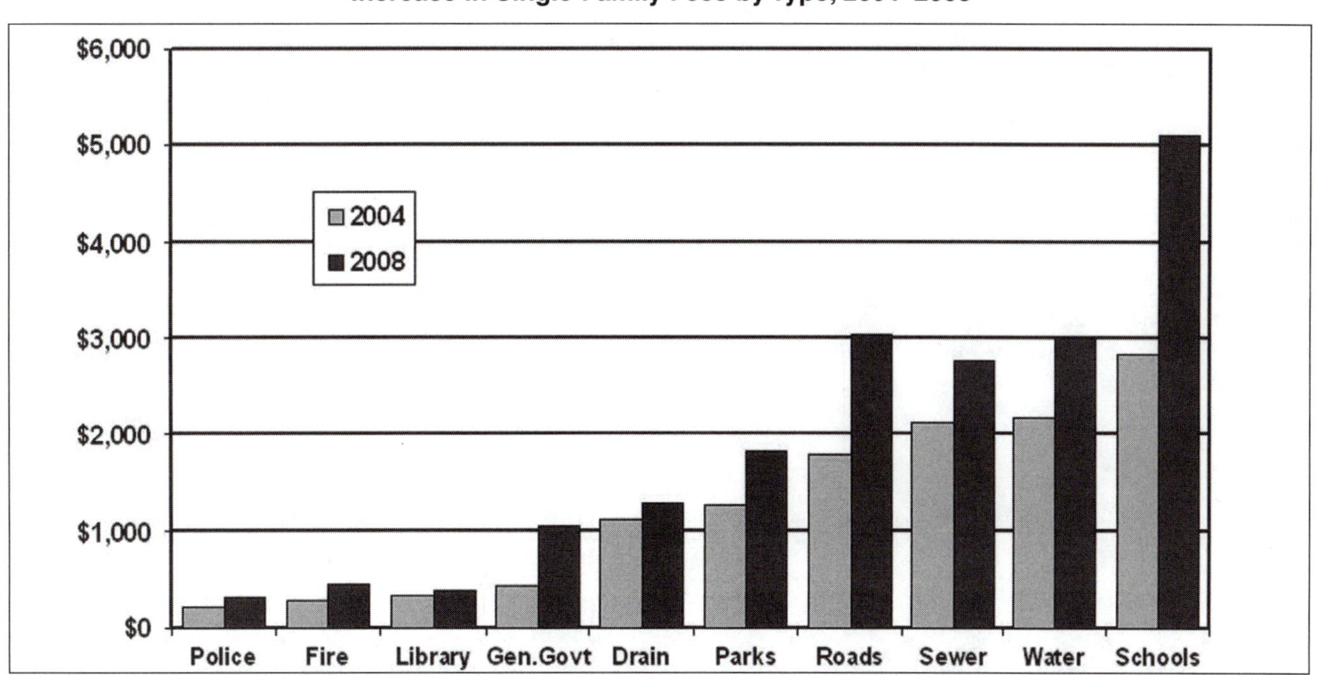

water and wastewater utilities. Much of this chapter summarizes impact fees based on a survey completed in 2008 (reported in Tables 2-1 through 2-5). Impact fee survey details for hundreds of communities across the U.S. for 2007 are reported in Table 2-6.

Over the last four years, utility fees increased at about twice the rate of inflation, while nonutility impact fees increased significantly more rapidly. On average, nonutility impact fees increased by about 76 percent, while construction costs increased by only about 18 percent. Total fees increased due to two prominent trends: adopting new fees and increasing existing fees. The increases were most pronounced in Florida where school fees, which saw the biggest increases, are becoming more common and are being aggressively increased. A more widespread factor was the increase in road impact fees, driven by increases in oil prices.

Over the last year, the pace of increase has slowed. Total nonutility fees charged by a constant sample of 279 jurisdictions went up only 8.8 percent. This more moderate rate of growth in the amount of impact fees charged may reflect the reluctance of governing bodies to increase fees or adopt new types of fees in the midst of the housing downturn.

Table 2-6
National Survey Appendix
Single-Family Unit (3-bedroom, 2,000-square-foot home on 10,000-square-foot lot at density of 4 units per acre and value of $200,000)

State	County	Jurisdiction	Total	Total Non-utility	Roads	Water	Sewer	Drain-age	Parks	Library	Fire	Police	General Govern-ment	Schools	Other
AR	Benton	Bentonville	$3,358	$762		$1,457	$1,139				$762				
AR	Benton	Lowell	$754	$504			$250				$504				
AR	Faulkner	Conway	$1,698	$1,698	$1,039				$659						
AR	Washington	Fayetteville	$1,455	$312		$308	$835				$150	$162			
AZ	Cochise	Sierra Vista	$4,604	$4,604	$1,390				$1,804	$553	$396	$461			
AZ	Gila	Payson	$6,167	$2,382	$1,235	$3,785			$647			$500			
AZ	Gila	Sedona	$9,214	$9,214	$1,804			$624	$6,249			$291	$246		
AZ	Maricopa	Avondale	$18,039	$7,295	$1,875	$5,251	$5,493		$2,501	$346	$996	$344	$929		$304
AZ	Maricopa	Buckeye	$7,412	$3,648	$319	$2,302	$1,462		$1,446	$252	$964	$417	$250		
AZ	Maricopa	Chandler	$13,587	$5,555	$2,353	$5,542	$2,490		$2,250		$362	$296			$294
AZ	Maricopa	Fountain Hills	$5,114	$5,114	$1,291				$2,192	$163	$99	$441	$928		
AZ	Maricopa	Gilbert	$14,633	$5,178	$306	$5,033	$4,422		$2,769		$883	$590	$630		
AZ	Maricopa	Glendale	$14,780	$5,790	$1,160	$6,660	$2,330		$2,072	$606	$409	$395	$847		$301
AZ	Maricopa	Goodyear	$12,709	$3,710	$824	$4,337	$4,662		$1,187	$229	$429	$323	$391		$327
AZ	Maricopa	Mesa	$5,763	$2,728		$1,011	$2,024	$158	$962	$424	$145	$226	$446		$367
AZ	Maricopa	Peoria	$17,025	$11,096	$6,588	$3,905	$2,024		$2,368	$396	$518	$392	$523		$311
AZ	Maricopa	Phoenix	$14,444	$7,304	$2,176	$4,694	$2,446		$4,018	$370	$322	$344	$74		
AZ	Maricopa	Scottsdale	$8,163	$906		$4,234	$3,023	$906							
AZ	Maricopa	Surprise	$9,050	$3,470	$885	$3,335	$2,245		$1,127	$266	$454	$424	$314		
AZ	Maricopa	Tempe	$2,824			$1,266	$1,558								
AZ	Mojave	Bullhead City	$721			$721									
AZ	Navajo	Show Low		$3,971	$687		$759	$2,525			$519	$168			
AZ	Pima	Pima County		$11,255	$6,142	$4,545		$5,113		$1,597					
AZ	Pima	Marana		$9,944	$7,613	$4,585	$2,331			$3,028					
AZ	Pima	Oro Valley		$5,114	$3,040	$3,040	$2,074								

Single-Family Unit (3-bedroom, 2,000-square-foot home on 10,000-square-foot lot at density of 4 units per acre and value of $200,000) *(continued)*

State	County	Jurisdiction	Total	Total Non-utility	Roads	Water	Sewer	Drain-age	Parks	Library	Fire	Police	General Govern-ment	Schools	Other
AZ	Pima	Tucson		$8,717	$7,189	$4,000	$1,528			$1,600		$469	$643		$477
AZ	Pinal	Apache Junction	$12,429	$9,508	$6,323	$921	$2,000		$1,801	$721		$294	$369		
AZ	Pinal	Casa Grande	$7,905	$5,516	$983		$2,389				$595	$284	$694		$2,960
AZ	Pinal	Eloy	$4,314	$1,720		$1,433	$1,161		$478	$134		$318	$790		
AZ	Pinal	Florence	$5,535	$3,765	$114	$777	$993		$1,205	$450	$483	$513	$745		$255
AZ	Pinal	Queen Creek	$14,158	$9,377	$459		$4,781		$5,142	$1,074	$655	$640	$1,407		
AZ	Yavapai	Yavapai County	$3,400	$3,400	$3,400										
AZ	Yavapai	Chino Valley	$10,089	$4,428	$2,948	$831	$4,830		$532	$144	$358	$295	$151		
AZ	Yavapai	Prescott	$11,737	$2,364	$469	$9,373			$1,116	$253	$167	$84	$275		
AZ	Yuma	Yuma	$16,130	$4,350	$1,756	$5,203	$6,577		$1,245		$110	$386	$329		$524
CA	Alameda	Fremont	$31,050	$31,050	$3,878				$23,636		$349		$3,187		
CA	Alameda	Hayward	$27,886	$19,143		$4,343	$4,400		$11,953					$5,240	$1,950
CA	Alameda	Livermore	$55,863	$29,088	$8,661	$22,775	$4,000	$1,852	$13,315					$5,260	
CA	Alameda	San Leandro	$21,147	$19,897	$1,048		$1,250		$13,168					$4,480	$1,201
CA	Contra Costa	Orinda	$20,872	$20,872	$4,718			$3,880	$12,274						
CA	El Dorado	El Dorado Co.	$38,237	$38,237	$23,101				$7,073		$2,200			$5,863	
CA	Fresno	Clovis	$19,832	$11,831	$7,486	$2,414	$5,587		$3,205		$434	$100			$606
CA	Kern	Bakersfield	$14,491	$11,691	$5,115		$2,800		$1,560					$4,480	$536
CA	Los Angeles	Lancaster	$12,103	$12,103	$2,478			$4,065	$3,211		$1,430		$119	$800	
CA	Los Angeles	Long Beach	$8,363	$8,285	$1,125		$78		$2,680					$4,480	
CA	Monterey	Salinas	$9,078	$5,678	$2,570		$3,400	$1,146	$1,962						
CA	Napa	St. Helena	$24,280	$10,740	$1,000	$7,200	$6,340	$1,280			$3,520	$4,940			
CA	Orange	Brea	$17,472	$4,927	$3,406	$12,545					$1,388	$133			
CA	Placer	Rocklin	$18,668	$18,668	$7,199			$293	$2,696			$6,380			$2,100
CA	Sacramento	Citrus Heights	$13,893	$6,793	$1,434		$7,100	varies	$1,079					$4,280	
CA	Sacramento	Elk Grove	$52,863	$33,159	$11,635	$11,004	$8,700	$9,870	$3,339	$394	$1,604	$838	$1,184		$4,295

Single-Family Unit (3-bedroom, 2,000-square-foot home on 10,000-square-foot lot at density of 4 units per acre and value of $200,000) *(continued)*

State	County	Jurisdiction	Total	Total Non-utility	Roads	Water	Sewer	Drain-age	Parks	Library	Fire	Police	General Govern-ment	Schools	Other
CA	Sacramento	Sacramento	$32,513	$24,132	$4,310	$1,281	$7,100		$6,923					$6,122	$6,777
CA	San Bernardino	Highland	$10,513	$10,513	$8,116			$732	$1,176	$107	$165	$34	$183		
CA	San Bernardino	Redlands	$6,082	$6,082	$1,838			$712		$1,032	$254	$655	$1,591		
CA	San Bernardino	Rialto	$16,649	$8,179	$2,234	$5,100	$3,370	$2,111	$2,709	$66	$390	$422	$247		
CA	San Diego	Carlsbad	$24,876	$15,948	$1,640	$7,881	$1,047	$660	$6,208						$7,440
CA	San Diego	Escondido	$30,002	$13,486	$2,193	$9,016	$7,500	$1,071	$4,129				$4,533		$1,560
CA	San Diego	San Diego	$23,620	$12,620		$6,876	$4,124								$12,620
CA	San Joaquin	Lodi	$24,125	$17,702	$3,500	$1,230	$5,193	$4,499	$6,794		$473	$484	$1,953		
CA	San Joaquin	Ripon	$55,148	$44,227	$8,994	$8,287	$2,634	$1,915	$12,888	$574	$1,372	$3,200	$2,442	$5,660	$7,182
CA	San Luis Obispo	Paso Robles	$23,242	$11,157	$4,520	$7,734	$4,351	$644	$3,750	$1,064	$746		$433		
CA	San Luis Obispo	San Luis Obispo	$46,292	$26,483	$4,496	$14,919	$4,890		$11,987						$10,000
CA	Santa Barbara	Carpinteria	$24,861	$24,861	$5,370			$2,429	$12,561		$380		$1,046	$3,075	
CA	Santa Barbara	Santa Maria	$27,407	$19,580	$9,436	$4,153	$3,674		$7,238	$962	$844	$764	$336		
CA	Santa Clara	Gilroy	$50,185	$32,784	$11,487	$5,128	$12,273	$155					$21,142		
CA	Santa Clara	Palo Alto	$41,533	$41,533	$930				$39,800	$803					
CA	Santa Cruz	Santa Cruz Co.	$12,102	$6,475	$2,475	$3,000	$2,627	$4,000							
CA	Santa Cruz	Scotts Valley	$19,877	$13,740	$4,240		$6,137	$275	$7,529	$630		$744	$322		
CA	Shasta	Redding	$21,825	$9,114	$4,601	$6,341	$6,370	$700	$3,679		$134				
CA	Solano	Vacaville	$44,482	$29,059	$8,190	$7,159	$8,264	$1,909	$3,941		$287	$639	$634	$8,486	$4,973
CA	Sonoma	Windsor	$36,224	$21,898	$7,795	$1,460	$12,866	$2,528	$9,816				$1,759		
CA	Ventura	Santa Paula	$21,974	$13,447	$2,230	$4,668	$3,859	$1,062	$5,716	$1,215	$615	$423	$990		$1,196
CA	Yolo	Davis	$23,263	$19,132	$6,149	$2,740	$1,391	$289	$4,491			$568	$2,075	$5,560	
CO	Adams	Adams Co.	$1,599	$1,599	$1,599										

Single-Family Unit (3-bedroom, 2,000-square-foot home on 10,000-square-foot lot at density of 4 units per acre and value of $200,000) *(continued)*

State	County	Jurisdiction	Total	Total Non-utility	Roads	Water	Sewer	Drain-age	Parks	Library	Fire	Police	General Govern-ment	Schools	Other
CO	Adams	Commerce City	$2,700	$2,700	$1,181				$900					$619	
CO	Boulder	Boulder	$23,326	$11,761	$1,978	$9,710	$1,855	$3,640	$2,242	$390	$209	$250	$332	$2,280	$440
CO	Eagle	Eagle Co.	$2,137	$2,137	$1,600						$537			varies	
CO	Eagle	Basalt	$11,867	$1,750	$1,750	$5,217	$4,900		varies					varies	
CO	El Paso	Colorado Springs	$16,100	$5,116		$9,323	$1,661	$1,803	$1,781					$1,532	
CO	Fremont	Canon City	$304	$304							$304				
CO	Jefferson	Jefferson Co.	$2,482	$2,482	$2,482										
CO	La Plata	Durango	$9,255	$2,153	$908	$5,582	$1,520		$300					$945	
CO	Larimer	Larimer Co.	$3,172	$3,172	$1,913				$1,259						
CO	Larimer	Loveland	$20,176	$13,104	$2,984	$4,632	$2,440	$689	$4,650	$898	$502	$590	$679	$1,382	$730
CO	Larimer	Ft. Collins	$20,943	$8,626	$2,581	$10,094	$2,223	$352	$3,336	$527	$189	$131	$239	$1,271	
CO	Mesa	Mesa Co.	$2,314	$2,314	$1,589				$150					$575	
CO	Pitkin	Pitkin Co.	$20,980	$20,980	$7,158				$13,287					$535	
CO	Weld	Weld Co.	$2,862	$2,862	$1,987			$300							$575
CO	Weld	Windsor	$17,519	$7,419	$1,993	$6,600	$3,500	$735	$4,691						
CO	Weld	Greeley	$5,433	$5,433	$1,571			$280	$3,174		$275	$133			
DE	New Castle	New Castle Co.	$9,321	$1,157			$8,164		$328	$138	$517	$62	$112		
FL	Alachua	Alachua Co.	$3,984	$2,508	$2,104	$461	$1,015		$252		$152				
FL	Brevard	Brevard Co.	$13,347	$9,187	$4,353	$1,903	$2,257			$64	$93			$4,445	$232
FL	Brevard	Cocoa	$10,133	$9,133	$4,353	$1,000				$64	$39			$4,445	$232
FL	Brevard	Melbourne	$9,454	$9,454	$3,884				$540	$64	$39		$250	$4,445	$232
FL	Brevard	Palm Bay	$9,774	$9,774	$4,098				$575	$64	$322	$38		$4,445	$232
FL	Brevard	Rockledge	$9,133	$9,133	$4,353					$64	$39			$4,445	$232
FL	Broward	Broward Co.	$2,718	$2,718	$457				$417					$1,844	
FL	Broward	Ft. Lauderdale	$4,219	$4,219					$2,375					$1,844	

Single-Family Unit (3-bedroom, 2,000-square-foot home on 10,000-square-foot lot at density of 4 units per acre and value of $200,000) *(continued)*

State	County	Jurisdiction	Total	Total Non-utility	Roads	Water	Sewer	Drain-age	Parks	Library	Fire	Police	General Govern-ment	Schools	Other
FL	Charlotte	Charlotte Co.	$8,380	$8,380	$5,080				$1,660	$160	$400	$300	$780		
FL	Citrus	Citrus Co.	$9,314	$9,314	$4,853				$723	$251	$497	$257	$625	$2,109	
FL	Clay	Clay Co.	$7,034	$7,034										$7,034	
FL	Collier	Collier Co.	$31,358	$24,428	$8,884	$3,415	$3,515		$3,299	$506	$1,195	$318	$807	$9,206	$213
FL	Dade	Miami/Dade Co.	$6,157	$6,157	$1,275				$1,912		$177	$345		$2,448	
FL	Dade	Miami	$10,547	$10,547					$6,818		$704	$164	$413	$2,448	
FL	DeSoto	DeSoto Co.	$9,212	$9,212	$2,534				$370	$163	$398	$538	$647	$4,562	
FL	Flagler	Flagler Co.	$5,307	$5,307	$1,438				$269					$3,600	
FL	Flagler	Palm Coast	$13,523	$8,613	$3,632	$2,430	$2,480		$1,196		$185			$3,600	
FL	Gilchrist	Gilchrist Co.	$3,500	$3,500	$1,750								$1,000	$750	
FL	Glades	Glades Co.	$8,143	$8,143	$3,363				$365		$93			$4,322	
FL	Hardee	Hardee Co.	$2,628	$2,628	$1,348				$292	$146	$193	$152	$349		$148
FL	Hendry	Hendry Co.	$7,591	$7,591	$2,490									$5,101	
FL	Hernando	Hernando Co.	$9,238	$9,238	$3,627				$501	$154	$229	$99	$362	$4,266	
FL	Highlands	Highlands Co.	$5,218	$5,218	$1,649				$189	$61	$190	$58		$2,901	$171
FL	Hillsborough	Hillsborough Co.	$7,428	$3,878	$1,475	$1,650	$1,900		$354		$49			$2,000	
FL	Hillsborough	Plant City	$8,543	$6,414	$2,627	$595	$1,534		$582	$538	$363	$304		$2,000	
FL	Hillsborough	Tampa	$3,581	$3,581	$1,581									$2,000	
FL	Indian River	Indian River Co.	$9,877	$9,877	$5,202				$1,463	$483	$278	$244	$206	$1,756	$245
FL	Lake	Lake Co.	$10,026	$10,026	$2,189				$222	$191	$369			$7,055	
FL	Lake	Eustis	$11,754	$8,232		$854	$2,668		$599	$293	$147	$138		$7,055	
FL	Lee	Lee Co.	$15,503	$15,503	$8,976				$1,479		$739			$4,309	
FL	Lee	Bonita Springs	$11,211	$11,211	$5,647				$872		$383			$4,309	
FL	Lee	Cape Coral	$14,287	$10,835	$3,347	$1,714	$1,738		$1,115		$575	$632		$4,309	$857
FL	Lee	Ft. Myers	$17,858	$13,869	$8,976	$2,023	$1,966				$584			$4,309	

Single-Family Unit (3-bedroom, 2,000-square-foot home on 10,000-square-foot lot at density of 4 units per acre and value of $200,000) *(continued)*

State	County	Jurisdiction	Total	Total Non-utility	Roads	Water	Sewer	Drain-age	Parks	Library	Fire	Police	General Govern-ment	Schools	Other
FL	Levy	Levy Co.	$1,249	$1,249	$1,046				$150		$53				
FL	Manatee	Manatee Co.	$15,529	$15,529	$7,013				$971		$582	$839		$6,124	
FL	Marion	Marion Co.	$5,714	$5,714	$5,462						$252				
FL	Martin	Martin Co.	$11,511	$11,511	$2,793				$2,345	$456	$346	$444	$572	$4,555	
FL	Monroe	Monroe Co.	$1,534	$1,534	$633				$340	$242	$105	$150			$64
FL	Nassau	Nassau Co.	$6,211	$6,211	$1,430				$553		$121	$150	$231	$3,726	
FL	Okaloosa	Destin	$760	$760	$471				$160	$108		$21			
FL	Orange	Orange Co.	$12,217	$12,217	$3,605				$1,206		$208	$198		$7,000	
FL	Orange	Apopka	$16,371	$10,085	$2,844	$2,444	$3,842		$241					$7,000	
FL	Orange	Maitland	$14,105	$10,315	$1,315	$900	$2,890		$2,000					$7,000	
FL	Orange	Oakland	$10,235	$9,435	$1,500	$700	$100		$350		$100	$150		$7,000	$335
FL	Orange	Ocoee	$19,388	$13,666	$3,969	$1,443	$4,279		$1,560		$636	$501		$7,000	
FL	Orange	Orlando	$12,933	$10,050	$2,900		$2,883				$150			$7,000	
FL	Orange	Winter Garden	$17,381	$14,036	$5,765	$1,310	$2,035		$671		$340	$260		$7,000	
FL	Osceola	Osceola Co.	$17,941	$17,941	$6,877				$924		$159			$9,981	
FL	Palm Beach	Palm Beach Co.	$11,368	$11,368	$4,822				$1,540	$161	$528	$171	$148	$3,998	
FL	Palm Beach	Palm Beach Gardens	$15,618	$13,562	$6,527				$3,649	$250	$559	$487	$148	$3,998	
FL	Pasco	Pasco Co.	$13,742	$11,686	$5,632	$556	$1,500		$892	$145	$420			$4,356	$241
FL	Pinellas	Pinellas Co.	$2,418	$2,066	$2,066	$352									
FL	Polk	Polk Co.	$13,415	$13,415	$6,048				$443	$197	$312	$278		$6,006	$131
FL	Polk	Lakeland	$16,269	$13,539	$6,048	$1,250	$1,480		$904		$272	$177		$6,006	$132
FL	Putnam	Putnam Co.	$7,023	$7,023	$2,290				$227		$159			$4,347	
FL	Santa Rosa	Santa Rosa Co.	$1,801	$1,801	$1,801										
FL	St. Johns	St. Johns Co.	$9,605	$9,605	$3,830				$778		$518	$194	$390	$3,895	
FL	St. Lucie	St. Lucie Co.	$8,729	$8,729	$2,027				$484	$193	$478	$183	$368	$4,996	
FL	Sarasota	Sarasota Co.	$16,954	$12,203	$5,774	$2,720	$2,031		$2,348	$380	$339	$195	$339	$2,032	$796
FL	Sarasota	North Port	$14,176	$12,036	$6,487	$860	$1,280		$2,163	$217	$639	$212	$217	$2,032	$69

Single-Family Unit (3-bedroom, 2,000-square-foot home on 10,000-square-foot lot at density of 4 units per acre and value of $200,000) *(continued)*

State	County	Jurisdiction	Total	Total Non-utility	Roads	Water	Sewer	Drain-age	Parks	Library	Fire	Police	General Govern-ment	Schools	Other
FL	Seminole	Seminole Co.	$2,635	$2,635	$1,025					$54	$172			$1,384	
FL	Seminole	Altamonte Springs	$2,651	$2,651	$607				$211	$91	$172	$186		$1,384	
FL	Seminole	Winter Springs	$9,924	$7,207	$3,167	$518	$2,199		$1,200		$700	$356	$400	$1,384	
FL	Sumter	Sumter Co.	$2,393	$2,393	$1,996						$397				
FL	Volusia	Volusia Co.	$9,108	$9,108	$2,174				$582		$287			$6,066	
FL	Volusia	Daytona Beach	$12,638	$11,019	$2,474	$697	$922		$1,376		$190	$323	$590	$6,066	
FL	Volusia	Deland	$11,386	$10,028	$2,174	$585	$773		$1,409		$82	$112	$185	$6,066	
FL	Volusia	Deltona	$11,380	$8,454	$502	$1,146	$1,780		$1,556		$214	$116		$6,066	
FL	Volusia	Edgewater	$12,898	$8,585	$1,426	$2,151	$2,162		$612		$331	$151		$6,066	
FL	Volusia	Ormond Beach	$12,595	$9,517	$2,306	$1,416	$1,662	$97	$1,048					$6,066	
FL	Volusia	Port Orange	$13,869	$10,937	$3,076	$1,457	$1,475		$1,525		$270			$6,066	
GA	Cherokee	Canton	$3,346	$3,346	$1,813				$1,054		$385	$94			
GA	Cherokee	Cherokee Co.	$1,645	$1,645	$252				$279	$212	$511	$332	$48		$11
GA	Forsyth	Forsyth Co.	$990	$990					$686	$116	$188				
GA	Fulton	Alpharetta	$1,940	$1,940	$1,131				$545		$264				
GA	Fulton	Atlanta	$1,544	$1,544	$987				$410		$114	$33			
GA	Fulton	Roswell	$2,058	$2,058	$162				$1,303		$533		$60		
HI	Honolulu	Honolulu	$1,836	$1,836	$1,836										
ID	Ada	Boise	$3,894	$3,894	$2,707				$1,187						
ID	Kootenai	Post Falls	$9,891	$2,668	$734	$1,966	$5,257		$1,818			$88			$28
IL	DeKalb	DeKalb (city)	$2,419	$2,419					$1,232					$1,187	
IL	DeKalb	Sandwich	$12,695	$5,395		$3,400	$3,900			$100	$500	$400	$1,050	$3,270	$75

Single-Family Unit (3-bedroom, 2,000-square-foot home on 10,000-square-foot lot at density of 4 units per acre and value of $200,000) *(continued)*

State	County	Jurisdiction	Total	Total Non-utility	Roads	Water	Sewer	Drain-age	Parks	Library	Fire	Police	General Govern-ment	Schools	Other
IL	DuPage	DuPage County	$624	$624	$624										
IL	Kane	Kane County	$691	$691	$691										
IN	Hamilton	Fishers	$5,150	$2,750	$1,680		$2,400		$1,070						
IN	Hamilton	Noblesville	$2,860	$2,860	$1,579				$1,281						
KS	Johnson	Lenexa	$3,794	$3,794	$2,479			$905	$410						
KS	Johnson	Olathe	$8,047	$2,902	$2,382	$2,400	$2,745		$520						
KS	Johnson	Overland Park	$2,341	$2,341	$2,341										
LA	E Baton Rouge	Baton Rouge	$2,350	$200	$200		$2,150								
LA	St. Tammany	St. Tammany Parish	$3,077	$3,077	$1,468			$1,609							
MD	Anne Arundel	Anne Arundel Co.	$4,904	$4,904	$969							$125		$3,810	
MD	Calvert	Calvert Co.	$12,950	$12,950	$3,500				$1,300					$7,800	$350
MD	Carroll	Carroll Co.	$6,836	$6,836					$533					$6,303	
MD	Charles	Charles Co.	$19,276	$11,400		$3,258	$4,618							$11,400	
MD	Frederick	Frederick Co.	$23,641	$13,341	$220	$4,300	$6,000			$823				$12,298	
MD	Harford	Harford Co.	$8,269	$8,269										$8,269	
MD	Howard	Howard Co.	$2,960	$1,760	$1,760	$600	$600								
MD	Montgomery	Montgomery Co.	$17,337	$14,283	$5,819	$1,344	$1,710							8464	
MD	Queen Anne's	Queen Anne's Co.	$7,639	$7,639					$1,033		$1,166			$5,440	
MD	St. Mary's	St. Mary's Co.	$4,500	$4,500	$450				$675					$3,375	
MO	Clay/Jackson	Kansas City	$711	$711	$711										

Single-Family Unit (3-bedroom, 2,000-square-foot home on 10,000-square-foot lot at density of 4 units per acre and value of $200,000) *(continued)*

State	County	Jurisdiction	Total	Total Non-utility	Roads	Water	Sewer	Drain-age	Parks	Library	Fire	Police	General Government	Schools	Other
MO	Jackson	Lee's Summit	$1,011	$1,011	$1,011										
MT	Gallatin	Bozeman	$7,160	$2,094	$1,904	$2,234	$2,832				$190				
NC	Chatham	Chatham Co.	$6,400	$2,900		$3,500								$2,900	
NC	Durham	Durham	$5,231	$3,155	$806	$1,161	$915		$349					$2,000	
NC	Orange	Orange Co.	$8,076	$3,450		$1,625	$3,001		$450					$3,000	
NC	Wake	Cary	$4,787	$1,243	$1,243	$1,372	$2,172								
NC	Wake	Raleigh	$5,745	$879	$418	$2,433	$2,433		$461						
NE	Lancaster	Lincoln	$4,685	$2,800	$2,466	$1,261	$624		$334						
NH	Hillsborough	Manchester	$2,923	$2,923							$190			$2,733	
NH	Merrimack	Concord	$4,362	$4,362	$1,722				$840					$1,800	
NH	Rockingham	Salem	$5,232	$5,232											
NH	Rockingham	Fremont	$3,761	$3,761										$3,761	
NM	Bernalillo	Albuquerque	$12,023	$7,786	$3,662	$2,421	$1,816	$1,290	$2,420			$414			
NM	Bernalillo	Bernalillo Co.	$2,962	$2,962	$1,309			$1,063	$305		$196				$89
NM	Dona Ana	Las Cruces	$3,269	$249		$1,855	$1,165		$249						
NM	Lincoln	Ruidoso	$4,508			$2,674	$1,834								
NM	Sandoval	Rio Rancho	$12,799	$7,890	$2,691	$2,611	$2,298	$3,570	$1,258		$339				$32
NM	Santa Fe	Santa Fe	$5,608	$2,860	$1,527	$2,013	$735		$1,128		$165	$40			
NM	Santa Fe	Santa Fe County	$550	$550							$550				
NM	Valencia	Los Lunas	$4,548	$2,171		$898	$1,479		$2,171						
NV	Churchill	Churchill County	$4,200	$4,200	$2,300				$1,000					$900	
NV	Clark	Las Vegas	$4,124	$1,546	$700		$2,578		$720						$126
NV	Clark	Mesquite	$3,432	$2,108	$982		$1,324		$1,000						$126

Single-Family Unit (3-bedroom, 2,000-square-foot home on 10,000-square-foot lot at density of 4 units per acre and value of $200,000) *(continued)*

State	County	Jurisdiction	Total	Total Non-utility	Roads	Water	Sewer	Drain-age	Parks	Library	Fire	Police	General Govern-ment	Schools	Other
NV	Placer	Truckee	$2,381	$2,381	$2,381										
NV	Washoe	Reno	$2,935	$2,935	$1,935				$1,000						
OH	Butler	Middletown	$500	$500					$500						
OH	Delaware	Delaware (city)	$13,103	$2,068		$5,650	$5,385		$1,226		$314	$162	$366		
OH	Warren	Hamilton Township	$6,153	$6,153	$3,964				$1,648		$335	$206			
OK	Cleveland	Moore	$1,347	$647	$647		$700								
OR	Clackamas	Clackamas Co.	$10,529	$8,074	$5,273	$205	$2,250		$2,801						
OR	Clackamas	West Linn	$20,641	$13,381	$4,897	$4,628	$2,632	$455	$8,029						
OR	Deschutes	Bend	$13,440	$7,906	$4,356	$3,496	$2,038		$3,550						
OR	Josephine	Grants Pass	$14,283	$9,146	$6,182	$2,597	$2,540	$412	$2,552						
OR	Lane	Eugene	$7,148	$3,420	$1,582	$2,167	$1,561	$493	$1,345						
OR	Lane	Springfield	$2,976	$1,923	$1,058		$1,053	$865							
OR	Marion	Salem	$12,216	$5,227	$1,815	$4,184	$2,805	$449	$2,963						
OR	Marion	Silverton	$14,664	$6,285	$3,705	$3,987	$4,392	$1,375	$1,205						
OR	Multnomah	Portland	$10,771	$5,726	$1,995	$1,787	$3,258	$614	$3,117						
OR	Washington	Tigard	$5,464	$3,062	$3,062	$2,402									
OR	Washington	Washington Co.	$4,650	$1,850	$1,350		$2,800	$500							
PA	Montgomery	Towamencin Twp.	$2,220	$2,220	$2,220		$1,711	$1,610	$1,000						$250
SC	Beaufort	Beaufort Co.	$1,529	$1,529	varies				$471	$553	$505				
SC	Beaufort	Hilton Head	$7,436	$1,996	$816	$2,400	$3,040		$627	$553					
SC	Berkeley	Mt. Pleasant	$6,581	$1,850	$958	$1,868	$2,863		$358		$231	$69			$234
TN	Rutherford	La Vergne	$5,045	$2,695	$884	$500	$1,850		$311						$1,500

Single-Family Unit (3-bedroom, 2,000-square-foot home on 10,000-square-foot lot at density of 4 units per acre and value of $200,000) *(continued)*

State	County	Jurisdiction	Total	Total Non-utility	Roads	Water	Sewer	Drain-age	Parks	Library	Fire	Police	General Government	Schools	Other
TN	Rutherford	Smyrna	$4,124	$4,124	$1,802				$253		$569				$1,500
TN	Sumner	Portland	$3,065	$3,065					$1,228					$1,400	$437
TN	Sumner	White House	$2,645	$2,645	$381				$396		$186	$282		$1,400	
TN	Williamson	Franklin	$7,817	$4,537	$1,617	$1,185	$2,095								$2,920
TN	Williamson	Nolensville	$6,912	$6,912	$2,912										$4,000
TX	Brazos	College Station	$1,387	$556		$550	$281		$556						
TX	Collin	Allen	$2,350	$650	$650	$1,200	$500								
TX	Collin	McKinney	$3,700	$2,300	$2,300	$938	$462								
TX	Denton	Denton	$4,887			$3,155	$1,732								
TX	Tarrant	Arlington	$2,633	$1,773	$670	$480	$380		$1,103						
TX	Tarrant	Colleyville	$5,321	$2,187	$2,187	$2,491	$643								
TX	Tarrant	Ft. Worth	$840			$616	$224								
TX	Williamson	Georgetown	$2,778			$1,531	$1,247								
UT	Cache	Logan	$2,451	$1,258	$669	$258	$935	$77			$118	$34			$360
UT	Davis	Layton	$6,132	$5,532	$2,399	$600		$759	$1,873		$501				
UT	Salt Lake	Draper	$8,841	$7,428	$1,749	$1,413		$1,161	$3,990		$310	$218			
UT	Salt Lake	Sandy City	$5,688	$4,159		$1,529		$905	$3,018		$165	$71			
UT	Salt Lake	West Jordan City	$10,964	$5,354	$1,891	$3,266	$2,344	$1,478	$1,633		$247	$105			
UT	Salt Lake	West Valley City	$2,565	$2,565	$846			$181	$1,381		$91	$66			
UT	Tooele	Tooele	$9,825	$3,990	$1,515	$4,320	$1,515		$2,125			$350			
UT	Utah	Provo	$6,413	$4,622	$887	$684	$1,107	$801	$2,934						
VA	Loudoun	Leesburg	$11,459			$4,481	$6,978								
VA	Stafford	Stafford Co.	$45,251	$38,151	$13,621	$3,600	$3,500		$5,049	$626	$807			$446	$17,602
VT	Chittenden	Burlington	$4,762	$4,762	$354				$1,346	$836	$404	$80			$1,742

Single-Family Unit (3-bedroom, 2,000-square-foot home on 10,000-square-foot lot at density of 4 units per acre and value of $200,000) *(continued)*

State	County	Jurisdiction	Total	Total Non-utility	Roads	Water	Sewer	Drain-age	Parks	Library	Fire	Police	General Government	Schools	Other
VT	Chittenden	Williston	$11,898	$11,898	$303				$827					$10,768	
WA	Clark	Vancouver	$8,149	$8,149	$1,883				$2,084					$4,181	
WA	Cowlitz	Woodland	$12,446	$5,396		$2,800	$4,250		$1,116		$1,530			$2,750	
WA	King	King Co.	$5,574	$5,574	$1,715									$3,859	
WA	King	Bellevue	$415	$415	$415										
WA	King	Bothell	$6,903	$3,438	$2,093	$2,020	$1,445		$1,345						
WA	King	Issaquqh	$12,497	$12,497	$2,444				$3,147		$622	$62	$86	$6,136	
WA	King	Kirkland	$11,801	$2,059	$966	$7,882	$1,860	$481	$612						
WA	Kitsap	Kitsap Co.	$2,165	$2,165	$571				$539					$1,055	
WA	Pierce	Pierce Co.	$4,849	$4,849	$1,759				$325					$2,765	
WA	Skagit	Anacortes	$12,315	$2,923	$900	$2,800	$6,592	$1,408	$615						
WA	Skagit	Burlington	$5,836	$3,228	$188		$2,608		$500		$150			$2,390	
WA	Snohomish	Snohomish Co.	$7,329	$7,329	$2,369				$544					$4,416	
WA	Thurston	Olympia	$9,099	$9,099	$1,896				$1,843		$318			$5,042	
WA	Thurston	Tumwater	$9,443	$5,994	$1,083		$3,449		$564		$203			$4,145	
WA	Whatcom	Bellingham	$16,025	$7,926	$1,229	$4,663	$3,436	$678	$4,808					$1,211	
WV	Jefferson	Jefferson Co.	$12,144	$12,144					$751		$603	$135		$10,655	
WI	Dane	Fitchburg	$4,775	$4,775					$4,275		$500				
WI	Jefferson	Oconomowoc	$4,590	$1,646	$94	$808	$2,136		$1,188		$198	$166			
WI	Ozaukee	Cedarburg	$5,512	$3,677		$1,299	$536		$2,215	$667		$796			
WI	St. Croix	Hudson	$2,839	$1,297		$1,177	$365	$785		$512					
		National Average	$10,496	$7,530	$2,867	$3,232	$2,885	$1,360	$2,497	$378	$418	$355	$1,118	$4,463	$1,448
		Sample Size	283	276	234	142	150	60	207	69	140	103	70	117	60
		National Avg w/o CA	$8,030	$5,772	$2,431	$2,535	$2,389	$931	$1,511	$326	$370	$270	$456	$4,408	$532
		Sample Size w/o CA	245	238	198	119	122	36	175	59	123	89	50	104	46

Single-Family Unit (3-bedroom, 2,000-square-foot home on 10,000-square-foot lot at density of 4 units per acre and value of $200,000) *(continued)*

State	County	Jurisdiction	Total	Total Non-utility	Roads	Water	Sewer	Drain-age	Parks	Library	Fire	Police	General Govern-ment	Schools	Other
State Average Fees (sample size)															
AR		4	$1,816	$819	$1,039	$883	$741	n/a	$659	n/a	$472	$162	n/a	n/a	n/a
AZ		31	$9,321	$5,072	$2,193	$3,221	$3,074	$563	$1,994	$385	$464	$387	$544	n/a	$612
CA		38	$26,392	$18,535	$5,267	$6,837	$5,047	$2,003	$7,890	$685	$768	$895	$2,775	$4,907	$4,460
CO		17	$9,598	$5,524	$2,218	$7,308	$2,586	$1,114	$3,252	$605	$336	$276	$417	$1,142	$582
DE		1	$9,321	$1,157	n/a	n/a	$8,164	n/a	$328	$138	$517	$62	$112	n/a	n/a
FL		71	$9,939	$8,657	$3,395	$1,354	$2,014	$97	$1,103	$206	$319	$255	$430	$4,574	$268
GA		6	$1,921	$1,921	$869	n/a	n/a	n/a	$713	$164	$333	$153	$54	n/a	$11
HI		1	$1,836	$1,836	$1,836	n/a	n/a	n/a	n/a	n/a	n/a	n/a	n/a	n/a	n/a
ID		2	$6,893	$3,281	$1,721	$1,966	$5,257	n/a	$1,503	n/a	n/a	$88	n/a	n/a	$28
IL		4	$4,107	$2,282	$658	$3,400	$3,900	n/a	$1,232	$100	$500	$400	$1,050	$2,229	$75
IN		2	$4,005	$2,805	$1,630	n/a	$2,400	n/a	$1,176	n/a	n/a	n/a	n/a	n/a	n/a
KS		3	$4,727	$3,012	$2,401	$2,400	$2,745	$905	$465	n/a	n/a	n/a	n/a	n/a	n/a
LA		2	$2,714	$1,639	$834	n/a	$2,150	$1,609	n/a	n/a	n/a	n/a	n/a	n/a	n/a
MD		10	$10,831	$8,588	$2,120	$2,376	$3,232	n/a	$885	$823	$1,166	$125	n/a	$7,462	$350
MO		2	$861	$861	$861	n/a	n/a	n/a	n/a	n/a	n/a	n/a	n/a	n/a	n/a
MT		1	$7,160	$2,094	$1,904	$2,234	$2,832	n/a	n/a	n/a	$190	n/a	n/a	n/a	n/a
NC		5	$6,048	$2,325	$822	$2,018	$2,130	n/a	$420	n/a	n/a	n/a	n/a	$2,633	n/a
NE		1	$4,685	$2,800	$2,466	$1,261	$624	n/a	$334	n/a	n/a	n/a	n/a	n/a	n/a
NH		4	$4,070	$4,070	$1,722	n/a	n/a	n/a	$840	n/a	$190	n/a	n/a	$2,765	n/a
NM		8	$5,783	$3,495	$2,297	$2,079	$1,555	$1,974	$1,255	n/a	$313	$227	n/a	n/a	$60
NV		5	$3,414	$2,634	$1,660	n/a	$1,951	n/a	$930	n/a	n/a	n/a	n/a	$900	$126
OH		3	$6,585	$2,907	$3,964	$5,650	$5,385	n/a	$1,125	n/a	$325	$184	$366	n/a	n/a
OK		1	$1,347	$647	$647	n/a	$700	n/a	n/a	n/a	n/a	n/a	n/a	n/a	n/a
OR		11	$10,617	$6,000	$3,207	$2,828	$2,533	$645	$3,195	n/a	n/a	n/a	n/a	n/a	n/a
PA		1	$2,220	$2,220	$2,220	n/a	$1,711	$1,610	$1,000	n/a	n/a	n/a	n/a	n/a	$250
SC		3	$5,182	$1,792	$887	$2,134	$2,952	n/a	$485	$553	$368	$69	n/a	n/a	$234
TN		6	$4,935	$3,996	$1,519	$843	$1,973	n/a	$547	n/a	$378	$282	n/a	$1,400	$2,071
TX		8	$2,987	$1,493	$1,452	$1,370	$684	n/a	$830	n/a	n/a	n/a	n/a	n/a	n/a
UT		8	$6,610	$4,364	$1,422	$1,724	$1,475	$766	$2,422	n/a	$239	$141	n/a	n/a	$360

Single-Family Unit (3-bedroom, 2,000-square-foot home on 10,000-square-foot lot at density of 4 units per acre and value of $200,000) *(continued)*

State	County	Jurisdiction	Total	Total Non-utility	Roads	Water	Sewer	Drain-age	Parks	Library	Fire	Police	General Govern-ment	Schools	Other
State Average Fees (sample size)															
VA		2	$28,355	$38,151	$13,621	$4,041	$5,239	n/a	$5,049	$626	$807	n/a	$446	$17,602	n/a
VT		2	$8,330	$8,330	$329	n/a	n/a	n/a	$1,087	$836	$404	$80	n/a	$6,255	n/a
WA		15	$8,323	$5,403	$1,394	$4,033	$3,377	$856	$1,388	n/a	$565	$62	$86	$3,450	n/a
WV		1	$12,144	$12,144	n/a	n/a	n/a	n/a	$751	n/a	$603	$135	n/a	$10,655	n/a
WI		4	$4,429	$2,849	$94	$1,095	$1,012	$785	$2,559	$589	$349	$481	n/a	n/a	n/a

Multifamily Unit (2-bedroom, 1,000-square-foot unit, density of 12 units per acre; $100,000 value; 7 2-inch water meters (2 for irrigation) for 240-unit complex)

State	County	Jurisdiction	Total	Total Non-utility	Roads	Water	Sewer	Drain-age	Parks	Library	Fire	Police	General Govern-ment	Schools	Other
AR	Benton	Bentonville	$1,748	$548		$340	$860				$548				
AR	Benton	Lowell	$415	$373			$42				$373				
AR	Faulkner	Conway	$1,218	$1,218	$771				$447						
AR	Washington	Fayetteville	$1,124	$312		$219	$593				$150	$162			
AZ	Cochise	Sierra Vista	$3,196	$0	$976				$1,246	$382	$274	$318			
AZ	Gila	Payson	$3,118	$2,235	$1,235	$883			$1,000						
AZ	Gila	Sedona	$7,310	$7,310	$1,267			$234	$5,350			$249	$210		
AZ	Maricopa	Avondale	$7,308	$5,167	$1,137	$1,225	$916		$1,970	$273	$785	$271	$731		
AZ	Maricopa	Buckeye	$3,179	$2,679	$166	$347	$153		$1,092	$190	$728	$315	$188		
AZ	Maricopa	Chandler	$8,191	$3,792	$1,546	$2,934	$1,465		$1,294	$0	$362	$296	$294		
AZ	Maricopa	Fountain Hills	$4,588	$4,588	$765				$2,192	$163	$99	$441	$928		
AZ	Maricopa	Gilbert	$10,662	$4,700	$215	$2,957	$3,005		$2,382		$883	$590	$630		
AZ	Maricopa	Glendale	$5,185	$3,898	$591	$1,030	$257		$1,555	$455	$307	$297	$635		$58
AZ	Maricopa	Goodyear	$4,440	$3,255	$571	$670	$515		$1,104	$213	$399	$300	$365		$303
AZ	Maricopa	Mesa	$3,685	$1,820		$576	$1,289	$84	$683	$301	$103	$160	$291		$198
AZ	Maricopa	Peoria	$8,056	$7,264	$4,626	$584	$208		$1,386	$232	$303	$229	$306		$182
AZ	Maricopa	Phoenix	$4,971	$4,239	$760	$299	$433	$2,198	$989	$120	$111	$49	$12		

Multifamily Unit (2-bedroom, 1,000-square-foot unit, density of 12 units per acre; $100,000 value; 7 2-inch water meters (2 for irrigation) for 240-unit complex) *(continued)*

State	County	Jurisdiction	Total	Total Non-utility	Roads	Water	Sewer	Drain-age	Parks	Library	Fire	Police	General Govern-ment	Schools	Other
AZ	Maricopa	Scottsdale	$5,253	$302		$2,428	$2,523	$302							
AZ	Maricopa	Surprise	$3,367	$2,613	$437	$513	$241		$948	$224	$382	$357	$265		
AZ	Maricopa	Tempe	$2,854			$1,266	$1,588								
AZ	Mojave	Bullhead City	$596			$596									
AZ	Navajo	Show Low	$3,302	$544		$759	$1,999		$411	$133					
AZ	Pima	Pima County	$5,761	$4,909	$3,409		$852		$1,500						
AZ	Pima	Marana	$8,157	$7,613	$4,585	$544			$3,028						
AZ	Pima	Oro Valley	$2,838	$2,280	$2,280	$558									
AZ	Pima	Tucson	$4,332	$3,975	$2,000	$357			$800		$346	$476			$353
AZ	Pinal	Apache Junction	$7,349	$7,190	$4,440	$107	$52		$1,555	$622		$254	$319		
AZ	Pinal	Casa Grande	$3,928	$3,671	$494		$257				$420	$199	$489		$2,069
AZ	Pinal	Eloy	$1,572	$1,246		$210	$116		$346	$97		$231	$572		
AZ	Pinal	Florence	$4,991	$3,221	$57	$777	$993		$1,032	$385	$414	$440	$638		$255
AZ	Pinal	Queen Creek	$6,689	$6,169	$302		$520		$3,383	$706	$431	$421	$926		
AZ	Yavapai	Yavapai County	$3,400	$3,400	$3,400										
AZ	Yavapai	Chino Valley	$3,992	$3,057	$1,577	$130	$805		$532	$144	$358	$295	$151		
AZ	Yavapai	Prescott	$14,021	$2,364	$469	$11,657			$1,116	$253	$167	$84	$275		
AZ	Yuma	Yuma	$5,159	$3,254	$1,209	$809	$1,096		$981		$87	$305	$259		$413
CA	Alameda	Fremont	$21,092	$21,092	$3,007				$15,732		$231		$2,122		
CA	Alameda	Hayward	$18,613	$13,683		$1,013	$3,917		$9,653					$2,620	$1,410
CA	Alameda	Livermore	$27,923	$19,542	$5,766	$5,314	$3,067	$936	$10,210					$2,630	
CA	Alameda	San Leandro	$16,964	$15,944	$1,048		$1,020		$11,510					$2,240	$1,146
CA	Contra Costa	Orinda	$13,551	$13,551	$2,942			$1,940	$8,669						

Multifamily Unit (2-bedroom, 1,000-square-foot unit, density of 12 units per acre; $100,000 value; 7 2-inch water meters (2 for irrigation) for 240-unit complex) *(continued)*

State	County	Jurisdiction	Total	Total Non-utility	Roads	Water	Sewer	Drain-age	Parks	Library	Fire	Police	General Govern-ment	Schools	Other
CA	El Dorado	El Dorado Co.	$26,168	$26,168	$15,064				$7,073		$1,100			$2,931	
CA	Fresno	Clovis	$12,025	$10,531	$6,238	$563	$931		$3,205		$434	$100			$554
CA	Kern	Bakersfield	$8,216	$6,434	$2,455		$1,782		$1,560					$2,240	$179
CA	Los Angeles	Lancaster	$8,538	$8,538	$2,311			$2,032	$2,961		$715		$119	$400	
CA	Los Angeles	Long Beach	$5,513	$5,435	$1,125		$78		$2,070					$2,240	
CA	Monterey	Salinas	$6,039	$3,100	$1,028		$2,939	$764	$1,308						
CA	Napa	St. Helena	$12,140	$5,370	$500	$3,600	$3,170	$640				$1,760	$2,470		
CA	Orange	Brea	$7,203	$4,276	$2,756	$2,927					$1,388	$133			
CA	Placer	Rocklin	$11,947	$11,947	$4,490			$116	$2,217				$3,727		$1,397
CA	Sacramento	Citrus Heights	$4,118	$4,118	$1,313			varies	$665				$2,140		
CA	Sacramento	Elk Grove	$37,946	$20,817	$6,898	$11,004	$6,125	$6,606	$2,465	$262	$1,097	$558	$791		$2,141
CA	Sacramento	Sacramento	$21,730	$16,135	$3,510	$270	$5,325		$4,455					$3,061	$5,109
CA	San Bernardino	Highland	$7,251	$7,251	$5,411			$261	$1,090	$99	$173	$34	$183		
CA	San Bernardino	Redlands	$5,135	$5,135	$1,299			$377		$1,032	$181	$655	$1,591		
CA	San Bernardino	Rialto	$10,057	$5,894	$1,546	$793	$3,370	$532	$2,116	$52	$413	$988	$247		
CA	San Diego	Carlsbad	$15,133	$13,644	$960	$1,314	$175	$220	$5,025						$7,440
CA	San Diego	Escondido	$17,424	$10,404	$1,314	$1,395	$5,625	$428	$4,129				$4,533		
CA	San Diego	San Diego	$13,640	$6,310		$3,206	$4,124								$6,310
CA	San Joaquin	Lodi	$21,286	$14,662	$3,558	$1,431	$5,193	$1,500	$6,341		$680	$761	$1,823		
CA	San Joaquin	Ripon	$32,989	$25,817	$4,647	$5,525	$1,647	$764	$8,056	$358	$915	$2,000	$1,866	$2,830	$4,381
CA	San Luis Obispo	Paso Robles	$20,503	$8,418	$2,974	$7,734	$4,351	$212	$3,245	$921	$633		$433		
CA	San Luis Obispo	San Luis Obispo	$33,103	$17,255	$3,334	$11,935	$3,913		$8,921						$5,000
CA	Santa Barbara	Carpinteria	$16,096	$16,096	$3,539			$864	$9,498		$380		$791	$1,025	

Multifamily Unit (2-bedroom, 1,000-square-foot unit, density of 12 units per acre; $100,000 value; 7 2-inch water meters (2 for irrigation) for 240-unit complex) *(continued)*

State	County	Jurisdiction	Total	Total Non-utility	Roads	Water	Sewer	Drain-age	Parks	Library	Fire	Police	General Government	Schools	Other
CA	Santa Barbara	Santa Maria	$18,117	$12,506	$5,216	$2,298	$3,313		$5,837	$481	$422	$382	$168		
CA	Santa Clara	Gilroy	$36,025	$27,309	$9,311	$2,074	$6,642	$88					$17,910		
CA	Santa Clara	Palo Alto	$28,400	$28,400	$930				$26,945	$525					
CA	Santa Cruz	Santa Cruz Co.	$9,360	$3,733	$1,733	$3,000	$2,627	$2,000							
CA	Santa Cruz	Scotts Valley	$14,570	$10,130	$2,516		$4,440	$138	$5,863	$547		$744	$322		
CA	Shasta	Redding	$19,144	$6,433	$3,128	$6,341	$6,370	$344	$2,868		$93				
CA	Solano	Vacaville	$28,817	$19,408	$5,077	$2,798	$6,611	$1,627	$2,710		$98	$557	$392	$4,243	$4,704
CA	Sonoma	Windsor	$24,819	$15,674	$5,162	$193	$8,952	$2,528	$6,771				$1,213		
CA	Ventura	Santa Paula	$21,005	$12,178	$1,489	$4,833	$3,994	$476	$5,918	$1,258	$454	$355	$990		$1,238
CA	Yolo	Davis	$14,600	$12,167	$3,769	$1,472	$961	$83	$3,428			$491	$1,616	$2,780	
CO	Adams	Adams Co.	$983	$983	$983										
CO	Adams	Commerce City	$1,191	$1,191	$726				$327				$138		
CO	Boulder	Boulder	$15,912	$6,657	$1,194	$7,770	$1,485	$1,820	$1,496	$260	$139	$166	$222	$1,140	$220
CO	Eagle	Eagle Co.	$1,646	$1,646	$1,109						$537		varies		
CO	Eagle	Basalt	$4,420	$2,260	$250	$2,160			varies				$2,010		
CO	El Paso	Colorado Springs	$10,960	$2,233		$7,066	$1,661	$601	$1,264				$368		
CO	Fremont	Canon City	$304	$304							$304				
CO	Jefferson	Jefferson Co.	$2,064	$2,064	$2,064										
CO	La Plata	Durango	$8,264	$1,162	$567	$5,582	$1,520		$300				$295		
CO	Larimer	Larimer Co.	$2,145	$2,145	$1,326				$819						
CO	Larimer	Loveland	$15,192	$11,185	$1,940	$1,755	$2,252	$250	$4,650	$898	$502	$590	$679	$946	$730
CO	Larimer	Ft. Collins	$12,417	$5,833	$1,662	$5,001	$1,583	$128	$2,467	$390	$140	$96	$177	$773	
CO	Mesa	Mesa Co.	$1,825	$1,825	$1,100				$150				$575		
CO	Pitkin	Pitkin Co.	$13,464	$13,464	$4,501				$8,858				$105		
CO	Weld	Weld Co.	$2,252	$2,252	$1,377			$300							$575

Multifamily Unit (2-bedroom, 1,000-square-foot unit, density of 12 units per acre; $100,000 value; 7 2-inch water meters (2 for irrigation) for 240-unit complex) *(continued)*

State	County	Jurisdiction	Total	Total Non-utility	Roads	Water	Sewer	Drain-age	Parks	Library	Fire	Police	General Govern-ment	Schools	Other
CO	Weld	Windsor	$8,009	$6,339	$1,381	$1,211	$459	$267	$4,691						
CO	Weld	Greeley	$3,790	$3,790	$1,082			$202	$2,221		$192	$93			
DE	New Castle	New Castle Co.	$6,025	$762			$5,263		$225	$95	$322	$43	$77		
FL	Alachua	Alachua Co.	$1,254	$1,254	$1,052				$126		$76				
FL	Brevard	Brevard Co.	$5,427	$5,427	$2,381					$38	$53			$2,794	$161
FL	Brevard	Cocoa	$6,526	$5,726	$2,677	$800				$38	$34			$2,794	$183
FL	Brevard	Melbourne	$6,185	$6,185	$2,463				$450	$38	$34		$223	$2,794	$183
FL	Brevard	Palm Bay	$6,338	$6,338	$2,701				$361	$38	$233	$28		$2,794	$183
FL	Brevard	Rockledge	$5,726	$5,726	$2,677					$38	$34			$2,794	$183
FL	Broward	Broward Co.	$2,135	$2,135	$275				$299					$1,561	
FL	Broward	Ft. Lauderdale	$3,436	$3,436					$1,875					$1,561	
FL	Charlotte	Charlotte Co.	$4,190	$4,190	$2,540				$830	$80	$200	$150	$390		
FL	Citrus	Citrus Co.	$7,900	$7,900	$3,133				$473	$173	$339	$178	$497	$3,107	
FL	Clay	Clay Co.	$3,236	$3,236										$3,236	
FL	Collier	Collier Co.	$20,061	$13,131	$6,210	$3,415	$3,515		$2,409	$368	$642	$172	$410	$2,862	$58
FL	Dade	Miami/Dade Co.	$4,184	$4,184	$960				$1,162		$187	$345		$1,530	
FL	Dade	Miami	$4,702	$4,702					$3,959		$409	$95	$239		
FL	DeSoto	DeSoto Co.	$2,713	$2,713	$1,412				$177	$78	$191	$257	$310	$288	
FL	Flagler	Flagler Co.	$2,600	$2,600	$1,400				$269					$931	
FL	Flagler	Palm Coast	$5,394	$4,414	$2,102	$567	$413		$1,196		$185			$931	
FL	Gilchrist	Gilchrist Co.	$3,500	$3,500	$1,750								$1,000	$750	
FL	Glades	Glades Co.	$5,524	$5,524	$2,369				$339		$64			$2,752	
FL	Hardee	Hardee Co.	$1,857	$1,857	$925				$111	$121	$161	$126	$290		$123
FL	Hendry	Hendry Co.	$5,922	$5,922	$1,729									$4,193	

Multifamily Unit (2-bedroom, 1,000-square-foot unit, density of 12 units per acre; $100,000 value; 7 2-inch water meters (2 for irrigation) for 240-unit complex) *(continued)*

State	County	Jurisdiction	Total	Total Non-utility	Roads	Water	Sewer	Drain-age	Parks	Library	Fire	Police	General Govern-ment	Schools	Other
FL	Hernando	Hernando Co.	$6,919	$6,919	$2,498				$395	$122	$181	$78	$285	$3,360	
FL	Highlands	Highlands Co.	$3,505	$3,505	$1,170				$131	$42	$131	$39		$1,874	$119
FL	Hillsborough	Hillsborough Co.	$4,853	$2,698	$1,022	$825	$1,330		$230		$49			$1,397	
FL	Hillsborough	Plant City	$6,576	$5,335	$2,415	$127	$1,114		$503	$486	$308	$226		$1,397	
FL	Hillsborough	Tampa	$2,212	$2,212	$815									$1,397	
FL	Indian River	Indian River Co.	$5,073	$5,073	$2,842				$844	$285	$176	$148	$121	$500	$157
FL	Lake	Lake Co.	$6,216	$6,216	$1,408				$171	$146	$231			$4,260	
FL	Lake	Eustis	$8,024	$5,102		$708	$2,214		$428	$210	$105	$99		$4,260	
FL	Lee	Lee Co.	$9,686	$9,686	$6,297				$1,109		$576			$1,704	
FL	Lee	Bonita Springs	$6,397	$6,397	$3,913				$539		$241			$1,704	
FL	Lee	Cape Coral	$8,984	$6,430	$2,347	$1,268	$1,286		$1,115		$575	$632		$1,704	$57
FL	Lee	Ft. Myers	$7,637	$4,218	$2,059	$1,734	$1,685				$455			$1,704	
FL	Levy	Levy Co.	$911	$911	$734				$124		$53				
FL	Manatee	Manatee Co.	$7,445	$7,445	$5,267				$592		$511	$511		$564	
FL	Marion	Marion Co.	$3,259	$3,259	$3,047						$212				
FL	Martin	Martin Co.	$11,066	$11,066	$2,688				$2,255	$438	$333	$428	$550	$4,374	
FL	Monroe	Monroe Co.	$1,331	$1,331	$430				$340	$242	$105	$150			$64
FL	Nassau	Nassau Co.	$5,596	$5,596	$984				$431		$110	$136	$210	$3,726	
FL	Okaloosa	Destin	$781	$781	$577				$113	$76		$15			
FL	Orange	Orange Co.	$7,448	$7,448	$2,527				$869		$182	$63		$3,807	
FL	Orange	Apopka	$12,331	$6,045	$1,997	$2,444	$3,842		$241					$3,807	
FL	Orange	Maitland	$5,398	$4,707	$794	$209	$482				$106			$3,807	
FL	Orange	Oakland	$7,042	$6,242	$1,500	$700	$100		$350		$100	$150		$3,807	$335
FL	Orange	Ocoee	$14,019	$9,253	$2,749	$1,202	$3,564		$1,560		$636	$501		$3,807	
FL	Orange	Orlando	$8,227	$5,964	$2,037		$2,263				$120			$3,807	

Multifamily Unit (2-bedroom, 1,000-square-foot unit, density of 12 units per acre; $100,000 value; 7 2-inch water meters (2 for irrigation) for 240-unit complex) *(continued)*

State	County	Jurisdiction	Total	Total Non-utility	Roads	Water	Sewer	Drain-age	Parks	Library	Fire	Police	General Govern-ment	Schools	Other
FL	Osceola	Osceola Co.	$11,531	$11,531	$4,126				$679		$159			$6,567	
FL	Palm Beach	Palm Beach Co.	$7,618	$7,618	$3,375				$1,778	$123	$248	$50	$113	$1,931	
FL	Palm Beach	Palm Beach Gardens	$10,733	$10,733	$4,629				$2,901	$148	$462	$549	$113	$1,931	
FL	Pasco	Pasco Co.	$8,235	$8,235	$5,176				$627	$97	$420			$1,674	$241
FL	Pinellas	Pinellas Co.	$1,596	$1,420	$1,420	$176									
FL	Polk	Polk Co.	$10,549	$10,549	$5,485				$337	$145	$254	$174		$4,082	$72
FL	Polk	Lakeland	$12,959	$10,859	$5,485	$1,000	$1,100		$896		$149	$175		$4,082	$72
FL	Putnam	Putnam Co.	$4,140	$4,140	$1,577				$187		$159			$2,217	
FL	Santa Rosa	Santa Rosa Co.	$1,265	$1,265	$1,265										
FL	St. Johns	St. Johns Co.	$6,905	$6,905	$3,096				$629		$418	$157	$315	$2,290	
FL	St. Lucie	St. Lucie Co.	$5,310	$5,310	$1,628				$431	$125	$97	$164	$329	$2,536	
FL	Sarasota	Sarasota Co.	$11,577	$8,251	$4,417	$1,904	$1,422		$1,794	$291	$259	$149	$259	$474	$608
FL	Sarasota	North Port	$8,837	$7,055	$4,551	$716	$1,066		$933	$291	$454	$150	$154	$474	$48
FL	Seminole	Seminole Co.	$1,550	$1,550	$685					$54	$172			$639	
FL	Seminole	Altamonte Springs	$1,659	$1,659	$421				$168	$91	$172	$168		$639	
FL	Seminole	Winter Springs	$7,795	$5,518	$2,224	$444	$1,833		$1,200		$700	$356	$400	$639	
FL	Sumter	Sumter Co.	$1,799	$1,799	$1,402						$397				
FL	Volusia	Volusia Co.	$8,440	$8,440	$1,506				$582		$287			$6,066	
FL	Volusia	Daytona Beach	$11,066	$9,447	$1,701	$697	$922		$934		$129	$218	$399	$6,066	
FL	Volusia	Deland	$8,632	$8,632	$1,506				$820		$79	$49	$112	$6,066	
FL	Volusia	Deltona	$9,914	$7,573	$489	$917	$1,424		$839		$116	$63		$6,066	
FL	Volusia	Edgewater	$12,112	$7,799	$1,054	$2,151	$2,162		$435		$144	$100		$6,066	
FL	Volusia	Ormond Beach	$10,035	$8,572	$1,638	$573	$890	$31	$837					$6,066	
FL	Volusia	Port Orange	$12,789	$9,857	$2,171	$1,457	$1,475		$1,350		$270			$6,066	

Multifamily Unit (2-bedroom, 1,000-square-foot unit, density of 12 units per acre; $100,000 value; 7 2-inch water meters (2 for irrigation) for 240-unit complex) *(continued)*

State	County	Jurisdiction	Total	Total Non-utility	Roads	Water	Sewer	Drain-age	Parks	Library	Fire	Police	General Govern-ment	Schools	Other
GA	Cherokee	Canton	$1,673	$1,673	$906				$527		$193	$47			
GA	Cherokee	Cherokee Co.	$1,564	$1,564	$174				$279	$212	$511	$332	$45		$11
GA	Forsyth	Forsyth Co.	$495	$495					$343	$58	$94				
GA	Fulton	Alpharetta	$1,722	$1,722	$1,123				$396		$203				
GA	Fulton	Atlanta	$857	$857	$470				$285		$79	$23			
GA	Fulton	Roswell	$1,828	$1,828	$110				$1,303		$362		$53		
HI	Honolulu	Honolulu	$1,245	$1,245	$1,245										
ID	Ada	Boise	$2,713	$2,713	$1,663				$1,050						
ID	Kootenai	Post Falls	$7,115	$2,668	$734	$308	$4,139		$1,818			$88			$28
IL	DeKalb	DeKalb (city)	$885	$885					$684					$201	
IL	DeKalb	Sandwich	$10,713	$3,413		$3,400	$3,900			$100	$500	$400	$1,050	$1,288	$75
IL	DuPage	DuPage County	$564	$564	$564										
IL	Kane	Kane County	$420	$420	$420										
IN	Hamilton	Fishers	$3,857	$2,177	$1,160		$1,680		$1,017						
IN	Hamilton	Noblesville	$2,198	$2,198	$1,109				$1,089						
KS	Johnson	Lenexa	$1,409	$1,409	$999				$410						
KS	Johnson	Olathe	$4,769	$1,344	$824	$1,600	$1,825		$520						
KS	Johnson	Overland Park	$780	$780	$780										
LA	E Baton Rouge	Baton Rouge	$1,385	$200	$200		$1,185								

Multifamily Unit (2-bedroom, 1,000-square-foot unit, density of 12 units per acre; $100,000 value; 7 2-inch water meters (2 for irrigation) for 240-unit complex) *(continued)*

State	County	Jurisdiction	Total	Total Non-utility	Roads	Water	Sewer	Drain-age	Parks	Library	Fire	Police	General Govern-ment	Schools	Other
LA	St Tammany	St Tammany Parish	$1,487	$1,487	$902			$585							
MD	Anne Arundel	Anne Arundel Co.	$2,492	$2,492	$693							$72		$1,727	
MD	Calvert	Calvert Co.	$7,750	$7,750	$3,500				$1,300					$2,600	$350
MD	Carroll	Carroll Co.	$2,787	$2,787					$530					$2,257	
MD	Charles	Charles Co.	$9,755	$8,227		$757	$771							$8,227	
MD	Frederick	Frederick Co.	$7,145	$2,510	$30	$1,935	$2,700			$517				$1,963	
MD	Harford	Harford Co.	$1,637	$1,637										$1,637	
MD	Howard	Howard Co.	$2,080	$880	$880	$600	$600								
MD	Montgomery	Montgomery Co.	$9,971	$7,935	$3,703	$896	$1,140							$4,232	
MD	Queen Anne's	Queen Anne's Co.	$4,757	$4,757					$851		$952			$2,954	
MD	St. Mary's	St. Mary's Co.	$4,500	$4,500	$450				$675					$3,375	
MO	Clay/Jackson	Kansas City	$435	$435	$435										
MO	Jackson	Lee's Summit	$621	$621	$621										
MT	Gallatin	Bozeman	$2,370	$1,377	$1,290	$521	$472				$87				
NC	Chatham	Chatham Co.	$1,417	$950		$467								$950	
NC	Durham	Durham	$2,243	$1,861	$495	$230	$152		$216					$1,150	
NC	Orange	Orange Co.	$5,648	$1,870		$1,133	$2,645		$450					$1,420	
NC	Wake	Cary	$3,621	$762	$762	$1,086	$1,773								
NC	Wake	Raleigh	$2,015	$590	$254	$784	$641		$336						

Multifamily Unit (2-bedroom, 1,000-square-foot unit, density of 12 units per acre; $100,000 value; 7 2-inch water meters (2 for irrigation) for 240-unit complex) *(continued)*

State	County	Jurisdiction	Total	Total Non-utility	Roads	Water	Sewer	Drain-age	Parks	Library	Fire	Police	General Govern-ment	Schools	Other
NE	Lancaster	Lincoln	$1,966	$1,701	$1,501	$196	$69		$200						
NH	Hillsborough	Manchester	$1,315	$1,315							$146			$1,169	
NH	Merrimack	Concord	$2,522	$2,522	$1,183				$535					$804	
NH	Rockingham	Salem	$2,923	$2,923											
NH	Rockingham	Fremont	$2,438	$2,438										$2,438	
NM	Bernalillo	Albuquerque	$4,161	$3,582	$1,520	$377	$202	$645	$1,210			$207			
NM	Bernalillo	Bernalillo Co.	$1,445	$1,445	$761			$354	$192		$66				$72
NM	Dona Ana	Las Cruces	$527	$175		$243	$109		$175						
NM	Lincoln	Ruidoso	$930			$624	$306								
NM	Sandoval	Rio Rancho	$4,914	$3,922	$1,887	$609	$383	$955	$832		$225				$23
NM	Santa Fe	Santa Fe	$3,399	$2,503	$1,485	$335	$561		$863		$94	$61			
NM	Santa Fe	Santa Fe County	$275	$275							$275				
NM	Valencia	Los Lunas	$2,373	$1,963		$189	$221		$1,963						
NV	Churchill	Churchill County	$4,200	$4,200	$2,300				$1,000					$900	
NV	Clark	Las Vegas	$2,838	$1,034	$628		$1,804		$360						$46
NV	Clark	Mesquite	$3,352	$2,028	$982		$1,324		$1,000						$46
NV	Placer	Truckee	$1,499	$1,499	$1,499										
NV	Washoe	Reno	$2,340	$2,340	$1,340				$1,000						
OH	Butler	Middletown	$500	$500					$500						
OH	Delaware	Delaware (city)	$3,511	$1,295		$1,318	$898		$767		$197	$101	$230		
OH	Warren	Hamilton Township	$4,005	$4,005	$2,782				$921		$187	$115			

Multifamily Unit (2-bedroom, 1,000-square-foot unit, density of 12 units per acre; $100,000 value; 7 2-inch water meters (2 for irrigation) for 240-unit complex) *(continued)*

State	County	Jurisdiction	Total	Total Non-utility	Roads	Water	Sewer	Drain-age	Parks	Library	Fire	Police	General Government	Schools	Other
OK	Cleveland	Moore	$1,347	$647	$647		$700								
OR	Clackamas	Clackamas Co.	$7,972	$7,549	$5,273	$48	$375		$2,276						
OR	Clackamas	West Linn	$11,684	$9,138	$3,006	$1,080	$1,466	$455	$5,677						
OR	Deschutes	Bend	$10,286	$5,859	$2,674	$2,797	$1,630		$3,185						
OR	Josephine	Grants Pass	$10,197	$7,034	$4,070	$1,537	$1,626	$412	$2,552						
OR	Lane	Eugene	$4,625	$2,792	$908	$506	$1,327	$34	$1,850						
OR	Lane	Springfield	$2,338	$1,435	$743		$903	$692							
OR	Marion	Salem	$6,987	$3,493	$1,274	$2,092	$1,402	$281	$1,937						
OR	Marion	Silverton	$5,982	$4,874	$2,294	$620	$488	$1,375	$1,205						
OR	Multnomah	Portland	$6,739	$3,716	$1,435	$417	$2,606	$254	$2,027						
OR	Washington	Tigard	$2,576	$2,016	$2,016	$560									
OR	Washington	Washington Co.	$3,564	$1,324	$824		$2,240	$500							
PA	Montgomery	Towamencin Twp.	$1,362	$1,362	$1,362		$1,425	$583	$1,000						$250
SC	Beaufort	Beaufort Co.	$1,445	$1,445	varies				$471	$553	$421				
SC	Beaufort	Hilton Head	$7,120	$1,680	$500	$2,400	$3,040		$627	$553					
SC	Berkeley	Mt. Pleasant	$2,295	$1,382	$664	$436	$477		$358		$231	$69			$60
TN	Rutherford	La Vergne	$4,751	$2,289	$543	$587	$1,875		$246						$1,500
TN	Rutherford	Smyrna	$3,182	$3,182	$1,095				$406		$181				$1,500
TN	Sumner	Portland	$1,931	$1,931					$907					$700	$324
TN	Sumner	White House	$1,492	$1,492	$258				$245		$115	$174		$700	
TN	Williamson	Franklin	$4,980	$2,356	$896	$948	$1,676								$1,460
TN	Williamson	Nolensville	$4,043	$4,043	$2,043										$2,000

Multifamily Unit (2-bedroom, 1,000-square-foot unit, density of 12 units per acre; $100,000 value; 7 2-inch water meters (2 for irrigation) for 240-unit complex) *(continued)*

State	County	Jurisdiction	Total	Total Non-utility	Roads	Water	Sewer	Drain-age	Parks	Library	Fire	Police	General Govern-ment	Schools	Other
TX	Brazos	College Station	$474	$452		$16	$6		$452						
TX	Collin	Allen	$763	$400	$400	$280	$83								
TX	Collin	McKinney	$715	$503	$503	$157	$55								
TX	Denton	Denton	$1,025			$736	$289								
TX	Tarrant	Arlington	$1,932	$1,773	$670	$107	$52		$1,103						
TX	Tarrant	Colleyville	$2,030	$1,342	$1,342	$581	$107								
TX	Tarrant	Ft. Worth	$180			$143	$37								
TX	Williamson	Georgetown	$565			$357	$208								
UT	Cache	Logan	$1,202	$986	$461	$60	$156	$37			$100	$28			$360
UT	Davis	Layton	$3,895	$3,647	$1,508	$248		$367	$1,381		$391				
UT	Salt Lake	Draper	$6,085	$5,003	$1,202	$1,082		$1,161	$2,463		$107	$70			
UT	Salt Lake	Sandy City	$3,324	$2,967		$357		$301	$2,536		$92	$38			
UT	Salt Lake	West Jordan City	$8,066	$3,596	$1,523	$2,602	$1,868	$493	$1,301		$196	$83			
UT	Salt Lake	West Valley City	$1,739	$1,739	$514			$181	$937		$62	$45			
UT	Tooele	Tooele	$3,361	$1,456		$1,523	$382		$1,250			$206			
UT	Utah	Provo	$5,006	$3,739	$591	$160	$1,107	$501	$2,647						
VA	Loudoun	Leesburg	$9,183			$3,583	$5,600								
VA	Stafford	Stafford Co.	$28,186	$21,086	$5,448	$3,600	$3,500		$6,219	$514	$662		$446	$7,797	
VT	Chittenden	Burlington	$2,381	$2,381	$177				$673	$418	$202	$40		$871	
VT	Chittenden	Williston	$4,400	$4,400	$186				$657					$3,557	
WA	Clark	Vancouver	$5,090	$5,090	$1,322				$1,523					$2,245	
WA	Cowlitz	Woodland	$3,432	$2,907		$280	$245		$831		$1,426			$650	
WA	King	King Co.	$1,975	$1,975	$950									$1,025	

Multifamily Unit (2-bedroom, 1,000-square-foot unit, density of 12 units per acre; $100,000 value; 7 2-inch water meters (2 for irrigation) for 240-unit complex) *(continued)*

State	County	Jurisdiction	Total	Total Non-utility	Roads	Water	Sewer	Drain-age	Parks	Library	Fire	Police	General Govern-ment	Schools	Other
WA	King	Bellevue	$218	$218	$218										
WA	King	Bothell	$2,744	$2,033	$1,271	$470	$241		$762						
WA	King	Issaquqh	$5,902	$5,902	$1,500				$2,189		$853	$49	$47	$1,264	
WA	King	Kirkland	$4,045	$1,016	$586	$1,839	$1,190		$430						
WA	Kitsap	Kitsap Co.	$1,245	$1,245	$374				$262					$609	
WA	Pierce	Pierce Co.	$2,374	$2,374	$1,046				$165					$1,162	
WA	Skagit	Anacortes	$4,393	$2,641	$900	$653	$1,099	$1,126	$615						
WA	Skagit	Burlington	$5,585	$3,499	$116		$2,086		$500		$254			$2,629	
WA	Snohomish	Snohomish Co.	$4,495	$4,495	$1,663				$376					$2,456	
WA	Thurston	Olympia	$4,306	$4,306	$1,091				$1,223		$159			$1,833	
WA	Thurston	Tumwater	$3,494	$3,422	$703		$72		$372		$101			$2,247	
WA	Whatcom	Bellingham	$7,113	$5,452	$755	$1,088	$573	$452	$3,524					$721	
WV	Jefferson	Jefferson Co.	$7,047	$7,047					$565		$454	$112		$5,916	
WI	Dane	Fitchburg	$4,404	$4,404					$3,904		$500				
WI	Jefferson	Oconomowoc	$2,052	$1,507	$94	$189	$356		$1,188		$121	$104			
WI	Ozaukee	Cedarburg	$3,216	$1,602		$1,299	$314		$745	$391		$466			
WI	St. Croix	Hudson	$1,775	$469		$941	$365	$366		$102					
		National Average	$6,533	$4,997	$1,922	$1,619	$1,696	$746	$1,917	$284	$316	$270	$867	$2,430	$1,006
		Sample Size	283	276	233	138	144	59	206	70	140	101	71	117	57
		National Avg w/o CA	$4,823	$3,755	$1,627	$1,239	$1,227	$529	$1,164	$240	$283	$204	$357	$2,432	$371
		Sample Size w/o CA	245	238	197	115	117	35	174	60	123	87	51	104	44

Multifamily Unit (2-bedroom, 1,000-square-foot unit, density of 12 units per acre; $100,000 value; 7 2-inch water meters (2 for irrigation) for 240-unit complex) *(continued)*

State	County	Jurisdiction	Total	Total Non-utility	Roads	Water	Sewer	Drain-age	Parks	Library	Fire	Police	General Government	Schools	Other
State Average Fees															
AR			$1,126	$613	$771	$280	$498	n/a	$447	n/a	$357	$162	n/a	n/a	n/a
AZ			$5,208	$3,681	$1,541	$1,342	$918	$705	$1,515	$272	$366	$299	$424	n/a	$479
CA			$17,558	$12,776	$3,538	$3,523	$3,728	$1,061	$6,016	$554	$553	$680	$2,165	$2,414	$3,155
CO			$6,167	$3,843	$1,417	$4,364	$1,493	$510	$2,477	$516	$302	$236	$359	$706	$508
DE			$6,025	$762	n/a	n/a	$5,263	n/a	$225	$95	$322	$43	$77	n/a	n/a
FL			$6,592	$5,734	$2,328	$1,092	$1,627	$31	$809	$158	$239	$196	$320	$2,848	$167
GA			$1,356	$1,356	$557	n/a	n/a	n/a	$522	$135	$240	$134	$49	n/a	$11
HI			$1,245	$1,245	$1,245	n/a	n/a	n/a	n/a	n/a	n/a	n/a	n/a	n/a	n/a
ID			$4,914	$2,690	$1,198	$308	$4,139	n/a	$1,434	n/a	n/a	$88	n/a	n/a	$28
IL			$3,146	$1,321	$492	$3,400	$3,900	n/a	$684	$100	$500	$400	$1,050	$745	$75
IN			$3,028	$2,188	$1,135	n/a	$1,680	n/a	$1,053	n/a	n/a	n/a	n/a	n/a	n/a
KS			$2,319	$1,178	$868	$1,600	$1,825	n/a	$465	n/a	n/a	n/a	n/a	n/a	n/a
LA			$1,436	$844	$551	n/a	$1,185	$585	n/a	n/a	n/a	n/a	n/a	n/a	n/a
MD			$5,287	$4,348	$1,543	$1,047	$1,303	n/a	$839	$517	$952	$72	n/a	$3,219	$350
MO			$528	$528	$528	n/a	n/a	n/a	n/a	n/a	n/a	n/a	n/a	n/a	n/a
MT			$2,370	$1,377	$1,290	$521	$472	n/a	n/a	n/a	$87	n/a	n/a	n/a	n/a
NC			$2,989	$1,207	$504	$740	$1,303	n/a	$334	n/a	n/a	n/a	n/a	$1,173	n/a
NE			$1,966	$1,701	$1,501	$196	$69	n/a	$200	n/a	n/a	n/a	n/a	n/a	n/a
NH			$2,300	$2,300	$1,183	n/a	n/a	n/a	$535	n/a	$146	n/a	n/a	$1,470	n/a
NM			$2,253	$1,981	$1,413	$396	$297	$651	$873	n/a	$165	$134	n/a	n/a	$47
NV			$2,846	$2,220	$1,350	n/a	$1,564	n/a	$840	n/a	n/a	n/a	n/a	$900	$46
OH			$2,672	$1,933	$2,782	$1,318	$898	n/a	$729	n/a	$192	$108	$230	n/a	n/a
OK			$1,347	$647	$647	n/a	$700	n/a	n/a	n/a	n/a	n/a	n/a	n/a	n/a
OR			$6,632	$4,475	$2,229	$1,073	$1,406	$500	$2,589	n/a	n/a	n/a	n/a	n/a	n/a
PA			$1,362	$1,362	$1,362	n/a	$1,425	$583	$1,000	n/a	n/a	n/a	n/a	n/a	$250
SC			$3,620	$1,502	$582	$1,418	$1,759	n/a	$485	$553	$326	$69	n/a	n/a	$60
TN			$3,397	$2,549	$967	$768	$1,776	n/a	$451	n/a	$148	$174	n/a	$700	$1,357
TX			$961	$894	$729	$297	$105	n/a	$778	n/a	n/a	n/a	n/a	n/a	n/a

Multifamily Unit (2-bedroom, 1,000-square-foot unit, density of 12 units per acre; $100,000 value; 7 2-inch water meters (2 for irrigation) for 240-unit complex) *(continued)*

State	County	Jurisdiction	Total	Total Non-utility	Roads	Water	Sewer	Drain-age	Parks	Library	Fire	Police	General Govern-ment	Schools	Other
UT			$4,085	$2,891	$966	$862	$878	$434	$1,788	n/a	$158	$78	n/a	n/a	$360
VA			$18,685	$21,086	$5,448	$3,592	$4,550	n/a	$6,219	$514	$662	n/a	$446	$7,797	n/a
VT			$3,391	$3,391	$182	n/a	n/a	n/a	$665	$418	$202	$40	n/a	$2,214	n/a
WA			$3,761	$3,105	$893	$866	$787	$789	$983	n/a	$559	$49	$47	$1,531	n/a
WV			$7,047	$7,047	n/a	n/a	n/a	n/a	$565	n/a	$454	$112	n/a	$5,916	n/a
WI			$2,862	$1,995	$94	$810	$345	$366	$1,946	$247	$311	$285	n/a	n/a	n/a

Retail per 1,000 square feet (100,000-square-foot shopping center; 0.15 floor area ratio; 3-inch water meter)

State	County	Jurisdiction	Total	Total Non-utility	Roads	Water	Sewer	Drain-age	Parks	Library	Fire	Police	General Govern-ment	Schools	Other
AR	Benton	Bentonville	$655	$240		$233	$182				$240				
AR	Benton	Lowell	$504	$455			$49				$455				
AR	Faulkner	Conway	$1,915	$1,915	$1,915										
AR	Washington	Fayetteville	$864	$681		$49	$134				$293	$388			
AZ	Cochise	Sierra Vista	$2,990	$2,990	$2,550						$220	$220			
AZ	Gila	Payson	$505			$505									
AZ	Gila	Sedona	$8,760	$8,760	$7,430			$500				$540	$290		
AZ	Maricopa	Avondale	$8,091	$6,934	$3,960	$562	$595				$723	$1,380	$871		
AZ	Maricopa	Buckeye	$4,741	$4,354	$1,314	$240	$148				$731	$2,126	$183		
AZ	Maricopa	Chandler	$7,347	$6,170	$5,630	$779	$398				$200	$170	$170		
AZ	Maricopa	Fountain Hills	$3,000	$3,000	$2,081						$62	$276	$581		
AZ	Maricopa	Gilbert	$3,628	$2,249	$1,154	$671	$708				$447	$315	$333		
AZ	Maricopa	Glendale	$6,754	$5,765	$4,131	$733	$256				$303	$578	$682		$71
AZ	Maricopa	Goodyear	$4,360	$3,370	$1,530	$477	$513				$200	$1,150	$270		$220
AZ	Maricopa	Mesa	$1,569	$1,083		$162	$324				$423	$660			
AZ	Maricopa	Peoria	$13,725	$13,128	$10,216	$399	$198				$433	$2,041	$438		
AZ	Maricopa	Phoenix	$7,691	$6,202	$3,922	$609	$880	$2,144				$61	$75		

Retail per 1,000 square feet (100,000-square-foot shopping center; 0.15 floor area ratio; 3-inch water meter) *(continued)*

State	County	Jurisdiction	Total	Total Non-utility	Roads	Water	Sewer	Drain-age	Parks	Library	Fire	Police	General Govern-ment	Schools	Other
AZ	Maricopa	Scottsdale	$1,716	$555		$677	$484	$555							
AZ	Maricopa	Surprise	$4,046	$3,457	$512	$356	$234					$1,053	$1,659	$233		
AZ	Maricopa	Tempe	$494			$222	$273								
AZ	Mojave	Bullhead City	$1,898			$1,898									
AZ	Navajo	Show Low	$501			$116	$385								
AZ	Pima	Pima County	$3,353	$2,535	$2,535		$818								
AZ	Pima	Marana	$350			$350									
AZ	Pima	Oro Valley	$698			$698									
AZ	Pima	Tucson	$5,447	$5,203	$3,976	$244					$269	$699			$259
AZ	Pinal	Apache Junction	$15,537	$15,070	$13,220	$147	$320					$1,740	$110		
AZ	Pinal	Casa Grande	$5,987	$5,708	$4,052		$279				$466	$748	$442		
AZ	Pinal	Eloy	$1,276	$1,020		$145	$112					$397	$623		
AZ	Pinal	Florence	$1,284	$1,095	$470	$83	$106				$325	$122	$178		
AZ	Pinal	Queen Creek	$5,656	$5,152	$2,819		$504				$1,040	$265	$1,028		
AZ	Yavapai	Yavapai County													
AZ	Yavapai	Chino Valley	$2,207	$1,350	$940	$84	$773				$180	$160	$70		
AZ	Yavapai	Prescott	$3,044	$1,544	$469	$1,500					$435	$365	$275		
AZ	Yuma	Yuma	$6,126	$4,466	$2,874	$607	$1,052				$192	$1,093	$265		$42
CA	Alameda	Fremont	$8,696	$8,696	$7,720						$129		$847		
CA	Alameda	Hayward	$5,719	$5,719		$695	$704							$360	$3,960
CA	Alameda	Livermore	$31,454	$31,454	$19,666	$3,644	$4,220	$936	$1,688					$420	$880
CA	Alameda	San Leandro	$3,920	$3,920	$3,250		$200							$360	$110
CA	Contra Costa	Orinda	$3,930	$3,930	$1,990			$1,940							
CA	El Dorado	El Dorado Co.	$20,964	$20,964	$19,444						$1,100			$420	

Retail per 1,000 square feet (100,000-square-foot shopping center; 0.15 floor area ratio; 3-inch water meter) *(continued)*

State	County	Jurisdiction	Total	Total Non-utility	Roads	Water	Sewer	Drain-age	Parks	Library	Fire	Police	General Govern-ment	Schools	Other
CA	Fresno	Clovis	$14,746	$13,466	$11,456	$386	$894		$1,450		$4	$1			$554
CA	Kern	Bakersfield	$1,196	$688	varies		$508							$360	$328
CA	Los Angeles	Lancaster	$2,952	$2,952	$1,530			$660			$715		$47		
CA	Los Angeles	Long Beach	$3,438	$3,360	$3,000		$78							$360	
CA	Monterey	Salinas	$7,855	$7,311	$6,570		$544	$741							
CA	Napa	St. Helena	$17,180	$9,050	$4,180	$4,340	$3,790	$640				$1,760	$2,470		
CA	Orange	Brea	$9,447	$7,440	$7,440	$2,007									
CA	Placer	Rocklin	$13,267	$13,267	$10,721			$106					$1,390		$1,050
CA	Sacramento	Citrus Heights	$6,876	$5,740	$4,450		$1,136	varies	$180					$340	$770
CA	Sacramento	Elk Grove	$20,278	$16,398	$11,850	$990	$2,889	$1,390	$780		$1,298	$130	$180		$770
CA	Sacramento	Sacramento	$49,478	$48,082	$8,590	$260	$1,136		$7,114					$420	$31,958
CA	San Bernardino	Highland	$8,673	$8,673	$8,149			$322			$99	$30	$73		
CA	San Bernardino	Redlands	$13,221	$13,221	$8,321			$678		$711	$336	$616	$2,560		
CA	San Bernardino	Rialto	$7,686	$6,340	$5,140	$510	$836	$620	$140		$240	$100	$100		
CA	San Diego	Carlsbad	$3,704	$2,741	$2,680	$795	$168	$61							
CA	San Diego	Escondido	$8,813	$6,650	$3,820	$883	$1,280	$700					$2,130		
CA	San Diego	San Diego	$1,483			$823	$660								
CA	San Joaquin	Lodi	$13,825	$12,512	$4,456	$482	$831	$3,663	$1,331		$778	$1,219	$1,064		
CA	San Joaquin	Ripon	$37,966	$32,299	$25,302	$2,533	$3,133	$2,000	$1,333		$762	$1,333	$797	$420	$352
CA	San Luis Obispo	Paso Robles	$6,261	$4,740	$4,190	$825	$696	$150			$330		$70		
CA	San Luis Obispo	San Luis Obispo	$15,876	$13,085	$13,085	$2,089	$702								
CA	Santa Barbara	Carpinteria	$30,444	$30,444	$26,620			$1,785	$1,630		$4		$30	$330	$45
CA	Santa Barbara	Santa Maria	$11,691	$9,134	$8,330	$1,246	$1,311		$26	$168	$60	$382	$168		
CA	Santa Clara	Palo Alto	$24,006	$24,006	$3,810				$3,983	$203					$16,010

Retail per 1,000 square feet (100,000-square-foot shopping center; 0.15 floor area ratio; 3-inch water meter) *(continued)*

State	County	Jurisdiction	Total	Total Non-utility	Roads	Water	Sewer	Drain-age	Parks	Library	Fire	Police	General Govern-ment	Schools	Other
CA	Santa Cruz	Santa Cruz Co.	$7,940	$7,940	$5,940	varies	varies	$2,000							
CA	Santa Cruz	Scotts Valley	$12,293	$12,293	$8,430		$982	$138				$2,614	$130		
CA	Shasta	Redding	$21,408	$21,408	$8,179	$6,341	$6,370	$438			$79				
CA	Solano	Vacaville	$11,730	$11,730	$4,428	$1,661	$1,650	$1,407			$176	$1,189	$355	$330	$534
CA	Sonoma	Windsor	$14,635	$14,635	$10,123	$117	$2,059	$2,043					$293		
CA	Ventura	Santa Paula	$4,888	$4,888	$2,095	$381	$300	$410	$165		$146	$934	$457		
CA	Yolo	Davis	$18,301	$18,301	$15,266	$647	varies	$111	$548			$589	$800	$340	
CO	Adams	Adams Co.	$2,131	$2,131	$2,131										
CO	Adams	Commerce City	$3,562	$3,562	$3,229			$333							
CO	Boulder	Boulder	$6,540	$4,690	$1,736	$1,554	$297	$1,820			$180	$180	$304		$470
CO	Eagle	Eagle Co.	$5,192	$5,192	$4,923						$269				
CO	Eagle	Basalt	$940	$250	$250	$690			varies						varies
CO	El Paso	Colorado Springs	$2,710	$953		$1,492	$266	$953							
CO	Fremont	Canon City	$152	$152							$152				
CO	Jefferson	Jefferson Co.	$5,390	$5,390	$5,390										
CO	La Plata	Durango	$2,850	$2,126	$2,126	$558	$166								
CO	Larimer	Larimer Co.	$5,870	$5,870	$5,870										
CO	Larimer	Loveland	$9,356	$8,553	$7,510	$803		$113			$260	$310	$360		
CO	Larimer	Ft. Collins	$12,451	$9,477	$8,534	$2,163	$811	$376			$202	$140	$225		
CO	Mesa	Mesa Co.	$2,448	$2,448	$2,448										
CO	Pitkin	Pitkin Co.	$41,018	$41,018	$12,143				$4,100						$24,775
CO	Weld	Weld Co.	$3,454	$3,454	$3,059			$300							$95
CO	Weld	Windsor	$8,629	$7,229	$6,065	$915	$485	$1,164							
CO	Weld	Greeley	$8,420	$8,420	$7,454			$298			$499	$170			
DE	New Castle	New Castle Co.	$1,603	$297			$1,306				$169	$33	$95		
FL	Alachua	Alachua Co.	$3,890	$3,890	$3,814						$76				

Retail per 1,000 square feet (100,000-square-foot shopping center; 0.15 floor area ratio; 3-inch water meter) *(continued)*

State	County	Jurisdiction	Total	Total Non-utility	Roads	Water	Sewer	Drain-age	Parks	Library	Fire	Police	General Govern-ment	Schools	Other
FL	Brevard	Brevard Co.	$5,516	$5,516	$5,270						$86				$160
FL	Brevard	Cocoa	$5,676	$5,516	$5,270	$160					$86				$160
FL	Brevard	Melbourne	$6,184	$6,184	$5,270						$86		$668		$160
FL	Brevard	Palm Bay	$10,066	$10,066	$9,549						$291	$66			$160
FL	Brevard	Rockledge	$5,516	$5,516	$5,270						$86				$160
FL	Broward	Broward Co.	$1,132	$1,132	$1,132										
FL	Broward	Ft. Lauderdale													
FL	Charlotte	Charlotte Co.	$11,476	$11,476	$10,585						$242	$178	$471		
FL	Citrus	Citrus Co.	$8,213	$8,213	$5,847						$775	$404	$1,188		
FL	Clay	Clay Co.													
FL	Collier	Collier Co.	$18,360	$16,177	$13,198	$1,076	$1,107				$802	$478	$1,135		$564
FL	Dade	Miami/Dade Co.	$1,521	$1,521	$991						$291	$239			
FL	Dade	Miami	$931	$931							$227	$609	$95		
FL	DeSoto	DeSoto Co.	$7,560	$7,560	$5,040						$200	$1,990	$330		
FL	Flagler	Flagler Co.	$1,997	$1,997	$1,997										
FL	Flagler	Palm Coast	$4,790	$4,004	$3,953	$389	$397				$51				
FL	Gilchrist	Gilchrist Co.	$560	$560	$500								$60		
FL	Glades	Glades Co.	$5,681	$5,681	$5,590						$91				
FL	Hardee	Hardee Co.	$2,753	$2,753	$1,531						$326	$152	$522		$222
FL	Hendry	Hendry Co.	$3,916	$3,916	$3,916										
FL	Hernando	Hernando Co.	$6,433	$6,433	$5,411						$350	$145	$527		
FL	Highlands	Highlands Co.	$2,736	$2,736	$2,455						$280				
FL	Hillsborough	Hillsborough Co.	$3,942	$3,374	$3,352	$264	$304				$22				
FL	Hillsborough	Plant City	$6,742	$6,418	$5,352	$78	$245				$533	$533			
FL	Hillsborough	Tampa	$3,797	$3,797	$3,797										

Retail per 1,000 square feet (100,000-square-foot shopping center; 0.15 floor area ratio; 3-inch water meter) *(continued)*

State	County	Jurisdiction	Total	Total Non-utility	Roads	Water	Sewer	Drain-age	Parks	Library	Fire	Police	General Govern-ment	Schools	Other
FL	Indian River	Indian River Co.	$10,828	$10,828	$7,813						$502	$439	$1,527		$547
FL	Lake	Lake Co.	$3,410	$3,410	$2,177						$1,233				
FL	Lake	Eustis	$2,101	$941		$280	$880				$485	$456			
FL	Lee	Lee Co.	$16,478	$16,478	$15,837						$641				
FL	Lee	Bonita Springs	$10,135	$10,135	$9,625						$510				
FL	Lee	Cape Coral	$6,715	$6,163	$5,709	$274	$278				$153	$163			$137
FL	Lee	Ft. Myers	$17,022	$16,357	$15,837	$337	$328				$520				
FL	Levy	Levy Co.	$1,790	$1,790	$1,710						$80				
FL	Manatee	Manatee Co.	$16,636	$16,636	$15,508						$299	$829			
FL	Marion	Marion Co.	$7,541	$7,541	$7,055						$486				
FL	Martin	Martin Co.	$10,347	$10,347	$8,420						$486	$625	$816		
FL	Monroe	Monroe Co.	$2,398	$2,398	$1,168						$64	$112			$1,054
FL	Nassau	Nassau Co.	$3,736	$3,736	$2,726						$245	$304	$460		
FL	Okaloosa	Destin	$9,448	$9,448	$9,400							$48			
FL	Orange	Orange Co.	$13,850	$13,850	$13,303						$231	$316			
FL	Orange	Apopka	$10,803	$9,797	$9,797	$391	$615								
FL	Orange	Maitland	$3,023	$2,417	$2,267	$144	$462				$150				
FL	Orange	Oakland	$12,426	$8,726	$7,370	$3,500	$200				$98	$358			$900
FL	Orange	Ocoee	$9,167	$7,261	$6,461	$481	$1,425				$470	$330			
FL	Orange	Orlando	$10,737	$10,737	$10,477						$260				
FL	Orange	Winter Garden	$9,016	$8,347	$7,237	$262	$407				$610	$500			
FL	Osceola	Osceola Co.	$16,690	$16,690	$16,690										
FL	Palm Beach	Palm Beach Co.	$6,767	$6,767	$6,256						$226	$71	$214		
FL	Palm Beach	Palm Beach Gardens	$12,016	$12,016	$11,087						$463	$252	$214		
FL	Pasco	Pasco Co.	$12,139	$12,139	$11,349						$549				$241
FL	Pinellas	Pinellas Co.	$3,683	$3,627	$3,627	$56									

Retail per 1,000 square feet (100,000-square-foot shopping center; 0.15 floor area ratio; 3-inch water meter) *(continued)*

State	County	Jurisdiction	Total	Total Non-utility	Roads	Water	Sewer	Drain-age	Parks	Library	Fire	Police	General Government	Schools	Other
FL	Polk	Polk Co.	$9,948	$9,948	$8,278						$190	$980			$500
FL	Polk	Lakeland	$12,343	$9,613	$8,278	$1,250	$1,480				$324	$511			$500
FL	Putnam	Putnam Co.	$1,550	$1,550	$1,280						$270				
FL	Santa Rosa	Santa Rosa Co.	$3,111	$3,111	$3,111										
FL	St .Johns	St. Johns Co.	$6,747	$6,747	$5,539						$10	$398	$800		
FL	St. Lucie	St. Lucie Co.	$3,179	$3,179	$1,445						$443	$756	$535		
FL	Sarasota	Sarasota Co.	$14,443	$13,493	$11,319	$544	$406				$442	$254	$441		$1,037
FL	Sarasota	North Port	$17,233	$17,233	$14,275						$1,770	$587	$601		
FL	Seminole	Seminole Co.	$2,901	$2,901	$2,741						$160				
FL	Seminole	Altamonte Springs	$2,936	$2,936	$2,283						$160	$493			
FL	Seminole	Winter Springs	$7,450	$7,015	$4,298	$83	$352				$1,300	$492	$925		
FL	Sumter	Sumter Co.	$6,425	$6,425	$5,915						$510				
FL	Volusia	Volusia Co.	$3,230	$3,230	$3,080						$150				
FL	Volusia	Daytona Beach	$6,247	$5,791	$3,850	$228	$228				$334	$568	$1,039		
FL	Volusia	Deland	$3,653	$3,653	$3,080						$22	$30	$521		
FL	Volusia	Deltona	$2,288	$1,176	$790	$435	$676				$250	$136			
FL	Volusia	Edgewater	$2,989	$2,299	$1,722	$344	$346				$241	$335			
FL	Volusia	Ormond Beach	$4,338	$3,846	$3,732	$227	$266	$114							
FL	Volusia	Port Orange	$6,434	$3,502	$3,302	$1,457	$1,475				$200				
GA	Cherokee	Canton	$2,644	$2,644	$2,256				$173		$173	$43			
GA	Cherokee	Cherokee Co.	$856	$856	$357						$284	$184	$25		$6
GA	Forsyth	Forsyth Co.	$216	$216							$216				
GA	Fulton	Alpharetta	$4,424	$4,424	$4,166				$14		$244				
GA	Fulton	Atlanta	$1,983	$1,983	$1,189				$584		$163	$47			
GA	Fulton	Roswell	$758	$758	$426						$310		$22		

Retail per 1,000 square feet (100,000-square-foot shopping center; 0.15 floor area ratio; 3-inch water meter) *(continued)*

State	County	Jurisdiction	Total	Total Non-utility	Roads	Water	Sewer	Drain-age	Parks	Library	Fire	Police	General Government	Schools	Other
HI	Honolulu	Honolulu	$4,053	$4,053	$4,053										
ID	Ada	Boise	$6,015	$6,015	$6,015										
ID	Kootenai	Post Falls	$3,546	$2,509	$2,233	$196	$841					$262			$14
IL	DeKalb	DeKalb (city)													
IL	DeKalb	Sandwich				$64	$114								
IL	DuPage	DuPage County	$916	$916	$916										
IL	Kane	Kane County	$1,010	$1,010	$1,010										
IN	Hamilton	Fishers	$6,826	$5,258	$5,258		$1,568								
IN	Hamilton	Noblesville	$7,085	$7,085	$7,085										
KS	Johnson	Lenexa	$3,989	$3,989	$2,783			$1,097	$108						
KS	Johnson	Olathe	$2,693	$1,947	$1,817	$347	$399		$130						
KS	Johnson	Overland Park	$1,433	$1,433	$1,433										
LA	E Baton Rouge	Baton Rouge	$608				$608								
LA	St. Tammany	St. Tammany Parish	$3,003	$3,003	$1,833			$1,170							
MD	Anne Arundel	Anne Arundel Co.	$3,021	$3,021	$2,568							$453			
MD	Calvert	Calvert Co.	$110	$110											$110
MD	Carroll	Carroll Co.													
MD	Charles	Charles Co.	$1,260			$519	$741								
MD	Frederick	Frederick Co.	$2,975	$750	$750	$929	$1,296								

Retail per 1,000 square feet (100,000-square-foot shopping center; 0.15 floor area ratio; 3-inch water meter) *(continued)*

State	County	Jurisdiction	Total	Total Non-utility	Roads	Water	Sewer	Drain-age	Parks	Library	Fire	Police	General Government	Schools	Other
MD	Harford	Harford Co.													
MD	Howard	Howard Co.	$2,080	$880	$880	$600	$600								
MD	Montgomery	Montgomery Co.	$5,562	$4,750	$4,750	$352	$460								
MD	Queen Anne's	Queen Anne's Co.	$1,090	$1,090							$1,090				
MD	St. Mary's	St. Mary's Co.													
MO	Clay/ Jackson	Kansas City	$1,458	$1,458	$1,458										
MO	Jackson	Lee's Summit	$2,254	$2,254	$2,254										
MT	Gallatin	Bozeman	$6,706	$5,895	$5,338	$357	$453				$557				
NC	Chatham	Chatham Co.	$300			$300									
NC	Durham	Durham	$3,203	$2,873	$2,873	$170	$160								
NC	Orange	Orange Co.	$1,332			$492	$840								
NC	Wake	Cary	$2,329	$1,341	$1,341	$385	$603								
NC	Wake	Raleigh	$2,828	$1,696	$1,696	$566	$566								
NE	Lancaster	Lincoln	$3,461	$3,260	$3,260	$134	$67								
NH	Hillsborough	Manchester													
NH	Merrimack	Concord	$3,680	$3,680	$3,680										
NH	Rockingham	Salem	$570	$570								$570			
NH	Rockingham	Fremont													
NM	Bernalillo	Albuquerque	$5,045	$4,593	$3,607	$258	$194	$645				$341			
NM	Bernalillo	Bernalillo Co.	$2,124	$2,124	$1,117			$650				$357			
NM	Dona Ana	Las Cruces	$296			$182	$114								
NM	Lincoln	Ruidoso	$721			$428	$293								

Retail per 1,000 square feet (100,000-square-foot shopping center; 0.15 floor area ratio; 3-inch water meter) *(continued)*

State	County	Jurisdiction	Total	Total Non-utility	Roads	Water	Sewer	Drain-age	Parks	Library	Fire	Police	General Govern-ment	Schools	Other
NM	Sandoval	Rio Rancho	$7,216	$6,430	$4,196	$418	$368	$1,430			$755				$49
NM	Santa Fe	Santa Fe	$4,590	$4,136	$3,893	$314	$140				$182	$61			
NM	Santa Fe	Santa Fe County	$460	$460							$460				
NM	Valencia	Los Lunas	$375			$146	$229								
NV	Churchill	Churchill County													
NV	Clark	Las Vegas	$1,246	$834	$750		$412								$84
NV	Clark	Mesquite	$1,294	$1,082	$998		$212								$84
NV	Placer	Truckee													
NV	Washoe	Reno	$3,519	$3,519	$3,519										
OH	Butler	Middletown													
OH	Delaware	Delaware (city)	$2,960	$1,194		$904	$862				$389	$456	$349		
OH	Warren	Hamilton Township	$7,962	$7,962	$7,265						$432	$265			
OK	Cleveland	Moore	$250	$250	$250										
OR	Clackamas	Clackamas Co.	$360	$0	varies		$360								
OR	Clackamas	West Linn	$13,632	$12,453	$12,297	$740	$439	$156							
OR	Deschutes	Bend	$9,976	$8,565	$8,565	$891	$520								
OR	Josephine	Grants Pass	$24,082	$23,260	$23,256	$416	$406	$4	varies						
OR	Lane	Eugene	$5,909	$5,312	$5,278	$347	$250	$34							
OR	Lane	Springfield	$5,420	$5,252	$2,945		$168	$2,307							
OR	Marion	Salem	$9,542	$8,424	$8,143	$669	$449	$281							
OR	Marion	Silverton	$5,837	$4,267	varies	$425	$1,145	$4,267							
OR	Multnomah	Portland	$3,963	$3,174	$2,920	$268	$521	$254							
OR	Washington	Tigard	$3,276	$2,916	$2,916	$360									
OR	Washington	Washington Co.	$5,565	$2,765	$2,265		$2,800	$500							

Retail per 1,000 square feet (100,000-square-foot shopping center; 0.15 floor area ratio; 3-inch water meter) *(continued)*

State	County	Jurisdiction	Total	Total Non-utility	Roads	Water	Sewer	Drain-age	Parks	Library	Fire	Police	General Govern-ment	Schools	Other
PA	Montgomery	Towamencin Twp.	$5,109	$5,109	$5,109		$342	$161	$500						$300
SC	Beaufort	Beaufort Co.	$55	$55	varies						$55				
SC	Beaufort	Hilton Head	$4,187	$3,317	$3,317	$384	$486								
SC	Berkeley	Mt. Pleasant	$3,925	$3,280	$2,840	$187	$458				$190	$120			$130
TN	Rutherford	La Vergne	$376			$80	$296								
TN	Rutherford	Smyrna	$3,013	$3,013	$2,438						$575				
TN	Sumner	Portland													$400
TN	Sumner	White House	$2,888	$2,888	$1,550						$532	$806			
TN	Williamson	Franklin	$6,623	$5,311	$3,541	$474	$838								$1,770
TN	Williamson	Nolensville	$2,849	$2,849	$849										$2,000
TX	Brazos	College Station	$133			$88	$45								
TX	Collin	Allen	$1,772	$1,500	$1,500	$192	$80								
TX	Collin	McKinney	$243	$75	$75	$113	$55								
TX	Denton	Denton	$855			$552	$303								
TX	Tarrant	Arlington	$1,635	$1,393	$1,393	$135	$107								
TX	Tarrant	Colleyville	$2,009	$1,508	$1,508	$399	$103								
TX	Tarrant	Ft. Worth	$146			$107	$39								
TX	Williamson	Georgetown	$444			$245	$199								
UT	Cache	Logan	$691	$511	$270	$39	$140	$90			$118	$33			
UT	Davis	Layton	$5,540	$5,396	$3,730	$144		$1,011			$655				
UT	Salt Lake	Draper	$7,119	$6,907	$5,859	$212		$371			$410	$267			
UT	Salt Lake	Sandy City	$1,529	$1,086		$443		$553	$78		$322	$133			
UT	Salt Lake	West Jordan City	$6,244	$5,545	$4,340	$407	$292	$905			$140	$160			
UT	Salt Lake	West Valley City	$1,797	$1,797	$1,343			$185			$156	$113			
UT	Tooele	Tooele	$798	$320		$354	$124					$320			

Retail per 1,000 square feet (100,000-square-foot shopping center; 0.15 floor area ratio; 3-inch water meter) *(continued)*

State	County	Jurisdiction	Total	Total Non-utility	Roads	Water	Sewer	Drain-age	Parks	Library	Fire	Police	General Government	Schools	Other
UT	Utah	Provo	$2,937	$2,657	$2,156	$103	$177	$501							
VA	Loudoun	Leesburg	$1,833			$717	$1,116								
VA	Stafford	Stafford Co.	$3,172	$2,036	$2,036	$576	$560								
VT	Chittenden	Burlington	$1,543	$1,543	$666				$380		$179	$318			
VT	Chittenden	Williston	$1,125	$1,125	$1,125										
WA	Clark	Vancouver	$8,451	$8,451	$8,451										
WA	Cowlitz	Woodland	$933	$510		$195	$228				$510				
WA	King	King Co.			varies										
WA	King	Bellevue	$707	$707	$707										
WA	King	Bothell	$3,853	$3,300	$3,300	$322	$231								
WA	King	Issaquqh	$6,811	$6,811	$5,990						$640	$151	$30		
WA	King	Kirkland	$3,079	$1,520	$1,520	$1,261	$298								
WA	Kitsap	Kitsap Co.	$811	$811	$811										
WA	Pierce	Pierce Co.	$2,151	$2,151	$2,151										
WA	Skagit	Anacortes	$5,256	$3,753		$448	$1,055	$3,753							
WA	Skagit	Burlington	$1,846	$1,326	$699		$520		$400		$227				
WA	Snohomish	Snohomish Co.	$9,035	$9,035	$9,035										
WA	Thurston	Olympia	$3,139	$3,139	$2,980						$159				
WA	Thurston	Tumwater	$2,363	$1,811	$1,710		$552				$101				
WA	Whatcom	Bellingham	$2,802	$1,507		$746	$550	$1,507							
WV	Jefferson	Jefferson Co.	$1,844	$1,844							$1,650	$194			
WI	Dane	Fitchburg	$100	$100							$100				
WI	Jefferson	Oconomowoc	$1,204	$733	$325	$129	$342				$204	$204			
WI	Ozaukee	Cedarburg	$2,314	$2,020		$208	$86					$2,020			
WI	St Croix	Hudson	$2,560	$673		$1,440	$447	$673							

Retail per 1,000 square feet (100,000-square-foot shopping center; 0.15 floor area ratio; 3-inch water meter) *(continued)*

State	County	Jurisdiction	Total	Total Non-utility	Roads	Water	Sewer	Drain-age	Parks	Library	Fire	Police	General Govern-ment	Schools	Other
		National Average	$6,039	$5,917	$5,150	$654	$671	$916	$1,132	$361	$368	$515	$568	$372	$2,059
		Sample Size	268	248	217	135	139	59	24	3	135	100	68	12	46
		National Avg w/o CA	$4,769	$4,680	$4,440	$494	$480	$881	$618		$365	$467	$450		$1,133
		Sample Size w/o CA	229	210	181	113	113	35	11		119	87	48		33
State Average Fees															
AR			$985	$823	$1,915	$141	$122	n/a	n/a	n/a	$329	$388	n/a	n/a	n/a
AZ			$4,426	$4,632	$3,609	$511	$446	$1,066	n/a	n/a	$428	$762	$375	n/a	$148
CA			$13,725	$12,974	$8,840	$1,476	$1,502	$967	$1,567	$361	$391	$838	$852	$372	$4,409
CO			$7,124	$6,524	$4,858	$1,168	$405	$718	$2,217	n/a	$260	$200	$296	n/a	$8,447
DE			$1,603	$297	n/a	n/a	$1,306	n/a	n/a	n/a	$169	$33	$95	n/a	n/a
FL			$7,040	$6,690	$6,064	$557	$594	$114	n/a	n/a	$352	$421	$623	n/a	$434
GA			$1,813	$1,813	$1,679	n/a	n/a	n/a	$257	n/a	$232	$91	$24	n/a	$6
HI			$4,053	$4,053	$4,053	n/a	n/a	n/a	n/a	n/a	n/a	n/a	n/a	n/a	n/a
ID			$4,780	$4,262	$4,124	$196	$841	n/a	n/a	n/a	n/a	$262	n/a	n/a	$14
IL			$963	$963	$963	$64	$114	n/a	n/a	n/a	n/a	n/a	n/a	n/a	n/a
IN			$6,955	$6,171	$6,171	n/a	$1,568	n/a	n/a	n/a	n/a	n/a	n/a	n/a	n/a
KS			$2,705	$2,456	$2,011	$347	$399	$1,097	$119	n/a	n/a	n/a	n/a	n/a	n/a
LA			$1,805	$3,003	$1,833	n/a	$608	$1,170	n/a	n/a	n/a	n/a	n/a	n/a	n/a
MD			$2,300	$1,767	$2,237	$600	$774	n/a	n/a	n/a	$1,090	$453	n/a	n/a	$110
MO			$1,856	$1,856	$1,856	n/a	n/a	n/a	n/a	n/a	n/a	n/a	n/a	n/a	n/a
MT			$6,706	$5,895	$5,338	$357	$453	n/a	n/a	n/a	$557	n/a	n/a	n/a	n/a
NC			$1,998	$1,970	$1,970	$383	$542	n/a	n/a	n/a	n/a	n/a	n/a	n/a	n/a
NE			$3,461	$3,260	$3,260	$134	$67	n/a	n/a	n/a	n/a	n/a	n/a	n/a	n/a
NH			$2,125	$2,125	$3,680	n/a	n/a	n/a	n/a	n/a	n/a	$570	n/a	n/a	n/a
NM			$2,603	$3,549	$3,203	$291	$223	$909	n/a	n/a	$438	$201	n/a	n/a	$49
NV			$2,020	$1,812	$1,756	n/a	$312	n/a	n/a	n/a	n/a	n/a	n/a	n/a	$84
OH			$5,461	$4,578	$7,265	$904	$862	n/a	n/a	n/a	$411	$361	$349	n/a	n/a

Retail per 1,000 square feet (100,000-square-foot shopping center; 0.15 floor area ratio; 3-inch water meter) *(continued)*

State	County	Jurisdiction	Total	Total Non-utility	Roads	Water	Sewer	Drain-age	Parks	Library	Fire	Police	General Government	Schools	Other
State Average Fees															
OK			$250	$250	$250	n/a	n/a	n/a	n/a	n/a	n/a	n/a	n/a	n/a	n/a
OR			$7,960	$6,944	$7,621	$515	$706	$975	n/a	n/a	n/a	n/a	n/a	n/a	n/a
PA			$5,109	$5,109	$5,109	n/a	$342	$161	$500	n/a	n/a	n/a	n/a	n/a	$300
SC			$2,722	$2,217	$3,079	$285	$472	n/a	n/a	n/a	$123	$120	n/a	n/a	$130
TN			$3,150	$3,515	$2,095	$277	$567	n/a	n/a	n/a	$554	$806	n/a	n/a	$1,390
TX			$905	$1,119	$1,119	$229	$116	n/a	n/a	n/a	n/a	n/a	n/a	n/a	n/a
UT			$3,332	$3,027	$2,950	$243	$183	$517	$78	n/a	$300	$171	n/a	n/a	n/a
VA			$2,503	$2,036	$2,036	$646	$838	n/a	n/a	n/a	n/a	n/a	n/a	n/a	n/a
VT			$1,334	$1,334	$896	n/a	n/a	n/a	$380	n/a	$179	$318	n/a	n/a	n/a
WA			$3,660	$3,202	$3,396	$594	$490	$2,630	$400	n/a	$327	$151	$30	n/a	n/a
WV			$1,844	$1,844	n/a	n/a	n/a	n/a	n/a	n/a	$1,650	$194	n/a	n/a	n/a
WI			$1,544	$881	$325	$592	$292	$673	n/a	n/a	$152	$1,112	n/a	n/a	n/a

Office per 1,000 square feet (100,000-square-foot general office building; 0.25 floor area ratio; 3-inch water meter)

State	County	Jurisdiction	Total	Total Non-utility	Roads	Water	Sewer	Drain-age	Parks	Library	Fire	Police	General Government	Schools	Other
AR	Benton	Bentonville	$775	$360		$233	$182				$360				
AR	Benton	Lowell	$698	$649			$49				$649				
AR	Faulkner	Conway	$1,280	$1,280	$1,280										
AR	Washington	Fayetteville	$864	$681		$49	$134				$293	$388			
AZ	Cochise	Sierra Vista	$1,180	$1,180	$1,030						$70	$80			
AZ	Gila	Payson	$757			$757									
AZ	Gila	Sedona	$3,410	$3,410	$2,520		$0	$300				$180	$410		
AZ	Maricopa	Avondale	$4,914	$3,757	$1,286	$562	$595				$1,067	$411	$993		
AZ	Maricopa	Buckeye	$2,902	$2,515	$445	$240	$148				$1,080	$720	$270		
AZ	Maricopa	Chandler	$5,177	$4,000	$3,460	$779	$398				$200	$170	$170		
AZ	Maricopa	Fountain Hills	$2,200	$2,200	$1,281						$62	$276	$581		

Office per 1,000 square feet (100,000-square-foot general office building; 0.25 floor area ratio; 3-inch water meter) *(continued)*

State	County	Jurisdiction	Total	Total Non-utility	Roads	Water	Sewer	Drainage	Parks	Library	Fire	Police	General Government	Schools	Other
AZ	Maricopa	Gilbert	$2,887	$1,508	$413	$671	$708				$447	$315	$333		
AZ	Maricopa	Glendale	$5,025	$4,036	$2,173	$733	$256				$447	$304	$1,007		$105
AZ	Maricopa	Goodyear	$3,630	$2,640	$900	$477	$513				$310	$680	$410		$340
AZ	Maricopa	Mesa	$1,046	$560		$162	$324				$219	$341			
AZ	Maricopa	Peoria	$6,833	$6,236	$4,260	$399	$198				$639	$691	$646		
AZ	Maricopa	Phoenix	$6,508	$5,912	$3,679	$244	$352	$2,145				$62	$26		
AZ	Maricopa	Scottsdale	$1,494	$333		$677	$484	$333							
AZ	Maricopa	Surprise	$3,670	$3,081	$687	$356	$234				$1,505	$556	$333		
AZ	Maricopa	Tempe	$494			$222	$273								
AZ	Mojave	Bullhead City	$1,898			$1,898									
AZ	Navajo	Show Low	$501			$116	$385								
AZ	Pima	Pima County	$2,267	$1,449	$1,449		$818								
AZ	Pima	Marana	$350			$350									
AZ	Pima	Oro Valley	$698			$698									
AZ	Pima	Tucson	$6,195	$5,951	$4,724	$244					$269	$699			$259
AZ	Pinal	Apache Junction	$5,477	$5,010	$4,330	$147	$320					$520	$160		
AZ	Pinal	Casa Grande	$3,190	$2,911	$1,361		$279				$666	$253	$631		
AZ	Pinal	Eloy	$1,167	$911		$145	$112					$133	$778		
AZ	Pinal	Florence	$1,287	$1,098	$269	$83	$106				$432	$161	$236		
AZ	Pinal	Queen Creek	$3,280	$2,776	$860		$504				$317	$81	$1,518		
AZ	Yavapai	Yavapai County													
AZ	Yavapai	Chino Valley	$2,207	$1,350	$940	$84	$773				$180	$160	$70		
AZ	Yavapai	Prescott	$3,044	$1,544	$469	$1,500					$435	$365	$275		
AZ	Yuma	Yuma	$3,995	$2,335	$1,243	$607	$1,052				$280	$366	$386		$60
CA	Alameda	Fremont	$11,380	$11,380	$9,820						$207		$1,353		
CA	Alameda	Hayward	$4,759	$4,759		$695	$704							$360	$3,000
CA	Alameda	Livermore	$27,367	$27,367	$15,167	$3,644	$4,220	$936	$2,414					$420	$566

Office per 1,000 square feet (100,000-square-foot general office building; 0.25 floor area ratio; 3-inch water meter) *(continued)*

State	County	Jurisdiction	Total	Total Non-utility	Roads	Water	Sewer	Drain-age	Parks	Library	Fire	Police	General Government	Schools	Other
CA	Alameda	San Leandro	$3,580	$3,580	$2,910		$200							$360	$110
CA	Contra Costa	Orinda	$3,930	$3,930	$1,990			$1,940							
CA	El Dorado	El Dorado Co.	$3,848	$3,848	$2,328						$1,100			$420	
CA	Fresno	Clovis	$10,163	$8,883	$6,874	$386	$894		$1,450		$4	$1			$554
CA	Kern	Bakersfield	$1,065	$557	varies		$508							$360	$197
CA	Los Angeles	Lancaster	$2,952	$2,952	$1,530			$660			$715		$47		
CA	Los Angeles	Long Beach	$2,438	$2,360	$2,000		$78							$360	
CA	Monterey	Salinas	$2,673	$2,129	$1,685		$544	$445							
CA	Napa	St. Helena	$12,580	$8,340	$3,470	$2,260	$1,980	$640				$1,760	$2,470		
CA	Orange	Brea	$9,447	$7,440	$7,440	$2,007									
CA	Placer	Rocklin	$15,691	$15,691	$12,667			$64					$1,910		$1,050
CA	Sacramento	Citrus Heights	$6,456	$5,320	$3,640		$1,136	varies	$370					$340	$970
CA	Sacramento	Elk Grove	$19,225	$15,933	$10,600	$990	$2,302	1435	$1,120		$1,298	$210	$300		$970
CA	Sacramento	Sacramento	$29,207	$27,811	$7,756	$260	$1,136		$7,114					$420	$12,521
CA	San Bernardino	Highland	$8,673	$8,673	$8,149			$322			$99	$30	$73		
CA	San Bernardino	Redlands	$6,687	$6,687	$2,133			$330		$711	$336	$616	$2,560		
CA	San Bernardino	Rialto	$6,351	$4,290	$3,090	$510	$1,551	$620	$140		$240	$100	$100		
CA	San Diego	Carlsbad	$2,163	$1,200	$1,139	$795	$168	$61							
CA	San Diego	Escondido	$5,913	$3,750	$920	$883	$1,280	$700					$2,130		
CA	San Diego	San Diego	$1,483			$823	$660								
CA	San Joaquin	Lodi	$11,054	$9,934	$4,203	$289	$831	$2,198	$1,348		$427	$661	$1,098		
CA	San Joaquin	Ripon	$15,704	$12,304	$7,247	$1,520	$1,880	$1,200	$800		$915	$800	$570	$420	$352
CA	San Luis Obispo	Paso Robles	$5,941	$4,420	$4,190	$825	$696	$150			$10		$70		
CA	San Luis Obispo	San Luis Obispo	$11,085	$8,294	$8,294	$2,089	$702								

Office per 1,000 square feet (100,000-square-foot general office building; 0.25 floor area ratio; 3-inch water meter) *(continued)*

State	County	Jurisdiction	Total	Total Non-utility	Roads	Water	Sewer	Drain-age	Parks	Library	Fire	Police	General Govern-ment	Schools	Other
CA	Santa Barbara	Carpinteria	$29,730	$29,730	$26,620			$1,071	$1,630		$4		$30	$330	$45
CA	Santa Barbara	Santa Maria	$7,893	$5,336	$4,532	$1,246	$1,311		$26	$168	$60	$382	$168		
CA	Santa Clara	Gilroy	$25,216	$22,432	$19,190	$820	$1,964	$168					$3,074		
CA	Santa Clara	Palo Alto	$24,006	$24,006	$3,810				$3,983	$203					$16,010
CA	Santa Cruz	Santa Cruz Co.	$6,365	$6,365	$4,365	varies	varies	$2,000							
CA	Santa Cruz	Scotts Valley	$11,196	$11,196	$8,430		$982	$138				$1,568	$78		
CA	Shasta	Redding	$20,067	$20,067	$6,835	$6,341	$6,370	$403			$119				
CA	Solano	Vacaville	$10,164	$10,164	$3,362	$1,661	$2,070	$844			$106	$629	$274	$330	$889
CA	Sonoma	Windsor	$10,015	$10,015	$6,124	$117	$2,059	$1,226					$489		
CA	Ventura	Santa Paula	$4,888	$4,888	$2,095	$381	$300	$410	$165		$146	$934	$457		
CA	Yolo	Davis	$6,986	$6,986	$3,947	$647	varies	$115	$548			$589	$800	$340	
CO	Adams	Adams Co.	$1,178	$1,178	$1,178										
CO	Adams	Commerce City	$1,941	$1,941	$1,741				$200						
CO	Boulder	Boulder	$6,540	$4,690	$1,736	$1,554	$297	$1,820			$180	$180	$304		$470
CO	Eagle	Eagle Co.	$2,156	$2,156	$1,887						$269				
CO	Eagle	Basalt	$1,285	$250	$250	$1,035			varies						varies
CO	El Paso	Colorado Springs	$2,329	$572		$1,492	$266	$572							
CO	Fremont	Canon City	$152	$152							$152				
CO	Jefferson	Jefferson Co.	$3,630	$3,630	$3,630										
CO	La Plata	Durango	$2,560	$1,836	$1,836	$558	$166								
CO	Larimer	Larimer Co.	$2,408	$2,408	$2,408										
CO	Larimer	Loveland	$6,046	$5,243	$4,200	$803		$113			$260	$310	$360		
CO	Larimer	Ft. Collins	$6,834	$3,860	$3,067	$2,163	$811	$226			$202	$140	$225		
CO	Mesa	Mesa Co.	$1,665	$1,665	$1,665										
CO	Pitkin	Weld Co.	$46,925	$46,925	$4,381				$4,100						$38,444

Office per 1,000 square feet (100,000-square-foot general office building; 0.25 floor area ratio; 3-inch water meter) *(continued)*

State	County	Jurisdiction	Total	Total Non-utility	Roads	Water	Sewer	Drain-age	Parks	Library	Fire	Police	General Government	Schools	Other
CO	Weld	Windsor	$4,607	$3,207	$2,509	$915	$485	$698							
CO	Weld	Greeley	$3,526	$3,526	$2,560			$254			$623	$89			
DE	New Castle	New Castle Co.	$1,759	$453			$1,306				$297	$14	$142		
FL	Alachua	Alachua Co.	$1,897	$1,897	$1,821						$76				
FL	Brevard	Brevard Co.	$5,110	$5,110	$5,058						$18				$34
FL	Brevard	Cocoa	$5,270	$5,110	$5,058	$160					$18				$34
FL	Brevard	Melbourne	$9,297	$9,297	$9,058						$18		$187		$34
FL	Brevard	Palm Bay	$6,404	$6,404	$6,174						$153	$43			$34
FL	Brevard	Rockledge	$5,110	$5,110	$5,058						$18				$34
FL	Broward	Broward Co.	$661	$661	$661										
FL	Broward	Ft. Lauderdale													
FL	Charlotte	Charlotte Co.	$4,939	$4,939	$4,417						$142	$104	$276		
FL	Citrus	Citrus Co.	$7,061	$7,061	$5,757						$427	$223	$655		
FL	Clay	Clay Co.													
FL	Collier	Collier Co.	$16,950	$14,767	$13,122	$1,076	$1,107				$693	$173	$557		$222
FL	Dade	Miami/Dade Co.	$2,632	$2,632	$2,154						$239	$239			
FL	Dade	Miami	$682	$682							$336	$206	$140		
FL	DeSoto	DeSoto Co.	$2,800	$2,800	$1,560						$280	$500	$460		
FL	Flagler	Flagler Co.	$1,500	$1,500	$1,500										
FL	Flagler	Palm Coast	$4,335	$3,549	$3,498	$389	$397				$51				
FL	Gilchrist	Gilchrist Co.	$560	$560	$500								$60		
FL	Glades	Glades Co.	$2,256	$2,256	$2,203						$53				
FL	Hardee	Hardee Co.	$2,366	$2,366	$1,961						$113	$50	$170		$72
FL	Hendry	Hendry Co.	$1,466	$1,466	$1,466										
FL	Hernando	Hernando Co.	$3,094	$3,094	$2,567						$181	$74	$272		
FL	Highlands	Highlands Co.	$2,558	$2,558	$2,403						$155				

Office per 1,000 square feet (100,000-square-foot general office building; 0.25 floor area ratio; 3-inch water meter) *(continued)*

State	County	Jurisdiction	Total	Total Non-utility	Roads	Water	Sewer	Drain-age	Parks	Library	Fire	Police	General Govern-ment	Schools	Other
FL	Hillsborough	Hillsborough Co.	$2,502	$1,934	$1,893	$264	$304				$41				
FL	Hillsborough	Plant City	$4,850	$4,526	$4,062	$78	$245				$262	$202			
FL	Hillsborough	Tampa	$3,425	$3,425	$3,425										
FL	Indian River	Indian River Co.	$6,300	$6,300	$5,326						$130	$114	$555		$175
FL	Lake	Lake Co.	$4,116	$4,116	$2,883						$1,233				
FL	Lake	Eustis	$2,426	$666		$430	$1,330				$343	$323			
FL	Lee	Lee Co.	$7,606	$7,606	$7,305						$301				
FL	Lee	Bonita Springs	$4,670	$4,670	$4,441						$229				
FL	Lee	Cape Coral	$3,640	$3,088	$2,634	$274	$278				$153	$163			$137
FL	Lee	Ft. Myers	$8,214	$7,549	$7,305	$337	$328				$244				
FL	Levy	Levy Co.	$898	$898	$818						$80				
FL	Manatee	Manatee Co.	$8,421	$8,421	$7,733						$442	$246			
FL	Marion	Marion Co.	$7,077	$7,077	$6,893						$184				
FL	Martin	Martin Co.	$3,943	$3,943	$3,210						$185	$238	$310		
FL	Monroe	Monroe Co.	$1,914	$1,914	$684						$64	$112			$1,054
FL	Nassau	Nassau Co.	$1,858	$1,858	$1,154						$169	$210	$324		
FL	Okaloosa	Destin	$1,896	$1,896	$1,871							$25			
FL	Orange	Orange Co.	$6,856	$6,856	$6,588						$189	$79			
FL	Orange	Apopka	$3,844	$2,838	$2,838	$391	$615								
FL	Orange	Maitland	$2,134	$1,528	$1,378	$144	$462				$150				
FL	Orange	Oakland	$7,313	$3,613	$2,250	$3,500	$200				$98	$365			$900
FL	Orange	Ocoee	$7,619	$5,708	$4,908	$482	$1,429				$470	$330			
FL	Orange	Orlando	$4,104	$4,104	$3,844						$260				
FL	Orange	Winter Garden	$6,246	$5,129	$4,019	$438	$680				$610	$500			
FL	Osceola	Osceola Co.	$9,020	$9,020	$9,020										
FL	Palm Beach	Palm Beach Co.	$2,359	$2,359	$2,026						$151	$64	$118		
FL	Palm Beach	Palm Beach Gardens	$3,344	$3,344	$2,745						$261	$220	$118		
FL	Pasco	Pasco Co	$8,711	$8,711	$7,921						$549				$241

Office per 1,000 square feet (100,000-square-foot general office building; 0.25 floor area ratio; 3-inch water meter) *(continued)*

State	County	Jurisdiction	Total	Total Non-utility	Roads	Water	Sewer	Drain-age	Parks	Library	Fire	Police	General Govern-ment	Schools	Other
FL	Pinellas	Pinellas Co.	$2,823	$2,767	$2,767	$56									
FL	Polk	Polk Co.	$9,220	$9,220	$7,320						$190	$1,520			$190
FL	Polk	Lakeland	$10,674	$7,944	$7,320	$1,250	$1,480				$280	$154			$190
FL	Putnam	Putnam Co.	$2,953	$2,953	$2,683						$270				
FL	Santa Rosa	Santa Rosa Co.	$1,356	$1,356	$1,356										
FL	St. Johns	St. Johns Co.	$5,400	$5,400	$4,798						$112	$163	$327		
FL	St. Lucie	St. Lucie Co.	$1,621	$1,621	$645						$282	$280	$414		
FL	Sarasota	Sarasota Co.	$7,831	$6,881	$6,008	$544	$406				$178	$102	$177		$416
FL	Sarasota	North Port	$9,823	$9,010	$7,461	$327	$486				$927	$307	$315		
FL	Seminole	Seminole Co.	$1,944	$1,944	$1,872						$72				
FL	Seminole	Altamonte Springs	$1,113	$1,113	$766						$72	$275			
FL	Seminole	Winter Springs	$7,927	$7,492	$4,775	$83	$352				$1,300	$492	$925		
FL	Sumter	Sumter Co.	$2,185	$2,185	$2,065						$120				
FL	Volusia	Volusia Co.	$2,460	$2,460	$2,310						$150				
FL	Volusia	Daytona Beach	$4,329	$3,873	$2,629	$228	$228				$214	$364	$666		
FL	Volusia	Deland	$2,705	$2,705	$2,310						$22	$30	$343		
FL	Volusia	Deltona	$1,936	$824	$520	$435	$676				$197	$107			
FL	Volusia	Edgewater	$2,716	$2,026	$1,658	$344	$346				$165	$202			
FL	Volusia	Ormond Beach	$3,073	$2,581	$2,489	$227	$266	$92							
FL	Volusia	Port Orange	$6,550	$3,618	$3,418	$1,457	$1,475				$200				
GA	Cherokee	Canton	$1,377	$1,377	$989				$173		$173	$43			
GA	Cherokee	Cherokee Co.	$1,241	$1,241	$266						$564	$366	$36		$9
GA	Forsyth	Forsyth Co.	$86	$86							$86				
GA	Fulton	Alpharetta	$1,423	$1,423	$1,211				$14		$198				
GA	Fulton	Atlanta	$1,935	$1,935	$1,608				$241		$67	$19			
GA	Fulton	Roswell	$924	$924	$280						$617		$27		
HI	Honolulu	Honolulu	$3,403	$3,403	$3,403										

Office per 1,000 square feet (100,000-square-foot general office building; 0.25 floor area ratio; 3-inch water meter) *(continued)*

State	County	Jurisdiction	Total	Total Non-utility	Roads	Water	Sewer	Drain-age	Parks	Library	Fire	Police	General Govern-ment	Schools	Other
ID	Ada	Boise	$4,614	$4,614	$4,614										
ID	Kootenai	Post Falls	$2,859	$1,822	$1,575	$196	$841					$233			$14
IL	DeKalb	DeKalb (city)													
IL	DeKalb	Sandwich	$178			$64	$114								
IL	DuPage	DuPage County	$2,114	$2,114	$2,114										
IL	Kane	Kane County	$1,308	$1,308	$1,308										
IN	Hamilton	Fishers	$2,527	$1,927	$1,927		$600								
IN	Hamilton	Noblesville	$1,817	$1,817	$1,817										
KS	Johnson	Lenexa	$2,502	$2,502	$1,297			$1,097	$108						
KS	Johnson	Olathe	$1,966	$1,220	$1,090	$347	$399		$130						
KS	Johnson	Overland Park	$860	$860	$860										
LA	E Baton Rouge	Baton Rouge	$608				$608								
LA	St. Tammany	St. Tammany Parish	$3,343	$3,343	$2,173			$1,170							
MD	Anne Arundel	Anne Arundel Co.	$1,746	$1,746	$1,628							$118			
MD	Calvert	Calvert Co.	$110	$110											$110
MD	Carroll	Carroll Co.													
MD	Charles	Charles Co.	$1,260			$519	$741								
MD	Frederick	Frederick Co.	$1,739	$750	$750	$413	$576								
MD	Harford	Harford Co.													
MD	Howard	Howard Co.	$2,080	$880	$880	$600	$600								
MD	Montgomery	Montgomery Co.	$6,112	$5,300	$5,300	$352	$460								
MD	Queen Anne's	Queen Anne's Co.	$1,550	$1,550							$1,550				

Office per 1,000 square feet (100,000-square-foot general office building; 0.25 floor area ratio; 3-inch water meter) *(continued)*

State	County	Jurisdiction	Total	Total Non-utility	Roads	Water	Sewer	Drain-age	Parks	Library	Fire	Police	General Govern-ment	Schools	Other
MD	St. Mary's	St. Mary's Co.													
MO	Clay/ Jackson	Kansas City	$1,049	$1,049	$1,049										
MO	Jackson	Lee's Summit	$895	$895	$895										
MT	Gallatin	Bozeman	$4,480	$3,669	$3,309	$357	$453				$360				
NC	Chatham	Chatham Co.	$300			$300									
NC	Durham	Durham	$2,022	$1,692	$1,692	$170	$160								
NC	Orange	Orange Co.	$1,332			$492	$840								
NC	Wake	Cary	$2,821	$1,833	$1,833	$385	$603								
NC	Wake	Raleigh	$1,728	$596	$596	$566	$566								
NE	Lancaster	Lincoln	$3,821	$3,620	$3,620	$134	$67								
NH	Hillsborough	Manchester													
NH	Merrimack	Concord	$1,390	$1,390	$1,390										
NH	Rockingham	Salem	$560	$560								$560			
NH	Rockingham	Fremont													
NM	Bernalillo	Albuquerque	$4,920	$4,468	$4,006	$258	$194	$387				$75			
NM	Bernalillo	Bernalillo Co.	$1,788	$1,788	$1,200			$390			$198				
NM	Dona Ana	Las Cruces	$296			$182	$114								
NM	Lincoln	Ruidoso	$721			$428	$293								
NM	Sandoval	Rio Rancho	$5,681	$4,895	$3,094	$418	$368	$1,430			$335				$36
NM	Santa Fe	Santa Fe	$2,888	$2,434	$2,191	$314	$140				$182	$61			
NM	Santa Fe	Santa Fe County	$335	$335							$335				
NM	Valencia	Los Lunas	$375			$146	$229								

Office per 1,000 square feet (100,000-square-foot general office building; 0.25 floor area ratio; 3-inch water meter) *(continued)*

State	County	Jurisdiction	Total	Total Non-utility	Roads	Water	Sewer	Drain-age	Parks	Library	Fire	Police	General Govern-ment	Schools	Other
NV	Churchill	Churchill County													
NV	Clark	Las Vegas	$1,265	$853	$769		$412								$84
NV	Clark	Mesquite	$1,310	$1,098	$1,014		$212								$84
NV	Placer	Truckee													
NV	Washoe	Reno	$1,891	$1,891	$1,891										
OH	Butler	Middletown													
OH	Delaware	Delaware (city)	$3,096	$1,330		$904	$862				$574	$240	$516		
OH	Warren	Hamilton Township	$4,956	$4,956	$4,562						$244	$150			
OK	Cleveland	Moore	$250	$250	$250										
OR	Clackamas	Clackamas Co.	$360	$0	varies		$360								
OR	Clackamas	West Linn	$7,689	$6,528	$6,372	$740	$421	$156							
OR	Deschutes	Bend	$5,416	$3,148	$3,148	$1,748	$520								
OR	Josephine	Grants Pass	$7,286	$6,464	$6,460	$416	$406	$4	varies						
OR	Lane	Eugene	$2,996	$2,399	$2,365	$347	$250	$34							
OR	Lane	Springfield	$2,647	$2,479	$1,095		$168	$1,384							
OR	Marion	Salem	$3,487	$2,369	$2,088	$669	$449	$281							
OR	Marion	Silverton	$5,837	$4,267	varies	$425	$1,145	$4,267							
OR	Multnomah	Portland	$4,053	$3,264	$3,010	$268	$521	$254							
OR	Washington	Tigard	$3,300	$2,940	$2,940	$360									
OR	Washington	Washington Co.	$4,838	$2,038	$1,538		$2,800	$500							
PA	Montgomery	Towamencin Twp.	$6,549	$3,274	$3,274		$571	$161	$500						$300
SC	Beaufort	Beaufort Co.	$55	$55	varies						$55				
SC	Beaufort	Hilton Head	$2,858	$1,988	$1,988	$384	$486								
SC	Berkeley	Mt. Pleasant	$2,185	$1,540	$1,100	$187	$458				$190	$120			$130

Office per 1,000 square feet (100,000-square-foot general office building; 0.25 floor area ratio; 3-inch water meter) *(continued)*

State	County	Jurisdiction	Total	Total Non-utility	Roads	Water	Sewer	Drain-age	Parks	Library	Fire	Police	General Govern-ment	Schools	Other
TN	Rutherford	La Vergne	$376			$80	$296								
TN	Rutherford	Smyrna	$2,997	$2,997	$2,650						$347				
TN	Sumner	Portland													$400
TN	Sumner	White House	$1,550	$1,550	$929						$247	$374			
TN	Williamson	Franklin	$5,798	$4,486	$2,716	$474	$838								$1,770
TN	Williamson	Nolensville	$2,753	$2,753	$753										$2,000
TX	Brazos	College Station	$133			$88	$45								
TX	Collin	Allen	$1,022	$750	$750	$192	$80								
TX	Collin	McKinney	$303	$134	$134	$113	$55								
TX	Denton	Denton	$855			$552	$303								
TX	Tarrant	Arlington	$1,495	$1,253	$1,253	$135	$107								
TX	Tarrant	Colleyville	$1,280	$779	$779	$399	$103								
TX	Tarrant	Ft. Worth	$146			$107	$39								
TX	Williamson	Georgetown	$444			$245	$199								
UT	Cache	Logan	$419	$239	$112	$39	$140	$47			$62	$18			
UT	Davis	Layton	$3,813	$3,669	$2,190	$144		$1,011			$468				
UT	Salt Lake	Draper	$3,329	$3,117	$2,331	$212		$137			$542	$107			
UT	Salt Lake	Sandy City	$1,115	$672		$443		$332	$49		$206	$85			
UT	Salt Lake	West Jordan City	$2,992	$2,293	$1,470	$407	$292	$543			$200	$80			
UT	Salt Lake	West Valley City	$1,547	$1,547	$1,245			$111			$111	$80			
UT	Tooele	Tooele	$798	$320		$354	$124					$320			
UT	Utah	Provo	$1,334	$1,053	$553	$103	$177	$501							
VA	Loudoun	Leesburg	$1,833			$717	$1,116								
VA	Stafford	Stafford Co.	$3,742	$2,606	$2,606	$576	$560								
VT	Chittenden	Burlington	$1,491	$1,491	$614				$380		$179	$318			

Office per 1,000 square feet (100,000-square-foot general office building; 0.25 floor area ratio; 3-inch water meter) *(continued)*

State	County	Jurisdiction	Total	Total Non-utility	Roads	Water	Sewer	Drain-age	Parks	Library	Fire	Police	General Govern-ment	Schools	Other
VT	Chittenden	Williston	$447	$447	$447										
WA	Clark	Vancouver	$2,167	$2,167	$2,167										
WA	Cowlitz	Woodland	$933	$510		$195	$228				$510				
WA	King	King Co.			varies										
WA	King	Bellevue	$874	$874	$874										
WA	King	Bothell	$5,033	$4,480	$4,480	$322	$231								
WA	King	Issaquqh	$3,541	$3,541	$3,240						$200	$71	$30		
WA	King	Kirkland	$3,629	$2,070	$2,070	$1,261	$298								
WA	Kitsap	Kitsap Co.	$384	$384	$384										
WA	Pierce	Pierce Co.	$1,795	$1,795	$1,795										
WA	Skagit	Anacortes	$3,755	$2,252		$448	$1,055	$2,252							
WA	Skagit	Burlington	$1,425	$905	$278		$520		$400		$227				
WA	Snohomish	Snohomish Co.	$2,318	$2,318	$2,318										
WA	Thurston	Olympia	$4,219	$4,219	$4,060						$159				
WA	Thurston	Tumwater	$2,973	$2,421	$2,320		$552				$101				
WA	Whatcom	Bellingham	$2,200	$904		$746	$550	$904							
WV	Jefferson	Jefferson Co.	$624	$624							$559	$65			
WI	Dane	Fitchburg	$100	$100							$100				
WI	Jefferson	Oconomowoc	$1,204	$733	$325	$129	$342				$204	$204			
WI	Ozaukee	Cedarburg	$2,314	$2,020		$208	$86					$2,020			
WI	St Croix	Hudson	$1,536	$404		$864	$268	$404							
		National Average	$4,242	$4,005	$3,192	$630	$637	$723	$1,142	$361	$314	$315	$534	$372	$1,863
		Sample Size	269	248	217	136	141	59	24	3	135	100	68	12	46
		National Avg w/o CA	$3,215	$2,987	$2,605	$496	$463	$703	$572		$307	$266	$380		$1,469
		Sample Size w/o CA	231	211	182	114	115	35	11		119	87	48		33

Office per 1,000 square feet (100,000-square-foot general office building; 0.25 floor area ratio; 3-inch water meter) *(continued)*

State	County	Jurisdiction	Total	Total Non-utility	Roads	Water	Sewer	Drain-age	Parks	Library	Fire	Police	General Govern-ment	Schools	Other
State Average Fees															
AR			$904	$743	$1,280	$141	$122	n/a	n/a	n/a	$434	$388	n/a	n/a	n/a
AZ			$2,923	$2,779	$1,799	$506	$401	$926	n/a	n/a	$479	$342	$486	n/a	$191
CA			$10,483	$9,811	$6,244	$1,327	$1,405	$753	$1,624	$361	$362	$637	$902	$372	$2,864
CO			$5,662	$5,041	$2,341	$1,217	$405	$569	$2,150	n/a	$281	$180	$296	n/a	$13,003
DE			$1,759	$453	n/a	n/a	$1,306	n/a	n/a	n/a	$297	$14	$142	n/a	n/a
FL			$4,506	$4,129	$3,736	$561	$623	$92	n/a	n/a	$250	$244	$351	n/a	$251
GA			$1,164	$1,164	$871	n/a	n/a	n/a	$143	n/a	$284	$143	$32	n/a	$9
HI			$3,403	$3,403	$3,403	n/a	n/a	n/a	n/a	n/a	n/a	n/a	n/a	n/a	n/a
ID			$3,736	$3,218	$3,094	$196	$841	n/a	n/a	n/a	n/a	$233	n/a	n/a	$14
IL			$1,200	$1,711	$1,711	$64	$114	n/a	n/a	n/a	n/a	n/a	n/a	n/a	n/a
IN			$2,172	$1,872	$1,872	n/a	$600	n/a	n/a	n/a	n/a	n/a	n/a	n/a	n/a
KS			$1,776	$1,528	$1,082	$347	$399	$1,097	$119	n/a	n/a	n/a	n/a	n/a	n/a
LA			$1,975	$3,343	$2,173	n/a	$608	$1,170	n/a	n/a	n/a	n/a	n/a	n/a	n/a
MD			$2,085	$1,723	$2,140	$471	$594	n/a	n/a	n/a	$1,550	$118	n/a	n/a	$110
MO			$972	$972	$972	n/a	n/a	n/a	n/a	n/a	n/a	n/a	n/a	n/a	n/a
MT			$4,480	$3,669	$3,309	$357	$453	n/a	n/a	n/a	$360	n/a	n/a	n/a	n/a
NC			$1,640	$1,374	$1,374	$383	$542	n/a	n/a	n/a	n/a	n/a	n/a	n/a	n/a
NE			$3,821	$3,620	$3,620	$134	$67	n/a	n/a	n/a	n/a	n/a	n/a	n/a	n/a
NH			$975	$975	$1,390	n/a	n/a	n/a	n/a	n/a	n/a	$560	n/a	n/a	n/a
NM			$2,126	$2,784	$2,623	$291	$223	$736	n/a	n/a	$262	$68	n/a	n/a	$36
NV			$1,489	$1,281	$1,225	n/a	$312	n/a	n/a	n/a	n/a	n/a	n/a	n/a	$84
OH			$4,026	$3,143	$4,562	$904	$862	n/a	n/a	n/a	$409	$195	$516	n/a	n/a
OK			$250	$250	$250	n/a	n/a	n/a	n/a	n/a	n/a	n/a	n/a	n/a	n/a
OR			$4,355	$3,263	$3,224	$622	$704	$860	n/a	n/a	n/a	n/a	n/a	n/a	n/a
PA			$6,549	$3,274	$3,274	n/a	$571	$161	$500	n/a	n/a	n/a	n/a	n/a	$300
SC			$1,699	$1,194	$1,544	$285	$472	n/a	n/a	n/a	$123	$120	n/a	n/a	$130
TN			$2,695	$2,947	$1,762	$277	$567	n/a	n/a	n/a	$297	$374	n/a	n/a	$1,390
TX			$710	$729	$729	$229	$116	n/a	n/a	n/a	n/a	n/a	n/a	n/a	n/a

Office per 1,000 square feet (100,000-square-foot general office building; 0.25 floor area ratio; 3-inch water meter) *(continued)*

State	County	Jurisdiction	Total	Total Non-utility	Roads	Water	Sewer	Drain-age	Parks	Library	Fire	Police	General Government	Schools	Other
State Average Fees															
UT			$1,918	$1,614	$1,317	$243	$183	$383	$49	n/a	$265	$115	n/a	n/a	n/a
VA			$2,788	$2,606	$2,606	$646	$838	n/a	n/a	n/a	n/a	n/a	n/a	n/a	n/a
VT			$969	$969	$531	n/a	n/a	n/a	$380	n/a	$179	$318	n/a	n/a	n/a
WA			$2,517	$2,060	$2,180	$594	$490	$1,578	$400	n/a	$239	$71	$30	n/a	n/a
WV			$624	$624	n/a	n/a	n/a	n/a	n/a	n/a	$559	$65	n/a	n/a	n/a
WI			$1,288	$814	$325	$400	$232	$404	n/a	n/a	$152	$1,112	n/a	n/a	n/a

Industrial per 1,000 square feet (100,000-square-foot building; 0.15 floor area ratio; 3-inch water meter)

State	County	Jurisdiction	Total	Total Non-utility	Roads	Water	Sewer	Drain-age	Parks	Library	Fire	Police	General Govern-ment	Schools	Other
AR	Benton	Bentonville	$635	$220		$233	$182				$220				
AR	Benton	Lowell	$469	$420			$49				$420				
AR	Faulkner	Conway	$808	$808	$808										
AR	Washington	Fayetteville	$455	$272		$49	$134				$117	$155			
AZ	Cochise	Sierra Vista	$690	$690	$610						$40	$40			
AZ	Gila	Payson	$505			$505									
AZ	Gila	Sedona	$2,170	$2,170	$1,310		$0	$500				$100	$260		
AZ	Maricopa	Avondale	$3,325	$2,168	$672	$562	$595				$668	$214	$614		
AZ	Maricopa	Buckeye	$1,840	$1,453	$232	$240	$148				$676	$376	$169		
AZ	Maricopa	Chandler	$4,207	$3,030	$2,490	$779	$398				$200	$170	$170		
AZ	Maricopa	Fountain Hills	$981	$981	$62						$62	$276	$581		
AZ	Maricopa	Gilbert	$2,767	$1,388	$293	$671	$708				$447	$315	$333		
AZ	Maricopa	Glendale	$3,364	$2,375	$1,228	$733	$256				$280	$171	$630		$66
AZ	Maricopa	Goodyear	$2,030	$1,040	$240	$477	$513				$180	$180	$240		$200
AZ	Maricopa	Mesa	$860	$374		$162	$324				$146	$228			
AZ	Maricopa	Peoria	$3,988	$3,391	$2,226	$399	$198				$400	$361	$404		
AZ	Maricopa	Phoenix	$3,659	$3,410	$1,102	$102	$147	$2,176			$45	$87			

Industrial per 1,000 square feet (100,000-square-foot building; 0.15 floor area ratio; 3-inch water meter) *(continued)*

State	County	Jurisdiction	Total	Total Non-utility	Roads	Water	Sewer	Drain-age	Parks	Library	Fire	Police	General Government	Schools	Other
AZ	Maricopa	Scottsdale	$1,716	$555		$677	$484	$555							
AZ	Maricopa	Surprise	$2,543	$1,954	$474	$356	$234				$973	$292	$215		
AZ	Maricopa	Tempe	$494			$222	$273								
AZ	Mojave	Bullhead City	$1,898			$1,898									
AZ	Navajo	Show Low	$501			$116	$385								
AZ	Pima	Pima County	$2,658	$1,840	$1,840		$818								
AZ	Pima	Marana	$350			$350									
AZ	Pima	Oro Valley	$698			$698									
AZ	Pima	Tucson	$3,510	$3,266	$2,039	$244					$269	$699			$259
AZ	Pinal	Apache Junction	$3,097	$2,630	$2,260	$147	$320					$270	$100		
AZ	Pinal	Casa Grande	$1,970	$1,691	$716		$279				$432	$135	$408		
AZ	Pinal	Eloy	$830	$574		$145	$112					$70	$504		
AZ	Pinal	Florence	$693	$504	$83	$83	$106				$218	$82	$121		
AZ	Pinal	Queen Creek	$2,165	$1,661	$486		$504				$179	$46	$950		
AZ	Yavapai	Yavapai County													
AZ	Yavapai	Chino Valley	$3,937	$3,080	$2,670	$84	$773				$180	$160	$70		
AZ	Yavapai	Prescott	$3,044	$1,544	$469	$1,500					$435	$365	$275		
AZ	Yuma	Yuma	$2,955	$1,295	$650	$607	$1,052				$175	$191	$241		$38
CA	Alameda	Fremont	$4,311	$4,311	$3,530						$104		$677		
CA	Alameda	Hayward	$3,199	$3,199		$695	$704							$360	$1,440
CA	Alameda	Livermore	$19,447	$19,447	$9,602	$3,644	$4,220	$936	$449					$420	$176
CA	Alameda	San Leandro	$1,600	$1,600	$930		$200							$360	$110
CA	Contra Costa	Orinda	$3,930	$3,930	$1,990			$1,940							
CA	El Dorado	El Dorado Co.	$2,998	$2,998	$1,478						$1,100		$420		
CA	Fresno	Clovis	$14,746	$13,466	$11,456	$386	$894		$1,450		$4	$1			$554
CA	Kern	Bakersfield	$1,196	$688	varies		$508							$360	$328
CA	Los Angeles	Lancaster	$2,012	$2,012	$590			$660			$715		$47		
CA	Los Angeles	Long Beach	$1,538	$1,460	$1,100		$78							$360	

Industrial per 1,000 square feet (100,000-square-foot building; 0.15 floor area ratio; 3-inch water meter) *(continued)*

State	County	Jurisdiction	Total	Total Non-utility	Roads	Water	Sewer	Drain-age	Parks	Library	Fire	Police	General Govern-ment	Schools	Other
CA	Monterey	Salinas	$2,351	$1,807	$1,066		$544	$741							
CA	Napa	St. Helena	$11,320	$5,700	$830	$3,000	$2,620	$640				$1,760	$2,470		
CA	Orange	Brea	$9,447	$7,440	$7,440	$2,007									
CA	Placer	Rocklin	$8,963	$8,963	$6,510			$106					$950		$1,397
CA	Sacramento	Citrus Heights	$5,816	$4,680	$3,640		$1,136	varies	$90					$340	$610
CA	Sacramento	Elk Grove	$12,648	$8,768	$6,310	$990	$2,889	$920	$380		$418	$60	$70		$610
CA	Sacramento	Sacramento	$19,241	$17,846	$3,417	$260	$1,136		$7,114					$420	$6,895
CA	San Bernardino	Highland	$5,550	$5,550	$5,101			$322			$24	$30	$73		
CA	San Bernardino	Redlands	$6,304	$6,304	$1,351			$762		$711	$304	$616	$2,560		
CA	San Bernardino	Rialto	$3,179	$2,530	$1,750	$510	$139	$550	$120		$10	$20	$80		
CA	San Diego	Carlsbad	$1,560	$597	$536	$795	$168	$61							
CA	San Diego	Escondido	$4,259	$2,750	$440	$883	$626	$700					$1,610		
CA	San Diego	San Diego	$1,483			$823	$660								
CA	San Joaquin	Lodi	$10,970	$9,943	$4,285	$196	$831	$3,663	$957		$185	$89	$765		
CA	San Joaquin	Ripon	$18,952	$11,952	$6,704	$2,533	$4,467	$2,400	$600		$506	$600	$370	$420	$352
CA	San Luis Obispo	Paso Robles	$540	$540	$250			$200			$10		$80		
CA	San Luis Obispo	San Luis Obispo	$8,576	$5,785	$5,785	$2,089	$702								
CA	Santa Barbara	Carpinteria	$16,044	$16,044	$12,670			$1,785	$1,180		$4		$30	$330	$45
CA	Santa Barbara	Santa Maria	$6,991	$4,434	$3,630	$1,246	$1,311		$26	$168	$60	$382	$168		
CA	Santa Clara	Gilroy	$21,677	$18,893	$5,037	$820	$1,964	$206					$13,650		
CA	Santa Clara	Palo Alto	$24,006	$24,006	$3,810				$3,983	$203					$16,010
CA	Santa Cruz	Santa Cruz Co.	$3,238	$3,238	$1,238	varies	varies	$2,000							
CA	Santa Cruz	Scotts Valley	$8,879	$8,879	$5,020		$982	$138				$2,614	$125		
CA	Shasta	Redding	$16,583	$16,583	$3,516	$6,341	$6,370	$293			$63				
CA	Solano	Vacaville	$15,040	$15,040	$2,460	$1,661	$8,264	$1,407			$176	$178	$191	$330	$373

Industrial per 1,000 square feet (100,000-square-foot building; 0.15 floor area ratio; 3-inch water meter) *(continued)*

State	County	Jurisdiction	Total	Total Non-utility	Roads	Water	Sewer	Drain-age	Parks	Library	Fire	Police	General Govern-ment	Schools	Other
CA	Sonoma	Windsor	$7,282	$7,282	$2,854	$117	$2,059	$2,043					$209		
CA	Ventura	Santa Paula	$2,669	$2,669	$733	$381	$300	$506	$192		$87	$13	$457		
CA	Yolo	Davis	$2,080	$2,080	$365	$647	varies	$111	$170			$224	$223	$340	
CO	Adams	Adams Co.	$776	$776	$776										
CO	Adams	Commerce City	$1,479	$1,479	$1,146				$333						
CO	Boulder	Boulder	$6,540	$4,690	$1,736	$1,554	$297	$1,820			$180	$180	$304		$470
CO	Eagle	Eagle Co.	$1,435	$1,435	$1,166						$269				
CO	Eagle	Basalt	$768	$250	$250	$518			varies						varies
CO	El Paso	Colorado Springs	$2,710	$953		$1,492	$266	$953							
CO	Fremont	Canon City	$152	$152							$152				
CO	Jefferson	Jefferson Co.	$1,560	$1,560	$1,560										
CO	La Plata	Durango	$1,488	$764	$764	$558	$166								
CO	Larimer	Larimer Co.	$1,392	$1,392	$1,392										
CO	Larimer	Loveland	$3,330	$2,526	$2,170	$803		$106			$70	$80	$100		
CO	Larimer	Ft. Collins	$5,355	$2,381	$1,849	$2,163	$811	$376			$56	$38	$62		
CO	Mesa	Mesa Co.	$1,155	$1,155	$1,155										
CO	Pitkin	Pitkin Co.	$16,273	$16,273	$2,519				$4,100						$9,654
CO	Weld	Weld Co.	$2,013	$2,013	$1,618			$300							$95
CO	Weld	Windsor	$4,012	$2,612	$1,448	$915	$485	$1,164							
CO	Weld	Greeley	$1,733	$1,733	$1,144			$136			$403	$50			
DE	New Castle	New Castle Co.	$1,578	$272			$1,306				$177	$7	$88		
FL	Alachua	Alachua Co.	$1,148	$1,148	$1,072						$76				
FL	Brevard	Brevard Co.	$5,110	$5,110	$5,058						$18				$34
FL	Brevard	Cocoa	$5,270	$5,110	$5,058	$160					$18				$34
FL	Brevard	Melbourne	$2,903	$2,903	$2,775						$18		$76		$34
FL	Brevard	Palm Bay	$3,121	$3,121	$2,911						$157	$19			$34
FL	Brevard	Rockledge	$5,110	$5,110	$5,058						$18				$34

Industrial per 1,000 square feet (100,000-square-foot building; 0.15 floor area ratio; 3-inch water meter) *(continued)*

State	County	Jurisdiction	Total	Total Non-utility	Roads	Water	Sewer	Drain-age	Parks	Library	Fire	Police	General Govern-ment	Schools	Other
FL	Broward	Broward Co.	$358	$358	$358										
FL	Broward	Ft. Lauderdale													
FL	Charlotte	Charlotte Co.	$4,232	$4,232	$3,911						$87	$64	$170		
FL	Citrus	Citrus Co.	$3,627	$3,627	$2,909						$235	$123	$360		
FL	Clay	Clay Co.													
FL	Collier	Collier Co.	$10,330	$8,147	$7,075	$1,076	$1,107				$644	$99	$298		$31
FL	Dade	Miami/Dade Co.	$1,475	$1,475	$1,070						$166	$239			
FL	Dade	Miami	$404	$404							$210	$107	$87		
FL	DeSoto	DeSoto Co.	$1,760	$1,760	$960						$190	$310	$300		
FL	Flagler	Flagler Co.	$794	$794	$794										
FL	Flagler	Palm Coast	$2,885	$2,099	$2,048	$389	$397				$51				
FL	Gilchrist	Gilchrist Co.	$560	$560	$500								$60		
FL	Glades	Glades Co.	$2,180	$2,180	$2,147						$33				
FL	Hardee	Hardee Co.	$751	$751	$634						$33	$14	$49		$21
FL	Hendry	Hendry Co.	$1,918	$1,918	$1,918										
FL	Hernando	Hernando Co.	$2,101	$2,101	$1,838						$90	$37	$136		
FL	Highlands	Highlands Co.	$1,248	$1,248	$1,166						$83				
FL	Hillsborough	Hillsborough Co.	$1,571	$1,003	$994	$264	$304				$9				
FL	Hillsborough	Plant City	$2,507	$2,183	$1,930	$78	$245				$139	$114			
FL	Hillsborough	Tampa	$1,359	$1,359	$1,359										
FL	Indian River	Indian River Co.	$3,845	$3,845	$2,797						$120	$105	$512		$311
FL	Lake	Lake Co.	$2,256	$2,256	$2,157						$99				
FL	Lake	Eustis	$2,127	$367		$430	$1,330				$189	$178			
FL	Lee	Lee Co.	$6,452	$6,452	$6,195						$257				
FL	Lee	Bonita Springs	$4,009	$4,009	$3,897						$112				
FL	Lee	Cape Coral	$3,316	$2,764	$2,310	$274	$278				$153	$163			$137
FL	Lee	Ft. Myers	$7,058	$6,393	$6,195	$337	$328				$198				
FL	Levy	Levy Co.	$789	$789	$709						$80				
FL	Manatee	Manatee Co.	$4,396	$4,396	$3,992						$276	$128			

Industrial per 1,000 square feet (100,000-square-foot building; 0.15 floor area ratio; 3-inch water meter) *(continued)*

State	County	Jurisdiction	Total	Total Non-utility	Roads	Water	Sewer	Drain-age	Parks	Library	Fire	Police	General Govern-ment	Schools	Other
FL	Marion	Marion Co.	$3,398	$3,398	$3,294						$104				
FL	Martin	Martin Co.	$2,837	$2,837	$2,403						$107	$137	$190		
FL	Monroe	Monroe Co.	$543	$543	$406						$64	$19			$54
FL	Nassau	Nassau Co.	$1,378	$1,378	$1,074						$73	$91	$140		
FL	Okaloosa	Destin	$1,036	$1,036	$1,030							$6			
FL	Orange	Orange Co.	$3,313	$3,313	$3,224						$41	$48			
FL	Orange	Apopka	$3,421	$2,415	$2,415	$391	$615								
FL	Orange	Maitland	$1,595	$989	$839	$144	$462				$150				
FL	Orange	Oakland	$6,256	$2,556	$1,200	$3,500	$200				$98	$358			$900
FL	Orange	Ocoee	$6,806	$4,129	$3,329	$675	$2,003				$470	$330			
FL	Orange	Orlando	$2,420	$2,420	$2,160						$260				
FL	Orange	Winter Garden	$3,177	$2,842	$1,732	$131	$204				$610	$500			
FL	Osceola	Osceola Co.	$5,882	$5,882	$5,882										
FL	Palm Beach	Palm Beach Co.	$1,263	$1,263	$1,064						$145	$5	$49		
FL	Palm Beach	Palm Beach Gardens	$1,915	$1,915	$1,432						$414	$20	$49		
FL	Pasco	Pasco Co.	$4,602	$4,602	$3,812						$549				$241
FL	Pinellas	Pinellas Co.	$1,470	$1,414	$1,414	$56									
FL	Polk	Polk Co.	$1,599	$1,599	$1,409						$30	$90			$70
FL	Polk	Lakeland	$4,413	$1,683	$1,409	$1,250	$1,480				$140	$64			$70
FL	Putnam	Putnam Co.	$1,568	$1,568	$1,338						$230				
FL	Santa Rosa	Santa Rosa Co.	$1,147	$1,147	$1,147										
FL	St. Johns	St. Johns Co.	$2,864	$2,864	$2,632						$15	$72	$145		
FL	St. Lucie	St. Lucie Co.	$397	$397	$185						$64	$53	$95		
FL	Sarasota	Sarasota Co.	$5,446	$4,496	$3,973	$544	$406				$106	$61	$106		$250
FL	Sarasota	North Port	$5,686	$5,686	$4,714						$581	$193	$198		
FL	Seminole	Seminole Co.	$768	$768	$762						$6				
FL	Seminole	Altamonte Springs	$537	$537	$442						$6	$89			
FL	Seminole	Winter Springs	$6,556	$6,121	$3,404	$83	$352				$1,300	$492	$925		
FL	Sumter	Sumter Co.	$1,395	$1,395	$1,305						$90				

Industrial per 1,000 square feet (100,000-square-foot building; 0.15 floor area ratio; 3-inch water meter) *(continued)*

State	County	Jurisdiction	Total	Total Non-utility	Roads	Water	Sewer	Drain-age	Parks	Library	Fire	Police	General Govern-ment	Schools	Other
FL	Volusia	Volusia Co.	$1,370	$1,370	$1,220						$150				
FL	Volusia	Daytona Beach	$2,665	$2,209	$1,421	$228	$228				$136	$230	$422		
FL	Volusia	Deland	$1,489	$1,489	$1,220						$51	$15	$203		
FL	Volusia	Deltona	$1,539	$427	$280	$435	$676				$95	$52			
FL	Volusia	Edgewater	$1,861	$1,171	$1,040	$344	$346				$12	$120			
FL	Volusia	Ormond Beach	$1,889	$1,397	$1,299	$227	$266	$98							
FL	Volusia	Port Orange	$5,009	$2,077	$1,877	$1,457	$1,475				$200				
GA	Cherokee	Canton	$522	$522	$134				$173		$173	$43			
GA	Cherokee	Cherokee Co.	$846	$846	$169						$393	$254	$24		$6
GA	Forsyth	Forsyth Co.	$52	$52							$52				
GA	Fulton	Alpharetta	$799	$799	$513				$14		$272				
GA	Fulton	Atlanta	$1,255	$1,255	$1,025				$169		$47	$14			
GA	Fulton	Roswell	$624	$624	$177						$429		$18		
HI	Honolulu	Honolulu	$2,019	$2,019	$2,019										
ID	Ada	Boise	$2,627	$2,627	$2,627										
ID	Kootenai	Post Falls	$1,505	$468	$446	$196	$841					$8			$14
IL	DeKalb	DeKalb (city)													
IL	DeKalb	Sandwich				$64	$114								
IL	DuPage	DuPage County	$1,049	$1,049	$1,049										
IL	Kane	Kane County	$862	$862	$862										
IN	Hamilton	Fishers	$1,350	$1,220	$1,220		$130								
IN	Hamilton	Noblesville	$1,150	$1,150	$1,150										

Industrial per 1,000 square feet (100,000-square-foot building; 0.15 floor area ratio; 3-inch water meter) *(continued)*

State	County	Jurisdiction	Total	Total Non-utility	Roads	Water	Sewer	Drain-age	Parks	Library	Fire	Police	General Govern-ment	Schools	Other
KS	Johnson	Lenexa	$2,797	$2,797	$1,591			$1,097	$108						
KS	Johnson	Olathe	$2,633	$1,887	$1,817	$347	$399		$70						
KS	Johnson	Overland Park	$1,433	$1,433	$1,433										
LA	E Baton Rouge	Baton Rouge	$608				$608								
LA	St. Tammany	St. Tammany Parish	$2,132	$2,132	$1,254			$878							
MD	Anne Arundel	Anne Arundel Co.	$471	$471	$451							$20			
MD	Calvert	Calvert Co.	$110	$110											$110
MD	Carroll	Carroll Co.													
MD	Charles	Charles Co.	$1,260			$519	$741								
MD	Frederick	Frederick Co.	$1,739	$750	$750	$413	$576								
MD	Harford	Harford Co.													
MD	Howard	Howard Co.	$1,640	$440	$440	$600	$600								
MD	Montgomery	Montgomery Co.	$3,462	$2,650	$2,650	$352	$460								
MD	Queen Anne's	Queen Anne's Co.	$1,000	$1,000							$1,000				
MD	St. Mary's	St. Mary's Co.													
MO	Clay/ Jackson	Kansas City	$647	$647	$647										
MO	Jackson	Lee's Summit	$689	$689	$689										
MT	Gallatin	Bozeman	$2,658	$1,847	$1,308	$357	$453				$539				
NC	Chatham	Chatham Co.	$300			$300									
NC	Durham	Durham	$921	$591	$591	$170	$160								
NC	Orange	Orange Co.	$1,332			$492	$840								

Industrial per 1,000 square feet (100,000-square-foot building; 0.15 floor area ratio; 3-inch water meter) *(continued)*

State	County	Jurisdiction	Total	Total Non-utility	Roads	Water	Sewer	Drain-age	Parks	Library	Fire	Police	General Government	Schools	Other
NC	Wake	Cary	$2,119	$1,131	$1,131	$385	$603								
NC	Wake	Raleigh	$1,378	$246	$246	$566	$566								
NE	Lancaster	Lincoln	$2,421	$2,220	$2,220	$134	$67								
NH	Hillsborough	Manchester													
NH	Merrimack	Concord	$890	$890	$890										
NH	Rockingham	Salem	$300	$300								$300			
NH	Rockingham	Fremont													
NM	Bernalillo	Albuquerque	$4,525	$4,073	$3,345	$258	$194	$645				$83			
NM	Bernalillo	Bernalillo Co.	$1,447	$1,447	$697			$650			$100				
NM	Dona Ana	Las Cruces	$296			$182	$114								
NM	Lincoln	Ruidoso	$721			$428	$293								
NM	Sandoval	Rio Rancho	$4,371	$3,585	$1,955	$418	$368	$1,430			$177				$23
NM	Santa Fe	Santa Fe	$2,254	$1,800	$1,557	$314	$140				$182	$61			
NM	Santa Fe	Santa Fe County	$460	$460							$460				
NM	Valencia	Los Lunas	$375			$146	$229								
NV	Churchill	Churchill County													
NV	Clark	Las Vegas	$1,103	$691	$607		$412								$84
NV	Clark	Mesquite	$1,449	$1,237	$1,153		$212								$84
NV	Placer	Truckee													
NV	Washoe	Reno	$1,199	$1,199	$1,199										
OH	Butler	Middletown													
OH	Delaware	Delaware (city)	$2,583	$817		$904	$862				$359	$135	$323		
OH	Warren	Hamilton Township	$3,759	$3,759	$3,512						$153	$94			

Industrial per 1,000 square feet (100,000-square-foot building; 0.15 floor area ratio; 3-inch water meter) *(continued)*

State	County	Jurisdiction	Total	Total Non-utility	Roads	Water	Sewer	Drain-age	Parks	Library	Fire	Police	General Govern-ment	Schools	Other
OK	Cleveland	Moore	$360	$360	$360										
OR	Clackamas	Clackamas Co.	$360	$0	varies		$360								
OR	Clackamas	West Linn	$7,689	$6,528	$6,372	$740	$421	$156							
OR	Deschutes	Bend	$5,637	$4,226	$4,226	$891	$520								
OR	Josephine	Grants Pass	$3,733	$2,911	$2,907	$416	$406	$4	varies						
OR	Lane	Eugene	$2,119	$1,522	$1,488	$347	$250	$34							
OR	Lane	Springfield	$3,207	$3,039	$732		$168	$2,307							
OR	Marion	Salem	$2,354	$1,603	$1,322	$302	$449	$281							
OR	Marion	Silverton	$4,692	$4,267	varies	$425	varies	$4,267							
OR	Multnomah	Portland	$2,943	$2,154	$1,900	$268	$521	$254							
OR	Washington	Tigard	$1,746	$1,386	$1,386	$360									
OR	Washington	Washington Co.	$4,206	$1,406	$906		$2,800	$500							
PA	Montgomery	Towamencin Twp.	$2,154	$2,154	$2,154		$171	$161	$500			.			$300
SC	Beaufort	Beaufort Co.	$55	$55	varies						$55				
SC	Beaufort	Hilton Head	$1,465	$595	$595	$384	$486								
SC	Berkeley	Mt. Pleasant	$1,695	$1,050	$700	$187	$458				$190	$30			$130
TN	Rutherford	La Vergne	$376			$80	$296								
TN	Rutherford	Smyrna	$1,830	$1,830	$1,625						$205				
TN	Sumner	Portland	$400	$400										$400	
TN	Sumner	White House	$977	$977	$278						$119	$180		$400	
TN	Williamson	Franklin	$4,579	$3,267	$1,497	$474	$838								$1,770
TN	Williamson	Nolensville	$2,498	$2,498	$498										$2,000
TX	Brazos	College Station	$133			$88	$45								
TX	Collin	Allen	$872	$600	$600	$192	$80								
TX	Collin	McKinney	$219	$51	$51	$113	$55								

Industrial per 1,000 square feet (100,000-square-foot building; 0.15 floor area ratio; 3-inch water meter) *(continued)*

State	County	Jurisdiction	Total	Total Non-utility	Roads	Water	Sewer	Drain-age	Parks	Library	Fire	Police	General Government	Schools	Other
TX	Denton	Denton	$855			$552	$303								
TX	Tarrant	Arlington	$715	$473	$473	$135	$107								
TX	Tarrant	Colleyville	$2,623	$2,122	$2,122	$399	$103								
TX	Tarrant	Ft. Worth	$146			$107	$39								
TX	Williamson	Georgetown	$444			$245	$199								
UT	Cache	Logan	$362	$183	$59	$39	$140	$79			$35	$10			
UT	Davis	Layton	$3,781	$3,637	$2,552	$144		$1,011			$74				
UT	Salt Lake	Draper	$1,796	$1,584	$1,275	$212		$228			$43	$38			
UT	Salt Lake	Sandy City	$1,211	$768		$443		$553	$31		$130	$54			
UT	Salt Lake	West Jordan City	$2,554	$1,855	$770	$407	$292	$905			$130	$50			
UT	Salt Lake	West Valley City	$1,086	$1,086	$815			$185			$50	$36			
UT	Tooele	Tooele	$798	$320		$354	$124					$320			
UT	Utah	Provo	$1,131	$851	$350	$103	$177	$501							
VA	Loudoun	Leesburg	$1,833			$717	$1,116								
VA	Stafford	Stafford Co.	$2,646	$1,510	$1,510	$576	$560								
VT	Chittenden	Burlington	$1,052	$1,052	$239				$318		$177	$318			
VT	Chittenden	Williston	$294	$294	$294										
WA	Clark	Vancouver	$1,372	$1,372	$1,372										
WA	Cowlitz	Woodland	$933	$510	varies	$195	$228				$510				
WA	King	King Co.	$588	$588	$588										
WA	King	Bellevue	$3,513	$2,960	$2,960	$322	$231								
WA	King	Bothell	$2,386	$2,386	$2,130						$200	$26	$30		
WA	King	Issaquqh	$2,386	$2,386	$2,130						$200	$26	$30		
WA	King	Kirkland	$2,929	$1,370	$1,370	$1,261	$298								

Industrial per 1,000 square feet (100,000-square-foot building; 0.15 floor area ratio; 3-inch water meter) *(continued)*

State	County	Jurisdiction	Total	Total Non-utility	Roads	Water	Sewer	Drain-age	Parks	Library	Fire	Police	General Government	Schools	Other
WA	Kitsap	Kitsap Co.	$197	$197	$197										
WA	Pierce	Pierce Co.	$1,582	$1,582	$1,582										
WA	Skagit	Anacortes	$5,256	$3,753		$448	$1,055	$3,753							
WA	Skagit	Burlington	$1,330	$810	$183		$520		$400		$227				
WA	Snohomish	Snohomish Co.	$1,467	$1,467	$1,467										
WA	Thurston	Olympia	$2,509	$2,509	$2,350						$159				
WA	Thurston	Tumwater	$2,183	$1,631	$1,530		$552				$101				
WA	Whatcom	Bellingham	$2,802	$1,507		$746	$550	$1,507							
WV	Jefferson	Jefferson Co.	$327	$327							$293	$34			
WI	Dane	Fitchburg	$125	$125							$125				
WI	Jefferson	Oconomowoc	$815	$344	$160	$129	$342				$93	$91			
WI	Ozaukee	Cedarburg	$2,314	$2,020		$208	$86					$2,020			
WI	St Croix	Hudson	$2,560	$673		$1,440	$447	$673							
		National Average	$3,025	$2,697	$1,936	$631	$685	$904	$955	$361	$214	$209	$546	$376	$1,032
		Sample Size	269	249	217	134	138	59	24	3	136	100	67	14	45
		National Avg w/o CA	$2,177	$1,878	$1,608	$482	$450	$864	$565	#DIV/0!	$211	$164	$251		$549
		Sample Size w/o CA	231	212	182	113	113	35	11	0	120	87	47		32

State Average Fees

State	County	Jurisdiction	Total	Total Non-utility	Roads	Water	Sewer	Drain-age	Parks	Library	Fire	Police	General Government	Schools	Other
AR			$592	$430	$808	$141	$122	n/a	n/a	n/a	$252	$155	n/a	n/a	n/a
AZ			$2,115	$1,794	$1,055	$490	$392	$1,077	n/a	n/a	$316	$219	$349	n/a	$141
CA			$8,174	$7,390	$3,641	$1,430	$1,751	$962	$1,285	$361	$236	$507	$1,240	$372	$2,223
CO			$3,069	$2,479	$1,380	$1,143	$405	$694	$2,217	n/a	$188	$87	$155	n/a	$3,406
DE			$1,578	$272	n/a	n/a	$1,306	n/a	n/a	n/a	$177	$7	$88	n/a	n/a
FL			$2,848	$2,483	$2,233	$567	$635	$98	n/a	n/a	$173	$132	$218	n/a	$150
GA			$683	$683	$404	n/a	n/a	n/a	$119	n/a	$228	$104	$21	n/a	$6

Industrial per 1,000 square feet (100,000-square-foot building; 0.15 floor area ratio; 3-inch water meter) *(continued)*

State	County	Jurisdiction	Total	Total Non-utility	Roads	Water	Sewer	Drain-age	Parks	Library	Fire	Police	General Govern-ment	Schools	Other
State Average Fees															
HI			$2,019	$2,019	$2,019	n/a	n/a	n/a	n/a	n/a	n/a	n/a	n/a	n/a	n/a
ID			$2,066	$1,547	$1,536	$196	$841	n/a	n/a	n/a	n/a	$8	n/a	n/a	$14
IL			$955	$955	$955	$64	$114	n/a	n/a	n/a	n/a	n/a	n/a	n/a	n/a
IN			$1,250	$1,185	$1,185	n/a	$130	n/a	n/a	n/a	n/a	n/a	n/a	n/a	n/a
KS			$2,288	$2,039	$1,614	$347	$399	$1,097	$89	n/a	n/a	n/a	n/a	n/a	n/a
LA			$1,370	$2,132	$1,254	n/a	$608	$878	n/a	n/a	n/a	n/a	n/a	n/a	n/a
MD			$1,383	$904	$1,073	$471	$594	n/a	n/a	n/a	$1,000	$20	n/a	n/a	$110
MO			$668	$668	$668	n/a	n/a	n/a	n/a	n/a	n/a	n/a	n/a	n/a	n/a
MT			$2,658	$1,847	$1,308	$357	$453	n/a	n/a	n/a	$539	n/a	n/a	n/a	n/a
NC			$1,210	$656	$656	$383	$542	n/a	n/a	n/a	n/a	n/a	n/a	n/a	n/a
NE			$2,421	$2,220	$2,220	$134	$67	n/a	n/a	n/a	n/a	n/a	n/a	n/a	n/a
NH			$595	$595	$890	n/a	n/a	n/a	n/a	n/a	n/a	$300	n/a	n/a	n/a
NM			$1,806	$2,273	$1,888	$291	$223	$909	n/a	n/a	$230	$72	n/a	n/a	$23
NV			$1,250	$1,042	$986	n/a	$312	n/a	n/a	n/a	n/a	n/a	n/a	n/a	$84
OH			$3,171	$2,288	$3,512	$904	$862	n/a	n/a	n/a	$256	$115	$323	n/a	n/a
OK			$360	$360	$360	n/a	n/a	n/a	n/a	n/a	n/a	n/a	n/a	n/a	n/a
OR			$3,517	$2,640	$2,360	$469	$655	$975	n/a	n/a	n/a	n/a	n/a	n/a	n/a
PA			$2,154	$2,154	$2,154	n/a	$171	$161	$500	n/a	n/a	n/a	n/a	n/a	$300
SC			$1,072	$567	$648	$285	$472	n/a	n/a	n/a	$123	$30	n/a	n/a	$130
TN			$1,777	$1,794	$975	$277	$567	n/a	n/a	n/a	$162	$180	n/a	$400	$1,885
TX			$751	$811	$811	$229	$116	n/a	n/a	n/a	n/a	n/a	n/a	n/a	n/a
UT			$1,590	$1,286	$970	$243	$183	$495	$31	n/a	$77	$85	n/a	n/a	n/a
VA			$2,240	$1,510	$1,510	$646	$838	n/a	n/a	n/a	n/a	n/a	n/a	n/a	n/a
VT			$673	$673	$267	n/a	n/a	n/a	$318	n/a	$177	$318	n/a	n/a	n/a
WA			$2,075	$1,617	$1,430	$594	$490	$2,630	$400	n/a	$239	$26	$30	n/a	n/a
WV			$327	$327	n/a	n/a	n/a	n/a	n/a	n/a	$293	$34	n/a	n/a	n/a
WI			$1,453	$790	$160	$592	$292	$673	n/a	n/a	$109	$1,056	n/a	n/a	n/a

Source: Clancy Mullen of Duncan and Associates. Information based on data collected substantually during 2007.

NOTES

1. Florida, Washington, and Maryland have extensive and significant school impact fees. California's school fees are widespread but are capped by state law at a relatively modest level.
2. *Engineering News-Record*, "Construction Cost Index" (October 2004 to October 2008).

3

Legal Principles
of Impact Fees

INTRODUCTION

In one form or another, impact fees now exist in nearly all states and are a common technique used to generate revenue for capital funding necessitated by new development.[1] To date, approximately half the states have enacted impact fee enabling legislation[2] and, in most other states, impact fees are enacted pursuant to home rule powers or pursuant to individual local government enablement. Impact fees are charges imposed by local governments that take the form of a predetermined monetary payment—a fee—and are generally levied against developers to fund capital expansion of large-scale public facilities and services. Such fees play an integral part in giving local governments the ability to cope with many burdens of rapid population growth, such as the need for new parks, roads, schools, jails, public buildings, sewer and water treatment facilities, and public safety (fire, police, and EMS facilities).[3]

Historically, it has been a primary function of state and local governments to construct, operate, maintain, and improve the basic physical infrastructure of American communities. However, as a result of three significant events in American history, this traditional approach began to break down. The first

of these events was the sharp rise in inflation in the 1970s[4] and the decimation of fixed-based taxes such as the motor fuel tax. The next was the federal government's fiscal retrenchment that began in 1982 and has continued since then, thus reducing the funds made available to local jurisdictions. The third factor leading to the breakdown of the traditional approach was the general hostility to the taxation of real property, thus forcing local jurisdictions to look elsewhere to fund the ever-increasing quantity and quality demands of constituents.[5] Because these factors were occurring at a time when the pace of urban development was increasing, both the demand for and the cost of investment in public infrastructure began to climb at a time when the available financial resources were falling. As a result, there arose an increasing need for investment concurrent with declining means.

Due to the lessening of federal and state funding for such infrastructure facilities as water pollution control and highway system expansion and repairs, an increasing share of the responsibility to pay for these and other public investments fell directly on local jurisdictions by default.[6] In order to assume control of providing these infrastructure needs, local governments were forced to pay the associated costs, commonly by raising local property taxes. In turn, they were then hit by the "taxpayer's revolt." Increasingly, local elected officials faced a public demand to increase public services without increasing taxes. After failing to remedy this dilemma through taxation, many jurisdictions looked to their police power as a means of addressing the problem.

In terms of the police power, most local governments have great discretion to regulate in order to protect the public's health, safety, and welfare. In contrast, local governments have almost no discretion in the exercise of their power to tax. It was natural, then, that local governments would turn to the police power, where they had discretion, in order to finance infrastructure needs.[7] Negative aspects of urban growth, including congestion and loss of quality of life that further growth and development would entail, provided the framework for invoking the police power to protect the public. Thus, in order to make up for public service funding lost as a result of the conditions mentioned above, local governments began to impose conditions on development that were consistent with the protection of the public's health, safety, and welfare. This was accomplished through the implementation of the impact fee.

To see how the impact fee originated, however, it is necessary to understand the division of public services that had arisen in American public administration, namely governmental and proprietary services. Governmental services were those needed in order to promote the health, safety, and welfare of the public but not provided for by private entities (e.g., police and fire protection and the maintenance of public roads and parks). Proprietary services, on the other hand, are those services created for the same purpose but which can be and frequently are provided by the private sector and for which service charges are imposed by the party performing the service (e.g., trash collection and water service).

Local governments had long charged for proprietary services, and these charges—often called "user fees"—were extremely common. These user charges were possible because the benefit of providing a service could be isolated to individual users and, if the individual user failed to pay the charge, the user could be excluded from use or consumption.[8] Governmental services, on the other hand, are classified differently because the cost of performing a service cannot be identified with a single user nor can individuals be easily excluded from use or benefit. Under this framework, initial proponents of the impact fee had the objective of applying the principles of public finance, which had hitherto been applied only to proprietary services, to governmental services. This type of application had the effect of reducing, if not eliminating, the distinction between proprietary and governmental services.[9]

The legal implications of enacting a program such as this were unknown at the time. Fearing that the fees would be seen as an unconstitutional tax, many impact fees to pay for governmental services were initially set very low. For example, the "land-use fee" used in Broward County, Florida,[10] imposed for road improvement, was $100 per residence. Even so, this particular charge was struck down by a Florida court as an unconstitutional tax.[11] The court based its holding on the theory that the fee exceeded the county's cost of regulation, which would have justified its collection.[12] This holding, like court holdings in many other states, demanded that fees or charges assessed under the police power for the impact of new development be no greater than the costs borne by the governmental entity in "regulating" new development; otherwise, such a fee would be considered a tax.

Ultimately, both the definition of regulation and a detailed accounting of the "costs of regulating" development allowed local governments to base the imposition of impact fees on the police power and avoid the tax label.[13] Once at this stage, local governments were able to have their impact fee programs classified as regulatory by demonstrating that new development creates the need for new and expanded facilities, and then collecting from new development its proportionate share of the cost of expanding facility capacity. Even though local governments labeled impact fees as regulatory, courts still required local governments to produce calculations and other data to support the reasonableness of their fees.[14]

EVOLUTION OF IMPACT FEES

Required dedication was the earliest significant land-use regulation developed to shift a portion of the capital expense burden to developers. The practice of local governments conditioning their approval of a subdivision plat upon the developer's agreement to provide and dedicate certain improvements is now a well-accepted part of subdivision regulation and is generally approved by the courts.[15]

The "in-lieu" fee was developed as a refinement of required dedications. For example, requiring each subdivision to dedicate land for educational purposes would not solve the problem of providing school facilities for developing suburban areas because the sites would often be inadequate in size and imperfectly located. The in-lieu fee sought to solve this problem by substituting a money payment for dedication of land when the local government determined that the latter was not feasible.[16]

Although the impact fee owes its origin to the impact analysis concepts of federal environmental law, it is functionally similar to the in-lieu fee in that both are required payments for capital facilities. In fact, the terms are sometimes used interchangeably.[17] Impact fees are, however, a more flexible approach to private funding of public infrastructure. Impact fees are designed to apportion the cost of new infrastructure among the new residents who create the need for these improvements. The fees, at least in theory, represent the pro rata share of the cost of providing a public service to an individual residential, commercial, or industrial unit.

The distinction between in-lieu fees and impact fees results in several decided advantages for impact fees. First, impact fees can be utilized to fund types of facilities and capital expenses, which are not normally the subject of dedication requirements and can more easily be applied to facilities to be constructed outside the development (extradevelopmental or system infrastructure) as well as those inside the development (intradevelopmental or project infrastructure). For example, since in-lieu fees are predicated on dedication requirements, they can be used only where required dedications can be appropriately utilized. In the case of sewer and water facilities, public safety facilities, and similar capital outlays, required dedications frequently are not an appropriate device for shifting a portion of the capital costs to the development because one facility (and parcel of land) can service a very wide area, and there is little need for additional land to extend these services.[18]

Second, impact fees can be applied to developments platted before the advent of required dedications or in-lieu fees and thus impose on new development its fair share of these capital costs. This advantage is particularly important in a state such as Florida, where hundreds of thousands of vacant lots were platted prior to the use of required dedications by local governments.[19]

A third advantage is that impact fees can be applied to condominium, apartment, commercial, and industrial developments, which create the need for extradevelopmental capital expenditures but which generally escape dedication or in-lieu fee requirements because of the small land area involved or the inapplicability of subdivision regulations.

Finally, impact fees can be collected when building permits are issued, when the growth creating a need for new capital facilities occurs, rather than at the time of platting.[20]

CONSTITUTIONALITY OF IMPACT FEES

Developer funding of public capital facilities—whether in-lieu fees, required dedications, or impact fees—has been justified on several theories. Shifting the burden of the cost of new facilities from the general public to the people who create the need for the facilities has been viewed as a logical and fair method of accommodating growth. Commentators have argued that, absent developer exactions, the developer may reap a windfall at the expense of the general public, which must bear the costs generated by the new development. Others have extolled the "privilege" theory, which holds that, in exchange for the privilege of developing, the developer must be responsible for the costs of public facilities necessary to service his/her project.[21]

In spite of these conceptual supports, impact fees are generally subjected to a two-tiered constitutional attack. The preliminary objection is that they are not authorized by state statute or constitution and therefore are void as ultra vires. If statutory authority is found or unneeded, the local impact fee ordinance is alternatively challenged as an unreasonable regulation exceeding the police power or as a disguised tax, which violates various state constitutional strictures.[22]

Additionally, impact fees have been challenged as discriminatory and a violation of equal protection principles, since different types of development may pay varying amounts and those who developed prior to the enactment of the impact fee may have made no contribution toward infrastructure. Finally, impact fees have been challenged as violations of property rights and therefore as regulatory "takings" without just compensation.[23]

LAND-USE REGULATION OR TAXATION?

Because impact fees are conceptually and functionally similar to dedications and other land-use regulations, they can be considered land-use regulations, which are generally considered valid exercises of the police power. Arguably, however, impact fees could also be classified as taxes, particularly if a court considers simplistic distinctions between taxes and regulations and does not look closely at the purposes of impact fees and the restrictions placed on their collection and use.

The choice a court makes between these two classifications is important, since this issue will often determine the validity of the exaction at issue. If the tax label is adopted, the impact fee will be invalidated unless express and specific statutory authorization for the tax exists. Even if statutory authorization is present, constitutional limitations on taxation may still invalidate the statute. Alternatively, if the impact fee is construed as a police power regulation, very broad legislative delegation will suffice.

The clear trend among state courts is to validate such extradevelopmental capital funding payment requirements as a valid exercise of the police power. Nonetheless, the issue will not go away and several recent cases return to the fee-versus-tax dispute, which was resolved many years ago in most states by judicial decision or impact fee enabling statutes.[24]

Those courts applying the tax label to impact fees either implicitly or expressly rely on two rationales. The first is a simplistic observation that impact fees are a positive exaction of funds and are therefore a tax. This criterion is an untenable basis for distinction because it exalts form over function. It ignores similar police power regulations, which mandate that the developer expend considerable funds for streets, sewers, and other capital project improvements within the development. Also, distinctions between impact fees and similar police power regulations, made on the basis that impact fees are imposed prior to the issuance of building permits rather than as part of the plat approval process, are distinctions without a difference. In either case, funds must be expended by the developer prior to development.

The second rationale used to label system infrastructure impact fees "taxes" is the theory that funds for educational, recreational, and public safety purposes cannot be raised under the police power.[25] This assertion is based on the conviction that such facilities should be financed solely from general revenues provided by the community as a whole. There is no constitutional mandate, however, that educational, recreational, and other facilities be underwritten by the general population

rather than by the new development creating the need for the additional improvements. Furthermore, this rationale employs an unduly restrictive and inflexible conception of local land-use regulatory power.[26]

Finally, some courts avoid this classification issue altogether by viewing some impact fees as charges for services rendered rather than as either police power regulations or invalid taxes. Impact fees under this analysis are generally upheld as authorized under general and broad statutory authority. Utah decisions, for example, have upheld sewer connection fees and similar charges as neither "taxes nor assessment but payments for services rendered."[27]

TESTS FOR IMPACT FEE VALIDITY

Two landmark decisions placed an almost insurmountable burden on local governments seeking money payments for system infrastructure capital spending from developers whose activities necessitated such expenditures. In *Pioneer Trust & Savings Bank v. Village of Mount Prospect*,[28] a developer challenged the validity of an ordinance requiring subdividers to dedicate one acre per 60 residential lots for schools, parks, and other public purposes. In determining whether required dedications or money payments for recreational or educational purposes represented a valid exercise of the police power, the Illinois Supreme Court propounded the "specifically and uniquely attributable test." The court focused on the origin of the need for the new facilities and held that, unless the village could prove that the demand for additional facilities was "specifically and uniquely attributable" to the particular subdivision, such requirements were an unreasonable regulation not authorized by the police power. Thus, where schools had become overcrowded because of the "total development of the community," the subdivider could not be compelled to help fund new facilities that his activity would necessitate.[29]

The New York court in *Gulest Associates, Inc. v. Town of Newburgh*[30] delineated a related and equally restrictive test. In that case, developers attacked an ordinance that charged in-lieu fees for recreational purposes. The amounts collected were to be used by the town for neighborhood park, playground, or recreational purposes including the acquisition of property. The court held that the money payment requirement was an unreasonable regulation tantamount to an unconstitutional taking because the funds collected were not used solely for the benefit of the residents of the particular subdivision charged but rather could be used in any section of town for any recreational purpose.[31]

In essence, the *Gulest* "direct benefit" test required that funds collected from required payments for capital expenditures be specifically tied to a benefit directly conferred on the home owners in the subdivision that was charged. If recreation fees were used to purchase a park outside the subdivision, the direct benefit test was not met and the ordinance was invalid.

Perhaps the reason for this initial restrictive approach was an underlying judicial suspicion that payment requirements for system capital expenditures were, in reality, a tax. Unlike zoning, payment requirements did not fit neatly into traditional conceptions of police power regulations. By applying the restrictive *Pioneer Trust* and *Gulest* tests, courts imposed the restrictive requirements of a special assessment on such payment requirements. This was consistent with perceiving them as a tax. Unfortunately, it effectively precluded their use for most system capital funding purposes. The *Pioneer Trust* and *Gulest* tests, therefore, quickly became difficult to reconcile with the planning and funding problems imposed on local governments by the constant acceleration of suburban growth. This restrictiveness also became difficult to rationalize with the judicial view of zoning ordinances as presumptively valid. As public policy concerns about the burden of economic growth became more evident, the state courts turned away from the stringent *Pioneer Trust* and *Gulest* standards. Although the results of these decisions are progressive, the measure of police power criteria developed by the courts is far from enlightening.

Some courts nominally retained the *Pioneer Trust* test but reached patently contrary results without any explanation of the discrepancy. Other courts adopted a privilege theory, under which granting the privilege to subdivide entitles local governments to require payments for extradevelopmental capital spending in return. The imposition of these payment requirements is viewed more as a part of a transaction than as an exercise of the police power. Still other courts have deferred to legislative judgments and eschewed constitutional analysis of such payment requirements.[32]

In contrast to these results-oriented techniques, the Wisconsin Supreme Court in *Jordan v. Village of Menomonee Falls*[33] suggested a more rational constitutional approach. A two-part "rational nexus" test of reasonableness for judging the validity of extradevelopmental impact and in-lieu fees can be discerned in the decision. In response to a developer's attack upon the ordinance as unauthorized by state statute and as an unconstitutional taking without just compensation, the *Jordan* court addressed the constitutionality of in-lieu fees for education and recreational purposes. After concluding that the fee payments were statutorily authorized, the court focused first on the *Pioneer Trust* "specifically and uniquely attributable" test.

The Wisconsin Supreme Court expressed concern that it was virtually impossible for a municipality to prove that money payment or land dedication requirements was assessed to meet a need solely generated by a particular subdivision. Suggesting a substitute test, the court held that money payment and dedication requirements for educational and recreational purposes were a valid exercise of the police power if there was a "reasonable connection" between the need for additional facilities and the growth generated by the subdivision. This first "rational nexus" was sufficiently established if the local government had generated the need to provide educational and recreational facilities for the benefit of this stream of new residents. In the absence of contrary evidence, such proof showed that the need for the facilities was sufficiently attributable to the activity of the particular developer to permit the collection of fees for financing required improvements.[34]

The *Jordan* court also rejected the *Gulest* direct benefit requirement, declining to treat the fees as a special assessment. It imposed no requirement that the ordinance restrict the funds to the purchase of school and park facilities that would directly benefit the assessed subdivision. Instead, the court concluded that the relationship between the expenditure of funds and the benefits accruing to the subdivision providing funds was a fact issue pertinent to the reasonableness of the payment requirement under the police power.

The *Jordan* court did not expressly define the "reasonableness" required in the expenditure of system capital funds; however, a second "rational nexus" was by implication required between the expenditure of the funds and benefits accruing to the subdivision. The court concluded that this second rational nexus was met if the fees were to be used exclusively for site acquisition, and the amount spent by the village in constructing additional school facilities was greater than the amounts collected from the developments creating the need for additional facilities.[35]

This second rational nexus requirement inferred from *Jordan*, therefore, is met if a local government can demonstrate that its actual or projected system capital expenditures earmarked for the substantial benefit of a series of developments are greater than the capital payments required of those developments. Such proof establishes a sufficient benefit to a particular subdivision in the stream of residential growth so that the system payment requirements may be deemed to be reasonable under the police power. The concept of benefits received is clearly distinct from the concept of needs attributable. As the *Jordan* court recognized, the benefit accruing to the development, although it need not be direct, is a necessary factor in analyzing the reasonableness of payment requirements for system infrastructure capital funding.

Another court addressing the difficult issue of reasonableness of an impact fee has identified seven factors to evaluate the validity of an impact fee. The Utah Supreme Court, in *Banberry Development Corp. v. South Jordan City*,[36] suggested the following as the most important factors for a local government to consider when determining the burden borne and to be borne by new development:

1. The cost of existing infrastructure;
2. The method of financing existing facilities (e.g., user charges, bonds, special assessments, general taxes, and federal grants);
3. The extent to which new developments and existing projects have already contributed to the cost of existing facilities (e.g., through property taxes and special assessments);
4. The extent of future contributions (e.g., user charges);
5. The extent to which developers may be entitled to credit because of required common facilities;
6. The extraordinary costs, if any, in providing service to new development; and
7. The time-price differential inherent in comparison of amounts paid at different times.

The *Banberry* criteria were promulgated in an attempt to deal with two problems of the proper cost apportionment in an impact fee rate determination. The first problem (recoupment) occurs because impact fees are sometimes required in situations in which a local government seeks to recoup a portion of money spent previously on capital facilities with excess capacity. The second problem (double charging) occurs when infrastructure is financed by more than one revenue source. These criteria are designed to ensure that developers pay their fair share and are not overcharged by local governments.[37]

EQUAL PROTECTION ISSUES

Another challenge to the validity of impact fees is that they violate the constitutional guarantees of equal protection. A fee levied only on new development, it is argued, denies the equal protection of the laws guaranteed by the U.S. Constitution. In an opinion letter addressing a proposed beach restoration impact fee, for example, the Maryland attorney general noted that developers of new beachfront projects (and therefore the ultimate buyers or lessees) would pay all of the cost of restoring the beachfront despite the fact that all residents would benefit by the restoration. However, the attorney general concluded that, since the plan was supported by a rational basis, an equal protection attack would probably not be successful.[38]

If a court accepts the principle of impact fees, it is likely to reject equal protection attacks. For example, in California, a city's impact fee plan was upheld as reasonable despite its varying rates for residential developers and builders.[39]

In *Ivy Steel and Wire Co. v. City of Jacksonville*,[40] the Jacksonville, Florida, ordinance at issue imposed a water pollution control charge on those persons connecting to the city sewer system after a specified date. Plaintiff challenged the ordinance on the theory that the equal protection clause of the U.S. Constitution was violated by the fact that those people connected before the specified date would be exempt while those who connected afterwards would have to pay the fee. The federal district court found no denial of equal protection.

The Florida Supreme Court considered but rejected an equal protection challenge in its landmark decision in *Contractors and Builders Assn. of Pinellas County v. City of Dunedin*,[41] which is discussed later in this chapter. The Supreme Court of Colorado also rejected an equal protection-based challenge in *City of Arvada v. City and County of Denver*.[42]

In *Cherokee County v. Greater Atlanta Home Builders Ass'n*,[43] Cherokee County's impact fee program, adopted pursuant to the Georgia Development Impact Fee Act, was challenged on equal protection grounds because the fees were imposed only on development within the unincorporated area of the county but also benefited development in the incorporated areas. The court upheld the fees and stated:

> The county's authority to require development approval through a building permit, however, is restricted to development in unincorporated portions of the county. OCGA Section 36-13-1. Thus, the General Assembly has limited Cherokee County's authority to impose impact fees to the unincorporated portions of the county. It has authorized but not required counties to enter into intergovernmental agreements with municipalities to jointly collect impact fees to pay for system improvements benefiting both. OCGA Section 36-71-11. … The county has imposed an impact fee on all new developments within the unincorporated portions of the county, which is all it has the power to do. It has not made a "classification" exempting incorporated developments from the fees, for by statute the county simply has no power or control over developments in municipal limits. The reason new developments in municipalities do not pay the fees is not because of any legislative distinction or action by the county, but results from decisions by the municipalities not to impose such fees and not to enter into optional intergovernmental agreements with the county regarding such.[44]

THE TAKING ISSUE: THE RATIONAL NEXUS TEST REVISITED?

Challenges by landowners that a land-use regulation constitutes a taking of property without compensation are frequently made. Certainly, many land-use regulations—including exactions—decrease the market value of land or the potential profits from its development. Nonetheless, the taking attack is one of the least successful and hardest to establish by landowners in suits against local governments. In theory, the concept does place limitations on the power of local governments to require exactions, and the issue is frequently raised in impact fee litigation.

The U.S. Supreme Court has admitted that it quite simply has been unable to develop any "'set' formula" for deciding whether there has been a taking.[45] The test used by the reviewing court indicates whether the regulation imposes too heavy an economic burden on the landowner to be sustained as an exercise of the police power. The requirement of the courts (i.e., that mandatory dedications, in-lieu fees, and impact fees benefit the developments paying them) seems at the same time a limitation within the taking jurisprudence and an answer to such a challenge. In other words, to be valid, such exactions must be required by and be of benefit to the development. If the exactions are for infrastructure necessitated by the development and are used to benefit it, then the regulation would arguably have not gone too far, since value would have been returned to the development by the provision of infrastructure. Linkage programs would seem to be the most susceptible of all exactions to a taking challenge since the link between the development and the benefit of the fees paid are at times less direct. Again, however, the reasonableness of the amount charged and the economic analysis of the connection between the development and the linkage program would seem to be the key.

Two cases decided by the U.S. Supreme Court set out the federal constitutional standards that must be met by programs requiring developer funding of infrastructure by way of required dedications or physical exactions: *Nollan v. California Coastal Commission*[46] and *Dolan v. City of Tigard*.[47] A look at *Dolan* will provide the opportunity to consider the effect of both cases on the rational nexus standards for impact fees.

In *Dolan v. City of Tigard*,[48] the Supreme Court of Oregon used the "reasonable relationship" test to uphold the validity of the city's requirement that a landowner dedicate land for improvement of a storm drainage system and for a bicycle/pedestrian pathway. The Oregon court considered its usage of the "reasonable relationship" test consistent with the "essential nexus" language contained in *Nollan*. In a 5-4 decision, the U.S. Supreme Court reversed the Oregon decision. Chief Justice Rehnquist, writing for the majority, first explained that the Court granted certiorari to resolve a question left open by *Nollan* "of what is the required degree of connection between the exactions imposed by the city and the projected impacts of the proposed development."[49]

Chief Justice Rehnquist went on to characterize the attack by the landowner Dolan on the constitutional validity of the city's actions as being grounded in the contention that the Supreme Court in *Nollan* "had abandoned the 'reasonable relationship' test in favor of a stricter 'essential nexus test'"[50] and further commented that the Supreme Court of Oregon had read *Nollan* "to mean that an exaction is reasonably related to an impact if the exaction serves the same purpose that a denial of the permit would serve."[51]

The majority had no problem, as it had in *Nollan*, finding an essential nexus between the governmental action and the governmental interest furthered by the permit condition, and therefore reached the second issue (i.e., "whether the degree of the exactions demanded by the city's permit conditions bear the required relationship to the projected impact of petitioner's proposed development"[52]).

In answering this question, the majority first turned to state court decisions because, as Chief Justice Rehnquist phrased it, "they have been dealing with this question a good deal longer than we have. …"[53] The examination of state court decisions began with *Billings Properties, Inc. v. Yellowstone County*[54] and *Jenad, Inc. v. Scarsdale*.[55] Without any discussion of what standard was used in those cases or why it was deficient, the majority opinion rejected the standard used as "too lax to adequately protect petitioner's right to just compensation if her property is taken for a public purpose."[56]

The opinion next turned to a case previously discussed, *Pioneer Trust & Savings Bank v. Village of Mount Prospect*,[57] and, in a comment of considerable potential importance to local governments that enact impact fee programs, concluded that the federal constitution does not require such exacting scrutiny as the *Pioneer Trust* court's "specific and uniquely attributable test" requires.

Chief Justice Rehnquist then turned to state court decisions of which he approved. One of these is *Jordan v. Village of Menomonee Falls*,[58] the important Wisconsin decision that established the dual rational nexus test. Surprisingly, the chief justice did not refer to the *Jordan* test by its usual name—the dual rational nexus test—but instead referred to it as a "form" of the reasonable relationship test. This part of the decision seems to leave us with the specific and uniquely attributable test being stricter than the Constitution requires, the "generalized statements as to the necessary connection between the required dedication and the proposed development"[59] required by a few state courts being too lax, and the form of the reasonable relationship test adopted by the majority of state courts being the constitutionally acceptable standard.

As previously stated, instead of calling the "acceptable test" the "dual rational nexus test," the Court comes up with a new label, to wit:

> We think the "reasonable relationship" test adopted by a majority of the state courts is closer to the federal constitutional norm than either of those previously discussed. But we do not adopt it as such partly because the term "reasonable relationship" seems confusingly similar to the term "rational basis" which describes the minimal level of scrutiny under the Equal Protection Clause of the Fourteenth Amendment. We

think a term such as "rough proportionality" best encapsulates what we hold to be the requirement of the Fifth Amendment. No precise mathematical calculation is required, but the city must make some sort of individualized determination that the dedication is related in nature and extend to the impact of the proposed development.[60]

To the extent that *Dolan* applies to impact fees, the majority may have actually liberalized the standard required of local governments in most states since Chief Justice Rehnquist concludes, "No precise mathematical calculation is required, but the city must make some effort to quantify its findings in support of … [its] dedication requirement."[61] Most state courts and statutes require local governments enacting impact fee and other exaction programs to have precise mathematical calculations and to make considerable efforts to quantify their findings.

Arizona and California courts, and a few others, have considered the applicability of *Nollan* and *Dolan* to developer funding fees. The Arizona and California cases intertwine. The Arizona Court of Appeals in *Home Builders Ass'n of Central Arizona v. City of Scottsdale*[62] deduced that the U.S. Supreme Court's remand of *Ehrlich v. City of Culver City*[63] (a case in which the city required a developer to pay an impact-type fee for recreational facilities when it sought approval to build apartments to replace a private tennis club) for reconsideration in light of the *Dolan* decision implied that the *Dolan* tests can apply to impact fee cases. However, the court of appeals proceeded to distinguish *Dolan* and determined that a *Dolan* analysis was not appropriate in the Scottsdale case:

> Unlike Tigard's ordinance, Scottsdale's [ordinance] allows its staff no discretion in setting the fees which are based upon a standardized schedule. The fees are tailored to the type of development involved and are uniform within each class of development. Because the fees are standardized and uniform, and because the ordinance permits no discretion in its application, a prospective developer may know precisely the fee that will be charged. The Scottsdale ordinance, therefore, does not permit a Dolan-like ad hoc, adjudicative determination.[64]

Although the Supreme Court of Arizona unanimously affirmed the court of appeals decision,[65] the court saw the *Dolan* issue somewhat differently. It agreed with the language just quoted but added:

We note, however, that there may be good reason to distinguish the Dolan adjudicative decision from the Scottsdale legislative one. Ehrlich v. City of Culver City * * * dramatically illustrates the differences between the two exactions. * * * On remand from the United States Supreme Court for reconsideration in light of Dolan, the California Supreme Court held the record insufficient to show that the fee was roughly proportional to the public burden of replacing recreational facilities that would be lost as a result of rezoning Ehrlich's property. The California court suggested that the Dolan analysis applied to cases of regulatory leveraging that occur when the landowner must bargain for approval of a particular use of its land. ... The risk of that sort of leveraging does not exist when the exaction is embodied in a generally applicable legislative decision.

Dolan may also be distinguished from our case on another ground. There, the city demanded that Mrs. Dolan cede a part of her property to the city a particularly invasive form of land regulation that the court believed justified increased judicial protection for the landowner. Here, Scottsdale seeks to impose a fee, a considerably more benign form of regulation.[66]

As indicated in the quoted language from the *Scottsdale* case above, following remand of its decision in *Ehrlich* by the U.S. Supreme Court, the California Court of Appeal, in a divided and unpublished decision, reaffirmed its earlier ruling in favor of *Ehrlich*. In a long, rambling decision made especially confusing by the "concurring in part—dissenting in part" statements of several justices, the Supreme Court of California reversed and remanded.[67]

The holding starts out with a direct statement responsive to the speculation over the impact of *Dolan*, to wit:

We conclude that the tests formulated by the high court in its Dolan and Nollan opinions for determining whether a compensable regulatory taking has occurred under the takings clause of the Fifth Amendment to the federal Constitution apply under the circumstances of this case, to the monetary exaction imposed by Culver City as a condition of approving plaintiff's request that the real property in suit be rezoned to permit the construction of a multiunit residential condominium. We thus reject the city's contention that the heightened taking clause standard formulated by the court in Nollan and Dolan applies only to cases in which the local land use authority requires the developer to dedicate real property to public use as a condition of the permit approval.[68]

Unfortunately for those seeking a clear answer to the speculation over the meaning of *Dolan*, the California court ties its above-quoted conclusion to its interpretation of the California Mitigation Fee Act.[69]

The Supreme Court of California revisited the issue in *San Remo Hotel v. City and County of San Francisco*,[70] which involved the required payment of a substantial in-lieu fee pursuant to the San Francisco Residential Hotel Unit Conversion and Demolition Ordinance regulating the conversion and demolition of single-room occupancy units. The court held that the heightened scrutiny requirements of *Nollan/Dolan* did not apply because the in-lieu fee was generally applicable and nondiscretionary.

In 2006, the Supreme Court of Washington weighed in on the applicability of *Nollan/Dolan*[71] principles to impact fees. In *City of Olympia v. Drebick*,[72] the amicus parties argued that *Nollan/Dolan* was the applicable standard and had been violated. The court totally and no doubt properly rejected this contention but with an analysis much less clear than some of its sister state supreme courts, such as those of Arizona and California.[73] The Washington Court of Appeals had found *Nollan/Dolan* not only applicable to the impact fees in question but also found the fees in violation of them. The state supreme court disagreed and opined as follows:

[T]he dissent takes the ... view that local governments must base GMA impact fees on individualized assessments of the direct impacts each new development will have on each improvement planned in a service area. ... The dissent does not explain that neither Nollan nor Dolan concerned the imposition of impact fees but addressed instead the authority of a local government to condition development approval on a property owner's dedication of a portion of land for public use; nor does the dissent mention that neither the United States Supreme Court nor this court has determined that the tests applied in Nollan and Dolan to evaluate land exactions must be extended to the consideration of fees imposed to mitigate the direct impacts of a new development, much less to the consideration of more general growth impact fees imposed pursuant to statutorily authorized local ordinances.[74]

The debate continues over whether or not and to what extent *Nollan/Dolan* principles of essential nexus and rough proportionality apply to all or some impact fees or only to required dedication (i.e., physical exactions). Four principal positions have emerged. Some advocate the full application of taking principles including *Nollan/Dolan* to impact fees and all other forms of exaction. Their position is based upon the assertion that the *Dolan* test is well established, it is logical in its outcome, and it seems to work reasonably well for both developers and local governments[75]; others consider that *Nollan/Dolan* should be applied only to mandatory dedication of land.[76]

A third position is that *Nollan/Dolan* should apply to administratively determined impact fees but not to those legislatively set.[77] This approach centers on the *Ehrlich* decision by the Supreme Court of California, previously discussed. A fourth view of the issue is that impact fees, and perhaps all exactions, should not be subject to the *Nollan/Dolan* test because, in virtually all states, they are subject to the dual rational nexus test. The dual rational nexus test is more stringent than *Nollan/Dolan*. It guarantees that exactions, which meet the dual rational nexus test, could not be takings. If an impact fee is valid (i.e., it satisfies the dual rational nexus test), then it cannot destroy property rights. If an impact fee violates the nexus test, it is invalid. Therefore, no takings analysis is appropriate or necessary.[78]

The relevance of *Nollan/Dolan* to required dedications and monetary exactions such as impact fees took a new twist with the 2005 decision of the U.S. Supreme Court in *Lingle v. Chevron, USA, Inc.*[79] In overruling *Agins*,[80] the *Lingle* Court retained the holdings of *Nollan* and *Dolan* but disclaimed the "substantially advances" rationale used in those opinions. While recognizing that "it might be argued that [the *Agins*] formula played a role in [those] decisions * * *, the rule those decisions established is entirely distinct"[81] from Agins's "substantially advances" test. Rather, the Court says, those cases "involved dedications of property so onerous that, outside the exactions context, they would be deemed per se physical takings"[82] under the *Loretto*[83] doctrine. Thus, whether an exaction is justified and thus exempt from *Loretto*'s per se takings rule depends on whether the exaction is a condition for the granting of development permission and that, qualitatively and quantitatively, the exaction is reasonably necessary to prevent or counteract anticipated adverse public effects of the proposed development.

Prior to *Lingle,* lower courts differed on the question of whether *Nollan* and *Dolan*'s intermediate scrutiny should be extended to regulations such as impact fees that do not cause physical invasions. By directly tying those cases to *Loretto*, and in disclaiming use of the "substantially advances test" to explain them, *Lingle* appears to answer that question in the negative. Without a threatened physical invasion, there is nothing to trigger *Loretto*, and no need for the government to raise the *Nollan/Dolan* nexus defenses.

A second reason that monetary charges do not raise takings issues is that nothing is taken for which the state could pay just compensation. As one court said, "applying the Takings Clause to regulations that merely require the payment of money is like saying the government can take money, but only if it pays it back. It is far more logical to conclude that a regulation of this sort violates due process by employing an irrational means and declare the fee void, than to let the government 'take' the money and then require it to 'pay' the money as compensation."[84]

Nollan and *Dolan* arose in adjudicatory settings, and the courts have grappled with whether the doctrine of those cases applies to legislative action as well. The legislative adjudicatory question arises because exactions are imposed on development in two distinct settings that may call for different levels of review. As Chief Justice Rehnquist said in *Dolan*, the burden is on a challenger to prove the invalidity of a generally applicable law but, where an adjudicative decision is made, the burden must switch to the government. Where property owners must bargain on a case-by-case basis, in what is essentially an adjudicatory setting, the safeguards of the open legislative process are lost, and concern arises that the individual may be compelled to give more than a fair share. Taking their cue from *Dolan*'s emphasis on the fact that the case involved an adjudicative decision, most lower courts in addressing the issue have found heightened scrutiny inapplicable to broad-based legislative conditions. Other courts take the position that heightened scrutiny applies to legislative as well as adjudicative acts. The question remains open and likely will continue to be disputed until the Court answers it.[85]

THE RELATIONSHIP OF IMPACT FEES TO THE COMPREHENSIVE PLAN

The reasonableness and proper exercise of the police power issues tie in with the concept of having impact fees based upon and an implementation of the local government's comprehensive plan. In short, it is easier to convince a judge of the reasonableness of an impact fee program if it is based upon and even required by specific comprehensive plan language.

Planning legislation in some states (e.g., Florida) requires all land-use regulations to be consistent with the comprehensive plan. Such a requirement makes impact fee and comprehensive plan consistency a necessity and not just a luxury.

The more specific the language in the comprehensive plan, the easier it is to make the consistency argument. The following language is suggested as the "bare bones" expression of the planning principles upon which impact fees are grounded:

- Land development shall not be permitted unless adequate capital facilities exist or are assured.
- Land development shall bear a proportionate cost of the provision of the new or expanded capital facilities required by such development.
- The imposition of impact fees and dedication requirements are the preferred methods of regulating land development in order to assure that it bears a proportionate share of the cost of capital facilities necessary to accommodate that development.

STATE AUTHORIZING LEGISLATION

The "tests" for impact fee validity discussed above relate primarily to basic land-use control and local government law principles. At least 27 states have statutory provisions authorizing or enabling impact fees.[86] These statutory provisions range from a few short paragraphs, which generally authorize all or certain local governments to adopt impact fees programs (e.g., Arizona) or briefly "solve" a very specific impact fee issue (e.g., Florida), to lengthy and comprehensive impact fee codes that cover most impact fee issues in considerable detail (e.g., Texas, Georgia, and New Mexico).[87] In most states, the relevant statutory provisions not only authorize impact fees but also establish requirements they must meet in order to be valid. Careful attention must therefore be paid to the express statutory language.

DRAFTING IMPACT FEES
TO PASS JUDICIAL SCRUTINY

The increasing number of judicial decisions and state statutory provisions authorizing impact fees has resulted in more numerous and more varied impact fee ordinances and comprehensive plan provisions. The attention of planners, judges, attorneys, and local government officials has shifted in many states from the issues of statutory authorization, constitutional validity, tax versus land regulatory change, and rational nexus to how to draft impact fee ordinances in order to bring them within the parameters for validity established by the courts. Drafting requirements vary according to the jurisdiction in question, but some generally applicable standards can be formulated. At this point, some of the general considerations will be discussed. The following basic list should be considered:

- An impact fee ordinance should expressly cite statutory authority for local government regulation of the substantive area selected.
- A need for service or improvements resulting from new development should be demonstrated.
- The fee charged must not exceed the cost of improvements.
- The improvements funded must adequately benefit the development that is the source of the fee (even if nonresidents of the development also benefit).
- In place of a rigid and inflexible formula for calculating the amount of the fee to be imposed on a particular development, a variance procedure should be included so that the local government may consider studies and data submitted by the developer to decrease his/her assessment.
- The expenditure of funds should be localized to the areas from which they were collected.

Cases from various jurisdictions give further indications of judicial requirements that will likely be imposed on impact fee-related ordinances. A decision by the Supreme Court of Arkansas[88] should prove to be a leading case in point. The city required a cash contribution from the plaintiff land developer of $85 per lot, which was to be invested by the city and eventually used for the acquisition and development of parks. The court held for the plaintiff on the basis that the city did not have a sufficiently definite plan for parks and park facilities to justify the contribution, and further noted that no provision was made for refund of the contributions if the area is not developed as expected.

Both of these points would seem to translate into principles that should be followed in formulating and drafting impact fee ordinances. The easiest with which to comply is the concern that provisions for refunds should be included in the ordinance so that the feepayor is entitled to get fees returned if they are not properly spent for the purposes for which they were collected within a reasonable period of time after their collection. The reasonableness of the time period should be tied to the capital funding planning period for the infrastructure in question. If, for example, the jurisdiction works with a five-year capital improvements program (CIP), that five-year period plus an extra year for flexibility should be stated as the refund period.

The more important requirement established by the Arkansas court is that money can be collected for capital expenditures only if there is a "reasonably definite" plan for its expenditure. What the court seems to be—and should be—requiring is that impact fee and related ordinances must implement comprehensive plans. Impact fees, it should be remembered, are land-use regulations, and thus their validity should be dependent upon their being an implementation of the local government's plan for capital facilities. If a fee is to be collected from new development for park acquisition or park facilities construction, then the jurisdiction should have a plan for parks as well as a standard for park facilities against which the validity and fairness of the park impact fee can be judged.

Careful earmarking and restriction of funds for expenditure for the benefit of the geographic areas from which they are collected also merit careful attention. Lee County, Florida, has addressed this concern in its Parks Impact Fee Ordinance by requiring that all impact fees will be deposited into "special trusts funds" to be used "exclusively for capital improvements within or for the benefit of the regional parks impact fee districts from which the funds were created."[89] Lee County's Roads Impact Fee Ordinance[90] similarly creates specific trust funds for the revenues collected from road impact fees. Montgomery County, Maryland, has likewise separated the revenues for its new road impact fees. The ordinance directs the County Department of Finance "to establish separate accounts for each impact fee area and … maintain records for each such account so that development impact fee funds collected can be segregated by the impact fee area of origin."[91]

Many state impact fee statutes require that local government impact fee ordinances establish "one or more" benefit districts or service areas. The goal is to ensure that impact fees are spent close enough to the developments that pay them so that the

second prong of the dual rational nexus test (i.e., the fees must be spent so as to benefit those who pay them) is respected. Since the statutes generally leave to the local government the decisions as to how many service areas or benefit districts are established, many local governments that are large in area establish only one district. This practice has led to allegations by feepayors that the districts are so large that impact fees can be spent so distant from the development that generates them that little if any benefit is received by them. Litigation has ensued. In *City of Olympia v. Drebick*,[92] for example, the feepayor unsuccessfully sought to have the city's road impact fee invalidated because the city had a single service/benefit area even though the city constituted 17 square miles.

The controversy over size of service areas/benefit districts led to statutory changes in the impact fee legislation in Georgia and Nevada in 2007. In 2006, the Georgia Legislature considered several bills that would have set a maximum area size for service areas but none were enacted. Instead, Georgia House Bill 232[93] was enacted in 2007 and, in effect, applies only to the City of Atlanta and only to road impact fees. It requires the city, when spending impact fees, to consider the proximity of the improvements to developments that have generated the fees and the improvements that will have the greatest effect on levels of service (LOSs) of the developments that have paid the fees. Nevada took a more direct approach in 2007 by enacting Nevada Assembly Bill 253,[94] which prohibits the use of single jurisdictionwide service areas for cities with fewer than 10,000 residents and counties with fewer than 15,000 residents.

The necessity of a "tie in" between the plan and the impact fee should be stressed in formulating the impact fee and the ordinance enacting it. The *City of Fayetteville*[95] decision emphasizes the necessity of wedding planning and law in the formulation, adoption, and implementation of impact fees designed to fund capital expenditures for infrastructure to service new development. A decision by the Supreme Court of Utah revisits the absolute necessity for careful and highly competent economic analysis in the impact fee formulation and implementation process. Ostensibly, *Lafferty v. Payson City*[96] simply reiterates the requirement discussed earlier in connection with the decision of the Supreme Court of Florida in *Dunedin*,[97] which states that impact fee monies must be earmarked so they can be spent only for the purpose for which they were collected. More important, however, the Supreme Court of Utah takes the opportunity in *Lafferty* to reemphasize the economic analysis it formulated in *Banberry* to guarantee that impact fees do not treat new residents unfairly "in determining the relative burden already borne and yet to be borne by newly developed properties."[98]

Complex and sophisticated economic analysis is required to assess the considerations deemed crucial by the Utah court. Nonetheless, courts in other jurisdictions will doubtless turn them into standards that impact fee calculation formulae must meet to be held valid. Even in jurisdictions in which the courts are less demanding, local developers, new residents, taxpayers, and others will doubtless require of their elected officials sound economic analysis to support impact fee programs.

IMPACT FEE USES

Impact fees are currently being used for a wide variety of public services and now represent a common fiscal tool used by local governments in funding public service infrastructure needs. Impact fees are assessed for the provision of water and sewer systems, roads, solid waste facilities, libraries, parks, schools, police and fire facilities, emergency medical facilities, environmental and habitat preservation, public hospitals, and even public cemeteries.[99]

The most common use for impact fees is in the funding of capital improvements for potable water and sanitary sewer facilities. Transportation services such as highways and bridges are the next most common type of impact fee.[100] No matter what the fee is used for, courts assess the validity of impact fees in large part on how fairly and accurately they reflect a new development's proportional share of the necessary infrastructure costs.[101] Because accuracy is a major factor in determining the reasonableness of an impact fee, impact fee programs require very careful economic analysis and planning to determine what public facilities will be provided, the cost of providing the infrastructure, and the proportion of that cost attributable to the individual unit of development on the infrastructure facilities.[102] Therefore, the most widely upheld and implemented impact fees are those based on data that indicate the desired LOS standards for a particular facility and calculate the cost of maintaining those standards in light of the increased demands created by new development.[103]

Today, impact fee formulae are the methods used to set impact fees and are based on the fundamental theory of the police power.[104] Once the formulae are developed, the actual impact fee is then derived by entering the data into the formulae. Impact fees can then be offset with credits[105] given by the local government to account for past payment for existing capital facilities, future tax and other payments by the development, and infrastructure and improvements to the land provided directly by the developer.[106]

One of the more common uses for impact fees is to fund the need for roads and highway systems brought on by new development. When visualizing how the formula may be set for an impact fee assessment, transportation network fees provide a useful example of how impact fees are calculated and assessed. One of the first steps in calculating this type of impact fee is to determine the level and quality of service that the local government wants to maintain or achieve—a desired LOS standard. Once this is established, formulae are then developed to determine the actual impact that a development will have on the particular facility (in this case, the highway system). For example, a shopping center will have a very different impact on the highway system than a single-family home. Differences such as this are then taken into consideration in determining the amount of the fee.

For roads specifically, the impact fee formulae begin by calculating the physical quantity of roads that must be built in order to protect public health, safety, and welfare from deterioration in the quality of service on public roads. This quantity of roads is physical and is measured in lane-miles or lane-feet of roadways.[107] It is calculated by multiplying the trip generation rate,[108] divided by two, times the average trip length, times the percent of new trips, all divided by the capacity of a lane-mile (or -foot) of roadway.[109] The attributable travel is also reduced to account for what are known as "captured" or "diverted" trips (i.e., trips that were already on the road and are not attributable to new development). This results in a number of vehicle-miles traveled (VMTs), the impact that may be attributed to new development. The next step is to calculate the cost of the road construction and to include credits.[110] The impact fee is then established based on the projected cost of new construction less any "credits" for dedications to which the developer may be entitled.

EXTENDING THE APPLICABILITY OF IMPACT FEES ACROSS THE DEVELOPMENT SPECTRUM

Not only must the scope of infrastructure be expanded to include "green" and "social" infrastructure in order to correctly assess the true costs and impacts of growth, but the types of development that cause impact and therefore should share in its provision must be expanded. For example, it is often the practice to confine developer funding requirements for parks and schools to residential development. This practice places an inequitable burden on residential developers because commercial and industrial developments also "use" school facilities (e.g., hurricane shelter, adult education, recreation, and libraries) and parks (e.g., corporate athletic teams, office picnics, and sports competitions).[111]

MAKING IMPACT FEES MORE SENSITIVE TO AFFORDABLE HOUSING AND OTHER SOCIETAL NEEDS

Impact fees are now a commonplace means of infrastructure finance. By requiring new land development to bear a proportionate cost of providing the new or expanded infrastructure, it will require and impact fees provide, in part, an answer to the dilemma faced by local governments when searching for sources of funding for capital expenditures. Now that impact fees have been widely accepted by the courts as regulatory measures, rather than unconstitutional taxes, they are widely seen as funding programs that reasonably allow local governments to maintain levels of capital facilities that can keep up with growth.

There are limitations, however, to the traditional use of impact fees. While they respond to the issues of location, availability, and provision of capital infrastructure with regard to new development, they are "largely unresponsive and even insensitive to the issue of the quantity and type of growth that should be allowed to occur."[112] Furthermore, the traditional impact fee fails to respond to other growth and development issues such as housing and employment needs.[113]

Partly in response to these shortcomings associated with the traditional impact fee, and partly because of the success of impact fees in raising funds for many infrastructure items, local governments have begun to explore the possibility of using the impact fee concept to fund "soft" or "social" infrastructure needs such as child care facilities and workforce or affordable housing,[114] art in public

places, and environmental mitigation programs.[115] Developer funding requirements designed to raise funds for "soft," "social," and now "green" infrastructure items are frequently referred to as "linkage fees."[116] Linkage fees charge developers a fee to provide for expanded services that are incurred by the community because of the new development.

> Underlying every linkage program is the fundamental concept that new downtown development is directly "linked" to a specific social need. The rationale is fairly simple: Not only does the actual construction of the commercial building create new construction jobs, but the increased office space attracts new businesses and workers to fill new jobs. The new workers need places to live, transit systems, day care facilities, and the like. From the perspective of linkage proponents, the new commercial development is directly linked both to new employment opportunities and to increased demand for improved municipal facilities and services.[117]

When first implemented, "linkage" fees were thought to be something distinct from "impact" fees.[118] *Nollan v. California Coastal Commission*[119] dealt the first blow to the perceived difference between linkage and impact fees by holding that a nexus was essential to any condition of development approval requiring a dedication. The Ninth Circuit further diminished any distinction in *Commercial Builders of Northern California v. City of Sacramento*[120] by applying essentially impact fee criteria to what was characterized as an affordable housing "linkage" requirement. The city ordinance conditioned nonresidential building permits upon the payment of a fee for housing to offset expenses associated with the influx of low-income workers for the new project. The developers argued that the ordinance was a taking because it placed the burden of paying for the housing upon the new development without a sufficient showing that nonresidential development contributed to the need for new low-income housing in proportion to that burden.

The court found no taking, however, as the fee was enacted only after a study revealed that the need for low-income housing would rise as a direct result of demand from workers on the new development. The court found that "[t]he burden assessed against the developers thus bears a rational relationship to a public cost closely associated with such development."[121] The court seemingly broadened its holding beyond the imposition of a fee for low-income housing when it stated that "[a] purely financial exaction, then, will not constitute a taking if it is made for the purpose of paying a social cost that is reasonably related to the activity against which the fee is assessed."[122]

Perhaps the most famous linkage case decided thus far is the New Jersey case, *Holmdel Builders' Ass'n v. Township of Holmdel*,[123] which upheld the imposition of fees on commercial and noninclusionary residential developments for the construction of low-income housing per the local government's responsibilities under the *Mt. Laurel* doctrine.[124]

Not all linkage fee programs have fared as well as those just discussed. In *San Telmo Assoc. v. City of Seattle*,[125] the Supreme Court of Washington had before it a Seattle housing preservation ordinance, which provided that property owners who wished to demolish low-income housing units had to replace a specified percentage of the housing to be demolished with other suitable housing or contribute to the city's low-income housing replacement fund. The court found the requirement to constitute an unauthorized tax.

Today, the weight of opinion is that there are no fundamental differences between "linkage" and "impact" fees, but the convention of labeling soft, social, or green impact payments "linkage" and applying the term "impact fee" to hard infrastructure remains. To the extent that any differences can be identified between linkage and impact, most linkage programs have a primary goal of problem mitigation or abatement rather than payment. Impact fees are almost the reverse, in that the expectation is that payment of the fee will be the primary means of compliance. A linkage program would identify a concern and require that the concern be abated or mitigated, and, if not abated or mitigated, a payment would be made and the proceeds derived would be used to abate or mitigate the problem. An impact program would require the payment of a specified amount, the proceeds of which would be used to construct specified public facilities, unless the individual elects to sufficiently mitigate or abate the problem by construction/ dedication of those facilities.

The list of issues raised in regard to the validity of linkage fees is almost identical to the list of issues regarding the validity of impact fees. These include authority of the local government to enact linkage programs,[126] illegal tax rather than land-use regulation,[127] violation of due process, equal protection or takings provisions of U.S. and state constitutions,[128] and the standard to be applied to govern the reasonableness of the exercise of the police power.

In this last regard, *Holmdel* is of particular interest since it held that linkage programs for low-income housing need not meet the rational nexus test:

> We conclude that the rational-nexus test is not apposite in determining the validity of inclusionary zoning devices generally or of affordable housing development fees in particular. * * * Inclusionary zoning through the imposition of development fees is permissible because such fees are conducive to the creation of realistic opportunities for the development of affordable housing; development fees are the functional equivalent of mandatory set-asides; and it is fair and reasonable to impose such fee requirements on private developers when they possess, enjoy, and consume land, which constitutes the primary resource for housing.[129]

A similar issue exists in regard to environmental mitigation fees, which are assessments made by local governments against new development to reimburse the community for the new development's proportionate negative impact on the community's environment.[130] Whether these fees will parallel impact fees or linkage programs and become another legally authorized and acceptable aspect of developer funding to offset the impact of development is also an issue of current and considerable importance.

CONCLUSION

As far as local governments are concerned, there seems to be no doubt that the impact analysis-oriented land regulatory measures referred to as "impact fees," "dedication requirements," and "in-lieu payments" provide at least a partial answer to local governments' capital funding dilemma by providing a means whereby local governments can require new land development to bear a proportionate cost of providing the new or expanded capital facilities required by new development. The judicial acceptance of impact fees and their characterization as land regulation charges have not come easily in many high-growth jurisdictions. Recent court decisions indicate an increasing judicial acceptance of impact fees and their role in land development regulations in general and growth management in particular.

In spite of increased judicial acceptance of impact fees, their formulation, drafting, and implementation are becoming more complicated as the courts are becoming more sophisticated and demanding in their scrutiny of such measures. Nonetheless, assiduous melding of legal, planning, and economic analyses offers hope to local governments pushed to the verge of bankruptcy by the infrastructure demands placed on them by considerable and sometimes rampant growth.

The important role that impact fees can now fill for local governments should, however, not obscure their limitations. They are largely unresponsive and even insensitive to the issue of the quantity and type of growth that should be allowed to occur. They are only responsive to the issue of location of new development in terms of the availability and provision of capital infrastructure. They are also inadequate to solve such socioeconomic issues such as housing and employment needs, which are so closely related to growth. These limitations are indicated by the phenomenon that, even though impact fees are quite new in their political and judicial acceptance, they have already been somewhat relegated to second place in the eyes of many planners and planning attorneys by linkage programs that seek to broaden the responsibility of the private sector for the ramifications of new development. Perhaps the most exciting developments in regard to impact fees in the near future will relate to their interrelationship with linkage programs and other developer funding requirements.

There are currently various approaches available to a local government that wishes to require developer funding of infrastructure. These include required dedications, in-lieu fees, user fees, impact fees, rezoning conditions, and linkage programs. The legal frameworks for these various approaches have developed in different time periods and in different contexts, and they are therefore often subjected to different standards and legal requirements. While treating them differently and in a parallel manner has probably been helpful in obtaining their legal and political acceptability, the time has come to "unify" them for several reasons.

First, from a developer perspective, there is a possibility that, by treating them differently, the developer may be required to make overlapping "contributions," which, unless proper credit for one against the other is given, the developer could end up paying more than once for the same impact. This is usually avoided through credit provisions of impact fee programs, which require previously made dedications or payments to be deducted from the impact fees otherwise due. Nonetheless, the coordination is not always clear or totally effective.

Secondly, in some jurisdictions, the funding required of the development may vary based on the stage in the development process that it is "collected" or required. This is not fair to either the developer (vis-a-vis other developers) or to the local government since, if they are mutually exclusive, the local government may not be able to collect for the total impact the development has on infrastructure needs.

Thirdly, treating them separately may limit the "options" of both the developer and the local government in making the contributions as palatable as possible to the developer and as economically effective as possible for the local government.

Finally, from a legal perspective, coordination and assimilation of the various methods should result in clearer and more consistent standards for the various approaches that will increase fairness and efficiency for developers and local governments.[131]

NOTES

1. A review of impact fee law for attorneys is found in Chapter 9, Juergensmeyer and Roberts (2007); see also Nicholas, Nelson, and Juergensmeyer (1991).
2. See Chapter 4 for a list of state enabling statutes; see also www.impactfees.com.
3. Juergensmeyer and Roberts (2007), Section 9.9.
4. For most of the country's history, inflation averaged 2 percent or less, with the periods of war being significant exceptions. Beginning in the 1960s and continuing through the 1980s, inflation existed at hitherto unprecedented rates, peaking at over 18 percent in the late 1970s. See U.S. Department of Labor, Bureau of Labor Statistics. [Accessed January 24, 2008] Available at www.bls.gov.
5. See generally Susskind (1983); Arthur C. Nelson, "And Then There Were Property Taxes: A Primer on Property Taxes, Economic Development, and Public Policy," Urban Land Institute Working Paper Series, Paper 661 (July 1998).
6. Both state governments and the federal government abandoned funding programs for public investments because of a sharp rise in cost. Furthermore, there was a greater burden on the local governments responsible for handling these matters because of required improvements to many infrastructure facilities, such as water pollution control facilities. See, e.g., The Water Pollution Control (Clean Water) Act, 33 U.S.C. Sections 1251 et seq. (1994).
7. See Chapter 1.
8. The water could be turned off or the trash left uncollected.
9. This distinction among types of services, while important in public administration, received little if

any judicial recognition. This may explain why the courts had little problem with applying "proprietary" review criteria to "governmental" functions.
10. The Fort Lauderdale-Hollywood metropolitan area.
11. See *Broward County v. Janis Development Corp.*, 311 So.2d 371 (Fla. 4th DCA 1975).
12. *Contractors and Builders Assn. of Pinellas County v. City of Dunedin*, 329 So.2d 314 (Fla. 1976).
13. The idea of regulation had to be expanded from the concept of simply imposing rules and standards to actually imposing fees not classified as taxes, for public health, safety, and welfare purposes.
14. In *Holmdel Builders' Ass'n v. Township of Holmdel*, 121 N.J. 550, 583 A.2d 277 (1990) the court distinguished taxation from regulatory fees. The court stated that, if the primary purpose of the fee was to raise general revenue, it was a tax. However, if the primary purpose was to "reimburse the municipality for services reasonably related to development, it was a permissible regulatory exaction." *Id.*
15. Heyman and Gilhool (1964), at 1119–57.
16. Juergensmeyer and Roberts (2007).
17. A hybrid form of the two has developed in Virginia where "proffers" combine many aspects of both by requiring developer payment of negotiated fees based on schedules tied to infrastructure provision costs.
18. See Nicholas, Nelson, and Juergensmeyer (1991), at 28–33.
19. Juergensmeyer (1988a), at 96–112.
20. Impact fees are also collected at one or more of the following stages of development: rezoning, platting, development order issuance, building permit issuance, and certificate of occupancy issuance. Collecting them late in the development process is best for the developer since he/she has no (or low) finance charges to pay on the impact fee amount. Local governments prefer collecting the fee as early as possible in the development process so that funds will be available to start construction in time to provide infrastructure when the development is completed. The conflicting preference of payors and payees has been resolved in most jurisdictions by providing for payment at the time a building permit is issued.
21. Hagman and Juergensmeyer (1986), Chapter 7.
22. Juergensmeyer and Blake (1981).
23. Juergensmeyer (1988b), at 51–65.
24. Recent decisions on point include *Mayor and Board of Aldermen, City of Ocean Springs v. Homebuilders Ass'n of Mississippi, Inc.*, 932 So.2d 44, 61 (Miss. 2006) (impact fees void because taxes); *Home Builders Association of Greater Des Moines v. City of West Des Moines*, 644 N.W.2d 339 (Iowa 2002) (impact fees taxes not regulatory fees); *HBA of Lincoln v. City of Lincoln*, 711 N.W.2d 871 (Neb. 2006) (impact fees "taxes" but city authorized by its charter to collect them); *Durham Land Owners Association v. County of Durham*, 630 S.E.2d 200, 208 (N.C.Ct.App. 2006), review denied, 633 S.E. 2d 678 (N.C. 2006) (county lacked authority to impose impact fee; no discussion of fee versus tax); *HomeBuilders Ass'n of Dayton v. City of Beavercreek*, 89 Ohio St.3d 121, 729 N.E.2d. 349 (2000) (impact fee valid under city's powers pursuant to Ohio Constitution); *City of Olympia v. Drebick*, 126 P.3d 802 (Wash. 2006), cert. denied, 127 S.Ct. 436 (2006) (Wash Sup. Ct. held city's transportation impact fee really excise tax and therefore not subject to dual rational nexus requirements). See Smith and Juergensmeyer (2007); Kristin B. Flood, "Who Should Pay for the Impact of New Development in Iowa: Developers or the Preexisting Community? Analysis of Home Builders Association of Greater Des Moines v. City of West Des Moines," 91 *Iowa L.Rev.* 751 (2006).
25. See *Home Builders Association of Greater Des Moines v. City of West Des Moines*, 644 N.W.2d 339 (Iowa 2002) (park impact fee found to be a tax; authority to promote the peace, safety, health, welfare, comfort, and convenience of its residents does not bestow broad powers for financing of local government activities).
26. See Nicholas, Nelson, and Juergensmeyer (1991), at 29–30.
27. *Ponderosa One Ltd. v. Salt Lake City Suburban Sanitary District*, 738 P.2d 635; 59 Utah Adv. Rep. 4; 1987 Utah LEXIS 723 citing *Murray City v. Board of Education Murray City*, 16 Utah 2d 115; 396 P.2d 628; 1964 Utah LEXIS 357.
28. 22 Ill.2d 375, 176 N.E.2d 799 (1961).
29. *Id.*
30. 25 Misc.2d 1004, 209 N.Y.S.2d 729 (1960), affirmed 15 A.D.2d 815, 225 N.Y.S.2d 538 (1962).
31. *Id.*
32. See Nicholas, Nelson, and Juergensmeyer (1991), at 31.
33. 28 Wis.2d 608, 137 N.W.2d 442 (1965), appeal dismissed 385 U.S. 4, 87 S.Ct. 36, 17 L.Ed.2d 3 (1966).
34. *Id.*
35. *Id.*
36. 631 P.2d 899 (Utah 1981).
37. See Nicholas, Nelson, and Juergensmeyer (1991), at 28–33.
38. Maryland Attorney General Opinion 86-018.
39. *Russ Building Partnership v. City and County of San Francisco*, 199 Cal.App.3d 1496, 246 Cal.Rptr. 21 (1987). See also *Northern Ill. Home Builders Ass'n v. County of Du Page*, 251 Ill.App.3d 494, 621 N.E.2d 1012 (Ill.App. 1991) (concluding no equal protection violation from differing fees), aff'd 165 Ill.2d 25, 649 N.E.2d 384 (Ill. 1995).
40. 401 F.Supp. 701 (M.D. Fla. 1975).
41. 329 So.2d 314 (Fla.1976), on remand 330 So.2d 744 (Fla.App.1976).

42. 663 P.2d 611; 1983 Colo. LEXIS 520 (1983).

43. 255 Ga.App. 764, 566 S.E.2d 470 (2002), cert. den. Ga. Supreme Court (Feb. 24, 2003).

44. *Id.*

45. *Penn Central Transportation Co. v. New York City*, 438 U.S. 104, 124, 98 S.Ct. 2646, 2659.

46. 483 U.S. 825, 107 S.Ct. 3141 (1987).

47. *Dolan v. City of Tigard*, 512 U.S. 374, 114 S.Ct. 2309 (1994).

48. 317 Or. 110, 854 P.2d 437 (1993).

49. 12 U.S. 377, 114 S.Ct. 2309, 2312, 129 L.Ed.2d 304 (1994).

50. *Id.* at 2315.

51. *Id.*

52. *Id.* at 2318.

53. 512 U.S. 389, 114 S.Ct. 2318.

54. 144 Mont. 25, 394 P.2d 182 (1964).

55. 18 N.Y.2d 78, 271 N.Y.S.2d 955, 218 N.E.2d 673 (1966). Also see Heyman and Gilhool (1964), 1119, 1146-55. Compare the following cases: *Montgomery v. Crossroads Land Co.*, 355 So.2d 363 (Ala.1978) (in-lieu fee a tax); *Venditti-Saravo, Inc. v. Hollywood*, 39 Fla.Supp. 121 (17th Cir. Ct.1973) (impact fee an invalid property tax); *Haugen v. Gleason*, 226 Or. 99, 103, 359 P.2d 108, 110 (1961) (in-lieu fee borders on tax); *Contractors and Builders Assn. of Pinellas County v. City of Dunedin*, 329 So.2d 314 (Fla.1976), on remand 330 So.2d 744 (Fla.App.1976) (impact fee properly earmarked not a tax); *Western Heights Land Corp. v. City of Fort Collins*, 14 Colo. 464, 362 P.2d 155 (1961) (not a tax because not intended to defray general municipal expenses); *Home Builders Ass'n of Greater Salt Lake v. Provo City*, 28 Utah 2d 402, 503 P.2d 451 (1972) (charge for services not a general revenue measure); *Call v. West Jordan*, 606 P.2d 217 (Utah 1979), on rehearing 614 P.2d 1257 (in-lieu fee not a tax but a form of planning).

56. 12 U.S. 377, 114 S.Ct. 2309, 2319, 129 L.Ed.2d 304 (1994).

57. 22 Ill.2d 375, 176 N.E.2d 799 (1961). (Note that the case has been reinterpreted by the Illinois courts in *Northern Ill. Home Builders v. County of Du Page*, 165 Ill.2d 25, 208 Ill.Dec. 328, 649 N.E.2d 384 (1995).

58. Note 33, supra.

59. 512 U.S. 374, 391, 114 S.Ct. 2309, 2319-20, 129 L.Ed.2d 304 (1994).

60. *Id.*

61. See *McCarthy v. City of Leawood*, 257 Kan. 566, 894 P.2d 836, 845 (1995) and *Clajon Production Corp. v. Petera*, 70 F.3d 1566 (10th Cir.1995), both finding *Dolan* inapplicable to nonphysical conditions. See *Commercial Builders of Northern California v. City of Sacramento*, 941 F.2d 872 (9th Cir. 1991), cert. denied 504 W.S. 931, 112 S.Ct. 1997, 118 L.Ed.2d 593 (1992) (*Nollan* inapplicable to fees). See also *Sparks v. Douglas County*, 127 Wash.2d 901, 904 P.2d 738 (Wash. 1995). ("Under Dolan, a land use regulation does not effect a taking if the local government shows by individualized determination that its exaction is 'roughly proportional' to the impact of the development.") For discussions of various cases on point, see David Callies, ed., *Takings: Land-Development Conditions and Regulatory Takings after Dolan and Lucas* (Chicago: American Bar Association, 1996); B. Gerry, "Parity Revisited: An Empirical Comparison of State and Lower Federal Court Interpretations of Nollan v. California Coastal Commission," 23 *Harv. J.L. & Pub. Pol'y* 233 (1999); R. Faus, "Exactions, Impact Fees and Dedications—Local Government Responses to Nollan/Dolan Takings Law Issues," 29 *Stetson. L.Rev.* 675 (2000).

62. 183 Ariz. 243, 902 P.2d 1347, 1352 (1995).

63. P.2d 429-50 (1996).

64. Note 62, supra.

65. 187 Ariz. 479, 930 P.2d 993 (1997), cert. denied 521 U.S. 1120, 117 S.Ct. 2512, 138 L.Ed.2d 1015 (1997).

66. *Id.* at 1000.

67. 12 Cal.4th 854, 50 Cal.Rptr.2d 242, 911 P.2d 429 (1996), cert. denied 519 U.S. 929, 117 S.Ct. 299, 136 L.Ed.2d 218 (1996).

68. *Id.* at 433.

69. "We arrive at this conclusion not by reference to the constitutional takings clause alone, but within the statutory framework presented by the Mitigation Fee Act. (Gov. Code, Section 66000 et seq.). ... We thus interpret the Act's 'reasonable relationship' standard, as applied to the development fee at issue in this case, as embodying the standard of review formulated by the high court in its Nollan and Dolan opinions. ... Applying this standard in this case, we conclude, first, that the city has met its burden of demonstrating the required connection or nexus between the rezoning ... and the imposition of a monetary exaction to be expended in support of recreational purposes as a means of mitigating that loss. We conclude, however, that the record before us is insufficient to sustain the city's determination that plaintiff pay a so-called mitigation fee of $280,000 as a condition for approval of his request that the property be rezoned to permit the construction of a condominium project. Because the city may be able to justify the imposition of some fee under the recently minted standard of Dolan, we follow the Oregon's Supreme Court's disposition in that case and direct that the cause be remanded to the city for additional proceedings in accordance with this opinion." *Id.*

70. 27 Cal.4th 643, 117 Cal.Rptr.2d 269, 41 P.3d 87 (2002).

71. Note 46, supra; note 47, supra.

72. 126 P.3d 802 (Wash. 2006), cert. denied, 127 S.Ct. 436 (2006) (Wash. Sup. Ct. held city's transportation impact fee really excise tax and therefore not subject to dual rational nexus). For a discussion of the *Drebick* case, see Smith and Juergensmeyer (2007).

73. See *Taking Sides on Takings Issues: Public and Private Perspectives* (Thomas E. Roberts, ed.) (Chicago: American Bar Association, 2002), Chapters 13–15.

74. 126 P.3d at 807–08.

75. See F. Bosselman, "Dolan Works, Taking Sides on Taking Issues" (T. Roberts, ed.) (Chicago: American Bar Association, 2002), Chapter 14. "The Dolan test is well established: it is logical in its outcome and it seems to work reasonably well for both developers and local governments. Let's not complicate the legal picture unnecessarily by imposing illogical limitations on the type of exactions to which the Dolan test applies." *Id*. at 353.

76. See N. Stroud, "A Review of Del Monte Dunes v. City of Monterrey and it Implications for Local Government Exactions," 15 *J. Land Use and Envtl. Law* 195 (1999).

77. See D. Curtin and C. Talbert, "Applying Nollan/Dolan to Impact Fees: A Case for the Ehrlich Approach," in *Taking Sides on Takings Issues* (T. Roberts, ed.) (Chicago: American Bar Association, 2002), Chapter 13.

78. Juergensmeyer and Nicholas (2002). "No takings analysis of dual rational nexus-based impact fees is appropriate or necessary. If an impact fee is valid, i.e., it satisfies the dual rational nexus test, then it cannot destroy property rights. If an impact fee violates the nexus test … it is invalid." *Id*. at 357.

79. 544 U.S. 528, 125 S. Ct. 2074 (2005).

80. *Agins v. Tiburon*, 447 U.S. 255, 100 S.Ct. 2138 (1980).

81. 544 U.S. 528, 125 S. Ct. 2074 (2005) at 2086.

82. 544 U.S. 528, 125 S. Ct. 2074 (2005) at 2087.

83. *Loretto v. Teleprompter Manhatten CATV Corp.*, 458 U.S. 419, 102 S.Ct. 3164 (1982).

84. *Small Property Owners of San Francisco v. City and County of San Francisco*, 141 Cal.App. 4th 1388, 47 Cal.Rptr.3d 121, 130, n.6 (2006).

85. The above discussion of the *Lingle* case is taken from Professor Roberts's discussion in Juergensmeyer and Roberts (2007), Section 10.5. (The numerous citations have been omitted.)

86. See Chapter 4.

87. See "2007 Impact Fee Enabling Acts" prepared by Clancy Mullen, AICP, of Duncan Associates of Austin, Texas. Updated material may be obtained from the Duncan Associates website: www.duncanplan .com and www.impactfees.com. See also Nicholas, Nelson, and Juergensmeyer (1991), Chapters 4 and 15; J. Bart Johnson and James van Hemert, *Development Impact Fees in the Rocky Mountain Region*, 2d ed. (Denver: Rocky Mountain Land Use Institute, University of Denver, 2006); J. Nicholas and D. Davidson, *Impact Fees in Hawaii: Implementing the State Law* (Honolulu: Land Use Research Foundation, 1992); Terry D. Morgan, "Recent Developments in the Law of Impact Fees with Special Attention to Legislation," 1990 Institute on Planning, Zoning, and Eminent Domain, Section 4; Terry D. Morgan, "State Impact Fee Legislation: Guidelines for Analysis," *Land Use L. & Zoning Dig.* (March 1990 and April 1990); Martin L. Leitner and Susan P. Schoettle, "A Survey of State Impact Fee Enabling Legislation," 25 *Urb. Law.* 491 (1993).

88. *City of Fayetteville v. IBI, Inc.*, 659 S.W.2d 505, 507 (Ark. 1983).

89. No. 85-24 (July 31, 1985).

90. No. 85-23 (July 31, 1985).

91. Montgomery County Council Bill No. 17-86, Section 49A-8(c) (July 29, 1986).

92. 126 P.3d 802 (Wash. 2006), cert. denied, 127 S.Ct. 436 (2006).

93. Codified as Official Code Georgia Annotated Section 36-71-2, 36-71-4, 36-71-5 and 36-71-8 (2007).

94. Codified as Nevada Statutes Section 278B.100 (2007).

95. *City of Fayetteville v. IBI, Inc.*, 280 Ark. 484, 659 S.W.2d 505 (Ark.1983).

96. 642 P.2d 376 (Utah 1982).

97. 329 So.2d 314 (Fla.1976), on remand 330 So.2d 744 (Fla.App.1976).

98. Note 36, supra.

99. This list is merely illustrative, not exhaustive. See generally Nicholas, Nelson, and Juergensmeyer (1991), at 2.

100. *Id*.

101. *Id*. at 82.

102. The forgiving language in *Dolan v. City of Tigard*, 512 U.S. 374, 114 S.Ct. 2309 (1994), that mathematical precision is not required, has not proven to be the case in impact fee challenges.

103. See *id*.

104. If the developer were required to pay for more impact than they actually cause, this would be a taking or a tax and consequently would be unconstitutional. Therefore, the role of the formulae is to accurately determine the cost of the impact.

105. It is unfortunate that, in impact fee methodology and literature, "credit" has two meanings. The first meaning refers to a reduction in the amount of an impact fee to reflect other funds the local government received devoted to that same facility or service. The second meaning refers to a donation or dedication of land and facilities that allows an individual to pay impact fees "in kind."

106. See Nicholas, Nelson, and Juergensmeyer (1991), at 98–107.

107. A lane-mile is a single lane of road, one mile long. A four-lane roadway one mile long is, therefore, four lane-miles.

108. Many jurisdictions use trip generation rates provided by the Institute of Transportation Engineers, although jurisdictions may elect to conduct their own trip generation studies.

109. The following is a general formula for roadway impact fee determination: (TRIP RATE/2) x TRIP LENGTH x PERCENT NEW TRIPS = ATTRIBUTABLE TRAVEL. (ATTRIBUTABLE TRAVEL/ROAD LANE CAPACITY) = NEW ROADS. (NEW ROADS (IN LANE-MILES)) x (CONSTRUCTION COST (IN LANE-MILES)) = CONSTRUCTION COSTS. (NEW ROADS (IN LANE-MILES)) x (RIGHT-OF-WAY COST (IN LANE-MILES)) = RIGHT-OF-WAY COSTS. (CONSTRUCTION COSTS) + (RIGHT-OF-WAY COSTS) = TOTAL COST. Following this computation, any credits the developer may possess will be subtracted from the total cost to obtain the impact fee.

110. Because roads are paid for in part by fuel taxes, new development should receive "credit" because it will generate and attract new attributable travel, thereby consuming fuel, the taxes on which will be used to pay for new roads. Because these taxes are paid annually and in perpetuity, it is necessary to consider future payments as well. "Credit" for the payment of past property taxes paid by the developer, which in part are used to fund the building of roads, should also be applied.

111. Smith and Juergensmeyer (2007).

112. Nicholas, Nelson, and Juergensmeyer (1991), at 48.

113. Andrews and Merriam (1988). See also Kayden and Pollard (1987), at 127, 128–29.

114. For a discussion of affordable housing as "social" infrastructure, see Marc T. Smith and Ruth L. Steiner, "Affordable Housing as an Adequate Public Facility," 36 *Val. U.L. Rev.* 443 (2002).

115. Juergensmeyer and Roberts (2007), at 442.

116. See generally Andrews and Merriam (1988).

117. Andrews and Merriam (1988), Chapter 19, at 228. See also Kayden and Pollard (1987), at 127.

118. See Connors and High (1987), at 69.

119. Note 71, supra.

120. 941 F.2d 872 (9th Cir. 1991), cert. denied 504 W.S. 931, 112 S.Ct. 1997, 118 L.Ed.2d 593 (1992).

121. *Id.* at 874.

122. *Id.* at 876. The *Commercial Builders* court also rejected the developer's contention that *Nollan* requires a more stringent taking standard, held that "Nollan does not stand for the proposition that an exaction ordinance will be upheld only where it can be shown that the development is directly responsible for the social ill in question. Rather, Nollan holds that where there is no evidence of a nexus between the development and that problem that the exaction seeks to address, the exaction cannot be upheld." *Id.*

123. 121 N.J. 550, 583 A.2d 277 (1990).

124. 67 N.J. 151, 336 A.2d 713 (1975) (Mt. Laurel I), appeal dismissed, cert. denied 423 U.S. 808, 96 S.Ct. 18, 46 L.Ed.2d 28 (1975).

125. 108 Wash.2d 20, 735 P.2d 673 (1987). See also *Sintra, Inc. v. City of Seattle*, 119 Wash.2d 1, 829 P.2d 765 (1992) (ordinance was found to be an illegal tax, and when the city persisted in applying the ordinance to other property, court found behavior which led to Section 1983 damages).

126. See Note 14, supra; *Bonan v. City of Boston*, 398 Mass. 315, 496 N.E.2d 640 (1986) (court did not reach issue of authority that was raised by lower court).

127. *San Telmo Assoc. v. City of Seattle*, 108 Wash.2d 20, 735 P.2d 673 (1987).

128. For a full discussion of due process, equal protection, and taking challenges, see William W. Merrill and Robert K. Lincoln, "Linkage Fees and Fair Share Regulations: Law and Method," 25 *Urb. Law* 223 (1993).

129. Note 120, supra.

130. See Ledman (1993), at 835; Nicholas, Juergensmeyer and Basse (1999), Part I, 7 *Env. Liab.* 27 ("Given the limitations of impact fees and Market-based environmental models, regulators may be able to combine advantages of both … [in] a new regulatory alternative, the environmental mitigation fee." *Id.* Part II at 71); Nicholas and Juergensmeyer (2003); Nelson, Nicholas, and Marsh (1992), at 1.

131. See "Infrastructure and the Law: Florida's Past, Present and Future" (Juergensmeyer (2008)).

4

State Impact Fee Enabling Acts

With Clancy Mullen

This chapter briefly summarizes state impact fee enabling acts, providing summary tables and examples of evolving state statutes. This information is useful to practitioners, since state statutes obviously affect local impact fee design. A broader purpose, however, is served by observing patterns in laws enacted by various states. Among other things, the enabling acts represent legislators' understanding of principles laid down by the courts. An understanding of case law can contribute to an understanding of the intent of the statutes, while the statutes themselves provide interpretations of the meaning of case law.

DISTRIBUTION OF ENABLING ACTS

Texas adopted the first general impact fee enabling act in 1987. To date, 27 states have adopted impact fee enabling legislation for impact fees other than water and wastewater. These acts have tended to embody the constitutional standards that have been developed by the courts. The distribution of those states is illustrated in Figure 4-1, while the enabling legislation is shown in Table 4-1.

Until 2006, Florida was the state with the largest amount of impact fee activity that had no state enabling legislation. Florida's legislation in 2006 is not a true enabling act however, since the authority of local governments to impose impact fees had been long established through case law. The

Figure 4-1
States With Enabling Acts

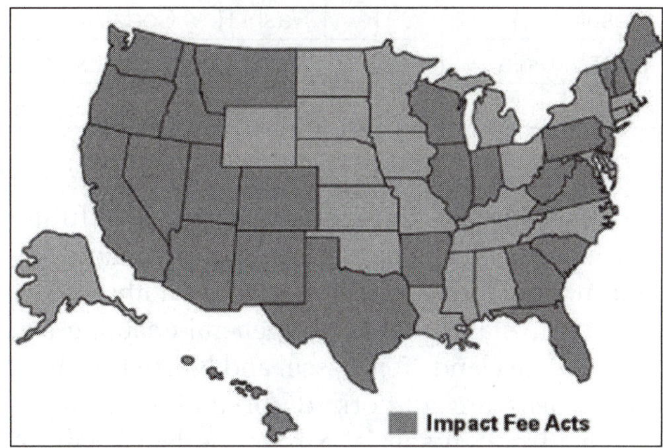

Courtesy of Clancy Mullen

Table 4-1
State Impact Fee Enabling Acts

State	Year	Citation
Arizona	1988	Ariz. Rev. Stat. Ann., Section 9 463.05 (cities), Section 11 1102 et seq. (counties)
Arkansas	2003	Arkansas Code, Section 14 56 103 (cities only)
California	1989	Cal. Gov't Code, Section 66000 et seq. (mitigation fee act); Section 66477 (Quimby Act for park dedication/fee in lieu); Section 17620 et. seq. (school fees)
Colorado	2001	Colo. Rev. Stat., Section 29 20 104.5; Section 29 1 801804 (earmarking requirements); Section 22 54 102 (school fee prohibition)
Florida	2007	Fla. Stat., Section 163.31801
Georgia	1990	Ga. Code Ann., Section 36 71 1 et seq.
Hawaii	1992	Haw. Rev. Stat., Section 46 141 et seq.; Section 264-121 et seq.
Idaho	1992	Idaho Code, Section 67 8201 et seq.
Illinois	1987	605 Ill. Comp. Stat. Ann., Section 5/5 901 et seq.
Indiana	1991	Ind. Code Ann., Section 36 7 4 1300 et seq.
Maine	1988	Me. Rev. State. Ann., Title 30 A, Section 4354
Montana	2005	Montana Code Annotated, Title 7, Chapter 6, Part 16
Nevada	1989	Nev. Rev. Stat., Section 278B
New Hampshire	1991	N.H. Rev. Stat. Ann., Section 674:21
New Jersey	1989	N.J. Perm. Stat., Section 27:1C 1 et seq.; Section 40:55D 42
New Mexico	1993	New Mexico Stat. Ann., Section 5 8 1 et seq.
Oregon	1991	Or. Rev. State, Section 223.297 et seq.
Pennsylvania	1990	Pa. Stat. Ann., Title 53, Section 10502 A et seq.
Rhode Island	2000	General Laws of Rhode Island, Section 45 22.4
South Carolina	1999	Code of Laws of S.C., Section 6 1 910 et seq.
Texas	1987	Tex. Local Gov't Code Ann., Title 12, Section 395.001 et seq.
Utah	1995	Utah Code, Section 11 36 101 et. seq.
Vermont	1989	Vt. Stat. Ann., Title 24, Section 5200 et seq.
Virginia	1990	Va. Code Ann., Section 15.2 2317 et seq.
Washington	1991	Wash. Rev. Code Ann., Section 82.02.050 et seq.
West Virginia	1990	W. Va. Code, Section 7 20 1 et seq.
Wisconsin	1993	Wis. Stats., Section 66.0617

legislation imposes only minimal requirements, but cities and counties in the state are wary that future legislatures will amend the law to impose more significant limitations on their impact fee authority.

In some states that lack a general enabling act, such as Maryland, Tennessee, and North Carolina, impact fees are authorized for individual jurisdictions through special acts of the legislature. A number of Maryland counties have been granted the authority to impose school impact fees, making Maryland the state with the fourth highest number of school impact fees, after California, Florida, and Washington. In Tennessee, cities with mayor aldermanic charters have the authority to impose impact fees without special authorizing legislation. In North Carolina, no new grants of impact fee authority have been approved by the legislature in years.

Virginia has a formalized system of developer exactions, known as "cash proffers," which function somewhat like impact fees. However, the proffer system does differ significantly in that there is no required nexus study or published fee schedule. Instead, developers "voluntarily" proffer land dedications, capital improvements, or cash payments as part of their application for rezoning, which may or may not be granted depending in part on case law while others elaborate on the guidelines more explicitly.

Almost all of the state enabling acts contain words or phrases that indicate that impact fees should only charge new developments for the capital costs they actually impose on the community. A number of different terms are used to express this sentiment. Arizona's act, for example, states that impact fees "must bear a reasonable relationship to the burden imposed … to provide additional necessary public services to the development."[1] Georgia's act states that new development cannot be required to pay "more than its proportionate share of the cost of public facilities needed to serve new growth."[2]

Many acts use multiple terms. For example, "proportionate share" is often defined as the cost of improvements that "reasonably relates" to the needs created by growth. The majority of the state acts use one or more of the terms "proportionate share," "reasonable relationship" (or "reasonably related" or "reasonably attributable"), or "necessitated by and attributable to," and so forth; however, only 11 states (California, Georgia, Hawaii, Idaho, Illinois, New Mexico, Pennsylvania, South Carolina, Utah, Vermont, and West Virginia) actually define the concept.

While there is virtual unanimity among the state acts that impact fees should only require new development to pay for the cost of improvements that are reasonably related to its impacts, not all of them are clear on exactly what this means. One of the things it should mean is that impact fees should not charge new development for a higher LOS than is provided to existing development. If the fees are based on a higher LOS than is provided to existing development in the community, other funding must be identified to remedy the existing deficiencies. This principle is expressed colloquially in the saying, "Impact fees should not be used to pay for the sins of the past." Not all of the enabling acts are clear on this point, but a majority of the acts do codify this principle in one way or another, as evidenced by the following examples:

Colorado: "No impact fee or other similar development charge shall be imposed to remedy any deficiency in capital facilities that exists without regard to the proposed development." (Section 29-20-104.5(2), Colo. Rev. Stat.)

Georgia: "Development impact fees shall be calculated on the basis of levels of service for public facilities that are adopted in the municipal or county comprehensive plan that are applicable to existing development as well as the new growth and development." (Section 36-71-4(c), Ga. Code Ann.).

Montana: "New development may not be held to a higher level of service than existing users unless there is a mechanism in place for the existing users to make improvements to the existing system to match the higher level of service." (Section 7-6-1602.5(d), Montana Code Ann.)

Utah: "… the local political subdivision may not impose an impact fee to cure deficiencies in public facilities serving existing development." (Section 11-36-202(4), Utah Code)

A corollary principle is that new development should not have to pay more than its proportionate share when multiple sources of payment are considered. This principle is often expressed informally as "new development should not be charged twice for the same facilities." Virtually all of the state enabling acts require construction credits for developments that make in-kind contributions, such as the dedication of property or construction of improvements. The reduction of impact fees on a case-by-case basis for a particular development to account for such contributions is known as a "construction credit." All but four of the 27 state acts explicitly require that developers be given reimbursements or credits for in-kind contributions for the same type of capital facility costs covered by the impact fee. South Carolina's act words this principle as follows:

> A developer required to pay a development impact fee may not be required to pay more than his proportionate share of the costs of the project, including the payment of money or contribution or dedication of land, or to oversize his facilities for use of others outside of the project without fair compensation or reimbursement. (Section 6-1-1000, Code of Laws of S.C.)

Other sources of payment could include future property taxes that will be generated by the new development and used to pay debt service on existing facilities, or sales tax revenues earmarked to remedy existing deficiencies in facilities serving existing development. Since there is no way to charge new development a lower property or sales tax rate than existing development, the solution is to reduce the impact fees by an amount equivalent to the future payments. Such a reduction is referred to as a "revenue credit." A majority of the state enabling acts explicitly require consideration of revenue credits. However, those acts that do mandate consideration of revenue credits often provide little guidance on how this should be accomplished. Georgia's act provides more guidance than most:

> Development impact fees shall be calculated on a basis which is net of credits for the present value of revenues that will be generated by new growth and development based on historical funding patterns and that are anticipated to be available to pay for system improvements, including taxes, assessments, user fees, and intergovernmental transfers. (Section 36-71-4(r), Ga. Code Ann.)

Most of the acts require credits only for future revenues that will be generated by the new development. However, six state acts require credits for past revenues generated before the property was developed as well. In most cases, such credits are limited to property taxes paid by vacant land and used to pay for the same type of facility.

The basic standards enunciated by the enabling acts for calculating impact fees are summarized in Table 4-2. Florida's act is the only one not to contain any guiding terms or standards, probably because these are well articulated in that state's case law.

Florida aside, it is interesting to note that there is no unanimity among the state acts on clearly spelling out even the most basic impact fee principles.

ELIGIBLE FACILITIES

One of the most important things that most enabling acts do is restrict the types of facilities for which impact fees may be imposed. The types of facilities that are eligible for impact fees in the various state acts are listed in Table 4-3. It would be more accurate to say that these are the types of impact fees that are not prohibited by the enabling acts.

An exception is water and wastewater impact fees. In most states, with or without impact fee enabling acts, local governments have the authority to require payment of a fee at the time of meter purchase or connection to the public utility system. The fact that the general impact fee enabling act in a state does not specifically authorize water and wastewater impact fees does not necessarily mean that such fees are prohibited. In fact, it is likely that such fees are authorized under a separate statute governing public utilities.

Table 4-2
Basic State Enabling Act Standards

State	Guiding Terms	No Higher Level of Service	Construction Credits	Revenue Credits	Past Credits
Arizona	reasonable relationship		explicit	explicit	
Arkansas	reasonably attributable				
California	reasonable relationship		explicit*	explicit*	
Colorado	directly related	explicit	explicit		
Florida	proportionate share**				
Georgia	proportionate share; reasonably related	explicit	explicit	explicit	
Hawaii	proportionate share; reasonably attributable	explicit	explicit	explicit	yes
Idaho	proportionate share; reasonably relates	explicit	explicit	explicit	
Illinois	proportionate share; specifically and uniquely attributable	explicit	explicit	explicit	yes
Indiana	proportionate share		explicit	explicit	
Maine	reasonably related		explicit		
Montana	proportionate share; reasonably relates	explicit	explicit	explicit	
Nevada	necessitated by and attributable to		explicit		
New Hampshire	proportionate share; reasonably related				

Table 4-2
Basic State Enabling Act Standards *(continued)*

State	Guiding Terms	No Higher Level of Service	Construction Credits	Revenue Credits	Past Credits
New Jersey	fair share; reasonably related	explicit	explicit		
New Mexico	proportionate share; necessitated by and attributable to		explicit		
Oregon	equitable share		explicit	explicit	
Pennsylvania	necessitated by and attributable to	explicit	explicit	explicit	
Rhode Island	proportionate share; reasonably relates	explicit	explicit		
South Carolina	proportionate share; reasonably relates	explicit	explicit	explicit	
Texas	necessitated by and attributable to	explicit	explicit	explicit	
Utah	proportionate share; roughly proportionate; reasonably related		explicit	explicit	yes
Vermont	proportionate share		explicit		
Virginia	necessitated by and attributable to		explicit	explicit	yes
Washington	proportionate share; reasonably related	explicit	explicit	explicit	yes
West Virginia	proportionate share; reasonably attributed	explicit	explicit	explicit	yes
Wisconsin	proportionate share	explicit	explicit		

* Developer credits explicit for road and park in-kind contributions; revenue credits explicit for special district taxes used to finance schools.
** Standard based on case law.

Table 4-3
Facilities Eligible for Impact Fees by State

State	Roads	Water	Sewer	Stormwater	Parks	Fire	Police	Library	Solid Waste	School
Arizona (cities)	■	■	■	■	■	■	■	■	■	
Arizona (counties)	■	■	■		■	■	■			
Arkansas (cities)	■	■	■	■	■	■	■	■		
California	■	■	■	■	■	■	■	■	■	■
Colorado	■	■	■	■	■	■	■	■	■	
Florida	■	■	■	■	■	■	■	■	■	■
Georgia	■	■	■	■	■	■	■	■		
Hawaii	■	■	■	■	■	■	■	■	■	■
Idaho	■	■	■	■	■	■	■			
Illinois	■									
Indiana	■	■	■	■	■					
Maine	■	■	■		■	■			■	
Montana	■	■	■	■	■	■	■	■	■	
Nevada	■	■	■	■	■	■	■			

Table 4-3
Facilities Eligible for Impact Fees by State *(continued)*

State	Roads	Water	Sewer	Stormwater	Parks	Fire	Police	Library	Solid Waste	School
New Hampshire	■	■	■	■	■	■	■	■	■	■
New Jersey	■	■	■	■						
New Mexico	■	■	■	■	■	■	■			
Oregon	■	■	■	■	■					
Pennsylvania	■									
Rhode Island	■	■	■	■	■	■	■	■	■	■
South Carolina	■	■	■	■	■	■	■			
Texas (cities)	■	■	■	■						
Utah	■	■	■	■	■	■	■			
Vermont	■	■	■	■	■	■	■	■	■	■
Virginia	■									
Washington	■				■	■				■
West Virginia	■	■	■	■	■	■	■			■
Wisconsin (cities)	■	■	■	■	■	■	■	■	■	

It is noteworthy that only eight states do not prohibit school impact fees. School impact fees are found almost exclusively in Florida, California, Washington, and Maryland (where they are authorized in some counties by special acts of the legislature). School impact fees tend to be high fees that are imposed only on residential development, and their prohibition in most of the country is an indication of both the controversy surrounding these fees and their political sensitivity.

PLANNING AND ANALYSIS REQUIREMENTS

For the most part, state legislation does not establish maximum fees that can be charged.[3] Instead, the state acts require, implicitly or explicitly, that a study or analysis be done to determine how to apply the "proportionate share" or other guiding standard in order to determine the maximum amounts that the local government can charge. The planning and analysis requirements of the various state impact fee enabling acts are summarized in Table 4-4. Note that seven of the 27 acts do not even explicitly require that a written analysis be performed. However, it is hard to imagine how compliance with the general impact fee principles expressed by the acts could be demonstrated without some kind of written report.

Many of the state acts require that the local government identify the "service area" where the impact fees will be collected based on the service provided to new development from a common set of facilities. Most acts require that impact fees collected within a service area must be spent on capital improvements within the same service area. In general, local governments are allowed broad discretion in defining service areas, which can cover the entire jurisdiction or only a subarea of the city or county. An exception is the Texas act, which limits service areas for transportation impact fees to no more than six miles.

Over two-thirds of the state acts require that the impact fees be based on a CIP. In some state acts, as in the original Texas act, the required "capital improvements plan" is both a list of projects to be funded with the impact fees and the written analysis used to calculate the impact fees. Some of these CIP requirements simply mandate that a list of projects be developed on which the fees will be spent. Arkansas's act, for example, requires that the municipality adopt a "capital plan," which is defined as:

Table 4-4
State Enabling Act Planning Requirements

State	Written Analysis	Service Areas	List of Projects	Growth Projections	Level-of-Service Standards
Arizona (cities)	yes				
Arizona (counties)	yes		yes		
Arkansas	yes		yes		yes
California	yes*		yes	yes*	
Colorado					
Florida					
Georgia	yes	yes	yes	yes	yes
Hawaii					yes
Idaho	yes	yes	yes	yes	yes
Illinois	yes	yes	yes	yes	yes
Indiana	yes		yes	yes	yes
Maine					
Montana	yes	yes	yes	yes	yes
Nevada	yes	yes	yes	yes	
New Hampshire					
New Jersey	yes		yes	yes	
New Mexico	yes	yes	yes	yes	
Oregon	yes		yes		
Pennsylvania	yes	yes	yes	yes	yes
Rhode Island	yes		yes		yes
South Carolina	yes	yes	yes	yes	yes
Texas	yes	yes	yes	yes	
Utah	yes	yes	yes		
Vermont	yes	yes	yes		yes
Virginia	yes	yes	yes	yes	
Washington		yes			
West Virginia					yes
Wisconsin	yes	yes	yes		

* Required for school impact fees only

... a description of new public facilities or of new capital improvements to existing public facilities or of previous capital improvements to public facilities that continue to provide capacity available for new development that includes cost estimates and capacity available to serve new development ... (Section 14 56 103(a)(1), Arkansas Code)

About half of the state acts require land-use projections that cover the same period as the capital plan. The combination of these two requirements— the capital plan and growth projections—would seem to imply that impact fees in these states must be calculated using a "plan-based" (or "improvements-driven") methodology. Such a methodology determines capital improvements needed to accommodate projected growth over a fixed planning horizon, then divides the total improvement cost by the projected growth in service units to determine the gross impact fee (without consideration of revenue credits).

Some states with these requirements, such as Texas, even specify that impact fees may not exceed the amount determined by dividing the costs of the capital improvements by the total number of projected service units. Yet, while these requirements do force the impact fee calculations to take the form of a plan-based methodology, in many cases the fees are actually based on the existing LOS or some other planning standard (see discussion of plan-based and standards-based methodologies in Chapter 9).

One cannot calculate an impact fee without at least an implicit LOS standard. Without such a standard, it would not be possible to determine the impact of a new development on the need for capital facilities. However, only about half of the state acts require that the local government explicitly describe the LOS standards on which the impact fees are based. (Some states that do not mandate explicit LOSs do prohibit the use of impact fees from being used to remedy existing deficiencies, which in turn implies the use of an LOS standard.)

In an ideal world, impact fees would always be based on extensive planning. However, many communities, especially smaller ones, do not have the resources to prepare long-range facility master plans, and it is possible to calculate defensible impact fees in the absence of such planning documents. Intentionally or not, state acts with extensive planning requirements may make it more difficult for communities to adopt impact fees.

SUBSTANTIVE REQUIREMENTS

A review of the state enabling acts reveals that, outside of the general principles and planning standards discussed above, there is little agreement about what form state regulation should take. State impact fee enabling acts impose both substantive and procedural requirements. Selected substantive provisions of the state acts are summarized in Table 4-5. The second column, showing the length of the various acts, illustrates that enabling acts range from brief grants of authority and statements of general principles (Arizona, Arkansas, Florida, Maine, Vermont, and Wisconsin) to the lengthy, detailed, and confusing provisions of California's legislation.

Table 4-5
State Enabling Act Substantive Provisions

State	Length (Word Count)	Time to Collect	Recoupment	Recalculation Requirement	Platting Locks in Fee?	Explicit Waivers	Waiver Funding Required?
Arizona	1,068	any time	yes				
Arkansas	1,634	certificate of occupancy	yes				
California	22,907	certificate of occupancy*	yes				
Colorado	3,980	any time				affordable housing	no
Florida	307	any time					
Georgia	3,757	building permit	yes		180 days	economic development	yes
Hawaii	2,017	building permit	yes				
Idaho	7,124	building permit			1 year	affordable housing	yes
Illinois	5,670	building permit/ certificate of occupancy					
Indiana	9,705	building permit			3 years	affordable housing	no
Maine	465	any time	yes	yes			
Montana	1,809	building permit	yes				

Table 4-5
State Enabling Act Substantive Provisions *(continued)*

State	Length (Word Count)	Time to Collect	Recoupment	Recalculation Requirement	Platting Locks in Fee?	Explicit Waivers	Waiver Funding Required?
Nevada	4,685	building permit		yes		schools	no
New Hampshire	2,356	certificate of occupancy	yes				
New Jersey	8,670	building permit					
New Mexico	6,575	building permit	yes	yes	4 years	affordable housing	unclear
Oregon	4,111	any time	yes				
Pennsylvania	6,115	building permit		yes		affordable housing/other	no
Rhode Island	1,942	certificate of occupancy	yes			general	no
South Carolina	4,571	building permit			forever	affordable housing	yes
Texas	8,641	building permit	yes		forever	affordable housing	no
Utah	4,818	any time	yes			affordable housing	yes
Vermont	1,229	any time	yes	yes		general	no
Virginia	1,893	certificate of occupancy		yes	forever		
Washington	2,064	any time	yes			general	yes
West Virginia	3,105	any time	yes			general	yes
Wisconsin	1,167	building permit				affordable housing	no

* Specified for residential development only

About one-third of the enabling acts allow impact fees to be collected at any time during the development process. Most of the others provide that impact fees cannot be collected prior to the building permit or certificate of occupancy.

A majority of the state acts explicitly allow local governments to recoup costs incurred prior to the development provided that the capacity is available to serve the development. It should be noted that recoupment fees are not necessarily prohibited by the state acts that do not explicitly authorize them. Rhode Island's act provides that the portion of an impact fee deemed recoupment is exempted from provisions requiring expenditure in eight years.[4] To the extent that the capital improvements for which the fees are paying has already been paid for, recoupment fees can be returned to the general fund or used for whatever purpose the local government chooses.

Several states, following Texas's early lead, have imposed a recalculation requirement. This provision mandates that the local government recalculate the impact fees after completion of the CIP, then refund any excess collected if actual costs were less than projected costs. This provision from the original Texas act was copied almost verbatim in several other acts. Texas has since repealed the provision. The provision is seldom applicable, since impact fees are usually updated before the completion of the entire capital plan.

Another type of provision pioneered by the Texas act stipulates that fees are assessed at platting and locked in for a period of time. In the Texas act, the fee schedule in effect at the time of final subdivision approval is the maximum fee that may be charged to development within the subdivision, regardless of when building construction actually occurs. Two other states have this same provision, while another four lock in the fee schedule in effect at the time of platting for one to four years.

While about half of the acts are silent on the issue of waivers or exemptions, the other half explicitly authorize local governments to waive impact fees for certain types of projects. Most of them limit waivers to affordable housing or, to a lesser extent, economic development projects. Of the acts that authorize waivers, about half require that the local government reimburse the impact fee fund from some other nonimpact fee revenue source.

PROCEDURAL REQUIREMENTS

In addition to substantive provisions, many impact fee enabling acts set forth procedural requirements for impact fee adoption and updating. Some of these procedural provisions are summarized in Table 4-6. Ten states require that an advisory committee be appointed to oversee the development of the impact fee system. The committee generally must have significant representation from the development community, most commonly 40 percent.

State acts generally require that impact fees be adopted by ordinance at a duly noticed public hearing. Many of the acts even specify the minimum time period that notice must be published before the public hearing is held. Four state acts specify the time period that must elapse between the adoption of an impact fee ordinance and the imposition of the new or increased impact fee (see "Fee Phase-in" column in Table 4-6).

A majority of state acts require that impact fee revenues be spent within a specified number of years or be refunded to the feepayor. These requirements range from five to 15 years, with six years being the most common. In states with refund requirements, local governments must keep records on fee payments to be able to track the payment and expenditure of fees on a first-in, first-out basis. In practice, however, refunds due to the failure to spend the money within the required time period are rare.

Most acts are silent on how frequently the fees must be updated. Of the less than one-third that require periodic updates, every five years is the most common requirement. Three states— California (school impact fees only), Nevada,

Table 4-6
State Enabling Act Procedural Provisions

| State | Advisory Committee | | Hearing Notice | Fee Phase-in | Spending Limit | Update Frequency | Administrative Fee |
	Size	Developer Representation					
Arizona (cities)			60 days	90 days			
Arizona (counties)			120 days	90 days			
Arkansas					7 years		
California			30 days	60 days	5 years		3%*
Colorado							
Florida				90 days			actual cost
Georgia	5-10	40%			6 years		3%
Hawaii			15 days		6 years		
Idaho	5+	2+	2 weeks		10 years	5 years	study cost
Illinois	10-20	40%	30 days		5 years	5 years	
Indiana	5-10	40%			6 years	5 years	5%
Maine							
Montana	N/A	1					
Nevada	5+	N/A	20 days		10 years	3 years	study cost
New Hampshire					6 years		

Table 4-6
State Enabling Act Procedural Provisions *(continued)*

State	Advisory Committee		Hearing Notice	Fee Phase-in	Spending Limit	Update Frequency	Administrative Fee
	Size	Developer Representation					
New Jersey							
New Mexico	5+	40%	zoning		7 years	5 years	3%
Oregon			90				study cost
Pennsylvania	7-15	40%	2 weeks				
Rhode Island					8 years		
South Carolina					5 years		
Texas	5+	40%	30 days		10 years	5 years	study cost
Utah			2 weeks		6 years		
Vermont					6 years		
Virginia	5-10	40%			15 years	2 years	
Washington					6 years		
West Virginia				60 days	6 years		
Wisconsin			1 week		7 years		

* School impact fee

and Oregon—have guidelines for indexing fees for inflation between periodic updates.

Several state acts authorize the use of a portion of impact fees collected to defray the cost of administering the impact fee system. Some set limits on the percentage of impact fees that can be used for this purpose, while others require that administrative fees be limited to actual administrative costs. Some limit the use of such fees to paying for the costs of preparing the impact fee study or CIP.

RECENT DEVELOPMENTS

Florida can now be said to have an impact fee act, although local governments in Florida have long had their authority to impose impact fees confirmed by the courts. The Florida Impact Fee Act, which became effective on June 14, 2006, imposes several minor requirements on local governments adopting or amending impact fee ordinances. The fees must be based on the most "recent and localized" data, administrative charges may not exceed actual administrative costs, and notice must be provided at least 90 days prior to the effective date of an impact fee ordinance. Local governments, however, remain concerned that a future legislature will impose more onerous restrictions.

Although Tennessee does not have a general enabling act, 13 counties and 15 cities have enacted impact fees or adequate facilities taxes, based either on home rule authority or special local acts.[5] Near the end of the 2006 legislative session, the Tennessee General Assembly passed the County Powers Relief Act, which was signed by the governor on June 20, 2006. It authorizes growth counties, as defined under the act, to enact a "county school facilities tax" of up to $1 per square foot on residential development. However, this new authority comes with some significant restrictions: It prohibits any new private acts for facilities taxes, and counties may not impose a school facilities tax unless they repeal any other impact fee or facilities tax. Earlier, the legislature passed a bill effective July 1, 2005 requiring "a statement disclosing the amount of any impact fees or adequate facilities taxes paid to any city or county" to be given to the purchaser at the first sale of residential properties.

The Wisconsin Legislature made some major retrenchments to the authority granted by that state's enabling act. Act 477, which became effective on June 13, 2006, prohibits counties from imposing impact fees (four counties had been assessing park impact fees), prohibits fees for recreational facilities other than parks and athletic fields, prohibits impact fees for vehicles, and prohibits fees in lieu of parkland dedication. It also prohibits impact fees from being collected prior to building permit issuance. Act 203, which became effective on April

10, 2006, requires fees to be refunded if not spent in seven years.

Montana adopted an impact fee enabling act in 2005. Senate Bill 185 was passed by the legislature on April 9, 2005, and was signed by the governor on April 19, 2005. It is relatively brief and has few restrictive provisions. A key provision, however, may be that the "impact fees imposed may not exceed a proportionate share of the costs incurred or to be incurred by the governmental entity."

Arkansas adopted an impact fee enabling act in 2003. Senate Bill 620 was passed by the legislature on April 16, 2003, and was signed by the governor as Act 1719 on April 22, 2003. The act only applies to municipalities and water or wastewater providers; it does not authorize impact fees for counties. It clarified the authority of cities to enact impact fees, which had not been firmly established before this. Like most state acts, it does not allow school impact fees. It is relatively short and has few requirements. Its only unusual feature is that it requires that the amount of the impact fee paid be itemized separately on the closing statements when property is sold. The original version of the bill, drafted at the behest of the state home builders association, had proposed that the fees for single-family homes actually be paid at the time of closing by the buyer, but this requirement was dropped in conference committee.

A CAUTIONARY TALE

State legislatures are becoming increasingly involved in regulating how local governments develop and impose impact fees. Because of the complexity of impact fee principles and practice, and the lack of understanding of the field by legislators, there is a real danger that attempts to impose more specific requirements may have negative unintended consequences.

For example, the Idaho Legislature amended that state's impact fee enabling act in 2002 in a way that was intended to favor Micron in its dispute with the Ada County Highway District. Micron had filed an independent assessment with the highway district for an expansion to its existing manufacturing facilities in Boise in which it claimed that it should get credit for all district property taxes, which it had paid in the past or the future, that were available for capital improvements. The amendments to the act, which became effective July 1, 2002, require local governments to calculate revenue credits in such a way that an existing business,

which expands its operations or builds a new facility, gets credit for past and future tax payments by the business within the same service area, even though the gross fee before credits is based only on the net increase in traffic generated by the expansion or new construction.

If interpreted as the act appears to intend, an existing business that expands or opens a new branch within the same service area would likely never pay a road impact fee; a business that does not have existing operations within a service area would be required to pay. Such an inequitable outcome would be subject to challenge as contrary to the enabling act's more general "proportionate-share" language. As a result, the amendments to the state act cast a cloud of uncertainty over how revenue credits should be calculated in Idaho.

TO THE FUTURE

From 1987 to 1993, there was a flurry of legislative activity as 20 states adopted impact fee enabling acts. This was an average of three new acts each year. Since then, seven additional states have adopted enabling legislation, which works out to about one new act every two years.

A major factor in the initial surge of impact fee acts was the support of builder groups that wanted impact fees that were being imposed by local governments under their police powers to be regulated. Now that virtually all states with significant growth and impact fee activity have enabling acts, one might expect builders and legislators' attention to shift to fine-tuning existing legislation.

To date, there have not been many significant amendments to existing enabling acts. The only state to expand the list of eligible facilities was Nevada, which added authority to impose impact fees for traffic signals, parks, and police and fire stations in 2001 (Utah's addition of ladder trucks in 2006 is so narrow that it does not count). Wisconsin became the first state to withdraw authority to impose impact fees when, in 2006, it repealed the authority of counties to impose fees and prohibited fees for major park improvements and public safety vehicles.

While it is difficult to generalize, there does seem to have been a hardening of resistance among development interests and legislators to granting additional impact fee authority or even allowing existing authority to continue to be available. This may be due, in part, to the increasing level of impact fees being charged (see Chapter 1). Evidence of this resistance is mounting.

The 2006 retrenchment of impact fee authority in Wisconsin is a prime example. Legislation in New Mexico, which attempted to retroactively prohibit Albuquerque's "growth tier" impact fee system, was narrowly defeated in 2005. The relatively benign Florida act was enacted only after a very restrictive version narrowly failed, and local governments in that state are now bracing for annual battles to preserve their relatively unfettered impact fee authority. Court decisions favorable to development interests in Mississippi and North Carolina in 2006 undermined home rule authority for impact fees in those states (see Chapter 3 for discussion of case law). In sum, future legislative battles seem likely to revolve around preserving, rather than expanding, impact fee authority.

Economic downturns will challenge acceptance of impact fee programs. Our earlier book on impact fees, *A Practitioners' Guide to Development Impact Fees* (Nicholas, Nelson, and Juergensmeyer (1991)), was published during a recession. That book was timely, however, in helping guide impact fee planning, design, and implementation as the nation recovered. Indeed, the nation saw unprecedented growth from 1992 through 2006. During this time, local governments also raised unprecedented tens of billions of dollars from impact fees to facilitate that growth.

This book is also being published during a recession, and we know of many communities (and a few states) that are considering rolling back impact fees, waiving them for the next year or longer, or repealing them altogether, either locally or through rescission of enabling legislation. While we sympathize with the concerns, such steps would be unwise. The nation continues to grow. When the economy recovers, states and local governments should not be in the situation of paying for infrastructure backlogs on top of new or expanded infrastructure to meet the demands of growth. Rolling back or waiving impact fees in the near term may also send incorrect political signals that local government did not need the revenue to begin with, thereby compromising the ability of local government to reinstate or raise impact fees. Finally, impact fees are based on analyses of growth patterns and the costs of serving new development; if they are arbitrarily adjusted for momentary convenience, they may cross the line in the eyes of courts to be viewed as a kind of tax and, if so, perhaps unauthorized.

As we look to the future, we need to be sure that impact fee programs are poised to facilitate growth when it occurs after the recession of the late 2000s or the next one, perhaps in many ways presented in this book.

NOTES

1. Section 9-463.05.B.4 (cities) and Section 11-1102.B.4 (counties), Ariz. Rev. Stat. Ann.
2. Section 36-71-1(b)(4), Ga. Code Ann.
3. The major exception is school impact fees in California, which are limited to $2.63 per square foot for residential buildings and $0.42 per square foot for commercial buildings. As of January 2006, the maximums are adjusted for inflation every two years.
4. Section 45-22.4-5(c), General Laws of Rhode Island.
5. Tennessee Association of Realtors. [Accessed on June 22, 2006] Available at www.tarnet.com/govaff/adqtaxdisc.html.

PART

2

Context

The local government planning and infrastructure policy **Context** for impact fees specifically, as well as for the whole range of proportionate-share development fees generally, is provided in **Part 2.** *Chapter 5* reviews the critical elements of impact fee combined lessons learned from professional practice tempered with case law and, in about half the states, enabling acts. *Chapter 6* addresses the importance of identifying various forms of credits against impact fees that need consideration. It includes a discussion of emerging credit issues. From the critical elements to the role of credits, we come to the planning connection in *Chapter 7*. The relationship of impact fees and other forms of proportionate-share development fees to policy has been addressed throughout Part 1 and in the first two chapters of Part 2, but this chapter fleshes out how to structure a planning foundation. Impact fees are predicated on measuring the impact of new development on the community, but different land uses have different levels of impact on facilities.

Chapter 8 describes several uniform measures that apply to all land uses and includes a method to ascribe impacts of different land uses where other uniform measures are not suitable. It presents a method to calculate "functional population" and introduces its potential for assessing nonresidential development its proportionate-share cost of facilities that are commonly assessed on only residential development (i.e., educational, library, and parks and recreational facilities). *Chapter 9* has three sections that review general methodological variations in impact fee design and focus on their features and differences; report findings from a selection of impact fee technical reports from a cross section of communities based on region, size, growth rates, and approach to calculating impact fees; and present a survey of communities focusing on variations in impact fee design. The chapter concludes that, when it comes to calculating proportionate-share development fees for any given community, "one size does not fit all."

5

Proportionate-Share Basics

With James B. Duncan and Clancy Mullen

"Impact fees" may be defined as one-time payments to help finance new or expanded infrastructure needed to mitigate the impacts of new development. The actual fee calculation process must be consistent with the "dual rational nexus" test (see Chapter 3). This test requires that there first be a relationship between new development and the new or expanded facilities required to serve it (the "impact") and second that the mitigation required of new development is proportionate to the cost (the "fee"). In a sense, impact fees are paid in lieu of new development mitigating the facility impact itself.

Over the better part of two generations, impact fees have evolved to become standardized in several respects based on important principles or proportionate-share principles. In 1990, the State of Georgia adopted one of the nation's first impact fee statutes (the Development Impact Fee Act of 1990). It is based on a collaboration involving county and municipal organizations, development interests, the authors, and Governor Joe Frank Harris (who received the American Planning Association's elected official of the year award in part for his role in this process). In many respects, the Georgia Act was then and continues to be based on best-practice principles, many of which preceded federal and state court decisions clarifying what those practices

are and how they need to be applied. The act was among the first, if not the first, to:

- Carefully define the term "proportionate share."
- Distinguish clearly among those facilities that new development must install to benefit principally itself ("project" improvements) and those that serve principally the community as a whole ("system" improvements).
- Allow for waivers of impact fees on affordable housing and economic development, provided local government identifies substitute nonimpact fee funds to offset the lost impact fee revenue.
- Frame how intergovernmental agreements could be made to facilitate interjurisdictional impact fees.
- Prescribe the process of adopting impact fees including notification, impact fee advisory committee composition and operation, and adoption procedures.
- Outline contents of an impact fee ordinance.
- Require a clear connection to the comprehensive plan and its capital facility element.
- Define important expenditure concepts such as when impact fee revenues need to be spent, knowing whether they have been expended

through encumbrance, and when impact fees revenues are presumed to have been spent.

This chapter reviews how the principles included in the Georgia Development Impact Fee Act are applied to Atlanta, Georgia, as a case study. In particular, in 1993, the City of Atlanta adopted a pioneering impact fee program that advanced professional practice in several important ways. For instance, it was among the first jurisdictions—and, at the time, the largest—to use functional population as a unit of impact measure. It also used recoupment revenues to finance all or part of the impact fees assessed on affordable housing. Much of the foregoing is adapted from Atlanta's impact fee technical report (Duncan, Morgan, and Standerfer [1986] and James B. Duncan & Associates, Nelson, et al. [1993]).

The Atlanta case study does more than merely address principles contained in the Georgia Act. It includes a discussion of several alternative impact fee calculation approaches, LOS standards, service area designs, and implementation issues. The case study thus provides a rich sense of the options about which many jurisdictions should deliberate before settling on a particular impact fee program.

OVERVIEW OF IMPACT FEE ANALYSIS

The Georgia Act outlines important impact fee calculation principles relating to proportionate share, plan-based versus standards-based calculations, and fee calculation methodology. The basic impact fee calculation steps are illustrated in Figure 5-1.

PROPORTIONATE-SHARE REQUIREMENT

The Georgia Act places many restrictions on the way in which impact fees are calculated. It establishes the principle that local governments may not charge developments more than a proportionate share of the cost of new facilities. "Proportionate share" is defined as "that portion of the cost of system improvements which is reasonably related to the service demands and needs of the project." The Georgia Act's proportionate-share rule assures consistency with the *rational nexus test*, which has been established through professional practice and case law (see Chapter 2).

There are various approaches to calculating impact fees and crediting development for past and future contributions made toward system improvements. The Georgia Act does not specify a single fee calculation method; however, it does identify some factors that must be taken into account. The most important rules for calculating impact fees include:

- *Levels of service*. Calculation of impact fees must be based on LOSs that are adopted in the local jurisdiction's comprehensive plan and applicable to existing development as well as new development. The LOS should be based on sound planning and apply uniformly.
- *Service areas*. Impact fees must be calculated and imposed based on service areas. Impact fees collected within a service area must be spent on the type of facility for which the fee was collected and within the service area in which it was collected.
- *Improvement costs*. Calculation of impact fees must be based on "actual system improvement costs or reasonable estimates of such costs." Obviously, basing impact fees on inflated or unrealistically high improvement cost estimates would violate proportionate-share criteria.

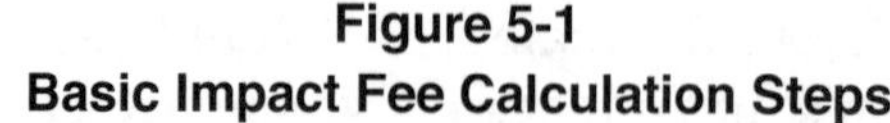

Figure 5-1
Basic Impact Fee Calculation Steps

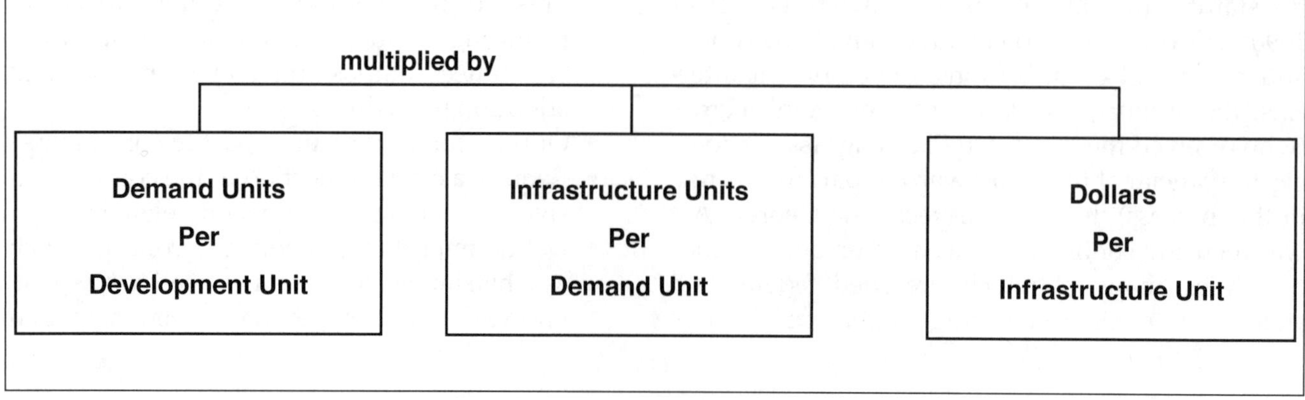

Figure courtesy of Dwayne Guthrie.

- *Revenue credits*. Calculation of impact fees must provide credits for the present value of future revenues "that will be generated by new development and that will be available to pay for system improvements."

PLAN-BASED VERSUS STANDARDS-BASED SYSTEMS

There are essentially two approaches in designing impact fee systems—"plan-based" and "standards-based"—both of which are valid under Georgia law. Under the plan-based approach, specific facilities are identified as necessary by a certain horizon year. The total cost of facilities is then prorated among anticipated units of growth during that same period. Use of this approach requires a very strong link between the design of the impact fee system and capital improvements programming. The weaknesses of the approach are that long-range growth projections are usually unreliable, and many assumptions are often required to convert from projections to future facility demand estimates. Due to these shortcomings, a standards-based approach has been used in this study.

Although some attempt must be made under the standards-based approach to show that programmed capital improvements are reasonably sufficient to meet projected demands, the estimated cost of those improvements and the growth projections do not directly determine the fee level. Instead, the standards-based approach determines the marginal cost to construct additional capacity and charges new development based on the capacity required to serve it, regardless of whether that capacity exists. Marginal cost can be determined based on the cost of and capacity created by typical past improvements, or on a list of potential or planned future improvements. Unlike the plan-based approach, however, the cost of past or future capital improvements is divided by the capacity created by the improvements, rather than by projected demand, to determine marginal costs on which the fees are based.

FEE CALCULATION METHODOLOGY

Regardless of whether a standards- or plan-based approach is used, the calculation of impact fees must follow essentially the same steps. They include an analysis of the following:

- *Capital cost*. The capital cost of constructing new capacity to serve new development has been calculated on a "per unit" basis. Under a standards-based approach, this is typically the marginal cost of an additional unit of capacity. Nonlocal funding sources have been excluded from these cost calculations or calculated as revenue credits.
- *Demand schedule*. For each land use (or, in the case of water and wastewater, each meter size), the demand generated per unit of development (e.g., dwelling unit or floor area) has been estimated and then multiplied by capital cost estimates to determine the total cost per unit of development.
- *Revenue credits*. The total capital cost has been reduced by the present value of future payments made by new development for the very facilities for which they are being assessed impact fees, such as through GO bonds retired by property taxes. The result is "net capital cost." This is the maximum impact fee that may be adopted by the city.

  This particular adjustment is needed to assure that new development is sheltered from the cost of paying for facilities twice— once through impact fees and again for other revenues it contributed for the same purpose. When revenues come from other than local government sources, such as federal or state agencies, it is common to reduce the gross impact costs by those revenue amounts. Another revenue credit would come in the form of discounting the stream of future payments, such as payments to retire bonds, that may be used to help finance facilities for which impact fees are assessed, as well as credit for past payments the property has already similarly paid before new development occurs. Chapter 10 reviews the details of these adjustments.
- *Construction credits*. For individual development projects, the fee calculated from the impact fee schedule may be reduced to credit new development for developer contributions made toward system improvements in compliance with past exaction requirements or as part of developer agreements. Such credits must be determined on a case-by-case basis.

POLICY FRAMEWORK

As applied to Atlanta, impact fees needed to be based on a consideration of the unique characteristics of the community. Unlike many cities that have adopted impact fees, Atlanta represents a largely developed central city that is surrounded by a large suburban area. As a result, most of the city's future growth will come in the form of redevelopment and infill rather than outward expansion.

Atlanta's daytime population—swollen by the in-migration of commuting employees, shoppers, and visitors—vastly exceeds its resident population, and future growth will be primarily of a nonresidential character. Much of the city's infrastructure is in need of replacement, and the expansion of certain facilities, such as the widening of roads, is severely constrained by the pattern of existing development. The community has experienced chronic fiscal problems in recent years, which have made it difficult to maintain existing infrastructure, much less expand to meet demands caused by growth. The city also has a significant low-income population, and affordable housing and economic development are big concerns.

While the impact fee program was based on sound technical analysis and complied with the Georgia Act, it also reflected local policy decisions. Based on an analysis of the city's characteristics and discussions with the citizens' Impact Fee Advisory Committee and staff Impact Fee Task Force, the consulting team recommended certain policies to guide the development of impact fees for the city.

- **Target nonresidential development**. Because it is expected that nonresidential development would constitute most future growth in the city, it was important to gauge the public facility demands posed by new nonresidential development. Most park impact fees, for example, assumed that only residential development generates new demands for parks. An analysis of park usage in Atlanta, however, provided significant evidence of park usage by nonresidential development. The methodology used in the park impact fee study therefore assessed both residential and nonresidential development. Atlanta thus became one of the nation's first jurisdictions, and by far the largest, to impose park impact fees on all development and not just residential development.
- **Minimize negative impacts on affordable housing and economic development**. While the Georgia Act authorizes exemptions for affordable housing and economic development, it also requires that the city find non-impact fee funds to pay the impact fees for the exempted development. This requirement, however, did not apply to water and wastewater connection fees, or to the parks and public safety impact fees because such fees recouped past investments (more on this below). Thus, only waivers of transportation impact fees would require replacement from nonimpact fee revenues.

- **Avoid current deficiencies**. It was found that existing facility deficiencies could be avoided by setting LOSs at or below current levels. Based on initial discussions with city staff, it was learned that, for many types of facilities, current service levels, though not ideal, were reasonably acceptable. If higher service levels were desired, they would create a deficiency in current service levels that would require new city investment from revenues other than impact fees to remedy. By adopting current service levels, few if any deficiencies were created. This avoided the need for using nonimpact fee funds to remedy deficiencies.

- **Recoup past investments**. The parks and public safety impact fees were designed to recoup past investments that created excess capacity in existing facilities to accommodate new growth. LOSs for these facilities were set below current levels, which thus created excess facility capacity. The value of this excess capacity was used as the basis for assessing recoupment impact fees, which, because they are reimbursements to the city for funds that have already been spent, could be used by the city in any appropriate manner.

  However, the city made the policy decision that a percentage of such recoupment fees would be set aside for reimbursement of same-facility impact fee exemptions, with the remainder earmarked for expenditure on the types of facilities, and in the service areas, for which they were collected. While this constrained the flexibility in the expenditure of these funds, the policy had important advantages over nonrecoupment impact fees. First, recoupment fees could be waived for affordable housing and economic development projects without replacing the waived fees with nonimpact fee revenues. Second, parks and police recoupment fees could be spent on improvements that would not qualify as system improvements under the 10-year-life and capacity-expansion requirements of the Georgia Act, such as the purchase of police cars or the replacement of a roof.

On the other hand, over the years since 1993, the city has actually been able to increase the number of its parks and raises its operational LOS standard for parks. This is because a substantial share of recoupment-based park impact fee revenue was leveraged with other revenue to expand the supply of parks. In effect, the policy has turned out to be a win-win situation for the city because affordable housing was sheltered from any adverse effects that park impact fees might have imposed, and the city was still able to expand park supply.

These principles guided the city's overall impact fee design process and implementation once adopted.

LEVEL-OF-SERVICE STANDARDS

The principal purpose in establishing LOS standards is to help meet the first prong of the dual rational nexus test. In effect, the LOS standard becomes the multiplier to estimate the impact of new development. If a community desires to have five acres of parks per 1,000 residents, it can project future population and thus future parkland needs, compare current park levels, and know how many acres of parkland would need to be added. It can also estimate the cost of this. On this point, the Georgia Act states that:

> Development impact fees shall be calculated based on *levels of service* for public facilities that are adopted in the municipal or county comprehensive plan that are applicable to existing development as well as the new growth and development. [Emphasis added.]

It defines "level of service" as a "measure of the relationship between service capacity and service demand for public facilities in terms of demand-to-capacity ratios or the comfort or convenience of use or both." If, for example, roadways are severely congested, the parks are overcrowded, and water rationing is required every summer, one would conclude that the LOS provided by these facilities is low. However, in some cases, a community might be willing to tolerate a relatively low LOS. This could be because a low LOS is less expensive to provide, or because it promotes another policy objective (i.e., congestion could encourage use of mass transit alternatives).

ADOPTED VERSUS EXISTING LEVELS OF SERVICE

A distinction should be made between the actual LOS, which can be measured at a given time, and the desired LOS. For the purpose of impact fees, the desired LOS was formally adopted in the city's comprehensive plan. The relationship between the adopted LOS that was used to calculate impact fees for new development and the actual LOS existing at the time of impact fee adoption had important implications in impact fee design. These implications are summarized in Table 5-1.

If a community establishes a desired LOS that is higher than the existing level, existing facilities will be found to be deficient when compared to the adopted standard. New developments will pay impact fees calculated on the cost to maintain the adopted LOS but will be sharing existing facilities that operate at a lower LOS. As the impact fees are spent, facilities will be upgraded and the LOS will improve for all users. However, new developments would not be receiving the LOS for which they are being charged, and existing users would be benefiting from the improved LOS paid for by new development.

Such a situation would clearly violate the "proportionate fair-share" intent of the Georgia Act, not to mention generally accepted impact fee practices. It would be inconsistent with the requirement that LOSs must be "applicable to existing development as well as the new growth and development," and inconsistent with the restriction on the use of impact fee revenues to finance "system improvements that

Table 5-1
Level-of-Service Standard

Characteristic	Adopted Level of Service Compared to Existing Level of Service		
	Below	Same	Higher
Impact fee level	Low	Moderate	High
Level of service	Decline	Maintain	Improve
Deficiencies	None	None	Must remedy
Excess capacity	Recoupment	None	None

create additional service available to serve new growth and development." Thus, if the city decided to adopt an LOS higher than the existing service level, it must find nonimpact fee revenue sources to upgrade existing facilities to the adopted service level. Such revenues would need to be available based on realistic projections to remedy any deficiencies over a reasonable period.

Adoption of a higher-than-existing LOS would result in higher impact fee revenues and improvement, over time, in the actual LOS provided. However, given the city's fiscal conditions at the time, it was determined that sufficient nonimpact fee funds could not be found to remedy the deficiencies in existing facilities that would be created. Consequently, the city decided to adopt LOSs that were at or below existing levels to avoid the creation of existing deficiencies.

At the other extreme, the city could adopt an LOS that was below the level currently provided. Such an approach would mean that existing facilities have excess capacity that would be available to serve new development. The Georgia Act specifically allows recoupment of the cost of constructing this excess capacity by authorizing "imposition of a development impact fee for system improvement costs previously incurred by a municipality or county to the extent that new growth and development will be serviced by the previously constructed system improvements."

Recoupment fees are akin to buy-in fees because they are based on recovering prior investments. They are also calculated and handled administratively in the same manner as any other impact fee except that, because such fees are collected to reimburse local governments for money they have already spent on infrastructure, they need not be earmarked for capital expansion expenditure. If facilities were built with outstanding bond issues or other debt instruments, impact fee revenues could be used to retire the debt. If the facilities have been paid for, the impact fee revenues may be returned to the general fund or used for any other purpose, including tax reductions. In the case of water and wastewater facilities, fee revenues could be returned to the respective enterprise funds. Like all fee calculation methods, recoupment must respect the general principles of not double-charging and adjusting credits to reflect the time value of money. The recoupment option therefore requires careful analysis of how and when each applicable capital project was originally financed.

While recoupment can be used for revenue enhancement, setting an artificially low LOS for this purpose alone would be short-sighted. While more of the sunk costs of existing facilities would be recaptured, impact fees collected for future system expansion would be limited to the costs of providing the lower LOS. In addition, the lower the LOS that is adopted, the lower the annual amount of impact fee revenues received.

The third option, of course, is to adopt an LOS that is identical to the existing LOS. In many ways, this is the simplest and most direct approach. It does not create any existing deficiencies or excess capacity, and simply charges new development the cost to maintain the LOS that existed prior to the development.

VARYING LEVEL OF SERVICE BY SERVICE AREAS

The Georgia Act anticipates the potential for different LOSs for different service areas within the same jurisdiction. For example, the city could be willing to tolerate higher levels of traffic congestion in the downtown area, where alternative transportation options such as mass transit are more readily available, than in outlying areas, where the automobile is the primary transportation mode. If there is a logical reason for providing more intensive services in a particular part of a jurisdiction, or constraints that prevent extending capital facilities to certain areas, it is best to state the reasons for the decisions a community has made in the comprehensive plan.

The possibility of recoupment fees as a revenue source created a situation where the city could be able to remedy existing deficiencies. For example, if the city established multiple service areas and adopted an LOS at the citywide average, the existing LOSs within the individual service areas could be either above or below the citywide average. Thus, some service areas would have deficiencies while others would have excess capacity. Until the excess capacity is used up, impact fee revenues collected in service areas with excess capacity could be used to remedy deficiencies in other service areas. Used in this way, impact fees could help bring about a more uniform LOS to all areas of the city. The city, however, decided to have a uniform LOS for all facilities.

LEVEL OF COST RECOVERY

Another issue that relates to the LOS is the level of cost recovery desired by the community. For a variety of reasons, many communities adopt impact fees at a level that is below the actual cost to serve new development. The impact fee level established in neighboring jurisdictions with which the community considers itself in competition for new development is often a major factor in such considerations.

There are basically two approaches to lowering impact fees. Probably the most common approach is to calculate the full cost to serve new development at the existing LOS standard, but then charge impact fees at a fixed percentage of the calculated cost. In the context of the Georgia Act, however, the city decided that a preferable approach would be to calculate the impact fees based on a lower-than-existing LOS. The city could then charge the full cost of the lower LOS, keep impact fees competitive with its neighbors, and have greater flexibility in the expenditure of the "recoupment" impact fee revenues.

SERVICE AREAS

Service areas are geographic areas used in the implementation of impact fee systems. The Georgia Act defines "service area" as:

... a geographic area defined by a municipality, county or intergovernmental agreement in which a defined set of public facilities provides service to development within the area. Service areas shall be designated on the basis of sound planning or engineering principles or both.

For each type of facility, a single service area encompassing the entire jurisdiction may be designated, or the jurisdiction may be divided into more than one service area. Designating multiple service areas has both drawbacks and advantages. The approach chosen by the city was to create the fewest number of service areas required to accomplish its objectives.

CRITERIA FOR DELINEATING SERVICE AREAS

The Georgia Act states that service area boundaries should be based on "sound engineering or planning criteria." Natural or environmental boundaries such as aquifer recharge areas, watersheds, or floodplains might be used in defining service areas. Planning considerations might include political divisions or utility service boundaries. Other planning considerations include traffic analysis zones, census tracts, facility maintenance districts, neighborhood planning units, and park or school

Table 5-2
Service Area Criteria for Atlanta, Georgia

Facility	Number Recommended	Area	Rationale
Transportation	1	City-wide	Fees are based only on arterial roadways that provide transportation service on a city-wide basis.
Water	1	City-wide	Water system operates as a pressurized, integrated system, with many redundancies for service reliability.
Wastewater	1	City-wide	Delineating separate service areas (drainage basins) will undermine security pledges to service debt incurred to build the systems. Moreover, "pump-overs" and other system "interconnects" cloud the delineation of service areas.
Parks and recreation	3	Southside Westside Northside	Focus is on medium-size community parks that serve more than one neighborhood, though not the entire city.
Public safety (police, fire, emergency medical service)	1	City-wide	Services are offered throughout the community on demand, at roughly the same response time and quality.

Source: Adapted from "Development Impact Fee Study for Atlanta, Georgia, 1993," by Duncan Associates with Arthur C. Nelson et al.

districts. Table 5-2 summarizes the service area rationale used by Atlanta.

Under the Georgia Act, service areas serve both as "assessment districts" and "benefit districts." These separate functions of service areas are discussed next.

SERVICE AREAS AS ASSESSMENT DISTRICTS

The use of service areas as "assessment districts" is reflected in the requirement of the Georgia Act that "impact fees shall be calculated and imposed on the basis of service areas." Different impact fee schedules may apply within different service areas, reflecting differences in desired LOS, the cost to construct facilities, or in the demand generated by new development.

In the case of road impact fees, for example, different impact fee schedules among service areas could reflect lower right-of-way costs in rural areas due to lower land values, lower construction costs in rural areas due to swale drainage, and longer average trip lengths in more remote areas. Besides these potential cost and demand differentials, different LOSs may be appropriate for different service areas. For example, as part of the growth management plans in several Florida counties, different LOSs adopted for subareas of the county reflect the relative availability of public transit alternatives.

SERVICE AREAS AS BENEFIT DISTRICTS

The use of service areas as "benefit districts" is consistent with the requirement of the Georgia Act that impact fee revenues must be spent within the service area from which they are collected. This provision is designed to ensure that the improvements constructed with impact fee funds provide reasonable benefit to fee-paying development. Thus, service areas assure that there is a reasonable relationship between the assessment of impact fees on new development and the delivery of facilities benefiting new development.

In their role as benefit districts, service area boundaries must be consistent with rational nexus principles. Service areas are intended to ensure that capital facilities are built within reasonable proximity to the new development and serve its residents or occupants. The actual distance from a development project to a capital improvement serving it is not important as long as a benefit link can be established.

Once service areas are established and impact fees are collected to help finance facilities within them, they will not be simple to change. Service areas will also limit the flexibility with which impact fees can be spent. A poorly drawn service area might include many proposed new facilities but not much developable area. Similarly, without proper planning, a particular service area might include considerable development potential but no new facilities. If service areas are too small, there may never be enough money for major improvements. On the other hand, if a service area is too large, some improvements may be so far from the contributing development that it is difficult to show reasonable benefit.

SERVICE AREAS APPLIED IN ATLANTA

Atlanta adopted a citywide impact fee service area for transportation, water, wastewater, and public safety, and divided the city into three service areas for parks and recreation impact fees. These service areas provide maximum flexibility in fee expenditures while also ensuring reasonable benefit to fee-paying developments. The rationale for service area design is summarized in Table 5-2.

PROCEDURAL ISSUES

In addition to the general planning and methodological requirements discussed above, impact fees are subject to many procedural requirements under the Georgia Act that have become standard practice nationally. Several of these requirements are discussed next.

FEE SCHEDULE

The Georgia Act requires that an impact fee ordinance contain a fee schedule, based on a proportionate fair-share methodology that specifies a fee per unit for various land-use types. For example, the schedule should specify the fee for each dwelling unit in a multifamily project, or for each 1,000 square feet of gross floor area in a shopping center. One fee schedule may apply within the local government's entire jurisdiction, or there may be different fee schedules applicable to various service areas. Payment of the impact fee according to the adopted fee schedule constitutes "full and complete payment of a project's proportionate share of system improvement costs," and no other contributions toward system improvements may be required.

INDIVIDUAL ASSESSMENTS

Besides a fee schedule, the Georgia Act requires that impact fee ordinances also contain provisions allowing developers the option of "individual assessments" of required impact fees for specific projects. Applicants who believe that their proposed developments are unique in their impacts are entitled to request individual assessments. The Georgia Act does not specify the nature of the individual assessment process, except that the process must conform to guidelines established in the impact fee ordinance. Many road impact fee ordinances, for example, require individual assessments to be prepared by a professional traffic engineer, and establish criteria for preparation and review of individual assessments. A fee may be charged to cover the administrative costs of reviewing an individual assessment. Generally, the final determination of an impact fee based on an individual assessment rests with an impact fee administrator.

APPEALS

The Georgia Act requires impact fee ordinances to provide for appeals of administrative determinations of the impact fee for a particular development project. The appeal may be to the governing body or another body designated in the impact fee ordinance. A developer also may pay an impact fee under protest to obtain development approval, while retaining the right to appeal and the right to any refund for any fees deemed illegally collected. The ordinance may provide an option for resolution of conflicts over the amount of the impact fee through binding arbitration. In general, there are two kinds of administrative decisions that are subject to appeal. First, applicants choosing to use the fee schedule may disagree with the administrative classification of the land use applicable to the proposed project. Second, applicants choosing an individual assessment may appeal the impact fee resulting from that process.

EXEMPTIONS AND WAIVERS

The Georgia Act allows for exemptions from the payment of impact fees for all or part of particular development projects that create "extraordinary economic development and employment growth or affordable housing." As with any system in which government collects revenues, various groups sometimes seek exemptions from local impact fees. Essentially, the Georgia General Assembly did the city and other Georgia jurisdictions a favor by specifying only two classes of activities that can be granted exemptions.

Federal agencies are usually exempt from payment of impact fees under the separation of powers doctrine, and the city is not able to compel payment by state agencies. Despite whether it can actually collect the fee, however, the city still assesses impact fees on all new development in order to comply with the Georgia Act. The policy supporting such exemptions is contained in the city's comprehensive plan. In addition, the exempt development's proportionate share of system improvements must be "funded through a revenue source other than development impact fees." This requirement makes it difficult to craft exemptions in jurisdictions like Atlanta that lack other revenue to cover the *proportionate share* of exempted facilities. The Georgia Act does not permit any waivers of this requirement; however, this requirement does not apply to "recoupment" impact fees.

States differ in treating such exemptions and waivers. New Mexico allows an outright exemption for qualifying affordable housing at the option of local government with the requirement for substitute revenue. Arizona requires all new development to be assessed but its statute is silent on exemptions or waivers. The policy supporting such exemption or waiver should be contained in the comprehensive plan, as Atlanta has done for its affordable housing and extraordinary economic development waivers. When developments that have actual impact are exempted or have their fees waived, such as affordable housing, the local government would be well advised to deal with how the forgone revenues will be replaced. The Georgia statute requires that replacement revenues be identified. The provision of replacement revenues provides some assurance that those paying impact fees will get the facilities for which they paid.

CONSTRUCTION CREDITS

Credits for in-kind or monetary contributions made by individual developers are often called "construction credits" to distinguish them from "revenue credits." Revenue credits reflect future payments common to all feepayors, such as property taxes or utility rates, and such credits are reflected in the impact fee schedule (see Chapter 6). In contrast, construction credits are deducted from impact fees calculated from the fee schedule on a case-by-case basis. The recommended practice is to provide reasonable credit for facilities a developer installs that are on the CIP and the basis for calculating the impact fee in the first place. When developments, such as affordable housing projects that have actual impact, are exempted or have their fees waived, the local government would be well advised to specify how the foregone revenues are provided from other nonimpact fee sources.

CREDIT FOR LAPSED APPROVALS

A somewhat different credit provision applies to instances where an impact fee has been paid and the building permit expires due to failure to proceed with development. The Georgia Act offers important guidance:

> … in the event a building permit is abandoned, credit shall be given for the present value of the development impact fee against future development impact fees for the same parcel of land. (O.C.G.A. 36-71-4(n))

Unlike the provision for preordinance credits, this provision makes clear that the credit runs with the land, not with the original feepayor. The "present value" language indicates that any interest earned on the impact fee should be included in the credit calculation.

COLLECTION OF FEES

The Georgia Act specifies that impact fees shall be paid at the time of issuance of a building permit or certificate of occupancy. This means that impact fees may not be required at the time of zoning, subdivision, or site plan approval.

There are three general reasons for requiring payment of impact fees prior to the issuance of either a building permit or certificate of occupancy. One is to prevent projects for which building permits have been issued, but that have not been completed or occupied, from avoiding payment of impact fees. The second is to ensure impact fee assessment and collection for a change of use that does not require a building permit but does increase demand on the system. The third is to allow impact fees to be assessed for shell buildings based on the intended use at the time, with the understanding that the fee will be reviewed at the time an ultimate user is found.

REFUNDS

There are two situations identified in the Georgia Act when impact fees must be refunded. The first occurs when an impact fee has been paid, and the first occurs when an impact fee has been paid, and the

capacity is available and service is denied. The second situation occurs when impact fees have been paid but not "encumbered" or construction has not begun within six years of payment. According to the Georgia Act, "encumber" means "to legally obligate by contract or otherwise commit to use by appropriation or other official act."

To determine whether impact fees paid by a particular project have been spent or encumbered, the Georgia Act specifies that impact fees are to be considered encumbered on a first-in, first-out basis. Upon determining that a right to a refund exists, the local jurisdiction must provide notice to the feepayor and publish such notice within 30 days of the expiration of the six-year period. An application for a refund must be made within one year of the expiration of the six-year period or the date of notice publication, whichever is later. Refunds must be made within 60 days of receipt of a valid application, and must include a pro rata share of the interest earned on the impact fee account.

Entitlement to refunds does not "run with the land." Refunds must be made to the person or entity that initially paid the impact fee unless the right to any refund has been expressly transferred to a successor in interest in the property. As a practical matter, communities rarely fail to expend fee revenue in a timely manner if service area definitions are broad enough to allow expenditure on a wide range of projects.

EXPENDITURE AND ACCOUNTING REQUIREMENTS

The Georgia Act provides that:

> Expenditures of development impact fees shall be made only for the categories of system improvements and in the service area for which the development impact fee was imposed as shown by the capital improvements element and as authorized by this chapter. (O.C.G.A. 36-71-8)

Impact fees are thus restricted to the category of facilities for which they were collected. Transportation impact fees, for example, may only be spent on "roads, streets and bridges, including rights-of-way, traffic signals, landscaping, and any local components of state or federal highways." Impact fee revenues also must be spent within the service area from which they were collected.

Moreover, impact fee funds are limited to capital improvements that expand system capacity and may not be spent on maintenance, personnel training, or other operating costs. The following types of costs are eligible for impact fee financing according to the Georgia Act:

- Planning, including cost of qualified staff or consultants to prepare capital improvements element (CIE);
- Design and engineering;
- Land acquisition, including related costs such as court costs and attorneys fees;
- Interest payments on bonds used to finance capital improvements; and
- Administration, limited to a maximum of 3 percent of total fee revenues.

The Georgia Act requires impact fee revenues to be maintained in interest-bearing accounts. Separate accounting records must be maintained for each type of facility and service area. Interest on impact fees is considered funds of the account and subject to the same expenditure limitations as direct impact fee payments. An annual report must be prepared describing, for each facility and service area, the amount of impact fees collected, encumbered, and spent during the preceding year.

Finally, the Georgia Act requires that impact fees be expended, which can include being encumbered, within six years of collection.

Consistent with impact fee practice that has evolved over the past two generations, the Georgia Act and Atlanta's implementation program earmarks impact fees for service areas, and expends those fees for the intended facilities within six years.

ADOPTION PROCEDURES

The Georgia Act requires two "duly noticed" public hearings on the proposed impact fee ordinance prior to adoption. The second hearing must be held at least two weeks after the first hearing. To ensure that those who are most directly affected by impact fees are involved in developing the impact fee system, the Georgia Act requires the establishment of a Development Impact Fee Advisory Committee. The committee must consist of five to 10 members, appointed by the local governing body, with at least 40 percent of the membership representing the development, building, and real estate industries. An existing appointed body meeting these criteria can serve as the Development Impact Fee Advisory Committee. However, the committee is advisory and no committee action is required prior to adoption of an ordinance.

SUMMARY

Proportionate-share principles are founded on the dual rational nexus test. The first element is met by demonstrating that new development affects facilities in ways that need mitigation, either through construction of facilities by such development or payment of impact fees in lieu. For their part, impact fees must be based on reasonable estimates of costs net of other revenues. Those other revenues may include funds from external sources, funds from dedicated local revenues, and other local funds to which new development may contribute. Chapter 6 is dedicated to these credit issues. Chapter 9 presents several alternative methodologies to meet the first test. Chapter 10 illustrates numerous examples of how these issues have been addressed by a number of communities across the United States.

The second element is met by demonstrating that new development paying impact fees receives a reasonable benefit in return that is proportionate to the fees paid. This is achieved through a planning system described in Chapter 7 and administrative procedures reviewed above. Chapters 10 through 13 also provide numerous specific examples of how administrative aspects are addressed, while Chapter 14 offers a model ordinance and Chapter 15 a model administrative code.

6

Credits

INTRODUCTION

This chapter addresses the issue of "credits" or the extent to which impact fees on new development should be reduced because of revenues it generates for the same purpose. There are, broadly, two forms of "credits" against impact fees. The first are "construction" credits, such as credit when a developer widens a road accessing a development where the road project would have been financed from impact fees. The second are "revenue" credits, as when property taxes from new development help retire GO debt incurred to construct the same type of facilities for which impact fees are assessed. The purpose of credits is to avoid collecting from new development more total revenues than is proportionate to its impact on the cost of facilities (also known as "double charging"). Let us consider the role of credits in calculating impact fees.

The general impact fee formula can be represented as:

$$\text{IMPACT FEE} =$$
$$(\text{DEMAND} \times \text{UNIT COST}) - \text{CREDIT}$$

Where:

DEMAND = the amount of capacity needed to accommodate new development, based on the existing or adopted LOS standard, or the associated need for service (e.g., VMT, fire stations per 1,000 population, acres of parks per 1,000 population, and library or other building square footage per 1,000 population)

UNIT COST = the cost per unit of demand based on the calculated value of the asset or set of improvements

CREDIT = the value of the future nonimpact fee revenues that growth will generate, which will also be used to pay for the capital facility expansion of that public infrastructure plus the value of any past or present contributions to the cost of capital facility expansion

The objective of credits is to achieve the equality of costs and revenues (as shown in Figure 6-1). If costs exceed revenues, the facility will be underfunded; if revenues exceed cost, the developer would be overcharged. Such an overcharge would be illegal and perhaps result in a voiding of the impact fee ordinance.[1] In this chapter, we will discuss how to achieve this equality.

The particular approach utilized in establishing an impact fee-reducing credit within the context of impact fee methodology will vary from fee to fee and from place to place. The courts have generally recognized that the local government imposing the fee is best able to evaluate the differing approaches.[2] However, several state enabling acts provide direction, which should be followed where it exists. The only limitation courts have imposed is that any methodology utilized must consider and

Figure 6-1
Relationship of Credits to Impact Fees

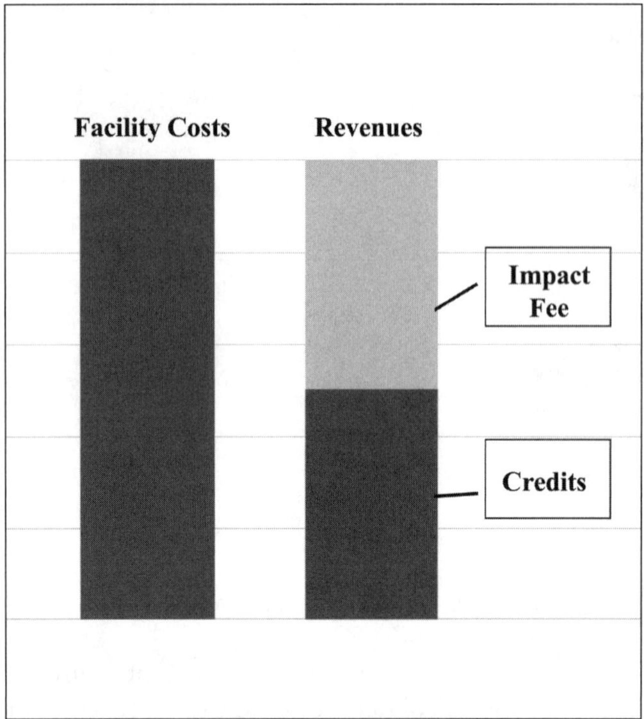

provide a credit for other revenues that are available and applied toward providing the same infrastructure for which the impact fee is collected. The objective of the credit is to avoid a windfall to existing residents at the expense of future taxpayers or residents.

In determining whether the payment of taxes or other revenues is required to be credited against the impact fee, it is only those revenues, which are dedicated to the funding of improvements that create additional capacity to serve that development, that are entitled to a credit under applicable law. Newly constructed development, just as existing development, pays a variety of taxes and revenues to the federal, state, and local governments. Those general revenues may be used for operations, maintenance, repair renovations, and even capital improvements. However, they are general revenues and are subject to annual appropriation by the governing body. No credit against impact fees is required because those revenues are not dedicated to capital facilities. However, those taxes and revenues that are dedicated to the provision of additional capacity in the same infrastructure system for which the impact fee is being collected are entitled to a credit under the laws of many states and this is consistent with professional practice nationally.

As developed through case law and embedded in the laws of several states, there is a two-pronged test as to whether taxes or other revenues must be credited against an impact fee, namely:

1. Whether the taxes or other revenues paid by that newly constructed development are legally available to fund the same infrastructure for which the impact fee is collected ("legally available" in this context means "not restricted or otherwise committed for purposes other than for what the impact fee was collected"); and

2. Whether those legally available taxes or other revenues are actually applied toward reducing the cost of the infrastructure requirements for the newly constructed development that pays the impact fee.

If a revenue source meets this two-pronged test, then a credit must be deducted from the capital cost determined in the impact fee calculation.

Impact fee methodologies may and frequently do vary in how they approach the consideration of credits. Some methodologies employ a more generous approach to credits—not necessarily because they are legally required, but rather for ease of administration, to avoid legal challenge, or based on direction from the elected officials. These approaches are valid and represent a judgment by the legislative body. However, merely because a more generous approach to credits is incorporated into a methodology, it does not mean that it is a legal requirement for a valid impact fee.

For example, some methodologies incorporate a credit for past taxes and revenues paid to a local government prior to the actual development of a property. Though such adjustments may be made in the calculation of an impact fee, they are not required to be credited unless it created capacity that is available to serve that property at the time it was developed. If these contributions were not applied to provide the capacity to serve any development on that property, then they are not a substitute for the impact fee and no credit is due. The relationship between impact fees and credits is illustrated in Figure 6-1.

An example may help to clarify this point. Anne Arundel County, Maryland, has a 5 percent credit in its school impact fee for past payment of property taxes by vacant land. This credit was included because the governing body felt that it was a matter of equity to recognize that owners of vacant land had contributed toward school capital costs in the past without placing any demands on the school system and without receiving any direct benefits from the provision of schools.[3]

Additionally, a variety of planning periods has been utilized to analyze credits from a newly developed property. The courts have granted local governments wide deference in the selection of the particular planning period to be utilized. However, the particular period selected should be consistent with the ultimate aim of the impact fee, which is to provide the necessary infrastructure to serve that development and to do so in a timely fashion. Therefore, there is an inherent connection between the use of impact fees and the requirements of growth management laws to provide the necessary infrastructure to serve a development concurrently with its impacts.

This chapter is devoted to the credit element of impact fee calculations. It includes an overview of various forms of credit and their applications, a review of calculating certain credits based on the *Banberry* factors reviewed in Chapter 3, including examples of applications, and the special case of development credits.

OVERVIEW OF FORMS OF CREDIT AND THEIR APPLICATIONS

As noted in Chapter 3, proportionate-share development fees should not generate more revenue than needed to provide the facilities required to accommodate development. Most state laws, where they exist, provide statutory language to this effect. One way to assure that this does not happen is to consider the extent to which new development must be given "credit" toward its proportionate-share cost of facilities. However, the word "credit" has several meanings, some leading to unfortunate confusion. The different forms of credit are briefly reviewed here.

Suppose a school serving 1,000 students costs $40 million (or $40,000 per student) to construct. Suppose also that the average home will have a student generation rate of 0.50, which equates to $20,000 in school capital costs per average home. This is considered the "gross impact cost." If no other revenues are available to help finance the school, this may also be the impact fee.

Now suppose that the state will pay $20 million of that cost but there are no other revenues available. The "net impact cost" is reduced from $40 million for the school and $40,000 per average home to $20 million and $20,000, respectively. If the local government chooses to set the impact fee at 100 percent of the net impact cost, the impact fee averages $20,000 per home.

Adjusting the impact cost by the "external credit" generated by the state assures that the impact fee does not generate more revenue than is needed to provide to the school, which would be a windfall to existing residents and taxpayers. If the external credit was not applied, and the impact fee averaged $40,000 per home, then $40 million would be collected from 2,000 new homes, but only $20 million would have been spent on the school by the local government. Where does the other $20 million go? Such an impact fee may be challenged as an unauthorized tax and, if successful, may be voided.

The term "external credit" is applied to all revenues available to finance the same facilities for which impact fees are used and from those coming from nonlocal government sources. Federal and state agencies are obvious sources of external credit, but the same may be said for other local governments. For example, a regional park district serving multiple jurisdictions may generate some revenues for the same parks that impact fees may help finance; the park district provides an external credit. Suppose that a local foundation, perhaps the Friends of the Library, offers to help finance library expansion otherwise financed in part from impact fees. This is another example of external credit.[4]

Sometimes a local government has a fixed source of revenue for facilities that may also be financed in part from impact fees. For example, we found that Albuquerque, New Mexico, had a special source of park improvement funds that could be applied to parks, thereby reducing park improvement costs. These funds would be a source of "local credit" that reduces the gross impact cost. Additionally, local governments commonly pledge revenues over time to finance facilities that may also be financed in part from impact fees. These can range from pay-as-you-go arrangements (e.g., a dedicated line item in the budget pledged to facility expansion, which may increase as the population or tax base grows) or debt financing (e.g., issuing bonds to build fire stations).

As new development occurs, it adds to the tax base and thus to available financial resources, which helps finance the expansion of capital facilities. If those facilities are also financed in part with impact fees, new development may be paying twice: once through taxes or other revenues it generates to finance facilities through pay-as-you-go or debt service approaches, and then a second time through impact fees.

To assure that new development is not paying more that its proportionate share of the cost of that facility, a "future revenue credit" is estimated and applied against the gross impact cost. For instance, Florida allows counties to pledge up to two mills of assessed property value to educational facility capital costs. If the entire amount is charged and applied to new school construction, then a new $200,000 home would be paying $400 per year toward school capital costs through this dedicated revenue.

For simplicity, if one assumes a level payment of $400 annually for 20 years, and if the long-term local government borrowing rate is 4 percent, then the present (discounted) value of this stream of revenues would be $5,436. This future revenue credit would be applied to the gross impact cost. The real calculation would not be done this way, however, since impact fee schedules should not be calculated based on each individual land use but rather for all applicable land uses.

Sometimes the site on which new development occurs will have helped finance facilities for which impact fees may be assessed. If all properties in an area were assessed the cost of a fire station, the vacant land on which a new subdivision is constructed has already helped finance fire facilities. An estimate of "past revenue credit" may be appropriate. Most of the discussion about past revenue credits relates to general revenue. Whether or not to grant general revenue credits, if not addressed by a state enabling act or case law, is a policy matter. If a decision is made to grant a past general revenue credit, there is no technically accurate way to estimate the appropriate amount. In practice, consultants (including the authors) reduce the gross impact cost by the percent of the local property tax assessment base that is in vacant land available for development. If the local assessed tax base is $1 billion, for instance, and vacant land available for development (i.e., not in farm-use zones) is $50 million, then the gross impact cost is reduced by 5 percent as a reasonable estimate of the past revenue credit.

Caution is urged, however, because past revenue credits are often inappropriate. This may be the case where no or a small share of the past revenue from vacant or underdeveloped land has gone to finance facilities. For example, water, wastewater, and stormwater utilities are typically financed from user fees, so a past revenue credit for these facilities is not normally necessary because users, rather than property owners, paid the cost. Transportation improvements are typically financed locally through gasoline or sales taxes, which are thus not creditable to vacant land. Sometimes vacant land is not even part of a municipality assessing impact fees until it is developed and then annexed to it. Past revenue credit may have few if any applications in any given situation.

In review, credit considerations result in the following adjustments to the gross impact cost:

$$\text{GROSS IMPACT COST} = (\text{DEMAND} \times \text{UNIT COST})$$

$$\text{NET IMPACT COST} = (\text{GROSS IMPACT COST} - \text{CREDITS}) -$$

$$\text{CREDITS} = (\text{EXTERNAL CREDIT} + \text{LOCAL CREDIT} + \text{FUTURE REVENUE CREDIT} + \text{PAST REVENUE CREDIT})$$

Where:

GROSS IMPACT COST is a function of:

DEMAND based on the adopted LOS (such as five acres of park per 1,000 residents) x

UNIT COST based on the cost per unit of provision (such as $100,000 per acre of parkland) or, in this example, $500 per resident (five acres x $100,000 per acre divided by 1,000 residents)

NET IMPACT COST is a function of:

CREDITS, which include

EXTERNAL CREDIT such as federal or state funds available to help acquire and develop parkland, and

LOCAL CREDIT such as funds the local government has available for park acquisition and development (for example, a fixed amount of money available from local government sources to help acquire and develop parkland), and

FUTURE REVENUE CREDIT such as the discounted (present value) of a bond issued to help finance park acquisition and development (for example, perhaps $1 million of the $2 million needed for park acquisition would be financed from bonds retired from property taxes, thus reducing the net impact cost by $1 million), and

PAST REVENUE CREDIT, which may be an estimate of the extent to which vacant land may have already helped finance parks through property taxes that helped retire park bonds—often simply reducing the gross impact cost by the percent of the local property tax base composed of vacant land planned and/or zoned for development

These considerations are made in calculating the impact fee schedule. There is another source of credit that is determined on a project-by-project basis. Sometimes a development contributes specifically to the same facility that is financed in part from impact fees the development also pays, such as making and dedicating road improvements. To prevent overcharging, a "development credit" may be needed against impact fees otherwise due.

PRINCIPLES FOR ESTIMATING
CREDIT WITH APPLICATIONS

Recall the *Banberry* factors from Chapter 3. Great emphasis is placed on the need to provide "consideration" to new development for past and future payments toward capital improvements costs. In *Banberry*, this consideration was broken down into several parts:

- The means by which existing facilities have been financed;
- The extent to which new development has already contributed to the cost of providing existing facilities;
- The extent to which existing development will, in the future, contribute to the cost of existing facilities in the form of property taxes or user fees; and
- The extent to which new development should receive credit for providing at its cost facilities the community has provided in the past without charge to other development in the service area.

Banberry and similar treatises tell us that total impact costs should not serve solely as the basis for determining the amount of impact fees. Rather, consideration should be given to what new developments provide toward capital improvements finance. This consideration should extend to existing as well as future improvements. The obvious point is that it would be patently unfair to require new development to pay some portion of either existing or future capital improvements and also require it to be totally responsible for the capital improvements costs that new development will need. This then returns to the matter of what new development has paid or will pay toward capital improvements costs.

DETERMINING HOW EXISTING FACILITIES WERE FINANCED AND HOW MUCH NEW DEVELOPMENT WILL PAY IN THE FUTURE

Existing development should be sheltered from the cost of facilities necessitated by new development. Conversely, new development should be sheltered from the cost of paying for facilities that will be paid in part by other sources of revenue. The beginning point in determining credits, both past and future, is an analysis of how existing capital improvements were financed.

Each means of financing employed should be classified in terms of whether development, which occurred after the improvements were made, was required to pay for such improvements prior to its construction (i.e., when it was still vacant land) and post development, either as user fees or taxes. The extent to which external funds were used to finance existing facilities is also an important step in the process. This can be ascertained from budget records.

Typical financing arrangements will include user charges, property taxes, other taxes, revenue bonds (retired by user fees or property taxes), and intergovernmental transfers (from state or federal agencies). Those same financing means may be available to help finance new or expanded facilities in the future. (See Table 6-1 for an example of sources of capital funds for a given facility.) The extent to which those sources were used to pay for past improvements, as well as the extent to which those same sources will be used in the future, should be ascertained. The objective is to come up with a distribution similar to that shown in Figure 6-1, which deals with the past. The next step is to determine what, if any, of these sources will be available in the future. Some of these sources are dedicated, such as grants, both GO and revenue bonds, and gas taxes; others are not.

Facilities using dedicated funding sources are the easiest with which to deal. Highways are a good example of such dedicated funding sources. In most states, road capital improvements and maintenance projects are financed with motor fuel taxes and other highway user charges. These receipts go into restricted funds and are used exclusively for transportation purposes. If traffic data exist, the amount that new development will pay into this fund may be determined. This is done by calculating traffic impact in terms of total miles of travel per year. This total annual mileage may then be divided by the average mileage per gallon to arrive at annual motor fuel consumption. The annual volume of

Table 6-1
Examples of Fund Sources for Capital Facilities

Sources of Capital Funds						
Facility Type	State/Federal Grants	General Obligation Bonds	Revenue Bonds	General Funds	Gas Taxes	Other
Utilities	40%	0%	60%	0%	0%	0%
Roads	35%	0%	0%	0%	65%	0%
Parks	20%	60%	0%	20%	0%	0%
Public safety	40%	50%	0%	5%	0%	5%

gallons consumed is then multiplied by the tax rate to arrive at annual receipts.

Reference to the reports of the various federal and state highway (transportation) departments will provide the split of these receipts between maintenance and capital improvements. Applying this split to the annual motor fuel tax payments will yield annual payments toward capital improvements in the form of motor fuel taxes. The present value of these annual payments would be the appropriate credit for motor fuel tax payments. Consider now how a credit for motor fuel payments is calculated. Suppose the parameters shown in Table 6-2 were used in making the calculations for the credit to an average single-family home.

Table 6-2 is used for illustration purposes only. In the present example, suppose that the cost to construct a road averages $2,000,000 per lane-mile. Further, suppose that the capacity of such a road is 7,200 vehicles per lane per day. The road cost per vehicular mile is $278. The home in Table 6-2 produced 22.5 vehicular miles per day on the local roads, so the cost of roads for that home would be $6,250. Its payment of motor fuel taxes, however, will cover about $1,583 of this cost, leaving a net impact cost of $4,667. This would be the impact fee. An example of a generalized formula for calculating the credit is shown in Table 6-3.

For most nonresidential and many residential land uses, road impact would be based on the size of the building in square feet of floor area. However, for some land uses, the impact measure would be different, such as rooms for hotels and motels and seating capacity for restaurants. The example shown here is thus illustrative to one example of a single residential unit. Chapter 10 shows in more detail how motor fuel credits are applied in specific case studies.

The example in Table 6-3 includes two important assumptions that are discussed here: the choice of the discount factor (also called the "capitalization rate") to bring the value of future revenue streams to the present, and the choice of the time period over which to discount the revenue flow (also called the "capitalization period").

Future values are discounted back to present value for two things: the time value of money and risk. The discount rate commonly used is the local government's long-term borrowing rate. Local governments can often borrow money by selling bonds at tax-exempt interest rates. The result is that local governments can borrow money less expensively than the private sector.

There are a number of sources for interest rates, although the best might be what the local government is paying. Using the borrowing cost at the discount rate implies that there is no risk associated with the future stream of funds. When that stream is a fixed-base payment, such as motor fuel taxes, which are based on cents per gallon, this might be reasonable. However, when the base can change, risk will exist. If the relevant stream of funds were sales tax receipts, the base can and will change over time.

The future rate of increase of sales tax receipts is much less certain than motor fuel taxes and thus some risk premium is warranted. How much of a risk premium would depend on the extent of the risk. It should be noted that there is relatively little risk associated with public tax receipts, thus it would be expected that risk premiums would be low. Fixed-based taxes are used in the example here and no risk premium is added.

The other issue is the discount period. Infrastructure is a long-term investment. It would follow that the discount period should also be long term. National impact fee practice typically uses a 20- or 25-year discount period. The longer the discount period, the greater the present value and the higher the credit against gross impact cost.

Table 6-2
Revenue Credit for Motor Fuel Taxes, Average Single-Family Home

Calculation Step	Figure
Average daily trip ends [a]	5.0
Miles per trip on local roads [a]	4.5
Average daily vehicular miles on local roads	22.5
Average annual miles [b]	16,436
Average miles per gallon [c]	17.0
Average annual gallons	966.84
Total motor fuel tax rate per gallon [d]	$0.25
Percent for capacity expansion [e]	50.00%
Cents for capacity expansion	$0.13
Average annual capacity expansion revenue	$120.85
Public long-term debt financing rate [f]	4.42%
Planning horizon, years	20
Present value factor [g]	13.10
Revenue credit	$1,583.03

Notes:
a. Rounded for simplicity. An average single-family home in a suburban setting will generate about 10 total daily weekday trips and the average trip will be about 9 miles. However, the "trips" are calculated as a vehicle leaving the home and then returning. To avoid double counting the same trip from the home to a destination, the residential trips are typically adjusted by 50%.
b. Based on 365.25 days per year, which includes leap year once every four years.
c. This is the fleet mileage including trucks (www.bts.gov/publications/transportation_indicators/september_2002/Environment/excel/Average_Motor_Vehicle_Miles_Per_Gallon.xls).
d. Illustrative state and local rate (federal rate excluded because federal motor fuel taxes typically help finance the federal highway system, while impact fees are typically used to help finance local roads).
e. Illustrative share of the motor fuel tax that is spent for capacity expansion (such as new lane-miles or road widening) and not repairs and replacement.
f. This is the average 20-year, long-term municipal bond rate as report by the Federal Reserve System (www.federalreserve.gov/releases/h15/data/monthly).
g. The formula in Excel is = PV(1,Financing Rate, Planning Horizon).

Table 6-3
General Road Impact Fee Calculation Model

IMPACT FEE = (VMT x COST per VMT) – CREDITS

Where:

VMT	=	Average daily trips (ADT) x % NEW x LENGTH ÷ 2
ADT	=	Trip ends during average weekday
% NEW	=	Percent of trips that are primary trips as opposed to pass-by or diverted trips
LENGTH	=	Average length of a trip on the major roadway system
÷ 2	=	Avoids double counting trips for origin and destination
COST per VMT	=	COST per LANE-MILE ÷ AVG LANE CAPACITY
COST per LANE-MILE	=	Average cost to add a new lane to the major roadway system
AVG LANE CAPACITY	=	Average daily capacity of a lane at desired level of service
CREDITS	=	[(VMT * 365.25) ÷ MPG] * $ per GAL x NPV
365.25	=	Days per year (used to convert daily VMT to annual VMT)
MPG	=	Miles per gallon, average for U.S. motor vehicle fleet
$ per GAL	=	Motor fuel tax rate x % to capital
NPV	=	Net present value factor (i.e., 13.1 for 20 years at 4.42% discount)

A 20-year period is reasonable because it reflects a typical 20-year planning horizon and the typical term of long-term bonds. A 25-year period is also reasonable because it reflects some long-term planning horizons, is equivalent to traditional notions of how many years a "generation" lasts, and is a common period of time for bonds. Shorter or longer periods of time may be reasonable based on local government borrowing history.

Often, capital expansion is financed from property tax revenue either on a pay-as-you-go basis or through long-term debt retired from property tax revenue. The following is an example of how the credit is calculated for this. The case is a law enforcement impact fee. The local government desires to maintain its current LOS of 2.13 sworn police offices per 1,000 functional residents (see Chapter 8 for calculating functional population). The gross impact cost per functional resident is summarized in Table 6-4.

In this case, the local government expanded its law enforcement facilities and funded it with GO debt. The bonds were issued two years ago and the facility was sized to serve future development. The following is a straightforward way to calculate the gross cost, credit, and net cost. Here, the gross cost is $200 per capita and the credit is $140.14, leaving a net cost of $59.86 per capita (as shown in Table 6-5).

There is another way to calculate this cost. The population of this subject jurisdiction is growing. As it grows, the jurisdiction will incur costs to provide law enforcement facilities. That growth will also spread the debt service obligation over a larger base (as seen in Table 6-6). The credit can also be calculated as the present value of the per capita debt service payments over the remaining life of the bonds (as shown in Table 6-7). This latter approach results in a smaller credit and thus a higher net cost. Either would be an acceptable methodology.

Grants are another common source of funding. To the extent that grants will be forthcoming, they should reduce the net costs and the impact fee because that portion of the facility cost is not borne by the jurisdiction. Problems arise when it is unclear that grants may be available or in what mount. Many look to the recent past, commonly five years, as a means to establish grant parameters. If, over the past five years, 15 percent of park capital costs have been paid by grants, it would be reasonable to assume that 15 percent of capital costs will be paid by grants in the future. If there is specific knowledge that future grants will be different from the past, certainly that knowledge could be used. The real problem is when we simply don't know. Grants have been available in the past, but they might not be available in the future. When faced with such a dilemma, recall San Francisco's plight. They assumed that no future Urban Mass Transportation Administration grants would be available for the Bay Area Rapid Transit (BART) system and then, several years later, they had to explain to the court what they did with the grant money that they received.

There can be many nuances to calculating future revenue credits. Chapters 6 and 10 indicate several approaches. Because there may be many forms of

Table 6-4
Law Enforcement Facility Gross Impact Cost Per Functional Resident

Item	Figure
Land cost per square foot of building	$50
Total building square footage	200,000
Total land cost	$10,000,000
Total building cost	$50,000,000
Total equipment cost	$40,000,000
Total capital cost	$100,000,000
General obligation bond	$75,000,000
Number of sworn police officers	250
Gross impact cost per police officer	$400,000
Sworn officers per 1,000 functional residents	2.00
Gross impact cost per functional resident	$800.00

Figures based on current replacement cost of existing facilities. A "functional resident" is a means of measuring population. It includes residents, commuters, and transients, all of which place demands on a jurisdiction's law enforcement infrastructure.

Table 6-5
Simple Future Revenue Credit and Net Impact Cost

Component/Calculation Step	Figure
Facility cost	$100,000,000
General obligation bond	$75,000,000
Interest rate	4.42%
Term	20
Years to maturity	18
Annual payment	$5,725,812
Population	500,000
Payment per capita per year	$11.45
Present value per capita	$140.14
Facility cost per capita	$200.00
Credit per capita	$140.14
Net cost per capita	$59.86

Table 6-6
Annual Future Revenue Credit

Years to Maturity	Payment	Population	Payment Per Capita
1	$5,725,812	500,000	$11.45
2	$5,725,812	510,000	$11.23
3	$5,725,812	520,200	$11.01
4	$5,725,812	530,604	$10.79
5	$5,725,812	541,216	$10.58
6	$5,725,812	552,040	$10.37
7	$5,725,812	563,081	$10.17
8	$5,725,812	574,343	$9.97
9	$5,725,812	585,830	$9.77
10	$5,725,812	597,546	$9.58
11	$5,725,812	609,497	$9.39
12	$5,725,812	621,687	$9.21
13	$5,725,812	634,121	$9.03
14	$5,725,812	646,803	$8.85
15	$5,725,812	659,739	$8.68
16	$5,725,812	672,934	$8.51
17	$5,725,812	686,393	$8.34
18	$5,725,812	700,121	$8.18
Present value			$121.78

Table 6-7
Cash Flow Future Revenue Credit and Net Impact Cost

Component/ Calculation Step	Figure
Facility cost	$100,000,000
General obligation bond	$75,000,000
Interest rate	4.42%
Term	20
Years to maturity	18
Annual payment	$5,725,812
Population	500,000
Payment per capita per year	$11.45
Present value per capita	$140.14
Facility cost per capita	$200.00
Credit per capita	$121.78
Net cost per capita	$78.22

future revenue credits attributable to new development, impact fee analysts need to be sure to identify all reasonable (and predictable) sources, and make reasoned efforts to consider their effect on proportionate-share development fees.

DETERMINING HOW MUCH NEW DEVELOPMENT HAS ALREADY PAID

Another time issue relates to past payments. The *Banberry* court wanted consideration of the extent to which new development had already contributed to the cost of existing facilities. Where such past payments can be identified, they should be dealt with in exactly the same manner as future payments.

The main difference is that interest would be paid rather than charged. However, interest would be payable only for those public facilities toward which new development had contributed and from which it received no benefit (i.e., use). Owners or developers of raw land have not paid user fees, sales and excise taxes, fuels, or other taxes or fees on that land. They do pay property taxes, however. If property taxes have been used to pay for the construction of existing facilities, even in part, new development could be credited for the value of those past payments.

For example, if new development, in the form of vacant land, paid toward parks, no benefit (use) would have been received. However, if new development contributed toward fire protection, benefit would have been received because vacant land also burns and benefits from fire protection. Common sense should be relied upon to determine whether new development has paid for various services and facilities and whether any benefit was derived. Additionally, some cutoff is needed for the consideration of past payments. Considering the past five to 10 years would appear to be reasonable.

Assume, for example, that property taxes have paid for approximately 20 percent of the cost of new roads in the past five years. Further assume that about 20 percent of the assessed property valuation of the community is in vacant land. Undeveloped land would, therefore, have contributed about 4 percent to the cost of constructing existing roads (20 percent of 20 percent). Assume further that none of those roads constructed in part with property taxes paid by vacant land will benefit the development of vacant land. The present value of those past contributions to new roads that will not benefit new development must be recouped when road impact fees are determined. This will usually mean lower road impact fees.

Any shortfall in revenue needed should come from nonimpact fee sources. In reality, the easiest way to do this administratively is for public officials to contribute general funds in an amount equivalent to the value of past contributions of vacant land to existing roads toward the construction of new roads benefiting new development. This will also result in some double payment by new development as its property taxes support the general fund.

However, the proportion of these double payments will likely be so low as to be meaningless. In the example above, it was shown that vacant land on which new development will be sited has paid for 4 percent of the cost of constructing roads solely for the benefit of existing development. If the community contributes an equivalent amount toward the construction of new roads benefiting new development, then the amount of that money that comes from vacant land through property taxes will be 0.16 percent (or 20 percent times 20 percent times 4 percent). In other words, very nearly all of the value of those past payments will, in effect, come from existing development. The figures shown here might suggest that the results are de minimis and thus unimportant. Regardless of the result, consideration in determining how what is becoming new development has contributed toward the cost of existing facilities is important and should not be ignored.

When those calculations are made, they must be in present value figures. This can be done in two ways. First, the current cost of constructing existing roads can be taken as the present value equivalent. If vacant land on which new development will be sited has historically contributed 4 percent to the cost of constructing roads benefiting existing development, then the present value of that stream of payments could simply be 4 percent of the current replacement cost of the roads built with property taxes. Second, the present value of the stream of those property tax contributions can be calculated making assumptions of appropriate time value of money.

Failure to look at how existing facilities were financed, and the extent to which what is becoming new development contributed to the cost of existing facilities, could jeopardize legal defensibility of impact fee programs. Moreover, grossly underestimating the magnitude of these funding sources through conservative assumptions may also fail court review. Consider the bar graph in Figure 6-2, which shows future credits and impact fees equaling the facility cost. If a past payment credit was due, the sum of the credits plus the impact fee would exceed the facility cost.

When is a past payment credit due? To the extent that new developments have already paid for existing facilities, through some dedicated source of revenue, a past payment credit may be due. A special assessment against land for water and sewer facilities would be a good example. The vacant land

has already paid some or even all of the cost of the facilities, and not incorporating those payments into the fee calculation would result in total charge to the development that exceeds costs. If such payments were in the form of paying general taxes, there is no requirement to reduce impact fees. All are required to pay general taxes, and the proceeds from general taxes are used for a variety of purposes.

There are many instances where what are commonly thought of as general taxes are in fact dedicated revenues. Debt service on GO bond issues is a property tax, but it is a property tax dedicated to a specific purpose. Florida's two mill tax for school capital facilities is also a dedicated property tax. Having a good inventory of how existing facilities were funded will greatly assist in determining what, if any, past payment credits may be due. It is also a help in dealing with future revenue credits. As mentioned above, some jurisdictions elect to give past payment credits for the payment of general taxes. While there is no question about a legislative body's authority to do this, it should be recognized that such credits will result in underfunding and either an increase of other funds or less infrastructure investment.

DEVELOPMENT CREDITS

Proportionate-share development fees need to consider external, local, and revenue credits as reviewed above. The role of "development credits" was also introduced above and will be addressed in more detail here.

Figure 6-2
Past and Future Credits in Relation to Impact Fees

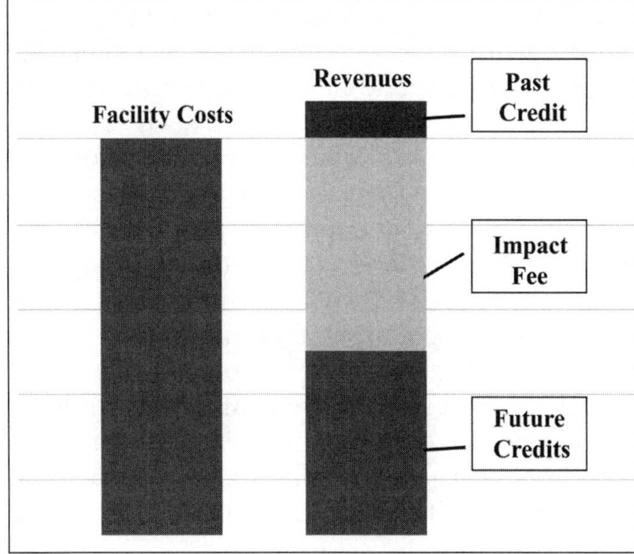

In some situations, development credits are needed because local codes mandate dedications of land or facilities as a condition of approval. A common example of a mandated dedication would be land for parks. If the development is dedicating land and paying impact fees for parks, then typically a value of the dedicated land is determined and used to reduce the impact fees otherwise assessed. Note that this is a credit against the net impact cost (assuming the impact fee is 100 percent of the net impact cost) and not against the gross impact cost. This is usually determined on a case-by-case basis. (See Chapters 14 and 15 for model language addressing this.)

In other situations, the development may offer to finance a facility and request a development credit against impact fees assessed. Whether and the extent to what is allowed is a matter of local policy. Generally, such credit is allowed when:

- The facility being constructed by the developer is already on the list of facilities to be financed from impact fees;
- The credit is applied only to facilities of the same type (such as a road impact fee credit for the cost of widening a road); and
- The credit is allowed for only up to the impact fees that would be assessed.

Suppose a developer proposes road improvements that are not on the list of capital improvements (e.g., improvement-driven methods) or used as the basis for calculating impact fees (e.g., standards-based impact fees that use future projects to calculate fees). Local officials will first need to determine if the proposed improvements should have been included in the list of projects on which the impact fees were based. If so, the relevant lists of projects on which impact fees were calculated would need to be amended to include the proposed improvements.

This can raise important issues, such as raising the impact fee by adding the projects proposed by the developer. The developer is obviously proposing that the new improvements offset current impact fee obligations. However, if the proposed projects were added to the basis for calculating impact fees, the credit should be against the higher fees and not the current, lower ones. It is possible that the proposed improvements should replace others already on the lists but, if this is the case, those projects need to be removed. If the new projects are roughly the same cost as the ones removed, then the impact fee would likely stay about the same.

Generally speaking, local officials need to have the discipline to avoid changing CIPs or other lists of projects on which impact fees are based. These lists are typically developed through a public participation process, and developers can participate in—and probably do so—more actively than other interests because of their stake in the planning, design, and financing of capital improvements. Local officials probably do not want to be perceived by the public or media as having gone around the process to modify the lists after they have been developed and approved.

This does not mean that developers proposing worthwhile improvements should not receive relief. There are two broad approaches to this. The first one, used by many jurisdictions, is called the "latecomer fee." Bozeman, Montana, uses this approach when developers propose projects that, while anticipated on the long term, are not included in current CIPs. Assuming all other features of the development are appropriate given local planning processes, Bozeman enters into an agreement with a developer to have the developer finance the improvements but then receive payments from future developers using the same facility based on a formula.

The second approach is having the developer finance the desired improvements while the local government goes through the process of amending the capital improvements lists and updating the impact fees. By prior agreement, if the proposed projects are added to the list, then credit is given based on the updated amount of the impact fees, perhaps not exceeding the impact fees. While there is some risk to the developer that the process might not result in the proposed projects being added to the list, chances are that, if staff and other local government officials endorse the changes, they will be adopted.

Suppose the project is on the relevant lists and the developer proposes to construct them at their cost, but the cost exceeds the impact fees that would be assessed. Should the local government provide reimbursement to the developer? Depending on the circumstances, the answer may be affirmative. However, this does not necessarily mean that local government writes a check to the developer for the amount in excess of the impact fees. Impact fees are in place largely because local governments do not have the funds readily available to make the needed improvements. Many local governments, however, reimburse the developer through future impact fee revenues collected within the same service area for the same category of facility for which development-based impact fee credit was given.

Another angle—transferable credits—is conceptually simple but administratively tedious. Suppose a developer installs improvements in excess of any impact fee credits, and that it may be unlikely that the developer could be reimbursed from future impact fee revenues or that local government chooses not to engage in that option. In some jurisdictions, the difference between the cost and the impact fees that would have been collected is allowed to be transferred to any other development within the same service area for the same class of facilities, perhaps subject to a time limit. The developer owning these transferable credits could sell them to other developers who then present the credits when it comes time for them to pay impact fees. The sale of transferable credits is often discounted 10 to 20 percent, recognizing the willingness of the credit owner to convert the credits into cash, and the buyer of the credits who may have to borrow funds to purchase them for use months or even years later.

The administrative part is tedious because local government needs to track the ownership of the credits and assess how much they are worth. When these programs first began, some local governments simply lost track of how much was outstanding in credit values or who had them. Disputes would arise when a developer would attempt to reduce impact fee assessments by the value of the credits they purchased from another developer. Lee and Palm Beach counties in Florida have evolved a reasonable system for awarding, tracking, and honoring transferable impact fee credits.

The area of impact fee credits continues to evolve. One area of concern that is not widely addressed is the extent to which credit is given when the impact fee itself is less than the net impact cost. Suppose a local government decides to assess impact fees at 50 percent of the net impact cost. If a developer constructs a project on the relevant list out of their pocket, does the developer receive a credit based on 100 percent of the cost or the level at which the impact fee is assessed?

Arguments can be made both ways, but it may be local government that finds it difficult to grant a credit for less than the cost simply because the fees assessed are less than they should be. While there may be no clear solution to this predicament, there may be two options. First, local government raises impact fees to their full level, thus assuring full credit if and when the credit issue arises. Second, a developer's offer is not accepted to make the improvements if they involve 100 percent credit against impact fess charged less than 100 percent of the net impact cost.

SUMMARY OBSERVATIONS

When payments cannot be identified, some other reasonable means, such as a percentage reduction, could be employed. It is important to keep in mind that the criterion is that impact fees should not exceed a proportionate share of the local government's costs in accommodating new development. In the vast majority of cases, these costs will occur in the future. Because the future is at issue, these amounts are likely to be unknown. However, exactitude is not the standard; reasonableness is. Due care to details, plus dedication to being reasonable, should result in proportionate-share calculations that will stand up to the established judicial standards.

The object of calculating credits is to establish an impact fee that is fair or equitable—where revenues are equal to but are no greater than costs. This fee should be structured so that existing taxes or user fees would not have to be raised in order to accommodate new development. Such fees should be limited to that amount and no more. It is important to continuously keep the objective of credit calculation in mind. Fairness, but not perfection, can be attained.

The methods set out above are attempts at integrating a degree of fairness—proportionality—into impact fee calculations. These methods are in use and have survived both political and legal challenges. These methods, however, will almost certainly end up being refined. Further case law and legislative actions will influence changes in the way impact fees are calculated. However, the analyst can rest assured that the future evolution of impact fees and fee methodology will be in the direction of attaining equity. Keeping fairness, equity, and proportionality as the goals should provide some degree of assurance that impact fees will not be the ones that provide the future case law on this subject.

Remember: The development industry will not litigate over an impact fee that it thinks is reasonable.

NOTES

1. Juergensmeyer and Nicholas (2002).
2. See *St. Johns County v. N.E. Builders Ass'n*, 583 So.2d 635 (Fla. 1991); *Sarasota County v. Sarasota Church of Christ, Inc.*, 667 So.2d 417 (Fla. 1995).
3. Anne Arundel County Code, Title 11, Subtitle 2, "Development Impact Fees."
4. A recent event is interesting on this issue. The Library Foundation of Martin County, Florida, provides "enhancements funds" to the library. The Library Foundation specifically directed that their "enhancement funds" not be used to offset or otherwise reduce Martin County's library impact fees. This directive was followed and no credit was given for those donations.

7

Impact Fees and the Planning Connection

It is clear that local governments throughout the country are increasingly using impact fees to help finance new and expanded facilities to serve new development. When based on a comprehensive plan, and used in conjunction with a CIP, impact fees can be an important tool for providing adequate infrastructure to accommodate growth.

It is important to understand that impact fees are a land-use planning implementation device. From the perspective of a developer, the impact fee is paid only when a development proposal is consistent with local zoning, subdivision, and other land-use regulations. From the perspective of local governments, impact fees are one of many financial elements of a CIP, which implements the long-range CIE, which is part of the long-range comprehensive plan. The relationship of impact fees to the comprehensive planning process is illustrated in Figure 7-1.

In this chapter, we review the linkages between planning, land-use regulations, and impact fees. We begin with what we consider an impact fee Magna Carta (Juergensmeyer and Roberts (2007)):

I. Land development shall not be permitted unless adequate capital facilities exist or are assured.

II. Land development shall bear a proportionate cost of the provision of new or expanded capital facilities required by such development.

III. The imposition of impact fees and dedication requirements are the preferred methods of regulating land development in order to assure that it bears a proportionate share of the cost of capital facilities necessary to accommodate that development and to promote and protect the healthy, safety, and general welfare.

Toward this general end, many state impact fee enabling acts require that local governments prepare comprehensive plans and CIPs to support impact fee policy. Georgia's statute, for example, provides:

Municipalities and counties that have adopted a comprehensive plan containing a capital improvements element are authorized to impose by ordinance development impact fees as a condition of development approval on all development pursuant to and in accordance with the provisions of this chapter. (Official Code Georgia Annotated 36-71-4)

Other states, such as New Mexico and Texas, substitute the terms "land-use assumptions" for "comprehensive plan," but there is very little practical difference. Even in the absence of enabling legislation requiring comprehensive plans and CIPs, in which Florida is a leading state, case law is clear about the role of those documents in justifying impact fees.

Figure 7-1
Impact Fees and the Planning Process

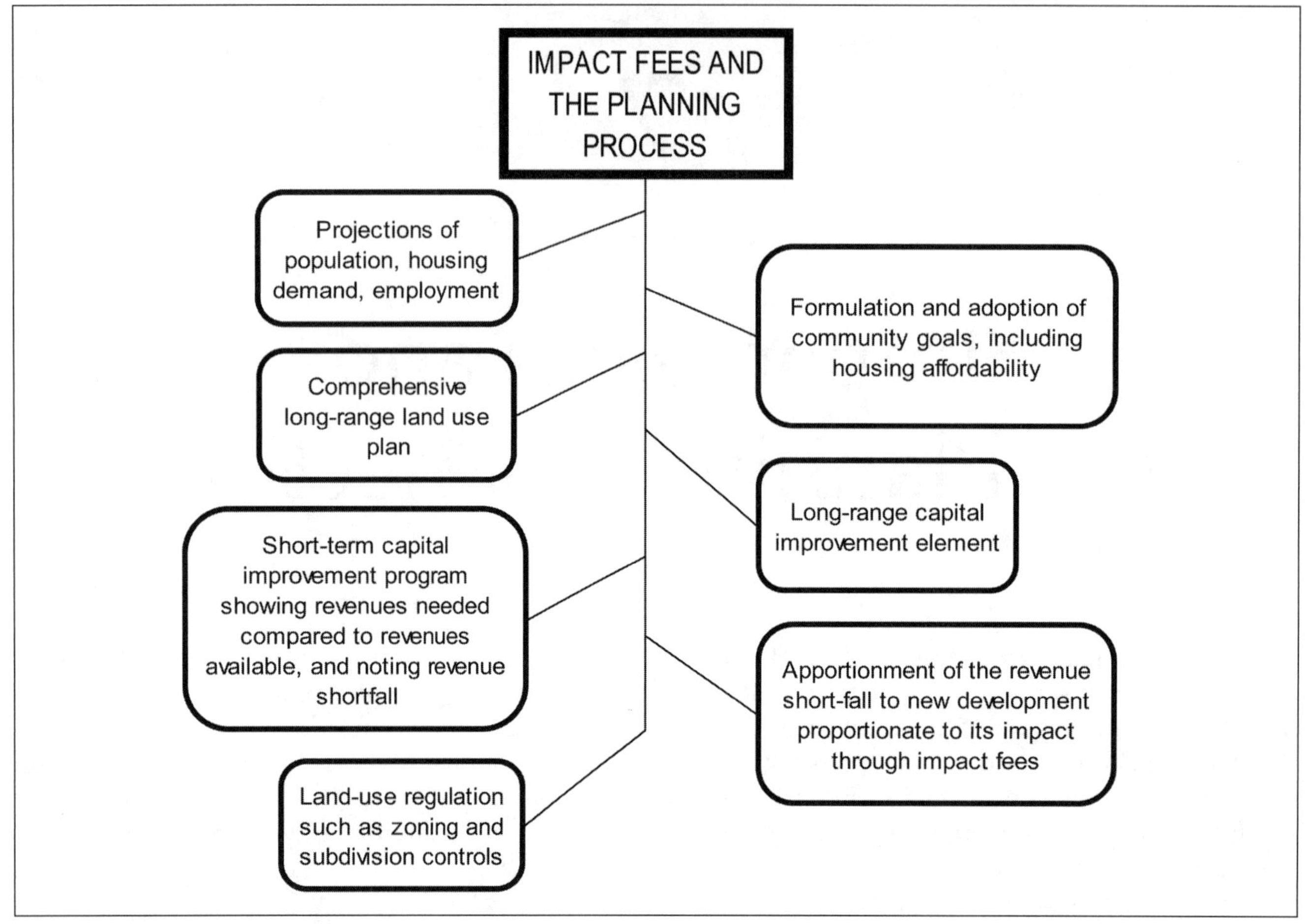

Courtesy of Newport Partners, LLC.

Impact fees need to be differentiated from other forms of exactions in the context of planning. Impact fees come nearly at the end of a planning and implementation process.[1] The legal logic for impact fees came initially through the exercise of local police powers provided in home rule charters, subdivision regulation authority, zoning enabling legislation, and utility statutes. Since they must be tied to regulation, they are sometimes called "regulatory impact fees." They must be based on the relationship between growth and its demand on facilities needed to serve it. They must also not exceed the "proportionate share" of the impact of growth on facilities. This is the foundation of the "dual rational nexus test" (see section on proportionate-share impact fees).

The Georgia Department of Community Affairs provides useful guidance on how this is established. Few other states require the kind of close link between the comprehensive plan and the impact fee analysis required in Georgia. The impact fee CIPs required in Texas and New Mexico, for example, are basically impact fee studies that include a list of capital improvements. Other states require various levels of planning to demonstrate the link between growth and the need for new or expanded capital facilities. We believe Georgia's approach offers a sound model to be emulated in practice

First, long-range projections of population, housing unit demand, and employment growth are made and adopted officially. This is typically over a 10- to 20-year planning horizon.

Second, community planning goals are established, which are designed to guide growth consistent with them. One or more goals may relate to housing affordability.

Third, a comprehensive, long-range (typically 10- to 20-year) land-use plan is prepared to help guide development to achieve planning goals.

Fourth, the projections are converted into facility demand. Suppose a community will double in population, adding 100,000 new residents over the planning horizon. Suppose also that it already has 500 acres of parkland, or five acres per 1,000 residents. Its current "level of service" is thus five acres per 1,000 residents. If the community is satisfied with the current LOS, it may adopt it as the official LOS standard. The next 500 acres of park are thus included generally in a long-range CIE.

The CIE is implemented by a CIP, which in Georgia is typically five to 10 years. This is the fifth step. In the case of parks, it shows the parkland acquisition and improvements projects needed over that period to accommodate new development. Costs are estimated and sources of revenue available to cover those costs are identified. These revenue sources may include federal, state, and local funds; gifts from foundations, civic groups, or individuals; and dedicated sources of revenue, such as a dedicated property tax used to expand park inventory. If there is a shortfall in revenue needed to fully fund the park CIP, impact fees are used to make up the gap.

Impact fees are themselves the sixth step of the planning and implementation process. Once the CIP gap has been identified, a process is undertaken to apportion the shortfall in revenues to benefit development. An impact fee schedule is developed and applied to land development permits, building permits, or certificates of occupancy as determined locally.

The last step in the process is designing and implementing land development regulations. Zoning and subdivision controls regulate the actual timing, shape, density, and other features of development, especially including residential development. Once a development has been deemed consistent with zoning and subdivision regulations, and others as locally required, it is then assessed impact fees proportionate to its impact on facilities as determined from the first five steps in the planning and implementation process.

IMPACT FEES AND EXACTIONS

The land-use regulatory step itself may include other forms of exactions. Suppose, for example, that land needs to be rezoned and then subdivided to meet a developer's objectives, presumably consistent with the goals and framework of the comprehensive land-use plan. The rezoning process may identify unique or unanticipated impacts of it on the community. These may include environmental, habitat, localized facility, and other impacts.

Comprehensive plans, CIEs, CIPs, and impact fees cannot anticipate all potential forms of development impacts, so it is the rezoning and subdivision stage that does so. For example, drainage, stream setback, buffers, access improvements, and utility extensions may be needed to assure the development mitigates impacts not covered by impact fees or other community-based investments shown in the CIP. Subdivision regulations also assure that on-site improvements are made at no or relatively little cost to the community—although those improvements are usually dedicated to the community for long-term maintenance after they are installed and accepted.

Rezoning and subdivision exactions are negotiated as part of the development approval process. After the rezoning (if needed) and subdivision final orders have been adopted, the developer then pays impact fees to mitigate the off-site facility impacts the final orders do not. The distinction here is that there is a two-stage development approval process: one that addresses unique and development-specific impacts, and the other that addresses communitywide development impacts on facilities.

Two qualifications are in order. About half the states have impact fee enabling statutes, but nearly all of them limit the use of impact fees to a list of facilities (see Chapter 4). Thus, if a development may impact on facilities for which impact fees are not or cannot be assessed, it may be required to mitigate its impact on those facilities through additional exactions. In addition, if a development exaction includes money or improvements to mitigate off-site improvements that would otherwise have been paid through impact fees, the development receives a credit against those impact fees to avoid double charging.

There is another set of "near impact fee" exactions that are commonly used. For example, many communities require a share of land within developments to be dedicated to the public for such uses as parks, school sites, and other facilities. Where a community park impact fee pays only for community- and regional-scale parks, but not local ones, mandatory land dedications for such local parks may not be subject to an impact fee credit. In states where school impact fees are not enabled or communities choose not to have them, mandatory land dedications for school sites—or in-lieu fees based on the land value—do not result in an impact fee credit.

There is probably room for improvement in how exactions other than impact fees are effected. In many communities, impact fees are a relatively minor part of the total package of development exactions. On-site infrastructure exactions, such as for subdivision improvements, are usually far larger in total cost than are impact fees. Thus, from the perspective of housing affordability, understanding the nature of how other exactions are negotiated or calculated is recommended. Often, exactions provide benefits to future development that are not recovered by the exacted development. In part, this is simple expediency on behalf of local government and even the developer because crafting a nonimpact system to recoup the value of infrastructure for the benefit of the exacted development can be complex, not to mention obligating local government to more burdens. Nonetheless, this book recommends that some effort be made to do so.

For example, perhaps so-called latecomer assessments should be allowed more liberally than they are at present. A "latecomer" assessment is a public-to-private agreement in which new development, benefiting from improvements installed by previous developments for its benefit, is assessed its proportionate share of the benefit value. The funds are collected by the local government—based on a formula akin to impact fees—and then rebated to the developer creating the benefits. Latecomer fees are allowed in many states but should be enabled by all and used more liberally in those that already have the authority. This is just another way in which to soften the effect of exactions on housing affordability.

Let us now review the larger planning steps needed to assure the role of impact fees as a regulatory device. Examples will be drawn from DeKalb County, Georgia, to illustrate key steps and analytic processes.

CAPITAL IMPROVEMENTS ELEMENT

It is recommended that a CIE is a prerequisite to implementing an impact fee program. A CIE should include all major types of community facilities and infrastructure, especially those for which impact fees may be assessed. The CIE should include the following features:

- Establish future service levels for categories of improvements to be financed with impact fees (service levels must be defined in quantifiable terms so that the local government's progress in attaining its stated service level goals can be measured);
- Delineate service areas, which will involve defining exactly where within its jurisdiction the specific capital facilities and service

levels will be provided during the planning period; and
- Show capital improvements costs and identify prospective funding sources including impact fees and separate improvements and costs by service area.

To be effective in guiding impact fee design, the CIE must include clearly defined service areas, LOS standards, and projections of needed facilities. In essence, the CIE should serve to strengthen the relationship between impact fees and public policy by clearly stating those policies and the role of impact fees in effecting them.

A local government should organize CIE components to ensure an orderly flow of information, rational analysis, and a clear understanding of the relationship between infrastructure expansion and the overall goals, strategies, and policies established in the comprehensive plan. For example, a plan might merge the CIE's schedule of improvements with the five- to 10-year CIP. The CIE should be written as a separate element of the plan, linking at least the population, economic development, housing, and land-use elements. The same principle applies to goal and policy statements. A policy exempting affordable housing projects from paying impact fees might be grouped with the other policies related to the housing element.

When a CIE is being added to an already approved plan, documentation should be included stating how data in other plan elements have been reconciled, amended, or updated. The best way to handle inconsistencies with a previously approved plan is to amend other plan elements while adding the CIE to remove or modify any information that has been superseded. However, if this is not practical for some reason, a local government should list by page or section any data or text that are no longer valid, and indicate why.

The CIE should also indicate how data from other elements have been used to arrive at the projects in the schedule of improvements, or indicate if more recent or specific data have been employed in developing the CIE. If a CIE is developed concurrently with the comprehensive plan, there should be no problem explaining the relationships between the CIE and information presented in other plan elements.

Problems may arise in assuring that CIEs added later are coordinated with the rest of the plan. Many states (e.g., California, Florida, Georgia, New Mexico, Oregon, Texas, and Washington) require internal consistency between the CIE and other plan (or land-use assumption) elements.

The CIE should be prepared following a three-step process, each of which is reviewed below:

1. Preparation of an inventory and assessment;
2. Determination of needs and goals; and
3. Development of an implementation strategy.

Appendix 7A illustrates the connection among planning, the CIE, and the CIP. It is from DeKalb County, Georgia, for its parks and recreation system, and is consistent with national practice.

LEVELS OF SERVICE

In review, "level of service" can be defined as a measure of the relationship between service capacity and service demand for public facilities in terms of demand-to-capacity ratios or the comfort or convenience of use, or both. Such standards serve as the basis for calculating the need for additional capacity to serve new development. Service level standards should relate capacity to demand and allow accurate assessment of progress toward attainment of service level goals. Service levels for different categories of capital facilities can be measured and expressed using a variety of relationships, units, and criteria.

Service level policies drive the capital facility planning process. To be consistent with impact fee principles, local governments must clearly define the LOS to be achieved and maintained for affected public facilities over the planning horizon. Establishing appropriate service levels is a policy decision that should be stated in the form of goals or policies within the plan and the CIE. The establishment of LOSs involves policy considerations that have been discussed in detail in the previous analysis.

Table 7-1 illustrates how a comprehensive plan may report adopted LOSs for all facilities subject to impact fees, and recommends appropriate action by the local government prior to adoption of impact fees. Recommended LOS standards are discussed in more detail in the individual studies.

SERVICE AREAS

Also as noted earlier, impact fee principles require that fees be assessed, collected, and spent within a "service area," which can be defined as a geographic area in which a defined set of public facilities provides service to development within the area.

The delineation of service areas helps to ensure that there is a reasonable relationship between the assessment of impact fees on new development and the delivery of facilities that benefit the development. They may cover all or part of a community; they may even span jurisdictional boundaries. Service areas for various categories of services or facilities may be completely different or they may overlap, but they must be based on sound engineering or planning criteria.

A number of factors may influence the delineation of services areas. Other considerations might include natural or environmental boundaries (such as aquifer recharge zones, watersheds, or floodplains), political divisions, utility service areas, traffic analysis zones, census tracts, facility maintenance districts, neighborhood planning units, or park and school district boundaries. Service areas also can be used to support growth management objectives, economic development strategies, or land-use patterns established in the

Table 7-1
Level-of-Service Standards

Facility	Level-of-Service Standard	Recommended Action
Transportation	None	Adopt 10,000 vehicles per lane-mile per day.
Libraries	None	Adopt 0.60 square feet per resident.
Parks and recreation	None	Adopt 3.50 acres of improved park and open space land per 1,000 residents based on the guidelines for a general mix of activities contained in the amended comprehensive plan.
Fire	None	Adopt one fire/emergency medical service (EMS) station per 25,000 residents distributed as a system throughout the county to sustain reasonable response times.
Police/EMS	None	Adopt 0.145 square feet per capita county-wide outside cities.

Source: Authors for DeKalb County, Georgia.

comprehensive plan's land-use element. In short, as long as the respective service areas are defined based on sound engineering and planning considerations, they will likely be considered valid.

Plans should include projections of total residential, commercial, and industrial development by service area. Where there is more than one service area for any given facility category, general land-use projections should be made for those service areas. Table 7-2 displays a way in which to report service areas in the comprehensive plan, summarizes the extent to which the plan delineates service areas, and recommends appropriate action prior to adoption of impact fees.

PROJECTIONS OF FACILITY NEEDS

To meet impact fee principles, facility needs associated with new development must be clearly identified. Needs assessments should be based on population projections and employment forecasts developed in the plan and tailored to individual facility categories. Such projections should take into account how extending or upgrading services to various areas within a jurisdiction might affect the local economy, as well as the rate, direction, and quality of development.

The provision of services to various areas should also be assessed in terms of impacts on natural and historic resources. Since growth often follows, or even hinges upon, the availability of infrastructure and public services, investments in these items will be a powerful force in realizing the community's future vision for development. Projections of facility needs should include:

- Current LOSs for all facilities for which impact fees are to be charged;
- Determination of whether existing service levels are adequate to meet current needs and an identification of major deficiencies or underutilized existing facilities;
- Description of variations in current service levels throughout the jurisdiction, such as geographic areas that differ in regard to available capacity, distribution systems, or quality of service delivery;
- Identification of any parts of the community where the provision of services is, or will be, limited by engineering, economic, or environmental factors;
- Identification of areas where new infrastructure will be needed to support local government's desired future land-use distribution and promote other goals established in the plan;
- Methodologies used in assessing capital facility capacity needs that are consistent with information provided in other plan elements, such as population projections, economic forecasts, established development densities for various housing types, and land use; and
- General description of infrastructure needs for the horizon of the comprehensive plan.

There is no one data source a community must use for planning. However, once these sources are chosen, they should be used as the basis for determining the projected needs listed in the CIE. The CIE should show how the infrastructure needs of the projected new population will be met. If the

Table 7-2
Service Area Delineation

Facility	Identified Service Areas	Recommended Action
Transportation	None	Adopt four service areas: 1. Inside I-285 and the I-85 Corridor 2. US 78 Corridor 3. I-20 Corridor 4. I-675 Corridor
Libraries	None	Adopt one county-wide benefit district.
Parks and recreation	None	Adopt one county-wide service area with three benefit districts for local and community-based parks and recreation improvements.
Fire	None	Adopt one county-wide service area.
Police/emergency medical service (EMS)	None	Adopt one county-wide service area for EMS and county-wide outside cities for police.

Source: Authors for DeKalb County, Georgia.

population and economic development elements of a community's plan support a slow growth scenario, while the CIE describes several infrastructure improvements projects aimed at fostering rapid growth, this would constitute an unacceptable internal inconsistency between the CIE and the rest of the plan.

The needs projection should include a description of infrastructure needs for the entire planning horizon of the comprehensive plan. Project costs and growth projections become more uncertain the further into the future they are extended. However, the CIE is required to anticipate long-range needs along with short-range priorities. When a community is building major facilities, it may be most cost effective to size some types of facilities to meet the needs of the projected population of 10 or 15 years into the future; other facilities may be designed to be developed in phases. Major capital facility needs for the entire planning period should be anticipated, even if they will not be addressed during the five-year period covered in the schedule of improvements.

While it may not be reasonable to define every project required to meet long-range needs, an overview or general indication of major infrastructure investments anticipated should be included in the CIE. For example, if a local government knows that a new highway is needed by the year 2015, this knowledge may affect the planning and placement of other infrastructure in the meantime.

Appendix 7A illustrates how a CIE may summarize the extent to which the community's comprehensive plan complies with the requirement to project future demand for all facilities subject to impact fees, and recommends appropriate action by the county prior to adoption of impact fees.

SCHEDULE OF IMPROVEMENTS

Impact fee principles also require that the CIE considers system improvements for the entire planning horizon of the comprehensive plan, which for many plans will be 20 years. This means that major long-range projects, which will be financed with impact fees but may not be initiated within five years of plan adoption, must be identified or described only in general terms. These projects will often be covered in sufficient detail in the community facilities element of the plan.

The specific capital improvements projects and funding sources listed in a schedule of improvements are not set in stone. If a given revenue source

does not materialize to complete a new facility, or priorities shift within a service area so that different projects take precedence at a later date, these changes can simply be reflected in the annual update of the schedule of improvements. On the other hand, changes in service area boundaries or modifications of officially adopted service levels are major policy shifts, which would require a plan amendment.

The more specific five- to 10-year CIP lists the projects to be initiated during that period. The CIP should identify the service area(s) of each capital improvements project and include a listing, by year, of all impact fee-related capital improvements to be undertaken over the CIP period, and a listing of all capital projects that will be required to upgrade service levels for existing development within each service area.

The listing of impact fee-related capital improvements to be undertaken over the CIP period should include:

- A brief description of each project (e.g., something as simple as "Widen Jones Road from two to four lanes from Broad Street to I-75" or "Build Fire Station Number 5 in Service Area One")
- Assignment of each project to a specific service area or areas
- Implementation time frame (i.e., anticipated start and completion dates). A breakdown of a project by phases should be included when the project phases will occur in different years, when part of the project will occur outside the short-term planning horizon, and when funding sources or responsible administrative entities are separate and distinct for various parts of a project.
- Amount of additional capacity that will be created to serve new development (if any). Since projects undertaken for the purpose of raising current service levels for existing development must be listed in the schedule of improvements, it is possible that none of the additional capacity of a listed project would be intended to serve new development. Ideally, a CIP should describe additional capacity to serve new development in terms of demand units. For example, "this treatment plant will accommodate 600 living unit equivalents." However, for some categories of infrastructure in which individual projects have an interactive effect on the

whole system of a service area, this may not be possible. The main idea is to indicate that the projects listed provide sufficient capacity to serve the projected demand in the particular service area.

Local governments should ensure that capital improvements projects proposed for each service area are consistent with any policies stated in the plan regarding the distribution of future growth or differential rates of growth among service areas. Appendix 7A illustrates how this may be done and recommends appropriate action prior to adoption of impact fees.

DESCRIPTION OF FUNDING SOURCES

The CIE should be as accurate as possible in estimating project costs and listing funding sources. If project costs are adjusted or financing strategies change, these changes should be addressed in the required yearly updates of scheduled improvements. To provide the most efficient use of public revenues, traditional financing methods will have to be adapted and combined with impact fees. Ideally, the combination of funding sources listed for each capital improvements project should only be established after consideration of various alternatives. The description of funding sources in the implementation strategy should represent the optimum combination that will be to the best advantage of the community.

The description of funding sources in the CIE must include the following considerations:
- Accurate total project costs for each capital improvements project listed in the schedule of improvements;
- An analysis of the percentage of each project's stated total cost that is directly attributable to adding capacity to serve new development; and
- A description of proposed sources of funds other than impact fees that are expected to make up the remaining portion of each project's cost.

If special studies are required to identify costs, and such studies cannot be conducted prior to the development of the CIE, the studies themselves should be listed as work items in the schedule of improvements along with the years when they will begin and be completed. If specific project costs are unknown, the community will need to examine cost data for similar recent projects, seek assistance from experts, or request information from other local governments that have installed comparable facilities.

Local governments are, to some extent, free to define "total project cost" as they deem appropriate. However, consistency must be demonstrated. A local government might establish service level goals that involve expenses which cannot be financed with impact fees, such as adding specialized equipment, vehicles, or personnel. In such a case, the total cost of reaching stated goals might include major costs that may be integral to expanding services but not classified as capital improvements or otherwise not eligible for impact fee financing.

The requirement that CIEs include an assessment of the percentage of total cost that is directly attributable to adding capacity to serve new development is intended to establish the portion of the total cost stated that is actually a "system improvements cost." The portion of the total cost designated as a system improvements cost represents the maximum amount eligible for impact fee financing. It is important to note, however, that CIE requirements do not require local governments to establish the percentage of the total cost that will be paid for by any particular financing source, including impact fees. As a matter of policy, some local governments may choose not to collect the entire costs of system improvements through impact fees. Although it will be important for a local government to calculate the portion of the total cost of each project that will be generated through impact fees when developing an impact fee schedule, presenting this level of detail on funding sources in the CIE is optional. An important nuance is that not all system improvements are fully attributable to growth. For example, a school improvement could add classrooms and also replace the existing roof, or part of a road expansion project could be attributed to a pre-existing deficiency.

Sometimes a capital cost is incurred by a local government for a specific development and is really a project improvement. Impact fees should not be used to finance project improvements. Thus, the funding source for such facilities must include other than impact fees. Where part of the facility is a project improvement but part is a system improvement, impact fees may be shown as a source of revenue for the system improvement. Ideally, the CIE would indicate the percent of each facility improvement that is a system improvement. Similarly, the CIE should indicate the percent of a system improvement that remedies deficiencies and identify other than impact fee revenues to finance deficiencies.

Since it is possible for local governments to recoup the cost of excess capacity remaining in existing systems, the present value of such existing capital improvements should be stated in the CIE as a total project cost. The existing capacity or demand units available to serve new development should be stated in the CIE rather than (or in addition to) the original capacity of the project, since some of the original capacity will have been absorbed between the time the capital improvement was built and the adoption of the CIE.

Funding sources are required to be more precisely described in the CIE than in the CIP. Instead of stating that additional funding will come from grants, for example, the CIE should include specific information on the source of grant funds. When "local government" revenues are to be used, the CIE should specify the actual budget source (i.e., general fund, special option sales tax, revenue bonds, private contributions, or other general categories of financing).

Capital improvements projects required to upgrade service levels for existing development must be included and identified in the CIP in order to demonstrate that a local government has planned to spend impact fees appropriately. This does not necessarily mean that each listed project will be built because flexibility needs to be maintained; however, it does mean that impact fee revenues collected from a service area will nonetheless be spent there for impact fee-eligible facilities within the time frame required.

RECOUPMENT

Local governments with excess capacity may charge impact fees to recover the cost of existing infrastructure that was built before the impact fee ordinance was adopted. This concept is often referred to as "recoupment." Impact fees that are based on the principle of recoupment require careful analysis of how and when each applicable capital project was originally financed since, like all fee calculation methodologies, recoupment fees must avoid double charging and include credits that reflect the time value of money.

A community's plan should clearly indicate whether impact fee revenue will be used to recover the costs of existing capital facilities with excess capacity. Local governments that plan to recover the cost of facilities or infrastructure already in

place should indicate their intention to do so in the CIE of the plan. Communities that use recoupment must also be prepared to document how much service capacity existed for each eligible facility or service at the time of plan adoption.

If a local government wishes to assess recoupment fees, it must establish a point-in-time estimate of the excess capacity remaining in capital facilities. The comprehensive plan should identify existing excess capacity for all facilities eligible for "recoupment" impact fees, and recommend appropriate action by the local government prior to adoption of fees.

RELATION OF IMPACT FEES TO COMMUNITY PLANNING GOALS

The plan itself must be based on community policies toward growth and development. Most plans that include impact fees do so in order to achieve more efficient provisions of facilities and services, containment of urban growth (which is also related to the preservation of important lands for nonurban use), and urban infill development. The relation of impact fees to community comprehensive land-use planning goals follows.

EFFICIENT PROVISION OF FACILITIES

Beyond predicting the timing, location, and dimensions of growth, and accommodating new development with appropriate facilities, communities increasingly require new development to be responsible for its proportionate share of the incremental cost of providing those facilities. Recall from Chapter 1 that communities, in the past, have enjoyed considerable subsidies for the installation of new capital facilities. The local contribution toward the cost of facilities such as water and sewer were relatively small. Communities readily extended those services to new development in order to grow, to build a tax base large enough to support community investment and the cost of maintenance, and to generally improve the local economic and fiscal bases.

However, communities would not charge the appropriate connection fees, which are used in many communities to cover some of the capital expansion costs. Inappropriate connection fees would include charging all new connections the same price, regardless of where the development was or how far it was from the facility providing necessary services (e.g., water and sewer treatment systems, schools, and certain roads). The result is that development that cost the community more to connect was charged less than its true cost, and development that cost the community less to connect was charged more than its true cost. As a result, development farther out was subsidized while development closer in was penalized.

As facilities were extended greater distances or designed with greater capacity based on subsidized demand signals than were efficient, construction and maintenance costs grew to a level that communities could no longer afford. Many communities reacted by imposing connection or facility expansion moratoria.

Development impact fees give communities some way in which to properly charge for the provision of facilities to new development based on the dimensions, location, and somewhat on the timing of that development. Typically, some development closer in would not be charged as much as development farther out. More importantly, by forcing development to account more fully for its facility costs, only development that generated benefits to the developer and tenants greater than the costs would proceed. Development that does not take place would result in inefficient use of facilities. Revenue raised by impact fees would be of such magnitude as to shelter existing development from the cost of extending facilities to new development, although all development pays for long-term O & M.

CONTAINMENT OF URBAN GROWTH

A related purpose of impact fees is thus the containment of urban growth, or rather the reduction or elimination of urban sprawl. When impact fees should be designed to reflect the incremental cost of extending facilities to new development, they should have the effect of discouraging development farther out and encouraging development closer in.

In fact, many cities impose impact fees only in newly developed areas and do not charge fees in developed areas. For example, San Diego, California, and Montgomery and Anne Arundel counties in Maryland assess relatively high impact fees in urbanizing areas but assess no impact fees in built-up areas where excess capacity remains. This has the effect of encouraging development inward.

In both situations, development outside urbanizing areas is severely restricted. No facilities are promised for those areas, at least until urban and urbanizing areas are suitably filled in. This has the effect of preserving open spaces near urban areas. This is an indirect consequence of an impact fee policy.

ENCOURAGEMENT AND ACCOMMODATION OF URBAN INFILL

While infill development in urban areas is encouraged, sometimes impact fees can be used to expand facility capacity in developed urban areas so that more intensive infill or urban redevelopment activities can be accommodated. For example, planning staff in New Orleans, Louisiana, informally considered expanding water, sewer, drainage, street, and other facility capacities in the built-up urban area to accommodate higher density housing and greater intensity nonresidential development.

Impact fees could be used to pay for a portion of the cost of expanding the current capacity of those facilities. Development proposed for sites dimensioned consistent with underlying zoning, which is based on current capacity conditions, would pay no impact fee. New development exceeding underlying zoning restrictions up to a level that could be accommodated by expanded facility capacities would pay a proportionate-share impact fee. Different scales of urban infill and redevelopment could thus be accommodated. Only that development larger than allowed by underlying zoning parameters, which generated benefits in excess of the impact fee (and related city exaction) costs, would be constructed.

SUMMARY COMMENT

Land-use planning and capital improvements programming provides the means for establishing the need for new facilities, the fact that new development generates the need and cost of those facilities, the source of revenues for those facilities, and the shortfall in revenue that must be made up by impact fees. The plan and CIP therefore provide for a court the opportunity to find the rational basis for the impact fee.

NOTE

1. For a review of the planning and impact fee process, see Kaiser and Burby (1988). See also Nicholas, Nelson, and Juergensmeyer (1991). For a general review of the land-use and facility planning process, see Edward Kaiser, David Godschalk, Philip Berke, and F. Stuart Chapin, *Urban Land Use Planning*, 4th ed. (Champaign-Urbana: University of Illinois Press, 2006).

APPENDIX 7A
SAMPLE CAPITAL
IMPROVEMENTS ELEMENT

This appendix presents amendments considered for the parks and recreation section of the capital improvements element of the DeKalb County, Georgia, comprehensive plan to implement impacts fees. It has been modified slightly to reflect national practice for illustration purposes. It also includes a five-year capital improvement program.

DEKALB COUNTY, GEORGIA
AMENDMENT TO THE
COMPREHENSIVE PLAN, 1995-2015
PARKS AND RECREATION SECTION
CAPITAL IMPROVEMENTS ELEMENT

This is an amendment to DeKalb County's comprehensive plan. It includes amendments to the Community Facilities Element and adds text regarding parks and recreation. This amendment also includes the components of the capital improvement element needed to support a parks and recreation impact fee. Such components include a description of the service area, levels of service, and a schedule of improvements to be funded with parks and recreation impact fees.

Inventory. The DeKalb County Parks and Recreation Department has prepared an updated inventory of all parks and recreation facilities. Major facilities are shown in Table 7A-1.

Service Area. The DeKalb County Parks and Recreation Department recommends a county-wide service area outside

municipalities (as shown in Figure 7A-1). Within this service area will be three benefit districts (as shown in Figure 7A-2).

Although only one service area is provided, there are three "benefit assessment" districts established (North, South, and East) (see Figure 7A-2). The benefit districts are based on the Department's maintenance district design, which itself is based on balancing park and recreation maintenance needs with responsiveness to particular needs of each district. The development impact fee consulting team recommends the establishment of benefit districts so that impact fees for parks and recreation collected in a given benefit district will be spent in that district.

The benefit districts are not "service areas" per the definition in the Development Impact Fee Act of 1990. Because North, South, and East park benefit districts are established, however, parks and recreation impact fees will be collected and placed in three separate parks and recreation impact fee trust funds corresponding to these three benefit districts. The amount of parks and recreation impact fees collected in these three different geographic areas will vary, depending on the amount of residential growth (i.e., number of housing units permitted). The exact fee amounts collected for each of the benefit districts cannot be forecasted with any certainty, since parks and recreation impact fees will also vary based on the types and sizes of housing units constructed.

Table 7A-1
Inventory of Parks and Recreational Facilities

Type of Facility	Number
Land	
Total land (acres)	5,036
Land Improvements	
Ballfields	112
Football	16
Soccer	34
Tennis courts	105
Multipurpose courts	50
Playground units	125
Parking lots	194
Golf course acres	496
Buildings	
Picnic shelters	87
Pools	12
Recreation centers	11
Tennis centers	2
Combined golf and tennis	1
Clubhouse	1

Source: DeKalb County Parks and Recreation Department (2004).

Figure 7A-1
Unincorporated DeKalb County Parks
and Recreation Service Area

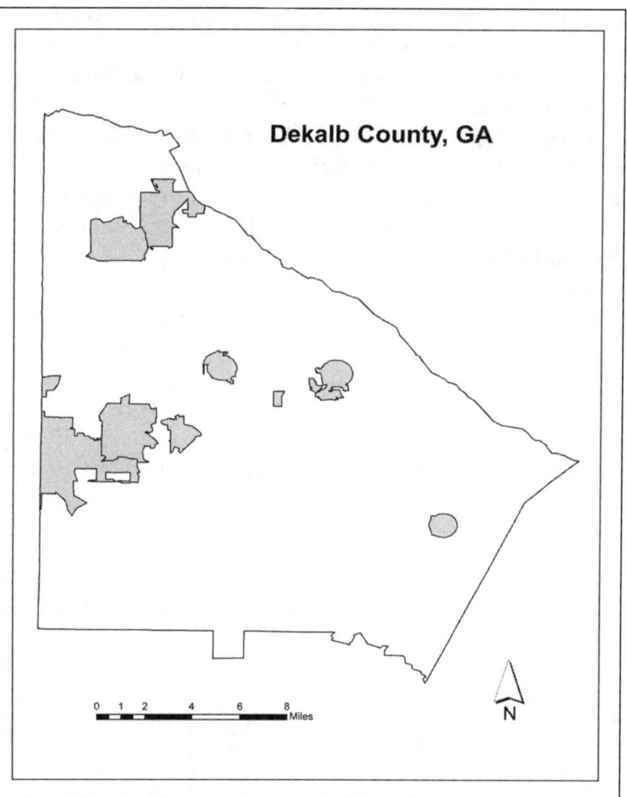

Municipalities have their own parks and recreational facilities, and so all incorporated areas of the county are excluded. The service area for parks and recreation impact fees is the unincorporated area of DeKalb County (see unshaded areas).

Figure 7A-2
Benefit Districts Within DeKalb County
Parks and Recreation Service Area

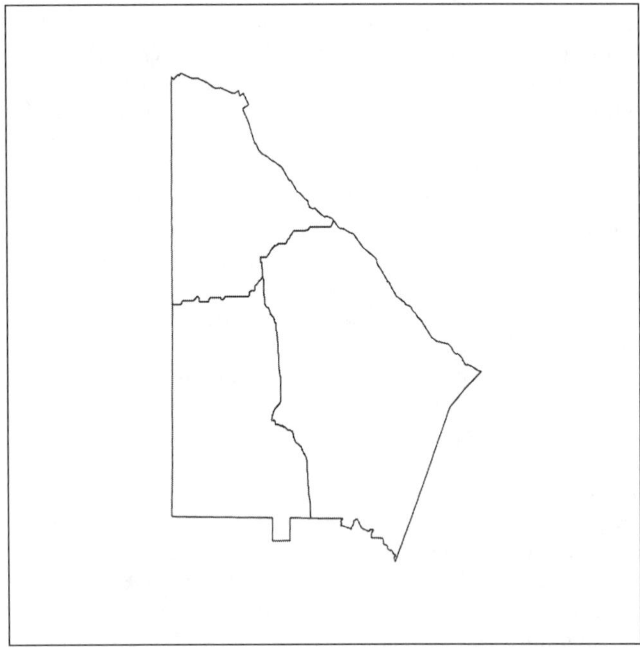

This division into benefit districts does not mean that improvements must be specified for each of the three benefit districts, however, nor do levels of service have to be maintained within each of the benefit districts, since there is only one service area. It is instructive to note, however, for purposes of proposing the schedule of improvements, that population is divided more or less evenly among the three benefit districts.

Level of Service. In 2000, EDAW prepared a Parks and Recreation Plan. The 2000 Recreation Strategic Plan was accepted but not adopted by the Board of Commissioners. The strategic plan sets forth a complicated level of service standard which lumps everything "green" together (e.g., tot lots plus Stone Mountain Park). Therefore, the level of service standards provided in the strategic plan (which were not adopted) is not recommended for use in the impact fee program.

The existing level of service for parks and recreation is determined on the basis of acres of parks and recreation lands per 1,000 unincorporated population. DeKalb County finds the existing level of service to be adequate and proposes to maintain the same existing level of service for future

Table 7A-2
Existing Parks and Recreation Level of Service

Level of Service	2004 Population	Total County Park Acreage	2004 Existing Level of Service, Parks, and Recreational Facilities
Unincorporated DeKalb County	610,693	5,036	8.25 developed acres per 1,000 residents

unincorporated populations, which is 8.25 developed acres per 1,000 unincorporated population (the level of service standard). Accordingly, the existing Level of Service is adequate to meet current needs.

Projection of Needs. A Parks Resource Management Study was completed which recommended a major maintenance program over ten years with a projected facility need of $26 million. That study included things such as HVAC replacements, re-roofing of centers, resurfacing tennis courts, and the like. Such needs are "maintenance and replacement" and not the types of projects that are intended to serve new growth and development and are therefore not impact fee-eligible.

The Parks and Recreation Strategic Plan (accepted by the Board of Commissioners September 12, 2000) provides some insight to future parks and recreation facility needs. The strategic plan outlines a broad facility capital plan, but it is not really project-specific. Some of the projects in the master plan were considered aggressive and have to be scaled back.

The county's comprehensive plan identifies some specific parks and recreation improvement projects which are reportedly from the strategic plan. According to staff, all (or virtually all) of the specific projects identified are no longer recommended and may have been proposed by individual citizens during the public participation process of the strategic plan. For those reasons, the specific projects included in the comprehensive plan are not included in the schedule of improvements for impact fees.

Table 7A-3 shows needs for park land at the adopted level of service standard of 8.25 acres of park land per 1,000 unincorporated residents.

To maintain the existing level of service of 8.25 acres per 1,000 unincorporated population (the level of service standard) in the future, the county will need to add 582 acres of park and recreation land to meet unincorporated

Table 7A-3
Projection of Parks and Recreational Facility Needs, 2005–2030, Unincorporated DeKalb County

	2004	2005	2009	2010	2015	2020	2025	2030
Unincorporated population	610,693	621,319	680,931	695,834	728,873	757,303	790,788	823,743
Acres needed (at 8.25 per 1,000 unincorporated population)	5,036	5,126	5,618	5,741	6,013	6,248	6,524	6,796
Acres to add to 2004 inventory (attributed to new growth)	0	90	582	705	977	1,212	1,488	1,760

population growth during the next five years, and by 2030, the county will need to add 1,760 acres of parks and recreation land.

Recommended Facility Prototypes. The county's Parks and Recreation Strategic Plan (2000) identifies typical facility types that are being built regionally and nationally, and which are useful in determining future capital facility projects. Based on input from the county's parks and recreation facility staff, and the 2000 strategic plan, the following major facility types and typical acreage requirements are provided.

Recreation Centers: (Land Requirement: 30 acres). Gymnasiums, game and dance rooms, offices, gathering, etc. Five new recreation centers were recommended by 2010.

Family Aquatic Centers: Warm water pools, in-water playgrounds, water slides, etc. According to department staff, aquatic centers could be built in conjunction with recreation centers as "multi-purpose" centers.

Ballfield or "Athletic" Complexes: (Land Requirement: 50-80 acres, depending on whether youth or adult patrons are served). Baseball, softball, football, soccer in 4-16 fields per complex. Staff modified this strategic plan recommendation to suggest a complex would consist of 5 baseball/softball fields in a "wagon wheel" configuration, and 7-9 soccer/ football fields.

Regional Parks: (Land Requirement: 500 or more acres). The strategic plan does not specifically include this type of facility, but it is multi-jurisdictional and would include Arabia Mountain and Fernbank Forest. Note: This is similar to the "Nature Preserves and Greenspace" (wildlife and plant habitat, greenways, passive spaces) recommended in the strategic plan.

Community Parks: (Land Requirement: 50 to 100 acres) (40 to 200 in the Strategic Plan) Active and passive spaces, which may include recreation centers, tennis courts, playgrounds, nature center, etc.

Neighborhood Parks: 15-30 acres (4 to 10 acres in the strategic plan) which may include playground, picnic facilities, walking paths, outdoor courts, dog park.

Mini-Parks: (Land Requirement: 4-5 acres) (not mentioned in the Strategic Plan). Such facilities generally provide only picnic and passive facilities. They are reportedly very costly to maintain and are therefore not recommended.

Historic Funding Patterns. The development impact fee consulting team met with county finance staff to discuss historic funding patterns. In 1997, the county's agreement with the voters over optional sales taxes was that no less than 80 percent of special sales tax would go to property tax relief. This means a maximum special sales tax allocation for capital funding of, at most, 20 percent. An estimated 91% of the special sales taxes has been used for property tax relief during the past 5-6 years.

A review of the county's 2003 annual budget reveals a capital projects budget of $392,573,442. The county has used its capital budget to fund necessary improvements to parks and recreation facilities. Parks and recreation received an appropriation from the capital projects budget of $136,267,784 beginning 1998. In addition, the county allocated $5,322,858 of HOST funds for parks and recreation improvements.

Capital Improvement Plan. The CIP is divided into the three benefit districts (North, South, and East). These three tables collectively constitute the schedule of improvements for parks and recreation. A total of 580 of developed acres of parks and recreation land are needed to meet the needs of the growing population between 2005 and 2009.

County Parks and Recreation Staff identified five multi-purpose centers (combination recreation center and aquatic complex) and provided the general areas where these should be located). This is also consistent with the recommendations of the Parks and Recreation Strategic Plan that five new recreation centers be constructed. Two of the multi-purpose centers are proposed in the north benefit district, one in the south, and two in the east.

The Parks and Recreation Strategic Plan 2000 placed great emphasis on the provision of soccer fields. Staff identified soccer fields in the north part of the county as a high priority. Staff suggested a need for 80 acres, and the schedule of improvements for the north benefit district provides 80 acres in two 40-acre complexes. A soccer complex will be constructed in the south and east benefit districts as well. One ballfield complex would be constructed in each of the three benefit districts.

In addition to the multi-purpose centers, soccer complexes, and ballfield complexes, community and neighborhood parks will be constructed in the south and east benefit districts, where population growth is highest, but not in the north district where land is much more expensive and land availability is scarce. The south and east benefit districts will each have one community park. The south benefit district will have one neighborhood park and the east benefit district will have two neighborhood parks.

Land acquisition slightly favors the east benefit district (210 acres) followed by the south (200 acres) and north (170 acres) benefit districts. The south benefit district is the smallest in land area and also includes the largest amount of incorporated area (which is outside the service area).

The schedule of improvements is shown individually for each benefit district in three separate tables (summarized below). Because all projects add parkland to the system above and beyond the existing level of service, each project in the schedule of improvements is 100 percent impact fee eligible.

Table 7A-4
Summary Schedule of Parks and Recreational Facility Improvements

	North Benefit District	South Benefit District	East Benefit District	All Benefit Districts
Acreage (580)	170	200	210	580
Multi-Purpose Centers (30 ac. ea.)	2	1	2	5
Soccer Complexes (40 ac. ea.)	2	1	1	4
Ballfield Complexes (30 ac. ea.)	1	1	1	3
Community Parks (50 ac. ea.)	None	1	1	2
Neighborhood Parks (15-30 ac. ea.)	None	3	2	5
Total Cost ($)	$13,677,590	$11,045,765	$13,319,670	$38,043,025

Table 7A-4a
Schedule of Parks and Recreational Facility Improvements Impact Fee-Eligible Projects, North Benefit District

Capital Improvement	2005	2006	2007	2008	2009	Total	Funding Sources
Soccer Complex 1 N: (North Benefit District) Acquire 40 acres of land and construct unlighted 9-field soccer complex in north part of county	$677,080 (land)	$2,475,000				$3,152,080	Impact Fees; Capital budget
Soccer Complex 2 N: (North Benefit District) Acquire 40 acres of land and construct 2nd unlighted 9-field soccer complex in north part of county	$677,080 (land)		2,475,000			$3,152,080	Impact Fees; Capital budget
Ballfield Complex 1 N: (North Benefit District) Acquire 30 acres of land and construct lighted 5-field baseball/ softball complex in north part of county	$507,810 (land)		$1,400,000			$1,907,810	Impact Fees; Capital budget
Multi-Purpose Center 1 N: (North Benefit District) Acquire 30 acres of land and construct center in Tucker area	$507,810 (land)			$2,225,000		$2,732,810	Impact Fees; Capital budget
Multi-Purpose Center 2 N: (North Benefit District) Acquire 30 acres of land and construct center in Buford Highway Corridor area		$507,810 (land)			$2,225,000	$2,732,810	Impact Fees; Capital budget
170 Acres	$2,369,780	$2,982,810	$3,875,000	$2,225,000	$2,225,000	$13,677,590	

All projects are 100% impact fee eligible.

Table 7A-4b
Schedule of Parks and Recreational Facility Improvements Impact Fee-Eligible Projects, South Benefit District

Capital Improvement	2005	2006	2007	2008	2009	Total	Funding Sources
Soccer Complex 1 S: (South Benefit District) Acquire 40 acres of land and construct unlighted 9-field soccer complex in south part of county	$677,080 (land)		$2,475,000			$3,152,080	Impact Fees; Capital budget
Neighborhood Park 1 S: (South Benefit District) Acquire 15 acres of land and construct improvements in south part of county	$253,905 (land)	$205,000				$458,905	Impact Fees; Capital budget
Neighborhood Park 2 S: (East Benefit District) Acquire 15 acres of land and construct improvements in east part of county	$253,905 (land)		$205,000			$458,905	Impact Fees; Capital budget
Multi-Purpose Center 1 S: (South Benefit District) Acquire 30 acres of land and construct center in central part of county (E. Ponce and N. Decatur in the Decatur area)	$507,810 (land)			$2,225,000		$2,732,810	Impact Fees; Capital budget
Community Park 1 S: (South Benefit District) Acquire 50 acres of land and construct improvement in high growth area of east part of county (target Census Tract 234.18)		$846,350 (land)			$1,030,000	$1,876,350	Impact Fees; Capital budget
Ballfield Complex 1 S: (South Benefit District) Acquire 30 acres of land and construct lighted 5-field baseball/softball complex in south part of county		$507,810 (land)			$1,400,000	$1,907,810	Impact Fees; Capital budget
Neighborhood Park 3 S: (South Benefit District) Acquire 20 acres of land and construct improvements in south part of county		$253,905 (land)		$205,000		$458,905	Impact Fees; Capital budget
200 Acres	$1,692,700	$1,813,065	$2,680,000	$2,430,000	$2,430,000	$11,045,765	

All projects are 100% impact fee eligible.

Table 7A-4c

Schedule of Parks and Recreational Facility Improvements Impact Fee-Eligible Projects, East Benefit District

Capital Improvement	2005	2006	2007	2008	2009	Total	Funding Sources
Soccer Complex 1 E: (East Benefit District) Acquire 40 acres of land and construct unlighted 9-field soccer complex in east part of county	$677,080 (land)		$2,475,000			$3,152,080	Impact Fees; Capital budget
Ballfield Complex 1 E: (East Benefit District) Acquire 30 acres of land and construct lighted 5-field baseball/softball complex in east part of county	$507,810 (land)	$1,400,000				$1,907,810	Impact Fees; Capital budget
Multi-Purpose Center 1 E: (East Benefit District) Acquire 30 acres of land and construct center at I-20 and Panola Road area	$507,810 (land)			$2,225,000		$2,732,810	Impact Fees; Capital budget
Neighborhood Park 1 E: (East Benefit District) Acquire 15 acres of land and construct improvements in east part of county	$253,905 (land)	$205,000				$458,905	Impact Fees; Capital budget
Neighborhood Park 2 E: (East Benefit District) Acquire 15 acres of land and construct improvements in east part of county	$253,905 (land)	$205,000				$458,905	Impact Fees; Capital budget
Community Park 1 E: (East Benefit District) Acquire 50 acres of land and construct improvement in high growth area in east part of county (target Census Tract 234.18)		$846,350 (land)		$1,030,000		$1,876,350	Impact Fees; Capital budget
Multi-Purpose Center 2 E: (East Benefit District) Acquire 30 acres of land and construct center in east area	$507,810 (land)				$2,225,000	$2,732,810	Impact Fees; Capital budget
210 Acres	$2,708,320	$2,656,350	$2,475,000	$3,255,000	$2,225,000	$13,319,670	

All projects are 100% impact fee eligible.

8

Uniform Measures of Impact

Impact fees are predicated on measuring the impact of new development on the community. Because different land uses have different levels of impact, it is important to find a way in which to render different impacts into a common figure. For water and wastewater facilities, for example, it is reasonably common to render impacts of different kinds of development to peak or average daily gallons of water or wastewater treatment per unit, such as a single-family home, an apartment, or 1,000 square feet of office space. Sometimes measuring impact is not easy to render into a uniform measure, such as the need for school facility capacity associated with new development. This chapter describes several uniform measures that apply to all land uses, as well as a method to ascribe impacts of different land uses where other uniform measures are not suitable.

COMMON MEASURES OF IMPACT

Establishing LOS standards is necessary to calculate impact fees. Some LOS standards are based on a standard level of consumption for a type of facility, such as five acres of parkland per 1,000 residents. Others are based on the planning policy for facility improvement, such as constructing a bridge to meet future needs 20 years from now, even though the bridge may have capacity to serve the demands of new development for much longer. In the first case, all new development is assessed based on its proportionate share of the cost to maintain five acres of parkland per 1,000 residents. In the second case, all new development is charged its proportionate share of the entire capacity of the bridge above that needed to accommodate the demand of existing development. For example, demand for water and wastewater service is usually based on a person's need for those services. People use water for a variety of purposes that, except for lawn irrigation, is invariable. School children need adequate space to perform, and school LOS standards are typically set by states, so there is little opportunity locally to change them. People need water and wastewater services and children need schools, and there is not much that policy may do to vary their consumption.[1] Table 8-1 summarizes common standards-based LOS indicators.

Plan-based LOS standards are different because the community has considerable discretion in deciding what they will be. A community, for example, may decide not to have any parks or 10 acres per 1,000 residents, or anything else in between or beyond. There may be standards recommended by national organizations, but they are not mandatory. In the area of fire service, state insurance service offices establish insurance ratings for communities based on a large number of factors, but it is up to the community to decide what rating it wishes to have based on its willingness to pay for different elements of a fire

Table 8-1
Facilities Applicable to Standards-Based Level-of-Service Standards

Facility	Impact Unit
Drainage	Impervious service creating runoff (subject to federal and state regulation)
Schools	Students served (subject to state regulation)
Wastewater	Gallons treated (subject to federal and state regulation)
Water	Gallons consumed (subject to state regulation)

system. Table 8-2 reviews facilities for which plan-based LOS standards are needed.

MEASURES OF IMPACT AND PLANNING

One of the purposes of establishing LOS standards is to project facility needs and plan for them. If a community has no standard for the number of park acres per 1,000 residents (or other base), it has no way of knowing how many parks to build. If it has five acres of parks per 1,000 residents and wants to sustain this LOS in the face of adding 10,000 new residents in 10 years, it will need to add 50 acres of parks to its inventory.

For standards-based facilities, there will be little room to vary the reality of what 10,000 new residents means—either the water system is expanded as needed to serve 10,000 new residents or those residents are not likely to move into the community.

However, for plan-based facilities, there is wide latitude.

THE NEED FOR COMMON MEASURES OF IMPACT

As a community grows, it will need to expand public facilities to meet new needs. The expansion needs of some facilities, such as water and wastewater, may be estimated using observed consumption patterns extrapolated into the future. The expansion needs for other facilities, however, may be more complicated.

For example, the demand for police and fire facilities varies by land use in ways that are not always clear. How many "units" of police service are needed to serve commercial, industrial, or single-family residential activities? A typical way to measure differences in demand across different land uses for public safety is to collect and analyze the

Table 8-2
Facilities Applicable to Plan-Based Level-of-Service Standards

Facility	Impact Unit
Animal control	From no facilities to whatever the community is willing to spend
Criminal justice (courts, jails, detention)	From no facilities to whatever the community is willing to spend
Emergency medical	From no service to high-quality service based in part on, for example, response time, professionalism of the force, equipment quality, distribution of facilities, and development patterns
Fire	From no service (ISO Rating 10) to best-quality service (ISO Rating 1) based in part on, for example, response time, professionalism of the force, equipment quality, water pressure, hydrant distribution, and building characteristics
Government buildings	From no facilities to whatever the community is willing to spend
Libraries	From no facilities to whatever the community is willing to spend
Parks and recreation	From no facilities to whatever the community is willing to spend
Police	From no service to high-quality service based in part on, for example, response time, professionalism of the force, equipment quality, distribution of facilities, and development patterns
Roads	Lane-mile capacity from free flowing to congestion
Transit	From no service to minimum headway on selected expressways, arterials, collectors, and other streets

nature of fire, police, and EMS calls over time. This is rarely done and is often prone to substantial error when such data are collected. In the case of jails, courts, and general government, it is virtually impossible to allocate demand based on observations. Unlike roads, water, wastewater, and drainage, which all have common ways of measuring impact (e.g., lane-miles for roads, gallons for water and wastewater, and impervious area for drainage), many facilities do not lend themselves obviously to a common impact measure.

A solution to this was developed by the authors in the 1980s and is now becoming commonly accepted practice: apportioning demand for facilities based on the "functional" population of the community.

Functional population is the equivalent number of people occupying space within a community on a 24-hour-per-day, seven-day-per-week basis. A person living and working in the community will have a functional population coefficient of 1.0. A person living in the community but working elsewhere may only spend 16 hours per day in the community on weekdays and 24 hours per day on weekends, for a functional population coefficient of 0.76 (128 hours presence divided by 168 hours in a week). A person commuting into the community to work five days per week would have a functional population coefficient of 0.24 (40 hours presence divided by 168 hours in a week). A person traveling into the community to shop at stores, perhaps averaging eight hours per week, would have a functional population coefficient of 0.05. Functional population thus tries to capture the presence of all people within the community—residents, workers, or visitors—to arrive at a total estimate of effective population that needs to be served.

By estimating the functional population per unit of land use across all major land uses in a community, the user can rationally estimate the demand for certain facilities and services in the present and in a future year. Estimating residential functional population is considerably easier than estimating functional population attributable to employment. Conceptually, residential functional population is the number of residents who occupy residential space on a 24-hour-per-day, seven-day-per-week basis.

How many hours per weekday and weekend day does the average resident occupy residential space? A rule of thumb assumes that half of a person's life is spent in residential space. This figure could be as high as two-thirds, depending on the population demographics and outdoor opportunities. For some population groups (e.g., retired persons, invalids, and prisoners), the figure approaches 100 percent. For Atlanta, Georgia, one author (Nelson) with James Duncan and Associates (1993) assumed the residential component of functional population was 0.67 during a 24-hour day. This differentiation allows for reasonably refined estimates of needs for particular facilities and associated land uses. For example, public safety facilities serve all residents, workers, and visitors to the community 24 hours per day. This approach has been adopted nationally among several impact fee consultants.

$$\text{FUNCTIONAL POPULATION}/1{,}000 \text{ SQ. FT.}$$
$$= (\text{EMPLOYEE HOURS}/1{,}000 \text{ SQ. FT.}$$
$$+ \text{VISITOR HOURS}/1{,}000 \text{ SQ. FT.})$$
$$\div 24 \text{ HOURS}/\text{DAY}$$

Where:

EMPLOYEE HOURS/1,000 sq. ft. = employees/ 1,000 sq. ft. x 8 hours/day

VISITOR HOURS /1,000 sq. ft. = visitors/1,000 sq. ft. x 1/2 hour visit

Visitors/1,000 sq. ft. = weekday average daily trips/1,000 sq. ft. x average vehicle occupancy – employees/1,000 sq. ft.

Weekday average daily trips /1,000 sq. ft. = one-way average daily trips (total trip ends ÷ 2)

A growing use of functional population is in the area of public safety. Clancy Mullen tested for the robustness of this approach over the traditional approach using calls by type and by land use where good data were collected. The analysis follows.

FIRE AND POLICE DEMAND MULTIPLIERS: CALLS FOR SERVICE VERSUS FUNCTIONAL POPULATION

Fire and police impact fees are based on two primary methodologies: calls for service and functional population. This brief report analyzes data from a number of impact fee studies to evaluate how closely fees based on functional population match those based on call data.

The calls-for-service approach is based on localized data on the land use from which calls for service originate and existing land uses. Dividing the calls for each land use by the amount of that land use yields calls per development unit (e.g., dwelling units or 1,000 square feet of building square footage). Annual calls per development unit, however, are unlikely to be comparable from one study to another. A large proportion of calls occur on roadways or are otherwise not able to be assigned directly to a land use. Some studies allocate these calls indirectly, based on trip generation or other factors, while other studies simply ignore them. In any case, what drives impact fee calculations is not the absolute number of calls but the relative number of calls from different land uses. For these reasons, this analysis converts the data into equivalent dwelling units (EDUs), which represent the demand for service from a typical, single-family detached dwelling.

The functional population approach is a more generalized approach, which presumes that the demand for public safety services is strongly related to the presence of people at the site of a land use. Functional population represents full-time equivalent people. For residential development, functional population is simply average household size times the percent of time people are assumed to spend at home (typically 50 or 67 percent). For nonresidential development, functional population is based on a rather complex formula involving trip generation rates, average vehicle occupancy, and average number of hours spent by visitors at the land use. Functional population can be based on 24-hour day or a 16-hour day (the 16-hour day is used to avoid assigning most demand to residential uses during nighttime hours, when most people are at home sleeping but nonresidential uses still need protecting). Functional population by land use can also be converted into EDUs.

Using the functional population formula and information on trip generation rates from the ITE manual (ITE (2003)), nonresidential functional population estimates per 1,000 square feet of gross floor area are calculated (as shown in Table 8-3).

The calls-for-service approach has the advantage of providing a very strong nexus between the impact fee and the demand for the service. It is grounded in localized data; however, this datum is not always available or reliable. Calls by land use may vary significantly from year to year, and the accuracy of land-use data may change over time. The combination of these factors may result in impact fee rates by land use changing drastically each time the fees are updated.

The functional population approach is less dependent on localized data. It only requires local data on average household size, which is readily available. Data on existing land uses are only required to determine the overall LOS and do not affect the calculation of EDUs per development unit. These characteristics make the functional population approach appropriate for communities without reliable calls-for-service data, or for whom stability of impact fee rates over time is more important than establishing the strongest nexus.

A problem with the functional population approach is that a number of assumptions must be made. Should the fees be based on a 24-hour day or a 16-hour day? What percent of time should people be assumed to spend at home? Should a typical visitor to a land use be assumed to spend half an hour or an hour? This analysis compares the results of various assumptions with the results of a number of studies based on call data in order to determine which set of assumptions most closely matches what we would get using call data.

EDUs based on calls for service were derived from a number of studies performed by several consultant firms. Fire call data are summarized in Table 8-4. The observed ranges are quite large.

Table 8-3
Nonresidential Functional Population

Land Use	Unit of Measure	Trip Rate	Persons Per Trip	Employees Per Unit	Visitors Per Unit	Functional Population Per Unit
Retail/ commercial	1,000 sq. ft.	21.47	1.80	1.96	36.69	1.418
Office	1,000 sq. ft.	5.51	1.14	3.31	2.97	1.165
Industrial	1,000 sq. ft.	3.48	1.14	2.08	1.89	0.733
Warehouse	1,000 sq. ft.	2.48	1.14	1.28	1.55	0.459

Source: Trip Rates are one-half average daily trip ends from Institute of Transportation Engineers (ITE) Trip Generation, *7th ed. (Washington, DC: ITE, 2003); Persons Per Trip are average vehicle occupancies from U.S. Department of Transportation,* National Household Travel Survey *(2001) for following trip purposes: shopping for retail, to work for office, industrial and warehouse; employees per 1,000 sq. ft. derived from trip rates per employee from ITE manual (retail employees per 1,000 sq. ft. from* America's Future Office Space Needs *(Washington, DC: National Association of Office and Industrial Parks, 1990), 22; Visitors Per Unit.*

Table 8-4
Summary of Fire Calls (Equivalent Dwelling Units)

Land Use	Unit	Number of Studies	Minimum	Maximum	Average
Single-family detached	Dwelling	7	1.00	1.00	1.00
Multifamily	Dwelling	7	0.34	1.00	0.68
Hotel/motel	Room	5	0.46	1.67	0.94
Retail/ commercial	1,000 sq. ft.	6	0.47	1.46	1.00
Office	1,000 sq. ft.	6	0.36	1.75	0.86
Industrial	1,000 sq. ft.	6	0.13	0.38	0.25
Warehouse	1,000 sq. ft.	4	0.09	0.35	0.20

Source: See Table 8-3.

For example, EDUs per 1,000 square feet for office development ranged from a low of 0.36 to a high of 1.75. This variation may be due to fundamental differences among communities, volatility in calls from one year to the next (especially for smaller communities), or inaccuracies in the call or land-use data. However, when one looks at the averages for all the studies analyzed, the results are what one might expect: a multifamily unit has less demand than a single-family unit, an office has somewhat less demand than retail, and industrial and warehouse uses require considerably less fire service than commercial or office uses.

Police call data are summarized in Table 8-5, and a similar pattern can be observed, with extremely wide variations in EDUs per development unit for individual land uses. Again, however, the averages for all the studies follow the expected pattern. A difference from the fire call data, however, is that multifamily units generate virtually the same number of calls as single-family units. The wide variation in multifamily EDUs per unit could be due to community characteristics (e.g., upscale town homes versus public housing projects), which would be expected to affect police calls more than fire/rescue calls.

In Table 8-6, EDUs based on functional population are presented using varying assumptions (67 percent versus 50 percent of average household size for residential EDUs; 16-hour versus 24-hour days; and one-hour visits versus half-hour visits). Functional population EDUs will vary based on the assumptions mentioned above, as well as on the average household size in the community. For this analysis, average household sizes for the State of Florida from the 2000 U.S. Census were used.

The multifamily EDU of 0.76 is in between the EDUs based on fire and police calls of 0.68 and 0.98. The nonresidential EDUs based on call data have a better fit with the 24-hour-day assumption rather

Table 8-5
Summary of Police Calls (Equivalent Dwelling Units)

Land Use	Unit	Number of Studies	Minimum	Maximum	Average
Single-family detached	Dwelling	14	1.00	1.00	1.00
Multifamily	Dwelling	14	0.32	1.98	0.98
Hotel/motel	Room	9	0.25	1.67	0.72
Retail/ commercial	1,000 sq. ft.	4	0.43	2.20	1.36
Office	1,000 sq. ft.	4	0.38	2.67	0.98
Industrial	1,000 sq. ft.	4	0.03	0.43	0.22
Warehouse	1,000 sq. ft.	2	0.07	0.24	0.16

Source: See Appendix 8A.

Table 8-6
Functional Population Equivalent Dwelling Units by Various Assumptions

Land Use	67% res. 24-hour day 1/2-hour visit	67% res. 24-hour day 1-hour visit	50% res. 24-hour day 1/2-hour visit	50% res. 24-hour day 1-hour visit	50% res. 16-hour day 1/2-hour visit	50% res. 16-hour day 1-hour visit
Single-family detached	1.00	1.00	1.00	1.00	1.00	1.00
Multifamily	0.76	0.76	0.76	0.76	0.76	0.76
Retail	0.78	1.20	1.04	1.60	1.56	2.40
Office	0.64	0.68	0.86	0.90	1.28	1.35
Industrial	0.40	0.43	0.54	0.57	0.81	0.85
Warehouse	0.25	0.27	0.34	0.36	0.51	0.54

Source: Assumptions in heading represent percent of average household size used in determining residential functional population, length of the day, and duration of a visit to the land use. Residential equivalent dwelling units (EDUs) based on Florida average household sizes from 2000 U.S. Census of 2.723 for single-family detached and 2.065 for multifamily; nonresidential EDUs based on functional population formula (adjusted by assumptions in heading of each column and single-family functional population).

than the 16-hour-day assumption. In general, they fit better with the assumption that 67 percent of time is spent at home, with retail and office fitting better with the one-hour-per-visit assumption.

This analysis suggests that a functional population approach can provide a reasonable representation of public safety demands for service, particularly if the following assumptions are used: average household size is multiplied by 67 percent to determine residential functional population, and nonresidential functional population is based on a 24-hour day. An assumption of one hour per visit seems to be more appropriate for retail and office uses than for industrial and warehouse uses.

Appendix 8A summarizes the studies used in this analysis.

EXTENSIONS OF FUNCTIONAL POPULATION: TOWARD TRULY UNIFORM IMPACT ASSESSMENTS

The functional population approach has been used for public safety, government buildings, jails and detention facilities, and other facilities. Thus, in addition to standards-based measures that apply across all land uses (excluding schools), functional population may be used for many facilities for which LOSs are established by policy. However, there is a class of facilities that remains assessed usually only on residential development, such as schools, libraries, and parks and recreational facilities. The conventional wisdom is that only residential development impacts these facilities and benefits exclusively from them. The conventional wisdom may warrant closer examination.

Remember that impact fees rest on three tenets:
1. New development impacts facilities.
2. New development benefits from facilities.
3. Proportionate-share assessment balances impact with benefit.

Regarding the first tenet, what is the actual source of impact on such facilities as schools, libraries, and parks and recreational facilities? Is it the new home bringing new school children impacting schools and are more residents impacting the other facilities, or is the source of the impact the jobs that attract newcomers to the community? Economic impact literature clearly states that jobs create the demand for households moving into communities (see, e.g., Bendavid-Val (1983)).

Economic base analysis, for instance, divides the economy into "export base" and "nonbasic" elements.[2] An export base job is one that exports goods and services outside the area for which it receives income, such as shipping cars built locally overseas. A nonbasic job is one serving the community and no one else, such as a local barber.[3] In this scheme, export base jobs attract households that require nonbasic jobs, which then attract more households that also need nonbasic jobs.

An export base to nonbasic job multiplier can be estimated showing the number of total jobs that one new export base job creates. It is also the case that usually the larger the number of jobs, the higher the community multiplier. Ultimately it is difficult to fully assign the impact of new development

Table 8-7
Functional Population Applied to Schools, Park and Recreational Facilities,
and Libraries (Illustrative Only)

Impact Measure	Conventional Apportionment to Residential Development Only	Broad Base Apportionment to All Development
School Facilities		
Students per home, FP	0.50	0.10
Net cost per student	$20,000	$20,000
Impact fee per home, FP	$10,000	$2,000
Parks		
Acres per 1,000 residents, FP	5.00	2.50
Net cost per acre	$100,000	$100,000
Impact fee per resident, FP	$500	$250
Libraries		
Sq. ft. per resident, FP	0.50	0.25
Net cost per sq. ft.	$400	$400
Impact fee per resident, FP	$200	$100

FP = functional population

from among export base jobs, nonbasic jobs, and households. Another analytic approach is known as "input-output analysis."[4] It is a widely used method for estimating multiplier effects associated with development, which treats the household as the outcome of economic change and not its source.[5]

Although some communities begin as bedroom communities, in others—where jobs are growing over time—jobs tend to redistribute more or less evenly across regions. Indeed, communities attempt to lure jobs into them in part to alter their bedroom community status. An argument could be made that it is not the new households but rather the new jobs that are the primary source of impact; arguably, the only kind of development that should pay impact fees. That is not the position recommended by the authors, but only an observation.

The second tenet is benefit. If firms creating new jobs are assigned the impact, do they also benefit? Economic development literature would appear consistent with the view that communities with higher quality facilities and services than others are often more successful in attracting economic development than communities with poor or degrading facilities and services.

Quality of life thus attracts firms that use quality of life to attract new workers. Quality facilities and services are at least an indirect benefit accruing to firms. A more direct benefit is having an educated workforce, which is something schools and libraries provide. Finally, research shows that firms often dominate in the use of certain parks and recreational facilities, and proximity to them makes them more competitive in attracting workers. The constitutional principle of rough proportionality does not require that a precise mathematical relationship be established to demonstrate that an exaction may benefit the exacted party.

While an argument can be posed that job-creating development is the sole source of impact, and that it benefits reasonably from facilities, it must be recognized that everyone—workers and their families—benefits from having facilities and services of sufficient quality and quantity to preserve the quality of life.

There is also a series of more direct benefits. Smith and Juergensmeyer (2007) observe that schools are commonly used for such things as adult education, community meetings and activities, private sector training programs, emergency shelters, and voting places. We have seen school facilities used for community theater, local government meetings, and public library functions. School athletic facilities are often used for public recreational purposes including business leagues and social functions. School libraries and computer labs are often used for private sector training purposes. It would seem that the potential list of activities for which schools may be used can be quite long, and public and private sector use of them is growing over time.

Given their broad benefit, both directly and indirectly, an argument can be made that school impact fees should be calculated based on functional population. The functional population approach may thus be a reasonable method to apportion the impact and the benefit across all land uses. Table 8-7 illustrates how this may be done. Impact fees for residential development would go down, while impact fees on nonresidential development would go up.

NOTES

1. This is an overstatement, of course, since policy can be used to reduce the water flushed through toilets and used in showers, for example. However, since all new homes have low-impact toilets and many come already installed with other water-conserving devices, what is left is the invariable demand for water consumption.
2. See Richard Klosterman, *Community Analysis and Planning Techniques* (Savage, MD: Rowman & Littlefield, 1987), for example.
3. There are nuances. The share of jobs used for cars sold to local residents is considered nonbasic, while the share of a barber's revenues attributable to clients traveling from outside the community is considered export base.
4. See Bendavid-Val (1983), for example.
5. See Bureau of Economic Analysis, RIMS-II (2001). This publication reports job-based multipliers for all 3 major economic sectors but reports 0 for the household sector.

Table 8A-1
Equivalent Dwelling Units Based on Fire Calls

Consultant	Jurisdiction	Year	Single-Family Unit	Multifamily Unit	Hotel/Motel Room	Retail 1,000 sq. ft.	Office 1,000 sq. ft.	Industrial 1,000 sq. ft.	Warehouse 1,000 sq. ft.	Public 1,000 sq. ft.	Residential Unit	Nonresidential 1,000 sq. ft.
Duncan	Lee Co., FL	2005	1.00	0.78	0.82	0.78	0.36	0.38	0.35	N/A		
Duncan	Colorado Springs, CO	2000	1.00	1.00	n/a	0.85	0.85	0.13	0.12	N/A		
Duncan	Mesa, AZ	2005	1.00	0.79								0.68
Duncan	Santa Fe, NM	2003									1.00	0.55
Tindale	Orange County, FL	2005	1.00	0.88	0.81	1.11	0.91	0.20	0.24	N/A		
Nicholas	Palm Bch County, FL	2003	1.00	0.50	1.67	0.47	0.38	0.29	0.09	N/A		
Rosenthal	Draper, UT	2004	1.00	0.34	0.46	1.32	1.75	0.14		2.43		
Rosenthal	Park City, UT	2001	1.00	0.49	0.96	1.46	0.88	0.36				
Eco & Plan Sys	Pagosa Springs, CO	2006									1.00	1.29
Giardina	Salt Lake City, UT	1999									1.00	0.60
Average			1.00	0.68	0.94	1.00	0.86	0.25	0.20	2.43	1.00	0.78

Table 8A-2
Equivalent Dwelling Units Based on Police Calls

Consultant	Jurisdiction	Year	Single-Family Unit	Multifamily Unit	Hotel/ Motel Room	Retail 1,000 sq. ft.	Office 1,000 sq. ft.	Industrial 1,000 sq. ft.	Warehouse 1,000 sq. ft.	Public 1,000 sq. ft.	Residential Unit	Nonresidential 1,000 sq. ft.
Duncan	Orange County, FL	2005	1.00	0.32	0.50	1.59	0.40	0.24	0.24	N/A		
Nicholas	Palm Beach County, FL	2003	1.00	0.34	0.41	0.43	0.38	0.03	0.07	N/A		
Rosenthal	Draper, UT	2004	1.00	0.32	1.67	1.22	0.49	0.17	n/a	0.16		
Duncan	Mesa, AZ	2005	1.00	0.84								0.74
Young	Collier County, FL	2004	1.00	0.55	1.10	2.20	2.67	0.43	n/a	N/A		
Giardina	Salt Lake City, UT	1999									1.00	0.62
Colgan	Orange County, FL	1994	1.00	1.98	0.91							
Colgan	Glendale, AZ	1995	1.00	1.60								
Colgan	Livermore, CA	1996	1.00	1.55	0.55							0.37
Colgan	Davie, FL	1996	1.00	0.55								
Colgan	Cedar City, UT	1996	1.00	0.56	0.58							
Colgan	Modesto, CA	1997	1.00	0.83	0.25							
Colgan	Moreno Valley, CA	1999	1.00	0.80								
Colgan	Temecula, CA	2002	1.00	1.77								
Colgan	Lompoc, CA	2003	1.00	1.67	0.56							
Average			1.00	0.98	0.72	1.36	0.98	0.22	0.16	0.16	1.00	0.58

9

Variations of Proportionate-Share Fee Design

This chapter has three sections. The first reviews general methodological variations in impact fee design, focusing on their features and differences. The second reports findings from a selection of impact fee technical reports from a cross section of communities based on region, size, growth rates, and approach to calculating impact fees. The third presents a survey of the Florida communities also focusing on variations in impact fee design. It was prepared for the Florida Legislature and captures a central theme: One size does not fit all.

GENERAL CALCULATION APPROACHES

This section reviews the main features of commonly used impact fee calculation approaches and then walks through a series of nuanced applications for water and wastewater impact fees to illustrate how robust the approaches are to addressing policy issues.

GENERAL METHODOLOGICAL APPROACHES

There are two generally accepted methodologies commonly used to formulate impact fee programs: the standards- and plan-based methodologies. These methodologies have evolved during the last 20 years and, while the majority of impact fees appear to be standards-based, both have been used to satisfy the requirements of the dual rational nexus test. While there are variations in the application of these methodologies, this section discusses the basic methodology, underlying assumptions, and implementation requirements of each methodology. This section also addresses the basic differences between the methodologies and how each of the methodologies furthers the implementation of the comprehensive plan and, in particular, the CIE.

Standards-Based Impact Fees

The standards-based methodology calculates impact fees based on the value of the increment of public infrastructure needed to meet the needs of new development. The value of the public infrastructure is usually developed by calculating the replacement cost of the existing public capital infrastructure. This value is then related to a facility-based standard (e.g., fire stations per 1,000 population, acres of parks per 1,000 population, and library or other building square footage per 1,000 population).

For transportation infrastructure, for example, the value of the infrastructure is calculated by looking to the typical types of recently built or planned road improvements that are representative of the transportation system. The analysis is based on the need for transportation improvements contained in transportation plans and programs that may include CIPs, comprehensive plan transportation elements, and long-range transportation plans. This resulting value of the transportation infrastructure is generally expressed in terms of cost per lane-mile or cost per vehicle-mile of capacity (VMC) added. Other facilities, such as parks, are measured in terms relevant to those facilities, such as value per acre and per capita. In the standards-based impact fee methodology, the key underlying supposition is that growth consumes some identifiable quantity of public infrastructure capacity, and the fee is based on the cost of providing that identified quantity.

Proponents of standards-based impact fees cite the flexibility to the government as a significant advantage to that approach. Specifically, a government that uses a standards-based impact fee can develop its CIP to include projects that directly respond to where growth and the need for the public infrastructure occur. The CIP list of improvements is reviewed annually, and that list can change as growth patterns change, resulting in new project priorities. Generally, these changes only occur in the out years of the CIP. Finally, it should be noted that ordinances that implement standards-based impact fees generally include a provision that ties the need for and benefit of impact fees to projects that must be included in the local government's CIP and comprehensive plan CIE.

Plan-Based Impact Fees

The plan-based (also known as "needs-based") methodology charges new development based on a specific set of capital improvements projects. This approach is usually based on a long-range master plan, which includes a list of future projects that are determined to be necessary to accommodate existing and future growth at the adopted LOS.

Under the plan-based approach, an analysis is usually made of the impact of any existing deficiencies. An adjustment is also made to account for deficiencies existing at the beginning of the planning period to assure that the cost of correcting those deficiencies is not shifted to new development. However, no adjustment is generally made for excess capacity built as part of the improvements list that is available at the end of the planning period, since the improvements-driven approach did not charge for the existing excess capacity that is available at the start of the planning period and that is consumed by new development. The implicit or explicit assumption is that there may be excess capacity in every infrastructure system and, as long as the amount or proportion of excess capacity at the end of the planning period is reasonably similar to what was there at the beginning, there is no need to make adjustments for excess capacity.

Proponents of the plan-based methodology indicate that this method provides a direct tie to the comprehensive plan, the CIE, and the CIP. In the plan-based methodology, the list of capital improvements used in the calculation of the cost component is usually the list of improvements included in the CIP and the local government's CIE. Proponents say that this methodology gives the development community assurance that the impact fees they pay are being spent on the specific improvements under which the impact fee was calculated. When the local government changes the list of capital improvements, the resulting impact fee should be recalculated using the new list of capital improvements. On the other hand, in practice, projects are added or removed from the CIP when needed to maximize delivery of facilities for reasons related to cost, refined analysis of needs, and the availability of other funds leveraged by (or leveraging) impact fees.

Finally, similar to ordinances for standards-based impact fees, plan-based impact fee ordinances also include provisions that tie the need for and benefit of impact fees to projects included in the local government's CIP and comprehensive plan CIE.

Differences Between Standards-Based and Plan-Based Impact Fees

The basic difference between standards-based and plan-based impact fees is that the standards-based impact fee charges new development based on the value of the capital asset being used by each unit of land use, whereas the plan-based impact fee charges new development based on the cost of a specific set of improvements and their associated cost per unit of land use. As indicated previously, the key underlying assumption for standards-based impact fees is that growth consumes some capacity of all public facilities and not just the new infrastructure being built.

In plan-based impact fees, growth is being charged based on a specific set of project improvements that the local government is planning to build through their adopted CIP. When the list of improvements in the CIP changes, the impact fee should be recalculated based on the new list of capital improvements.

At times, studies use a method that is a combination of the standards-based and plan-based methods. For example, some plan-based transportation impact fees include calculations that result in using only the share of the cost of a roadway improvement projected to be consumed by future traffic over the planning period. When this is done, the plan-based impact fee functions are closer to standards-based impact fee methodology.

In summary, both methods have been used successfully and satisfy the requirements of the dual rational nexus test. In the next sections, we will illustrate how the majority of the impact fees use the standards-based methodology. Additionally, each approach tends to be more applicable in particular situations. The inherent flexibility of the standards-based approach allows the jurisdiction to match impact fee receipts to specific projects as the needs for specific projects are identified. Plan-based systems are more inflexible and are more applicable to those situations where specific needed improvements can be identified well in advance and impact fees can be tailored to those specific needs. Experience has shown that both approaches are valuable tools of capital improvements planning and funding.

The Impact Fee Formula and Basic Implementation Considerations

The general impact fee formula can be represented as:

$$\text{IMPACT FEE} = (\text{DEMAND} \times \text{UNIT COST}) - \text{CREDIT}$$

Where:

DEMAND = the amount of capacity needed to accommodate new development, based on the existing or adopted LOS standard, or the associated need for service (e.g., VMT, fire stations per 1,000 population, acres of parks per 1,000 population, and library or other building square footage per 1,000 population)

UNIT COST = the cost per unit of capacity or demand based on the calculated value of the asset or set of improvements

CREDIT = the value of the future nonimpact fee revenues that growth will generate, which will also be used to pay for the capital facility expansion of that public infrastructure

Regardless of which methodology is used in the impact fee study, there are certain criteria and procedures that need to be followed in developing and implementing impact fee programs. These include, but are not limited to, the following:

- Local governments must establish LOS standards for each impact fee program area.
- Local governments must apply the same LOS standard to both existing and new development.
- An "existing deficiency" is created when a local government establishes an LOS standard that is greater than the current LOS.
- New development cannot be charged impact fees designed to correct an existing deficiency. To charge new development based on an LOS standard higher than what exists today, the local government must have a financial plan (nonimpact fee revenue sources) to eliminate the existing deficiency within a reasonable amount of time (generally during a CIP cycle, but there is no absolute time limit).
- Facility costs should be reflective of recently built projects, current bids, and architects and engineers' estimates of project costs.
- Credits (discussed more thoroughly in Chapter 6) should reflect the additional nonimpact fee revenues reasonably expected to be generated by new development being charged the impact fee, when such revenues are used for the same infrastructure for which impact fees are being charged.

There are many other policy-related issues that are addressed as each community updates and implements impact fees. These policy issues are unique to each community and are reflected in the impact fee technical analysis.

APPLICATIONS OF VARIATIONS TO WATER AND WASTEWATER IMPACT FEES

The following shows how standards- and plan-based approaches may be intermingled and adapted to meet certain policy objectives. While this discussion is applicable primarily to water and wastewater impact fees, some elements have applicability to other facilities. The follow specific approaches will be reviewed:

- Growth-related cost allocation method
- Recoupment value method (also known as the "buy-in" method)
- Replacement cost method
- Marginal cost method

Table 9-1
Alternative Wastewater System Development
Charge Methods Basic Assumptions

Assumptions	Figure
System capacity, 2004 (gallons)	42,000,000
Capacity before 2001 expansions (gallons)	40,000,000
Recent and planned expansions, 2001–2009 (gallons)	8,000,000
Total existing and planned capacity	48,000,000
Capacity used, 2001	24,700,000
Excess capacity, 2001	15,300,000
ERU factor (gallons)	246
New development demand, 2004–2009 (gallons)	5,100,000
Total replacement cost	$176,962,255
System-wide replacement cost	$126,536,568
Growth-related replacement cost	$12,218,206
Total fixed asset value, 2004	$106,649,330
System-wide fixed asset value	$93,966,655
Growth-related fixed asset value, since 2001	$11,971,730
CIP improvements, 2004–2009	$194,180,655
System-wide CIP improvements, 2004–2009	$25,275,000
CIP growth-related improvements, 2004–2009	$133,334,907

ERU = equivalent residential unit
CIP = capital improvements program

- Average cost method
- Systemwide and growth-related cost attribution method

To best understand the differences among the different calculation methods, it is important to compare the outcomes of systems development charges (SDCs) with a common set of assumptions. For any given system, these categories of assumptions are known or can be readily determined. Suppose that, for one community, these assumptions have characteristics as shown in Table 9-1 as they apply to a wastewater system.

The meaning of each assumption in Table 9-1 is described below:

System capacity, 2004 (gallons): This is the community's capacity to treat wastewater on an average daily or peak daily basis for the current year.

Capacity before 2001 expansions (gallons): Suppose the community embarked on a program to expand the current system to accommodate new development in 2001. Prior to such expansion, the community had a level of capacity that served existing development, although its pre-expansion capacity may have included some excess capacity able to accommodate new development. The year 2001 can be considered the base year for calculating SDCs under some methods described below.

Recent and planned expansions, 2001–2009 (gallons): Suppose the community has a long-range plan to expand capacity to some level between 2001 and 2009, after which it has no plans for further expansion. This is a kind of "build out" capacity, although the network accessing this build out capacity may take several years beyond 2009 to install.

Total existing and planned capacity: This is the total capacity anticipated to be in place at the end of an expansion period, which is 2009 in this example.

Capacity used, 2001: This is the average or peak daily demand during the base year.

Excess capacity, 2001: This is the difference between base year capacity (before expansion) and average or peak daily demand during the base year. This is the amount of treatment capacity since system expansion to accommodate new development.

ERU factor (gallons): This is the ERU factor that will be used to calculate impact fees by ERU for each method.

New development demand, 2004–2009 (gallons): This is an estimate of the change in system demand attributed to new development during the period of the CIP during 2004 and 2009.

Total replacement cost: This is the amount of money required to replace the entire system that is currently in place, irrespective of how the system was financed in the past. In this example, it is assumed that only local financing has been used to finance the system and its planned expansions.

Systemwide replacement cost: This is the cost of replacing elements of the system that serve all development, whether new or existing.

Growth-related replacement cost: This is the cost of replacing elements of the system that substantially serve only new development.

Total fixed asset value, 2004: This is the replacement cost of the entire system less accumulated depreciation.

Systemwide fixed asset value: This is the fixed asset value of that share of the system that serves all development, whether new or existing.

Growth-related fixed asset value, since 2001: This is the fixed asset value of that share of the system that substantially serves only new development since 2001, the base year of analysis for calculation methods of some SDCs. This would include, for example, expansions to wastewater treatment installed between 2001 and the current year.

CIP improvements, 2004–2009: This is the total cost of installing improvements to accommodate existing and anticipated development during a typical six-year CIP from 2004 to 2009.

Systemwide CIP improvements, 2004–2009: This is the share of CIP improvements that serves all development, whether new or existing. An example may be upgrades to treatment systems to comply with new environmental regulations, or replacement of a pump station installed 30 years ago.

CIP growth-related improvements, 2004–2009: This is the share of CIP improvements that substantially serves new development. This would include, for example, planned expansions to wastewater treatment.

Growth-Related Cost Allocation Method

The growth-related cost allocation method (presented in Table 9-2) applies all costs reflected in the CIP to new growth expected to occur during the CIP. The principal advantage of this method is its simplicity, but there are important pitfalls.

If the CIP includes considerable expansion of capacity that will benefit users beyond 2009, the entire costs of such expansion are borne only by new connections occurring between 2004 and 2009. The impact fees would be too high and would violate rational nexus principles because the capacity needed to accommodate new development is less than the capacity of new development financed. Alternatively, if the CIP includes

Table 9-2
Growth-Related Cost Allocation Method

Calculation Consideration	Amount
CIP improvements, 2004–2009	$194,180,655
New development demand, 2004–2009 (gallons)	5,100,000
Cost allocation cost per gallon	$38.07
ERU factor (gallons)	246
Growth-related-based impact fee per ERU	$9,365.22

CIP = capital improvements program
ERU = equivalent residential unit

Table 9-3
Recoupment Value Method

Calculation Consideration	Amount
Total fixed asset value, 2004	$106,649,330
System capacity, 2004 (gallons)	42,000,000
Recoupment value per gallon	$2.54
ERU factor (gallons)	246
Recoupment-based impact fee per ERU	$624.84

ERU = equivalent residential unit

no major expansions, in part because prior CIPs financed such expansions, new development is paying less than its proportionate share of the system capacity it uses.

About the only circumstance under which the growth-related method is appropriate is when the system being installed is a complete package, and the period of time over which costs are related to growth is the build out period. This condition usually does not hold for most communities, so the growth-related cost allocation approach is usually inappropriate.

Recoupment Value Method

The recoupment value method (see Table 9-3) essentially results in new development reimbursing existing development for new development's proportionate share of the cost of existing improvements, based on total system treatment capacity available in the current year. Recoupment is based only on the fixed asset value of the entire system. It does not distinguish among improvements made mostly for the benefit of new development, nor does it consider the cost of expanding system capacity to accommodate new development. As such, the recoupment approach will usually result in impact fees lower than the cost of accommodating new development.

This method is popular among developers who therefore pay considerably lower fees than other methods that more accurately reflect the real costs of accommodating development. It may also be popular among elected officials who see the recoupment fee as a way to keep costs on new development (including "economic" development) low. However, it will be the existing taxpayers and ratepayers who finance much, if not all, of the real costs of accommodating development.

About the only circumstance under which this approach reasonably reflects the cost of accommodating new development is when the system has been completely built out, possesses substantial excess capacity to accommodate new development on an infill basis, and is in no need of major system upgrades.

Replacement Cost Method

The replacement cost method (see Table 9-4) is conceptually similar to the recoupment value method, except that it is based on the cost of replacing the entire system presently in place. The result is slightly higher impact fees than calculated under the recoupment value method; otherwise, it suffers from the same limitations. This method is often used to estimate the cost of expanding the system, assuming that expansion costs would be comparable to replacement costs. Unlike the recoupment, it does not depreciate the value of assets based on age since it is used to estimate the cost of expanding capacity. Under this scenario, the impact fee reasonably reflects the costs of providing service to new development on an incremental or marginal basis. Moreover, if expansion costs are in fact reasonably close to replacement costs on a per-unit basis, this approach is also reasonable.

Marginal Cost Method

"Marginal cost" is defined as the cost of providing the next unit of development. The replacement value method is a form of marginal costing, but only when expansion costs to accommodate new development are reasonably close to replacement costs on a per-unit-of-demand basis.

Marginal cost is usually considered the cost per unit of expanding system capacity and the system

Table 9-4
Replacement Cost Method

Calculation Consideration	Amount
Total replacement cost	$176,962,255
System capacity, 2004 (gallons)	42,000,000
Replacement value per gallon, 2004	$4.21
ERU factor (gallons)	246
Replacement cost-based systems development charges per ERU	$1,035.66

ERU = equivalent residential unit

Table 9-5
Marginal Cost Method

Calculation Consideration	Amount
Growth-related fixed asset value, since 2001	$12,218,206
CIP growth-related improvements, 2004–2009	$133,334,907
Total growth-related marginal cost	$145,553,113
Recent and planned expansions, 2001–2009 (gallons)	8,000,000
Growth-related marginal cost per gallon	$18.19
ERU factor (gallons)	246
Marginal cost-based impact fee per ERU	$4,474.74

CIP = capital improvements program
ERU = equivalent residential unit

network on a per-unit basis to accommodate new development. There are two practical limitations with this approach. First, while the cost to expand treatment capacity to accommodate new development may be fairly easily determined, the cost of providing the network by which new development accesses treatment is less certain. Second, the approach does not usually consider facilities installed in the past that may be used by new development.

Marginal cost is defined here as being composed of two parts resulting in growth-related marginal costs. The first part is the asset value of existing growth-related facilities installed since the base year of 2001. These are facilities that have been installed in the past to serve new development but adjusted to reflect depreciation. This is the recoupment value component. The second part is the cost of installing CIP growth-related facilities. These two figures are summed and then divided by the total treatment capacity added to the system since the base year of 2001 (shown in Table 9-5).

There remain important shortcomings to this formulation of marginal cost analysis. For example, it does not consider the role of existing excess capacity in serving new development. If the costs of providing excess capacity are substantially less than the costs of expanding capacity, it is possible that new development would be paying more than its proportionate share of the cost of service actually received. As such, as new development absorbs

<table>
<tr><td colspan="2" align="center">Table 9-6
Average Cost Method</td></tr>
<tr><th>Calculation Consideration</th><th>Amount</th></tr>
<tr><td>Total replacement cost</td><td>$176,962,255</td></tr>
<tr><td>Total CIP expenditures</td><td>$194,180,655</td></tr>
<tr><td>Total costs</td><td>$371,142,910</td></tr>
<tr><td>Total existing and planned capacity, 2009</td><td>48,000,000</td></tr>
<tr><td>Average cost per gallon</td><td>$7.73</td></tr>
<tr><td>ERU factor (gallons)</td><td>246</td></tr>
<tr><td>Average cost-based impact fee per ERU</td><td>$1,901.58</td></tr>
</table>

CIP = capital improvements program
ERU = equivalent residential unit

<table>
<tr><td colspan="2" align="center">Table 9-7
Total Cost Attribution Method</td></tr>
<tr><th>Calculation Consideration</th><th>Amount</th></tr>
<tr><td>System-wide fixed asset value</td><td>$93,966,655</td></tr>
<tr><td>System-wide CIP improvements, 2004–2009</td><td>$25,275,000</td></tr>
<tr><td>Total system-wide value</td><td>$119,241,655</td></tr>
<tr><td>Pre expansion capacity (gallons)</td><td>48,000,000</td></tr>
<tr><td>System-wide value and cost per gallon</td><td>$2.48</td></tr>
<tr><td>Growth-related asset value</td><td>$11,971,730</td></tr>
<tr><td>CIP growth-related improvements, 2004–2009</td><td>$133,334,907</td></tr>
<tr><td>Total growth-related asset value and CIP improvements</td><td>$145,306,637</td></tr>
<tr><td>Total capacity for new development since 2001</td><td>23,300,000</td></tr>
<tr><td>CIP improvements per gallon based on excess capacity</td><td>$6.24</td></tr>
<tr><td>Asset value and CIP improvements per gallon</td><td>$8.72</td></tr>
<tr><td>ERU factor (gallons)</td><td>246</td></tr>
<tr><td>Total cost attribution-based impact fee per ERU</td><td>$2,145.12</td></tr>
</table>

CIP = capital improvements program
ERU = equivalent residential unit

excess capacity, which was purchased at a lower cost than new capacity, total revenues generated will exceed total costs. This would be inconsistent with rational nexus criteria. In addition, this approach does not account for the possibility that other elements of the system, not reflected in these particular marginal cost calculations, may nonetheless accommodate new development.

The marginal cost method is highly appropriate to those situations where there is little or no excess capacity, new development is not likely to use existing facilities that serve existing development, and the CIP reflects the total costs of serving new development using expanded treatment capacity. These conditions are not likely to be found in many communities.

Average Cost Method

The average cost method (see Table 9-6) is like the marginal cost method except that, instead of allocating costs to new development, the costs of replacing and expanding the entire system are considered in relation to the total capacity of the system to accommodate development, both existing and new. While it may appear to address some of the shortcomings of the marginal cost method reviewed above, it can have the effect of underestimating the costs of accommodating new development if new treatment capacity costs considerably more than replacing existing capacity. On the other hand, if expansion costs are lower than replacing existing capacity, more revenue would be collected than needed to accommodate new development.

As in the case of marginal cost analysis, average cost analysis is based on replacement or expansion costs, not asset values that include depreciation.

The average cost approach is suitable only when the costs of expansion are similar to the costs of replacing the existing system on a per-unit basis. It is more often the case that average costs are less than the costs of accommodating new development, and so revenues received would not cover revenues needed.

Total Cost Attribution Method

The total cost attribution method (see Table 9-7) considers both the contribution of systemwide facilities and growth-related facilities to the accommodation of new development. This has the advantage of accounting for the impact of new development on systemwide facilities, which serve both existing and new development. The method also allocates growth-related asset value and CIP improvements to capacity expansion as well as excess capacity. This recognizes that delivery of excess capacity often requires extension of lines, installation of pumps,

Table 9-8
Summary of Methods

Method	Impact Fee/ ERU
Growth-related cost allocation method	$9,365.22
Recoupment value method	$624.84
Replacement cost method	$1,185.72
Marginal cost method	$4,474.74
Average cost method	$1,901.58
Total cost attribution method	$2,145.12

ERU = equivalent residential unit

and construction of related facilities to accommodate new development. Asset value is used since CIP improvements will, over time, offset any depreciation of those assets.

The total cost allocation method is perhaps the most suitable approach to calculating system development charges. It combines all the elements of the rational nexus criteria, including how existing facilities were financed, the costs of accommodating new development, and the time value of money. However, modifications of the method are possible, such as substituting systemwide asset value and growth-related asset value with systemwide replacement cost and growth-related replacement cost.

Summary

Table 9-8 summarizes these six impact fee calculation methods. Each may be appropriate under particular circumstances. However, the total cost allocation method is probably the most suitable method to most systems in use today.

REVIEW OF IMPACT FEE PROGRAMS SELECTED NATIONALLY

This section reviews findings from a detailed content analysis of impact fees from a selection of 67 communities across the nation. The purpose is not to illustrate that one size fits all but rather that, when considering such things as local conditions, planning goals and policies, and development patterns, the impact fee "solution" used in one community is not necessarily suitable for the next. The methodologies vary considerably by geography and complexity. One thing many have in common is that they were prepared by some of the nation's most prominent impact fee firms.[1]

Table 9-9
Jurisdictions Selected for Content Analysis of Impact Fee Studies

State	Local Government
AZ	Avondale
	Buckeye
	Chandler
	Fountain Hills
	Gilbert
	Glendale
	Goodyear
	Mesa
	Peoria
	Sedona
	Surprise
	Tucson
AR	Bentonville
	Conway
	Fayetteville
CA	Calimesa
	Gilroy
	San Diego-Serra Mesa
	Sutter County
	Yuba City
	Yucaipa
CO	Larimer County
DE	New Castle County
FL	Clay County
	Collier County
	Lake County
	Lee County
	Manatee County
	Mount Dora
	Osceola County
	Palm Beach Gardens
	Pasco County
	Seminole County
GA	Atlanta
	Cherokee County
	Forsyth County
	Henry County
	Kennesaw
	Rockdale County
ID	Post Falls
	Sandpoint

Table 9-9
Jurisdictions Selected for Content Analysis
of Impact Fee Studies (*continued*)

State	Local Government
MD	Calvert County
	Charles County
	Frederick County
	Queen Anne's County
NE	Lincoln
NV	Las Vegas
NH	Fremont
	Manchester
	Windham
NM	Bernalillo County
	Rio Rancho
NC	Cary
	Durham County
	Orange County
OH	Delaware
OR	Salem
	Tigard
	West Linn
RI	East Greenwich
TN	La Vergne
	Smyrna
TX	Denton
UT	Sandy City
	West Valley City
WA	Bothell
	Pierce County

JURISDICTIONS SELECTED (67 TOTAL)

Jurisdictions were not selected based on formal sampling because there is no census of jurisdictions for which impact fees are assessed. Jurisdictions were selected for their geographic, size, and consultant variations. For jurisdictions with multiple technical reports or multiple consultants, the most recent is listed. For some jurisdictions, the ordinance was the only data source. The methodology outlined in the technical report(s) may or may not have actually been adopted in part or in full by the jurisdiction.

INSTANCES OF EACH FEE TYPE (263 TOTAL)

- Parks and recreation and open space and trails: 52
- Fire and EMS and E911 communications: 40
- Roads and traffic signals and transit: 37
- Police and criminal justice and combined public safety: 35
- Libraries: 21
- Water infrastructure and water resources: 20
- Government buildings and public facilities and combined public infrastructure: 18
- Wastewater: 15
- Schools: 12
- Stormwater/drainage: 10
- Other (sanitation, solid waste, animal control): 3

Jurisdiction Population Breakdown (2000 Census)

- { 50,000: 27
- 50,000-100,000: 9
- 100,000-200,000: 13
- 200,000-500,000: 14
- { 500,000: 4

Jurisdiction Type Breakdown

Urban/suburban/rural designation is given based on the jurisdiction's location in relation to Census 2000 metropolitan statistical areas (MSAs) or combined metropolitan statistical areas (CMSAs). If a jurisdiction is the major city of an MSA or one of the major cities constituting a CMSA, it is classified as "urban." If a jurisdiction is or lies within a county that is part of an MSA or CMSA, but is not or does not contain a major city of that MSA or CMSA, it is classified as "suburban." If a jurisdiction is not within any MSA or CMSA, it is classified as "rural." If the jurisdiction is a county that does contain a major city of an MSA or CMSA, it is classified as "mixed," since the county would contain the major city as well as suburban jurisdictions.

- City/town: 44
- County: 23
- Urban: 12
- Suburban: 46
- Rural: 4
- Mixed: 5

State Legal Environment

- Specific enabling legislation (Dillon's rule state): 43
- Specific enabling legislation (home rule state): 8
- No specific enabling legislation (home rule state): 11
- No specific enabling legislation (Dillon's rule state): 5

PARKS AND RECREATION, OPEN SPACE, AND TRAILS (52)

Assessment Distribution
- Residential only: 42
- Includes nonresidential uses: 10

Residential Differentiation
- Differentiation by residential type and size: 3
- Differentiation by size only: 1
- Differentiation by type only: 37
- No residential differentiation: 11

Type Differentiation—Number of Categories
- 2 categories: 12
- 3 categories: 20
- 4 categories: 4
- 5 categories: 4

Service Areas
- One service area: 45
- Multiple service areas: 7

Method
- Cost recovery/buy-in: 1
- Standards-based expansion: 26
- Plan-based: 8
- Combination buy-in/standards-based: 4
- Combination buy-in/plan-based: 0
- Combination standards-based/plan-based: 4
- Combination all three: 0
- Indeterminate: 9

Level-of-Service Measure Units

The number of occurrences may not match the total number of fee examples due to multiple LOS standards within a single fee.
- Acres: 69
- Dollars (replacement cost/expenditure): 47
- Square feet (recreational facilities): 2
- Vehicles and equipment: 2
- Number of recreational facilities: 1
- Linear feet (trails): 1
- Miles (trails): 1

Residential Demand Unit Cost Unit
- Person/resident: 31
- Dwelling unit: 10
- EDU/single-family equivalent (SFE): 8
- Functional or seasonal population: 2
- VMT: 1 (trails fee)

FIRE, EMERGENCY MEDICAL SERVICE, AND E911 COMMUNICATIONS (40)

Assessment Distribution
- Residential only: 1
- Includes nonresidential uses: 39

Residential Differentiation
- Differentiation by residential type and size: 0
- Differentiation by size only: 0
- Differentiation by type only: 29
- No residential differentiation: 11

Type Differentiation—Number of Categories
- 2 categories: 9
- 3 categories: 13
- 4 categories: 5
- 5 categories: 1
- 6 categories: 1

Service Areas
- One service area: 39
- Multiple service areas: 1

Method
- Cost recovery/buy-in: 1
- Standards-based expansion: 21
- Plan-based: 2
- Combination buy-in/standards-based: 2
- Combination buy-in/plan-based: 0
- Combination standards-based/plan-based: 6
- Combination all three: 0
- Indeterminate: 8

Level-of-Service Measure Units

The number of occurrences may not match the total number of fee examples due to multiple LOS standards within a single fee.
- Dollars (replacement cost/expenditure): 63
- Vehicles/apparatus: 14
- Square feet (station/communications buildings): 14
- Acres (station sites): 4
- Stations: 2
- Communications equipment: 1

Residential Demand Unit Cost Unit
- Person/resident: 17
- Dwelling unit: 10
- Service demand unit/service call/incident: 5
- EDU/SFE: 4
- Functional or day-night population: 4

ROADS, TRAFFIC SIGNALS, AND TRANSIT (37)

Assessment Distribution
- Residential only: 0
- Includes nonresidential uses: 37

Residential Differentiation

- Differentiation by residential type and size: 3
- Differentiation by size only: 0
- Differentiation by type only: 32
- No residential differentiation: 2

Type Differentiation—Number of Categories

- 2 categories: 12
- 3 categories: 12
- 4 categories: 6
- 5 categories: 4
- 5 categories: 1

Service Areas

- One service area: 31
- Multiple service areas: 6

Method

- Cost recovery/buy-in: 0
- Standards-based expansion: 7
- Plan-based: 18
- Combination buy-in/standards-based: 0
- Combination buy-in/plan-based: 2
- Combination standards-based/plan-based: 4
- Combination all three: 1
- Indeterminate: 5

Level-of-Service Measure Units

The number of occurrences may not match the total number of fee examples due to multiple LOS standards within a single fee.
- Dollars (replacement cost/expenditure): 38
  - Per trip: 23
  - Per VMT: 15
- VMC (per VMT): 9
- Trips (per lane-mile): 3
- Vehicles (per lane-mile): 1
- Traffic signals (per VMT): 1

Residential Demand Unit Cost Unit

- Trip (includes both peak-hour and average daily): 22
- VMT: 13
- EDU/SFE: 1
- Dwelling unit: 1

POLICE AND CRIMINAL JUSTICE OR COMBINED PUBLIC SAFETY (35)

Assessment Distribution
- Residential only: 0
- Includes nonresidential uses: 35

Residential Differentiation

- Differentiation by residential type and size: 0
- Differentiation by size only: 0
- Differentiation by type only: 24
- No residential differentiation: 11

Type Differentiation—Number of Categories

- 2 categories: 7
- 3 categories: 8
- 4 categories: 7
- 5 categories: 2

Service Areas

- One service area: 34
- Multiple service areas: 1

Method

- Cost recovery/buy-in: 0
- Standards-based expansion: 15
- Plan-based: 5
- Combination buy-in/standards-based: 4
- Combination buy-in/plan-based: 0
- Combination standards-based/plan-based: 9
- Combination all three: 0
- Indeterminate: 2

Level-of-Service Measure Units

The number of occurrences may not match the total number of fee examples due to multiple LOS standards within a single fee.
- Dollars (replacement cost/expenditure): 53
- Square feet (station or justice/corrections facility buildings): 21
- Vehicles: 6
- Acres (station or justice/corrections facility sites): 3
- Communications equipment: 1

Residential Demand Unit Cost Unit

- Person/resident: 16
- Dwelling unit: 9
- Functional or day-night population: 7
- Service demand unit/service call/incident: 2
- EDU/SFE: 1

LIBRARIES (21)

Assessment Distribution

- Residential only: 21
- Includes nonresidential uses: 0

Residential Differentiation

- Differentiation by residential type and size: 0
- Differentiation by size only: 0
- Differentiation by type only: 14
- No residential differentiation: 7

Type Differentiation—Number of Categories

- 2 categories: 5
- 3 categories: 6
- 4 categories: 2
- 5 categories: 1

Service Areas

- One service area: 21
- Multiple service areas: 0

Method

- Cost recovery/buy-in: 0
- Standards-based expansion: 10
- Plan-based: 2
- Combination buy-in/standards-based: 0
- Combination buy-in/plan-based: 0
- Combination standards-based/plan-based: 2
- Combination all three: 0
- Indeterminate: 7

Level-of-Service Measure Units

The number of occurrences may not match the total number of fee examples due to multiple LOS standards within a single fee.
- Square feet (library buildings): 15
- Books/volumes: 15
- Dollars (replacement cost/expenditure): 12
- Acres (library sites): 3
- Support vehicles: 1
- Computer facilities: 1

Residential Demand Unit Cost Unit

- Person/resident: 14
- Dwelling unit: 5
- EDU/SFE: 2

WATER INFRASTRUCTURE AND WATER RESOURCES (20)

Assessment Distribution

- Residential only: 0
- Includes nonresidential uses: 20

Residential Differentiation

Thirteen of the fees are assessed using meter categorizations as opposed to dwelling unit.
- Differentiation by residential type and size: 2
- Differentiation by size only: 0
- Differentiation by type only: 4
- No residential differentiation: 14

Type Differentiation—Number of Categories

- 2 categories: 3
- 3 categories: 2
- 4 categories: 1
- 5 categories: 0

Service Areas

- One service area: 19
- Multiple service areas: 1

Method

- Cost recovery/buy-in: 3
- Standards-based expansion: 4
- Plan-based: 7
- Combination buy-in/standards-based: 0
- Combination buy-in/plan-based: 2
- Combination standards-based/plan-based: 2
- Combination all three: 2
- Indeterminate: 0

Level-of-Service Measure Units

The number of occurrences may not match the total number of fee examples due to multiple LOS standards within a single fee.
- Gallons per day: 32
  - Per EDU/SFE: 26
  - Per customer/meter: 4
  - Per other unit: 2
- Dollars (replacement cost/expenditure): 11
  - Per EDU/SFE: 6
  - Per customer/meter: 2
  - Per other unit: 3

Residential Demand Unit Cost Unit

- EDU/SFE: 18
- Gallon per day: 2

GOVERNMENT BUILDINGS AND PUBLIC FACILITIES AND COMBINED PUBLIC INFRASTRUCTURE (18)

Assessment Distribution

- Residential only: 2
- Includes nonresidential uses: 16

Residential Differentiation

- Differentiation by type and size: 0
- Differentiation by size only: 0
- Differentiation by type only: 12
- No residential differentiation: 6

Type Differentiation—Number of Categories

- 2 categories: 2
- 3 categories: 7
- 4 categories: 2
- 5 categories: 1

Service Areas

- One service area: 17
- Multiple service areas: 1

Method

- Cost recovery/buy-in: 0
- Standards-based expansion: 9
- Plan-based: 3
- Combination buy-in/standards-based: 1
- Combination buy-in/plan-based: 0
- Combination standards-based/plan-based: 4
- Combination all three: 0
- Indeterminate: 1

Level-of-Service Measure Units

The number of occurrences may not match the total number of fee examples due to multiple LOS standards within a single fee.

- Dollars (replacement cost/expenditure): 24
- Square feet (buildings): 7
- Support vehicles: 3
- Acres (building sites): 2

Residential Demand Unit Cost Unit

- Person/resident: 11
- Dwelling unit: 3
- Acre: 2
- EDU/SFE: 1
- Square foot: 1

WASTEWATER (15)

Assessment Distribution

- Residential only: 0
- Includes nonresidential uses: 15

Residential Differentiation

Eight of the fees are assessed using meter categorizations as opposed to dwelling unit.

- Differentiation by type and size: 2
- Differentiation by size only: 0

- Differentiation by type only: 4
- No residential differentiation: 9

Type Differentiation—Number of Categories

- 2 categories: 3
- 3 categories: 2
- 4 categories: 1
- 5 categories: 0

Service Areas

- One service area: 13
- Multiple service areas: 2

Method

- Cost recovery/buy-in: 1
- Standards-based expansion: 3
- Plan-based: 5
- Combination buy-in/standards-based: 40
- Combination buy-in/plan-based: 1
- Combination standards-based/plan-based: 3
- Combination all three: 1
- Indeterminate: 1

Level-of-Service Measure Units

The number of occurrences may not match the total number of fee examples due to multiple LOS standards within a single fee.

- Gallons per day: 18
  - Per EDU/SFE: 12
  - Per customer/meter: 2
  - Per other unit: 4
- Dollars (replacement cost/expenditure): 9
  - Per EDU/SFE: 3
  - Per customer/meter: 5
  - Per other unit: 1

Residential Demand Unit Cost Unit

- EDU/SFE: 12
- Gallon per day: 2
- Person: 1

SCHOOLS (12)

Assessment Distribution (Outside California Only)

- Residential only: 12
- Includes nonresidential uses: 0

Residential Differentiation

- Differentiation by type and size: 0
- Differentiation by size only: 0
- Differentiation by type only: 12
- No residential differentiation: 0

Type Differentiation—Number of Categories

- 2 categories: 4
- 3 categories: 5
- 4 categories: 2
- 5 categories: 0
- 6 categories: 1

Service Areas

- One service area: 11
- Multiple service areas: 1

Method

- Cost recovery/buy-in: 0
- Standards-based expansion: 11
- Plan-based: 0
- Combination buy-in/standards-based: 0
- Combination buy-in/plan-based: 1
- Combination standards-based/plan-based: 0
- Combination all three: 0
- Indeterminate: 0

Level-of-Service Measure Units

The number of occurrences may not match the total number of fee examples due to multiple LOS standards within a single fee.
- Dollars (replacement cost/expenditure): 36
- Square feet (school and support buildings): 28
- Acres (school sites): 23
- Relocatable classrooms: 14
- Buses: 3
- Support vehicles: 1

Residential Demand Unit Cost Unit

- Student: 11
- EDU/SFE: 1

STORMWATER/DRAINAGE (10)

Assessment Distribution
- Residential only: 0
- Includes nonresidential uses: 10

Residential Differentiation

Six of the fees are assessed per acre of land area as opposed to per dwelling unit.
- Differentiation by type and size: 1
- Differentiation by size only: 0
- Differentiation by type only: 3
- No residential differentiation: 6

Type Differentiation—Number of Categories

One methodology calculates each fee separately based on land use and other factors.

- 2 categories: 1
- 3 categories: 3
- 4 categories: 0
- 5 categories: 0

Service Areas

- One service area: 7
- Multiple service areas: 3

Method

- Cost recovery/buy-in: 1
- Standards-based expansion: 2
- Plan-based: 4
- Combination buy-in/standards-based: 0
- Combination buy-in/plan-based: 2
- Combination standards-based/plan-based: 0
- Combination all three: 0
- Indeterminate: 1

Level-of-Service Measure Units

The number of occurrences may not match the total number of fee examples due to multiple LOS standards within a single fee.
- Dollars: 19
  - Per acre: 13
  - Per service demand unit (e.g., takes into account soil type): 5
  - Per other unit: 1

Residential Demand Unit Cost Unit

- Acre: 4
- Service demand unit: 4
- EDU/SFE: 2

FLORIDA IMPACT FEE SURVEY FINDINGS

In 2006, Florida surveyed local governments to understand how extensively impact fees were being used, their variation, calculation methodologies, variations in administrative procedures, whether special provisions were made for affordable housing, and other issues. The following are answers to selected survey questions that provide perspective on how impact fees vary across one state where they have been pioneered and used for more than a generation.

NOTE

1. We are indebted to Darren Smith for this analysis conducted while he was a graduate research assistant at Virginia Tech on a contract for the National Apartment Association (NAA). We are indebted to the NAA for support leading to this analysis.

Question 1: Please indicate the type of impact fee, the adoption date, the legal citation, and most recent revision/amendment date for each current impact fee.		
Response Categories	**Number**	**Percent**
Parks/recreation	55	18.8
Sewer/wastewater	31	10.6
Education	8	2.7
Emergency medical service	8	2.7
Fire	39	13.3
Water	17	5.8
General government	5	1.7
Libraries	16	5.5
Transportation	23	7.9
Police	15	5.1
Roads	15	5.1
Schools	19	6.5
Various combinations of the above responses	30	10.2
Other	12	4.1
Total	**293**	**100**

Question 2: Please indicate each type of new impact fee that your government intends to adopt within the next year.		
Response Categories	**Number**	**Percent**
Public safety	2	.7
Parks and recreation	2	.7
Law enforcement	1	.3
Fire	1	.3
Solid waste	1	.3
None	5	1.7
No response	281	96
Total	**293**	**100**

Question 3: Indicate the geographical boundaries of the impact fee below (if your jurisdiction is a county).		
Response Categories	**Number**	**Percent**
County-wide	91	54.5
Entire unincorporated area	34	20.3
Portion of the unincorporated area	5	3.0
Unincorporated area with some municipalities included	29	17.4
Other	8	4.8
Total	**167**	**100**

Question 3a: If your jurisdiction is a municipality:		
Response Categories	**Number**	**Percent**
City-wide	108	89.3
Portion of city	1	.8
Other	9	7.4
No response	3	2.5
Total	**121**	**100**

Question 3b: If your jurisdiction is a special district:		
Response Categories	**Number**	**Percent**
Other	5	100
Total	**5**	**100**

Question 4: Prior to the formal process of passing, amending, and/or enacting this impact fee ordinance, what method was utilized to notice and discuss the proposal?		
Response Categories	**Number**	**Percent**
Public hearing	80	27.3
Workshop	0	0
Other	5	1.7
Public hearing, workshop, other	98	33.4
Public hearing, workshop	71	24.3
Public hearing, other	24	8.2
Workshop, other	2	.7
No response	13	4.4
Total	**293**	**100**

Question 4a: Please specify how notice of actions described in Question 4 is authorized or required.		
Response Categories	**Number**	**Percent**
Local ordinance	80	27.3
Operating procedure	0	0
Resolution	5	1.7
Other	98	33.4
Various combinations of the above responses	71	24.3
No response	39	13.3
Total	**293**	**100**

Question 4b: Identify the times between the notice of the fee and fee adoption, as well as the time between fee adoption and effective date.

Time between the notice of the fee and fee adoption.

Response Categories	Number	Percent
7–40 days	115	39.2
41–75 days	34	11.6
76–120 days	3	1
121–210 days	24	8.2
1 month	2	.7
1.5 years	9	3.1
Other	32	10.9
No response	74	25.3
Total	**293**	**100**

Question 4c: Identify the time between fee adoption and effective date.

Response Categories	Number	Percent
Upon adoption	12	4.1
1–20 days	27	9.3
21–40 days	46	15.7
41–60 days	42	14.3
61–80 days	2	.7
81–100 days	14	4.8
101–120 days	3	1
121–140 days	1	.3
141–150 days	4	1.4
6 months	4	1.4
Other	32	10.9
No response	106	36.1
Total	**293**	**100**

Question 5. How are affected parties notified of impending changes in impact fee payment schedules?

Response Categories	Number	Percent
Various forms of advertising, TV, Internet, newspaper, postings	117	40.0
Letter	8	2.7
Meetings with stakeholders	8	2.7
Public hearings	34	11.6
Other	22	7.5
Various combinations of the above responses	76	25.9
No response	28	9.6
Total	**293**	**100**

Question 6c. Please specify the method for determining the administrative fee.		
Response Categories	**Number**	**Percent**
Percentage of the impact fee without a fee cap	8	5.8
Percentage of the impact fee with a fee cap	38	27.5
Flat rate charged per payment transaction	92	66.7
Total	**138**	**100**

Question 6d. What is the administrative fee collected on a typical single-family dwelling?		
Response Categories	**Number**	**Percent**
0%	6	6.3
1%	1	1
1.5%	4	4.2
2%	11	11.6
2.25%	3	3.2
2.7%	2	2.2
3%	66	69.5
4%	1	1
5%	1	1
Total	**95**	**100**

Question 6e. What is the administrative fee collected on a typical commercial building?		
Response Categories	**Number**	**Percent**
0%	6	8.5
2%	9	12.9
2.25%	1	1.4
3%	51	73
4%	1	1.4
5%	1	1.4
6%	1	1.4
Total	**70**	**100**

Question 7. Indicate at what point in the development process the impact fee is assessed.		
Response Categories	**Number**	**Percent**
Subdivision plat approval	16	5.4
Building permit issuance	223	76.1
Zoning change approval	0	0
Certificate of occupancy issuance	4	1.4
Time of connection to facility	6	2.1
Other	25	8.6
Various combinations of the above responses	11	3.7
No response	8	2.7
Total	**293**	**100**

Question 8. Indicate at what point in the development process the impact fee is due.

Response Categories	Number	Percent
Subdivision plat approval	8	2.7
Building permit issuance	170	58
Zoning change approval	0	0
Certificate of occupancy issuance	60	20.4
Time of connection to facility	14	4.9
Other	13	4.5
Various combinations of the above responses	22	7.5
No response	6	2.0
Total	**293**	**100**

Question 9. Indicate at what point in the development process the impact fee is collected.

Response Categories	Number	Percent
Subdivision plat approval	8	2.7
Building permit issuance	171	58.4
Zoning change approval	0	0
Certificate of occupancy issuance	52	17.7
Time of connection to facility	16	5.5
Other	14	4.8
Various combinations of the above responses	26	8.9
No response	6	2.0
Total	**293**	**100**

Question 10. Indicate each circumstance under which deferral of this impact fee is authorized.

Response Categories	Number	Percent
No deferral allowed	188	64.1
When payment is secured by lien	37	12.7
Other	58	19.8
No response	10	3.4
Total	**293**	**100**

Question 11. Indicate the event or action to which the collection is deferred.

Response Categories	Number	Percent
Issuance of certificate of occupancy	48	16.4
Issuance of building permit	15	5.1
Other	28	9.6
No response	202	68.9
Total	**293**	**100**

Question 12. Indicate the type of land use that this impact is levied upon.		
Response Categories	**Number**	**Percent**
Residential	87	29.7
Commercial	1	.3
Industrial	0	0
Residential, commercial, industrial	124	42.3
Other	0	0
Various combinations of the above responses	75	25.7
No response	6	2.0
Total	**293**	**100**

Question 13. Indicate the length of time after collection of this impact fee that the revenue must be spent.		
Response Categories	**Number**	**Percent**
No time limit	96	32.8
5–10 years	179	61.1
Other	3	1.0
No response	15	5.1
Total	**293**	**100**

Question 14. Indicate each type of credit authorized as an alternative to a cash impact fee payment.		
Response Categories	**Number**	**Percent**
None	68	23.2
Land donations	19	6.6
Improvements within development boundaries	1	.3
Improvements outside development boundaries	2	.6
Ad valorem taxes generated by development	0	0
Proportionate share mitigation	0	0
Other	5	1.8
Various combinations of the above responses	189	64.4
No response	9	3.1
Total	**293**	**100**

Question 14a. Do you charge proportionate share mitigation?		
Response Categories	**Number**	**Percent**
Yes	21	7.2
No	238	81.2
No response	34	11.6
Total	**293**	**100**

Question 14b. Are payers of the proportionate share mitigation given a credit for any portion of that payment towards this impact fee?		
Response Categories	**Number**	**Percent**
Yes	14	66.7
No	7	33.3
Total	**21**	**100**

Question 15: Indicate each type of capital outlay currently earmarked for this impact fee.		
Response Categories	**Number**	**Percent**
Building new facilities to serve new development ONLY	26	8.9
Upgrading existing facilities to serve new development ONLY	7	2.4
Recovering a portion of a facility's cost already built to serve new development ONLY	3	1.0
New capital development ONLY	6	2.1
Other ONLY	9	3.1
Various combinations of the above responses	234	79.9
No response	8	2.7
Total	**293**	**100**

Question 16: Indicate what provisions, if any, this impact fee ordinance contains related to affordable housing.		
Response Categories	**Number**	**Percent**
No relevant provisions ONLY	184	62.8
All of fee is waived ONLY	19	6.5
Portion of fee is waived ONLY	26	8.9
Fee is lower ONLY	6	2.0
Other ONLY	33	11.3
Various combinations of the above responses	19	6.5
No response	6	2.0
Total	**293**	**100**

Question 16a: If the impact fee is waived or lowered for affordable housing, how is the lost revenue recovered?		
Response Categories	**Number**	**Percent**
County pays	9	11.4
Federal subsidy	2	2.5
General revenue funds	8	10.1
Local property taxes	2	2.5
Not addressed, collected, or recovered	29	36.7
School district funds	2	2.5
SHIP or HOME monies	8	10.1
State	2	2.5
Trust fund	12	15.2
Other response	5	6.3
Total	**79**	**100**

Question 16b: At what point in the development is the lost revenue recovered or waived?		
Response Categories	Number	Percent
Building permit issuance	23	31.5
Certificate of occupancy issuance	22	30.1
Subdivision plat approval	1	1.4
Other response	27	37.0
Total	**73**	**100**

Question 16c: Who initiates the process to recover the lost revenues?		
Response Categories	Number	Percent
Applicant	3	4.8
Board of county commissioners	43	68.3
Building contractor	5	7.9
Community housing or code enforcement departments	3	4.8
Municipality	3	4.8
School board	5	7.9
Other response	1	1.6
Total	**63**	**100**

Question 17: How do you account for and report impact fee collections and expenditures?		
Response Categories	Number	Percent
Accounting system by project	21	7.2
Annual report ONLY	15	5.1
Annual report and budget	5	1.7
Budget ONLY	3	1.0
Separate fund accounts ONLY	117	39.9
Separate fund accounts and annual report	25	8.5
Separate fund accounts and budget	40	13.7
Separate fund accounts and monthly report	16	5.5
Separate fund accounts and other	5	1.7
Other response	40	13.7
No response	6	2.0
Total	**293**	**10**

Question 17a: What monitoring mechanism is in place to assure that fee collections are expended according to the initial impact fee study or plan on which the fee was based?		
Response Categories	Number	Percent
Annual report ONLY	61	20.8
Annual report and budget	15	5.1
Budget ONLY	79	27.0
None	3	1.0
Separate accounts ONLY	18	6.1
Other response	96	32.8
No response	21	7.2
Total	**293**	**100**

Question 17b: Has the monitoring mechanism been successful in ensuring that the projects are completed within the time frame required?

Response Categories	Number	Percent
No	7	2.4
Yes	214	73.0
No response	72	24.6
Total	**293**	**100**

Question 18: Has this impact fee been challenged in court since 1991?

Response Categories	Number	Percent
No	269	91.8
Yes	13	4.4
No response	11	3.8
Total	**293**	**100**

Question 19a: Is the impact fee amount based upon or tied to the level-of-service standard identified in the comprehensive plan for the type of facility for which the fee is levied?

Response Categories	Number	Percent
No	82	28.0
Yes	157	53.6
Other response	2	0.7
No response	52	17.7
Total	**293**	**100**

Question 20: Please state the importance of this impact fee to fund the infrastructure needed to address the impacts of development and meet statutory requirements for concurrency.

Response Categories	Number	Percent
Primary importance	206	70.3
Secondary importance	53	18.1
Other response	6	2.0
No response	28	9.6
Total	**293**	**100**

Question 21: Please specify the amount of this impact revenue for:

Fiscal Year 2003–04—Cash Collected

Response Categories	Number	Percent
$0	3	1.0
$1 to $99,999	61	20.8
$100,000 to $999,999	86	29.4
$1,000,000 to $9,999,999	66	22.5
$10,000,000 or more	23	7.8
New fee	5	1.7
No response	49	16.7
Total	**293**	**100**

Question 21 (continued): Please indicate the value of credits allowed:		
Fiscal Year 2003–04—Cash Value of Alternative Credits Used		
Response Categories	**Number**	**Percent**
$0	40	13.7
$1 to $99,999	9	3.1
$100,000 to $999,999	13	4.4
$1,000,000 to $9,999,999	10	3.4
$10,000,000 or more	2	0.7
No response	219	74.7
Total	**293**	**100**

Question 21 (continued): Please specify the amount of this impact revenue for:		
Fiscal Year 2004–05 Budgeted—Cash		
Response Categories	**Number**	**Percent**
$0	4	1.4
$1 to $99,999	61	20.8
$100,000 to $999,999	85	29.0
$1,000,000 to $9,999,999	61	20.8
$10,000,000 or more	27	9.2
No response	55	18.8
Total	**293**	**100**

Question 22: Indicate if this impact fee is used to secure debt issuance.		
Response Categories	**Number**	**Percent**
Not used to secure debt	235	80.2
Primary pledge	14	4.8
Secondary pledge	15	5.1
Both primary and secondary pledges	1	0.3
No response	28	9.6
Total	**293**	**100**

Question 23: What is the total cost of the capital outlay projects receiving revenue from this impact fee?		
Estimated		
Response Categories	**Number**	**Percent**
$0	3	1.0
Less than $1,000,000	32	10.9
$1,000,000 to $9,999,999	50	17.1
$10,000,000 to $99,999,999	45	15.4
$100,000,000 or more	24	8.2
No response	139	47.4
Total	**293**	**100**

Question 23 *(continued)*: What is the total cost of the capital outlay projects receiving revenue from this impact fee?		
Actual		
Response Categories	**Number**	**Percent**
$0	6	2.0
Less than $1,000,000	16	5.5
$1,000,000 to $9,999,999	9	3.1
$10,000,000 to $99,999,999	6	2.0
$100,000,000 or more	2	0.7
No response	254	86.7
Total	**293**	**100**

Question 24: What proportion or percent of the total cost of the capital outlay project referred to in Question 23 will actually be paid for by this impact fee?		
Response Categories	**Number**	**Percent**
1% to 25%	55	18.8
26% to 50%	35	11.9
51% to 75%	23	7.8
76% to 100%	60	20.5
Other response	3	1.0
No response	117	39.9
Total	**293**	**100**

Question 25: Please indicate the amount of this impact fee for a 2,000 sq. ft., three-bedroom, two-bath, single-family home.		
Response Categories	**Number**	**Percent**
Zero	4	1.4
$1 to $999	158	53.9
$1,000 to $1,999	38	13.0
$2,000 to $2,999	26	8.9
$3,000 to $3,999	17	5.8
$4,000 to $4,999	6	2.0
$5,000 or more	11	3.8
Varies	2	0.7
No response	31	10.6
Total	**293**	**100**

Question 26: What are the criteria and methodology used for the determination of the amount of this impact fee?		
Response Categories	**Number**	**Percent**
Formula, proportionate share, or ratio	123	42.0
Consultant's study, impact fee study, or schedule	96	32.8
Consumption-based methodology, business type, or usage capacity (in the context of the survey, "consumption-based" is equivalent to "standards-based" as used in this book)	19	6.5
Meter size	4	1.4
Dual rational nexus test	4	1.4
Other response	11	3.8
No response	36	12.3
Total	**293**	**100**

Question 26a: How often is the impact fee study updated?		
Response Categories	**Number**	**Percent**
Annually	16	5.5
Every 2 years	51	17.4
Every 3–5 years	111	37.9
Every 6–9 years	1	0.3
Every 10 or more years	8	2.7
Other response	14	4.8
No response	92	31.4
Total	**293**	**100**

Question 26b: Is each and every impact fee increase accompanied by a new study?		
Response Categories	**Number**	**Percent**
No	42	14.3
Yes	198	67.6
No response	53	18.1
Total	**293**	**100**

Question 27: Please indicate if this impact fee is applied in more than one zone.		
Response Categories	**Number**	**Percent**
One zone	175	59.7
Two or more zones	84	28.7
No response	34	11.6
Total	**293**	**100**

Question 27a: If the response to Question 27 was two or more zones, please indicate if the impact fee schedules are identical or not identical.		
Response Categories	**Number**	**Percent**
Identical	65	77.4
Not identical	13	15.5
No response	6	7.1
Total	**84**	**100**

3

Applications

Part 3 presents, in detail, many current and evolving **Applications** of proportionate-share development fees. *Chapter 10* starts by reviewing impact fee technical reports prepared for numerous communities throughout the nation for such standard facility types as utilities, roads, schools, public safety, and parks and recreational facilities. The selection of case studies, however, illustrates underlying themes in emerging practice: tailoring impact fees to encourage infill and redevelopment; more appropriately assessing new development at the urban fringe for its marginal costs; and refining impact fee calculations to better account for equity concerns. *Chapter 11* extends the proportionate-share logic behind impact fees to "social infrastructure" such as affordable (including workforce) housing, day care centers, public art, and other socially beneficial investments. The chapter presents the foundations of proportionate-share development fees assessed on commercial development for workforce housing production, shows how proportionate-share principles may be applied to both residential and commercial development to produce workforce housing, and reviews applications of proportionate-share development fees for other forms of social infrastructure. Proportionate-share development fee applications for "green infrastructure" are explored in *Chapter 12*, which necessarily devotes discussions to legal issues flavored with applications. Applying the proportionate-share method to green infrastructure may be the next wave of activity in these planning, policy, financial, and legal areas. New development impacts facilities in more ways than just requiring new or expanded facilities to serve it; it may create more new demands for O & M than it generates in new revenues to offset. *Chapter 13* explores ways in which the proportionate-share development fee methodology may be used to help close this financial gap.

10

Proportionate-Share Fees for Physical Infrastructure

The most common use of impact fees is for physical infrastructure, which applies to any public facility but not its operation or maintenance (O & M). Most impact fee enabling acts limit impact fees to a list of physical infrastructure and do not allow their use for O & M. This chapter has two sections. The first illustrates the decision steps necessary to consider whether impact fees are needed. If they are, the second section reviews a wide range of approaches to craft impact fee programs for a variety of public facilities.

ARE IMPACT FEES NEEDED?

For a variety of political, legal, and pragmatic reasons, impact fees are often seen as the most flexible option to address facility financing needs even though, for the most part, other funding alternatives may be superior (see Nelson (1988a)). Nonetheless, it is important to consider alternatives first to be sure that the impact fee choice is the best available option. The decision charts for specific facilities that follow are designed to help practitioners make rational decisions on potential funding mechanisms and consider if impact fees meet their needs. They should be used as a guide in the decision-making process. The decision charts are not exclusive to the facilities noted but are only illustrative for all facilities that have the potential to be financed in part by impact fees. The decision charts include:

- Public safety facilities (Figure 10-1) (fire, police, EMS, and related)
- Water-based utilities (Figure 10-2) (water, wastewater and stormwater/drainage, and related)
- Public amenity facilities (Figure 10-3) (parks, recreation, library, civic, and related)
- Transportation facilities (Figure 10-4) (streets of all kinds, bicycle and pedestrian ways, transit, and related)

If the determination is made that impact fees are needed, examples of how they may be calculated for a range of facilities are reviewed in the next section.

IMPACT FEES FOR PUBLIC FACILITIES

There is no single way to calculate defensible impact fees and, indeed, approaches will vary by the kind of facility involved, unique community characteristics, the role of other sources of financing and how they may be credited to new development if needed, the comprehensive plan,

Figure 10-1
Decision Chart for Public Safety Facilities

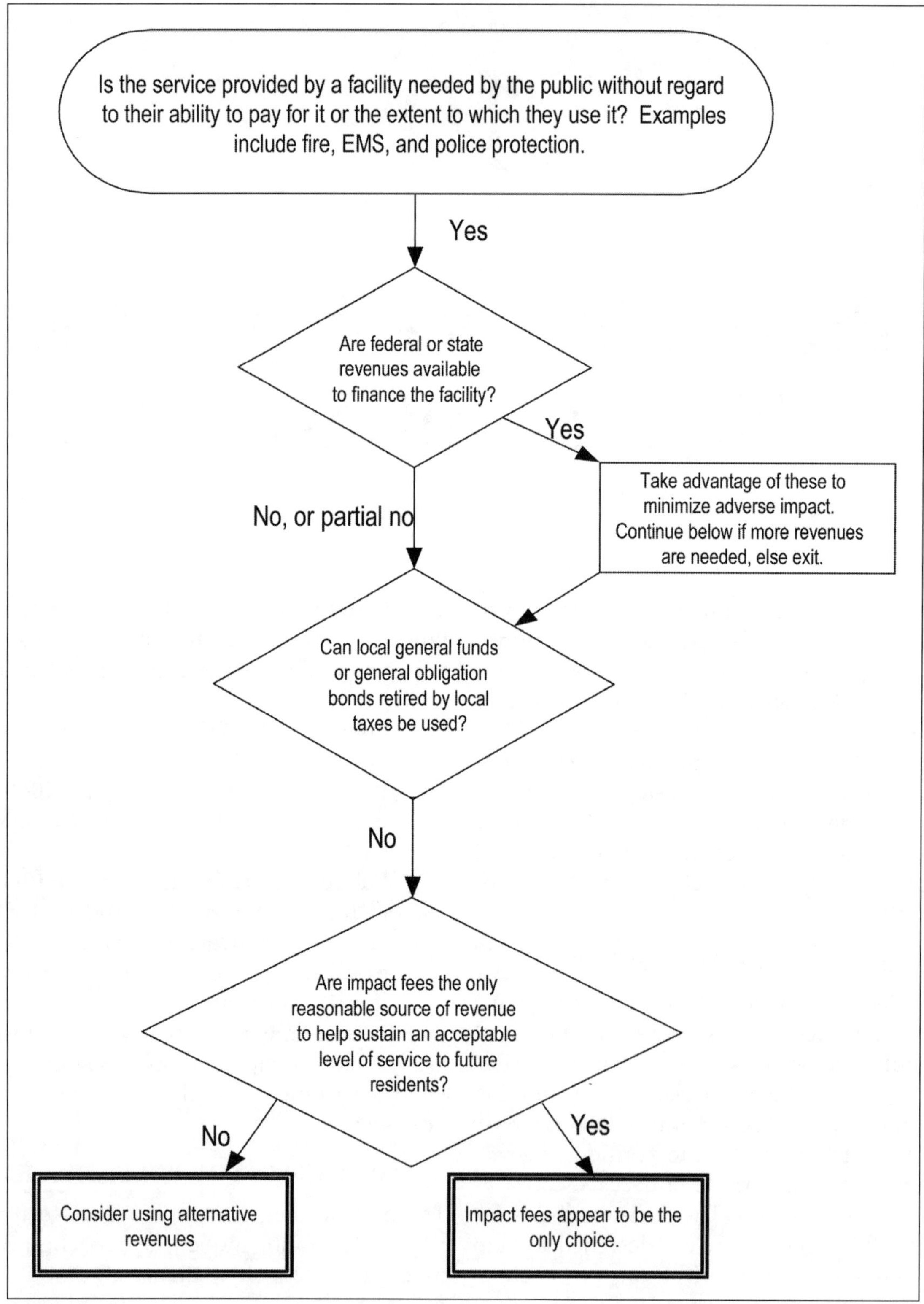

Courtesy of Newport Partners, LLC.

Figure 10-2
Decision Chart for Water-Based Utilities

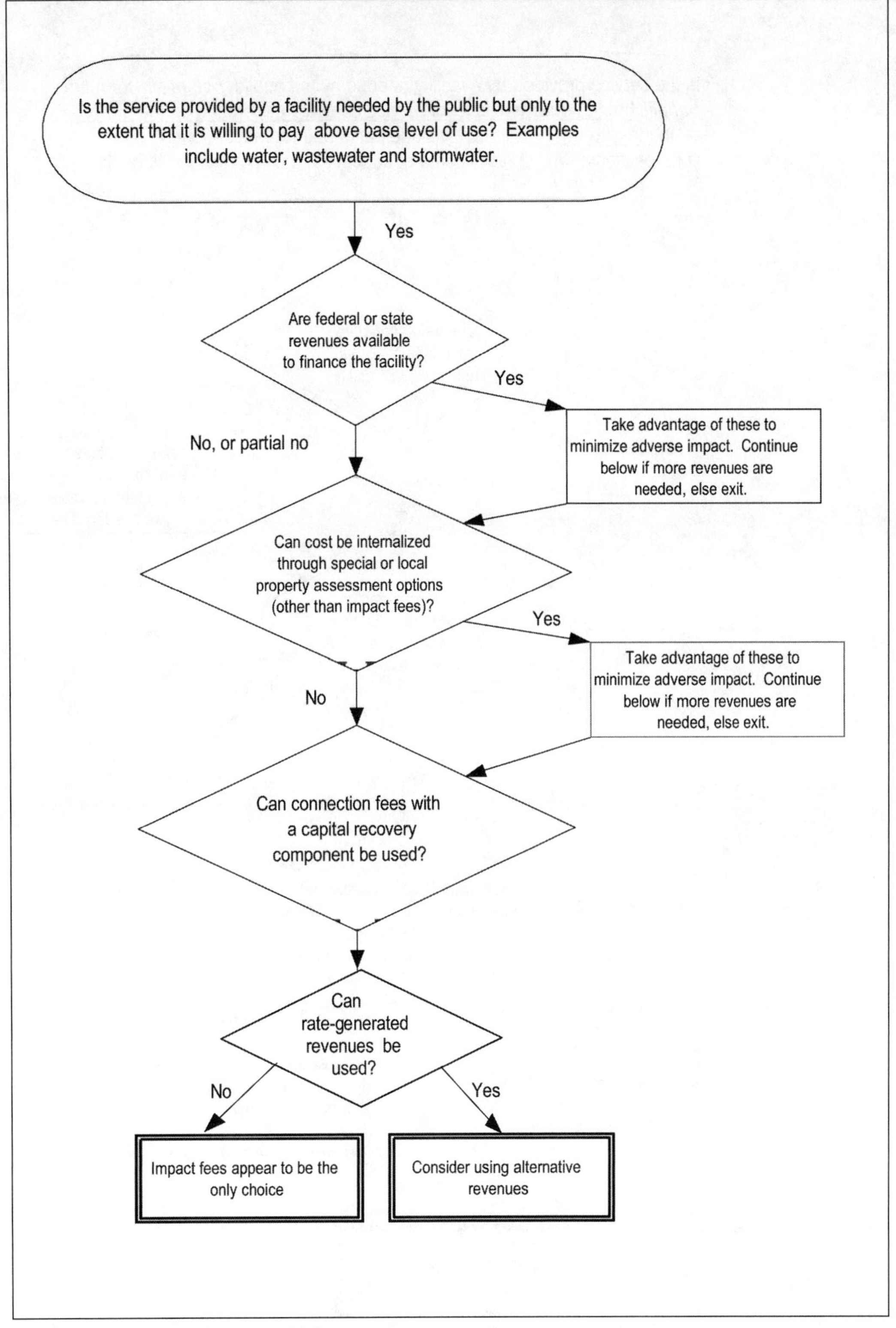

Courtesy of Newport Partners, LLC.

Figure 10-3
Decision Chart for Public Amenity Facilities

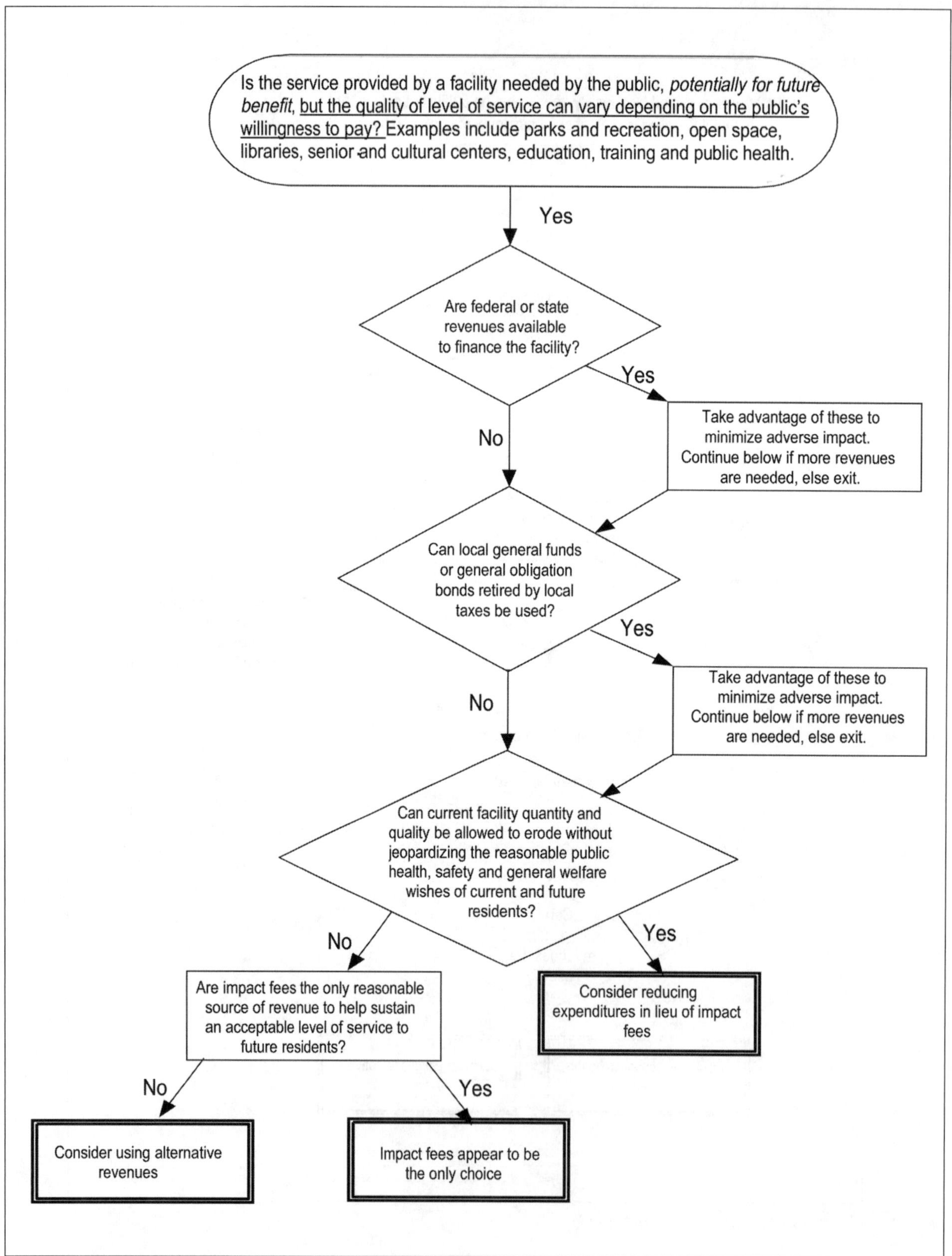

Courtesy of Newport Partners, LLC.

Figure 10-4
Decision Chart for Transportation Facilities

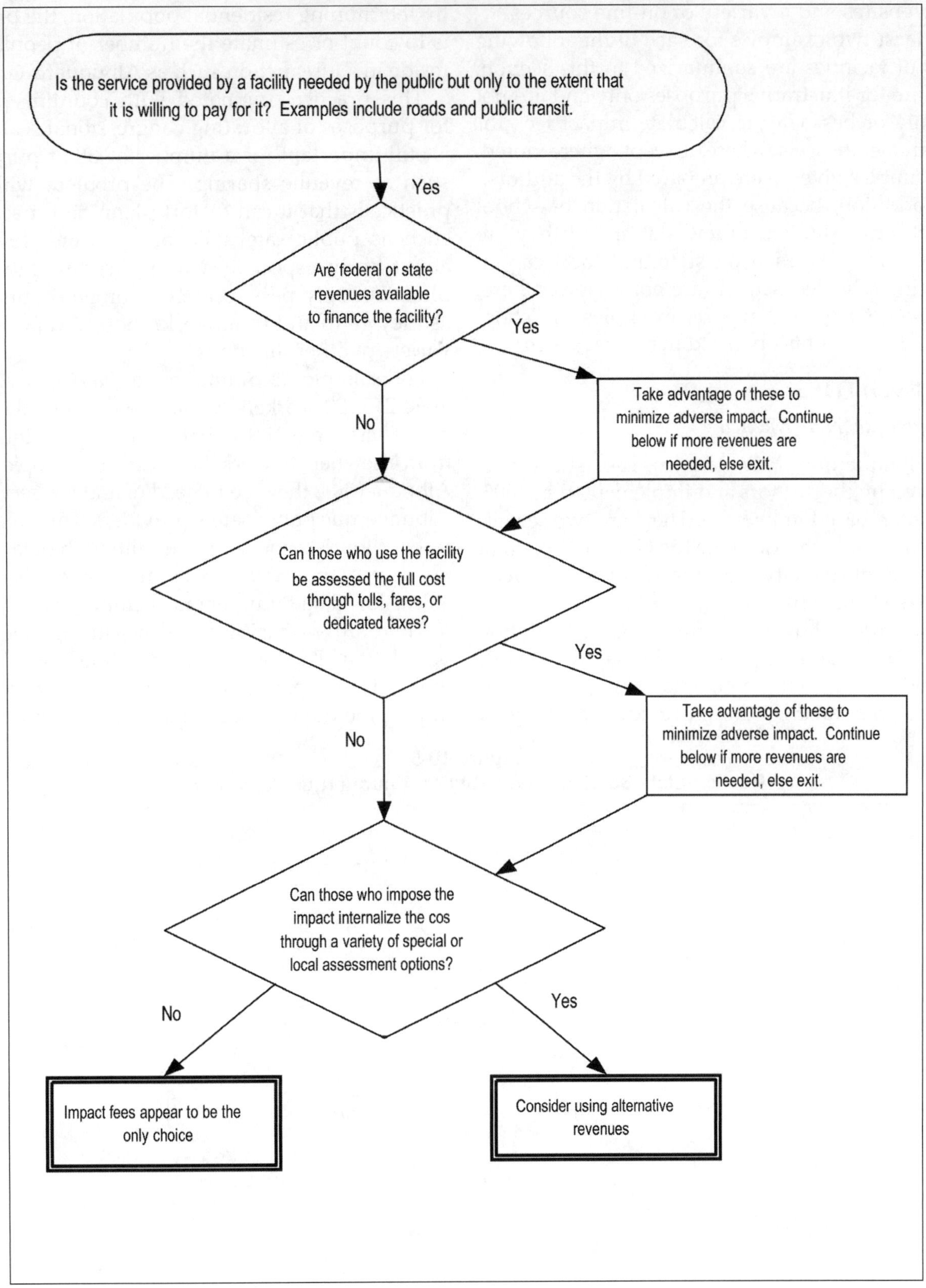

Courtesy of Newport Partners, LLC.

and many other factors. Examples of impact fee programs can be found in hundreds of community websites and a variety of on-line sources.[1]

At least two examples for each of the following kinds of facilities are summarized in this section. They are for illustrative purposes only and are not the only or best way to calculate impact fees for similar facilities elsewhere. Except where noted, the examples given were prepared by the authors.

In addition, because the calculation of school impact fees is limited to few states, and they are highly nuanced based on state and local capital financing schemes, schools are not reviewed here. However, Chapter 2 reports examples of school impact fee amounts observed in several states.

FIRE FACILITIES

Albuquerque, New Mexico

The Albuquerque, New Mexico, case study was prepared by the authors and implemented in 2005. It is a plan-based impact fee. There are two service areas (one for each side of the Rio Grande River that runs through the city) and the fees vary between them (see Figure 10-5).

Table 10-1 shows the functional population served by Albuquerque's public safety providers and the growth in functional population to be accommodated by those providers to the year

2025. Functional population is somewhat different from the usual concept of residential population. In determining residential population, the practice is to count or estimate the number of people who reside in a jurisdiction such as Albuquerque.

This practice originated with counting people for purposes of allocating congressional seats, and is still important for a number of other purposes, such as revenue sharing. The problem with this practice is that it can distort planning for services such as public safety. People can and do move about freely, especially within a community. People commonly pass local government boundaries as they go to and from work, shop, and perform a variety of other functions.

For example, according to the 2000 Census, there were 215,222 workers within the City of Albuquerque. There were 31,978 that came into Albuquerque from elsewhere to work. Because those people are in Albuquerque, they are in need of and are served by Albuquerque public safety providers. This is equally true for tourists and shoppers, although data on the numbers of these individuals are not as easily attainable as the data for numbers of employees.

There are two basic ways of measuring functional population. The first is the "daytime" population, which is the population that would be present during the daytime, conceptually as of noon. The

Figure 10-5
Public Safety Service Areas, City of Albuquerque, New Mexico

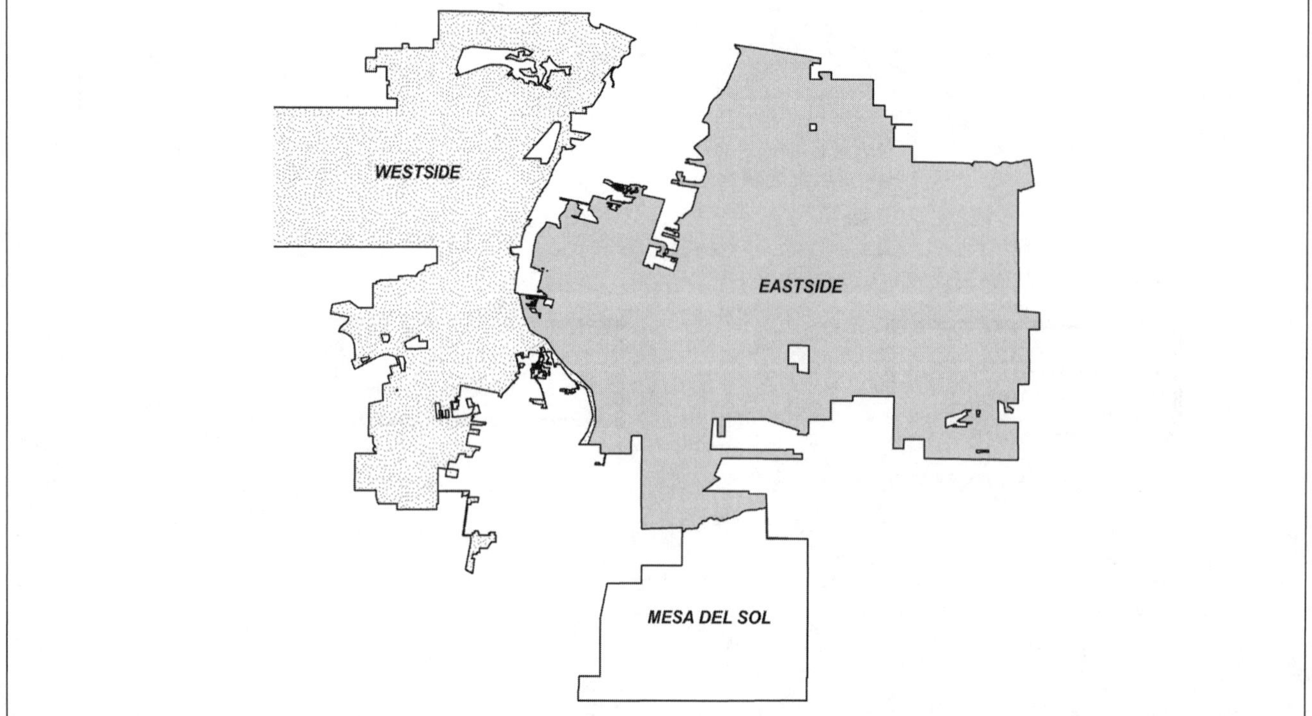

Table 10-1
Functional Population

Year	East Side	West Side	Total City
2004	409,724	102,477	512,201
2015	434,939	140,245	575,184
2025	457,715	166,257	623,972
Growth 2004–2025	47,991	63,779	111,770
Growth rate	0.53%	2.33%	0.94%

second is "24/7" population. This approach averages commuters, tourists, and imported shoppers with Albuquerque residents. The functional population measurement employed herein is the 24/7 equivalent population.

Albuquerque is divided into two public safety service areas: East Side and West Side. These service areas are divided by the Rio Grande River and are illustrated on the map at the end of this report.

Table 10-1 shows the 2004, 2015, and 2025 functional populations for Albuquerque. The 2004 functional population of 512,201 can be contrasted with a resident population of 476,973 in 2004 (City of Albuquerque). The number of people coming into Albuquerque can explain the difference.

Table 10-2 shows functional population by type of development. Here, functional population is shown as an allocation of the population among various land-use types per 1,000 square feet of floor area. This table expresses the extent to which particular land uses place demands on Albuquerque's public safety providers.

Table 10-3 shows the LOS for fire and emergency protection, which is approximately one station for every 20,000 people on the West Side and 23,000 on the East Side.

Table 10-4 sets out the needed fire and emergency protection improvements required to maintain the existing LOSs to 2025. Improvements to 2015 are the focus of the impact fee program, even though the city uses a longer planning horizon. This time limit is set in the statute.

Table 10-5 shows the total fire and emergency protection improvement costs from Table 10-3 as per capita costs of $237.45 for the East Side and $143.86 on the West Side, and then expresses those costs on the basis of individual land uses.

These calculations are based on the projections of needed improvements to 2025. This period is used in order to avoid attributing more than a proportionate share of costs to earlier development. Earlier development refers to the development between 2005 and 2015.

PARKS

Two park impact fee case studies are presented. The first is for Albuquerque, where the park impact fee design includes seven services and the fees vary from a few hundred dollars to more than $4,000 for a home larger than 2,500 square feet. It is a plan-based approach that does not recoup or involve a "buy-in" element reflecting the value of existing parks with excess capacity.

The second case study is Atlanta, Georgia, prepared by one of the authors (Nelson) as part of a team headed by James Duncan and Associates. It includes a buy-in component that is used to help offset impact fees on affordable housing. The chief purpose of presenting it as a case study here is that

Table 10-2
Functional Population by Type of Development Based
on Population 24 Hours Per Day, Seven Days Per Week

Type of Development	Functional Occupants	Unit of Measurement
Residential (average size: 1,886 sq. ft.)	0.743	Per 1,000 sq. ft.
Single-family detached	1.668	Per dwelling
Single-family attached	1.213	Per dwelling
Multifamily	0.929	Per dwelling
Mobile home	1.370	Per dwelling
All units	1.401	Per dwelling
Industrial	0.300	Per 1,000 sq. ft.
Offices	0.268	Per 1,000 sq. ft.
Retail	1.224	Per 1,000 sq. ft.

Table 10-3
Level of Service for Fire and Emergency Protection

Year	Area Served	24/7 Functional Population	Stations	Persons Served Per Station
2004	East Side	409,724	17	24,101
	West Side	102,477	6	17,080
2015	East Side	426,149	19	22,429
	West Side	131,017	8	16,377
2025	East Side	457,715	20	22,886
	West Side	166,257	8	20,782

Table 10-4
Needed Fire and Emergency Capital Improvements

Year Needed	Projected New Fire Station	Area Served	Station Construction Cost	Apparatus Cost	Total Cost
2008	Station 22	East Side	$3,293,381	$842,242	$4,135,623
2011	Station 23	East Side	$3,186,340	$814,867	$4,001,207
2011	Station 24	West Side	$3,047,389	$779,332	$3,826,721
2015	Station 25	West Side	$2,830,590	$2,517,833	$5,348,423
2022	Station 26	East Side	$2,594,875	$663,607	$3,258,482
Total					$20,570,456

All costs as of March 2004.

Source: Albuquerque Fire Department (January 2004).

Table 10-5
Cost Per Capita and Per Unit Fire and Emergency Protection

Per Capita Costs		
Description	**East Side**	**West Side**
Total needed improvements to 2025	$11,395,311	$9,175,144
New functional population by 2025	47,991	63,779
Cost per functional person	$237.45	$143.86

Unit Costs Per 1,000 Sq. Ft.			
Type of Development	**Occupants Per 1,000 Sq. Ft.**	**East Side**	**West Side**
Residential	0.743	$176.37	$106.86
Industrial	0.300	$71.22	$43.15
Offices	0.268	$63.72	$38.60
Retail	1.224	$290.70	$176.12

Table 10-6
Park and Recreation and Open Space
Trail Level of Service by Service Area

Service Area	Park and Recreation Acres Per 1,000 Residents	Open Space Trail Feet Per 1,000 Residents
Academy/NE	2.60	0.251
Central/University	2.60	0.251
Foothills/SE	2.60	0.251
North Albuquerque	2.60	0.251
North Valley/I-25	2.60	0.251
SW Mesa	2.60	0.251
NW Mesa/Volcano	2.60	0.251
City	2.60	0.251

Source: Authors based on analysis of City of Albuquerque adopted level-of-service standards.

the fee is applied to all land uses and not just residential, which is the normal assessment base.

Albuquerque, New Mexico

Albuquerque provides parks and recreation, open space, and trail opportunities to its residents. Open space and trail opportunities are provided citywide, while parks and recreational facilities are provided in a more localized fashion, serving seven service areas (as illustrated in Table 10-6, which shows the LOS standard adopted for each).

There are two important contributions the Albuquerque program makes to impact fee practice. The first is that the fees are assessed based on the size of the dwelling unit. This is consistent with analysis that shows on average that larger homes have more occupants than smaller ones and thus create more impacts. By calibrating the fee to house size, the fee itself is more closely related to the proportionate-share test and helps reduce potentially adverse effects of impact fees on housing affordability.

The second contribution is that, where there is excess capacity in park facilities, the city has decided not to seek reimbursement through the buy-in approach but rather to encourage infill and redevelopment where that excess capacity exists. This is consistent with the city's Planned Growth Strategies policy, which encourages development and redevelopment in "full-served" areas (i.e., areas with excess facility capacity). Thus, impact fees vary from a few hundred dollars where adequate local park facilities exist (but also considering citywide fees for open spaces and trails) to more than $4,000 for a 2,500-square-foot home where they do not. (Compare the service area map,

Figure 10-6
Service Areas for Parks and Recreation Impact Fees, City of Albuquerque, New Mexico

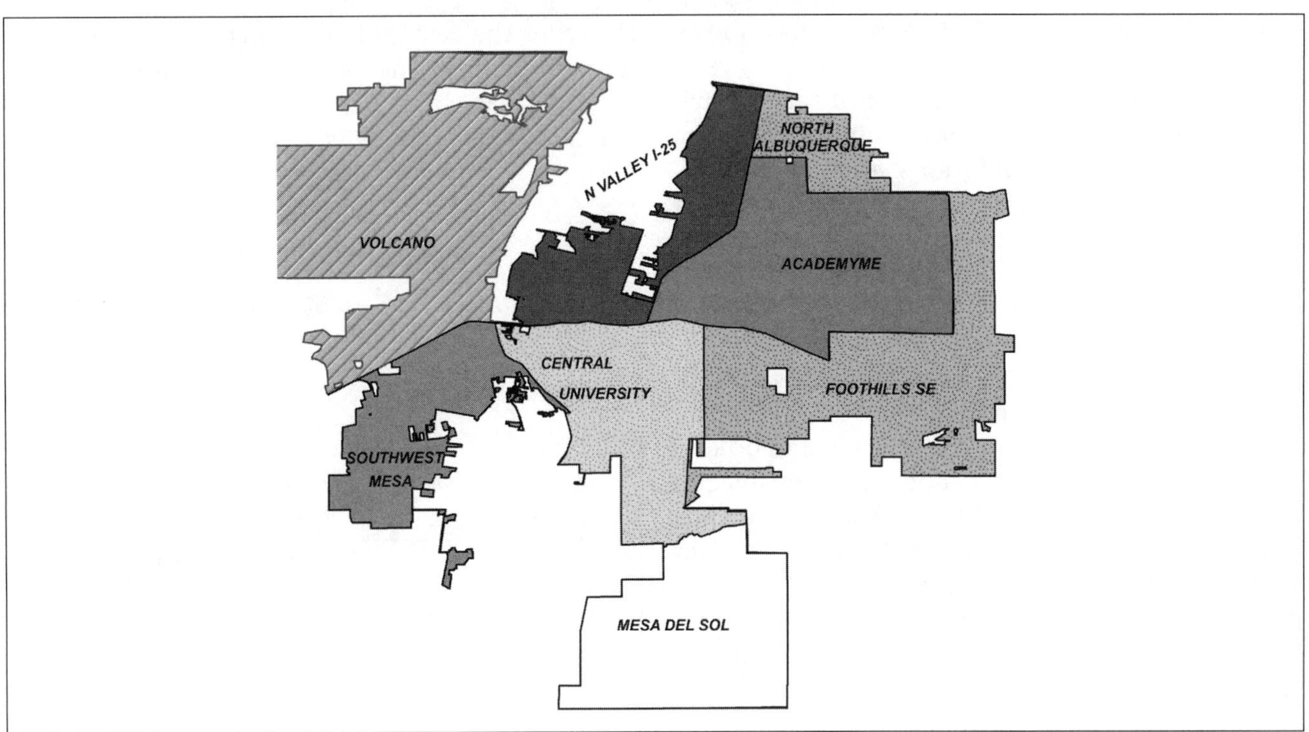

Table 10-7
Population and Housing 2004 to 2025 by Cash in Lieu and Service Area Within Current City Limits

Cash in Lieu and Park Service Area	Population			Housing Units		
	2004	2011	2025	2004	2011	2025
Academy/NE	**130,078**	**131,391**	**130,899**	**62,991**	**64,807**	**66,498**
Academy	61,071	61,219	60,715	30,347	30,890	31,470
Far NE Heights	34,749	34,905	34,088	15,817	16,105	16,129
Near NE Heights	34,258	35,267	36,096	16,827	17,812	18,899
Central/University	**52,985**	**53,590**	**56,604**	**25,129**	**26,098**	**28,966**
Central City	25,827	26,016	27,282	11,813	12,478	13,562
Tijeras	1,661	1,621	1,583	572	567	568
University	25,497	25,953	27,739	12,744	13,053	14,836
Foothills/SE	**120,097**	**121,707**	**123,512**	**56,609**	**58,326**	**60,652**
Foothills	21,431	22,220	23,645	9,487	9,898	10,625
East Central	71,820	72,668	73,408	35,190	36,293	37,759
Far East Heights	26,846	26,819	26,459	11,932	12,135	12,268
North Albuquerque	**22,731**	**25,778**	**30,449**	**8,496**	**9,956**	**12,702**
N Valley/I-25	**29,373**	**32,011**	**35,799**	**12,257**	**13,585**	**16,104**
North Valley	23,697	24,098	26,076	9,997	10,332	11,580
Panamerican	5,676	7,913	9,723	2,260	3,253	4,524
SW Mesa	**46,845**	**59,578**	**74,264**	**16,759**	**22,214**	**30,150**
NW Mesa/Volcano	**74,852**	**96,342**	**117,329**	**30,442**	**40,154**	**50,279**
NW Mesa	69,221	85,987	99,335	28,213	36,062	43,045
Volcano	5,631	10,356	17,994	2,229	4,092	7,234
Total in service areas	**476,961**	**520,398**	**577,622**	**212,683**	**235,140**	**268,784**

Bold rows are service areas with cash in lieu collection areas summing to them.

Figure 10-6, with the impact fee schedule, Tables 10-7 and 10-8.)

Analysis of demand for parks and recreational facilities begins with "land-use assumptions" (the term for land-use assumptions applied in New Mexico and several other states pursuant to impact fee enabling legislation). Because parks and recreation staff, combined with local planners and consultants, determined that parks and recreational facility impact fees should be based on seven service areas (see Figure 10-6), the land-use assumptions for each are shown on Table 10-7. This table sets out the population growth to be accommodated by parks, trails, open spaces, and recreational facilities to the year 2025. The City of Albuquerque has been employing a set of designated areas for "cash in lieu" of park dedication program for several years. As there are 16 cash in lieu collection areas, these existing areas do not lend themselves to becoming efficient neighborhood and community park service areas.

However, the cash in lieu areas can be aggregated into efficient neighborhood and community park service areas. Table 10-7 shows the 2004 population and housing units with the projected 2011 and

Table 10-8
Dwelling Unit Occupancies

Service Area	2004	2011	2025
Academy/NE	2.065	2.027	1.968
Central/University	2.109	2.053	1.954
Foothills/SE	2.122	2.087	2.036
North Albuquerque	2.675	2.589	2.397
North Valley/I-25	2.396	2.356	2.223
SW Mesa	2.795	2.682	2.463
NW Mesa/Volcano	2.459	2.399	2.334
City	2.243	2.213	2.149

Based on analysis of City of Albuquerque land-use projections.

Table 10-9
Existing Level of Service, 2004

Service Area	Total Acres	Developed Acres	Population	Developed Acres Per 1,000 People
Local Parks (Neighborhood and Community				
Academy/NE	317.56	291.07	130,078	2.238
Central/University	228.67	215.93	52,985	4.075
Foothills/SE	366.97	319.36	120,097	2.659
North Albuquerque	110.94	51.94	22,731	2.285
North Valley/I-25	68.91	64.95	29,373	2.211
SW Mesa	193.60	112.07	46,845	2.392
NW Mesa/Volcano	326.54	217.52	74,852	2.906
Total city parks	1,613.18	1,272.84	476,961	2.669
Trails	119.79	119.79	476,961	0.251
Open space	28,282	28,282	476,961	59.295

Source: Albuquerque Department of Parks & Recreation (2004).

2025 dwelling units by cash in lieu and park service area.

One area of the city that is not presently within a park service area is Mesa del Sol. This area is projected to receive little development to 2010. After 2010, Mesa del Sol is projected to receive substantial development. As development pressures in Mesa del Sol increase, it would be appropriate to add it as a separate park service area.

New Mexico's Development Fees Act requires that the time horizon for impact fee programs be no more than 10 years. Albuquerque's planning program extends beyond this time horizon and the LOSs are directed toward the 2025 time horizon. The proposed park, recreation, trail, and open space CIP will be set out for the 2011 time horizon.

The number of dwelling units in Albuquerque is growing more rapidly than new residents. The result is that the number of persons per new dwelling unit is quite low. Table 10-8 shows these data for Albuquerque. It is necessary for any impact fee to be consistent with the city's land-use assumptions. Since park, recreation, trail, and open space impact fees will be charged for new residential construction, it follows that measuring the occupancy per new residential unit is relevant in assessing the demand for areas and facilities.

Table 10-9 shows the existing LOS for the city as a whole and for the service areas. Trails and open spaces serve the entire City of Albuquerque without regard to service area, while neighborhood and community parks serve their respective service

areas. Therefore, the same LOS for trails and open spaces will be applied to all local park service areas of the city. In Table 10-9, the LOS is calculated using developed acres. This would make the undeveloped park acres available for future development that would serve future populations.

Table 10-10 shows the existing provision of recreational facilities. The ratios listed in it are not

Table 10-10
Existing Provision of Recreational Facilities, 2004

Recreational Facilities	Description	Total Number	Number Per 10,000 People
Baseball fields	Lit	3	0.629
	Youth	45	9.434
Swimming pools	Indoor	5	1.048
	Outdoor	8	1.677
Basketball	Full	59	12.370
	Half	67	14.047
Play areas		165	34.593
Tennis courts	Lit	25	5.241
	Unlit	108	22.643
Skate facility		1	0.210
Softball fields	Lit	18	3.774
	Unlit	14	2.935
Recreation fields		114	23.901

Source: City of Albuquerque (January 2004).

Table 10-11
Local Park Need and Availability

Park Service Area	2004 Population	LOS: Acres Per 1,000 People	2004 Developed Acres Needed at 2.60 LOS	2004 Developed Acres Available	2004 Developed Acres Deficient	2004 Developed Acres Surplus
Academy/NE	130,078	2.60	338.20	291.07	47.13	0.00
Central/ University	52,985	2.60	137.76	215.93	0.00	78.17
Foothills/SE	120,097	2.60	312.25	319.36	0.00	7.11
North Albuquerque	22,731	2.60	59.10	51.94	7.16	0.00
North Valley/I-25	29,373	2.60	76.37	64.95	11.42	0.00
SW Mesa	46,845	2.60	121.80	112.07	9.73	0.00
NW Mesa/ Volcano	74,852	2.60	194.62	217.52	0.00	22.90
Total	476,961	2.60	1,240.10	1,272.84	75.44	108.18

Park Service Area	2025 Population	2025 Needed Developed Acres at 2.60 LOS	2025 Needed Additional Developed Acres at 2.60 LOS	Undeveloped Acres Available in Inventory	Acres to Be Acquired	Net Acres to Be Developed
Academy/NE	130,899	340.34	2.13	26.49	0.00	2.13
Central/ University	56,604	147.17	0.00	12.74	0.00	0.00
Foothills/SE	123,512	321.13	8.88	47.61	0.00	1.77
North Albuquerque	30,449	79.17	20.07	59.00	0.00	20.07
North Valley/I-25	35,799	93.08	16.71	3.95	12.76	16.71
SW Mesa	74,264	193.09	71.29	81.53	0.00	71.29
NW Mesa/ Volcano	117,329	305.06	110.44	109.02	0.00	87.54
Total	568,856	1,479.04	229.52	340.34	12.76	199.51

LOS = level of service

considered to be LOSs because the recreational needs of a community like Albuquerque will change over time. While the mix of individual facilities will change, the need for facilities themselves will not change. These data are used to establish a recreational facility cost guideline, which will be used in the calculation of fiscal impact. Virtually all recreational facilities are provided at and in conjunction with local parks. Therefore, the cost of recreational facilities is expressed as a cost per local park acre.

Table 10-11 summarizes Albuquerque's need for local parks at present and by 2025. This table expresses need at a citywide LOS of 2.60 acres per 1,000 people. The city needs to add 229.52 acres of local parks in order to serve the future community at 2.60 acres per 1,000 people. Due to the high inventory of parkland, only 14.18 acres of land will have to be acquired. In fact, there is a surplus of land in most service areas. Note that, if the number of existing acres is added to the calculated deficiency, the resulting sum exceeds the citywide need. This occurs because deficiencies are determined on an individual service-area basis.

Table 10-12
Cash in Lieu Balances and Land Acquisition Cost, 2004

Cash In Lieu and Park Service Area	Cash in Lieu Balance			Land Cost Per Acre Total
	Land Acquisition	**Development**	**Total**	
Academy/NE	**$23,121**	**$89,797**	**$112,918**	**$125,000**
Academy	$1,521	$5,322	$6,843	$125,000
Far Northeast Heights	$19,757	$13,560	$33,317	$125,000
Near NE Heights	$1,843	$70,915	$72,758	$125,000
Central/University	**$17,133**	**$11,097**	**$28,230**	**$110,000**
Central City	$7,488	$10,944	$18,432	$100,000
Tijeras	$0	$0	$0	$125,000
University	$9,645	$153	$9,798	$105,000
Foothills/SE	**$152,225**	**$116,288**	**$268,513**	**$105,000**
Foothills	$89,377	$36,468	$125,845	$105,000
East Central	$61,112	$55,931	$117,043	$105,000
Far East Heights	$1,736	$23,889	$25,625	$105,000
North Albuquerque	**$267,654**	**$5,042**	**$272,696**	**$125,000**
North Valley/I-25	**$129,775**	**$359,687**	**$489,462**	**$122,500**
North Valley	$126,791	$83,404	$210,195	$120,000
Panamerican Corridor	$2,984	$276,283	$279,267	$125,000
SW Mesa	**$688,099**	**$17,883**	**$705,982**	**$72,000**
NW Mesa/Volcano	**$833,532**	**$3,208**	**$836,740**	**$120,000**
Northwest Mesa	$739,963	$279	$740,242	$120,000
Volcano NW	$93,569	$2,929	$96,498	$120,000
Totals	**$2,111,539**	**$603,002**	**$2,714,541**	

The city has been collecting cash in lieu of parkland dedications. These collections have been maintained in cash in lieu area accounts. Table 10-12 shows the existing balances by cash in lieu and local park service areas. These funds are available to provide parks within the designated local park service area. They will first be used to reduce any existing deficiency. Any remaining balances will be applied to reduce assignable costs and presumably any impact fees. Table 10-12 also shows the anticipated cost of acquiring parkland by service area.

Table 10-13 sets out per capita costs to provide parks in Albuquerque. These costs will be applied in order to calculate the cost of accommodating new development with parks and recreation areas.

Albuquerque has been employing a variety of funding sources to acquire and develop parks. Most significant have been grants and GO bonds. Table 10-14 summarizes historic and anticipated sources of capital funding by type of park. The significant anticipated shift is away from the use of GO bond funding of parks, trails, and open space. The anticipated sources of funding will be applied and appropriate credits calculated that will reduce assignable costs.

Table 10-15 applies the data contained in all of the tables to calculate the need for parks, recreation, trails, and open space, and the cost of providing those facilities by service area. Table 10-16 adds adjustments to reflect the cash in lieu balances and also calculates deficiencies by service area. Table 10-17 summarizes the conclusions from Table 10-15 together with the CIP for park development (not shown). The CIP includes nonimpact fee revenue to remedy deficiencies in the service areas.

These data show net park, trail, and open space costs for per-dwelling-unit and per-square-foot-of-floor-area basis by service area. Note that the recommended open space portion of the fee has been reduced to about 66 percent of attributable cost because projected open space fee receipts would generate more revenue than the expected cost of

Table 10-13
Gross Costs Per Capita

Local Parks	Costs
Academy/NE	$1,042.62
Central/University	$0
Foothills/SE	$207.49
North Albuquerque	$1,042.62
North Valley/I-25	$1,285.80
SW Mesa	$1,042.62
NW Mesa/Volcano	$830.45
Trails	
Existing acres	119.79
Population served	476,961
Acres per 1,000	0.251
Cost Per Acre	
Acquisition	$43,560
Development	$43,560
Cost per capita	$21.88
Open Spaces	
Existing acres	28,282.00
Population served	476,961
Acres per 1,000	59.295
Cost Per Acre	
Acquisition	$12,200
Development	included
Cost per capita	$723.40

Table 10-14
Historic and Anticipated Funding

Revenue Source	Historic	Anticipated
Local Parks		
Grants	6.75%	6.8%
GO bonds	82.31%	20.0%
Trails		
Grants	Unknown	6.8%
GO bonds	Unknown	20.0%
Open Space		
Grants	Unknown	6.8%
GO bonds	33.0%	20.0%

GO = general obligation

proposed improvements. The City of Albuquerque may adopt park, recreation, trail, and open space impact fees that do not exceed the amounts shown in Table 10-17 or in Table 10-18, which expresses the amounts by unit size ranges. However, assessment based on actual size in square feet is recommended. Of course, the council is free to adopt fees that are lower than these amounts. This presentation presumes that the implementing ordinance will direct any impact fees collected to the appropriate service area trust fund, and provide appropriate direction and limitation on the uses of impact fees collected.

Atlanta, Georgia

In 1993, the City of Atlanta, Georgia, became the first major U.S. jurisdiction to use the functional population approach to design its parks and recreation impact fees. It reasoned:

> It is people who create the demand for recreation facilities, not houses or businesses. In a sense, businesses are simply people in another facet of their daily lives. The parks and recreation impact fee will be based on the number of "full-time equivalent" people present in the city, a subarea of the city, or at the site of a land use. This "full-time equivalent" population is represented by the concept of "functional population."[3]

The city also determined that there were additional reasons for choosing the functional population basis. Its consultants found that more than 90 percent of the reservations made for ballfields of all types citywide were made by business or related nonresidential land uses. About 60 percent of the reservations for major picnic facilities were made by business or related nonresidential land uses. While it is normally assumed that only residents use parks, the reservation data clearly show the extent to which nonresidential development uses local parks. The functional population approach was deemed to provide improved attribution of benefits and burdens for providing parks and recreational facilities, and thus became the basis for assessing parks and recreational facility impact fees.

Atlanta went further to pioneer the use of recoupment-based impact fees to reduce the impact fees assessed on affordable housing. What follows is the design of the park impact fee program itself. Notice that the impact fee for residential land uses varies by type of unit but not size. Professional impact fee practice has since evolved to the point where impact fees are assessed based on the size of the residential dwelling unit, often in square feet of heated and cooled living area. Table 10-19 shows the park and recreational facility impact fee schedule for all new development in Atlanta's Northside park

Table 10-15
Park, Recreation, Trail, and Open Space Impact Costs by Service Areas

Service Area	Academy/NE	Central/ University	Foothills/SE	North Albuquerque	North Valley/I-25	SW Mesa	NW Mesa/ Volcano
Local Parks (Neighborhood and Community)							
Level of service per 1,000 people	2.600	2.600	2.600	2.600	2.600	2.600	2.600
Needed additional acres	2.13	0.00	8.88	20.07	16.71	71.29	110.44
Acres available in inventory	26.49	12.74	47.61	59.00	3.95	81.53	109.02
Acres to be acquired	0.00	0.00	0.00	0.00	12.76	0.00	0.00
Acquisition cost per acre	$125,000	$110,000	$105,000	$125,000	$122,500	$72,000	$120,000
Acquisition cost	$0	$0	$0	$0	$1,562,708	$0	0.00
Acres to be developed	2.13	0.00	8.88	20.07	16.71	71.29	110.44
Existing surplus	0.00	78.17	7.11	0.00	0.00	0.00	22.90
Net acres to be developed	2.13	0.00	1.77	20.07	16.71	71.29	87.54
Development cost per acre	$175,000	$175,000	$175,000	$175,000	$175,000	$175,000	$175,000
Development cost	$373,555	$0	$309,225	$3,511,690	$2,923,830	$12,475,645	$15,319,465
Facilities cost per acre	$226,007	$226,007	$226,007	$226,007	$226,007	$226,007	$226,007
Facilities cost	$482,434	$0	$399,354	$4,535,228	$3,776,027	$16,111,871	$19,784,567
Total cost local parks	$855,989	$0	$708,579	$8,046,918	$8,262,565	$28,587,516	$35,274,864
Cost per capita	$1,042.62	$0	$207.49	$1,042.62	$1,285.80	$1,042.62	$830.45
Less grants	($70.41)	$0	($14.01)	($70.41)	($86.84)	($70.41)	($56.08)
Less bond credit	($208.52)	$0	($41.50)	($208.52)	($257.16)	($208.52)	($166.09)
Net local park cost	**$763.69**	**$0**	**$151.98**	**$763.69**	**$941.80**	**$763.69**	**$608.28**
Trails							
Cost per capita	$21.88	$21.88	$21.88	$21.88	$21.88	$21.88	$21.88
Less grants	($1.48)	($1.48)	($1.48)	($1.48)	($1.48)	($1.48)	($1.48)
Less bond credit	($4.38)	($4.38)	($4.38)	($4.38)	($4.38)	($4.38)	($4.38)
Net trails cost	**$16.03**	**$16.03**	**$16.03**	**$16.03**	**$16.03**	**$16.03**	**$16.03**

Table 10-16
Park, Recreation, Trail, and Open Space Credits and Deficiencies by Service Area

Service Area	Academy/NE	Central/ University	Foothills/SE	North Albuquerque	North Valley/I-25	SW Mesa	NW Mesa/ Volcano
Open Space							
Cost per capita	$723.40	$723.40	$723.40	$723.40	$723.40	$723.40	$723.40
Less grants	($48.85)	($48.85)	($48.85)	($48.85)	($48.85)	($48.85)	($48.85)
Less bond credit	($144.68)	($144.68)	($144.68)	($144.68)	($144.68)	($144.68)	($144.68)
Net open space cost	*$529.87*	*$529.87*	*$529.87*	*$529.87*	*$529.87*	*$529.87*	*$529.87*
Net costs per capita	**$1,309.59**	**$545.89**	**$697.88**	**$1,309.59**	**$1,487.69**	**$1,309.58**	**$1,154.17**
Unit occupancy	**2.027**	**2.053**	**2.087**	**2.589**	**2.356**	**2.682**	**2.399**
Net costs per unit	**$2,654.52**	**$1,120.72**	**$1,456.47**	**$3,390.50**	**$3,505.01**	**$3,512.29**	**$2,768.86**
Unallocated cash in lieu balance	**$0**	**$28,230**	**$268,513**	**$0**	**$0**	**$0**	**$836,740**
New units 2004–2011	**1,816**	**969**	**1,717**	**1,460**	**1,328**	**5,455**	**9,712**
Unallocated cash in lieu balance per new unit after 2004	**($0.00)**	**($29.14)**	**($156.39)**	**($0.00)**	**($0.00)**	**($0.00)**	**($86.15)**
Final cost per unit	**$2,654.52**	**$1,091.59**	**$1,300.08**	**$3,390.50**	**$3,505.01**	**$3,512.29**	**$2,682.71**
Deficiencies in 2004							
Acres deficient Cost per acre	47.13	0.00	0.00	7.16	11.42	9.73	0.00
Acquisition	$125,000	$110,000	$105,000	$125,000	$122,500	$72,000	$120,000
Development	$175,000	$175,000	$175,000	$175,000	$175,000	$175,000	$175,000
Facilities	$226,007	$226,007	$226,007	$226,007	$226,007	$226,007	$226,007
Existing deficiency	$24,792,950	$0	$0	$3,766,207	$5,975,879	$4,602,354	$0
Cash in lieu balance	$112,918	$28,230	$268,513	$272,696	$489,462	$740,242	$836,740
Net deficiency	$24,680,032	$0	$0	$3,493,511	$5,486,417	$3,862,112	$0
Total city deficiencies	**$37,522,072**						

Table 10-17
Park, Trail, and Open Space Impact Fees Per Dwelling Unit and Per Square Foot of Floor Area

Service Area	Local Parks	Trails	Open Spaces (64% of Attributable Cost)	Total	Per Sq. Ft. (Based on a 1,886 Sq. Ft. House)
Academy/NE	$1,547.99	$32.49	$716.85	$2,297.33	$1.22
Central/University	$0.00	$32.05	$707.18	$739.22	$0.39
Foothills/SE	$283.13	$29.86	$658.82	$971.81	$0.52
North Albuquerque	$1,977.18	$41.49	$915.61	$2,934.28	$1.55
North Valley/I-25	$2,218.88	$37.76	$833.21	$3,089.85	$1.63
SW Mesa	$2,048.21	$42.98	$948.50	$3,039.69	$1.61
NW Mesa/Volcano	$1,413.86	$37.25	$822.01	$2,273.12	$1.21

Table 10-18
Impact Fee Per Dwelling by Size of Dwelling Example

Service Area	Under 1,500 Sq. Ft. (1,200 Used)	1,500-2,500 Sq. Ft. (2,000 used)	Over 2,500 Sq. Ft. (3,000 Used)
Academy/NE	$1,461.77	$2,436.28	$3,654.41
Central/University	$466.88	$778.13	$1,167.19
Foothills/SE	$620.43	$1,034.04	$1,551.07
North Albuquerque	$1,861.65	$3,102.74	$4,654.12
North Valley/I-25	$1,961.08	$3,268.47	$4,902.71
SW Mesa	$1,930.02	$3,216.70	$4,825.05
NW Mesa/Volcano	$1,450.08	$2,416.80	$3,625.20

Table 10-19
Parks and Recreation Impact Fee Schedule, Northside Service Area

Land Use	Unit	Functional Population Per Unit	Acres Per 1,000	Acres Per Unit	Cost Per Acre	Net Cost Per Unit	Impact Fee
Residential and Institutional							
Single family	Dwelling	1.60	5.75	0.0092	$89,047	$819	$491
Multifamily	Dwelling	1.11	5.75	0.0064	$89,047	$570	$342
Hotel/motel	Room	0.72	5.75	0.0041	$89,047	$365	$219
Elementary school	1,000 sq. ft.	1.71	5.75	0.0098	$89,047	$873	$524
High school	1,000 sq. ft.	1.74	5.75	0.0100	$89,047	$890	$534
Church	1,000 sq. ft.	0.74	5.75	0.0043	$89,047	$383	$230
Hospital	1,000 sq. ft.	1.86	5.75	0.0107	$89,047	$953	$572
Nursing home	1,000 sq. ft.	1.36	5.75	0.0078	$89,047	$695	$417
Office							
< 50,000 sq. ft.	1,000 sq. ft.	1.04	5.75	0.0060	$89,047	$534	$320
< 100,000 sq. ft.	1,000 sq. ft.	0.99	5.75	0.0057	$89,047	$508	$305
< 200,000 sq. ft.	1,000 sq. ft.	0.94	5.75	0.0054	$89,047	$481	$289
< 500,000 sq. ft.	1,000 sq. ft.	0.90	5.75	0.0052	$89,047	$463	$278
500,000 sq. ft.+	1,000 sq. ft.	0.87	5.75	0.0050	$89,047	$445	$267

Table 10-19
Parks and Recreation Impact Fee Schedule, Northside Service Area (*continued*)

Land Use	Unit	Functional Population Per Unit	Acres Per 1,000	Acres Per Unit	Cost Per Acre	Net Cost Per Unit	Impact Fee
Commercial							
< 100,000 sq. ft.	1,000 sq. ft.	2.78	5.75	0.0160	$89,047	$1,425	$855
< 200,000 sq. ft.	1,000 sq. ft.	2.28	5.75	0.0131	$89,047	$1,167	$700
< 300,000 sq. ft.	1,000 sq. ft.	2.08	5.75	0.0120	$89,047	$1,069	$641
< 400,000 sq. ft.	1,000 sq. ft.	1.90	5.75	0.0109	$89,047	$971	$583
< 500,000 sq. ft.	1,000 sq. ft.	1.81	5.75	0.0104	$89,047	$926	$556
< 600,000 sq. ft.	1,000 sq. ft.	1.73	5.75	0.0099	$89,047	$882	$529
< 1,000,000 sq. ft.	1,000 sq. ft.	1.57	5.75	0.0090	$89,047	$801	$481
1,000,000 sq. ft.+	1,000 sq. ft.	1.45	5.75	0.0083	$89,047	$739	$443
Industrial							
Industry	1,000 sq. ft.	0.66	5.75	0.0038	$89,047	$338	$203
Warehouse	1,000 sq. ft.	0.37	5.75	0.0021	$89,047	$187	$112

Source: James Duncan and Associates, Arthur C. Nelson, et al. (1993).

Table 10-20
Land-Use Assumptions, Canton, Georgia

Land-Use Assumption Category	1996	2000	2002	2015	Build Out
Population	5,167	7,709	9,711	43,563	58,523
Households	1,811	2,702	3,404	15,269	20,512
Persons per	2.853	2.853	2.853	2.853	2.853
Dwelling units	1,930	2,879	3,627	16,269	21,856
Occupied	1,811	2,702	3,404	15,269	20,512
Residential acres	1,892.37	1,919.33	2,159.58	4,648.29	5,464.00
Commercial acres	334.79	499.50	560.86	1,191.00	1,400.00
Office/professional acres	36.67	54.71	83.43	1,295.63	1,523.00
Industrial acres	317.25	473.33	413.25	171.00	171.00
Public and quasi-public	1,056.99	1,056.99	987.35	634.00	634.00
Agriculture acres	28.70	—	—	—	—
Vacant acres	5,525.23	5,188.14	4,987.54	1,252.08	—
Total acres	9,192.00	9,192.00	9,192.00	9,192.00	9,192.00
Dwelling units per acre	1.02	1.50	1.68	3.50	4.00
Nonresidential floor area per acre					8,712
Living area per residential unit					1,575

service area (one of three park service areas in the city).

Canton, Georgia

Canton, Georgia, illustrates the logical progression of broadening the base of impact fees conventionally charged only on residential development. Working with the Metropolitan Atlanta Home Builder Association and City of Canton officials, two of the authors (Nicholas and Juergensmeyer) devised a park facility impact fee that is paid by all new development. The fee is also assessed on the size of the project in square feet. Because of its small size, and the fact that all residents, workers, and visitors have reasonable access to all parks and recreational facilities throughout the city, there is one service area for those facilities. A summary of how the fee was calculated follows.

Table 10-20 sets out the land-use assumptions for the City of Canton. These developmental parameters were employed in developing the park, recreation, and open space CIP, and the park, recreation, and open space development impact fees.

Table 10-21 contains the short-term CIP for parks, recreation, and open spaces. These parks, recreation, and open space improvements, planned to be made during 2002–2006, will serve the anticipated growth of Canton to 2015.

The improvement program contained in Table 10-21 involves an increase in the LOS to the existing residents of Canton. Simple fairness and the law hold against shifting the cost for increasing the LOS for existing residents to new development in the form of impact fees. Therefore, it is necessary to identify the existing deficiency and to make sure that the cost of remedying that deficiency is not charged to new development.

The projected revenues to fund the parks, recreation, and open space improvement program are shown in Table 10-22.

An LOS analysis is contained in Table 10-23. The City of Canton has a park, recreation, and open space LOS of 5.280 acres per 1,000 residents. At this LOS, there is an existing deficit of 46.27 acres. The estimated cost of rectifying this deficiency is $7,881,998. The estimated cost of providing parks, recreation, and open spaces to new development is $30,443,600. It is anticipated that a GO bond issue will pay the preponderance of both components. If it further anticipated that impact fees will be used to pay debt service on the bonds.

The development to be served by these improvements is the new development occurring between 2002 and 2015 (as shown in Table 10-24).

It was anticipated that a GO bond issue will cover a substantial portion of the cost of the park,

Table 10-21
Park, Recreation, and Open Space Improvement Program, City of Canton, 2002–2006

Improvement	2002	2003	2004	2005	2006	Total
Community Center Land	$1,000,000					$1,000,000
Community Center Building	$4,500,000	$4,500,000				$9,000,000
Etowah Regional Greenway:						
Land Acquisition	$750,000					
Phase IA I-575 to Mill # 2		$6,690,432				
Phase II Multi-Use			$2,281,182			
Phase III Mill # 2 to Waleska St			$4,643,002			
Phase IV Waleska St to Marietta Hwy				$2,437,441		
Phase V Waleska St to Harmon Field					$5,192,863	
Other & Contingency					$5,530,678	$26,775,598
Brown Park	$100,000					$100,000
Crissler Park	$250,000					$250,000

Table 10-21
Park, Recreation, and Open Space Improvement Program, City of Canton, 2002–2006 (*continued*)

Improvement	2002	2003	2004	2005	2006	Total
Boling Park	$150,000	$150,000	$150,000			$450,000
Total	$6,750,000	$11,340,432	$7,074,184	$2,437,441	$10,723,541	$38,325,598
Additional acres						225.00
Cost per acre						$170,336

Source: City of Canton (January 2002) and Etowah River Greenway Master Plan, Section 3 (May 18, 2000).

Table 10-22
Park, Recreation, and Open Space, Capital Revenues, City of Canton, 2002–2006

Total improvement cost	$38,325,598
Sources of revenue	
General fund	900,000
Community development block grant	100,000
Transportation enhancement funds	1,200,000
Canton building authority	1,093,750
General obligation bond issue	$35,031,848

Table 10-23
Level of Service for City of Canton

	Acres	
Park	**Existing**	**Future**
Brown	1.000	1.000
Scout	0.667	0.667
Central	0.333	0.333
Crisler	0.500	0.500
Canton Theatre	0.500	0.500
Etowah Greenway	2.000	150.000
Boling	—	77.000
Total	5.000	230.000
Population	9,711	43,563
Acres per 1,000	0.515	5.280
Deficiency		
2002 acres at 5.280	51.27	
2002 actual acres	5.00	
Deficiency	46.27	
Deficiency as % of new	20.57%	
Cost of deficiency	$7,881,998	
Cost of growth	$30,443,600	

Table 10-24
Development in Canton, 2002 and 2015

Development	Existing	New
Population	9,711	33,852
Households	3,404	11,865
Dwelling units	3,627	12,642
Nonresidential acres	1,803	1,489
Nonresidential floor area	15,704,537	12,972,159

Source: Canton Land Use Assumptions (2002).

Table 10-25
Projected Tax Base, City of Canton, 1996–2025

Year	Net Taxable Values
1996	$131,910,125
1997	144,163,332
1998	183,333,205
1999	209,230,721
2000	244,241,949
2001	281,936,827
2002	334,305,573
2003	392,178,440
2004	459,209,544
2005	536,773,714
2006	626,445,126
2007	730,025,498
2008	849,576,213
2009	987,454,887

Table 10-25
Projected Tax Base, City of Canton, 1996–2025 (continued)

Year	Net Taxable Values
2010	1,146,357,001
2011	1,329,363,293
2012	1,539,993,681
2013	1,782,268,614
2014	2,060,778,872
2015	2,380,764,941
2016	2,448,545,455
2017	2,516,325,969
2018	2,584,106,483
2019	2,651,886,997
2020	2,719,667,511
2021	2,787,448,025
2022	2,855,228,539

Table 10-26
Bond Issue Debt Service, City of Canton, 2002–2021

Year	Proceeds	Principal Payment	Interest Payment	From Impact Fees	From Taxes	Balance	Payment Per Capita
2002*	3,343,750			171,850		0	
2003	11,792,179			403,239	0	12,971,397	$0.00
2004		726,398	583,713	452,556	454,316	12,971,397	$37.14
2005	8,588,476	368,769	976,154	507,675	837,249	21,692,322	$60.97
2006		533,089	959,560	569,563	923,086	21,323,553	$59.90
2007	6,298,869	554,384	1,247,365	639,187	1,162,562	27,719,219	$67.21
2008		814,945	1,222,418	717,514	1,319,849	27,164,835	$67.98
2009	6,708,633	843,235	1,517,822	805,511	1,555,546	33,729,386	$71.39
2010		1,216,788	1,479,877	904,145	1,792,519	32,886,151	$73.29
2011		1,583,468	1,425,121	1,014,383	1,994,207	31,669,363	$72.65
2012		1,805,154	1,353,865	1,139,126	2,019,893	30,085,895	$65.56
2013		2,262,459	1,272,633	1,278,374	2,256,719	28,280,742	$65.26
2014		3,122,194	1,170,823	1,434,061	2,858,956	26,018,282	$73.66
2015		3,205,452	1,030,324	1,610,055	2,625,721	22,896,088	$60.27
2016		2,953,595	886,079	0	3,839,674	19,690,636	$88.14
2017		3,180,038	753,167	0	3,933,205	16,737,041	$90.29
2018		3,389,251	610,065	0	3,999,316	13,557,003	$91.81
2019		3,558,713	457,549	0	4,016,262	10,167,752	$92.19
2020		3,304,519	297,407	0	3,601,926	6,609,039	$82.68
2021		3,304,519	148,703	0	3,453,223	3,304,519	$79.27
Totals	33,388,156	36,726,972	17,392,645	11,475,389	42,644,228	399,474,618	$1,299.66
Present value							$737.84

* Not from bond issue

Table 10-27
Parks Bond Parameters

Component	Figure
Bond proceeds	$35,031,848
Issuance cost	10%
Prepaid interest	$1,000,000
Total value	$39,635,032
Interest rate	4.50%
Term in years	20
Issued	2003
Real interest rate	1.00%
Discount rate	5.50%

recreation, and open space improvement program. While the city will be pledging full faith and credit on this bond issue, it is anticipated that a portion of the bond issue will be paid in part by impact fees. Table 10-25 shows the projected taxable value of Canton over the life of this assumed bond issue. These taxable values were estimated using a per capita time trend regression equation[4] for 1996 to 2001, and then projecting that per capita trend to 2025. The per capita value was then multiplied by the projected population to arrive at estimated taxable values.

Table 10-26 shows the estimated bond debt service payments used in these calculations.

These calculations are for an assumed bond issue. It is likely that a series of bonds will be used rather than a single issue. Such a series would minimize city cost and provide revenue when needed. This calculation uses a portion of the bond proceeds to pay interest in the early years in order to keep the debt service rate fewer than two mills. In

fact, the average millage to service this estimated debt is $1.3 per $1,000 of value.

Table 10-27 shows the parameters used in structuring the anticipated bond.

Prevailing municipal interest rates as of Jan. 25, 2002, were incorporated. Future debt service payments were discounted back to 2002 using the 4.5 percent cost of money plus a 1 percent real interest rate.

The debt service cost per capita for 2002 residents is $1,299.66, and the present value of that amount, discounted at 5.5 percent, is $737.84. This means that each 2002 resident of Canton, either existing or new, will pay $1,299.66 toward the cost of park improvements in the form of bond debt service payments. It would follow that the 9,711 existing residents would pay (present value) $737.84 each toward the cost of parks through bond debt service payments. Existing residents also pay the $3,293,750 in currently available funds, $339.16 per capita. Thus, existing residents will pay an estimated $1,077 toward Canton park improvements.

Table 10-28
Growth Costs

Capital Costs	New	Existing
Improvements	$30,443,600	$7,881,998
Adjustments	$0	$0
Net cost	$30,443,600	$7,881,998
Finance costs	$0	$0
Total growth cost	$42,054,887	$12,064,730
New population	33,852	9,711
Cost per capita	$1,242.33	$1,242.33
Nonbond credit per capita		$339.16
Bond credit per capita	$737.84	$737.84
Net cost per capita	$504.49	$165.33

Table 10-28
Growth Costs (*continued*)

Cost Assignment	New	Existing
Residential	85.71%	85.71%
Nonresidential	14.29%	14.29%
Residential cost assignment	$17,077,952	$1,605,583
Residential cost per capita	$432.42	$141.71
Persons per household	2.853	2.853
Cost per dwelling	$1,233.74	$404.31
Impact fee per dwelling unit	$829.42	
Impact fee per residential foot	$0.527	
Nonresidential cost assignment	$2,439,707	$229,369
Cost per foot	$0.188	$0.015
Impact fee per nonresidential foot	$0.173	

Table 10-28 calculates the gross and net costs of providing park, recreation, and open spaces to new developments in Canton on a per capita basis. The net cost is net of a credit for payments on the bond issue.

Table 10-28 divides net costs between existing and new developments and between residential and nonresidential developments. Canton park usage data show that nonresidential (i.e., business) usage of Canton parks is 14 percent. It would follow that net park cost would be divided on the basis of 14 percent assignable to nonresidential development and 86 percent assignable to residential development.

Table 10-28 shows that there is an existing deficiency of 1,834,952 ($1,605,583 for residential development and $229,369 for nonresidential development). An impact fee of $0.527 per foot for residential developments and $0.173 per foot for nonresidential developments would equalize the relative fiscal burdens between existing and new development. These fees were adopted and are now collected on all new residential and nonresidential development.

LIBRARIES

This section uses a relatively uncomplicated facility—libraries—to calculate impact fees and walks through the conventional calculation steps. The example

Table 10-29
Library Facilities and Materials

Level of Service Measure	LOS Standard
Square feet per weighted resident	0.60
Materials per weighted resident	2.00

is of the library impact fee program in Martin County, Florida.

Martin County, Florida

The Martin County Comprehensive Growth Management Plan establishes an LOS of 0.60 square feet of library facilities per "weighted" resident, which includes peak season residents. The service area is the entire county. Table 10-29 elaborates on the LOS standard.

Martin County's library impact fee program uses the plan-based approach, and the cost of expanding its system to meet new development needs is shown in Table 10-30.

In addition to building space, Martin County has an LOS related to library materials (as shown in Table 10-31).

The capital facility development impact fee is based on the following general formula:

NET IMPACT COST = {[TOTAL IMPACT COST] – [PAST REVENUE CREDIT] – [NONLOCAL SHARE] – [FUTURE REVENUE CREDIT]}

Where:

TOTAL IMPACT COST = the cost to provide a unit of facility to a unit of impact, such as 2.0 volumes and 0.60 square feet of space to a weighted resident

PAST REVENUE CREDIT = the percent of the taxable value of the county that is composed of vacant buildable land (thus excluding agricultural land), times the LOCAL IMPACT COST

NONLOCAL SHARE = the share of the TOTAL IMPACT COST that the Martin County CIP for fiscal years 1999–2003 indicates is reasonably available to

Table 10-30
Library Facility Costs

Library	Facility Sq. Ft.	Cost
Main—New Stuart	38,000	$7,078,000
Indiantown	10,000	$1,000,000
Hobe Sound	10,900	$1,600,000
Jensen Beach	10,000	$1,600,000
Port Salerno	15,000	$2,500,000
Total	83,900	$13,778,000
Cost per square foot		$164.22
Land, Main		$470,000
Land, Hobe Sound		$499,875
Total land		$969,875
Facility square feet	48,900	
Land cost per square foot		$19.83
Total cost per square foot		$184.05

finance the facilities. The report text identifies those revenues where applicable. The resulting figure is known as the LOCAL IMPACT COST.

FUTURE REVENUE CREDIT = the share of future taxes paid by new development that helps finance facilities for which impact fees are assessed

NET IMPACT COST = the difference among the TOTAL IMPACT COST, PAST REVENUE CREDIT, NONLOCAL SHARE, and FUTURE REVENUE CREDIT

Table 10-32 calculates the net impact cost per 24-hour functional resident, while Table 10-33 apportions the net impact cost to land uses.

GOVERNMENT BUILDINGS

Collier County, Florida

Collier County provides the case study for calculating a governmental buildings impact fee. It was developed by one of the authors (Nelson) as part of a team headed by Tindale-Oliver & Associates. Collier County provides a variety of buildings that are used to provide government services to businesses and residents that are not included in other impact fee program areas. A review of the county's General Government Buildings inventory and other impact fee program areas indicates that the buildings to include in this impact fee are court, health, other government services, related support, and mixed purpose facilities located throughout the county. Because these facilities service the county as a whole, the service area was considered all of Collier County, including the population of its municipalities. The following is a summary of the impact fee calculation steps.

The Collier County CIE requires capital demand estimates be based on the general formula:

$$Q = (S \times D) - I$$

Where:

Q = the quantity of facility (in square feet) needed to be built or expanded over the planning horizon

S = the standard of service (in square feet per person) for the facility

D = the projected demand, such as population, to be served at the end of the planning horizon

I = the current inventory of facilities in square feet

Table 10-32
Net Library Facility Impact Cost

Consideration	Figure
Total impact cost per weighted resident	
Facility cost	$110.43
Materials cost	$66.56
Total impact cost	$176.99
Percent past revenue credit	8.08%
Amount past revenue credit	$14.30
Total revenues	$6,667,000
Nonlocal revenues	$1,170,000
Nonlocal percent	17.55%
Credit for nonlocal funds	$31.06
Dedicated materials revenue, annual	$144,000
Weighted residents, 1998	129,797
Revenue per resident	$1.11
Capitalization rate	6.00%
Capitalization period, years	20
Credit per functional resident	$12.73
Total revenue credits	$57.81
Net impact cost per weighted resident	$118.90

Table 10-31
Net Library Materials Impact Cost

Consideration	Figure
Materials cost per volume	$33.28
Volumes per weighted resident	2.00
Facility impact cost/weighted resident	$66.56

Table 10-33
Net Impact Cost Schedule

Residential Land Use	Impact Unit	Weighted Residents	Net Impact Cost at $118.90 Per Impact Unit
Residential Occupied			
800 sq. ft. and under	Dwelling	1.520	$180.73
801 to 1,100 sq. ft.	Dwelling	2.265	$269.29
1,101 to 2,300 sq. ft.	Dwelling	2.354	$279.91
2,301 sq. ft. and over	Dwelling	2.434	$289.40
Residential Transient, Assisted			
Hotel	Room	0.808	$96.02
Motel	Room	0.808	$96.02
Nursing home	Bed	1.188	$141.20
Adult congregate living facility	Bed	1.188	$141.20

Because General Government Building facilities serve all residents, workers, and visitors, more than the population needs to be considered. The "functional" weekday daytime population approach for daytime-use facilities is used to establish a common unit of demand across different land uses (see Chapter 8 for uniform measures of demand). Calculating functional population entails three steps. The first is establishing the inventory of General Government Buildings in the base and planning horizon years. The county provided its current inventory, which establishes a baseline inventory for General Public Buildings for 2003. In addition, the county's 1998 Master Plan provides the inventory to 2017 (as summarized in Table 10-34).

Table 10-34
General Government Building Inventory, 2003 and 2017

Year	Sq. Ft.
2003	667,163
2017	1,168,739
Difference	501,576

Source: Collier County 2003 Inventory List and 1998 Master Plan.

Because of high seasonal variations in population, the next step is to calculate the weighted population. This begins with baseline (2003) and projected (2017) population, including seasonal residents, and employment. These figures are shown in Table 10-35.

In the third step, the figures in Table 10-36 are converted into functional residents. Table 10-37 shows the weighting factors used to adjust resident weighted population and employment into functional weekday daytime population.

Developing the residential component of functional resident population is simpler than the nonresidential component. It is generally assumed that people spend one-half to two-thirds of their time at home and the rest of each 24-hour day away from their place of residence. For the purposes of this analysis, it was assumed that, on average, people spend approximately 12 hours (50 percent) of each 24-hour day at their place of residence.

Developing estimates of functional residents for nonresidential land uses is more complicated than for residential land uses given the varying characteristics of nonresidential land uses. Nelson and Nicholas originally introduced a method for estimating functional resident population, now used internationally.[5] This method uses trip generation data from the ITE's *Trip Generation* (ITE (2003)) information on the number of employees per impact unit (such as per 1,000 square feet of space, per student, and per automobile service bay), passengers per vehicle, and length of time spent at the land use. Specific calculations include:

- Total one-way trips per impact unit (ITE trips times 50 percent, to avoid double counting entering and existing trips as two trips)
- Employees per impact unit, based on Arthur C. Nelson's *Planners' Estimating Guide* (Chicago: American Planning Association, 2004)
- Visitors per impact units based on occupants per trip minus journey-to-work-based occupants per trip
- Worker hours per week per impact unit (e.g., workers times nine hours per day times five days in a work week)
- Visitor hours per week per impact unit (visitors times number of hours per day times relevant days in a week)
- Functional residents (total hours occupied divided by hours in the week, which is 11 hours per day times five days per week in the case of government building (i.e., total

Table 10-35
Baseline Population and Employment Data

Data Category	2003	2017
Population Data Category		
Year-round population	299,479	502,439
Seasonal peak population	106,145	167,403
Weighted residents	334,506	557,682
Employment Data Category		
Natural resources	12,148	14,202
Construction	14,814	18,026
Manufacturing	3,562	4,664
TCU	3,337	4,055
Wholesale	3,843	5,007
Retail	28,709	39,404
FIRE	16,483	19,392
Business and professional services	54,521	78,805
Government	11,149	15,906
Total employment	148,566	199,462

TCU = transportation, communications, and utilities
FIRE = finance, insurance, and real estate
Figures may not add due to rounding.

Source: Population figures are obtained from Collier County Comprehensive Planning Section. Employment figures are from Woods and Poole.

hours government buildings tend to be open to service))

Table 10-37 uses the functional population coefficient estimates obtained from Table 10-36 to calculate the total functional population for 2003 and 2017.

Table 10-38 provides the 2003 LOS and projected 2017 LOS in relation to weighted population. The weighted resident figures are adapted from the county's comprehensive planning estimates. Although the analysis will be based on functional population, figures in Table 10-38 provide the county with a tool to check their LOS in future years since it is easier for the county to estimate the weighted population as opposed to functional population.

The next consideration addresses the cost to construct new General Government Building facility space. The costs considered include construction (including land), engineering, architectural services, parking, landscaping, heating and cooling facilities, and related expenses. Based on the estimated value of buildings and land provided by the county, an average figure of $189.09 per square foot of building cost and $26.21 of land cost per square foot of building are used.

It should be noted that the square footage included in this calculation is only the space for the primary buildings, excluding the related support facilities. However, the cost used in the calculation of the building construction does in fact include the cost of the necessary support facilities.

Table 10-39 reports these figures as applied to the recommended LOS standard, 2.1 square feet per functional resident. The resulting cost is $452 per functional resident.

To avoid overcharging or double payments, a final set of calculations is undertaken. These include reducing the impact cost to reflect external revenues exclusive of impact fees (from federal, state, and nongovernment local sources) that may be available to help finance facilities, as well as credit to reflect the future and past contributions to facilities accommodating new development. Collier County's government buildings are financed solely from local sources on a pay-as-you-go basis out of its general fund. However, new development will increase the general fund so a credit was considered for this.

Table 10-36
Functional Population Coefficients

Land-Use Category	Impact Unit	ITE	Employees Per Unit	In-Place Employee Percent	One-Way Trips Per Employee	Occupants Per Trip	Journey-to-Work-Based Occupants Per Trip	Employee, Student Hours	Visitors	Visitor Hours Per Trip	Days Per Week	Functional Population Per Resident and Employee
Total residents	Res. unit											0.5000
Natural resources	N/A	N/A	N/A	N/A	N/A	N/A	N/A	N/A	N/A	N/A	N/A	0.2500
Construction	1,000 sq. ft.	110	3.47	25.0%	0.434	1.20	1.14	9.0	0.09	1.0	5	0.8205
Manufacturing	1,000 sq. ft.	140	1.64	100.0%	0.820	1.37	1.14	9.0	0.31	1.0	5	0.8353
TCU	1,000 sq. ft.	110	3.61	100.0%	1.805	1.20	1.14	9.0	0.39	1.0	5	0.8280
Wholesale trade	1,000 sq. ft.	150	1.43	100.0%	0.716	1.30	1.14	9.0	0.16	1.0	5	0.8286
Retail trade	1,000 sq. ft.	820	1.48	100.0%	20.328	1.74	1.14	9.0	18.10	1.0	5	1.9270
FIRE	1,000 sq. ft.	710	2.85	100.0%	1.427	1.20	1.14	9.0	0.24	1.0	5	0.8260
Services	1,000 sq. ft.	710	2.85	100.0%	1.427	1.20	1.14	9.0	0.24	1.0	5	0.8260
Government	1,000 sq. ft.	730	2.98	100.0%	1.488	1.20	1.14	9.0	0.27	1.0	5	0.8263

ITE = Institute of Transportation Engineers
TCU = transportation, communications, and utilities
FIRE = finance, insurance, and real estate
Persons per trip based on:
- Retail occupants per car based on the "1995 Nationwide Personal Transportation Study" (Washington, DC: Bureau of Transportation Statistics, U.S. Department of Transportation, 1999), 27.
- Construction, TCU, and office-related including government based on ITE Code 714 (1.2 occupants/trip), ITE Code 760 (1.19 occupants/trip).
- Manufacturing based on ITE Code 140 (1.37 occupants/trip).
- Average vehicle occupancy and journey-to-work average vehicle occupancy from the "1995 Nationwide Personal Transportation Study" (Washington, DC: Bureau of Transportation Statistics, U.S. Department of Transportation, 1999), 27.
- Trips per retail employee from the following table: Weighted Retail Scale Trip Rate Share Trips Neighborhood < 50k sq. ft. 87.31 40.0% 34.92 Community 50k-250k sq. ft. 49.15 30.0% 14.74 Regional 250k-500k sq. ft. 38.37 20.0% 7.67 Super Reg. 500k-1,000k sq. ft. 29.96 10.0% 3.00 Sum of Weighted Trips/2 30.17 Employees Per 1,000 sq. ft. 1.48 Trips Per Employee 20.33.
- In-Place Employee Percent is estimated by Growth Management, Inc.

Table 10-37
Functional Population, 2003 and 2017

Residents and Employees Land-Use Category	Functional Population 2003	Functional Population 2003	Residents and Employees 2017	Functional Population 2017
Weighted residents	334,506	167,253	557,682	278,841
Employment				
Natural resource	12,148	3,037	14,202	3,551
Construction	14,814	12,156	18,026	14,791
Manufacturing	3,562	2,975	4,664	3,896
TCU	3,337	2,763	4,055	3,358
Wholesale trade	3,843	3,184	5,007	4,149
Retail trade	28,709	55,321	39,404	75,931
FIRE	16,483	13,614	19,392	16,017
Services	54,521	45,032	78,805	65,090
Government	11,149	9,213	15,906	13,143
Total employment	148,566	147,295	199,462	199,925
Functional population total		**314,549**		**478,766**

TCU = transportation, communications, and utilities
FIRE = finance, insurance, and real estate

Source: Collier County Comprehensive Planning Section.

Table 10-38
Observed and Projected General Government Building Level of Service, 2003 and 2017

Weighted Year	Sq. Ft.	Residents	Sq. Ft. Per Resident
2003	667,163[1]	334,506[3]	2.0
2017	1,168,739[2]	557,682[3]	2.1

Sources:
  1. Collier County 2003 Inventory List.
  2. 1998 Master Plan.
  3. Collier County Comprehensive Planning Section.

Table 10-39
General Government Facilities Impact Cost Per Functional Resident

Calculation Steps	Figure*
1. Level of service—sq. ft. per functional resident	2.1
2. Estimated replacement cost per sq. ft., 2003	$189.09
3. Land cost per sq. ft. of building, 2003	$26.21
4. Total cost per sq. ft. of building, 2003	$215.30
5. Impact cost per functional resident	$452.14

* Figures may not multiply due to rounding.

Table 10-40
New Development Share of Total Development

Year	Residents	Share of Base-Year Development to All Development	Cumulative New Development Share of Total Development After Base Year
0	203,616	100.0%	0.0%
1	214,820	97.4%	2.6%
2	226,025	94.8%	5.2%
3	237,229	92.1%	7.9%
4	248,434	89.5%	10.5%
5	259,638	86.9%	13.1%
6	270,843	84.3%	15.7%
7	282,047	81.7%	18.3%
8	293,252	79.0%	21.0%
9	304,456	76.4%	23.6%
10	315,661	73.8%	26.2%
11	326,865	71.2%	28.8%
12	338,070	68.6%	31.4%
13	349,274	65.9%	34.1%
14	360,479	63.3%	36.7%
15	371,683	60.7%	39.3%
16	382,888	58.1%	41.9%
17	394,092	55.5%	44.5%
18	405,296	52.8%	47.2%
19	416,501	50.2%	49.8%
20	427,705	47.6%	52.4%
Weighted development share		73.8%	26.2%

Credit for future payments made by new development for General Government Building facilities is the next consideration. The question posed here is the extent to which new development will contribute to the overall general revenue base over the next 20 years. Table 10-40 shows that, assuming constant annual growth from 2003 through 2023, new development's share of total development will be about 26.2 percent. Impact cost will be reduced by this factor to account for new revenue generated by new development that may flow into the general fund and be used to help finance General Government Building facilities.

The last consideration is for past payments. Here, the share of total buildable vacant land (i.e., residential, commercial, and industrial) to total assessed value is reviewed to develop the percentage of the vacant land assessment to the total county assessment. Table 10-41 indicates that the vacant land assessment is about 6 percent of total assessed value. Table 10-42 summarizes the analysis to generate the net impact cost per functional resident.

It should be noted that using 26.2 percent credit for the new development's share assumes that in the future a large percentage of government buildings will be built through debt service or other nonimpact fee funding sources and represents a very conservative estimate. If the county makes a policy decision to not use bonds or other funding sources for government building financing, the credit would be lower and the fees would be higher.

Demand for General Government Building facilities should be apportioned based on functional residents. Among commercial, industrial, and retail structures, impact fees will be assessed based on size, usually in units of 1,000 square feet

Table 10-41
Assessed Property Value, 2003

Land Use Improved	Assessed Value
Single family	$23,216,191,956
Residential condominiums	$18,482,991,472
Cooperatives	$380,932,621
Improved commercial	$3,509,382,606
Improved industrial	$618,968,496
	$46,208,467,151
Agriculture, Other	
Agriculture	$228,454,428
Other	$6,323,505,356
	$6,551,959,784
Vacant	
Residential vacant	$2,648,921,583
Vacant commercial	$448,014,219
Vacant industrial	$101,828,563
Vacant other	$3,198,764,365
County-wide total land value	$55,959,191,300
Vacant land as percent	5.72%

Source: Summation of assessor data.

Table 10-42
Impact Cost Per Functional Resident

Calculation Steps	Figure*
Impact Cost Analysis	
Impact cost per functional resident	$452.14
Credit Analysis	
External, nonlocal government credit	0.00%
Future share of revenue stream	26.20%
Past share of revenue stream	5.72%
Total credit percent	31.91%
Total credit amount	$144.29
Net impact cost per functional resident	**$307.85**

* Figures may not multiply due to rounding.

of building space. The same should be done for residential development. Consider the following relationships between house size, measured as number of bedrooms, and number of occupants presented in Table 10-43.

There is a certain amount of consistency across the nation in terms of the number of people living in single-family detached housing (including manufactured homes) and house size, number of bedrooms, bedrooms per occupant, and household size. We also know statistically from census data that larger homes have more people in them than smaller homes. This relationship tends to flatten out at about 3,000 square feet of living area. There

are always anecdotes about some larger units occupied by very few people—as few as one in some mansions—and about some smaller units occupied by many people, such as large or extended families in one- or two-bedroom apartments, but these tend to be the statistical outliers. In Collier County, it was found that there were 1.19 persons per 1,000 square feet for all residential units except for manufactured homes, which had 2.16 persons per 1,000 square feet. Based on the analysis, the impact fee for government buildings in Collier County is those shown in Table 10-44.

DRAINAGE

Albuquerque, New Mexico

The authors led a team of consultants who developed impact fees for the City of Albuquerque. One of the team members, Integrated Utilities Group, Inc. (IUG), developed the impact fees for the city's stormwater/drainage system (drainage) consistent with the city's Planned Growth Strategy (PGS). The following sections present the legal bases for the

Table 10-43
Relationship Between House Size and Occupancy Level Status
(Nation, Urban, Suburban, and South), 2001

Detached Housing Unit Data	Nation	Urban	Suburban	South
House size	1,737	1,767	1,771	1,663
Bedrooms	2.75	2.68	2.85	2.79
Average sq. ft. per person	720	719	722	720
Average bedrooms per person	1.08	1.05	1.07	1.12
Median household size (all occupied units)	2.55	2.54	2.66	2.50

Source: American Housing Survey (2001).

city's drainage impact fee, the methodology used to calculate the impact fee, the service areas where the fee will be applied, the data for the study, the analyses conducted by the study, and the results. Not reported for brevity is the CIP used partially as the foundation for calculating the fees.

The LOS for facilities to be included in the drainage impact fee is defined by the 100-year storm event. The facilities in the project listing are for those structures and channels that encompass improvements to the major facilities. Local improvements, such as street drainage and lot drainage, are not included in this listing. Such local improvements will remain the responsibility of the developer.

IUG developed a methodology that met the requirements of both the state statutes and the city's PGS. IUG used land-use assumptions by drainage area based on city council-approved land-use assumptions, assigning drainage projects to the appropriate (nexus-based) drainage service areas, evaluating impervious area changes based on the PGS proposed land-use changes for 2025 in each service area, using Albuquerque's Development Process Manual to calculate the service units based on impervious area, and calculating the drainage impact fees based on this information.

This overall methodology complies with the cost theory that is being implemented in Albuquerque. It identifies the full cost of new drainage facilities to support growth. It also identifies a mechanism for including the net equity from existing facilities, which were previously constructed to serve growth. This method is known locally as the "full marginal cost" method. It is commonly known as, and is consistent with, the "buy-in" method. The buy-in method consists of two portions: a reimbursement fee (for net equity in excess capacity in existing facilities) and a capital fee to cover the construction of projects specifically needed to support growth. UG implemented the methodology in conjunction with city staff to achieve the following results.

The underlying state legislation and the city's PGS both require that a rational nexus exist between the impact fee being assigned and the development area or development project that bears the impact fee.

This principle, when applied to drainage, leads to a basin-based or basin-grouped approach. Thus, developing areas within the same basin or group of basins must pay for the projects that supply the increased drainage capacity required to serve the project or group of projects. IUG worked with city

Figure 10-7
Albuquerque Drainage Service Areas

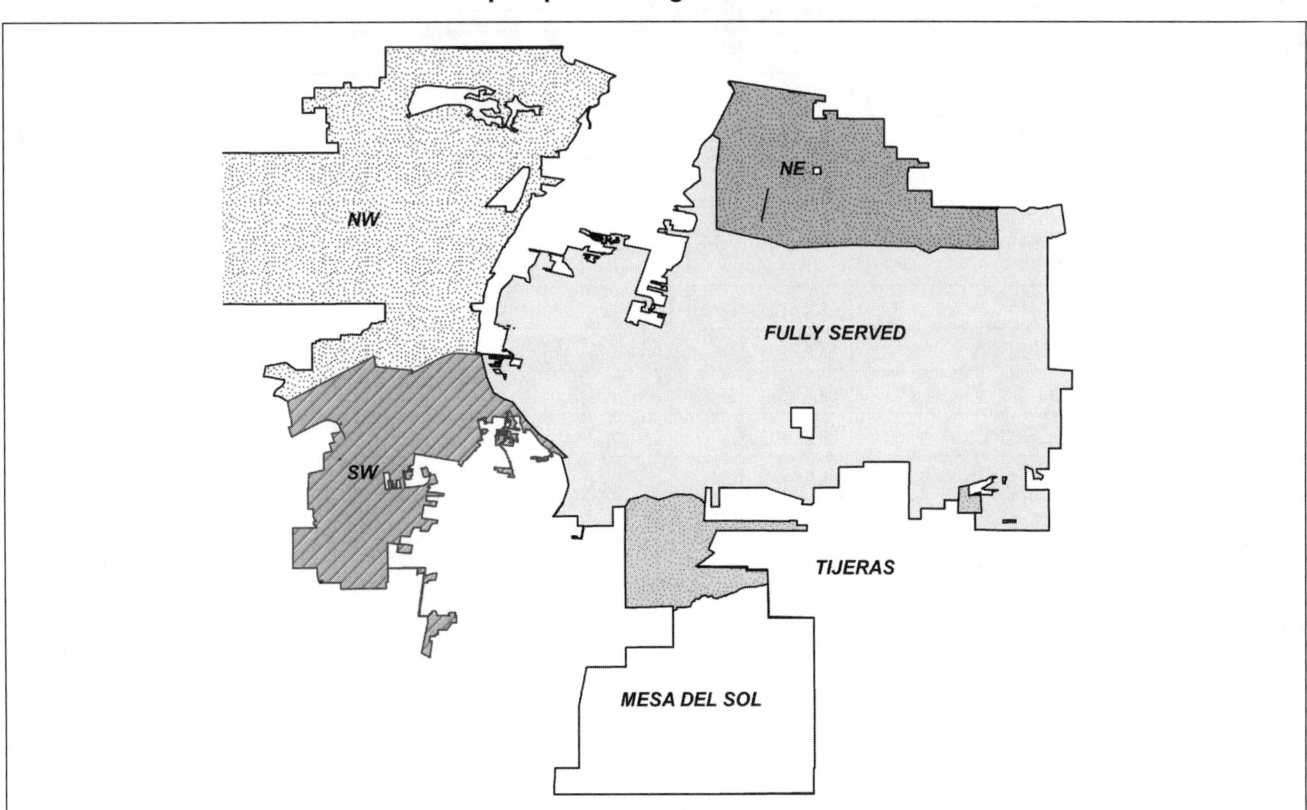

Table 10-44
Net Impact Fee Schedule

Land Use	Impact Unit	Weekday Functional Residents	Net Impact Cost at $308 Per Functional Resident
Residential			
Residential	1,000 sq. ft.	0.57	$175.47
Manufactured home	1,000 sq. ft.	1.03	$317.08
Transient, Assisted, Group			
Hotel/motel	Room	0.95	$292.45
Nursing home/ACLF	Bed	1.23	$378.65
Recreational			
Marina	Berths	0.32	$98.51
Golf course	18 holes	34.52	$10,626.86
Movie theater with matinee	Screen	11.81	$3,635.67
Institutions			
Hospital	1,000 sq. ft.	2.98	$917.38
Elementary school	Student	0.74	$227.81
Middle school	Student	1.05	$323.24
High school	Student	1.30	$400.20
Junior/community college	Student	0.38	$116.98
University/college	Student	0.67	$206.26
Church	1,000 sq. ft.	1.10	$338.63
Day care center	Student	0.88	$270.90
Office and Financial			
Office 50,000 sq. ft. or less	1,000 sq. ft.	3.84	$1,182.13
Office 50,001-100,000 sq. ft.	1,000 sq. ft.	3.27	$1,006.66
Office 100,001-200,000 sq. ft.	1,000 sq. ft.	2.78	$855.81
Office 200,001-400,000 sq. ft.	1,000 sq. ft.	2.37	$729.60
Office greater than 400,000 sq. ft.	1,000 sq. ft.	2.16	$664.95
Medical office	1,000 sq. ft.	4.83	$1,486.90
Retail, Gross Sq. Ft.			
Specialty retail	1,000 sq. ft.	5.04	$1,551.55
Retail 50,000 sfgla or less	1,000 sq. ft.	6.06	$1,865.55
Retail 50,001-100,000 sfgla	1,000 sq. ft.	5.60	$1,723.94
Retail 100,001-150,000 sfgla	1,000 sq. ft.	6.15	$1,893.26
Retail 150,001-200,000 sfgla	1,000 sq. ft.	5.70	$1,754.73
Retail 200,001-400,000 sfgla	1,000 sq. ft.	4.80	$1,477.66
Retail 400,001-600,000 sfgla	1,000 sq. ft.	5.01	$1,542.31
Retail 600,001-1,000,000 sfgla	1,000 sq. ft.	4.95	$1,523.84
Retail over 1,000,000 sfgla	1,000 sq. ft.	4.25	$1,308.35
Pharmacy/drug store w/drive-thru	1,000 sq. ft.	4.19	$1,289.88
Home improvement superstore	1,000 sq. ft.	4.30	$1,323.74

Table 10-44
Net Impact Fee Schedule (*continued*)

Land Use	Impact Unit	Weekday Functional Residents	Net Impact Cost at $308 Per Functional Resident
Retail, Gross Sq. Ft. (*continued*)			
Quality restaurant	1,000 sq. ft.	13.86	$4,266.75
High-turnover restaurant	1,000 sq. ft.	15.32	$4,716.21
Fast-food restaurant w/drive-thru	1,000 sq. ft.	16.25	$5,002.51
Gas/service station	Fuel pumps	3.53	$1,086.70
Quick lube	Bays	2.40	$738.83
Supermarket	1,000 sq. ft.	5.56	$1,711.63
Convenience store	1,000 sq. ft.	9.08	$2,795.25
Convenience store w/gas	Fuel pumps	9.27	$2,853.74
Convenience/gas/fast-food store	1,000 sq. ft.	13.76	$4,235.97
Auto repair	1,000 sq. ft.	6.42	$1,976.37
Tire store	Bays	3.32	$1,022.05
New and used car sales	1,000 sq. ft.	4.03	$1,240.62
Self-service car wash	Bays	4.07	$1,252.94
Bank/savings walk-in	1,000 sq. ft.	5.61	$1,727.02
Bank/savings drive-in	1,000 sq. ft.	4.90	$1,508.45
Industrial			
General industrial	1,000 sq. ft.	1.88	$578.75
Business park	1,000 sq. ft.	4.54	$1,397.62
Mini-warehouse	1,000 sq. ft.	0.16	$49.26

ACLF = adult congregate living facility
sfgla = square feet gross leasable area

staff to identify basins and basin groups based on the city's previous drainage studies and basins used for National Pollution Discharge Elimination System compliance.

Figure 10-7 presents the five areas identified for drainage impact fee analysis within the current city limits. Each of the areas is described briefly below.

Northwest area: This area includes the area in the northwest corner of the current city limits. It extends to the west as far as the Double Eagle Airport. The river is the eastern boundary. The southern boundary of the area is the Ladera Channel and associated upstream diversions just north of Interstate 40. The total size of this area is approximately 15,500 acres.

Southwest area: The southwest area is the remaining part within the current city limits on the west side of the river. The total size of this area is approximately 9,000 acres.

Far northeast area: The far northeast service area extends from the northern city limits south to the northern boundary of the fully served area. The size of this area is approximately 11,700 acres.

Tijeras Arroyo area: This single-basin drainage area drains across the airport and Kirtland Air Force Base. The size of this area is approximately 2,600 acres.

Fully served area: A large portion of the city (approximately 40,200 acres) is identified as the fully served area and is excluded from the application of impact fees. The fully served area is the area studied by the three main city drainage studies between 1981 and 1987. The existing drainage system in the fully served area provides drainage to this largely built-up area. However, the systems are dated with numerous hydraulic deficiencies and rehabilitation needs. Therefore, no impact fees were calculated for this area.

In January 1997, the city, along with Albuquerque Metropolitan Arroyo Flood Control Agency (AMAFCA), prepared a comprehensive list of drainage projects that would be needed for the next 25

Table 10-45
Funding for Recent Drainage Projects

Cost Element	2000	2001	2002	2003	2004
City CIP (GO bond money)	$5,287,835	$6,572,968	$10,063,018	$6,794,116	$8,000,000
CIAC	$21,225,165	$14,944,282	$18,430,982	$24,643,884	$15,138,000
Total capital costs	$26,513,000	$21,517,250	$28,494,000	$31,438,000	$23,138,000
City equity based on bond repayment schedule	$0	$0	$0	$0	$0

CIP = capital improvements program
GO = general obligation
CIAC = contributions in aid of construction

years. The projects were identified as those that would correct hydraulic deficiencies, conduct rehabilitation of aging facilities, and serve growth. This comprehensive listing of projects was taken from the 19 drainage plans that had been done at the time. Two additional recent west side drainage studies that were completed in 1999 and 2000 were added for completeness. The projects from the studies listed in Attachment 1 were selected and sorted by drainage analysis area. For each project, a short description is listed along with the updated capital cost, city grid assignment by zone map, and drainage study identification.

AMAFCA's projects are funded separately from city funding sources even though a significant source of the combined funding comes from the development community. There may be cases where projects are jointly funded. When this happens, the city's funds for these joint projects, and those that are used to add capacity, are tracked separately and are included in the capital project list.

IUG and city staff reviewed the project listings and removed those projects that were either for rehabilitation of existing structures or were to address currently deficient facilities. Following the culling of the ineligible projects, the remaining projects were entered into a geographic information system database and allocated to the areas shown in Figure 10-7.

City drainage project financial records were reviewed for recently (since 2000) completed city drainage projects. IUG limited this review to projects within the last five years since data prior to that time were not available. The city has only been classifying drainage capital projects by use (e.g., rehabilitation, deficiency correction, growth, and mandate) since 2001. Table 10-45 shows the total city drainage expenditures for capital projects from the last five years with stated revenue sources.

IUG's review established that the costs of recently completed drainage projects were sufficiently detailed to identify the new capacity portion of the costs separate from the total project cost. However, none of these capital costs could be assigned to the reimbursement portion of the impact fee. The reason for this result is that the city GO bonds used for the city portion of the project funding were still in the interest-payment-only portion of the repayment schedule. Therefore, the city has not yet accumulated net equity in the recently completed projects that could be applied to the impact fee. However, over time, the city will build equity ownership in the drainage facility assets. Thus, the reimbursement component of the impact fee might then increase from the currently computed zero value to a positive number.

IUG recommended that, in the future, the reimbursement portion of the drainage impact fee be expanded to include all drainage fixed assets with remaining excess capacity to serve new growth by drainage service area for possible inclusion of future as-built costs into the impact fee structure. This analysis should be repeated approximately every two years to update the buy-in analysis for city-funded projects that relate to the support of growth.

IUG also recommended that the city consider a revision to its bond repayment practices to accelerate the accumulation of net equity in such drainage projects. The existing net equity data should be compiled by drainage service area and added to the updated growth improvement portion of the drainage impact fee when net equity is earnzed by the city in the projects.

The impact fee calculation is based on previously identified drainage areas as well as on the full marginal cost of new capacity projects. The fee is based on the cumulative costs divided by the total number of expected service units to be developed in the drainage service area. Information was obtained from the Mid-Region Council of Governments related to the existing land-use conditions in 2000 and planned citywide 2025 growth. This information was analyzed and reduced to the service areas.

Table 10-46 presents the drainage impact fees resulting from these analyses. These impact fees are based on actual project analyses and city-adopted land-use projections.

The fee is thus based on additional impervious surface area attributable to new development. In the fully served area, there are no drainage impact fees, while in the northwest area, the fees for a home resulting in 4,000 square feet of impervious surface (for the home, driveway, patio, associated right-of-way, and other factors) would be $1,290 (($14,052 divided by 43,560) times 4,000).

TRANSPORTATION—STREETS

Two transportation impact fees—both for streets—are presented in this section. The first is a traditional approach developed for Martin County, Florida, by one of the authors (Nelson); the second was developed for Albuquerque, New Mexico, by Tindale-Oliver & Associates as part of the author's team, to recognize substantial differences in costs among several areas of the city.

Martin County, Florida

Martin County, Florida, has been assessing development impact fees for road facilities since the 1980s. The county used to have service areas for each of the four municipalities plus 12 others located throughout the incorporated county. Numerous service areas pose the potential disadvantage of being insufficiently large to generate meaningful amounts of revenue for projects. Borrowing back and forth among service areas can be done, but this poses administrative burdens. The county wished

to reconsider its service area design, and reviewing its process for doing so is instructive here.

Customarily, service areas are drawn to reflect the likelihood that new development paying impact fees will benefit reasonably from their expenditure. Impact fees used to build or expand a bridge, providing the only feasible access to an area regardless of the size of the territory, would easily pass muster. A small road—serving essentially local traffic, located far away from new development, and constructed in part from impact fees paid by that development—is less obvious. What is reasonable?

Martin County is essentially flat and, although there are islands and peninsulas, there are few other major barriers separating the county into physically unique subareas. Certain roads are probably used by every county resident regardless of where they live, since they provide access to the local community college, major shopping districts, medical facilities, and places of work. Even people living and working in, say, Indiantown, depend on county roads 10 or more miles away for many shopping, personal service, business, and related needs.

Furthermore, an origin destination study suggested the reasonable proposition that county roads are used by residents countywide. Although there may be segments where certain county roads are not likely to be used by any given county resident, they are probably the exception to this general observation. The county found that, given travel characteristics reported in this study, there are sufficient reasons for making the entire county one service area for road facility development impact fee purposes, including:

- Regardless of where they live, it appears that most, if not all, county residents use roads in the urban area for shopping, medical services,

Table 10-46
City of Albuquerque, Planned Growth Strategy Implementation, Proposed Drainage Impact Fees

Service Area	CIP Project Costs, June 2004 ($)	Total Basin Area (Acres)	Anticipated Service Units 2000–2025	Total Cost Per Service Unit ($/Service Unit)
Northwest	$55,015,528	15,490	3,915	$14,052
Southwest	$35,393,166	9,021	2,757	$12,836
Fully served	$0	40,250	2,009	$0
Tijeras Arroyo	$2,933,604	2,611	221	$13,290
Far Northeast	$15,044,434	11,753	1,474	$10,208

CIP = capital improvements program

personal and business purposes, and recreation when visiting the ocean.

- Travel characteristics of rural residents indicate that many work in the urban area and, in any event, use roads in the urban area routinely for shopping, personal service, beach-related recreation, and other purposes.
- Urban residents use rural roads for recreational driving, shopping for seasonal vegetables and fruits at wayside stands, visiting county parks and waterways, and traveling to Lake Okeechobee and other inland recreational opportunities.

However, because the Comprehensive Growth Management Plan clearly separates urban from rural land uses, it seemed reasonable to create two countywide transportation service areas outside the cities but also to retain the four service areas for the cities themselves.

The next issue to consider is the LOS. The Comprehensive Growth Management Plan provides for LOS C in rural areas and LOS D in urban areas. However, the county reconsidered this in favor of a single countywide LOS D for the following reasons:

- Reducing rural road capacity to LOS C relative to urban road capacity, set at LOS D could foster construction of more rural roads that would have the effect of encouraging urban sprawl into rural areas.
- Management of development is achieved more effectively through land-use measures than through manipulating service standards.

Another LOS question relates to choosing between link-specific and systemwide geographical areas. A "link-specific" approach would require all roadway links to function at a minimum operational level. The trouble with this approach is that there will almost always be some roadway facilities that are deficient with respect to such an approach. In contrast, a "systemwide" approach is based on a measure designed to summarize the overall operating condition of the major roadway system. This has the planning advantage of encouraging development in areas where capacity exists and discouraging it in areas where congestion occurs.

The exception to the systemwide approach is a special class of transportation facilities: bridges and causeways. Because of their expense and role as a conduit through which regional traffic passes, connecting communities to one another, they need to be considered separately. However, much, if not all, of the funding for those facilities comes from state and federal sources, not Martin County.

Two LOS standards were thus adopted:

1. A systemwide LOS approach for county roads based on LOS D.
2. For bridges and causeways, a link-specific LOS approach of E.

The transportation impact fee is calculated pursuant to the plan-based approach. From the total impact cost, one must consider how facilities are financed to arrive at net impact cost. This is done using the following general formula:

NET IMPACT COST = {[TOTAL IMPACT COST] − [PAST REVENUE CREDIT] − [NONLOCAL SHARE] − [FUTURE REVENUE CREDIT]}

Where:

TOTAL IMPACT COST = the cost to provide a unit of facility to a unit of impact, which in this study is LOS D for roads

PAST REVENUE CREDIT = an adjustment to reflect contributions to facilities made in the past by new development (not relevant in the case of transportation facilities)

NONLOCAL SHARE = the share of the TOTAL IMPACT COST that the Martin County CIP for fiscal years 1999–2003 indicates is reasonably available to finance the facilities. This study identifies those revenues where applicable.

FUTURE REVENUE CREDIT = the share of future taxes paid by new development that help finance facilities for which impact fees are assessed. In the case of transportation, this is mostly the gasoline tax.

NET IMPACT COST = the difference among the TOTAL IMPACT COST, PAST REVENUE CREDIT, NONLOCAL SHARE, and FUTURE REVENUE CREDIT

Table 10-47 shows the planned improvements that form the basis for impact fee calculation. Table 10-48 adjusts total costs by subtracting nonlocal revenues, resulting in local impact cost per lane-mile and per trip-mile.

Credit for new revenues that new development generates, which help finance the very roads impact fees may, is now considered. In Martin County, transportation facilities are financed principally from federal, state, and county gasoline taxes. Estimating tax revenue per gallon applied to transportation facilities is a two-step process. The first step is shown in Table 10-49, which shows the

Table 10-47
Road Facility Capacity and Cost Analysis

Road Improve-ment, CIP FY 1999–2003	New Lanes	Miles	Lane-Miles	Capa-city Per Mile	New Capacity	Total Cost	Nonlocal Amount	Land Share
Willoughby Blvd. 2 Lane: Salerno-Cove	2	0.50	1.00	15,800	7,900	$3,345,000	$590,000	$1,120,000
Western Palm City Corridor Expansion	2	5.00	10.00	15,800	79,000	$11,210,000	$0	$4,350,000
Green River Parkway	4	3.00	12.00	33,500	100,500	$8,370,000	$50,000	$2,700,000
Indian Street 4 Lane	2	1.00	2.00	17,700	17,700	$3,050,000	$0	$500,000
CR A1A, Monterey Road/Indian Street	2	1.20	2.40	17,700	21,240	$3,300,000	$0	$300,000
Market Place Corridor SR 76/ Com. Ave. 2 Lane @ 2/3 share	2	1.33	2.67	15,800	21,067	$2,075,000	$0	$600,000
Market Place Corridor SR 76/ Com. Ave. 4 Lane @ 1/3 share	4	0.67	2.67	33,500	22,333	$2,075,000	$0	$600,000
Willoughby Blvd. 4 Lane: US 1 Monterey	4	0.90	3.60	33,500	30,150	$4,000,000	$0	$1,700,000
Seabranch Blvd. 2 Lane	2	2.00	4.00	15,800	31,600	$2,000,000	$0	$250,000
Willoughby Blvd. Cove Road	4	2.50	10.00	17,700	44,250	$4,900,000	$0	$2,500,000
Willoughby Blvd. Bridge Road	2	3.50	7.00	15,800	55,300	$3,600,000	$0	$2,000,000
Total		21.60	57.33		431,040	$47,925,000	$640,000	$16,620,000
Cost per lane-mile						$835,901	1.34%	34.68%
Cost per trip-mile						$111.18		

CIP FY = capital improvements program fiscal year

Source: Martin County Growth Management Department.

monthly annual county-generated gasoline tax revenues and average revenues generated per penny of county gasoline tax.

The second step involves inventorying the use of county, state, and federal funds for capital reported in the County Capital Improvement Plan, which, when divided by average county revenue generated per penny from Table 10-48, is the total local, state, and federal gasoline taxes per gallon used for Martin County transportation facilities (shown in Table 10-50).

The next step in the process is calculating the local impact cost per land use (as shown in Table 10-51). This information will be used in Table 10-52 to calculate the impact fee for the same land uses. Note that, for residential land uses, variation is possible by size of the residential unit. The last step in the process is subtracting the local cost per lane-mile by the present value of the gasoline tax revenues that new development will generate per lane-mile. This calculation is shown for each land use with the resulting impact fee in the last column of Table 10-52.

Albuquerque, New Mexico

The City of Albuquerque's PGS, adopted by ordinance and resolution, calls for the creation of a

Table 10-48
Road Facility Local Impact Cost

Consideration	Figure
Facility cost per trip-mile	$111.18
Percent nonlocal share	1.34%
Amount nonlocal share	$1.48
Local impact cost per trip-mile	$109.70

development impact fee program to fund the cost of growth. The transportation impact fee study is used to help fulfill the plan's objectives.

The study uses a standards-based impact cost methodology. In the case of a standards-based impact cost analysis, it is assumed that new development consumes some roadway capacity on all roads, both existing and required new ones, regardless of whether the roads are among those that are planned for improvements.

The cost component of a standards-based impact cost is developed based on a review of historical project costs and typical capacity expansion projects, which are programmed in cost-affordable long- and short-range roadway facilities (or capital) improvements programs. A net impact cost schedule and the necessary support material utilized in its calculation are included in this document.

The general equation used to compute the roadway facility net impact cost for a given land use is:

$$(\text{UNIT DEMAND} \times \text{UNIT COST}) - \text{OFFSETS} = \text{NET IMPACT COST}$$

Figure 10-8
Transportation Impact Fee
Service Areas, City of Albuquerque

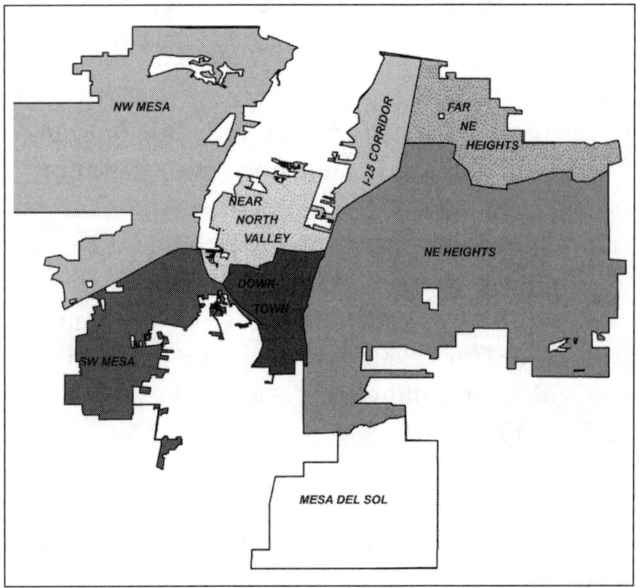

Table 10-49
Gasoline Tax Credit Amount Per Gallon, Estimation of Revenues Per Penny of Gasoline Tax

Month in Fiscal Year	County Gas Taxes Received
October	$270,463
November	$353,959
December	$344,925
January	$377,084
February	$368,135
March	$354,432
April	$419,176
May	$403,673
June	$398,926
July	$409,474
August	$348,179
September	$381,621
Total	$4,430,047
County gasoline tax per gallon	$0.08
Gasoline tax revenue per penny	$553,756

Source: "Local Government Tax Distribution by County, Office of Research and Analysis," monthly reports accessed via http://sun6.dms.state.fl.us/dor/tables/html for the relevant fiscal year.

The "demand" for travel placed on the roadway facility system is usually expressed in vehicle-miles or lane-miles of roadway capacity consumed. The cost of building capacity is typically expressed in dollars per vehicle-mile or lane-mile of roadway capacity. The "offsets" represent an estimate of the annual revenues generated by the development that are allocated to roadway construction or facilities expansion. Thus, the total net impact cost represents an "up front" payment for a portion of the cost to replace the roadway facilities consumed by a development.

Standards-based impact cost analyses must be based on a specific LOS or capacity provided by roadways. One decision to make is whether to base the analysis on peak or average daily impacts. The evening peak hour was selected based on the following criteria:

- The heaviest demand of service typically occurs during this hour;
- Roadways are sized during the planning process to serve the demand that occurs during the PM peak hour; and

Table 10-50
Estimation of Gasoline Tax Used for New or Expanded Facilities

Transportation Improvement Component	Project	County Gas Tax	State Funds[1]	Total[2]
County 6 year CIE/CIP projects[3]	90E CP 037	$550,000	$225,000	$775,000
	97E CP 016	$450,000		$450,000
	92E CP 016	$2,740,000	$362,000	$3,102,000
	90E CP 005	$1,050,000		$1,050,000
	90E CP 041	$3,050,000		$3,050,000
	95E CO 016		$1,500,000	$1,500,000
	92E CP 017	$750,000		$750,000
	SR 714	$3,375,000	$18,650,000	$22,025,000
	US 1	$350,000	$1,000,000	$1,350,000
	92E CP 041	$130,000	$90,000	$220,000
	92E CP 015		$3,700,000	$3,700,000
	Total	$12,445,000	$21,827,000	$34,272,000
Annual 5 year average				$6,854,400
Fox Brown Road annual debt service[4]				$650,000
Series 1993 bonds, annual average[5]				$627,139
Total annual average				$8,131,539
Gasoline tax revenue per penny				$553,756
Cents per gallon				$0.1468

CIE = capital improvements element
CIP = capital improvements program
Notes:
1. Assumes all state funds from gas tax.
2. Revenues that require unique funds, such as bridges, are excluded.
3. Resurfacing, maintenance projects excluded.
4. Martin County Capital Improvement Program.
5. Optional gas tax refunding revenue bonds.

Figure 10-9
Ratio of Existing to Growth Revenues, 2004–2025

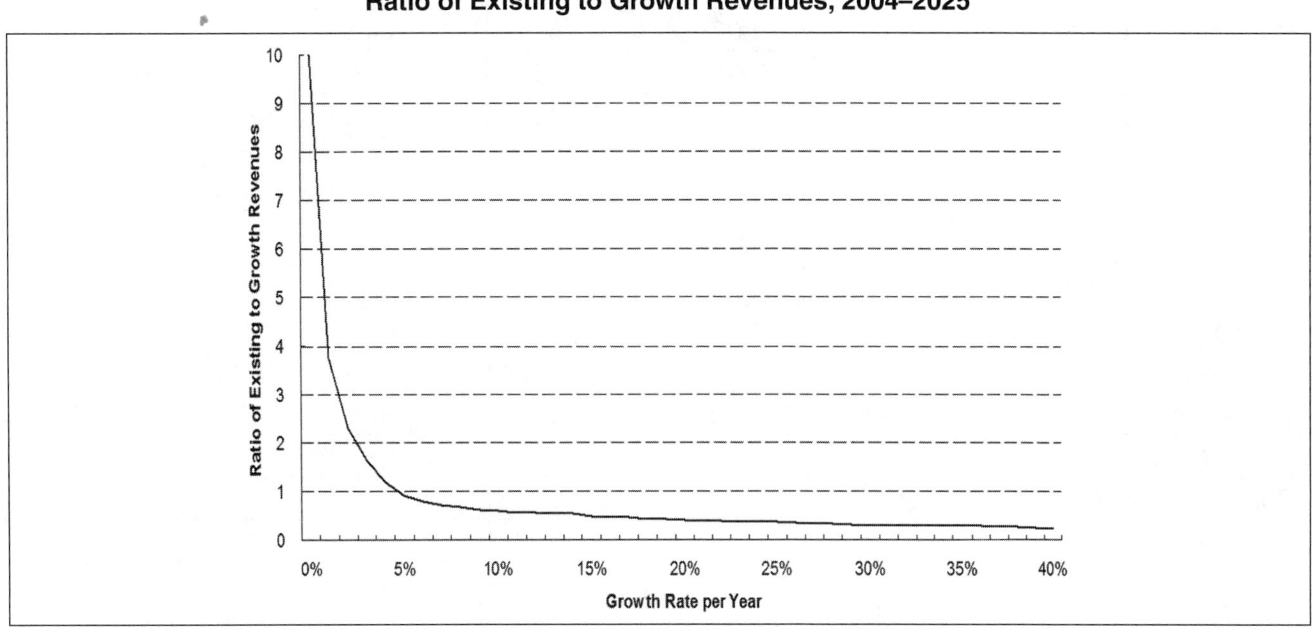

Table 10-51
Impact Cost Calculation

Land Use	Impact Units	One Way Trip-Miles at 50.00%	Percent New Trips	Daily Trip-Miles	Impact Cost Per Trip at $109.70
Residential Occupied					
800 sq. ft. and under	Dwelling	18.55	100%	18.55	$2,034.81
801-1,100 sq. ft.	Dwelling	27.64	100%	27.64	$3,031.86
1,101-2,300 sq. ft.	Dwelling	29.33	100%	29.33	$3,217.36
2,301 sq. ft. and over	Dwelling	30.32	100%	30.32	$3,326.42
Residential Transient, Assisted, Group					
Hotel	Room	22.68	66%	14.97	$1,642.01
Motel	Room	10.95	77%	8.43	$925.05
Nursing home	Bed	3.28	89%	2.92	$320.12
ACLF	Bed	3.14	72%	2.26	$247.74
Office and Financial					
Medical office	1,000 sq. ft.	83.46	87%	72.61	$7,964.98
Bank	1,000 sq. ft.	183.90	47%	86.43	$9,481.51
Bank w/drive In	1,000 sq. ft.	311.68	47%	146.49	$16,069.73
Office under 10,000 gross sq. ft.	1,000 sq. ft.	46.79	92%	43.05	$4,722.34
Office over 10,000 gross sq. ft.	1,000 sq. ft.	27.43	92%	25.23	$2,767.91
Industrial					
Manufacturing	1,000 sq. ft.	7.89	92%	7.26	$796.79
Warehouse	1,000 sq. ft.	10.09	92%	9.28	$1,017.89
Mini warehouse	1,000 sq. ft.	5.17	92%	4.75	$521.46
General industrial	1,000 sq. ft.	14.41	92%	13.25	$1,453.83
Retail					
Retail under 10,000 gross sq. ft.	1,000 sq. ft.	149.42	48%	71.72	$7,867.93
Retail 10,001-50,000 gross sq. ft.	1,000 sq. ft.	89.19	59%	52.62	$5,772.39
Retail 50,001-100,000 gross sq. ft.	1,000 sq. ft.	68.76	64%	44.01	$4,827.62
Retail 100,001-200,000 gross sq. ft.	1,000 sq. ft.	55.21	69%	38.10	$4,179.35
Retail over 200,000 gross sq. ft.	1,000 sq. ft.	49.36	75%	37.02	$4,060.98
Gas station	Pump	163.94	23%	37.71	$4,136.34
New, used auto sales, repair	1,000 sq. ft.	79.02	79%	62.43	$6,848.33
Restaurant	1,000 sq. ft.	127.58	77%	98.24	$10,776.62
Fast-food restaurant	1,000 sq. ft.	422.20	59%	249.10	$27,326.30
Car wash	1,000 sq. ft.	131.30	69%	90.60	$9,938.41
Convenience store with gas	1,000 sq. ft.	541.50	29%	157.03	$17,226.70
Convenience store with gas and fast food	1,000 sq. ft.	357.85	33%	118.09	$12,954.54
Recreational					
Golf course, per hole	Hole	69.52	90%	62.57	$6,863.74
Racquet club	1,000 sq. ft.	33.34	94%	31.34	$3,437.97
Park	Acres	4.08	90%	3.68	$403.30

Table 10-51
Impact Cost Calculation *(continued)*

Land Use	Impact Units	One Way Trip-Miles at 50.00%	Percent New Trips	Daily Trip-Miles	Impact Cost Per Trip at $109.70
Recreational (*continued*)					
Tennis court	Courts	60.38	90%	54.34	$5,961.13
Marina	Berths	5.76	94%	5.41	$593.72
Governmental					
Post office	1,000 sq. ft.	223.60	35%	78.26	$8,585.15
Library	1,000 sq. ft.	111.60	85%	94.86	$10,406.52
Government office	1,000 sq. ft.	142.40	92%	131.01	$14,371.43
Miscellaneous					
Day care center	1,000 sq. ft.	80.30	73%	58.62	$6,430.43
Hospital	1,000 sq. ft.	38.08	77%	29.32	$3,216.57
Veterinary clinic	1,000 sq. ft.	17.00	70%	11.90	$1,305.43
Church	1,000 sq. ft.	20.33	90%	18.29	$2,006.89
Movie theater with matinee	Screens	167.77	87%	145.96	$16,011.53

ACLF = adult congregate living facility

Table 10-52
Net Impact Cost Calculation

Land Use	Impact Unit	Year Miles at 365.25[1]	Gallons at 16.91[2]	Annual Revenue at $0.1468[3]	NPV Credit at 6.00% at 20 Years[4]	Net Road Impact Cost[5]
Residential Occupied						
800 sq. ft. and under	Dwelling	6,775	401	$58.83	$674.81	$1,360.00
801-1,100 sq. ft.	Dwelling	10,095	597	$87.66	$1,005.46	$2,026.40
1,101-2,300 sq. ft.	Dwelling	10,712	633	$93.02	$1,066.98	$2,150.38
2,301 sq. ft. and over	Dwelling	11,075	655	$96.18	$1,103.14	$2,223.27
Residential Transient, Assisted, Group						
Hotel	Room	5,467	323	$47.48	$544.54	$1,097.47
Motel	Room	3,080	182	$26.75	$306.77	$618.27
Nursing home	Bed	1,066	63	$9.26	$106.16	$213.96
ACLF	Bed	825	49	$7.16	$82.16	$165.58
Office and Financial						
Medical office	1,000 sq. ft.	26,520	1,568	$230.29	$2,641.44	$5,323.54
Bank	1,000 sq. ft.	31,569	1,867	$274.14	$3,144.37	$6,337.14
Bank w/drive In	1,000 sq. ft.	53,505	3,164	$464.63	$5,329.23	$10,740.50
Office under 10,000 gross sq. ft.	1,000 sq. ft.	15,723	930	$136.54	$1,566.08	$3,156.26
Office over 10,000 gross sq. ft.	1,000 sq. ft.	9,216	545	$80.03	$917.93	$1,849.98
Industrial						
Manufacturing	1,000 sq. ft.	2,653	157	$23.04	$264.24	$532.55
Warehouse	1,000 sq. ft.	3,389	200	$29.43	$337.56	$680.33
Mini warehouse	1,000 sq. ft.	1,736	103	$15.08	$172.93	$348.53
General industrial	1,000 sq. ft.	4,841	286	$42.03	$482.14	$971.69

Table 10-52
Net Impact Cost Calculation *(continued)*

Land Use	Impact Unit	Year Miles at 365.25[1]	Gallons at 16.91[2]	Annual Revenue at $0.1468[3]	NPV Credit at 6.00% at 20 Years[4]	Net Road Impact Cost[5]
Retail						
Retail under 10,000 gross sq. ft.	1,000 sq. ft.	26,197	1,549	$227.49	$2,609.25	$5,258.68
Retail 10,001-50,000 gross sq. ft.	1,000 sq. ft.	19,219	1,137	$166.90	$1,914.30	$3,858.08
Retail 50,001-100,000 gross sq. ft.	1,000 sq. ft.	16,074	951	$139.58	$1,600.99	$3,226.63
Retail 100,001-200,000 gross sq. ft.	1,000 sq. ft.	13,915	823	$120.84	$1,386.00	$2,793.34
Retail over 200,000 gross sq. ft.	1,000 sq. ft.	13,521	800	$117.42	$1,346.75	$2,714.23
Gas station	Pump	13,772	814	$119.59	$1,371.74	$2,764.60
New, used auto sales, repair	1,000 sq. ft.	22,802	1,348	$198.01	$2,271.12	$4,577.21
Restaurant	1,000 sq. ft.	35,881	2,122	$311.59	$3,573.87	$7,202.76
Fast-food restaurant	1,000 sq. ft.	90,984	5,380	$790.09	$9,062.26	$18,264.04
Car wash	1,000 sq. ft.	33,090	1,957	$287.35	$3,295.89	$6,642.52
Convenience store with gas	1,000 sq. ft.	57,357	3,392	$498.08	$5,712.91	$11,513.78
Convenience store with gas and fast food	1,000 sq. ft.	43,133	2,551	$374.56	$4,296.13	$8,658.41
Recreational						
Golf course	Hole	22,853	1,351	$198.45	$2,276.23	$4,587.51
Racquet club	1,000 sq. ft.	11,447	677	$99.40	$1,140.14	$2,297.83
Park	Acres	1,343	79	$11.66	$133.75	$269.55
Tennis court	Courts	19,848	1,174	$172.35	$1,976.90	$3,984.23
Marina	Berths	1,977	117	$17.17	$196.90	$396.83
Governmental						
Post office	1,000 sq. ft.	28,585	1,690	$248.22	$2,847.11	$5,738.05
Governmental						
Library	1,000 sq. ft.	34,649	2,049	$300.89	$3,451.13	$6,955.39
Government office	1,000 sq. ft.	47,850	2,830	$415.52	$4,766.02	$9,605.41
Miscellaneous						
Day care center	1,000 sq. ft.	21,410	1,266	$185.92	$2,132.53	$4,297.89
Hospital	1,000 sq. ft.	10,710	633	$93.00	$1,066.72	$2,149.86
Veterinary clinic	1,000 sq. ft.	4,346	257	$37.74	$432.92	$872.51
Church	1,000 sq. ft.	6,682	395	$58.03	$665.55	$1,341.34
Movie theater with matinee	Screens	53,311	3,153	$462.94	$5,309.93	$10,701.61

ACLF = adult congregate living facility

Notes:
1. [DAILY TRIP-MILES x 365.25 DAYS IN AVERAGE YEAR].
2. Adapted from "1997 National Transportation Statistics," Bureau of Transportation Statistics. Formula: [ANNUAL MILES / MILES PER GALLON].
3. Effective gasoline local, state, and federal gasoline tax per gallon for capital purposes. Formula: [GALLONS CONSUMED x GAS TAX PER GALLON].
4. Annual gas tax capitalized over 20 years (the standard long-term land-use and facility planning horizon) at 6.00% (roughly the long-term treasury rate).
5. [IMPACT COST – REVENUE CREDIT].

Table 10-53
Estimated Cost Per Lane-Mile by Service Area Within the City of Albuquerque, 2002–2025

Service Area	Number of Projects	Total Cost	Lane-Miles Added	Average Lane-Mile Cost
Downtown	N/A	N/A	N/A	N/A
NE Heights	4	$32,449,228	19.88	$1,632,255
Near North Valley	1	$7,690,710	4.54	$1,693,989
Far NE Heights	3	$12,393,267	6.18	$2,005,383
I-25 Corridor	2	$8,571,585	5.06	$1,693,989
NW Mesa	36	$173,059,625	85.20	$2,031,216
SW Mesa	23	$90,139,480	45.50	$1,981,087
Total	69	$324,303,894	166.36	$1,949,410

Table 10-54
Equivalent Pennies of Gas Tax Proxy Revenue

Gas Tax Proxy Revenues	Equivalent Pennies (Distribution)
State gross receipts tax	$0.007
Local GO bond financed from property taxes	$0.023
Quarter-cent sales tax	$0.007
Total	$0.037

GO = general obligation

Table 10-55
Growth Rates and Revenue Generation Factors by Service Area, 2004–2025

Service Area	Annual Percent Growth*	Existing Development Revenue Generation Factor
Downtown	0.38%	27.37
NE Heights	0.27%	38.91
Near North Valley	0.55%	19.11
Far NE Heights	1.05%	9.95
I-25 Corridor	1.91%	5.46
NW Mesa	3.21%	3.26
SW Mesa	3.56%	2.93

* The annual percent growth is calculated based on existing development, so it is not assumed to be compounded annually.

Table 10-56
Vehicle-Miles of Capacity, Vehicle-Miles Traveled, and Population Change by Service Area, 2000–2025

Service Area	2000–2025 Change (Percent)			
	VMC	VMT	Population	Employment
Downtown	0.01%	25.47%	1.78%	17.34%
NE Heights	3.41%	16.05%	3.08%	14.41%
Near North Valley	5.99%	34.43%	11.19%	19.91%
Far NE Heights	3.81%	26.81%	22.06%	47.91%
I-25 Corridor	9.01%	24.48%	144.15%	37.79%
NW Mesa	20.58%	61.31%	74.65%	116.15%
SW Mesa	12.01%	80.15%	81.23%	154.03%

VMC = vehicle-mile of capacity
VMT = vehicle-mile traveled

- Roadway capacity can be more precisely defined on an hourly basis.

Working with local transportation officials and planners, it was determined that the city should have the following seven service areas for transportation:

1. Downtown
2. NE Heights
3. Near North Valley
4. Far NE Heights
5. I-25 Corridor
6. NW Mesa
7. SW Mesa

The reason is that not all the areas of the city are expected to have the same amount of growth in development (and, therefore, in roadway facilities demand and capacity needs) over the next 20 or more years. These service areas are shown on Figure 10-8. The costs associated with roads, with respect to roadway facilities capacity improvements within each of the service areas in the city, are shown in Table 10-53.

Credits are now considered. New development generates new revenue that may be used to finance the same transportation facilities that impact fees may. It is important to recognize the new revenue that a given development generates (i.e., the gas tax proxy offset). It is also important to recognize the comparative ability of existing and future development to generate revenues for capital improvements (i.e., offset based on the existing/new development revenue ratio), which is based on the rate of growth occurring within the community.

Roads are financed from state transfers of gross receipts tax revenues, GO bonds retired by property tax levies, and a quarter-cent sales tax dedicated to roads. Analysis reported in Table 10-54 shows the equivalent gasoline tax credit that is considered. Later analysis will use these revenues as credits.

Normally the ratio of existing development-based revenue as a contribution to the underlying base of existing revenue is not considered (i.e., in a slow-growing area that may substantially have much of its transportation infrastructure in place, existing development may generate revenue that is transferred to support new construction in a fast-growing area where such infrastructure is not in place). This relationship is illustrated in Figure 10-9 for the 21-year period of analysis.

For example, for a 1 percent annual growth rate, the revenues generated by existing development make up about 88 percent of the total revenues generated by all development (existing plus new) during the 21-year period. In fact, existing revenues are 7.45 times the revenues generated by the new growth. This indicates that revenues for capital from growth are just a small percentage of the revenue generated by existing development during the 21-year time period. However, if the growth rate is 7.5 percent, the revenues generated by growth represent a significant portion of the total revenues (50 percent). This indicates that, at this growth rate, the revenues generated by growth play an equal role in determining the ability of existing development to absorb growth.

Table 10-55 shows the seven different service areas, their growth rates based on land-use assumptions, and the corresponding factors that have been developed to reflect the ratios between the revenues generated by existing development and

Table 10-57
Estimated Capacity Added Per Lane-Mile and Cost Per Vehicle-Mile
of Capacity Added by Service Area, 2002–2025

Service Area	Lane-Miles Added	Added VMC	Total Cost
Downtown	N/A	N/A	N/A
NE Heights	19.88	11,536	$32,449,228
Near North Valley	4.54	2,951	$7,690,710
Far NE Heights	6.18	4,017	$12,393,267
I-25 Corridor	5.06	3,289	$8,571,585
NW Mesa	85.20	71,665	$173,059,625
SW Mesa	45.50	35,094	$90,139,480
Total	166.36	128,552	$324,303,894
Weighted average capacity added and cost per VMC		773	$2,523

VMC = vehicle-mile of capacity

ITE LUC	Land Use	Unit	Service Area						
			Down-town	NE Heights	Near North Valley	Far NE Heights	I-25 Corridor	NW Mesa	SW Mesa
Residential									
210	Single-family detached/ mobile home individual lot								
	Less than 1,500 sq. ft.	DU	$0	$0	$0	$1,069	$2,113	$2,626	$2,702
	1,500-2,499 sq. ft.	DU	$0	$0	$0	$1,585	$3,160	$3,933	$4,046
	2,500 sq. ft. or larger	DU	$0	$0	$0	$1,754	$3,521	$4,388	$4,516
220	Multifamily	DU	$0	$0	$0	$512	$1,276	$1,651	$1,706
230	Condominium/ town house	DU	$0	$0	$0	$218	$885	$1,212	$1,260
240	Mobile home park	DU	$0	$0	$0	$765	$1,344	$1,629	$1,671
251	Retirement home	DU	$0	$0	$0	$74	$335	$462	$481
253	Congregate care facility (attached)	DU	$0	$0	$0	$67	$193	$255	$264
Lodging									
310	Hotel	Room	$0	$0	$0	$0	$869	$1,306	$1,371
320	Motel	Room	$0	$0	$0	$336	$837	$1,082	$1,119
416	RV park	RV space	$0	$0	$0	$441	$1,025	$1,312	$1,354
Recreation									
430	Golf course	Hole	$0	$0	$0	$3,513	$8,206	$10,510	$10,848
411	General recreation (city park)	Acres	$0	$0	$0	$162	$374	$478	$493
444	Movie theaters w/matinee	Screen	$0	$0	$0	$4,644	$9,422	$11,768	$12,112
492	Racquet club/ health club/ spa/dance studio	1,000 sq. ft.	$0	$0	$0	$6,231	$10,440	$12,507	$12,810
495	Community center	1,000 sq. ft.	$0	$0	$0	$2,769	$5,818	$7,316	$7,535
Institutional									
610	Hospital	1,000 sq. ft.	$0	$0	$0	$954	$2,902	$3,858	$3,998

Table 10-58
City of Albuquerque—Net Impact Cost Schedule (continued)

ITE LUC	Land Use	Unit	Service Area						
			Down-town	NE Heights	Near North Valley	Far NE Heights	I-25 Corridor	NW Mesa	SW Mesa
Institutional (continued)									
520	Elementary school	Student	$0	$0	$265	$502	$618	$675	$683
522	Middle school	Student	$0	$0	$252	$630	$814	$905	$919
530	High school	Student	$0	$0	$141	$551	$752	$850	$865
540	Junior/ community college	Student	$0	$0	$0	$146	$329	$419	$432
550	University	Student	$0	$0	$0	$299	$661	$839	$865
560	Church	1,000 sq. ft.	$0	$0	$318	$2,208	$3,134	$3,589	$3,656
566	Cemetery	Acres	$0	$0	$521	$2,324	$3,208	$3,642	$3,706
Office									
710	Under 50,000 sq. ft.	1,000 sq. ft.	$0	$0	$0	$2,076	$4,412	$5,559	$5,727
	50,000-100,000 sq. ft.	1,000 sq. ft.	$0	$0	$0	$1,612	$3,427	$4,318	$4,449
	100,001-200,000 sq. ft.	1,000 sq. ft.	$0	$0	$0	$1,375	$2,922	$3,681	$3,793
	200,001-400,000 sq. ft.	1,000 sq. ft.	$0	$0	$0	$1,172	$2,491	$3,139	$3,234
	Greater than 400,000 sq. ft.	1,000 sq. ft.	$0	$0	$0	$999	$2,124	$2,676	$2,757
770	Business park	1,000 sq. ft.	$0	$0	$0	$1,277	$2,895	$3,689	$3,806
Retail									
820	Under 100,000 gross sq. ft.	1,000 sq. ft.	$0	$0	$0	$200	$2,760	$4,016	$4,201
	100,000-400,000 gross sq. ft.	1,000 sq. ft.	$0	$0	$0	$662	$2,894	$3,990	$4,151
	400,001-800,000 gross sq. ft.	1,000 sq. ft.	$0	$0	$0	$792	$2,920	$3,965	$4,118
	Greater than 800,000 gross sq. ft.	1,000 sq. ft.	$0	$0	$0	$875	$2,932	$3,942	$4,090
931	Quality restaurant	1,000 sq. ft.	$1	$0	$0	$3,448	$9,458	$12,409	$12,843
934	Fast-food restaurant w/ drive-thru	1,000 sq. ft.	$2	$0	$0	$5,594	$25,755	$35,654	$37,107

Table 10-58
City of Albuquerque—Net Impact Cost Schedule (continued)

ITE LUC	Land Use	Unit	Service Area						
			Down-town	NE Heights	Near North Valley	Far NE Heights	I-25 Corridor	NW Mesa	SW Mesa
Retail (continued)									
841	New/used auto sales	1,000 sq. ft.	$0	$0	$0	$444	$3,758	$5,385	$5,624
850	Supermarket	1,000 sq. ft.	$0	$0	$0	$2,135	$4,580	$5,781	$5,957
853	Convenience store with gas pumps	1,000 sq. ft.	$1	$0	$0	$0	$6,461	$12,476	$13,359
862	Home improvement superstore	1,000 sq. ft.	$0	$0	$0	$2,170	$5,031	$6,436	$6,642
881	Pharmacy/ drug store w/ drive-thru	1,000 sq. ft.	$0	$0	$0	$1,082	$2,885	$3,771	$3,901
890	Furniture store	1,000 sq. ft.	$0	$0	$0	$411	$849	$1,064	$1,096
Industry									
110	General light industrial/ utilities	1,000 sq. ft.	$0	$0	$395	$2,187	$3,065	$3,496	$3,559
120	General heavy industrial	1,000 sq. ft.	$0	$1,045	$1,879	$2,264	$2,453	$2,546	$2,560
130	Industrial park	1,000 sq. ft.	$0	$0	$0	$1,308	$2,185	$2,616	$2,679
140	Manufacturing	1,000 sq. ft.	$0	$0	$850	$1,832	$2,313	$2,550	$2,584
150	Warehouse	1,000 sq. ft.	$0	$0	$0	$921	$1,546	$1,852	$1,897
151	Mini-warehouse	1,000 sq. ft.	$0	$0	$0	$394	$709	$864	$886

ITE LUC = Institute of Transportation Engineers Land Use Code
DU = dwelling unit

the revenues that will be generated by future development.

Evident in Table 10-55, for example, is that the anticipated growth in the Far NE Heights service area results in a revenue generation factor of 9.95. This factor indicates that, during the period from 2004 to 2025, the existing development in the service area is going to produce 9.95 times more revenue than the new development that will occur in the service area during this same time. These new revenues may offset the need to raise and spend impact fees for new roads in that service area.

To help further illustrate the implications of this relationship, Table 10-56 shows the VMC, VMT, population, and employment growth for the 2000–2025 period. Obviously, some areas are increasing their need for transportation facilities at a far faster rate than others.

Table 10-57 illustrates the differences in capacity among the service areas. Based on the analysis, a weighted average of 773 vehicle-miles of PM peak capacity added was calculated. In addition, the cost to add one VMC was calculated to be $2,523.

The impact fee schedule for Albuquerque is shown in Table 10-58. The schedule includes credits based on the gasoline tax equivalent (calculated similarly to that for Martin County, Florida) and reflects the contribution among service areas of existing development's share of service area-specific transportation-related revenue.

OBSERVATIONS

These case studies represent very different approaches to calculating impact fees for very different facilities, but they also show a common theme. Rational nexus and proportionate-share concepts are robust and can apply broadly. How broadly they can be considered will be shown in the next several chapters.

NOTES

1. One source that may be useful to practitioners and others is maintained by the National Impact Fee Roundtable at www.impactfee.org.
2. All those examples are from DeKalb County, Georgia, also prepared by the authors with the transportation impact fee analysis conducted by Tindale-Oliver & Associates.
3. James Duncan and Associates, Arthur C. Nelson, et al., "City of Atlanta Impact Fee Study" (Feb. 19, 1993), 4–5.
4. The regression equation is: Per Capita Taxable Value = $25,089 + ($1,556 * Time Since 1996). This regression equation has an r^2 of .909, thus indicating that time explains 91 percent of the variation of per capita taxable values. The T Statistics for the intercept is 38 and the T Statistics for the independent variable Time is 7.1. These statistics are significant at above 99 percent.
5. The analysis used the following publication as guidance: Arthur C. Nelson and James C. Nicholas, "Estimating Functional Population for Facility Planning," *Journal of Urban Planning and Development* 118(2): 45–58 (1992).

11

Proportionate-Share Fees for Social Infrastructure

New development can create demands on more than physical infrastructure. Chief among these is housing. In many metropolitan areas, a great deal of new development creates new jobs at income levels that are insufficient to afford even minimal housing. Worse, school teachers, fire fighters, police officers, nurses, and others who form the social fabric of communities cannot afford to live in new homes that are being built. A growing number of communities are recognizing that while development is mostly good, it may not benefit everyone proportionately. Additionally, because of declining federal and state aid combined with revenue limitations, many communities are looking to the source of impact—new development—to help offset socially undesirable impacts of that development.

This chapter reviews how proportionate-share development fee methodology may be used to expand "social" infrastructure such as affordable housing, day care centers, public art, and other socially beneficial investments. Its focus is mostly on housing, but it will touch on the other forms of social infrastructure.

The chapter has three sections. The first presents the foundations of proportionate-share development fees assessed on commercial development for workforce housing production. It includes a summary of national experience with such "workforce housing linkage" fees. The second section shows how proportionate-share principles may be applied to both residential and commercial development to produce workforce housing. The third section reviews other applications of proportionate-share development fees for other forms of social infrastructure.

PROPORTIONATE-SHARE PRINCIPLES TO PROVIDE WORKFORCE HOUSING FROM COMMERCIAL DEVELOPMENT

There is little practical difference between "linkage fees" and "impact fees" except for the type of facility that is financed. Impact fees are used to help finance physical infrastructure that benefits new development. Linkage fees are used to address socially desirable infrastructure that also provides benefits to new development but in a different way.

Where impact fees help provide the streets, fire stations, and water lines, the role of linkage fees is to address the housing occupied by low- and moderate-income workers, commonly also located near to where they work. The basic premise of impact fees is that new development should pay for at least a portion of the cost of providing the services that new development needs to proceed. The basic premise of linkage is that new development should provide some type of resources to abate social problems that are aggravated (or caused by) by new development, such as the additional need for day care facilities and housing within the means of the workforce. One difference is that impact fees commonly lead to a payment, while linkage commonly results in actual provision rather than payment of money.

There are other similarities. Linkage fees are most defensible when based on the very same proportionate-share principles as impact fees. To illustrate, the case of San Francisco's downtown office building linkage fee is reviewed. The analytic steps are common to proportionate-share analyses. San Francisco's current program is much more complex than the one it established in the 1980s, but the original formulation provides a very clear, concise appreciation of the proportionate-share method.[1]

Housing is becoming increasingly unaffordable. In 1995, the median household could afford the median resale home and come close to affording the median new home. Following 2000, this parity disappeared. Both new and existing home prices greatly outpaced median income. The causes of this phenomenon are many and varied, but the fact remains that nationally housing is scarce to working people and getting scarcer. In many states and areas, the problem is worse.

As might be expected, there is a positive correlation between median household income and median housing prices (see Table 11-2). Interestingly, the data in Table 11-1 show that there is no correlation at all between the change in median house price and the change in median household income. This indicates that the assumption that incomes will rise with development is becoming less and less of a reality. Many have concluded that, in order to continue receiving the benefits of development, something must be done for workforce housing. "Workforce" is usually defined as economically active households. Some take this stance on moral or ethical grounds while others take the position that continued economic development requires an increase in the labor force. Still others point to the cost and consequences of the long commuting trip when people "drive until they qualify."

Table 11-2 shows median household income, annual housing starts, median resale prices, changes in employment, and changes in population by state. Statistical analyses of these indicate that:

- There is a positive correlation between median household income and median sales prices

Table 11-1
Home Price Trends, 1993–2006

Year	Median Resale	New Home Median Price	Median Household Income	Housing Affordability *
1993		$126,500	$31,241	$104,137
1994		$130,000	$32,264	$107,547
1995	$110,500	$133,900	$34,076	$113,587
1996	$115,800	$140,000	$35,492	$118,307
1997	$121,800	$146,000	$37,005	$123,350
1998	$128,400	$152,500	$38,885	$129,617
1999	$133,300	$161,000	$40,696	$135,653
2000	$139,000	$169,000	$41,990	$139,967
2001	$147,800	$175,200	$42,228	$140,760
2002	$156,200	$187,600	$42,409	$141,363
2003	$178,800	$195,000	$43,318	$144,393
2004	$195,400	$221,000	$44,334	$147,780
2005	$219,600	$240,900	$46,326	$154,420
2006	$219,800	$246,500	$48,201	$160,670
Growth rate	6.45%	5.70%	3.20%	3.20%

* Affordability calculated at 30% of household income.

Source: Florida Board of Realtors and National Association of Realtors; Bureau of the Census, current construction reports.

Table 11-2
Income, Housing Starts, Resale Prices, and Employment and Population Change by State

Year	Median House-hold Income	2005 Housing Starts	Median Resale Price	Change from 2004 to 2005	
				Employment	Population
Alabama	$36,879	20.9	$210,205	27	31
Alaska	$56,234	2.3	$388,125	14	6
Arizona	$44,282	61.9	$263,400	36	207
Arkansas	$34,999	13.6	$198,750	66	29
California	$53,629	165.0	$926,250	406	313
Colorado	$50,652	36.8	$356,619	12	65
Connecticut	$60,941	8.5	$598,000	26	7
Delaware	$52,499	5.9	$384,000	12	13
Florida	$42,433	173.6	$390,000	380	402
Georgia	$45,604	86.1	$236,050	68	197
Hawaii	$58,112	6.5	$896,875	33	14
Idaho	$41,443	13.1	$249,889	44	35
Illinois	$50,260	58.5	$296,334	105	52
Indiana	$43,993	39.4	$182,130	41	43
Iowa	$43,609	14.6	$201,158	40	12
Kansas	$42,920	13.8	$201,250	3	10
Kentucky	$37,369	20.4	$213,779	9	32
Louisiana	$36,729	18.0	$242,375	36	12
Maine	$42,801	6.8	$219,250	14	4
Maryland	$61,592	27.1	$419,850	50	36
Massachusetts	$57,184	16.0	$579,375	-23	-3
Michigan	$46,039	51.7	$225,475	29	7
Minnesota	$52,024	39.0	$405,200	14	32
Mississippi	$32,938	12.8	$215,900	-14	16
Missouri	$41,974	27.5	$200,000	-1	45
Montana	$39,301	2.9	$193,572	13	8
Nebraska	$43,849	10.0	$200,000	-8	11
Nevada	$49,169	36.1	$399,000	49	80
New Hampshire	$56,768	7.0	$349,125	13	9
New Jersey	$61,672	26.5	$524,102	93	27
New Mexico	$37,492	10.3	$436,625	38	25
New York	$49,480	38.8	$402,333	107	24
North Carolina	$40,729	71.1	$216,359	59	141
North Dakota	$41,030	3.4	$186,010	0	-1
Ohio	$43,493	49.7	$202,750	47	9
Oklahoma	$37,063	14.3	$171,038	25	21
Oregon	$42,944	19.6	$357,233	22	50
Pennsylvania	$44,537	39.4	$310,667	65	28
Rhode Island	$51,458	2.4	$565,000	13	-5

Table 11-2
Income, Housing Starts, Resale Prices, and Employment and Population Change by State (*continued*)

Year	Median House-hold Income	2005 Housing Starts	Median Resale Price	Change from 2004 to 2005	
				Employment	Population
South Carolina	$39,316	33.4	$253,938	-3	52
South Dakota	$40,310	4.9	$171,625	-2	5
Tennessee	$38,874	34.2	$209,938	-39	70
Texas	$42,139	154.9	$193,059	298	411
Utah	$47,934	19.9	$330,625	41	69
Vermont	$45,686	2.7	$310,000	2	2
Virginia	$54,240	51.8	$355,949	164	92
Washington	$49,262	38.3	$358,750	74	86
West Virginia	$33,452	5.4	$162,667	5	3
Wisconsin	$47,105	36.7	$224,675	-35	29
Wyoming	$46,202	2.2	$213,166	2	3
United States	$46,242	1,656		2,478	2,869

Source: U.S. Census Bureau, "Income, Earnings, and Poverty" from the 2005 American Community Survey, series ACS-01; Statistical Abstract of the U.S. (Washington, DC: U.S. Department of Commerce, Census Bureau, 2007). Median resale prices from data provided by Coldwell Banker Home Price Comparison Index.

(i.e., states with higher median incomes also have higher sales prices);

- There is no correlation between median household income and changes in jobs or changes in population (i.e., states with more new jobs do not have higher incomes);
- There is no correlation between housing starts and median household income (i.e., states with higher incomes do not have more housing starts);
- There is statistically significant correlation between changes in population and changes in jobs (i.e., states with greater increases in population also have large increases in new jobs); and
- There are significant correlations between housing starts and changes in population and employment (i.e., increased population leads to increased demand for labor and housing). It would also be true that states with larger increases in new jobs will have larger increases in population and demand for housing.

Therefore, increases in population and housing appear to have material impacts on new jobs but no relationship with individual income. Since housing affordability is an income problem, increased growth would appear to aggravate rather than solve the problem. The City of San Francisco was among the first to address housing linkage in 1981.

The premise of San Francisco's housing linkage program is that, in some situations, construction of new office buildings in attractive downtown locations attracts more workers downtown as well as many who wish to work close to where they live and who can outbid existing, lower income households for downtown housing. Lower income households, many of which provide the support services required of downtown development, are displaced and some move entirely out of downtown. The aim of housing mitigation linkage fees is to collect fees from office buildings whose workers may displace existing residents, and then use that money to generate new, subsidized, low- and moderate-income housing. In this way, households that might have been displaced by new downtown development may nonetheless be able to live downtown.

Calculations for linkage are based on assumptions of new housing demand generated by new downtown office development. Those assumptions are based on detailed studies of local and regional housing market conditions as well as surveys of downtown office use and demand. Step-by-step review of the San Francisco housing linkage program will show its rational nexus characteristics.

The discussion begins with a review of the analytic steps involved in constructing Table 11-3,

Table 11-3
Housing Mitigation Requirements, Households Required

Row	Calculation	Result
A	Office space in new development (000s)	2,000 sq. ft.
B	Office space demolished (000s)	1,000 sq. ft.
C	Net addition of office space (000s)	1,000 sq. ft.
D	Employment density factor	268 sq. ft. per employee
E	Net addition of office employees	3,731 employees
F	Local employment ratio	31%
G	Net increase in local employment	1,157 employees
H	Percentage of new local employees occupying new housing	45%
I	Employees in new housing	521 employees
J	Average local employees per household	1.35 employees per household
K	Net new housing units needed	386 units
L	Net new units per 1,000 sq. ft. of new space	0.385572 units per 1,000 sq. ft.

which shows the nexus between downtown office construction and the need for new housing. In Row A, the amount of new office space expected to be constructed downtown over the planning period (typically 10 to 20 years) is reported. Row B is an estimate of the amount of existing space that is expected to be demolished to make room for new development. Row C is the net new office space expected over the planning period. Be sure you either input the number given or a different number.

Employee density (square feet per employee) is shown in Row D. This example shows a typical 250 square feet per employee plus a vacancy factor of 5 percent. Row E thus shows the total number of new downtown employees expected due to new office construction over the planning period.

The next several steps show how to relate new downtown employees with demand for new housing in the city. Row F shows the percent of new employees who are expected to move into the community. In this example during the 1980s, only 31 percent of the new office employees will actually move to the community. This information can only be ascertained through survey research, as was done by San Francisco. Row G then converts this percentage to the number of new employees expected to live downtown. This figure cannot be directly converted to new housing units; it is only the net addition of workers who live in the community.

The next step is to estimate the percentage of new workers choosing to live downtown who will occupy new housing and not existing housing. From the forecast of a San Francisco downtown plan environmental impact report, it was estimated that 55 percent of the increase in employed residents throughout the city between 1980 and 2000 would occur because of an increase in the number of workers per household in San Francisco without any change in the total number of households and housing stock. This means that 45 percent of the estimated increase in citywide employment would be attributable to a net addition of households in the city occupying new housing units. By applying the same percentages to new office employees, it was estimated that 45 percent of the increase in new office workers choosing to live in the city would occupy new housing units. The percent of new employees needing new housing units is reported in Row H and new units needed are reported in Row I.

However, many households have multiple office workers. In Row J, the estimate of the number of workers per household for the city is given. In the 1980s, it was 1.35 in San Francisco. Row K converts this ratio to an adjusted number of low- and moderate-income households that will be displaced by new office employees (in this example, 386 units). Row L converts Row K to an impact figure showing the number of new housing units needed for new and displaced households per 1,000 square feet of net downtown office space constructed over the planning period.

The objective of the housing linkage impact fee is to generate revenues sufficient to subsidize the construction of new housing units for new workers, although it is also assumed that all low- and moderate-income households displaced by new office employment will fill the pool of new housing if that housing is affordable. The next step is thus the distribution of new housing demand by income category. Table 11-4 presents the income category definitions and Table 11-5 reports the distribution of new households by the U.S. Department of Housing and Urban Development regional income category (for 1981).

The next four tables estimate the amount of subsidy needed to provide new housing units to new office employees, and presumably those existing households displaced by new office employees in the same percentages. Since housing is provided both for sale and for rent, subsidies for both kinds of housing are estimated. The subsidy is then converted to square feet of net office space construction.

Table 11-6 reports the average cost of constructing the average new home in San Francisco in 1984, the typical percent of gross income spent on mortgage and expenses during the first year of homeownership, the typical mortgage period, the prevailing long-term fixed mortgage rate, the down payment, the annual property tax as a percent of new home cost, and the annual insurance and association dues as a percent of new home cost.

With this information, the subsidy needed to provide new households with affordable homes for purchase can be calculated. The subsidy can be converted to a per-square-foot figure that may be assessed on net office space constructed (shown in Table 11-7).

Table 11-8 shows the average cost to construct the average rental housing unit in San Francisco, gross income to rent ratio typical for the area in 1984, and the local gross rent multiplier.

Table 11-9 shows the subsidy needed to provide new households with affordable rental housing. A

linkage fee per square foot of new office development is also calculated.

The linkage fees needed in the middle 1980s ranged between $9.55 and $10.47 per square foot. As there were no federal, state, or regional funds for the same purpose, there was no offset to this amount nor were new revenues generated by new development dedicated to the provision of housing. There was justification to assess the entire amount—about $10.00 per square foot (at a time when typical commercial office building construction was about $100 per square foot), but the city decided to assess half the justifiable rate of $5 per square foot.

Housing linkage programs are founded on the basic principles noted above to establish the nexus between new development and its impact on housing. Table 11-10 shows the range of use around the county

Table 11-5
Distribution of New Households by Income Category

New Household Distribution by HUD Income Categories	Percent	Number
50% of HUD median income	20%	77 households
80% of HUD median income	21%	81 households
120% of HUD median income	8%	31 households
150% of HUD median income	7%	27 households
165% of HUD median income	44%	170 households
Total		368 households

HUD = U.S. Department of Housing and Urban Development

Table 11-4
Definition of Income Category for Subsidy Calculations

Category	Income Range
50%	0% to 74% of HUD median household income
80%	75% to 99% of HUD median household income
120%	100% to 134% of HUD median household income
150%	135% to 164% of HUD median household income
165%	165% or more of HUD median household income

HUD = U.S. Department of Housing and Urban Development

Table 11-6
Cost to Produce Additional Households—For Sale

Average cost of new home (1981)	$100,000
Gross income spent on housing	38%
Mortgage period in years	30
Interest rate	13.00%
Down payment (percent of new home cost)	10.00%
Annual property taxes (percent of new home cost)	1.25%
Insurance/dues (percent of new home cost)	$1,200

Table 11-7
Subsidy Required—For Sale Housing, With Linkage Fee Estimate

Income Category	House Value Afforded	Subsidy Needed	Total Units
50% of HUD median income	$30,565	$69,440	77
80% of HUD median income	$53,923	$45,600	81
120% of HUD median income	$85,067	$13,800	31
150% of HUD median income	$108,425	$0	27
165% of HUD median income	$120,104	$0	170
Total subsidy	$9,545,855		
Linkage fee	$9.55 per sq. ft.		

HUD = U.S. Department of Housing and Urban Development

based on program design features, while Table 11-11 reports commercial housing linkage fees during the early 2000s. Appendix 11A reports experience with workforce housing linkage fees in California.

PROPORTIONATE-SHARE PRINCIPLES TO PROVIDE WORKFORCE HOUSING FROM RESIDENTIAL DEVELOPMENT

In some and perhaps a growing share of communities, commercial development as well as residential development puts pressure on supplying affordable housing. The case study of Collier County, Florida (prepared by James C. Nicholas), is instructive.

Housing is expensive in Collier County. Two of the consequences of high housing prices are higher rates of commuting and time committed to commuting. The 2000 Census found that 16 percent of Collier County employees commuted into the county[2] and 31 percent of all workers traveled 30 minutes or more to get to work.[3] Table 11-12 shows the median resale prices of existing single-family homes in Collier County, in Florida, and in the United States. During this period, the Collier median price grew at an annual rate of 9.1 percent, contrasted with 8.4 percent for the State of Florida and 6.6 percent for the United States as a whole.

Figure 11-1 visually presents these data. There has been a nationwide trend toward higher home prices. This trend has been especially apparent in growing areas such as Florida and Collier County. The causes of these price increases are many and varied. House

Table 11-8
Cost to Produce Additional Households—Rental

Assumption	Figure
Average cost of new rental unit (1984)	$100,000
Gross income spent on housing	30%
Gross rent multiplier (1984)	7.5

prices, like any good, are set in the market by forces of supply and demand. There is ample evidence that the supply of housing has greatly increased in Collier County, in Florida, and in the United States; thus, the resulting prices could not be the result of supply restriction. Rather, the demand for housing has increased and increased sharply, beyond the increase in supply. A number of factors have gone into this increase, most importantly:

- The demographic structure of American households together with the transition of the "Baby Boomers" toward preretirement and retirement;
- Very substantial reductions in interest rates, thus reducing the cost of home ownership;
- The relatively poor performance of financial investments, especially the stock and bond markets;
- The favorable tax treatment according home ownership, especially second or vacation home ownership, and
- The desirability of Collier County.

This list is intended to be illustrative rather than exhaustive. The point is that demand for housing, especially in resort-type areas such as Collier County, has greatly increased. During the decade of the 1990s, the annual average number of dwelling units built in Collier County was 5,037. Since 2000, the annual average number of dwellings constructed has averaged 7,333, 46 percent higher than the 1990s. Even though supply increased, prices have risen significantly. The dip in prices during 2006 is the much discussed "decline" in the housing market.

For Florida and the United States, there has been no decline from prices observed in 2005 levels, and the apparent decline in Collier County prices is likely due to seasonal fluctuations. Nevertheless, housing prices are abating locally, statewide, and

Table 11-9
Subsidy Required—Rental Housing With Linkage Fee Estimate

Income Category	House Value Afforded	Subsidy Needed	Total Units
50% of HUD median income	$30,752	$69,248	77
80% of HUD median income	$49,203	$50,797	81
120% of HUD median income	$73,805	$26,196	31
150% of HUD median income	$ 92,256	$7,744	27
165% of HUD median income	$101,481	$0	170
Total subsidy	$10,470,112		
Linkage fee	$10.47 per sq. ft.		

HUD = U.S. Department of Housing and Urban Development

Table 11-10
Linkage Program Variables

Variable	Policy Options	Considerations
Development category	Commercial (e.g., retail, office, and hotel)	Projected job growth within each type ideally including wage levels
	Institutional	Jobs/affordable housing impact of any projected location/ expansion of such institutions as universities and hospitals
	Residential (high value)	High-value residential developments can create a need for domestic workers.
	Industrial	Projected job growth ideally including wage levels
Rate	Ranges (at time of this survey) from $0.50 to $13.00 per sq. ft.	Cost of meeting affordable housing demand generated by new jobs
Payment timing	Immediate, or phased in as a project builds out; sometimes payment may be extended over time	How soon will the effects of new development be felt in the local housing market?
Use of funds	Affordable housing; jobs training; child care	Funds must be used based on the benefits for which they were calculated, such as affordable housing where the fee is calculated based on affordable housing impact.
Proximity requirement	Neighborhoods closer to commercial growth	Workers benefit when living in neighborhoods near the firms where they work.
Exemptions	Based on policy	Exemptions should not be allowed unless they meet other policy objectives that on balance offset the revenues lost. However, smaller developments falling below job-creation thresholds are often exempted as having de minimis impacts.

Source: Adapted from LISC. http://www.policylink.org/EDTK/Linkage/default.html.

Table 11-11
Linkage Programs Around the Country

City, Year Adopted	Development Assessed	Rate Per Square Foot	Exemptions	Unique Features
Boston, 1987	Office Retail Hotels Institutions	$8.62 ($7.18 for housing; $1.44 for job training)	Under 100,000 sq. ft.	Allows for seven-year extended payment period
Berkeley, 1993	Office Retail Other commercial and institutional	$5.00 ($4.00 for housing; $1.00 for child care) $2.50 ($2.00 for housing; $0.50 for child care)	Under 7,500 sq. ft.	Rate schedule is ceiling with options for reduced fees.
Cambridge, 1988	Office Retail Hotels Institutions	$3.28	Variable	Option to build affordable housing units of "equivalent benefit" in lieu of fees.
Sacramento, 1989	Office	$0.99		Provides exemptions to retail for financial hardship.
	Hotel	$0.94		
	Research and development	$0.84		
	Commercial, retail	$0.76		
	Manufacturing	$0.62		
	Warehouse	$0.27		
San Diego, 1990	Office	$1.06		
	Hotel	$0.60		
	Research and development	$0.75		
	Retail	$0.60		
	Manufacturing	$0.60		
	Warehouse	$0.60		
San Francisco, 1981	Entertainment	$13.95	Under 25,000 square feet	
	Hotel	$11.21		
	Office	$14.96		
	Research and development	$9.97		
	Retail	$13.95		
Seattle, 1989	Commercial	$20 per sq. ft. in excess of underlying floor area ratio allowance or construction of comparable affordable housing		Voluntary program

Source: Adapted from LISC. http://www.policylink.org/EDTK/Linkage/default.html.

Table 11-12
Median Resale Price of a Single-Family Home

Year	Collier	Florida	U.S.
1993	$149,500	$87,100	$0
1994	$144,800	$87,800	$0
1995	$149,000	$87,700	$110,500
1996	$172,200	$91,800	$115,800
1997	$164,000	$95,800	$121,800
1998	$176,000	$101,500	$128,400
1999	$209,300	$108,400	$133,300
2000	$237,400	$115,900	$139,000
2001	$237,500	$126,600	$147,800
2002	$263,700	$141,700	$156,200
2003	$297,200	$158,400	$178,800
2004	$371,700	$181,900	$195,400
2005	$482,400	$235,100	$219,600
2006 *	$469,100	$248,400	$219.800

* September

Source: Florida Board of Realtors and National Association of Realtors.

Figure 11-1
Median House Price: Collier, Florida, and U.S.

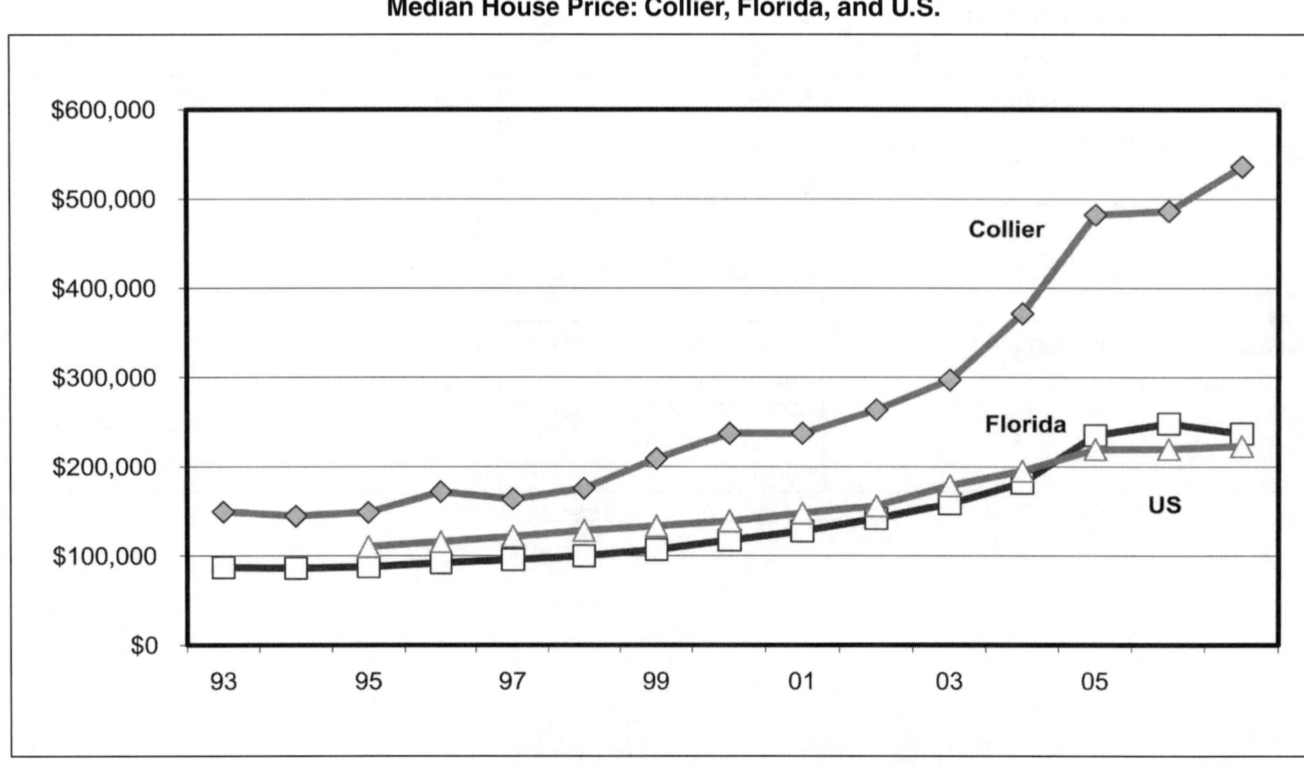

Table 11-13
Collier County and Florida Housing Resales by Month, 2003–2006

Year, Month		Collier				Florida			
		Sales	**Median Price**	**Percent Change in Sales**	**Percent Change in Price**	**Sales**	**Median Price**	**Percent Change in Sales**	**Percent Change in Price**
	Sep	351	$272,100			18,222	$158,800		
	Oct	387	$349,100			14,934	$174,100		
	Nov	278	$321,700			10,322	$172,500		
	Dec	341	$323,300			18,384	$161,100		
2004	Jan	321	$392,400			12,520	$168,100		
	Feb	373	$389,000			16,127	$162,300		
	Mar	435	$334,000			21,610	$168,400		
	Apr	529	$389,100			23,375	$173,900		
	May	416	$365,600			23,107	$181,300		
	Jun	615	$430,700			26,791	$189,700		
	Jul	388	$346,500			23,554	$186,700		
	Aug	390	$397,300			20,294	$189,500		
	Sep	333	$338,200	-5.1%	24.3%	14,803	$194,700	-18.8%	22.6%
	Oct	303	$357,500	-21.7%	2.4%	16,811	$190,800	12.6%	9.6%
	Nov	355	$369,900	27.7%	15.0%	17,116	$192,400	65.8%	11.5%
	Dec	388	$355,400	13.8%	9.9%	20,684	$195,900	12.5%	21.6%
2005	Jan	394	$497,900	22.7%	26.9%	15,567	$204,900	24.3%	21.9%
	Feb	434	$498,400	16.4%	28.1%	17,562	$201,400	8.9%	24.1%
	Mar	540	$430,800	24.1%	29.0%	24,045	$212,300	11.3%	26.1%
	Apr	540	$477,100	2.1%	22.6%	23,537	$218,600	0.7%	25.7%
	May	476	$488,900	14.4%	33.7%	24,069	$230,800	4.2%	27.3%
	Jun	528	$491,400	-14.1%	14.1%	25,455	$248,700	-5.0%	31.1%
	Jul	459	$490,400	18.3%	41.5%	21,669	$252,300	-8.0%	35.1%
	Aug	472	$500,800	21.0%	26.1%	21,318	$246,500	5.0%	30.1%
	Sep	350	$472,300	5.1%	39.7%	20,368	$247,800	37.6%	27.3%
	Oct	254	$495,500	-16.2%	38.6%	16,029	$241,000	-4.7%	26.3%
	Nov	333	$479,800	-6.2%	29.7%	17,219	$250,500	0.6%	30.2%
	Dec	668	$377,700	72.2%	6.3%	17,505	$247,000	-15.4%	26.1%
2006	Jan	580	$376,300	47.2%	-24.4%	12,815	$248,600	-17.7%	21.3%
	Feb	603	$492,300	38.9%	-1.2%	13,539	$244,200	-22.9%	21.3%
	Mar	371	$383,100	-31.3%	-11.1%	18,881	$248,200	-21.5%	16.9%
	Apr	274	$374,500	-49.3%	-21.5%	16,392	$249,700	-30.4%	14.2%
	May	313	$507,900	-34.2%	3.9%	18,680	$256,400	-22.4%	11.1%
	Jun	274	$451,500	-48.1%	-8.1%	18,089	$257,800	-28.9%	3.7%
	Jul	227	$461,800	-50.5%	-5.8%	14,451	$250,800	-33.3%	-0.6%
	Aug	259	$469,100	-45.1%	-6.3%	14,736	$248,400	-30.9%	0.8%
	Sep	236	$446,900	-32.6%	-5.4%	13,485	$243,900	-33.8%	-1.6%
2005	Highest	Aug	$500,800			July	$252,300		

Table 11-13
Collier County and Florida Housing Resales by Month, 2003–2006 *(continued)*

Year, Month			Collier			Florida			
				Median Price	Percent Change in			Median Price	Percent Change in	
		Sales			Sales	Price	Sales		Sales	Price
2005	Lowest	Dec	$377,700				Feb	$201,400		
2006	Highest	May	$507,900				June	$257,800		
	Lowest	Apr	$374,500				Sept	$243,900		

Source: Florida Board of Realtors.

nationally. It is not possible to project the extent of the possible decline. A closer look at Collier County sales data shows that ups and downs are normal. Table 11-13 shows monthly sales for the county and for the state. Year-to-year percentage changes are also shown. Wide swings are the norm. There are many factors that lead to such swings, including the state of the economy.

To this point, 2006 sales prices are within the range of those seen in 2005. For the state, 2006 prices are above those of 2005. Figures 11-2 and 11-3 show Collier County's monthly sales and median prices. Trend lines have been inserted. The fact that both the number of sales and median prices are under the trend would indicate that there is lessened demand and that prices are actually dropping. Given the normalcy of swings, it is now impossible to determine the extent of the declines. The year-over-year percentage changes would suggest a decline in price of 6 to 8 percent, with the dramatic changes in early 2006 likely due more to shifts within the market than to absolute declines.

Table 11-14 shows median household income together with median prices of existing single-family homes and an affordability limit calculated as 30 percent of median income devoted to housing. Figures 11-4 and 11-5 graph these data.

Figure 11-4 shows that there was rough parity between the affordability limit and median prices through 2002. Since then, a gap has existed and is getting bigger each year. The decline in median income following 2001 is probably due to the national economic recession, although it has yet to return to prior levels.

These data confirm that there is a housing affordability problem in Collier County and that the problem is getting worse with the passage of time. The causes of this problem are many and varied. Most are beyond the ability of local officials to influence. The recent declines in prices have stabilized the affordability problem. In order for market forces

Table 11-14
Median Household Income, Resale Prices, and Affordability Limits, Collier County

Year	Median Income	Resale Price	Affordability Limit
1996	$48,800	$172,200	$162,667
1997	$51,300	$164,000	$171,000
1998	$54,100	$176,000	$180,333
1999	$54,518	$209,300	$181,727
2000	$59,100	$237,400	$197,000
2001	$65,000	$237,500	$216,667
2002	$69,800	$263,700	$232,667
2003	$61,400	$297,200	$204,667
2004	$63,300	$371,700	$211,000
2005	$63,300	$482,400	$211,000
2006 *	$66,100	$446,900	$220,333

* September

Sources: U.S. Department of Housing & Urban Development and Florida Board of Realtors.

Figure 11-2
Collier Monthly Sales

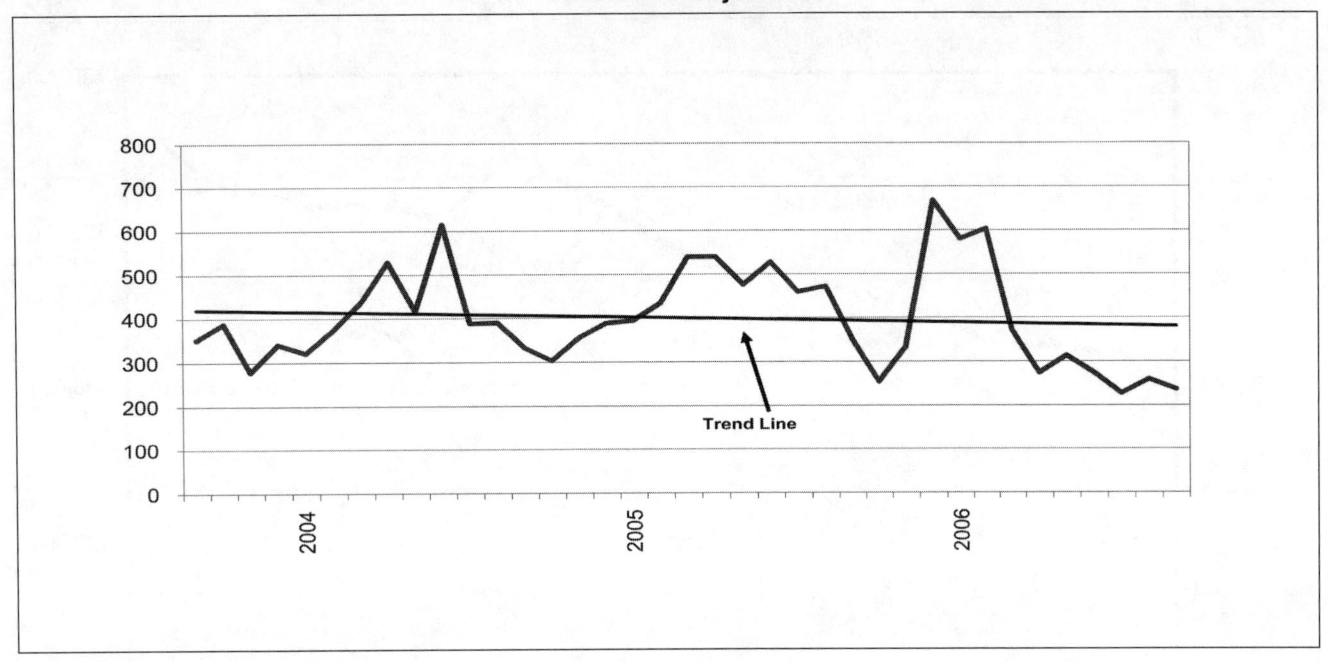

to reinstitute affordability of the median home to the median household income, median prices would have to fall by 50.7 percent (from $446,900 to $220,300). Such a decline is not foreseen.

Table 11-15 shows annual earnings of employees by industry for Collier County for 2001, 2004, and 2005. Also shown are Collier County earnings as a percent of annual earnings for the State of Florida. On average, Collier earnings tend to approximate those of the state, with some notable exceptions. One point is obvious: With Collier employee earnings approximating that of the state's, the higher Collier County housing prices will exert greater problems in Collier County than seen elsewhere in the State of Florida.

Table 11-16 applies the 2004 to 2005 rate of change to 2005 earnings to project Collier County annual employee earnings to December 2006. These data will be used for the subsequent calculations in this report. Additionally, employee household earnings are also projected to December 2006.

The typical economically active household has more than one person employed. Table 11-17 shows the number of employed persons per household

Figure 11-3
Median Price of Existing Homes

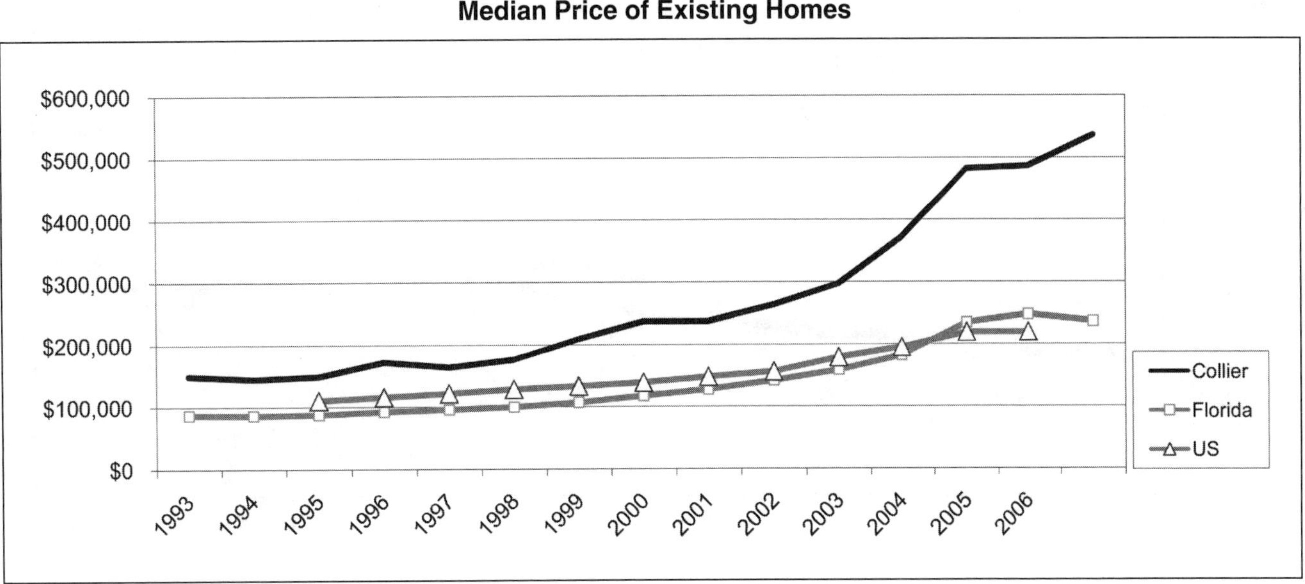

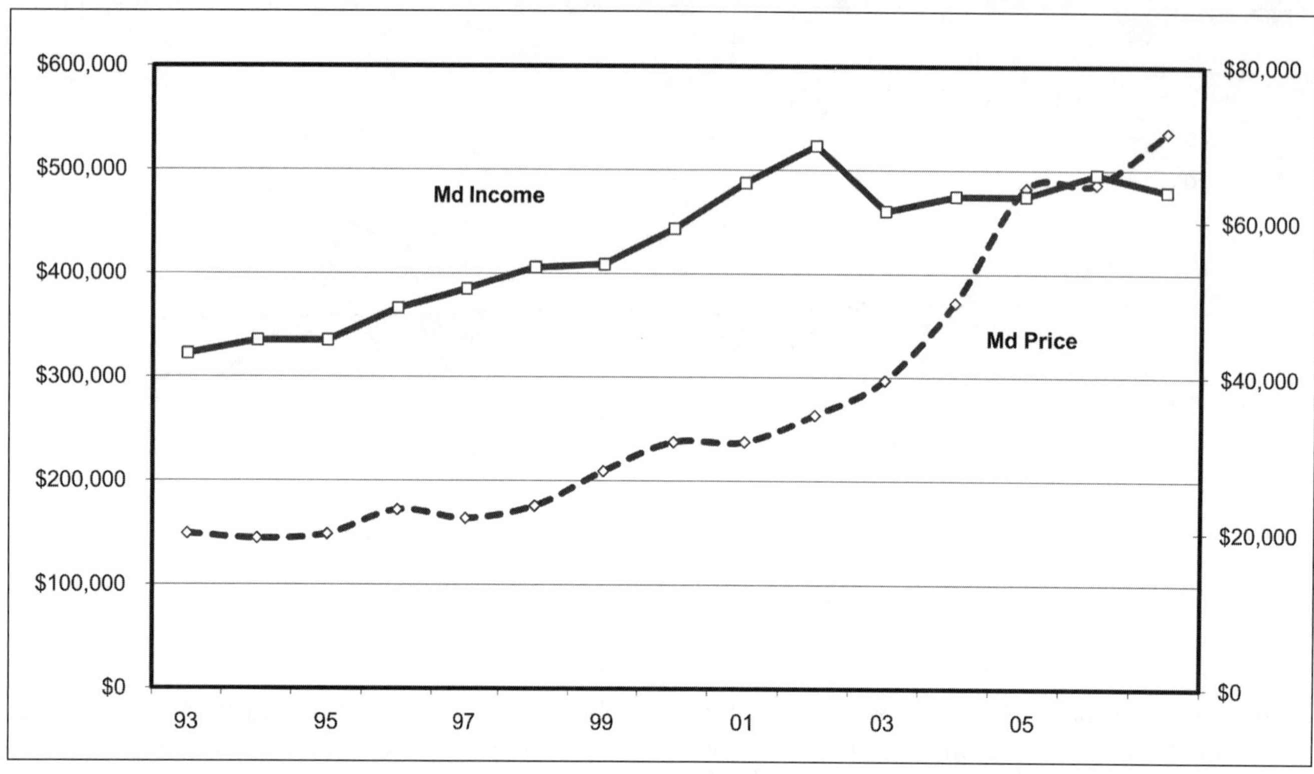

Figure 11-4
Existing Home Prices and Median Income, Collier County

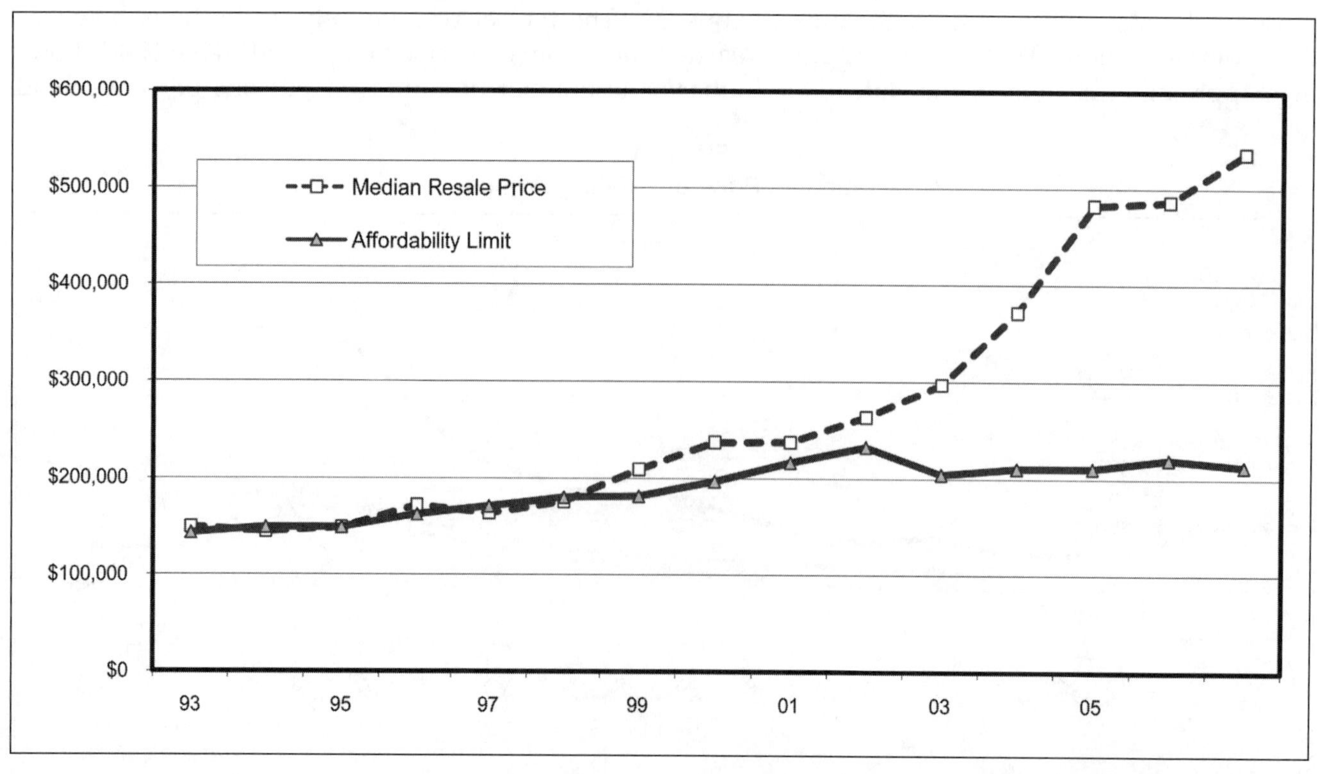

Figure 11-5
Collier County Housing Affordability

Table 11-15
Annual Earnings by Industry, Collier County

Industry Title	Collier County Annual Wage			Collier as Percent of State of Florida		
	2001	2004	2005	2001	2004	2005
Total, all industries	$30,838	$34,874	$38,179	97.7%	99.2%	103.8%
Goods-producing	$28,964	$32,450	$35,613	85.1%	86.7%	91.8%
Agriculture, forestry, fishing, and hunting	$14,673	$17,388	$18,173	74.2%	79.3%	79.0%
Construction	$35,165	$37,762	$40,298	104.6%	102.8%	105.1%
Manufacturing	$33,116	$37,971	$41,410	87.2%	89.4%	95.4%
Service-providing	$31,365	$35,524	$38,930	100.6%	102.1%	106.8%
TTU	$27,095	$32,168	$33,356	89.5%	96.5%	96.5%
Wholesale trade	$42,311	$52,328	$54,227	92.7%	103.9%	102.8%
Retail trade	$23,919	$27,669	$28,450	105.7%	111.6%	110.2%
Transportation and warehousing	$33,203	$40,405	$41,011	92.4%	100.3%	100.7%
Information	$44,922	$47,340	$49,341	97.0%	93.2%	93.5%
Financial activities	$51,734	$56,471	$69,540	120.3%	114.1%	132.2%
Finance and insurance	$63,555	$69,338	$91,195	129.8%	123.6%	153.8%
Real estate and rental and leasing	$34,922	$38,745	$42,708	115.4%	108.3%	109.6%
Professional and business services	$38,333	$38,676	$48,624	116.8%	105.3%	124.0%
Education and health services	$34,421	$40,575	$42,123	105.9%	111.1%	110.8%
Health care and social assistance	$35,679	$42,009	$43,315	104.8%	109.2%	109.1%
Leisure and hospitality	$20,852	$24,206	$25,728	122.8%	130.6%	132.3%
Accommodation and food services	$18,443	$20,346	$21,194	126.7%	127.6%	125.2%
Other services	$22,866	$25,696	$26,486	102.8%	104.3%	102.7%
Public administration	$37,219	$43,199	$44,780	100.0%	100.1%	100.4%

TTU = trade, transportation, and utilities

Source: Florida Labor Market Statistics (September 2006).

in Collier County. To get household earnings, the earnings of the individual are increased by the expected earnings for the other individual within the household. The average economically active household has 1.42 employed persons. This is the primary individual plus 0.42 others. The 0.42 is multiplied by the average earnings of all employed persons ($41,797), which is then added to the earnings of the primary individual to get household income. These data are shown in Table 11-17.

The prices of Collier County residences were shown in Table 11-14. Many of these residences could be considered to be luxurious and not what one would expect to be the residence of the typical member of Collier County's workforce. Additionally, the concern addressed herein is entry housing for members of the workforce that are in the lower segment of the earnings spectrum. It is expected that such dwellings would tend to be small and Spartan. Table 11-18 shows the expectation with respect to Collier County entry workforce housing.

The three housing types in Table 11-18 are organized into three categories. Category 1 is intended for those Collier County households earning less than 80 percent of median household income ($66,100). Category 2 is intended for those earning between 80 and 120 percent of median household income. Category 3 is intended for those earning

Table 11-16
Employment and Household Earnings by Industry, Collier County, 2006

Industry Title	NAICS* Code	Average Employment	Annual Wage 2005	Annual Wage 2006	Household Earnings
Total, all industries	10	129,308	$38,179	$41,797	$59,338
Goods-producing	101	29,298	$35,613	$39,084	$56,625
Agriculture, forestry, fishing, and hunting	11	6,365	$18,173	$18,993	$36,534
Construction	1012	19,707	$40,298	$43,004	$60,545
Manufacturing	1013	3,226	$41,410	$45,160	$62,702
Service-providing	102	100,010	$38,930	$42,663	$60,204
TTU	1021	24,011	$33,356	$34,588	$52,129
Wholesale trade	42	3,219	$54,227	$56,195	$73,736
Retail trade	44-45	18,550	$28,450	$29,253	$46,794
Transportation and warehousing	48-49	2,004	$41,011	$41,626	$59,167
Information	1022	1,796	$49,341	$51,427	$68,968
Financial activities	1023	7,535	$69,540	$85,634	$103,175
Finance and insurance	52	4,170	$91,195	$119,942	$137,483
Real estate and rental and leasing	53	3,365	$42,708	$47,076	$64,617
Professional and business services	1024	14,440	$48,624	$61,131	$78,672
Education and health services	1025	19,804	$42,123	$43,730	$61,271
Health care and social assistance	62	12,989	$43,315	$44,662	$62,203
Leisure and hospitality	1026	21,835	$25,728	$27,346	$44,887
Accommodation and food services	72	15,396	$21,194	$22,077	$39,618
Other services	1027	4,888	$26,486	$27,300	$44,841
Public administration	1028	5,492	$44,780	$46,419	$63,960

TTU = trade, transportation, and utilities

* North American Industrial Classification System (NAICS) is a system of classifying industries for purposes of data collection, reporting, and analysis.

Source: Florida Labor Market Statistics (September 2006).

more than 120 percent of median household income but still needing assistance. The categories are differentiated by the weighting of housing type (as shown in Table 11-18).

Table 11-19 shows the incomes necessary to afford the units set out in Table 11-18. These incomes are both individual and household. Only home ownership is shown here. These results are easily translated into rental equivalents if rental housing is the goal.

All new developments will have impacts on the need for workforce housing. The first will be the housing needs of the workers employed on a continuing basis to operate and maintain residences. The second is the housing needs of employees to operate and maintain places of business.

Table 11-17
Employees Per Household, Collier County

Calculation Step	Collier County
Total households	103,126
With earnings	70,298
Without earnings	32,828
Employed	99,800
Employed per economically active household	1.42

Employment data used here reflect total nonagricultural employment, as shown in previous tables.

Source: Bureau of the Census, American Factfinder and Florida Agency for Workforce Innovation, Labor Market Statistics.

Table 11-18
Entry-Level Workforce Housing, Collier County

	Multifamily Small	Multifamily Medium	Town Home
Cost Detail			
Land	$77,509	$77,509	$40,688
Building	$70,660	$114,830	$220,253
Other	$42,831	$77,661	$58,059
Floor area	800	1,300	1,990
Cost per sq. ft.	$239	$208	$160
Total	$191,000	$270,000	$319,000
	Category 1	**Category 2**	**Category 3**
Multifamily small	80%	25%	10%
Multifamily medium	10%	50%	15%
Town home	10%	25%	75%
Average cost/price	$211,700	$262,500	$298,850

Source: Fishkind & Associates (November 2006).

Table 11-19
Income Needed to Afford Housing

Calculation of Affordability	Category 1	Category 2	Category 3
Purchase or production price	$211,700	$262,500	$298,850
Down payment	3.00%	3.00%	3.00%
Loan term	30	30	30
Interest rate	5.78%	5.78%	5.78%
Points	2.00%	2.00%	2.00%
Mortgage insurance percent	0.60%	0.60%	0.60%
Taxes and insurance percent	1.83%	1.83%	1.83%
Other closing costs	3.00%	3.00%	3.00%
Cash to close	$16,809	$20,843	$23,729
Mortgage	$205,349	$254,625	$289,885
Mortgage payment	$1,202	$1,491	$1,697
Mortgage insurance amount	$103	$127	$145
Taxes and insurance amount	$236	$301	$348
Total monthly	$1,541	$1,919	$2,190
Maximum monthly expense to income	30.00%	30.00%	30.00%
Minimum monthly income	$5,135	$6,398	$7,302
Annual income	$61,624	$76,776	$87,619
Income to price ratio	29.11%	29.25%	29.32%
Workers per household	1.420	1.420	1.420
Income per worker	$43,407	$54,080	$61,718
Annual rental equivalent	$21,170	$26,250	$29,885

There is concern for a group of employees commonly referred to as "critical employees." Although the definition varies from community to community, in Collier County critical employees include public school teachers, police officers (including the jail), and firefighters, which include emergency medical technicians and paramedics. New developments will cause demands for additional critical employees who will face housing affordability issues.

Once a residence has been constructed, it must be operated and maintained. Some people do much of the O & M activities themselves while others do not. The residential survey conducted by RRC, Incorporated, found that the average number of full-time equivalent employees per residential unit in Collier County was 0.0952. This is 198 person-hours per residence per year devoted to O & M by employed persons. The assignment of employees to the residential sector is shown in Table 11-20. Critical employees (i.e., school teachers, law enforcement, and fire/rescue personnel) are also assigned to residences (as shown in Table 11-20).

Table 11-20
Employment Assignable to Residences

Industry	Employees	
	Total	**Per Unit**
O & M		
Construction		
Building finishing	1,282	0.007
Other contractors	1,709	0.010
Financial Activities		
Property management	427	0.002
Miscellaneous real estate and finance	427	0.002
Professional and Business Services		
Services to buildings and dwellings (cleaning and landscaping)	5,126	0.029
Waste collection	1,282	0.007
Education and Health Services		
Health services	1,282	0.007
Social services	1,282	0.007
Other Services		
Repair and maintenance	854	0.005
Personal and laundry services	1,282	0.007
Private household services	1,709	0.010
Other	427	0.002
Total O & M	17,087	0.095
Critical Employees		
Education and Health Services		
Educational services	2,841	0.016
Public Administration		
Police protection	800	0.004
Fire protection	800	0.004
Total critical employees	4,441	0.025
Total all employees	21,528	0.120

O & M = operations and maintenance
Critical employees, survey of Collier County critical employers (November 2006).

Source: Residential Employees, RRC, Incorporated.

The annual earnings of these employees are shown in Table 11-21. This table presents the weighted average of O & M employee earnings. The weighting is by the number of employees in the individual employment category (as shown in Table 11-21).

The household of the average O & M employee is expected to receive $65,657 in annual earnings. This is 99 percent of the median of $66,100. The necessary income data from Table 11-21 show that the typical O & M worker will be able to afford to pay $225,556 for housing, $36,944 short of the need (as illustrated in Table 11-22).

The RRC, Incorporated survey also determined how many O & M workers are required by type and size of residence. The results of this survey show that homes occupied full time have fewer O & M employees than vacation or second homes, and that larger homes require more employees than do smaller. A regression equation yielded the following formulae for the number of O & M employees, and the data resulting from these formulae are in Table 11-23.

EMPLOYEES—FULL TIME OCCUPIED =
-0.0566 + (.00007186 * AREA IN SQ. FT.) – (.07982)

EMPLOYEES—PART TIME OCCUPIED =
-0.0566 + (.00007186 * AREA IN SQ. FT.)

The regression results show that residences occupied by full-time residents are largely self-supplying until 2,000 feet in floor area, and then outside help is sought. The same is found for vacation or second homes, except outside help is sought after 1,000 feet of floor area. As both units get larger, the number of employees needed to operate and maintain the dwelling gets larger. Using the data shown in Tables 11-22 and 11-23, Table 11-24 estimates the number of residential employees by unit size.

While the statistical analysis indicated that assistance needed for second homes is greater, for the purpose of this study it is assumed that all residences in Collier County are occupied by full-time residents. The fire/rescue and law enforcement personnel included are for Collier County, the cities of Naples and Marco Island, and the independent fire districts. The number of critical employees and their earnings exclude those that are in support or supervisory roles. School principals, fire chiefs, and police captains are not included, thus focusing attention on those in the lower ranks.

Tables 11-25, 11-26, and 11-27 present the critical employee data. Table 11-25 shows that there are 0.0178 teachers per 1,000 square feet of residential floor area, or one public school teacher per 56,228 feet of residential floor area. The average salary for individual teachers is $50,830 and $68,371 per teacher household. The average teacher household will require $27,621 to afford housing, or $0.49 per square foot of residential floor area.

Table 11-26 presents data for fire and rescue personnel as well as population data. These data show the number of fire and rescue personnel per 1,000 square feet for both residential and nonresidential development.

Table 11-27 presents fire and rescue employee earnings data. The average individual salary is $48,168,

Table 11-21
Residential Operations and Maintenance, Employee Earnings

Calculation Step		Figure
Total dwelling units		188,651
O & M employees per unit		0.0952
Total O & M employees		17,960
O & M Employee Earnings	**Individual**	**Weight**
Construction	$43,004	0.18
Financial activities	$85,634	0.05
Professional and business services	$61,131	0.38
Education and health services	$43,730	0.15
Other services	$27,300	0.25
Weighted average	$48,116	1.00
Employees per household		1.420
Employee household earnings		$65,657

O & M = operations and maintenance

Table 11-22
Residential Operations and
Maintenance, Employee Assistance

Calculation Step	Figure
Weighted average	$48,116
Employees per household	1.420
Employee household earnings	$65,657
Housing affordability	$225,556
Available housing cost	$262,500
Assistance needed	$36,944

which converts to household income of $65,709. These households can afford $225,733, which is $36,767 short of the need. Table 11-27 also shows this shortage, referred to as a gap, per square foot of floor area for residential and nonresidential development.

The data for law enforcement are shown in Table 11-28. As with other critical employees, the number of employees is calculated on the basis of floor area, here differentiated between residential and nonresidential, with nonresidential further classified by type of use. Table 11-29 shows the earnings of law enforcement personnel. The average is $53,042 for the individual officer and $70,583 for the officer's household. The average household can afford $242,478 for housing, which is $20,022 short of the need. Table 11-29 shows this gap on a per-square-foot basis for the various land uses.

Table 11-24
Residential Employees by Size of Residence

Floor Area	O & M Employees	Households	Assistance Needed
500	0.000	0.000	$0
750	0.000	0.000	$0
1,000	0.000	0.000	$0
1,500	0.000	0.000	$0
2,000	0.007	0.005	$190
2,500	0.043	0.030	$1,125
3,000	0.079	0.056	$2,060
3,500	0.115	0.081	$2,995
4,000	0.151	0.106	$3,930
4,500	0.187	0.132	$4,865
5,000	0.223	0.157	$5,800

O & M = operations and maintenance

Table 11-30 brings together the O & M employees with the critical employees, and presents total assistance needed by size of residence.

The sizes shown are illustrative. The assistance would be calculated on the basis of the actual heated or air-conditioned space of the residence. The amount charged would be charged per square foot for the size grouping of the residence times the actual number of square feet. For example, a home with 1,250 square feet would

Table 11-23
Operations and Maintenance Employees,
by Type and Size of Residence

Floor Area	Resident Employees	Households	Vacation or Second Employees	Households
500	0.000	0.000	0.000	0.000
750	0.000	0.000	0.000	0.000
1,000	0.000	0.000	0.015	0.011
1,500	0.000	0.000	0.051	0.036
2,000	0.007	0.005	0.087	0.061
2,500	0.043	0.030	0.123	0.087
3,000	0.079	0.056	0.159	0.112
3,500	0.115	0.081	0.195	0.137
4,000	0.151	0.106	0.231	0.163
4,500	0.187	0.132	0.267	0.188
5,000	0.223	0.157	0.303	0.213

Table 11-25
Critical Employees—School Teachers

Calculation Step		Figure
Teachers 2006–07		2,841
Percent residential		100%
Total floor area		159,745,423
Teachers per 1,000 sq. ft.		0.0178
Base salary	Individual	Household
Bachelor of arts degree	$39,198	$56,739
Master's degree	$40,893	$58,434
Average salary	$50,830	$68,371
Salary used	$50,830	$68,371
Affordability limit		$234,879
Workforce housing cost		$262,500
Gap		$27,621
Gap per sq. ft. of residential floor area		$0.49

Source: School District of Collier County.

Table 11-26
Critical Employees—Fire and Rescue

Fire and Rescue	Employees	Population
City of Naples	55	22,490
City of Marco Island	33	15,647
Everglades	0	527
North Naples	144	91,119
Golden Gate	53	77,027
East Naples	144	72,641
Immokalee	17	25,351
Big Corkscrew	23	9,797
Isle of Capri	3	1,963
Ochopee	9	2,574
Total	481	319,136
Allocation	**Percent**	**Per 1,000 Sq. Ft.**
Residential	74.1%	0.00182
Nonresidential	25.9%	0.00294
Government		0.00294
Industrial		0.00294
Institutional		0.00294
Office		0.00294
Retail		0.00294
Tourist		0.00294

Source: Tindale-Oliver & Associates, "2005 Fire/Rescue Services Impact Fee Update Report" (January 2006).

Table 11-27
Critical Employees—Fire and Rescue Wages

Calculation Step	Individual	Household
Starting salary	$32,633	$50,174
Average salary	$48,168	$65,709
Salary used	$48,168	$65,709
Affordability limit		$225,733
Workforce housing cost		$262,500
Gap		$36,767
Gap per sq. ft. of floor area		
Residential		$0.07
Nonresidential		
Government		$0.11
Industrial		$0.11
Institutional		$0.11
Office		$0.11
Retail		$0.11
Tourist		$0.11

Source: Collier County (October 2006).

Table 11-28
Critical Employees—Law Enforcement

Law Enforcement	Officers
Sheriff	
Patrol	600
Jail	300
Naples	80
Marco Island	32
Total	1,012

Allocation	Officers	Per 1,000 Sq. Ft.
Residential	821	0.00830
Nonresidential		
Government	24	0.00298
Industrial	19	0.00179
Institutional	3	0.00075
Office	8	0.00298
Retail	123	0.00894
Tourist	14	0.00170

Source: Tindale-Oliver, "Collier County Law Enforcement Update" (May 8, 2006), 13f.

Table 11-29
Critical Employees—Law Enforcement Wages

Calculation Step	Assumption	Figure
Base salary		
Starting salary	$39,153	$56,694
Average salary	$53,042	$70,583
Salary used	$53,042	$70,583
Affordability limit		$242,478
Workforce housing cost		$262,500
Gap		$20,022
Gap per sq. ft. of floor area		
Residential		$0.17
Nonresidential		
Government		$0.06
Industrial		$0. 04
Institutional		$0.01
Office		$0.06
Retail		$0.18
Tourist		$0.03

Source: Collier County (October 2006).

Table 11-30
Residential Employees by Size of Residence

Floor Area	O & M Assistance Needed	Critical Employees			Assistance Needed	Total Assistance
		Teachers	Fire	Police		
500	$0	$246	$34	$83	$362	$362
750	$0	$368	$50	$125	$543	$543
1,000	$0	$491	$67	$166	$725	$725
1,500	$0	$737	$101	$249	$1,087	$1,087
2,000	$190	$982	$134	$333	$1,449	$1,639
2,500	$1,125	$1,228	$168	$416	$1,811	$2,936
3,000	$2,060	$1,474	$201	$499	$2,174	$4,233
3,500	$2,995	$1,719	$235	$582	$2,536	$5,531
4,000	$3,930	$1,965	$268	$665	$2,898	$6,828
4,500	$4,865	$2,211	$302	$748	$3,260	$8,125
5,000	$5,800	$2,456	$335	$831	$3,623	$9,422

O & M = operations and maintenance

Table 11-31
Employment in Collier County, 2001–2005

Industry Title	2001	2002	2003	2004	2005
Total, all industries	110,241	114,497	115,802	121,216	129,308
Goods-producing	24,234	24,243	23,597	25,658	29,298
Natural resources and mining	7,043	7,190	6,714	6,719	6,365
Agriculture, forestry, fishing, and hunting	6,983	7,130	6,660	6,660	6,310
Construction	14,284	14,255	14,263	16,127	19,707
Manufacturing	2,908	2,798	2,620	2,812	3,226
Service-providing	86,006	90,254	92,205	95,558	100,010
TTU	22,031	22,432	22,137	22,750	24,011
Wholesale trade	2,575	2,787	2,609	2,742	3,219
Retail trade	17,217	17,357	17,389	17,850	18,550
Transportation and warehousing	1,962	1,962	1,829	1,877	2,004
Utilities	277	327	310	281	238
Information	1,706	1,687	1,683	1,814	1,796
Financial activities	6,055	6,343	6,485	6,784	7,535
Finance and insurance	3,555	3,750	3,863	3,931	4,170
Real estate and rental and leasing	2,500	2,593	2,622	2,853	3,365
Professional and business services	12,493	13,364	14,171	15,374	14,440
Education and health services	17,076	18,148	18,879	18,713	19,804
Health care and social assistance	11,043	11,683	12,256	12,259	12,989
Leisure and hospitality	17,300	18,257	18,814	19,934	21,835
Accommodation and food services	11,989	12,720	13,070	14,035	15,396
Other services	4,561	4,814	4,706	4,603	4,888
Public administration	4,666	5,008	5,204	5,441	5,492
Unclassified	118	202	126	145	211

TTU = trade, transportation, and utilities

Source: Florida Agency for Workforce Innovation, Labor Market Statistics, Quarterly Census of Employment and Wages, various years (www.labormarketinfo.com/library/qcew.htm).

result in a need for assistance of $906, which is $0.725 (the cost per foot for the 1,000- to 1,500-foot category) times 1,250 square feet.

NONRESIDENTIAL DEVELOPMENT

Table 11-31 shows historic employment in Collier County by industry, using the North American Industrial Classification System. Table 11-31 shows the number of new jobs in Collier County by industry. The largest number of new jobs is in construction (5,423), which is 30 percent of all new jobs. The second largest is accommodation and food services, with 3,407 new jobs, which is 19 percent of the total. A problem is that many of these new jobs are in the lower wage industries, most significantly retail trade and tourism. Table 11-32 shows all industries in terms of their contribution to employment growth. Table 11-16 contained average employee and household earnings by industry for Collier County as of December 2006.

The assignment of employees to sectors is shown in Table 11-33. The industrial sectors were assigned to the 10 land-use categories, based on the description of employment activities related to land uses and related principles found in the *Standard Industrial Classification Manual*,[4] the classic *Land Use Information Systems*,[5] *Planner's Estimating Guide: Projecting Land-Use and Facility Needs*,[6] and *Standard Land Use Coding Manual*.[7] The percentage assignment of employment for each industry to the corresponding land-use categories is set out in Table 11-33. The O & M employees and critical employees discussed in the previous section are assigned in Table 11-33 to residences rather than to an industrial category.

The assignment percentages were multiplied by the employees by industry shown in Table 11-31 to get employees by land use by year for Collier County. These employees by land use were divided into the total floor area by type of land use to get floor area per employee. These data are shown in Table 11-34.

The earnings data from Table 11-16 are used in conjunction with employment data by land use from Table 11-34 to estimate annual earned income per household by land use of the household head. These data are shown in Table 11-35. These household incomes will be used in analyzing the ability of workforce households to afford housing in Collier County.

The RRC survey of Collier County employers determined the employees per unit of land use. Thus, there are two bases for determining employees per unit of land use. The first is the estimation using employment data; the second is the RRC survey of Collier County employers. Table 11-36 shows the results of the two efforts. Generally, the RRC survey found higher ratios of employees per land use than the estimate from employment data. However, in most instances, there is substantial agreement between the two methods. An apparent exception is bars/restaurants, but bars and restaurants are

Table 11-32
New Jobs in Collier County, 2001–2005

Industry Title	New Jobs	Percent of Total
Construction	5,423	30.5%
Manufacturing	318	1.8%
Wholesale trade	644	3.6%
Retail trade	1,333	7.5%
Transportation and warehousing	42	0.2%
Information	90	0.5%
Finance and insurance	615	3.5%
Real estate and rental and leasing	865	4.9%
Professional and business services	1,947	10.9%
Health care and social assistance	1,946	10.9%
Accommodation and food services	3,407	19.2%
Other services	327	1.8%
Public administration	826	4.6%
Total	17,783	100.0%

Table 11-33
Distribution of Employees to Land Uses

	Government	Industrial	Institutional	Office	Other	Retail	Tourist	Residence	Critical Employee	No Location
Construction		15.0%		10.0%				15.17%		59.8%
Manufacturing		75.0%		15.0%	10.0%					
Wholesale trade		70.0%		10.0%		20.0%				
Retail trade						90.0%	10.0%			
TTU	15.0%	50.0%		15.0%	10.0%	10.0%				
Information		35.0%		45.0%	10.0%	10.0%				
Financial activities		10.0%	20.0%	50.6%		8.1%		11.34%		
Professional and business services		10.0%	10.0%	20.6%		5.0%	10.0%	44.37%		
Educational and health services	20.0%		13.7%	19.7%		5.0%		27.29%	14.35%	
Leisure and hospitality					10.0%	20.0%	70.0%			
Other services			5.2%	7.1%			9.0%	78.65%		
Government	40.0%			10.0%				29.13%	27.18%	
Mining, agricultural, and other										100.0%

TTU = trade, transportation, and utilities

Table 11-34
Floor Area Per Employee, Collier County

	2001	2002	2003	2004	2005	Typical
Government						
Floor area	6,055,105	6,264,233	6,405,840	6,943,622	7,313,164	
Employment	5,617	5,998	5,913	6,243	6,494	
Sq. ft. per employee	1,077.91	1,044.40	1,083.42	1,112.28	1,126.16	1,089.79
Industrial						
Floor area	8,918,712	9,436,119	9,912,783	10,337,847	10,571,681	
Employment	9,698	9,966	8,769	10,377	11,576	
Sq. ft. per employee	919.69	946.85	1,130.38	996.21	913.25	976.01
Institutional						
Floor area	3,573,849	3,523,398	3,963,140	4,196,497	4,502,542	
Employment	5,037	5,342	5,545	5,697	5,918	
Sq. ft. per employee	709.54	659.61	714.69	736.58	760.78	717.50
Office						
Floor area	2,600,659	2,578,207	2,414,006	2,544,743	2,602,769	
Employment	13,017	13,628	13,667	14,606	15,506	
Sq. ft. per employee	199.78	189.18	176.63	174.23	167.86	180.91
Retail						
Floor area	12,112,802	12,477,163	12,871,377	13,406,009	13,464,486	
Employment	21,834	22,332	22,318	23,251	24,432	
Sq. ft. per employee	554.78	558.72	576.74	576.57	551.10	563.49
Tourist						
Floor area	6,985,100	7,123,437	7,980,617	8,127,216	8,263,059	
Employment	15,491	16,285	16,749	17,690	19,023	
Sq. ft. per employee	450.90	437.42	476.47	459.41	434.36	451.42
All						
Floor area	42,411,274	42,999,631	46,174,286	48,037,963	48,351,569	
Employment	110,535	114,812	116,130	121,558	129,653	
Sq. ft. per employee	383.69	374.52	397.61	395.19	372.93	384.65

Sources: Table 11-31 and Collier County Property Appraiser (2006).

Table 11-35
Earned Household Income by Land Use, Collier County

Land Use	Household Income
Government	$61,707
Industrial	$62,110
Institutional	$75,481
Office	$72,003
Other	$48,906
Retail	$50,312
Tourist	$47,636
Residence	$61,957
Critical employees	$62,197
No location	$36,534
All	$55,597

Sources: Tables 11-16 and 11-34.

Table 11-36
Employment Per 1,000 Sq. Ft. Survey Results and Estimate

RRC Land-Use Category	RRC Result	Employment Estimate	Used
Bar/restaurant	12.6	1.775	1.775
Construction	5.4		
Education	1.3	1.394	1.300
Finance/banking	7.1	5.528	5.528
Government/transportation/public utilities	1.1	0.918	0.918
Lodging/hotel (0.7 per room)	1.28	2.215	1.280
Professional services	2.7		
Personal/commercial services	5.2	5.528	3.333
Real estate/property management	2.1		
Retail sales	1.9	1.775	1.775
Recreation/entertainment	3.3	2.215	2.215
Other	0.6		
Manufacturing	2.3	1.025	1.025
Overall	2.5	2.600	

The office ratio used is the average of RRC, Incorporated's professional services, personal/commercial services and real estate/property management. Where there is no general land-use category corresponding to the RRC category, the field is left blank.

Source: RRC, Incorporated, Collier County Employment Survey (August 2006).

not distinct land-use classifications. For the actual calculations of workforce housing needs, the RRC or the estimate from employment will be used, whichever is lower.

Table 11-37 calculates the total workforce housing gap on the basis of square footage of floor area (the inverse of the data in Table 11-36). These calculations start with employee household incomes by land-use type from Table 11-35. The upper affordably limit is calculated by dividing the employee household income by 0.29109, which is the ratio of housing price to necessary income from Table 11-19. The cost of workforce housing was set out in Table 11-18. The gap is simply the workforce housing cost less the upper affordability limit. The assistance needs for employees is the gap per household divided by the number of square feet of floor area per household. The critical employee costs from Tables 11-28 and 11-29 are added to employee needs to arrive at total needs per square foot of floor area by land-use type.

Housing categories were assigned to land uses on the basis of the income associated with those uses as contrasted with Collier County median income. Government, industrial, institutional, and office uses were assigned Category 2 because all of the incomes fell within 80 to 120 percent of median income. Retail and tourist uses were assigned Category 1 because incomes fell below 80 percent of median income.

Implementation of a workforce housing mitigation impact fee would be effected through an ordinance. Appendix 11B provides an ordinance approach considered for Destin, Florida.

PROPORTIONATE-SHARE DEVELOPMENT FEES FOR OTHER SOCIAL INFRASTRUCTURE

The principles of proportionate-share development fees can and are being applied to other types of social infrastructure, such as day care, job training (as a kind of educational facility impact fee), and public art. Generally, so long as these types of development fees meet proportionate-share principles, they may be defensible and, under some circumstances (e.g., discretionary land-use approval or state environmental impact assessment regulations), even given state impact fee enabling legislation that may otherwise restrict the use of impact fees to a certain range of facilities.

Table 11-37
Nonresidential Housing Affordability Gap by Land Use, Collier County

	Government	Industrial	Institutional	Office	Retail	Tourist
Employees						
Employees per 1,000 sq. ft.	0.918	1.025	1.300	3.333	1.775	1.280
Sq. ft. per employee	1,090	976	769	300	563	781
Sq. ft. per household	1,547	1,386	1,092	426	800	1,109
Income per household	$61,707	$62,110	$75,481	$72,003	$50,312	$47,636
Upper affordability limit	$211,986	$213,371	$259,304	$247,355	$172,841	$163,647
Workforce housing cost	$262,500	$262,500	$262,500	$262,500	$211,700	$211,700
Gap	$50,514	$49,129	$3,196	$15,145	$38,859	$48,053
Gap per sq. ft.	$32.65	$35.46	$2.93	$35.56	$48.58	$43.32
Critical Employees						
Teachers	$0.00	$0.00	$0.00	$0.00	$0.00	$0.00
Fire/rescue	$0.11	$0.11	$0.11	$0.11	$0.11	$0.11
Law enforcement	$0.06	$0.04	$0.01	$0.06	$0.18	$0.03
Total per sq. ft.	**$32.82**	**$35.60**	**$3.05**	**$35.73**	**$48.86**	**$43.46**

CONCLUDING OBSERVATIONS

There is no question that workforce housing affordability is a serious problem. The 2007 housing slump has seen some decline in housing prices, but such declines are minor when seen in light of the gap between what working households can afford and housing costs. A failure to address such problems will ultimately result in a loss of economic vitality of such areas.

Nationally, all governments are attempting to limit expenditures in response to the public's demand for lower taxes. This does not alter or limit needs, such

Table 11-38
Affordable Units, Density, and Profit

Units to be built	35	50	70
Affordable units	0	8	18
Land cost	$2,000,000	$2,000,000	$2,000,000
Construction cost	$4,287,500	$7,043,750	$10,718,750
Total finance costs	$321,563	$528,281	$803,906
Other costs	$495,680	$717,902	$1,014,199
Total project costs	$7,104,742	$10,289,934	$14,536,855
Proceeds from Sales			
Market-rate units	$7,875,000	$10,125,000	$14,175,000
Affordable units	$0	$937,500	$2,187,500
Total proceeds	$7,875,000	$11,062,500	$16,362,500
Profit/loss	$770,258	$772,566	$1,825,645
Return	10.8%	7.5%	12.6%

as for affordable housing. It does mean that new and different approaches to addressing workforce and affordable housing issues will have to be explored. The discussion here has focused on the nexus aspect of this issue, but there are other aspects. Incentives can be offered that will mitigate and even totally offset any increased cost of development resulting from the linkage program. Table 11-38 shows simply how profit cannot only be restored but enhanced, even when the market price of units will diminish with density. There are a number of incentives that could be offered to encourage the private provision of less-than-market-rate units.

NOTES

1. This discussion is based on the San Francisco, California, Downtown Office Development—Housing Mitigation Linkage Fee program background study prepared by Linda L. Hausrath, reported in "Economic Basis for Linking Jobs and Housing in San Francisco," published in the *Journal of the American Planning Association* (Spring 1988).

2. 2000 Census, "Commuters to Collier County, Florida Agency from Workforce Innovation."

3. 2000 Census, Table P31 for Collier County. Available at http://factfinder.census.gov.

4. *Standard Industrial Classification Manual* (Washington, D.C.: U.S. Department of Labor, U.S. Government Printing Office, 1987).

5. Marion Clawson, *Land Use Information* (Washington, D.C.: Resources for the Future, 1965).

6. A. C. Nelson, *Planner's Estimating Guide: Projecting Land-Use and Facility Needs* (Chicago: American Planning Association, 2004).

7. *Standard Land Use Coding Manual* (Washington, D.C.: Urban Renewal Administration and Bureau of Public Roads, Government Printing Office, 1965).

APPENDIX 11A

WORKFORCE HOUSING LINKAGE
PROGRAMS IN CALIFORNIA

The tables in this section report analysis by Keyser Marston
Associates, Inc., on the extent of workforce housing linkage
fees used throughout California in the early 2000s prepared
for the city of Walnut Creek, California.

Table 11A-1
Jobs-Housing Balance Linkage Programs for High-Fee Cities, California

Jurisdiction	Year Adopted/ Updated	Current Fee Levels Per Sq. Ft.	Thresholds and Exemptions	Build Option/ Other	Market Strength	Comments
City of Palo Alto	1984 updated in March 2002	• Commercial and industrial $15.58	No minimum threshold. Churches; colleges and universities; commercial rec-reation; hospitals, convalescent facili-ties; private clubs, lodges, fraternal organizations; private educational facilities; and public facilities are exempt.	Yes	Very substantial	Fee is adjusted annually based on CPI.
City and County of San Francisco	1981 updated fees in 2002	• Office $14.96 • Hotel $11.21 • Retail $13.95	25,000 gross sq. ft. threshold. Excludes redevel-opment areas and port	Yes, may con-tribute land for housing.	Very substantial	$40 million raised
City of Menlo Park	1998	• Commercial and industrial $10.00 • Warehousing, printing, assem-bly $5.45.	10,000 gross sq. ft. threshold. Churches, private clubs, lodges, fraternal organiza-tions and public facilities are exempt.	Yes, may pro-vide housing on- or off-site.	Very substantial	Fee is adjusted annually based on CPI.

PI = Consumer Price Index
Source: www.walnut-creek.org/citygov/depts/cd/housing/linkfee.asp

Table 11A-2
Jobs-Housing Balance Linkage Programs for Medium-Fee Cities, California

Jurisdiction	Year Adopted/ Updated	Current Fee Levels Per Sq. Ft.	Thresholds and Exemptions	Build Option/Other	Market Strength	Comments
City of Santa Monica	1984 updated fees in 2002	• Office only • $4.37 per sq. ft. for first 15,000 sq. ft. • $9.72 per sq. ft. in excess of 15,000 sq. ft.	15,000 sq. ft. exemption for new construction, 10,000 sq. ft. exemption for additions.	N/A	Very substantial	Includes fee for open space as well. Fees adjusted quarterly based on CPI. No comprehensive update since adoption.
City of Sunnyvale	1984 updated in 2003	• Industrial and office $8	Applies only to the portion of the project that is in excess of allowable FAR (typically 0.35:1).	N/A	Very substantial	Fee had not changed since the 1980s, until fee was recently raised from $7.19.
County of Marin	2003	• Office/R & D $7.19 • Retail/restaurant $5.40 • Warehouse $1.95 • Hotel/motel $1,746 per room • Manufacturing $3.74	No minimum threshold.	Yes, preferred.	Substantial	
City of Mountain View	2001	• Office/industrial $6.00 • Hotel $2.00 • Retail $2.00	Fee is 50% less if building meets thresholds: Office < 10,000 sq. ft. Hotel < 25,000 sq. ft. Retail < 25,000 sq. ft	Yes	Very substantial	
City of Walnut Creek	2005	• Office, retail, hotel, and medical $5.00	First 500 sq. ft. no fee applied.	Yes	Very substantial	
Town of Corte Madera	2001	• Office $4.79 • R & D lab $3.20 • Light industrial $2.79 • Warehouse $0.40 • Retail $8.38 • Commercial services $1.20 • Restaurant $4.39 • Hotel $1.20	No minimum threshold.	N/A	Substantial	
City of Oakland	2002	• Office/warehouse $4.00	25,000 sq. ft. exemption	Yes, can build units equal to total eligible sq. ft. times .0004	Moderate	Fee due in three installments. Fee adjusted with an annual escalator tied to residential construction cost increases.

Table 11A-2
Jobs-Housing Balance Linkage Programs for Medium-Fee Cities, California (continued)

Jurisdiction	Year Adopted/ Updated	Current Fee Levels Per Sq. Ft.	Thresholds and Exemptions	Build Option/Other	Market Strength	Comments
City of Berkeley	1993	• All commercial $4.00 • Industrial $2.00	7,500 sq. ft. threshold	Yes	Substantial	Fee has not changed since 1993; may negotiate fee downward based on hardship or reduced impact.
City of St. Helena	2004	• Office $3.40 • Commercial/retail $4.30 • Hotel $3.14 • Winery/industrial $1.05	Small child care facilities, churches, nonprofits, vineyards, and public facilities are exempt.	Yes, subject to city council approval.	Substantial	

CPI = Consumer Price Index
FAR = floor area ratio
R & D = research and development
Source: www.walnut-creek.org/citygov/depts/cd/housing/linkfee.asp

Table 11A-3
Jobs-Housing Balance Linkage Programs for Low-Fee Cities, California

Jurisdiction	Year Adopted/ Updated	Current Fee Levels Per Sq. Ft.	Thresholds and Exemptions	Build Option/Other	Market Strength	Comments
City of Alameda	1989	• Office $3.63 • Retail $1.84 • Warehouse $0.63 • Hotel/motel $931 per room	No minimum threshold	Yes, program specifies number of units per 100,000 sq. ft.	Moderate	Fee may be adjusted by CPI.
City of West Hollywood	1986	• Nonresidential $2.85	N/A	N/A	Substantial	Fees adjusted by CPI each year.
City of Pleasanton		• Commercial, office, and industrial $2.31	No minimum threshold	N/A	Moderate	Fee increased in 2003.
City of Cupertino	1993	• Office and industrial $2.25	No minimum threshold	N/A	Very substantial	Fee is adjusted annually based on CPI. Update in process.
City of Petaluma	2003	• Commercial $2.08 * • Industrial $2.15 * • Retail $3.59 * (see comment in last column)	Fee is 50% less if located in redevelopment project area.	N/A	Moderate/ substantial	* Fee phased in over three years beginning 2005. Fees listed are full fees, starting in 2007.
County of Napa (also City of Napa)	County updated 2004; City 1999	• Office $2.00 • Hotel $3.00 • Retail $2.00 • Industrial $1.00 • Warehouse $0.80	No minimum threshold. Nonprofits are exempt.	Units or land dedication; on a case-by-case basis.	Moderate/ substantial	There is a companion fee of 1% of construction costs on all residential construction. Napa City rates not updated to these levels yet.

Table 11A-3
Jobs-Housing Balance Linkage Programs for Low-Fee Cities, California (*continued*)

Jurisdiction	Year Adopted/ Updated	Current Fee Levels Per Sq. Ft.	Thresholds and Exemptions	Build Option/Other	Market Strength	Comments
City of Sacramento	1989; most recent update 2005	• Office $1.79 • Hotel $1.70 • R & D $1.52 • Commercial $1.43 • Manufacturing $1.12 • Warehouse/office $0.65 • Warehouse $0.49	No minimum threshold. Service uses operated by nonprofits are exempt	Pay 20% fee plus build at reduced nexus (not meaningful given amount of fee).	Moderate	Fees listed in effect as of July 2005. North Natomas area has separate fee structure.
City of San Diego	1990 fees reduced in mid 90s; have not been readjusted	• Office $1.06 • Hotel $0.64 • R & D $0.80 • Retail $0.64 • Manufacturing $0.64 • Warehouse $0.27	No minimum threshold. No exempted uses. Does exclude some geographic areas.	Can dedicate land or air rights in lieu of fee.	Substantial	Since 1990, $33 million raised. Update in process. Office proposed to go to $1.50-$1.80 range.
City of Livermore	1999	• Retail $0.81 • Service retail $0.61 • Office $0.52 • Hotel $397 per room • Manufacturing $0.25 • Warehouse $0.07 • Business park $0.52 • Heavy industrial $0.26 • Light industrial $0.16	No minimum threshold. Church; private or public schools.	Yes, negotiated on a case-by-case basis.	Moderate	
City of Folsom	2002	• Office, retail, light industrial, heavy industrial, and manufacturing $1.20 • Up to 200,000 sq. ft., 100% of fee • 200,000-250,000 sq. ft., 75% of fee • 250,000-300,000 sq. ft., 50% of fee • 300,000 and up, 25% of fee	No minimum threshold. Select nonprofits, small child care centers, churches, mini-storage, parking garages, private schools, etc.	Yes, provide new or rehab housing affordable to very low and low-income households. Also, land dedication.	Moderate/ substantial	Fee is adjusted annually based on construction cost index.
County of Sacramento	1989	• Office $0.97 • Hotel $0.92 • R & D $0.82 • Commercial $0.77 • Manufacturing $0.61 • Indoor recreational centers $0.50 • Warehouse $0.26	No minimum threshold. Service uses operated by nonprofits are exempt.	Pay 20% fee plus build at reduced nexus (not meaningful given amount of fee).	Moderate	Currently in the process of updating.

Table 11A-3
Jobs-Housing Balance Linkage Programs for Low-Fee Cities, California *(continued)*

Jurisdiction	Year Adopted/ Updated	Current Fee Levels Per Sq. Ft.	Thresholds and Exemptions	Build Option/Other	Market Strength	Comments
City of Elk Grove	1988 (inherited from county when incorporated)	$30 flat fee plus: • Office $0.97 • Hotel $0.92 • R & D $0.82 • Commercial $0.77 • Manufacturing $0.61 • Indoor recreational centers $0.50 • Warehouse $0.26		No minimum threshold. Membership organizations (churches, nonprofits, etc.), mini-storage, car storage, marinas, car washes, private parking garages, and agricultural uses exempt.	Pay 20% fee plus build at reduced nexus (not meaningful given amount of fee).	Moderate
City of Rancho Cordova	1988 (inherited from county when incorporated)	$30-$100 flat fee plus: • Office $0.97 • Hotel $0.92 • R & D $0.82 • Commercial $0.77 • Manufacturing $0.61 • Indoor recreational centers $0.50 • Warehouse $0.26		No minimum threshold.	No build option, but developer can dedicate land to city in lieu of fee.	Moderate
City of Citrus Heights		• Office $0.97 • Hotel $0.92 • R & D $0.82 • Commercial $0.77 • Manufacturing $0.61 • Warehouse $0.26	No minimum threshold. Agriculture, auto smog inspections, car storage, private parking garage, mini-storage, churches, nonprofit membership organizations.		Moderate	

CPI = Consumer Price Index

R & D = research and development

Source: www.walnut-creek.org/citygov/depts/cd/housing/linkfee.asp

APPENDIX 11B

SAMPLE WORKFORCE HOUSING MITIGATION IMPACT FEE ORDINANCE

The following is an approach to implementing a workforce housing mitigation impact fee considered by Destin, Florida.

ORDINANCE NO. 2007 -- ___

AN ORDINANCE OF THE CITY OF DESTIN, FLORIDA; AMENDING CERTAIN LAND DEVELOPMENT REGULATIONS BY CREATING AN ORDINANCE RELATING TO THE REGULATION OF THE USE AND DEVELOPMENT OF LAND IN THE CITY OF DESTIN, FLORIDA, BY IMPOSING ATTAINABLE WORKFORCE HOUSING STANDARDS ON LAND DEVELOPMENT FOR THE PROVISION OF ATTAINABLE WORKFORCE HOUSING NECESSITATED BY SUCH NEW DEVELOPMENTS; PROVIDING FOR FINDINGS; PROVIDING FOR PURPOSE; PROVIDING FOR AUTHORITY; PROVIDING FOR TECHNICAL SUPPORT; PROVIDING FOR APPLICABILITY; PROVIDING FOR EXEMPTIONS; PROVIDING FOR PROCEDURES; PROVIDING ATTAINABLE WORKFORCE HOUSING STANDARDS; PROVIDING FOR INDEPENDENT CALCULATION FOR ALTERNATIVE MITIGATION; PROVIDING FOR COLLECTION AND ACCOUNTING FOR ATTAINABLE WORKFORCE HOUSING FEES IN-LIEU; PROVIDING FOR DEFINITIONS; PROVIDING FOR SEVERABILITY; PROVIDING FOR THE REPEAL OF ALL CODE PROVISIONS AND ORDINANCES INCONSISTENT WITH THIS ORDINANCE; PROVIDING FOR INCLUSION IN THE CITY CODE; AND PROVIDING FOR THE TRANSMITTAL OF THIS ORDINANCE TO THE SECRETARY OF STATE.

WHEREAS, pursuant to the Local Government Comprehensive Planning and Land Development Regulation Act the City of Destin has provided a housing element in its *Comprehensive Plan*, which includes provisions related to the current and future housing needs of the City; and

WHEREAS, the City has prepared and adopted *The City of Destin Attainable Workforce Housing Study* (hereinafter *Attainable Workforce Housing Study*), dated May 2007, attached as "Exhibit A" and incorporated herein by reference, that identifies there is a workforce housing attainability problem in the City; and

WHEREAS, as *The City of Destin Attainable Workforce Housing Study* demonstrates, beginning in 2000, significant increases in housing prices within Destin have made private housing unattainable to most working residents of the City, and forced a number of residents to move outside of Destin; and

WHEREAS, the *Attainable Workforce Housing Study* demonstrates the jobs that are expected to be created by much of the new development and re-development in the City are expected to pay wages that make market rate housing in the City unattainable; and

WHEREAS, there is a concern that an essential component of the City's community character will be damaged or lost since most of the workforce and their families will no longer reside in the community, attend schools in the community, participate in local civic organizations, worship in the community, act as emergency services volunteers, or express their ideas at the ballot box; and

WHEREAS, to address this serious community problem and to maintain the long-term sustainability of the City's economy and the character of the community, the City Council has established the goal of providing housing in the City to ___ percent (___%) of the local workforce and their families, at prices they can afford; and

WHEREAS, in part to accomplish these objectives, the City Council adopts these Attainable Workforce Housing Standards in this ordinance; and

WHEREAS, the City Council finds that the provisions of this Ordinance are intended to advance the public health, safety, and welfare of the citizens of the City.

NOW, THEREFORE, BE IT ORDAINED BY THE CITY COUNCIL OF DESTIN, FLORIDA, AS FOLLOWS:

SECTION 1: FINDINGS.

The City Council of the City of Destin, finds that:

A. **The City of Destin Needs a Resident Workforce to Ensure Sustainable Local Economy**.

One of the overarching goals of the City and its *Comprehensive Plan* is to maintain a balanced and sustainable local economy that supports the City as a destination resort. Maintenance of a balanced and sustainable local economy requires the availability of a stable and qualified workforce.

B. **Ensuring Workforce and Their Families Live in the City Is Important for Maintaining Community Character**.

A second important goal of the City and its *Comprehensive Plan* is to maintain and enhance the City's community character, including the social, economic, and political fabric, and general sense of community that occurs when persons and families who work in the community, live in the community, attend schools in the community, participate in civic organizations in the community, worship in the community, and vote in the community. One of the primary factors that has allowed this special sense of community, and the maintenance of the City's community character is that for many years the cost of housing was attainable to those persons living and working in the City.

C. **Provide Adequate Affordable Housing**.

Another goal of the *Comprehensive Plan* is to ensure there is an adequate supply of affordable and attainable housing to the City's workforce at prices they can reasonably afford.

D. **Housing Costs Have Outpaced Ability of Workforce to Afford Housing**.

Beginning in 2002, there has been a rise in housing prices that has made private housing unattainable to many working residents of the City.

E. **Unattainability of Housing Has Been Documented**.

Review of state and national census and other wage and labor data, in conjunction with Okaloosa County and City real estate sales data, demonstrate the amount of housing within the price ranges that are attainable to the City's workforce has been declining since 2002 to the point there are now only a very limited number of market units available today at prices the workforce in the City can afford.

F. **Forced Out-Migration of Workers and Their Families**.

The unattainability of workforce housing within Destin has or will soon result in a number of persons employed in the City and their families being forced to move from the City. Data outlined in *The Attainable Workforce Housing Study* demonstrate the following:

1. From 2000 to 2005, the gap between median household incomes and median housing costs in the City increased to the point that housing is not attainable to workforce households in Destin earning the area median income as evidenced by the following:

a. In 2000, the cost of a median priced home in the City amounted to 430 percent of the annual income of a household, which had a median household income.

b. By 2003, a household with a median annual income would have to spend 563 percent of its annual income for a median priced home.

c. In 2006, that same household would have to spend 911 percent of its income for that same home.

d. Sales of homes under $400,000 went from 851 in the year 2003, to 385 in the year 2005.

2. The estimated earnings of households of persons employed in Destin approximate but rarely exceed the area median household income, confirming that Destin housing is typically unavailable to those employed in Destin.

G. **Deterioration of Local Workforce and the Local Economy**.

This lack of attainable workforce housing has placed increasing stress on the capacity of the local community to maintain a viable workforce. Estimates indicate this problem will worsen in the future, potentially affecting the long-term sustainability of the local economy unless additional housing is provided within price ranges that are attainable by the workforce.

H. **Deterioration of Community Character**.

If these present trends continue an essential component of the City's community character will be damaged since most of the workforce and their families will no longer reside in the community, attend schools in the community, participate in local civic organizations, worship in the community, act as emergency services volunteers, or express their ideas at the ballot box.

I. *Attainable Workforce Housing Goal*.

To address this serious community problem and to maintain the long-term sustainability of the City's and county's economy and the character of the community, the City Council has established the goal of providing attainable housing in the City to _____ percent (_____%) of the local workforce and their families, at prices they can afford.

SECTION 2: PURPOSE.

The purpose of these Attainable Workforce Housing Standards is to ensure there is an attainable supply of housing for _____ percent of the City's workforce, and their families. This is done through these standards by:

1. Requiring attainable workforce housing be provided for all new development or re-development in an amount proportionate to the need for attainable workforce housing that development or re-development creates; or

2. The payment of a fee in-lieu or the donation of land for attainable housing in an amount proportionate to the need for attainable workforce housing the development or re-development creates.

SECTION 3: AUTHORITY.

The City has the authority to adopt these Attainable Workforce Housing Standards in accordance with Article VIII of the Florida Constitution (1968) and by Florida Statutes, Chapter 166 generally and Sections 166.04151, Chapter 163 generally and Section 163.3177 (6)(f).

SECTION 4: TECHNICAL SUPPORT.

The technical support and analysis upon which these Attainable Workforce Housing Standards are established are based on the *Attainable Workforce Housing Study*.

SECTION 5: APPLICABILITY.

The standards of these Attainable Workforce Housing Standards shall apply to the development or re-development of all lands within the City of Destin, unless exempted pursuant to this ordinance.

SECTION 6: DEFINITIONS.

For the purposes of this Division, the following terms shall have the following meanings.

A. **Attainable Workforce Housing Unit** means a dwelling unit which is provided for a person employed in the City of Destin and their families, either through sale or rent, at prices that are restricted to ensure the unit is maintained as attainable to persons employed in the City.

B. **All Other Residential Unit(s)** means all other residential units not classified as Units Occupied by Full-Time Residents of the City of Destin.

C. **Applicant** means the person, persons or entity that applies to the City of Destin for site plan or plat approval.

D. **Attainable Workforce Housing Study** means the document providing the technical support and analysis upon which these Attainable Workforce Housing Standards are established. It is titled *The City of Destin Attainable Workforce Housing Study*, May 2007.

E. **Attainable Workforce Housing Trust Account** means the account established in accordance with Section 11 A.: *Attainable Workforce Housing Trust Account*, to ensure the in-lieu fees collected pursuant to this ordinance are designated and used for attainable workforce housing units attributable to Employee-Generating Development that paid the in-lieu fees.

F. **Average Just Value** means the mean or average estimate of market value for Vacant Residential Lands in the City, as determined by the Okaloosa County, Florida Property Appraiser. The Average Just Value is the quotient of the calculation where the numerator is the sum of the Just Value for all Vacant Residential Lands and the denominator is the total number of parcels categorized as Vacant Residential Lands in the City.

G. **Building Permit** means that development permit issued by the City before any building or construction activity can be initiated on a parcel of land.

H. **City Manager** means the City Manager of the City of Destin or his/her designee, appointed to carry out the responsibilities of this Ordinance.

I. **Comprehensive Plan** means the Comprehensive Plan of the City of Destin.

J. **Council or City Council** means the elected legislative body of Destin.

K. **Development** has the meaning provided in Section 380.04, Fla. Stat.

L. **Employee Generating Development** means residential or nonresidential development designed or intended to permit a use of the land that will increase the size of residential units, contain more dwelling units or nonresidential development than the then existing use of the land, or the making of any material change in the use of any structure or land in a manner that creates an additional need for attainable workforce housing units, unless exempted pursuant to this ordinance.

M. **Existing Use** is the highest intensity use on a parcel or site within the last 12 months.

N. **Expansion or Redevelopment of Existing Uses** means the expansion or redevelopment of buildings on a parcel that were existing on the effective date of this Ordinance.

O. **Fair Market Value** means the value of land that is determined as part of a provision of land for attainable workforce housing in accordance with Section 9 E.: *Conveyance of Land*. Fair market value shall be established through an appraisal provided by a State of Florida licensed real estate appraiser, or an appraiser who is a member of the American Institute of Real Estate Appraisers or the Society of Real Estate Appraisers.

P. **Full Time Residents** are individuals or households that maintain their domicile within the City of Destin and who reside within Destin for more than six (6) months per year.

Q. **Governmental uses** include but are not limited to military facilities; parks and recreational areas; governmental office buildings; and other publicly owned facilities.

R. **Independent Calculation for Alternative Mitigation Study** means a study prepared by an applicant in accordance with Section 10: *Independent Calculation Study for Alternative Mitigation*.

S. **Industrial uses** include but are not limited to manufacturing; lumber yards; warehousing and distribution terminals; equipment and materials storage facilities; and other similar uses.

T. **Institutional uses** include but are not limited to churches; private schools; colleges; daycares; privately owned hospitals; homes for the aged; orphanages; clubs; cultural organizations; and other similar uses.

U. **Land** shall have the same meaning as set forth in Section 380.031(7), Fla. Stat.

V. **Market Rate Housing** is private housing within the City of Destin that is available for sale or rent to individuals or households without housing assistance from any public or non-profit entity.

W. **Maximum Extent Practicable** means no feasible or practical alternative exists, as determined by the City Manager, and all possible efforts to comply with the relevant standards or minimize potential harmful or adverse impacts have been undertaken by an applicant. Economic considerations may be taken into account but shall not be the overriding factor determining "maximum extent practicable."

X. **Office uses** include but are not limited to professional and non-professional office buildings, offices of financial institutions, professional services buildings, and insurance company offices; and other similar uses.

Y. **Person** means an individual, corporation, governmental agency, business trust, estate, trust, partnership, association, two or more persons having a joint or common interest, or any other entity.

Z. **Part Time Residents** are individuals or households that maintain their domicile outside of the City of Destin and who reside within Destin for less than six (6) months per year.

AA. **Retail uses** include but are not limited to stores, department stores, supermarkets, supercenters, shopping centers, restaurants, bars and night clubs, repair service shops, service stations, auto sales and repair, parking lots, and wholesale or discount outlets; and other similar uses.

BB. **Tourist uses** include but are not limited to amusement parks, theatres; auditoriums; nightclubs; bowling alleys; tourist attractions; camps; race tracks; golf courses; hotels, "beds and breakfasts," motels and ancillary spaces within hotels or motels such as restaurants and shops; and other similar uses.

CC. **Unit(s) Occupied by Full-Time Residents** means a residential unit that an applicant/developer can ensure will be occupied full-time by a resident of Destin.

DD. **Vacant Residential Land** means land that is categorized by the Okaloosa County, Florida Property Appraiser as "vacant residential land," and that is defined as being vacant, subdivided land available for development of single-family dwelling unit(s).

SECTION 7: EXEMPTIONS.

The following development shall be exempted from these Attainable Workforce Housing Standards:

A. **Construction of an Attainable Dwelling Unit**.

The construction of a dwelling unit that is deed restricted to ensure it is maintained as an attainable workforce housing unit.

B. Development of Residential Units Less Than 1,000 Square Feet.

Development or re-development of a residential unit that measures less than 1,000 square feet in heated or air-conditioned floor area upon completion of development or re-development provided that this dwelling is intended for occupancy by permanent full time residents and not as a second or vacation home.

C. Redevelopment, Remodeling or Expansion of Preexisting Residential Use.

Redevelopment, remodeling or expansion of a legally preexisting residential use of land if the redevelopment, remodeling or expansion does not increase the area of the nonresidential use that existed on the effective date of this Ordinance by more than 100 square feet of heated or air-conditioned area floor area.

D. Redevelopment, Remodeling or Expansion of Preexisting Nonresidential Use.

Redevelopment, remodeling or expansion of a legally preexisting nonresidential use if:

1. The use is not changed to a different category listed in Attachment C, and;

2. The redevelopment, remodeling or expansion does not increase the area of the nonresidential use that existed on the effective date of this Ordinance by more than 100 square feet of gross leasable floor area.

E. Temporary Uses.

Development of a temporary use, as listed in the Destin Land Development Code.

F. Attainable Workforce Housing Development.

Attainable workforce housing developments designed and administered to meet the purposes of this Ordinance. This may include projects developed or sponsored by non-profit organizations.

SECTION 8: PROCEDURES.

A. Submission of Attainable Workforce Housing Mitigation Plan.

An applicant for a subdivision, site plan or similar approval for any Employee Generating Development not exempted in accordance with Section 7: *Exemptions*, shall submit an Attainable Workforce Housing Mitigation Plan to the City Manager concurrent with the development application.

B. Contents of Attainable Workforce Housing Mitigation Plan.

The contents of the Attainable Workforce Housing Mitigation Plan shall include the following:

1. **Attainable Workforce Housing Need.**

Calculation of the need for attainable workforce housing created by the Employee Generating Development based on the requirements of Section 9: *Attainable Workforce Housing Standards*.

2. **Method**.

The method by which attainable workforce housing is to be provided to comply with the requirements of Section 9: *Attainable Workforce Housing Standards* by means of on-site or off-site construction of units, conversion of free market units, payment of a fee in-lieu, conveyance of land for attainable housing, or a combination of the above, and appropriate justification for the proposed mitigation method.

3. **Construction of Attainable Workforce Units**.

If attainable workforce housing units are to be constructed (either on or off-site), the Attainable Workforce Housing Mitigation Plan shall include:

a. *Conceptual Site Plan.*

A conceptual site plan and building floor plan (if applicable) illustrating the number of attainable workforce units proposed, the type and nature of those units, their location in relation to the other residential or non-residential developments on the site and surrounding land uses, and the number and size of bedrooms of each unit.

b. *Summary of Attainable Units.*

A summary of the number of attainable workforce units, the number and size of bedrooms of each unit, the rental/sale mix, and the sales price or rent for each unit.

c. *Restrictions.*

The proposed restrictions to be placed on the attainable workforce units to ensure they remain attainable to the workforce.

4. **Conversion of Free Market to Attainable Workforce Housing**.

If existing free market units are proposed to be converted to attainable workforce housing units, the Mitigation Plan shall include:

a. *Site Plan.*

Identification of the location and construction quality of the free market units that are proposed to be converted to attainable workforce housing units.

b. *Summary of Attainable Units.*

A summary of the number of free market units that will be converted to attainable workforce units, the number and size of bedrooms of each unit, the rental/sale mix, and the sales price or rent for each unit.

c. *Restrictions.*

The proposed restrictions to be placed on the units to ensure they remain attainable workforce units.

5. **Land Conveyance**.

If land is to be conveyed, the Mitigation Plan shall include:

a. *Survey.*

A survey depicting the location, size and topography of the land proposed for conveyance.

b. *Title Report.*

A title report demonstrating clear title, physical and legal access, liens, easements, and other information necessary to fully describe the legal status of the property to be conveyed.

c. ***Appropriate for Development of Attainable Workforce Housing Units.***

Verification that the conditions of the land, any restrictions on title to the land (such as covenants and easements) and these regulations allow the development of residential units on the land, and that the site can generally be developed for attainable workforce housing.

d. ***Appraisal.***

An appraisal of the fair market value of the land.

e. ***Other Information.***

Any additional information or studies determined by the City Manager to be necessary to verify the suitability of the land for attainable workforce housing units.

6. **Payment of In-Lieu Fee.**

If payment of a fee in-lieu is proposed, the Mitigation Plan shall include a commitment by the applicant that the appropriate attainable workforce housing mitigation fee will be paid at the time of the issuance of building permits and in the amount required at the time of the request for the issuance of building permits. The Payments in-lieu fees are to be found in Attachments B and C, except as modified by the annual update as provided for in Section: 9 F.2 of this ordinance. Ninety days after the adoption of this ordinance, the Payments In-Lieu shown in Schedules B1 and C1, attached hereto in Exhibits B and C, are the amounts of payments in-lieu to be paid. One-year and 90 days after the adoption of this ordinance the payments in-lieu shown in Schedules B2 and C2, attached hereto in Exhibits B and C, are the amounts of payments in-lieu to be paid.

7. **Attainable Workforce Housing Agreement.**

An Attainable Workforce Housing Agreement (hereinafter "Agreement") in which the applicant agrees to implement the Attainable Workforce Housing Mitigation Plan. The Agreement shall be in a form approved by the City Attorney, and shall include the following:

a. ***Construction of Units.***

If the Attainable Workforce Housing Mitigation Plan proposes the construction of attainable workforce housing units, the Agreement shall identify: the location, number, type and size of the units to be constructed; sales and/or rental terms; occupancy requirements; a timetable for completion of the units; construction specifications; and the restrictions to be placed on the units to ensure their permanent affordability to the workforce.

b. ***Conversion of Units.***

If the Attainable Workforce Housing Mitigation Plan proposes the conversion of free market units to attainable workforce housing units, the Agreement shall identify: the location, number, type and size of the units to be converted; sales and/or rental terms; occupancy requirements; a timetable for conversion of the units; and the restrictions to be placed on the units to ensure their permanent affordability.

c. ***In-Lieu Fees.***

If the Attainable Workforce Housing Mitigation Plan proposes the payment of in-lieu fees, the Agreement shall provide the commitment by the applicant that the fees will be paid at the time of issuance of building permits.

d. ***Conveyance of Land.***

If the Attainable Workforce Housing Mitigation Plan proposes the conveyance of land, the Agreement shall identify the land to be conveyed, its fair market value, and the time at which the land will be conveyed to the City.

e. ***Combination of Mitigation Methods.***

If the Attainable Workforce Housing Mitigation Plan proposes a combination of mitigation methods (construction of units, conversion of units, conveyance of land, or in-lieu fees), the Agreement shall identify the appropriate provisions for each method of mitigation.

f. ***Plan to be Recorded & Run with the Land.***

Once approved pursuant to the procedures established by this Ordinance, the Attainable Workforce Housing Mitigation Plan shall be recorded, shall run with the land, and shall be binding upon and enforceable by the City of Destin against the parties thereto and all subsequent owners of any interest in the land subject to the Plan.

8. **Review of Attainable Workforce Housing Mitigation Plan.**

a. ***General.***

The procedures for review of the Attainable Workforce Housing Mitigation Plan shall be the same as those for the Site Plan or plat with which it is submitted.

b. ***Timing of Review and Approval.***

The Attainable Workforce Housing Mitigation Plan shall be approved, approved with conditions, or disapproved by the City Manager, based on the standards in Section 9: *Attainable Workforce Housing Standards*. A decision on the Attainable Workforce Housing Mitigation Plan shall be made prior to a decision on the Site Plan or plat with which it is submitted. A Site Plan or plat shall not be approved without an Attainable Workforce Housing Mitigation Plan approved in accordance with the procedures and standards of this Section.

c. ***Amendment.***

An approved Attainable Workforce Housing Mitigation Plan may be amended or modified only in accordance with the procedures and standards established for its original approval.

SECTION 9: ATTAINABLE WORKFORCE HOUSING STANDARDS.

A. **General Requirements.**

1. **Mitigate Attainable Workforce Housing Demand.**

Each Employee Generating Development not exempted by Section 7: *Exemptions*, shall mitigate the demand for attainable workforce housing created by the development by one or a combination of the methods identified below. The City Manager shall approve, approve with conditions, or disapprove the method of mitigation in accordance with the standards of this section.

a. *Construction of Attainable Workforce Housing On Site.*

Attainable workforce housing units shall be constructed on the site of the Employee Generating Development unless the City Manager finds the provision of attainable workforce housing on-site is impracticable pursuant to Section 9.B.1: *Construction of Attainable Workforce Housing On-Site Impractical.*

b. *Impractical to Construct On-Site.*

If it is determined it is impracticable to provide attainable workforce housing on-site in accordance with Section 9.B.1: *Construction of Attainable Workforce Housing On-Site Impractical*, the housing shall be provided either off-site, through the conversion of free-market to attainable workforce housing units, the dedication of land for attainable workforce housing, through payment of an in-lieu fee, or through assignment of responsibility to a non-profit provider. This shall be done through the applicant making an offer of mitigation, and the City Manager reviewing and accepting the most appropriate mitigation option, based on the standards of this section and the attainable workforce housing goals of the City and the goals, objectives, and policies of the Comprehensive Plan.

c. *Less Than One Attainable Unit.*

If the attainable workforce housing requirement results in less than one (1) housing unit, or a fraction of a required attainable workforce housing unit, the City Manager shall accept a fee in-lieu, pursuant to Section 9.F, *Payment of Fee In-Lieu.*

2. **Amount of Attainable Workforce Housing Required**.

a. *Residential Development.*

All Employee Generating Residential Development not exempted by Section 7: *Exemptions*, shall provide attainable workforce housing for _____ percent of the number of employee households generated by the Employee Generating Residential Development. All residential units, except units which the applicant/developer can ensure will be occupied full-time by residents (hereinafter "All Other Units") shall provide attainable workforce housing at the ratios shown in Table 11B-1.

Residential units which the applicant/developer can ensure will be occupied full-time by a resident (hereinafter "Units Occupied by Full-Time Residents") shall provide attainable workforce housing at the ratios shown in Table 11B-2.

For applications that do not include plans identifying the size of the residential units proposed to be built, the size of the residential units shall be estimated based on the average size of residential units in existing subdivisions of comparably sized and valued lots within the City.

b. *Non-Residential Development.*

All Employee Generating Non-Residential Development not exempted by Section 7: *Exemptions*, shall provide attainable workforce housing for _____ percent of the number of employee households generated by the Employee Generating Non-Residential Development at the ratios shown in Table 11B-3.

Table 11B-1
Residential Units for Non-Full-Time Residents

Unit Size FT²	Residential Units for Non-Full-Time Residents	
500 or Less	0.01	attainable units for each market unit
501-750	0.03	attainable units for each market unit
751-1,000	0.07	attainable units for each market unit
1,001-1,500	0.12	attainable units for each market unit
1,501-2000	0.16	attainable units for each market unit
2,001-2,500	0.19	attainable units for each market unit
2,501-3,000	0.22	attainable units for each market unit
3,001-3,500	0.24	attainable units for each market unit
3,501-4,000	0.26	attainable units for each market unit
4,001 or more	0.28	attainable units for each market unit

Table 11B-2
Residential Units for Full-Time Residents

Unit Size FT²	Residential Units for Full-Time Residents	
500 or Less	0	attainable units for each market unit
501-750	0	attainable units for each market unit
751-1,000	0.01	attainable units for each market unit
1,001-1,500	0.04	attainable units for each market unit
1,501-2000	0.08	attainable units for each market unit
2,001-2,500	0.11	attainable units for each market unit
2,501-3,000	0.14	attainable units for each market unit
3,001-3,500	0.16	attainable units for each market unit
3,501-4,000	0.18	attainable units for each market unit
4,001 or more	0.20	attainable units for each market unit

Table 11B-3
Attainable Units Per Square Feet of Floor Area

Land Use	Attainable Units Per Square Feet of Floor Area		
Government	1 attainable unit for each	909	square feet of floor area
Industrial	1 attainable unit for each	1,286	square feet of floor area
Institutional	1 attainable unit for each	1,027	square feet of floor area
Office	1 attainable unit for each	585	square feet of floor area
Retail	1 attainable unit for each	990	square feet of floor area
Tourist	1 attainable unit for each	1,023	square feet of floor area

c. *Unspecified Uses.*

If proposed Employee Generating Development for nonresidential development is not specified in the formula, the City Manager shall use the employee generation rate of the most comparable category in the formula, or require the developer to conduct an independent calculation for alternative mitigation as provided for in Section 10: *Independent Calculation for Alternative Mitigation*, to determine the appropriate attainable workforce housing requirement.

d. *Change of Use.*

The attainable workforce housing required for nonresidential development when a new use replaces an existing use shall be calculated based on the incremental increase, if any, in the number of employees.

3. Remodels, Redevelopment and Expansion of Existing Uses.

The attainable workforce housing requirement for a remodel, re-development or expansion of an existing use, not exempted by Section 7: *Exemptions*, shall be calculated based on the incremental increase in the size (in gross area) of the residential unit, the increase in the number of residential units (and their size in gross area), or gross leasable floor area of a nonresidential use, whichever is applicable.

4. Income Categories, Sales Price and Rental Rate.

In determining the mitigation requirement, attainable workforce housing units shall be distributed and priced for workforce families whose incomes are less than one hundred and forty (140) percent of the median income for a City family of four (4).

5. Construction and Occupancy.

The construction and occupancy of all attainable housing units shall comply with the following.

a. *Sales and Rental Terms, Size, Type, and Occupancy.*

All attainable workforce housing units constructed shall comply with the sales and/or rental terms, appreciation rates, and size, type, and occupancy requirements as established by the City Council by resolution, which may be changed from time to time.

b. *Other Restrictions.*

All attainable workforce units shall comply with all other requirements as established by the City Council by resolution, which may be changed from time to time, to ensure they are maintained, occupied and owned/rented as attainable workforce housing units.

6. Timing of Occupancy.

All attainable workforce housing units shall be ready for occupancy no later than the date of the initial occupancy of the Employee Generating Development for which the housing is constructed. If the development is approved for phases, then the attainable workforce housing units may be constructed in proportion to the phases of the development for which the attainable workforce units are constructed.

7. Prior Agreement.

Any agreement by a developer to provide attainable workforce housing as a condition of development approval prior to the effective date of this Ordinance shall be implemented under the terms of such agreement, and the provision of the prior agreed upon attainable workforce housing by the developer shall be offset against any additional attainable workforce housing required pursuant to the terms of this section.

B. Construction of Attainable Workforce Housing On-Site Impractical.

Attainable workforce housing shall be constructed on the site of the Employee Generating Development unless the City Manager determines it impractical by making one (1) or more of the following findings:

1. Inconsistent with Comprehensive Plan.

It is inconsistent with the *Comprehensive Plan* goals, objectives, or policies.

2. Proximity to Employment, Schools, and Commercial Services.

It is not proximate to existing or planned employment, schools, and commercial services.

3. It Complies with Development Code.

The applicant has attempted, to the maximum extent practicable, to design the attainable workforce housing on-site, and it does not comply with this development code.

4. Federal or State Requirements.

The attainable workforce housing units cannot be designed and located so as to comply with federal or state law.

5. Opportunity to Combine with Other Attainable Units.

An opportunity exists to construct the units in conjunction with another attainable workforce housing project at an off-site location that would result in more efficient production of attainable workforce housing or the location of the units at a place that is better suited for attainable workforce housing, based on the goals, objectives, and polices of the *Comprehensive Plan*.

6. Incompatible with Surrounding Land Uses.

The attainable workforce housing units located on-site would be incompatible with the surrounding lands because of conflicting uses, architectural style, or bulk.

7. Less Than One Unit.

The number of persons required to be housed in attainable workforce housing results in less than one (1) housing unit.

C. Construction of Workforce Housing at Off-site Location.

If the City Manager finds it is impracticable to construct attainable units on the site of the Employee Generating Development, the applicant may offer the units be provided off-site, if the location is suitable. A proposed off-site location shall be considered suitable for attainable workforce housing units if it complies with the following:

1. Complies with Comprehensive Plan Goals.

Development of attainable workforce housing on the site is consistent with the goals, objectives, and policies of the *Comprehensive Plan*.

2. Proximity to Employment, Schools, and Commercial Services.

The site is proximate to existing or planned employment, schools, and commercial services.

3. Federal or State Requirements.

The attainable workforce housing units can be designed and located so as to comply with federal or state law.

4. Compatible with Surrounding Uses.

The attainable workforce units can be designed and built in a way that is compatible with surrounding land uses.

D. Conversion of Free Market to Attainable Workforce Housing Units.

The City Manager may accept an offer by the applicant to convert existing free market units to restricted attainable workforce housing units if those comply with the following:

1. Complies with Comprehensive Plan Goals.

The converted units are consistent with the goals, objectives, and policies of the *Comprehensive Plan*.

2. Proximity to Employment, Schools, and Commercial Services.

The converted units are proximate to existing or planned employment, schools, and commercial services.

3. Federal or State Requirements.

The converted units are in compliance with federal or state law.

4. Compatible with Surrounding Uses.

The converted units are designed and built in a way that is compatible with surrounding land uses.

E. Conveyance of Land.

1. General.

The City Manager may accept the offer by the applicant to convey land for attainable workforce housing, in an amount that is comparable to the attainable workforce housing need created by the development.

a. *Appropriateness of Land for Conveyance.*

The land offered for attainable workforce housing shall comply with the following:

1. *Consistent with Comprehensive Plan.*

It shall accommodate attainable workforce housing in a way that is consistent with the goals, objectives, and policies of the *Comprehensive Plan*.

2. *Locate Near Services.*

It shall be proximate to existing or planned employment, schools, and commercial services.

3. *Allowed by Land Development Code.*

It shall be located on the site in a way that complies with the City of Destin, Land Development Code.

b. *Establishment of Fair Market Value.*

The fair market value of the land to be conveyed shall be established, and shall be comparable to the cost to mitigate the need for attainable workforce housing attributable to the development.

1. *Preliminary Market Value.*

Fair market value shall be established on a preliminary basis at the time the Attainable Workforce Housing Mitigation Plan is reviewed.

2. *Final Fair Market Value.*

Fair market value shall be confirmed at the time of review and approval of the Site Plan or plat for the free market portion of the development.

3. *Value Net of Commission.*

Fair market value shall be net of any customary real estate commissions for the sale of the land.

c. *Time of Conveyance.*

Land conveyance shall occur concurrent with approval of the Site Plan or plat, unless the City Manager approves other arrangements with financial assurances in the Attainable Workforce Housing Agreement.

d. *Use of Land.*

Land conveyed shall be used for the development of attainable workforce housing units, except conveyed land may be sold by the City in accordance with Section 9.E.3, *Sale of Land*.

2. Sale of Land.

The Council is permitted to sell land conveyed for attainable workforce housing if it better assists the City in meeting its attainable workforce housing goals and if:

a. *Proceeds Placed in Attainable Workforce Housing Trust Account.*

All proceeds from the sale of the land are placed in the Attainable Workforce Housing Trust Account (Section 11.A: *Attainable Workforce Housing Trust Account*).

b. *Use of Proceeds.*

The proceeds from the sale of the land and any interest accrued thereon are used only for subsidizing or constructing attainable workforce housing.

F. Payment of a Fee In-Lieu.

If the City Manager finds it is impracticable to construct attainable units on the site and the applicant elects not to propose off-site provision or conveyance of land for attainable workforce housing, the applicant may offer to mitigate for attainable workforce housing through payment of an in-lieu fee pursuant to this section.

1. Fee Amount.

The in-lieu fees for residential development vary based on the size of the residential unit. The fees for nonresidential development vary, based on the size (gross leasable floor area) and type of nonresidential development. The in-lieu fee formula schedule for residential development is attached hereto as Exhibit B, and incorporated herein by reference. The in-lieu fee formula shall be used to calculate the in-lieu fee for nonresidential development. The in-lieu fee schedule for nonresidential development is attached hereto as Exhibit C, and incorporated herein by reference. The in-lieu fee formula shall be used to calculate the in-lieu fee that will be paid at the time of the issuance of building permits. The in-lieu fee schedules shall be updated annually following the procedures set out in 2, below.

2. **Annual Update of Subsidy and Fee Schedule**.

Prior to September 1, 2008, and on September 1 of each following year, the subsidy amount used in the in-lieu fee formulas for residential (Exhibit B) and nonresidential (Exhibit C) development shall be modified in order to reflect any appropriate adjustments of current land and construction costs. For each annual adjustment, the in-lieu fees shall be multiplied by a fraction, the numerator of which is the Average Just Value per parcel for Vacant Residential land as shown in the most recent tax roll of the City of Destin as prepared by the Okaloosa County Property Appraiser in the current year and the denominator of which is the Average Just Value per parcel of Vacant Residential land for the period of one year prior to the period reflected in the numerator. The new in-lieu fee shall be applicable beginning December 1, 2008, and on December 1 of each following year.

3. **Payment of In-Lieu Fee**.

The fee in-lieu required by this ordinance shall be paid prior to issuance of a Building Permit.

G. **Assignment of Responsibility to a Non-Profit Provider**.

The City of Destin will allow the transfer of responsibility for all or part the obligation to provide attainable workforce housing to a non-profit provider if:

1. The non-profit attainable housing provider has been approved by the City of Destin as a provider of attainable workforce housing, pursuant to a service provider agreement approved by the City Council;

2. The City is made a party to the agreement between the applicant and the non-profit provider and the agreement has been approved by the City Council; and

3. The non-profit provider will accept all responsibilities and obligations originally borne by the applicant for the provision of attainable workforce housing.

SECTION 10: INDEPENDENT CALCULATION FOR ALTERNATIVE MITIGATION.

A. **Applicability**.

1. An applicant may elect to prepare an independent calculation for alternative mitigation if the applicant believes the nature, timing, or location of the proposed Employee Generating Development is likely to generate less need for attainable workforce housing than otherwise required in this section.

2. If the City Manager determines a proposed use is not a use included in Exhibits B and C, the number of employees generated by the proposed use and the required amount of attainable workforce housing shall be computed by an independent calculation for alternative mitigation pursuant to this subsection.

B. **Applicant to Prepare**.

The applicant shall prepare the independent calculation for alternative mitigation.

C. **Portion Subject to Study and Method of Study**.

1. **Portion Subject to Study**.

The independent calculation for alternative mitigation may provide alternative data in one or both of two areas:

a. *Employees*.

The number of employees generated by the proposed use, and/or;

b. *Timing or Rate of Occupancy*.

The timing or rate of occupancy for employees in attainable workforce housing units.

2. **Method**.

The applicant shall use generally accepted principles and methods and verifiable local information and data, and other appropriate materials to support the employee generation data or the occupancy rates.

D. **Procedure**.

1. **Submission of Application**.

An independent calculation for alternative mitigation shall be submitted concurrent with an application for an Attainable Workforce Housing Mitigation Plan in a form established by the City Manager and made available to the public.

a. *Review*.

Within thirty (30) calendar days of receipt of the application, the City Manager shall determine if the application is complete and includes data in sufficient detail to evaluate the independent calculation for alternative mitigation.

b. *Determination*.

If the City Manager determines the application is not sufficient, a written notice shall be mailed to the applicant specifying the deficiencies. No further action shall be taken on the application until the deficiencies are remedied. When the application is determined sufficient, it shall be reviewed pursuant to the procedures and standards of this section. If the applicant fails to correct the deficiencies within sixty (60) calendar days, the application shall be considered withdrawn.

c. *Review of Application*.

Within thirty (30) calendar days of the submission of a sufficient application, the City Manager shall review the independent calculation for alternative mitigation and render a decision on the required amount of attainable workforce housing pursuant to Section 10.E, *Independent Calculation for Alternative Mitigation Standards*.

E. Independent Calculation for Alternative Mitigation Standards.

The City Manager shall approve, approve with modifications, or deny the independent calculation for alternative mitigation based on generally recognized principles and methodologies of impact analysis and the accuracy of the data, information, and assumptions used to prepare the independent calculation. If the independent calculation is approved or approved with modifications, the amount of attainable workforce housing required for the Employee Generating Development will be adjusted, consistent with the City Manager's decision and any such adjustment shall be set forth in the Attainable Workforce Housing Agreement which shall be made a part of the Attainable Workforce Housing Mitigation Plan.

SECTION 11: COLLECTION AND ACCOUNTING FOR ATTAINABLE WORKFORCE HOUSING FEES IN-LIEU.

A. Attainable Workforce Housing Trust Account.

1. Trust Account Established.

For the purpose of ensuring that any fees in-lieu collected are spent for attainable workforce housing that will mitigate the demand for attainable workforce housing created by the applicant, an interest-bearing Attainable Workforce Housing Trust Account is established.

2. Fees Deposited into Account.

All fees collected by the City pursuant to this ordinance shall be immediately deposited into the Attainable Workforce Housing Trust Account.

3. Interest Bearing.

All proceeds in the Attainable Workforce Housing Trust Account not immediately necessary for expenditure shall be invested in an interest-bearing account. All income derived from these investments shall be retained in the trust account until spent or refunded.

4. Limitations on Expenditures.

All funds deposited into the Attainable Workforce Housing Trust Account and accrued interest shall be expended only for the purposes of planning, subsidizing or developing attainable workforce housing units within the City.

B. Refund of Fee In-Lieu.

1. Seven Year Limit.

A fee in-lieu collected pursuant to ordinance shall be returned upon written request to the then present owner of the development for which a fee was paid if the fee has not been spent within seven (7) years from the date the fee was paid, along with interest of four (4) percent per annum. Notwithstanding, if the Council has earmarked the funds for expenditure on a specific attainable workforce housing project, the Council may extend the time period by up to three (3) more years.

2. Written Request.

To obtain the refund, the present owner must submit a written request to the City Manager within one (1) year from the end of the seventh (7th) year from the date payment was received, or within one (1) year from the end of the time this refund requirement is extended by the Council pursuant to Section 11.B.1: *Seven Year Limit*.

C. Payments Determined.

For the purpose of this section, fee payments shall be deemed spent on the basis that the first (1st) payment in shall be the first (1st) payment out.

D. Refunds for Expired Permits.

Any fee in-lieu for an Employee Generating Development for which approval has expired due to non-commencement of construction, may be refunded upon a written request from the then owner of the property for which the fee was paid. Said request shall be submitted to the City Manager within three (3) months of the date of the expiration of approval and be accompanied by proof of ownership of the property and a copy of the receipt verifying payment of the fee.

SECTION 12: SEVERABILITY.

The provisions of this Ordinance are declared to be severable and if any section, sentence, clause or phrase of this Ordinance is held to be invalid or unconstitutional, such decision shall not affect the validity of the remaining sections, sentences, clauses, and phrases of this Ordinance but they shall remain in effect, it being the legislative intent that this Ordinance shall stand notwithstanding the invalidity of any part.

SECTION 13: REPEAL OF CONFLICTING PROVISIONS.

The provisions of the City Code and all ordinances or parts of ordinances in conflict with the provisions of this Ordinance are hereby repealed.

SECTION 14: INCLUSION IN THE CODE.

It is the intention of the City Council, and it is hereby ordained that the provisions of this Ordinance shall become a part of the Destin, Florida, Code of Ordinances; that the sections of this Ordinance may be renumbered or re-lettered to accomplish such intentions; and that the word "Ordinance" shall be changed to "Section" or other appropriate word.

EFFECTIVE DATE.

This Ordinance shall be effective ninety (90) days after passage by the Destin City Council.

The foregoing Ordinance was offered by _____________ who moved for its adoption on first reading. This motion was seconded by _____________ and upon being put to a vote, the vote was as follows:

PASSED on the first reading this ________ day of _______, 2007.

The foregoing Ordinance was offered by _______________, who moved its adoption on second reading. The motion was seconded by _________________, and upon being put to a vote, the vote was as follows:

PASSED AND ADOPTED on the second reading this _______day of________, 2007.

____

MAYOR

ATTEST:

____

CITY CLERK

APPROVED AS TO FORM AND LEGALITY

____

CITY ATTORNEY

EXHIBIT A: THE DESTIN ATTAINABLE WORKFORCE HOUSING STUDY

[Study Inserted Here]

EXHIBIT B: RESIDENTIAL IN-LIEU FEE SCHEDULE

Schedule B1 Residential Payment In-Lieu Fee at 25%			
Residential	**Unit**	**At 25%**	
		Full Time	**Part Time**
< 500 sq. ft.	Dwelling	$0.00	$13.56
500-749 sq. ft.	Dwelling	$0.00	$25.34
750-999 sq. ft.	Dwelling	$0.00	$42.85
1,000-1,499 sq. ft.	Dwelling	$42.64	$66.13
1,500-1,999 sq. ft.	Dwelling	$67.26	$91.93
2,000-2,999 sq. ft.	Dwelling	$60.01	$76.92
3,000-3,999 sq. ft.	Dwelling	$141.78	$174.68
4,000 sq. ft. or more	Dwelling	$162.20	$194.43

Schedule B2 Residential Payment In-Lieu Fee at 50%			
Residential	**Unit**	**At 50%**	
		Full Time	**Part Time**
< 500 sq. ft.	Dwelling	$0.00	$27.12
500-749 sq. ft.	Dwelling	$0.00	$50.68
750-999 sq. ft.	Dwelling	$0.00	$85.71
1,000-1,499 sq. ft.	Dwelling	$85.27	$132.27
1,500-1,999 sq. ft.	Dwelling	$134.52	$183.87
2,000-2,999 sq. ft.	Dwelling	$120.01	$153.85
3,000-3,999 sq. ft.	Dwelling	$283.56	$349.36
4,000 sq. ft. or more	Dwelling	$324.40	$388.86

EXHIBIT C: NONRESIDENTIAL IN-LIEU FEE SCHEDULE

Schedule C1 Nonresidential Payment In-Lieu Fees 25%		
	Unit	**At 25%**
Retail/Commercial		
Shopping Center	sq. ft.	$6.80
Discount Superstore	sq. ft.	$6.80
Bank, Walk-in	sq. ft.	$2.86
Bank, Drive-in	sq. ft.	$2.86
Supermarket	sq. ft.	$6.80
Convenience Market	sq. ft.	$6.80
Golf Course (public)	acre	study
Marina	berth	study
Racquet/Health Club	sq. ft.	study
Restaurant, Fast Food	sq. ft.	$6.80
Restaurant, High Turnover	sq. ft.	$6.80
Restaurant, Sit Down	sq. ft.	$6.80
Service Station	sq. ft.	$6.80
Office Institutional		
Office, General	sq. ft.	$2.86
Hospital	sq. ft.	$0.00
Nursing Home	sq. ft.	$0.00
Place of Worship	sq. ft.	$0.00
School/College (private)	sq. ft.	$0.00
Industrial		
General Light Industrial	sq. ft.	$0.00
Warehouse/Storage	sq. ft.	$0.00
Mini-Warehouse	sq. ft.	$0.00
Tourist		
Hotels and Motels	sq. ft.	$26.33
RV Parks	acre	$46,080

Schedule C2 Nonresidential Payment In-Lieu Fees 50%	Unit	At 50%
Retail/Commercial		
Shopping Center	sq. ft.	$13.60
Discount Superstore	sq. ft.	$13.60
Bank, Walk-in	sq. ft.	$5.71
Bank, Drive-in	sq. ft.	$5.71
Supermarket	sq. ft.	$13.60
Convenience Market	sq. ft.	$13.60
Golf Course (Public)	acre	
Marina	berth	
Racquet/Health Club	sq. ft.	
Restaurant, Fast Food	sq. ft.	$13.60
Restaurant, High Turnover	sq. ft.	$13.60
Restaurant, Sit Down	sq. ft.	$13.60
Service Station	sq. ft.	$13.60
Office Institutional		
Office, General	sq. ft.	$5.71
Hospital	sq. ft.	$0.00
Nursing Home	sq. ft.	$0.00
Place of Worship	sq. ft.	$0.00
School/College (private)	sq. ft.	$0.00
Industrial		
General Light Industrial	sq. ft.	$0.00
Warehouse/Storage	sq. ft.	$0.00
Mini-Warehouse	sq. ft.	$0.00
Tourist		
Hotels and Motels	sq. ft.	$52.66
RV Parks	acre	$92,159

12

Proportionate-Share Environmental Mitigation Fees for Green Infrastructure

This chapter consists of three sections. The first discusses the need to preserve and protect green infrastructure in the development context, and the economic and legal basis for attributing a portion of the cost of such protection to new development through environmental mitigation fees. The discussion and analysis are based on that contained in Nicholas and Juergensmeyer (2003). The next consists of a study prepared for St. Lucie County, Florida, to formulate an environmental lands impact fee program. The last section presents an approach to implement the St. Lucie program through an ordinance to establish an environmental lands impact fee program (see Appendix 12A).

LEGAL AND ECONOMIC FOUNDATIONS

INTRODUCTION

Present environmental problems facing the world today clearly show that past techniques used for environmental protection have failed to mitigate environmental degradation. The decline of the environment—signified by rising air pollution, water pollution, and deforestation—shows the inherent tension between economically profitable ventures and environmental protection. This is the tragedy: Environmental preservation tends to be "unprofitable" while environmental degradation tends to be "cheaper." In essence, it is cheaper for a private party to pollute than to protect environmental resources. This construct, however, which arises as a result of concern with the "bottom line," exists separately from the social and natural features that society might wish to have considered.

However, what if environmental conservation were profitable? Can we move toward regulatory paradigms where the profit motive works toward preservation? Adam Smith told us that "it is not from the benevolence of the butcher, the brewer or the baker that we expect our dinner, but from their regard to their self-interest. We address ourselves not to their humanity, but to their self-love, and never talk to them of our necessities, but of their advantages" (Smith (1999), 50). There are—and could be many more—scenarios in which private parties can find certain environmental protection and preservation activities in their own economic self-interest.

When considering alternative methods from those presently used, it is first necessary to realize that technology and progress are both a cause and a potential solution to the decline of the environment. Modern technology has produced many of the pollutants and wastes that today cause much of the environmental degradation plaguing the world's ecosystems. Technology, and the accumulated knowledge that goes along with this technology, are helping to create alternative production techniques and systems that can better protect, preserve, and even enhance our environment.

The implementation of alternative techniques employed to preserve our natural systems are clearly not costless, however. Additionally, protecting natural systems will have further costs, typically as foregone development opportunities. The enactment of regulations requiring environmental preservation has done little to protect natural systems, especially after it was learned that the penalties for violating such regulations were minimal.

Often, new techniques to protect the environment increase development costs even if they add value or lower future costs (such as protecting property from hurricanes or floods). One way to protect environmental interests is to create economic incentives that achieve desired levels of environmental protection. The purpose of this chapter is to examine this incentive-based approach to environmental protection through the use of mitigation programs funded by an environmental impact mitigation fee. An environmental mitigation fee combines some techniques being used in the United States and other countries to compensate society for the impact of pollution and land development.

The first section of this chapter will explain and discuss one of these techniques—the development impact fee—and will discuss how the impact fee has evolved over the years to help mitigate the effects of new development. The second section will then discuss other market-based regulatory schemes and how they have been used to combat environmental degradation. This section will focus attention on tradable emissions programs and, more importantly, wetland mitigation programs. The third section will then discuss how these different programs and techniques can be combined to create an environmental impact mitigation fee that is based on a market-based approach so as to make it a profitable venture to protect the environment. Because this chapter may break new ground in the application of proportionate-share fees, substantial legal foundation is laid.

FOUNDATIONS FOR PROPORTIONATE-SHARE ENVIRONMENTAL MITIGATION FEES

In one form or another, impact fees now exist in all 50 states and are a common technique used to generate revenue for capital funding necessitated by new development (Juergensmeyer and Roberts (2007)); Nicholas, Nelson, and Juergensmeyer (1991)). Impact fees are charges imposed by local governments that take the form of a predetermined monetary payment—a fee—and are generally levied against developers to fund capital expansion of large-scale public facilities and services necessitated by new development (Denbo (1994)). Such fees play an integral part in giving local governments the ability to cope with many burdens of rapid population growth, such as the need for new parks, roads, schools, jails, public buildings, sewer and water treatment facilities, and public safety (fire, police, and EMS) facilities (Juergensmeyer and Roberts (2007)).

Historically, it has been a primary function of state and local governments to construct, operate, maintain, and improve the basic physical infrastructure of American communities. However, as a result of three significant events in American history, this traditional approach began to break down.

The first of these events was the sharp rise in inflation in the 1970s[1] and the decimation of fixed-based taxes, such as the motor fuel tax. The next was the federal fiscal retrenchment that began in 1982 and has continued since then, thus reducing the funds made available to local jurisdictions. The third factor leading to the breakdown of the traditional approach was the general hostility to the taxation of real property, thus forcing local jurisdictions to look elsewhere to fund the ever-increasing demands to constituents (Susskind (1983)). Because these factors were occurring at a time when the pace of urban development was increasing, both the demand for and the cost of investment in public infrastructure began to climb at a time when the available financial resources were falling. As a result, there arose an increasing need for investment concurrent with declining means.

Due to the lessening of federal and state funding for such infrastructure facilities as water pollution control and highway system expansion and repairs, an increasing share of the responsibility to pay for these and other public investments fell directly on the local jurisdictions by default.[2] In order to assume control of providing these infrastructure needs, local governments were forced to pay the associated costs, commonly by raising local property taxes. In turn, they were then hit by the "taxpayer's revolt." Increasingly, local elected officials faced a public demand to increase public services without increasing taxes. After failing to remedy this dilemma through taxation, many jurisdictions looked to their police powers as a means of addressing the problem.

In terms of the police power, most local governments have great discretion to regulate in order to protect the public's health, safety, and welfare. In contrast, local governments have almost no discretion in the exercise of their power to tax. It was natural, then, that local governments would turn to the police power, where they had discretion, in order to finance infrastructure needs (Nicholas, Nelson, and Juergensmeyer (1991)). Negative aspects of urban growth, including congestion and loss of "quality of life" that further growth and development would entail, provided the framework for invoking the police power to protect the public. Thus, in order to make up for public service funding lost as a result of the conditions mentioned above, local governments began to impose conditions on development that were consistent with the protection of the public's health, safety, and welfare. This was accomplished through the implementation of the impact fee.

In order to see how the impact fee originated, however, it is first necessary to bring up the division of public services that had arisen in American public administration: governmental and proprietary services. Governmental services were those needed in order to promote the health, safety, and welfare of the public, but not offered by private entities. Examples of these types of services are police and fire protection as well as the maintenance of public roads and parks. Proprietary services, on the other hand, are those services created for the same purpose but can be and frequently are provided by the private sector and for which service charges are imposed by the party performing the service. Examples of this are trash collection and water service.

Local governments had long charged for proprietary services, and these charges (called "user fees") were extremely common. These user charges were possible because the benefit of providing a service could be isolated to individual users, and if the individual user failed to pay the charge, the user could be excluded from use or consumption. Governmental services, on the other hand, are classified differently because the cost of performing a service cannot be identified with a single user. This type of application would, in the end, have the effect of reducing, if not totally eliminating, the distinction between proprietary and governmental services.[3]

The legal implications of enacting a plan such as this were unknown at the time. Many, fearing that these fees would be seen as an unconstitutional tax, initially set impact fees to pay for governmental services very low. For example, the "land-use fee" used in Broward County, Florida (the Fort Lauderdale-Hollywood metropolitan area), imposed for road improvement was $100 per residence. Even so, this particular charge was struck down by the Florida Supreme Court as an unconstitutional tax.[4]

The court based its holding on the theory that the fee exceeded the county's "cost of regulation, which was supposed to justify their collection."[5] This holding, like court holdings in many other states, demanded that fees or charges assessed under the police power for the impact of new development be no greater than the costs borne by the governmental entity in "regulating" new development; otherwise, such a fee would be considered a tax.

Ultimately, both the definition of regulation and a detailed accounting of the "costs of regulating" development allowed local governments to base the imposition of impact fees on the police power and avoid the tax label. The idea of regulation had to be expanded from the concept of simply imposing rules and standards to actually imposing fees not classified as taxes, for health, safety, and welfare purposes. Once at this stage, local governments were able to have their impact fee programs classified as regulatory by demonstrating that new development creates the need for new and expanded facilities, and then collecting from new development its proportionate share of the cost of expanding facility capacity. Even though local governments labeled impact fees as regulatory, courts still required local governments to produce calculations and other data to support the reasonableness of their fees.[6]

The courts then devised several tests for reasonable "fees" as distinct from unreasonable regulations or unconstitutional taxes (Juergensmeyer and Nicholas (2002)). California's "reasonable relations"[7] and

Illinois's "specifically and uniquely attributable"[8] have evolved to be closer to the dual rational nexus test followed in many states and indirectly blessed by Justice Scalia in *Nollan*.[9]

The objective of all of these tests was to assure a rational relationship between the demands of new development and assessments against it. Today the dual rational nexus test tends to be followed in most states because of its consistency with the "essential nexus" requirement of *Nollan* (see Chapter 3). The rational nexus test was designed to ensure that impact fees imposed on a new development are proportionate to the facilities and services needed as a result of the new development as well as with the benefits received by the new development.

Thus, two prongs must be met before an impact fee will pass the rational nexus test:

1. Impact fees may be no more that the government's infrastructure costs, which are reasonably attributable to the new development; and

2. The development required to pay the fee must derive some benefit from the use of the fees collected (Juergensmeyer and Roberts (2007)).

If the two prongs of this test are not met, however, the impact fee in question has at times been deemed an unconstitutional taking, entitling the property owner to monetary damages.[10] Whether impact fees failing to meet rational nexus criteria are unconstitutional takings of private property or illegal taxes is a matter of current debate, with these authors aligned on the illegal tax side of the argument (Juergensmeyer and Nicholas (2002)).

IMPACT FEE USES

Impact fees are currently being used for a wide variety of public services, and now represent a common tool used by local governments in funding public service infrastructure needs. Indeed, in one form or another, impact fees exist in all states and have existed for a number of years. Impact fees are assessed for the provision of water and sewer systems, roads, solid waste facilities, libraries, parks, schools, police and fire facilities, emergency medical facilities, environmental and habitat preservation, public hospitals, and even public cemeteries. This list is merely illustrative (see Nicholas, Nelson, and Juergensmeyer (1991)). The most common use for impact fees is in the funding of capital improvements for potable water and sanitary sewer facilities, with transportation services, including highways and roads, being the next most common type of impact fee.

No matter what the fee is used for, courts assess the validity of impact fees in large part on how fairly and accurately they reflect a new development's proportional share of the necessary infrastructure costs. Because accuracy is a major factor in determining the reasonableness of an impact fee, impact fee programs require very careful economic analysis and planning to determine what public facilities will be provided, the cost of providing the infrastructure, and the proportion of that cost attributable to the individual unit of development on the infrastructure facilities.[11] Therefore, the most widely upheld and implemented impact fees are those that are based on data that indicate the desired LOS standards for a particular facility and calculate the cost of maintaining those standards in light of the increased demands created by new development.

Today, impact fee formulae are the methods used to set impact fees and are based on the fundamental theory of the police power. If the developer were required to pay for more impact than they actually cause, this would be a taking or a tax and would therefore be unconstitutional. Therefore, the role of the formulae is to accurately determine the cost of the impact. Once the formulae are developed, the actual impact fee is then derived by entering the data into the formulae. Impact fees can then be offset with credits[12] given by the local government to account for past payment for existing capital facilities, future tax and other payments by the development, and infrastructure and improvements to the land provided directly by the developer (Nicholas, Nelson, and Juergensmeyer (1991), 98–107).

One of the more common uses for impact fees is to fund the need for roads and highway systems brought on by new development. When visualizing how the formula may be set for an impact fee assessment, transportation network fees provide a useful example of how impact fees are calculated and assessed. One of the first steps in calculating this type of impact fee is to determine the level and quality of service that the local government wants to maintain or achieve—a desired LOS standard. Once this is established, formulae are then developed to determine the actual impact that a development will have on the particular facility—in this case, the highway system. For example, a shopping center will have a very different impact on the highway system than a single-family home will have.

Differences such as this are then considered in determining the amount of the fee.

For roads specifically, the impact fee formulae begin by calculating the physical quantity of roads that must be built in order to protect public health, safety, and welfare from deterioration in the quality of service on public roads. This quantity of roads is physical and is measured in lane-miles or lane-feet of roadways. It is usually calculated by multiplying the trip generation rate, divided by two (to adjust for the same trip to and from a destination), times the average trip length, times the percent of new trips, all divided by the capacity of a lane-mile (or lane-foot) of roadway (see Chapter 10 for examples).

The attributable travel is also reduced to account for what are known as "captured" or "diverted" trips (i.e., trips that were already on the road and are not attributable to new development). This results in a number of VMTs, the impact that may be attributed to new development. The next step is to calculate the cost of the road construction and include credits (see Chapters 6 and 10 for discussion). The impact fee is then established based on the projected cost of new construction less any "credits" for dedications to which the developer may be entitled.

IMPACT FEE EVALUATION AND FUTURE USES FOR THE FRAMEWORK

Impact fees are now a commonplace means of infrastructure finance. Requiring new land development to bear a proportionate cost of providing the new or expanded infrastructure it will require, impact fees provide in part an answer to the dilemma faced by local governments when searching for sources of funding for capital expenditures. Now that impact fees have been widely accepted by the courts as regulatory measures, rather than unconstitutional taxes, they are widely seen as funding programs that reasonably allow local governments to maintain levels of capital facilities that can keep up with growth.

There are limitations, however, to the traditional use of impact fees. While they respond to the issues of location, availability, and provision of capital infrastructure with regard to new development, they are "largely unresponsive and even insensitive to the issue of the quantity and type of growth that should be allowed to occur" (Nicholas, Nelson, and Juergensmeyer (1991), 48). Furthermore,

the traditional impact fee fails to respond to other growth and development issues such as housing and employment needs (Andrews and Merriam (1988); Kayden and Pollard (1987)).

Partly in response to these shortcomings associated with the traditional impact fee, and partly because of the success of impact fees in raising funds for many infrastructure items, many local governments have begun to explore the possibility of using the idea of the impact fee to fund "soft" or "social" infrastructure needs, such as "child care facilities, low income or 'affordable housing' housing, art in public places, and environmental mitigation programs" (Juergensmeyer and Roberts (2007), 442).

These types of funding requirements—designed to raise funds for "soft," "social," and now "green" infrastructure items—are usually referred to as "linkage fees" (Andrews and Merriam (1988), 41). When first implemented, linkage fees were thought to be something distinct from "impact fees" (Connors and High (1987)). *Nollan v. California Coastal Commission*[13] dealt the first blow to the perceived difference between linkage and impact fees by holding that a nexus was essential to any condition of development approval requiring a dedication. The Ninth Circuit further diminished any distinction in *Commercial Builders of Northern California v. City of Sacramento*[14] by applying what were essentially "impact fee" criteria to what was characterized as an affordable housing "linkage" requirement. Today, the weight of opinion is that there are no fundamental differences between "linkage" and "impact" fees, but the convention of naming "soft," "social," or "green" impact payments "linkage," and applying "impact" to "hard" infrastructure, remains.

To the extent that any differences can be identified between "linkage" and "impact," most linkage programs have a primary goal of problem mitigation or abatement rather than payment. Impact fees are almost the reverse in that the expectation is that payment of the fee will be the primary means of compliance. A "linkage" program would identify a "concern" and require that the "concern" be abated or mitigated and, if not abated or mitigated, a payment would be made and the proceeds derived would be used to abate or mitigate the problem. An "impact" program would require the payment of a specified amount, the proceeds of which would be used to construct specified public facilities, unless the individual elects to sufficiently mitigate or abate the problem by construction/dedication of those facilities.

MARKET-BASED APPROACH TO ENVIRONMENTAL REGULATION

Many local governments are now exploring the possibility of requiring developers to account for soft infrastructure needs through linkage programs (Merriam (1999)). The use of such protocols to protect the environment would signify a shift from command and control regulations that have employed to control environmental degradation in the past.[15] Command and control regulation, or traditional regulation of the environment, has long been criticized as being too rigid, inefficient, and ineffective (Frieden (1979)). While this traditional regulatory method may have valid and useful applications, the drawbacks of the scheme have led many to believe that a market-based regulatory framework is needed in order to better protect environmental resources (Ackerman and Stewart (1985)).

For the purposes of this book, the term "market-based regulation" refers to the more recent environmental reforms that attempt to use market forces—Adam Smith's "invisible hand"—more extensively than in traditional regulations. This is done by making the desired end, in this case environmental protection, in somebody's economic interest, meaning that someone must profit from environmental protection.

One of the main goals of market-based pollution control programs is to reduce the cost of complying with environmental regulations. One way that a market-based regulatory framework allows for this is to allow the "polluter," not the regulators, to determine the most efficient means of reducing pollution (Polesetsky (1995)). The polluter is not given a choice with respect to the end—pollution abatement or environmental protection—but the polluter is given a choice on how best to achieve that end. One of the choices is to hire another (a "mitigator") —to achieve the desired end on behalf of the polluter.

TRADABLE EMISSIONS PROGRAMS

One of the more prominent types of market-based environmental regulation is the tradable emission. The goal of most tradable emissions programs, unlike impact fees, is to reduce the total amount of existing pollution rather than justly compensating society for the costs associated with new pollution. Another goal of this type of program is to improve the efficiency of meeting environmental regulations, thus making more stringent pollution or environmental standards economically feasible than with a traditional regulatory format.[16]

The typical tradable emissions program begins with regulations setting a cap—an upper limit—on the total amount of emissions for a particular region and for a specific type of air pollution. The regulator then allocates a number of tradable emissions credits to polluters, not to exceed the cap for that region. Polluters are allowed to continue to pollute up to that authorized by their credits or sell the credits they possess to other polluters in the same program.

The flexibility of the program is seen in the fact that the regulator does not specify the means by which the polluter attains the level of pollution set by the number of credits held. Instead, the polluter can reach this level by whatever means they think are most efficient and effective (McGee and Block (1994)). Thus, tradable emissions credits can increase efficiency by encouraging entrepreneurs to develop better pollution control devices and substitute pollution abatement for pollution by credit, while selling pollution credits, potentially for a profit (Polesetsky (1995), 369). In this manner, someone profits from pollution abatement. Contrast this situation with the typical command and control situation: As long as the polluter stays under the preset limit, there is no profit in pollution reductions.

Tradable Emissions in Action: California's RECLAIM

California's Regional Clean Air Incentives Market (RECLAIM) is currently one of the largest trading programs operating in the world (Leyden (1998)). This program was first adopted in 1993 to reduce air pollution in the Los Angeles area—the region with the most air pollution in the United States.[17] In order to combat this problem, RECLAIM was implemented in 1993 in order to reduce existing pollution by targeting reductions in stationary sources of nitrogen oxide and sulfur dioxide. This was to be accomplished by creating a market in tradable emissions credits that would achieve the same level of pollution reduction as targeted by traditional regulations already in place (Leyden (1998), 160).

Because of political pressures and economic forces at work in the area at the time, the goals of RECLAIM were twofold: to attain high air-quality goals while reducing the costs of pollution control.[18] The basis of the tradable emissions program for RECLAIM was to give each existing polluting facility a mass allocation of pollution credits—in effect, a right to pollute—based on emissions during prior years (Selmi (1998)). Each of the credits allocated represents one pound of emissions of one particular pollutant and has a term of one year.[19] New facilities, however, do not receive any emissions credits and must purchase the credits from other facilities (Polesetsky (1995)).

Pursuant to the number of emissions credits given to a facility, the polluter's yearly pollution may not exceed the amount of tradable emissions credits that it holds (Johnson and Pekelney (1996)). The program's flexibility can be seen in the fact that the polluter is then given the choice of how that emissions cap would be most efficiently met. If the polluter is able to reduce air pollution to levels below the individual cap set for it, it may then sell any excess credits it owns to another facility that has insufficient credits to meet its emissions rate limits.[20] This option allows some facilities to maintain pollution levels at their current rate despite reductions in the overall emissions cap for that facility by buying excess credits from another facility. While it is apparent how this method potentially saves the polluter in cost, the South Coast Air Quality Management District (SCAQMD) must also reduce the emissions cap on each facility every year in order to fulfill the second goal of the tradable emissions program: attaining high air-quality goals (Leyden (1998), 160).

Reports show that RECLAIM was initially successful in achieving many of its goals. By 1999, six years after the implementation of RECLAIM, results looked promising. RECLAIM had high compliance rates of over 90 percent, and over $35 million in credits had been traded (Leyden (1998), 164). By 2003, emissions of nitrogen oxide were expected to be reduced by 17 tons per day, and the projected costs of meeting these reductions were reduced by almost half in comparison to projected costs of meeting the same reduction under the traditional regulatory framework (from $139 million to $80 million annually) (*Id.*). Recently, however, the effectiveness of the program has been called into question.

In November 2002, the EPA for District Nine (including Southern California) issued a report evaluating the effectiveness of RECLAIM. The evaluation of the program was conducted after the EPA discovered that the price of tradable emissions credits had risen drastically during 2000 and 2001, while at the same time some facilities under RECLAIM had a very difficult time meeting emissions standards.[21]

In the EPA's final report, it found different factors that may have led to a decrease in the efficiency of the RECLAIM program. One of the largest problems found with the program is that it was unable to react to certain political and economic externalities that may have driven the price of credits to a point where it became difficult for polluters to afford to trade credits. Indeed, the EPA's report found the energy demand in Southern California during 2000 had the unforeseen effect of causing a spike in the price of tradable credits, which in turn put a strain on the market (US EPA (2002)). Even so, the EPA did find that RECLAIM as a whole had been effective in reducing costs for polluters to comply with regulations in large part because "facilities were able to minimize costs by controlling emissions using the least costly methods" (*Id.*).

Evaluation of Tradable Emissions Programs

Despite the advantages of tradable emissions programs, it is clear that they are not a perfect solution to air pollution. Externalities, such as the political and economic climate on local, state, and national levels, can have unforeseen impacts on the effectiveness of such a program. These climates must support pollution reduction requirements and require stringent reductions in overall pollution for such a plan to work effectively (Leyden (1998), 161). A clear baseline of allowable pollution that protects the environment must be set, from which credits can then be traded (Powers (1998)).

Some commentators consider this type of program to be a quick fix rather than a long-term solution to environmental regulation because many tradable emissions programs fail to provide an incentive for continuous pollution reduction (Dreisen (1998), 323). In essence, once a polluter has met pollution requirements set by the regulating body, no incentive remains to further reduce pollution—as one commentator states, the "equilibrium point" (*Id.*). Even when trading programs have succeeded in reducing air pollution by setting pollution caps at levels substantially lower than existing pollution levels, these programs will not encourage further reduction once the equilibrium point has been met (*Id.*, at 317). There is no longer a profit in pollution reduction. Putting a profit in further pollution reduction would address this shortcoming.

Another criticism of the program is that it focuses more on the concerns of reducing costs for industry while ignoring the health of people who live near polluting facilities. There is a concern that many pollution credits will be traded into poorer neighborhoods, resulting in higher emissions in areas with less political power (Schuyler (1995)). On the other hand, Leyden ((1998), 163) argues that RECLAIM has not resulted in increased pollution to any particular geographic area.

Mitigation: Programs for Prevention of Loss of Wetlands

While the issue of air quality remains a hot topic, rising to the forefront in the environmental community of late is the issue of preventing the loss of wetlands as a result of development. This issue came to the forefront in 1989 when President George H. W. Bush declared a "no net loss" of wetlands goal.[22] This goal was again reaffirmed in 1993 when President Bill Clinton expressed support for an "interim goal of no overall loss of the nation's remaining wetlands, and the long-term goal of increasing the quality and quantity of the nation's wetland resource base" (White House Council of Environmental Quality (1993)). A variety of federal, state, and local laws and regulations now affect development in wetlands areas (Dennison (1997)). The goal of these laws and regulations is similar to the goal of impact fees: The developer should compensate for the development's burden on the environment. Unlike emissions trading, however, wetlands mitigation regulations apply principally to new developers as opposed to existing industrial polluters.

Federal Wetlands Regulation

The main federal laws that regulate wetlands development activities are the National Environmental Policy Act (NEPA) and Sections 401 and 404 of the Clean Water Act (CWA) (Dennison (1997), 33). Following the passage of NEPA, which required federal agencies to consider the environmental impact of proposed development, Congress amended the CWA (*Id.*). The CWA Section 404 program now provides the primary federal authority for protecting the nation's wetlands.

Section 404 is jointly implemented and enforced by the U.S. EPA and the U.S. Army Corps of Engineers (Army Corps), and requires that "wetland damage due to development should be avoided, lessened, or compensated in descending order of preference" (Roth (1998)).

Through Section 404, the Army Corps regulates the discharge of dredged or fill materials through a permitting process. Even if the dredge-and-fill permit is granted, however, the Army Corps's role in the development process is not over. As mentioned earlier, it is a national goal—a goal adopted by the Army Corps—for a "no net loss of wetlands."[23] Therefore, the Army Corps may require changes to the plans of a project and will usually require some wetlands mitigation measure to offset the negative impact of development on wetlands habitats (Juergensmeyer and Roberts (2007), 626).

Even with the restrictive nature of the regulations, federal agencies and private property owners have traded thousands of acres worth millions of dollars, with the result being the preservation of substantial environmentally sensitive areas (Merriam (1999)). Oftentimes, the Army Corps's requirements of mitigation are a result of state wetlands mitigation.

State Wetlands Regulation

Before Section 404 dredge-and-fill permits are even considered by the Army Corps, all necessary state wetlands approvals must be secured.[24] The degree of state wetlands regulation by law ranges from minimal to stringent. A number of states have enacted enabling laws that grant the authority to enact wetlands protection ordinances to local governments. "Thus, a landowner or developer may need to comply with three layers of regulation from federal, state, and local authorities" (Dennison and Berry (1993)). Even so, participation in state and local wetlands mitigation programs will often satisfy the mitigation requirements on which a Section 404 permit approval is conditioned.

Forms of Mitigation: Wetlands Mitigation Banking

The Army Corps and many states have allowed a wide range of mitigation measures, including: (1) increased public access to the area; (2) acquisition of other wetlands to provide enhanced protection, or acquisition with a management commitment; (3) restoration or creation of wetlands, either as general compensation or as replacement for a specific habitat type; (4) indemnification or direct monetary payment for lost wetlands values; and (5) mitigation banking (compensatory off-site wetlands restoration or creation) (Dennison (1997), 291).

Approaches (1) and (2), above, are no longer permitted by states or the Army Corps "unless the goal of increased public access is compensation for lost public recreational opportunities or the acquisition includes enhancement or assurance of proper management to compensate for last wetland values" (*Id.*). In contrast, the mitigation banking option (option (5)) is increasingly being implemented as the mitigation method of choice. Like air emissions trading, mitigation banking is a market-based regulation program designed to create an alternative means of environmental preservation by combining investment opportunities with environmental concerns (Dunec (1998)). In the United States today, there are over 100 mitigation banks either operating or proposed.

The basic premise behind mitigation banking is mitigation done outside the area in which the development is planned (off-site mitigation). This type of mitigation allows the developer or a polluter to pay another firm to take over the responsibility for mitigation. This allows a developer whose project is assessed as having a certain number of units of environmental impact to pay a private company, which has already purchased land identified for conservation in the comprehensive plan equal to the units of environmental impact assessed on the project. The incentive for such a program to the developer is that the private mitigation company may be able to offer this service at a price that is less than what it would cost the developer to pursue other means of mitigation.

The typical mitigation bank involves the creation of wetlands from an upland area, but banking has been expanded to include other compensatory activities, such as restoring or enhancing degraded wetlands or providing more stringent protection for wetlands threatened by human activities not subject to regulatory control.

There are two key aspects that distinguish mitigation banking from other forms of mitigation programs. First, banking attempts to construct mitigation areas, or banked wetlands, far in advance of anticipated development impacts in an area. This is one of the key attractions to mitigation banking (i.e., fully functional bank wetlands will be attained by the time impacts are contemplated). Second, banks are generally large in area to provide this trading service for a number of different contemplated impacts rather than through case-by-case processes associated with traditional mitigation programs. Thus, banking consolidates many small fragmented mitigation projects into fewer, much larger contiguous sites.

The general process of mitigation banking is usually initiated when the need for a bank is identified by a governmental planning agency, developer, or other party anticipating future mitigation needs in a given area. A requirement for all banks is that a corporate, nonprofit, or governmental "sponsor" acquires or possesses a long-term interest in a large piece of land. The land must then be suitable to support the anticipated functional needs of a wetlands habitat.

There are typically four types of wetlands mitigation banks, which are classified on the basis of the nature of the sponsors and credit users or purchasers. The first type is typically known as a "single-user wetlands mitigation bank," where the bank is developed and exclusively used by "a single public or private entity to provide for its own mitigation needs" (Whitsitt (1997), 454) The next type of bank is known as a "public/commercial" or "public/private" type bank, which is owned by the government and sells mitigation credits to the general public (*Id.*, at 455).[25] Another type of mitigation bank is known as a "private/private" or "private/commercial" (entrepreneurial) bank, which sells mitigation credits to the general public but is privately owned and operated.

The ownership and management of mitigation banks are open to innovative arrangements. Perhaps the most interesting partnership in the country is that found at the Monastery of the Holy Spirit in Conyers, Georgia. The Trappist monks there joined with a Savannah-based company, Wetlands Environmental Technologies, to form a mitigation bank. The company spent $2 million restoring 500 acres of destroyed wetlands on the monastery's property and is now recouping its investment through the sale of wetlands credits. The monastery considers itself to have profited financially and spiritually from the arrangement (Duffy (2003)).

Mitigation banks are designed to either replace anticipated functional losses within a specified trading area or replace identified historical functional losses with an area. The regulating agency then values the bank by quantifying the created or restored wetlands functions in terms of "credits." The calculation of these credits may be done simply by the amount of acreage and the wetlands type, or by quantifying habitat, physical and biological functions, and social values (Turner and Gannon (1999)). The total credits allocated to a bank are based on the difference in the quality of the ecosystem before and after the bank is established. The regulating agency then undertakes a substantial permitting process, establishing the bank's goals, ownership, location, size, wetlands and other resource types included, trading area, crediting methods and accounting procedures, performance and success criteria, monitoring and reporting protocol, contingency plans, financial assurances, long-term responsibility, and detailed construction plans.

The next step involves the projection of anticipated, unavoidable impacts of development through which applicants can purchase credits from the mitigation bank to make up for the projected wetlands losses (or "debits") that the development will create (*Id.*).

Evaluation of Existing Wetlands Mitigation Banking Programs

Many believe that wetlands mitigation programs are helping to lay the framework for future market-based regulations and have innumerable positive aspects. On the other hand, some believe that this type of mitigation bank is unsuccessful in mitigating the harms created by new development. However, it is clear that successful mitigation banks offer larger, ecologically superior wetlands areas, an attractive alternative to "postage-sized," on-site mitigation projects, which often fail.

Whitsitt ((1997): 459–60) gives four reasons for on-site mitigation failure: (1) the isolated and fragmented nature of replacement wetlands, which makes them vulnerable to functional degradation; (2) the lack of a federal regulatory requirement that permitted developers must maintain successful mitigation sites; (3) the lack of sufficient technical expertise by regulatory agencies to evaluate a large number of diverse mitigation plans adequately; and (4) the lack of regulatory agencies to oversee and enforce mitigation construction and to conduct site monitoring. Even so, many environmentalists continue to argue that off-site mitigation does not confront the importance of wetlands functions to the particular site. To develop that site, they might argue, is to destroy the wetland's relationship to other wetlands, sources of groundwater and surface water, and adjacent uplands (Dennison and Berry (1993), 301).

Other advantages to mitigation banking can be seen from the perspective of the developer. By purchasing or using existing mitigation credits, they are able to save the time and expense involved in designing, implementing, and maintaining specific mitigation plans for each project (Whitsitt (1997)). On the regulatory side, mitigation banks are advantageous to state and local authorities because they allow for increased efficiency of review and compliance monitoring (Brumbaugh (nd)). Others see the mitigation bank as superior to other types of mitigation because it generally includes greater portions of viable ecosystems for fish and wildlife; removes from the reach of developers the aquatic resources provided by wetlands; and, perhaps most importantly, "results in mitigation being performed in advance of, rather than subsequent to, wetland conversion projects" (*Id.*).

Advance mitigation has two principal benefits. First, advance mitigation eliminates concerns that, once a permit is granted, mitigation may never take place. Perhaps more importantly, however, mitigation banking shows promise as a step toward moving past a "no net loss" attitude and actually realizing a gain in wetlands (Whitsitt (1997), 477).

JOINING FORCES: IMPACT FEES, LINKAGE, AND ENVIRONMENTAL MITIGATION FEES

Nicholas, Juergensmeyer and Basse (1999) have expressed their concept of environmental mitigation fees, especially in the European context. It is applied here to the U.S. environmental linkage programs, which combine the principles of market-based regulation, such as those underlying tradable emissions and wetlands mitigation banking, with the principles of impact fees, which may provide economic incentives for developers to actually increase conservation as opposed to merely maintaining the environmental status quo. Such a program could be packaged in an environmental mitigation fee.

Although some local governments have attempted to establish similar "linkage fees" in order to finance other "social" or "soft" infrastructure needs, a more overarching plan is needed in order to establish a program that is likely to harness market forces to make environmental protection possible while at the same time limiting available attacks on such a program. The purpose of this section is to examine the use of an environmental mitigation fee using the implementation standards that have guided the use of impact fees and, at the same time, attempt to guide environmental regulation to a more market-based approach.

The goal of an environmental mitigation fee should be to move away from the on-site regulatory framework and toward a more broad-based and long-range approach to environmental protection. Historically, mitigation of the ecological impact of development and pollution has been addressed on a case-by-case basis (Nelson, Nicholas, and Marsh (1992)). Each development or polluting facility has been required to minimize its own impact on site, or mitigate its impact through some regulatorily approved means. This can result in fragmented scraps of habitat that may not assure an adequate critical mass, and it may not be the best place for the habitat in the long term (*Id.*, at 99). Through the use of an environmental mitigation fee, solutions to many of these problems could be more readily available. This, however, requires long-range planning of environmental goals.

A first step is to expand the context of the "environment." The concept of the environment in mitigation and tradable emissions is wetlands destruction or air pollution. While these are certainly components of the environment and its protection, the environment of concern is much greater. It includes wetlands, habitat, and clean air and water, but it also includes trees and open spaces as well as sites with cultural and historical significance. It would include places to walk or just sit by a stream. In sum, the environment includes those places that should be left as they are or restored to what they were, if degraded.

For instance, in the context of habitat preservation, critical and intact habitat must be identified at an early stage. Identified land, perhaps the furthest away from being developed, can be purchased, thus preventing fragmentation of habitats. We have seen this to some extent with wetlands mitigation banking, but an environmental mitigation fee program would need to be more farsighted than those banking operations in effect now. Just as long-range plans play an important role in terms of habitat mitigation, in the pollution control context, long-range pollution prevention and clean-up plans help establish the validity and success of an environmental mitigation fee program.

As we have seen with impact fees, however, environmental mitigation fees would need very careful impact analysis in order to make them feasible and defensible. Comprehensive plans should guide the assessment of impact of any development or polluting activity. Government regulators would then determine the units of environmental impact associated with a new or existing project and multiply the number of units by a price per unit. Again, however, it is instructive to look at the framework for the impact fee as a guide. For instance, polluters would probably object to paying a fee for pollution that is below the regulatory limit already established for their facility, just as the citizens of Broward County, Florida, attacked the land-use fee, claiming that the fee was an unconstitutional tax.[26]

Assuming that the mitigation fee imposed does not exceed the cost of regulation, however, the above formula would then determine the environmental mitigation fee for that project. At this point, the developer would have three choices. First, the polluter or developer can simply pay the environmental mitigation fee and proceed with the project. The funds derived from these fees would be used to purchase habitat that has been identified in the comprehensive plan, or for pollution prevention and clean-up projects also identified in a pollution control-oriented comprehensive plan. Second, the developer can reduce the environmental impact of the project to a point at which the activity is still profitable but the environmental impact is significantly less, thereby reducing the amount of payment required pursuant to the mitigation fee. Third, the polluter can pay another firm to mitigate the impact elsewhere. The last option is very similar to tradable emissions programs and wetlands mitigation programs. However, there are significant differences among these existing regulatory programs and an environmental mitigation fee.

One of the main differences between an environmental mitigation fee program and programs that are already in place is that existing programs do not incorporate a fee for the impact of existing pollution or development. Whereas a tradable emissions program might set a cap based on what is considered an acceptable level of pollution, and wetlands mitigation fees do not take into account already decimated wetlands, an environmental mitigation fee would set the baseline at zero. This means that all pollution and development, whether or not "legal" under the current regulatory framework, is assessed based on the societal impact to the environment. This would force polluters or developers to consider the environmental impact when designing a project.

Market forces would take over, however, because the polluter or developer is then allowed to pay another firm to take over the responsibility for mitigation and for complying with the comprehensive plan. The incentive for this is that a private mitigation company may be able to offer this service at a price that is less than the environmental mitigation fee.

Legal Ramifications of Environmental Mitigation Fees as an Option

While this type of program doesn't at first glance appear to be anything other than an exercise of the police power, it is important to understand that mitigation fee programs must be able to avoid the labels of an "unconstitutional tax" or a "taking." The avoidance of these labels is best accomplished by the application of the dual rational nexus test. In terms of environmental mitigation fees, the idea is in essence the same as with the impact fee: Development can be charged a proportionate share of the impact cost of the development on the environment, just as they are now legally charged under impact fee programs for impacts that development has on roads, parks, schools, and other hard infrastructure items. They cannot be charged any more than their proportionate share, however. The next step is to ensure that a regulatory program is established to accomplish the goals for which it is collected.

For the limited number of jurisdictions that have adopted an environmental fee mitigation program, the second prong of the dual rational nexus test is the one in which planning is lacking. In order for a mitigation fee program to function as it should, long-range plans and goals should be established. The dilemmas encountered when such plans are not in place can be seen in the Connecticut Supreme Court case of *Branhaven Plaza v. Inland Wetlands Comm'n of Branford*.[27]

In *Branhaven*, a developer wanted to build a convenience store on a parcel of land with some very minor and very small wetlands areas. Initially, the developer offered to build a bigger wetland off-site. The local government agreed, but then changed its mind over fears that there were flood control problems with the proposal. In response to this, the developer offered to spend $25,000 to construct an off-site wetland and to donate to the local government $25,000 worth of engineering services. The local government agreed, but many people in the community objected to the building of the convenience store on the grounds that only paying money to be able to destroy the on-site wetlands

was an inadequate and unacceptable way of satisfying the mitigation requirements.

The court ended up striking down the fee, but not because they did not want to allow for off-site mitigation or the imposition of a mitigation fee. The court struck down the fee on the basis that there were no comprehensive plans and goals for how the money was to be spent. Neither the developer, the planning commission, nor the local government authority had formulated a proposal for the creation of new wetlands or the enhancement of existing wetlands. They were not acting in accordance with a comprehensive plan (Haar (1955)). This result clearly shows the importance of creating a comprehensive plan and long-range goals for environmental quality, including spending fees collected for environmental mitigation.

Implementing the Program

The first and perhaps most important step in the implementation of an environmental mitigation fee program is the establishment of a comprehensive environmental preservation or pollution control plan as part of the comprehensive plan. All implementing actions would then be in accordance with a comprehensive plan, with all the luster that "accordance" or "consistency" adds. In preparing such a plan, local governments should conduct studies to show the impact that proposed development might have on the environment (Ledman (1993)). After conducting the studies, local governments should craft development performance standards that reflect the need for, the nature of, and the extent of the need for environmental mitigation. These standards should be derived from the comprehensive plan and then be implemented in accordance with that plan (*Id.*).

The more difficult aspect of implementation will be first defining and then identifying the nexus between new development and the need for environmental protection and preservation. If an impact fee model is followed, some type of quantitative nexus between new development and environmental damage would be needed. If the new development was not in or adjacent to environmentally sensitive areas, such a relationship may be difficult to establish[28] and, lacking such a nexus, a traditional "hard" impact fee approach may stretch present knowledge.

SUMMARY PERSPECTIVE

What is the environment and how is it impacted by new development? We tend to think of the environment as places where water collects and wild things, especially threatened or endangered wild things, live. Under this definition, environmental nexi would have to be direct impacts of new development on wetlands or habitat. However, is not the environment more than just wetlands and habitat? Doesn't it include trees that may or may not be home to red cockaded woodpeckers? Does it include open areas where children and their dogs can explore? Is not the environment inclusive of unpaved places? Under this expansive view of the environment, any alteration to a natural area, especially by adding impervious surfaces, would be an environmental impact calling for mitigation.

CASE STUDY APPLICATION

This section includes the technical analysis combined with numerous planning and policy considerations leading to the calculation of an environmental mitigation impact fee for St. Lucie County, Florida.

The rapid growth and development of Florida has inevitably resulted in a loss of natural areas. As growth continues, the concern with the loss of natural areas is growing. The Florida State Comprehensive Plan establishes an environmental goal:

> Florida shall protect and acquire unique natural habitats and ecological systems, such as wetlands, tropical hardwood hammocks, palm hammocks, and virgin longleaf pine forests, and restore degraded natural systems to a functional condition. [187.201(10) Florida Statutes]

A number of policies that are intended to implement this goal are set out in the State Comprehensive Plan. These policies include [that state and local government should]:

1. CONSERVE FORESTS, WETLANDS, FISH, MARINE LIFE, AND WILDLIFE TO MAINTAIN THEIR ENVIRONMENTAL, ECONOMIC, AESTHETIC, AND RECREATIONAL VALUES.

2. ACQUIRE, RETAIN, MANAGE, AND INVENTORY PUBLIC LANDS TO PROVIDE RECREATION, CONSERVATION, AND RELATED PUBLIC BENEFITS.

3. PROHIBIT THE DESTRUCTION OF ENDANGERED SPECIES AND PROTECT THEIR HABITATS.

4. ESTABLISH AN INTEGRATED REGULATORY PROGRAM TO ASSURE THE SURVIVAL OF ENDANGERED AND THREATENED SPECIES WITHIN THE STATE.

10. EMPHASIZE THE ACQUISITION AND MAINTENANCE OF ECOLOGICALLY INTACT SYSTEMS IN ALL LAND AND WATER PLANNING, MANAGEMENT, AND REGULATION.

11. EXPAND STATE AND LOCAL EFFORTS TO PROVIDE RECREATIONAL OPPORTUNITIES TO URBAN AREAS, INCLUDING THE DEVELOPMENT OF ACTIVITY-BASED PARKS.

12. PROTECT AND EXPAND PARK SYSTEMS THROUGHOUT THE STATE.

13. ENCOURAGE THE USE OF PUBLIC AND PRIVATE FINANCIAL AND OTHER RESOURCES FOR THE DEVELOPMENT OF RECREATIONAL OPPORTUNITIES AT THE STATE AND LOCAL LEVELS.

St. Lucie County is required, by Chapter 163, to develop and implement plans and land development regulations that are consistent with these and other state goals and policies.

The Conservation Element of St. Lucie County established the following goal:

> Goal 8.1   The natural recourses of St. Lucie County shall be protected, appropriately used, or conserved in a manner which maximizes their functions and values.

A component of the county's efforts to achieve this goal is:

> Objective 8.1.8   The County shall protect native upland habitats, and shall prevent the net loss of listed species and their habitat. This shall be accomplished through the County Environmentally Significant Lands Acquisition program, ongoing natural resource protection programs and the implementation of land development regulations.

Policy 8.1.8.11 implements this objective:

> Policy 8.1.8.11   The County shall continue to support the County Land Acquisition Selection Committee whose function is to utilize the 1992 Upland and Wetland Inventory and federal, state, and local resources, to formulate a master acquisition list of land having native upland habitat. The overall objective is to ensure the preservation of a minimum of 12,500 acres of the 1992 remaining native upland habitat, with the highest priority being those classified as endangered or threatened as well as those having habitats that are facing destruction as a result of urban development and which recognizes relationships to those areas *of native habitat already under public and/or private preservation.*

It is the clearly established policy of St. Lucie County to protect natural resources. One means of this protection is the acquisition of natural areas for the protection of those areas and for the benefit of the public.

The county's acquisition program combines two objectives. The first is the preservation of natural areas for the benefit of the environment and the natural inhabitants of those areas. The second objective is to preserve these natural areas as places of public recreation. In this manner, the environmental and recreational objectives of the county are both being achieved. All of the natural areas now owned by the county, and those designated for acquisition, are now or will be open to the public and made accessible by the provision of parking, trails, and water paths.

ENVIRONMENTALLY SIGNIFICANT LANDS IN ST. LUCIE COUNTY

The current inventory of natural lands owned and to be acquired by St. Lucie County is shown in Table 12-1. This inventory includes:

Current ownership	6,969.6 acres
Pending acquisitions	322.7 acres
Future acquisitions	1,606.3 acres
Grand total	8,898.6 acres

These properties serve the dual purpose of habitat preservation and public recreation. The LOS is calculated on the basis of current ownership and pending acquisitions (7,292 acres).

LEVEL OF SERVICE

It is conventional to measure recreational LOSs in terms of acres per 1,000 residents. Table 12-2 shows the past and projected population of St. Lucie County.

In 2006, the existing inventory of conservation lands with recreational functions is 7,292 acres. The resulting existing LOS is 28.6 acres per 1,000 population. Table 12-3 shows this existing provision and the need for additional lands as the population expands. The county will need to add 2,931 acres of conservation lands by 2015 to meet the passive recreational needs of the growing population.

Table 12-4 summarizes the environmental lands LOS for St. Lucie County. The costs to acquire land shown in Table 12-4 are taken from the data in Table 12-1. Two points are clear: (1) the cost of land is

Table 12-1
Environmentally Significant Lands Program, St. Lucie County

Project	Acres	ESL Funds	Matching Funds	Cost to Acquire
Purchased Sites (Actual Costs)				
Ancient Oaks (White City)	48.00	$543,043	$228,390	$771,433
Blind Creek (S. Hutchinson Island) (1)	409.00	$3,627,914	$9,388,126	$13,016,040
Bluefield Ranch (Trail Ridge)	3,285.00	$1,720,313	$1,690,931	$3,411,244
Brefrank Tract (Avalon St Pk Add.)	45.00	$500,000	$2,100,000	$2,600,000
Indrio North Savannahs	278.00	$1,110,081	$950,997	$2,061,078
Kings Island (N. Hutchinson Island)	173.00	$212,929	$466,214	$679,143
North Fork of the St. Lucie River FCT	150.00	$624,722	$861,908	$1,486,630
North Fork of the St. Lucie River CARL	601.00	$1,442,493	$2,990,291	$4,432,784
North Fork-Platt's Creek (2)	86.00	$31,585	0	$31,585
Ocean Bay (S. Hutchinson Island)	27.00	$326,495	$1,623,380	$1,949,875
Paleo Hammock (Western SLC)	80.00	$272,470	$237,400	$509,870
Queens Island (N. Hutchinson Island)	255.00	$755,358	$3,725,529	$4,480,887
St. Lucie Pinelands	746.00	$641,323	$631,885	$1,273,208
South Savannas	1.00	$58,589	$0	$58,589
Walton Scrub Homestead	33.00	$29,223	$1,095,000	$1,124,223
Westmoreland/PSL	38	$337,990	$2,329,935	$2,667,925
St. Lucie Village	60	$58,642	$2,158,156	$2,216,798

Table 12-1
Environmentally Significant Lands Program, St. Lucie County (*continued*)

Project	Acres	ESL Funds	Matching Funds	Cost to Acquire
Purchased Sites (Actual Costs) (*continued*)				
Indrio Scrub Preserve	13	$251,579	$471,500	$723,079
DJ Wilcox (Indrio Blueway)	105	$724,845	$990,000	$1,714,845
Sheraton Scrub Preserve	56	$428,468	$662,468	$1,090,936
St. Lucie Village-MRC	32	$8,018	$0	$8,018
Paleo Hammock Addition	340	$2,491,284	$2,491,283	$4,982,567
Ten Mile Creek West	8.6	$171,394	$284,485	$455,879
Ten Mile Creek East	100	$667,425	$2,475,000	$3,142,425
Subtotal	6,969.6	$17,036,183	$37,852,878	$54,889,061
Pending Negotiations (Est. $)				
Hackberry Hammock	232	$5,287,500	$3,398,750	$8,686,250
Heathcote I	45	$1,397,862	$4,193,585	$5,591,447
Heathcote II	45.7	$3,201,250	$3,201,250	$6,402,500
Subtotal	322.7	$9,886,612	$10,793,585	$20,680,197
Pending Matching Funds (Est. $)				
Airport Greenway	10.5	$394,125	$394,125	$788,250
Old Dixie Greenway	19.14	$717,750	$717,750	$1,435,500
S. Indrio Greenway	7.9	$281,250	$281,250	$562,500
Bluefield	200	$2,500,000	$2,500,000	$5,000,000
Indrio Savannahs	150	$7,430,000	$7,430,000	$14,860,000
Pinelands Greenway	100	$1,250,000	$1,250,000	$2,500,000
Pinelands Addition	647.95	$8,099,375	$8,099,375	$16,198,750
Indrio Blueway North	170.95	$1,734,500	$1,734,500	$3,469,000
Golf Course	17.4	$652,500	$652,500	$1,305,000
Eden Cemetery	1.82	$100,000	$100,000	$200,000
Heathcote III	50	$1,625,000	$4,875,000	$6,500,000
Subtotal	1606.3	$24,784,500	$28,034,500	$52,819,000
Grand total	8898.6	$51,707,295	$76,680,963	$128,388,258
Historic cost per acre				$14,811.82
Future				

ESL = Environmentally Significant Lands

Acquisition costs are the cost actually incurred when the property was acquired.

Source: St Lucie County, Environmental Resources Department (February and August 2006).

rising, and (2) the availability of matching funds is not being maintained. These two factors may well be interrelated.

Over the next nine years, St. Lucie County will need to add 2,931 acres of environmental land to maintain the LOS. At 28.6 acres per 1,000 population, needed lands for environmental conservation and passive recreation amount to 2,931 acres, with an expected cost of $26.5 million after matching funds (as shown in Table 12-5).

Table 12-2
Historic and Projected Population, St. Lucie County

	St Lucie County		St Lucie County
1980	87,182	1998	184,242
1981	93,705	1999	188,327
1982	99,705	2000	192,695
1983	104,673	2001	198,211
1984	109,833	2002	205,340
1985	114,738	2003	214,031
1986	119,960	2004	226,816
1987	126,105	2005*	240,000
1988	132,416	2006*	255,000
1989	139,655	2007*	270,000
1990	150,171	2008*	285,000
1991	155,368	2009*	300,000
1992	159,302	2010*	315,000
1993	163,831	2011*	323,500
1994	167,833	2012*	332,000
1995	172,212	2013*	340,500
1996	176,272	2014*	349,000
1997	180,338	2015*	357,500

* Estimated

Sources: University of Florida, Bureau of Economic & Business Research and St. Lucie County.

Table 12-3
Population and Conservation Lands, St. Lucie County

	Population	Conservation Acres Needed
2000	192,695	7,292
2001	198,211	7,721
2002	205,340	8,150
2003	214,031	8,579
2004	226,816	9,008
2005	240,000	9,251
2006	255,000	9,494
2007	270,000	9,737
2008	285,000	9,980
2009	300,000	10,224
2010	315,000	7,292
2011	323,500	7,721
2012	332,000	8,150
2013	340,500	8,579
2014	349,000	9,008
2015	357,500	9,251

Table 12-4
Environmental Lands Level of Service

Existing lands	6,969.60
Pending acquisitions	322.70
Total	7,292.30
Population served	255,000
Level of service	28.60
Historic cost per acre	$14,812
% matching	70.22%
Historic local cost per acre	$4,411
Historic cost per capita	$126.13
Projected cost per acre	$17,892
% matching	50.63%
Projected local cost per acre	$9,058
Projected cost per capita	$259.04

Table 12-5
Needed Environmental Lands, St. Lucie County

Population 2006	255,000
Population 2015	357,500
Change	102,500
Environmental lands level of service	28.60
Acres needed	2,931.22
Cost per acre	$17,892
Acquisition cost	$52,445,694
Anticipated matching funds	$26,552,059
Net cost	$25,893,634

Table 12-6
Dwelling Occupancy Characteristics,
St. Lucie County, 2000

Population	192,695
Households	76,933
Average household size	2.505
Dwelling units	91,262
Occupied	76,933
Total vacant	14,329
For rent	2,264
For sale only	1,440
Rented or sold, not occupied	441
For seasonal, recreational, or occasional use	9,056
For migrant workers	20
Other vacant	1,108
Total seasonal and other	10,184
Seasonal population	23,471
Peak population	216,166
Total used units	87,117
Persons per unit	2.481

Source: Bureau of the Census, American Factfinder
(http://factfinder.census.gov/servlet).

GROWTH COST OF ENVIRONMENTAL LAND ACQUISITION

From Table 12-4, it can be seen that the unmet cost of environmental land acquisition to meet the needs of a growing population is $180.30 per capita. Table 12-6 shows the occupancies of St. Lucie County dwelling units from the 2000 Census. The showing here is that dwelling units in St. Lucie County have an expected occupancy of 2.481 persons.

Table 12-7 present occupancies by type of dwelling unit and multiplies the number of people expected to be in occupancy, times the per capita net cost of environmental land acquisition, to get environmental land acquisition cost per dwelling unit.

Table 12-7
Environmental Land Cost Per Unit

Land-Use Type (Unit)	Occupancy	Cost Per Unit
Single family	2.656	$687.99
Mobile home/recreational vehicle	1.739	$613.59
Multifamily 3+ stories	2.369	$259.04
Multifamily 1- and 2-story	2.369	$613.59
Hotel/motel, room	1.776	$460.06
Bed and breakfast, room	1.776	$460.06
All other residential	2.656	$687.99
Average	2.481	

NOTES

1. For most of the country's history, inflation averaged 2 percent or less, with the periods of war being significant exceptions. Beginning in the 1960s and continuing through the 1980s, inflation existed at hitherto unprecedented rates, peaking at over 18 percent in the late 1970s. See U.S. Department of Labor, Bureau of Labor Statistics. Available at www.bls.gov.

2. Both the state and the federal government abandoned funding programs for public investments because of a sharp rise in cost. Furthermore, there were more burdens on the local governments responsible for handling these matters because of required improvements to many infrastructure facilities, such as water pollution control facilities. See, e.g., The Water Pollution Control (Clean Water) Act, 33 U.S.C. Sections 1251 et seq. (1994).

3. This distinction a mong types of services, while important in public administration, received little if any judicial recognition. This may explain why the courts had little problem with applying "proprietary" review criteria to "governmental" functions.

4. See *Broward County v. Janis Development Corp.*, 311 So.2d 371 (Fla. 4th DCA 1975).

5. *Contractors and Builders Assn. of Pinellas County v. City of Dunedin*, 329 So.2d 314 (Fla.1976), on remand 330 So.2d 744 (Fla.App.1976).

6. In *Holmdel Builders' Ass'n. v. Township of Holmdel*, 121 N.J. 550, 583 A.2d 277 (1990), the court distinguished taxation from regulatory fees. The court stated that, if the primary purpose of the fee was to raise general revenue, it was a tax. However, if the primary purpose was to "reimburse the municipality for services reasonably related to development, it [was] a permissible regulatory exaction." *Id.*

7. First seen in *Ayers v. City Council of City of Los Angeles*, 34 Cal.2d 31; 207 P.2d 1 (1949).

8. *Pioneer Trust & Savings Bank v. Village of Mount Prospect*, 22 Ill.2d 375, 176 N.E.2d 799 (1961).

9. *Nollan v. California Coastal Commission*, 483 U.S. 825, 107 S.Ct. 3141 (1987).

10. There are three general theories under which courts have held that taking by regulation has occurred: (1) that a taking by invasion has occurred; (2) when a regulation significantly diminishes the value of the private property; and (3) when the requirements placed upon a landowner do not substantially advance the purpose of the regulation. In terms of impact fees, developers most often advance the third theory listed. If, however, an impact fee has fulfilled the nexus requirement of the dual rational nexus test, it will generally withstand this type of challenge (Juergensmeyer and Roberts (2007)).

11. The forgiving language in *Dolan v. City of Tigard*, 512 U.S. 374, 114 S.Ct. 2309 (1994) (that mathematical precision is not required) has not proven to be the case in impact fee challenges.

12. It is unfortunate that, in impact fee methodology and literature, "credit" has two meanings. The first refers to a reduction in the amount of an impact fee to reflect other funds devoted to that same facility or service. The second meaning refers to a donation or dedication of land and facilities that allow an individual to pay impact fees "in kind" (see Chapter 6).

13. Note 9, supra.

14. 941 F.2d 872 (9th Cir. 1991), cert. denied 504 W.S. 931, 112 S.Ct. 1997, 118 L.Ed.2d 593 (1992).

15. The "command and control" form of environmental protection refers to mandated environmental controls instituted after the enactment of the National Environmental Policy Act (1969) and subsequent acts such as the Clean Air Act and the Clean Water Act in the 1970s (Hahn and Stavins (1991)).

16. In theory, the cost savings produced through more efficient measures of meeting environmental regulatory standards would allow for more stringent standards to be set, an important aspect of the program for those interested in reducing pollution, not reducing costs for industry. (Hahn and Stavins (1991)).

17. *Alliance of Small Emitters/Metals Industry et al. v. South Coast Air Quality Management District*, 60 Cal. App. 4th 55, 57 (Cal.App. 2d 1997).

18. Leading up to the implementation of RECLAIM, the agency in charge of air quality management in the area—the South Coast Air Quality Management District (SCAQMD)—was under pressure to find an alternative to reduce air pollution. At the same time, the Los Angeles area was experiencing a severe economic recession (Johnson and Pekelney (1996)). Thus, businesses were seeking more cost-effective means of meeting environmental regulations because of the high costs of meeting the requirements of traditional regulations (Leyden (1998), 160).

19. SCAQMD Rule 2007(c)(1).

20. Note 17, supra.

21. See "Region 9 Air Problems: EPA's Evaluation of the RECLAIM Program in the South Coast Air Quality Management District," U.S. Environmental Protection Agency (November 2002). Available at www.epa.gov/Region9/air/reclaim/index.html.

22. "President's message to the Congress Transmitting the Fiscal Year 1990 Budget, Building a Better America," 25 Weekly Comp. Pres. Doc. 184 (February 9, 1989).

23. See "Memorandum of Agreement Between EPA and Dept. of Army Concerning the Determination of Mitigation Under the Clean Water Act Section 404(b)(1)," Guidelines, 55 Fed. Reg. 9210, 9211 (March 12, 1990).

24. See 33 CFR 320.4(j). Under the Clean Water Act Section 404 program, individual states may adopt and administer their own wetlands protection programs, which must be approved by the Army Corps. Once the program has been approved, the state, rather than the Army Corps, may issue Section 404 permits directly. The EPA, however, retains veto power to withdraw the state's Section 404 permitting authority if regulatory and statutory requirements are not followed (Dennison (1997), 62).
25. An offshoot of the public/private type bank can be seen in the State of Florida. In this variation, it is possible for the state to own the land on which the bank is to be created, but arises when the state lacks the funding or the impetus to administer the bank. In this situation, even though the state owns the land, a private company can put up bids for the credits, and then the state and the private administering company split the mitigation proceeds resulting from the sale of credits. Phone conversation on March, 25, 2003, with Sheri Lewin, employee of "Mitigation Marketing." E-mail: sheri@mitigation marketing.com; phone: 407-481-0677.
26. See Chapter 3. The courts, as stated earlier, struck down this impact fee, basing its decision on the fact that the fee exceeded the county's cost of regulation, "which was supposed to justify their collection."
27. 251 Conn. 269, 740 A.2d 847 (1999).
28. It would appear that terrestrial ecological science is not yet able to establish a statistical nexus between off-site development and ecological damage.

APPENDIX 12A

ENVIRONMENTAL LANDS IMPACT FEE DRAFT ORDINANCE

This section includes sample ordinance language implementing an environmental mitigation impact fee. Although designed for use by a specific Florida jurisdiction, the construction concepts and logic may be broadly applied.

ORDINANCE NO. 07-021
AN ORDINANCE AMENDING ___________ OF THE ST. LUCIE COUNTY CODE AND COMPILED LAWS BY ADDING AN ENVIRONMENTAL LANDS IMPACT FEE ORDINANCE

AN ORDINANCE RELATING TO THE REGULATION OF THE USE AND DEVELOPMENT OF LAND IN ST. LUCIE COUNTY, FLORIDA; IMPOSING AN ENVIRONMENTAL LANDS IMPACT FEE ON LAND DEVELOPMENT IN ST. LUCIE COUNTY FOR THE PROTECTION AND PROVISION OF ENVIRONMENTAL LANDS NECESSITATED BY SUCH NEW DEVELOP-MENT; STATING THE AUTHORITY FOR ADOPTION OF THE ORDINANCE; MAKING LEGISLATIVE FINDINGS; PROVIDING DEFINITIONS; PROVIDING A SHORT TITLE AND APPLICABILITY; PROVIDING INTENTS AND PURPOSES; PROVIDING RULES OF CONSTRUC-TION; PROVIDING DEFINITIONS; PROVIDING FOR THE COMPUTATION OF THE AMOUNT OF THE ENVIRONMENTAL LANDS IMPACT FEE; PROVIDING FOR THE PAYMENT OF AN ENVIRONMENTAL LANDS IMPACT FEE; PROVIDING FOR THE ESTABLISH-MENT OF AN ENVIRONMENTAL LANDS IMPACT FEE DISTRICT; PROVIDING FOR THE ESTABLISHMENT OF AN ENVIRONMENTAL LANDS IMPACT FEE TRUST FUND; PROVIDING FOR THE USE OF FUNDS; PRO-VIDING FOR THE REFUND OF FEES PAID; PROVID-ING FOR EXEMPTIONS AND CREDITS; PROVIDING FOR INDEPENDENT PROPERTY APPRAISALS AND REVIEW OF PROPERTY APPRAISALS; PROVIDING FOR REVIEW AND AUTOMATIC ADJUSTMENT OF THE FEE SCHEDULE; PROVIDING FOR APPEALS; PROVIDING A PENALTY PROVISION; PROVIDING FOR SEVERABIL-ITY; PROVIDING AN EFFECTIVE DATE.

WHEREAS, the Board of County Commissioners of St. Lucie County, Florida, has made the following determinations:

(a) On ___________, 2007 the Local Planning Agency/St. Lucie County Planning and Zoning Commission held a public hearing on the proposed ordinance after publishing two notices in The Port St. Lucie News and The Tribune at least ten (10) days prior to the hearing and determined that the proposed ordinance was consistent with the St. Lucie County Comprehensive Plan.

(b) On ___________, 2007, this Board held its first public hearing on the proposed ordinance, after publishing a notice of such hearing in The Tribune and the Port St. Lucie News on ___________, 2007.

(c) On ___________, 2007, this Board held its second public hearing on the proposed ordinance, after publishing a notice of such hearing in The Tribune and the Port St. Lucie News on ___________, 2007.

(d) The Board of County Commissioners has reviewed and accepted a Report entitled "An Environmental Lands Acquisition Impact Fee," by Dr. James Nicholas dated January 8, 2007.

(e) The Environmental Lands Impact Fee is consistent with the general purpose, goals, objectives, and standards of the St. Lucie County Comprehensive Plan and is in the best interest of the health, safety, and public welfare of the citizens of St. Lucie County, Florida.

NOW, THEREFORE, be it ordained by the Board of County Commissioners of St. Lucie County:

Section 1. Short title, authority, and applicability.

(a) This ordinance shall be known and may be cited as the "Environmental Lands Impact Fee Ordinance."

(b) The Board of County Commissioners of St. Lucie County has the authority to adopt this ordinance pursuant to Article VIII of the Constitution of the State of Florida and to Chapter 125 and sections 163.3201 and 163.3202(3) Florida Statutes.

(c) Pursuant to section 125.01(1)(f), Florida Statutes, St. Lucie County has the power to preserve and protect Environmental Lands in the county. St. Lucie County provides Environmental Lands in the incorporated and unincorporated areas of St. Lucie County. Development within the cities impacts the capital needs for protection and provision of Environmental Lands in the county.

(d) St. Lucie County must collect Environmental Lands impact fees within the incorporated and unincorporated areas of St. Lucie County in order to preserve and protect county Environmental Lands that adequately serve the needs of all county residents including the residents of the cities.

(e) This article shall apply to all areas of St. Lucie County, even in the absence of interlocal agreements with the affected municipalities.

Section 2. Intents, purposes, and findings.

(a) This chapter is intended to implement and be consistent with the goals, objectives and policies of the St. Lucie County Comprehensive Plan.

(b) The purpose of this chapter is to regulate the use and development of land so as to assure that new development bears a proportionate share of the cost of capital expenditures necessary to preserve and protect Environmental Lands in St. Lucie County as contemplated by the St. Lucie County Comprehensive Plan.

(c) The Florida Legislature through the enactment of Section 163.3202, Local Government Comprehensive Planning and Land Development Regulation Act and Section 380.06(16) of the Environmental Land and Water Management Act, Florida Statutes, Chapters 163 and 380, respectively, has sought to encourage local governments to enact impact fees as a part of their land development regulation program and, more specifically, Florida Statutes Chapter 163.31801 has established requirements for their enactment..

(d) The protection and provision of Environmental Lands in the county is designed and intended to provide preservation of natural areas, habitat preservation and areas for passive recreational opportunities for all citizens of the county, in both unincorporated and incorporated areas. Therefore, placing a fair share of the burden of the cost

Table 12A-1
Environmental Lands Impact Fee Countywide Assessment

Land Use Type	Unit of Measure	Impact Fee
Residential		
Single-family	Per dwelling unit	$687.99
Mobile home/RV unit (park only)	Per pad	$613.59
Multi-family 1 and 2 floors	Per dwelling unit	$259.04
Multi-family 3+ floors	Per dwelling unit	$613.59
Hotel/motel	Per room	$460.06
Bed and breakfast (guest rooms)	Per room	$460.06
All other residential	Per dwelling unit	$687.99

Note: The fee schedule shown in this table is subject to annual revision based upon the provisions of section 18 of this article.

of providing capital expenditures for the protection and provision of Environmental Lands on land development within municipal areas constitutes a county purpose.

(e) All new residential construction within the county in both unincorporated and incorporated areas impacts the need for protection and provision of Environmental Lands. Accordingly, the protection and provision of environmental lands benefits all residents of the county, including residents of municipalities, and is in the best interest of the public's health, safety, and welfare.

(f) The protection and provision of Environmental Lands pursuant to this Environmental Lands Impact Fee Ordinance are designed to work in conjunction with and be compatible with the ongoing St. Lucie County Environmentally Significant Land Acquisition Program.

(g) The methodology used to calculate the impact fees imposed by this ordinance is based upon the most recent and localized data available for St. Lucie County as required by Florida Statutes Chapter 163.31801.

Section 3. Rules of construction.

(a) The provisions of this article shall be liberally construed so as to effectively carry out its purpose in the interest of the public health, safety, and welfare.

(b) For the purposes of administration and enforcement of this article, unless otherwise stated in this article, the following rules of construction shall apply to the text of this article:

(1) In case of any difference of meaning or implication between the text of this article and any caption, illustration, summary table, or illustrative table, the text shall control.

(2) The word "shall" is always mandatory and not discretionary; the word "may" is permissive.

(3) Words used in the present tense shall include the future; and words used in the singular number shall include the plural, and the plural the singular, unless the context clearly indicates the contrary.

(4) The phrase "used for" includes "arranged for," "designed for," "maintained for," or "occupied for."

(5) The word "person" includes an individual, a corporation, a partnership, an incorporated association, or any other similar entity.

(6) Unless the context clearly indicates the contrary, where a regulation involves two (2) or more items, conditions, provisions, or events connected by the conjunction "and,"

"or" or "either … or," the conjunction shall be interpreted as follows:

a. "And" indicates that all the connected terms, conditions, provisions or events shall apply.

b. "Or" indicates that the connected items, conditions, provisions or events may apply singly or in any combination.

c. "Either … or" indicates that the connected items, conditions, provisions or events shall apply singly but not in combination.

(7) The word "includes" shall not limit a term to the specific example but is intended to extend its meaning to all other instances or circumstances of like kind or character.

(8) Unless the context clearly indicates to the contrary, the terms "protection and provision of Environmental Lands" shall have the same meaning as given in the St. Lucie County Comprehensive Plan.

(9) "County administrator" means the county administrator or whoever he/she may designate to carry out the administration of this article.

(10) Unless the context clearly indicates to the contrary, all land use terminology in this article shall have the same meaning as it has in the St. Lucie County Land Development Code.

Section 4. Definitions.

(a) *Capital improvement* includes Environmental Lands planning, land acquisition, remediation of degraded environmentally significant lands, removal of exotic plants, the provision of vehicular and non-vehicular access, site improvements, buildings, and equipment, but excludes maintenance and operation.

(b) *Feepayer* is a person commencing a land development activity by applying for the issuance of a building permit or electrical permit for a mobile home park or recreational vehicle park for a type of land development activity specified in section 6 of this article.

(c) *Environmental Lands* means "outdoor preserve areas," "natural area preserves," "conservation/open space area," and "environmentally significant land" as defined and identified in the St. Lucie County Comprehensive Plan and in the study entitled "An Environmental Lands Acquisition Impact Fee," by Dr. James Nicholas dated January 8, 2007.

Section 5. Imposition of Environmental Lands impact fee.

(a) Any person who, ninety days or more after the effective date of this article, seeks to develop land within

St. Lucie County by applying for the issuance of a building permit for one of the residential land use types specified in section 6 of this article or an electrical permit for a mobile home park or recreational vehicle park shall be required to pay an Environmental Lands impact fee in the manner and amount set forth in this article.

(b) No building permit for any residential land use types specified in section 7 of this article nor electrical permit for a mobile home park or recreational vehicle park shall be issued unless and until the Environmental Lands impact fee hereby required has been paid as provided in section 7 of this article.

Section 6. Computation of the amount of environmental Lands impact fee.

(a) At the option of the feepayer, the amount of the fee may be determined by the following fee schedule:

If the type of residential development activity for which a building permit or electrical permit for a mobile home park or recreational vehicle park which is being applied for is not specified on the above fee schedule, the county administrator shall use the fee applicable to the most nearly comparable type of land use on the above fee schedule.

(b) The person applying for the issuance of a building permit or electrical permit for a mobile home park or recreational vehicle park may, at his option, submit evidence to the county administrator indicating that the fees set out in subsection

(a) above are not appropriate for his particular development. Based upon convincing and competent evidence, the county administrator may adjust the fee to that appropriate for the particular development.

Section 7. Payment of fee.

(a) The feepayer shall pay the fee to the county administrator at any time prior to the issuance of a building permit or electrical permit for a recreational vehicle park or mobile home park.

(b) In the event the developer proposes to dedicate environmental lands, the provisions of sections 9, 10 & 11 shall apply. The portion of the fee represented by the property dedications or acquisitions shall be deemed paid only when the dedicated or acquired property is officially accepted by the county or other appropriate governmental entity.

If Environmental Lands impact fees are owed, no development permits of any type may be issued for the building or structure in question while the fee remains unpaid. The county administrator may authorize the initiation of any action as permitted by law or equity to collect the unpaid fees.

Section 8. Alternative collection mechanism.

In the event the Environmental Lands impact fees are not paid prior to the issuance of a building permit because of mistake or inadvertence or in the event a municipality has not agreed to assist in the collection of those Environmental Lands impact fees imposed within municipal boundaries, the county shall proceed to collect the Environmental Lands impact fees as follows:

(a) The county shall serve, by certified mail, return receipt requested, an impact fee statement notice upon the feepayer at the address set forth in the application for a building permit, and the owner at the address appearing on the most recent records maintained by the property appraiser of the county. The county shall also attach a copy of the impact fee statement notice to the building permit posted at the site of the land development activity if construction has commenced. Service of the impact fee statement notice shall be deemed notice that the impact fees are due and service shall be deemed effective on the date the return receipt indicates the notice was received by either the feepayer of the owner of the property, whichever occurs first. The impact fee statement notice shall contain the legal description of the property and shall advise the feepayer and owner as follows:

(1) The amount due and the general purpose for which the Environmental Lands impact fees were imposed;

(2) That a hearing before the board of county commissioners may be requested within thirty (30) calendar days from the receipt of the impact fee statement notice, by making application at the office of the county administrator;

(3) That the Environmental Lands impact fees shall be delinquent if not paid and received by the county within sixty (60) calendar days of the date the impact fee statement notice was received, excluding the date of receipt, or if a hearing is not scheduled and, upon becoming delinquent, shall be subject to the imposition of a delinquent fee and interest on the unpaid amount until paid;

(4) That in the event the Environmental Lands impact fees become delinquent a lien against the property for which the building permit was secured shall be recorded in the official records of the county.

(b) The Environmental Lands impact fees shall be delinquent if, within sixty (60) calendar days from the date of the receipt of the impact fee statement notice by either the feepayer or the owner or the date said notice was attached to the building permit, neither the Environmental Lands impact fees have been paid and received by the county nor a hearing requested. In the event a hearing is requested within the time period allowed, the Environmental Lands impact fees shall become delinquent if not paid within thirty (30) calendar days from the date the board of county commissioners determined the amount of Environmental Lands impact fees due upon the conclusion of such hearing. Upon becoming delinquent, a delinquency fee equal to ten (10) percent of the total Environmental Lands impact fees imposed shall be assessed. Such total Environmental Lands impact fees, plus the delinquency fee, shall bear interest at the statutory rate for final judgments calculated on a calendar-day basis, until paid.

(c) Should the Environmental Lands impact fees become delinquent, as set forth above, the county shall serve, by certified mail, return receipt requested, a "Notice of Lien" upon the delinquent feepayer at the address indicated in the application for a building permit and upon the owner of the property at the address appearing on the most recent records maintained by the property appraiser of the county. The notice of lien shall notify the delinquent feepayer and owner that due to their failure to pay the Environmental Lands impact fees, the county shall file a claim of lien with the clerk of the circuit court.

(d) Upon mailing the notice of lien, the county attorney shall file a claim of lien with the clerk of the circuit court for recording in the official records of the county. The claim of lien shall contain the legal description of the property, the amount of the delinquent impact fees and the date of their imposition. Once recorded, the claim of lien shall constitute a lien against the property described therein. The county attorney shall proceed expeditiously to collect, foreclose or otherwise enforce said lien.

(e) After the expiration of one (1) year from the date of recording the claim of lien, as provided herein, a suit may be filed to foreclose said lien. Such foreclosure proceedings shall be instituted, conducted and enforced in conformity with the procedures for the foreclosure of municipal special assessment liens, as set forth in F.S. §§ 173.04 through 173.12, inclusive, which provisions are hereby incorporated herein in their entirety to the same extent as if such provisions were set forth herein verbatim. Attorney's fees and costs incurred by the county in the foreclosure proceedings shall be recoverable.

(f) The liens for delinquent impact fees imposed hereunder shall remain liens, coequal with the liens of all state, county, district and municipal taxes and superior in dignity to all other liens and claims, until paid.

(g) The collection and enforcement procedures set forth in this section shall be cumulative with, supplemental to and in addition to, any applicable procedures provided in any other ordinances or administrative regulations of the county or any other applicable law or administrative regulation of the State of Florida. Failure of the county to follow the procedure set forth in this section shall not constitute a waiver of its rights to proceed under any other applicable procedure.

(h) In the event that the property for which the building permit is issued is located within a municipality that has not agreed to assist in the collection of the Environmental Lands impact fee, a feepayer that pays the Environmental Lands impact fee directly to the county prior to the receipt of an impact fee statement notice, shall be entitled to a ten (10) percent reduction in the amount of the Environmental Lands impact fee due.

(i) In the event that the alternative collection mechanism contained herein is utilized by the county to collect the delinquent Environmental Lands impact fee and that collection procedure results in an inequitable burden as a result of the particular terms and provisions of the construction or loan contract of the feepayer, then such feepayer may petition the county administrator for relief. The county administrator may make such adjustments to the collection process to address such adverse impacts resulting from the use of the alternative collection procedure. The feepayer shall have a right of review of the decision of the county administrator to the board of county commissioners.

Section 9. Credits.

(a) *Scope*. Any person who shall commence any Environmental Lands impact generating land development activity may apply for a credit against the required Environmental Lands impact fee for any contribution, construction, or dedication of land made by such person or a predecessor in interest and accepted and received by St. Lucie County, the appropriate local municipality, state or federal agency for Environmental Lands facilities that are creditable pursuant to this section. Consistent with the standards of this section, an application may be made for credit for any contribution, construction or dedication made in St. Lucie County as required by a development order issued by St. Lucie County, the City of Fort Pierce, the City of Port St. Lucie, or St. Lucie Village pursuant to its local development regulations or F.S. § 380.06, or any additional development condition imposed by the Florida Land and Water Adjudicatory Commission on a development of regional impact to the extent the contribution, payment, construction or dedication meets the same needs as the Environmental Lands impact fee.

(b) *General*. Any person desiring an Environmental Lands impact fee credit, who proposes to make any contribution, construction or dedication of an Environmental Lands facility that is consistent with the county's comprehensive plan or the adopted Comprehensive Plan of Ft. Pierce, Port St. Lucie or St. Lucie Village, shall first obtain from the board of county commissioners an approval that the proposed contribution, construction or dedication is considered to be eligible for an Environmental Lands impact fee credit. Upon the determination by the board that the proposed contribution, construction or dedication is eligible for an Environmental Lands impact fee credit, the final amount of the credit shall be determined upon the submission of a request for Environmental Lands impact fee credit and the entering into of a formal Environmental Lands impact fee credit agreement.

(c) *Relationship of Environmental Lands impact fee to development of regional impact*. Pursuant to F.S. § 380.06(16), the value of Environmental Lands required pursuant to a county or city approved development order shall be credited against the Environmental Lands impact fee.

(d) *General standards for issuing Environmental Lands impact fee credit*. Prior to the issuance of any credits against the Environmental Lands impact fee, the person who contributed or dedicated Environmental Lands shall enter into an impact fee credit agreement with the board of county commissioners. The following provisions are the general rules for the award of credit, supplemented and provided in this section:

(1) Credit for contributions, payments, construction or dedications of the Environmental Lands impact fee shall not be transferable as a credit against other impact fees imposed for purposes other than protection and provision of Environmental Lands.

(2) If allowed by the credit agreement, credits may be assigned to successors in interest provided the county receives a copy of the written agreement signed by both the assignor and the assignee that has been recorded in the public records of St. Lucie County, Florida.

(3) No credit shall exceed the amount due for the Environmental Lands impact fee.

(4) No credit shall be given for dedications prior to _________, 2007.

(e) *Specific standards*. Credits against Environmental Lands impact fees otherwise payable shall be allowed only under the following conditions.

(1) *County need*. The contribution, payment, construction or dedication shall meet an Environmental Lands capital need identified in the county's comprehensive plan or in the adopted comprehensive plan of Ft. Pierce, Port St. Lucie or St. Lucie Village. No credit shall be given for capital improvements that do not meet an Environmental Lands capital need identified in the county's comprehensive plan or in the adopted comprehensive plan of Ft. Pierce, Port St. Lucie or St. Lucie Village.

(2) *Environmental lands dedication*. Credit for the dedication of environmental lands shall be valued at one hundred twenty (120) percent of the most recent assessed value by the county property appraiser plus the reasonable cost, as

determined by the county administrator, of any survey, closing costs or title information provided by the feepayer to the county at the request of the county. Credit for the dedication of environmental lands shall be provided when the property has been conveyed at no charge to, and accepted by, St. Lucie County, Ft. Pierce, Port St. Lucie or St. Lucie Village, in a manner satisfactory to the board of county commissioners or the appropriate local municipality.

If the feepayer shall opt not to have the property dedication credit determined as set out above, then the amount of credit shall be determined by the board of county commissioners based on an independent property appraisal, as described in section __________ of this article, prepared by an individual both a member of the appraisal institute (MAI) and a state certified general appraiser acceptable to the board of county commissioners, that is paid for by the feepayer. At the option of the board, the board may request a review appraisal, as described in section 1-15-40 of this article provided that in the event the value established by the independent appraisal exceeds one hundred twenty (120) percent of the assessed value by more than twenty-five (25) percent, the board shall request a review appraisal.

In the event the board determines to request a review appraisal and the determination of the value is the same or greater than value determined by the independent appraiser, then the county shall bear the cost of the review appraisal. If the determination of the value by the review appraiser is less than the value determined by the independent appraiser, then the feepayer shall pay for the cost of the review appraisal. Any independent or review appraisal submitted pursuant to this subsection shall be subject to review of methodology and technical accuracy at the discretion of the county administrator.

(3) *Application procedure.* Applicants for credit for construction of Environmental Lands improvements shall submit documentation of the actual engineering and construction costs to the county administrator or his designee. The county administrator or his designee shall determine credit for Environmental Lands construction based upon these costs or upon alternative engineering and construction cost estimates if the county administrator or his designee determines that such costs submitted are excessive or incomplete.

(f) *Time of claim; waiver.* Any claim for credit must be made no later than the time of application for a building permit or an electrical permit. Any claim not so made shall be deemed waived.

Section 10. Independent Property Appraisal.

If the feepayer shall opt not to have the value of any property dedication determined as set out in section 1-15-38(e)(3), the amount of credit shall be determined by the board of county commissioners based on an independent property appraisal (IPA), prepared by an individual who is both a member of the appraisal institute (MAI) and a state certified general appraiser acceptable to the board of county commissioners, that is paid for by the feepayer. An "independent property appraisal" is an appraisal report containing the following:

(1) *Purpose of appraisal.* The purpose of the appraisal, which includes a statement of value to be estimated and the rights or interest being appraised.

(2) *Legal description of property.*

(3) *Description of parent property.* Description of the parent property to be appraised will include:

a. Names of apparent owner of each interest being evaluated.

b. Location of property.

c. Total area of property in acres or square feet.

d. Area of each interest in property being acquired in acres or square feet.

e. A minimum of five (5) years delineation of title.

f. Present use and zoning.

g. Utilities.

h. Type and condition of improvements and special features that may add to or detract from the value of the property.

(4) *Highest and best use.* The highest and best use of the property on which the appraisal is based before the acquisition of rights and interests to be acquired and the highest and best use of the remainder after the acquisition when a partial taking is involved. In either instance, if the existing use is not the premise on which the valuation is based, the appraisal will contain an explanation justifying the determination that the property is available and adaptable for a different highest and best use and there is demand for that use in the market.

(5) *Before and after valuation.* The "before and after" method of valuation as interpreted by Florida law will be used in partial donations or special benefits to the residue land or improvements.

(6) *Approaches to value.* The appraisal should include all applicable approaches to value. If an approach is not considered applicable, the appraiser must state why. All pertinent calculations used in developing the approaches will be shown.

a. In the market approach, the appraisal report will contain a direct comparison of pertinent comparable sales to the property being appraised. The appraiser must include a statement setting forth his analysis and reasoning for each item of adjustment to comparable sales.

b. Where the income (capitalization) approach is used, there must be documentation to support the income, expenses, interest rate, capitalization rate, discount rate, or any other factors used in the analysis. Where it is determined that the market rental income is different from the existing or contract income, the increase or decrease must be explained and supported by market information.

c. Where the cost approach is utilized, the appraisal report must contain the specific source of cost data, remaining economic life, and an explanation of each type of accrued depreciation.

(7) *Appraisal of after value.* The appraisal of the after value must be supported to the same extent as the appraisal of the before value. This support should include one (1) or more of the following:

a. Sales comparable to the remainder properties.

b. Sales of comparable properties from which there have been similar donations or acquisitions for like usages.

c. Development of the income approach on properties which show economic loss or gain as a result of similar acquisition or taking for like usages.

d. Public sales of comparable lands by the state or other public agencies.

e. In the event the data described in subsections a. through d. above are not available, the appraisal will so state and give the appraiser's reasoning for his value estimate.

(8) *Difference between before and after*. The difference between the before and after appraisal will represent the value of the property to be acquired including the damages to the remainder property. The appraiser will separately analyze and tabulate the difference showing a reasonable allocation to lane improvements, and damages.

(9) *More than one (1) approach used*. Where two (2) or more of the approaches of value are used, the appraisal will show the correlation of the separate indications of value derived by each approach along with a reasonable explanation for the final conclusion of value. This correlation will be included for both before and after appraisals.

(10) *Photographs*. All appraisals should include identified photographs of the subject property including all principal aboveground improvements or unusual features affecting the value of the property to be taken or damaged.

(11) *Sketch or plat*. Appraisal reports for whole takings will contain a sketch or plat of the property showing boundary dimensions, location of improvements and other significant features of the property. For partial takings, the sketch or plat will also show the area to be acquired, relation of the improvements to the taking area and area of each remainder.

(12) *Comparable sales*. Each appraisal report will contain or make reference to the comparable sales which were used in arriving at the fair market value.

a. The appraiser must state the date of sale, names of parties to the transaction, consideration paid, financing, conditions of sale and with whom these were verified, the location, total area, type of improvements, appraiser's estimate of highest and best use at the date of sale, zoning and any other data pertinent to the analysis and evaluation thereof.

b. If the appraiser is unable to verify the financing and conditions of sale from the usual sources such as buyer, seller, broker, title or escrow company, etc., he will so state.

c. Pertinent comparable sales data should include identified photographs of all principal aboveground improvements or unusual features affecting the value of the comparable.

(13) *Inspection of properties*. All property appraised and the comparable sales which were relied upon in arriving at the fair market value estimate will be personally inspected in the field by the appraiser and all dates of inspection will be shown in the appraisal report.

(14) *Date of valuation*. The effective date to which the valuation applies.

(15) *Limiting conditions*. Statement of appropriate contingent and limiting conditions, if any.

(16) *Certification and signature*. The certification, signature, and date of signature of the appraiser.

Section 11. Property review appraisal.

At the option of the board, the board may request a review appraisal of the independent property appraisal (IPA), provided that in the event the value established by the independent property appraisal exceeds one hundred twenty (120) percent of the assessed value by more than twenty-five (25) percent, the board shall require a review appraisal. A "review appraisal" shall comply with the following procedures:

(1) The reviewing appraiser will field inspect the property appraised and the comparable sales considered by the appraiser in arriving at either or both, as appropriate, the fair market value of the whole property and of the remainder.

(2) The reviewing appraiser will examine the appraisal reports to determine that they:

a. Comply with the provisions of this section.

b. Follow accepted appraisal principles and techniques in the valuation of real property in accordance with existing state law.

c. Contain or make reference to the information necessary to explain, substantiate and thereby document the conclusions and estimates of value and/or just compensations identified therein.

d. Include consideration of compensable items, damages and benefits, but do not include compensation for items, damages and benefits noncompensable under state law.

e. Contain an identification or listing of the buildings, structures and other improvements on the land as well as the fixtures which the appraiser considered to be a part of the real property to be acquired.

f. Contain the estimated fair market value for or resulting from the acquisition, and where appropriate, in the case of a partial acquisition, either in the report or in a separate statement, a reasonable allocation of the estimate of the fair market value for the real property acquired and for damages to remaining real property.

(3) Prior to finalizing his estimate of just compensation, the reviewing appraiser will request and obtain corrections or revisions of appraisal reports which do not substantially meet the requirements set forth in this section. These will be documented and retained in the parcel file.

(4) The reviewing appraiser may supplement an appraisal report with corrections of minor mathematical errors where such errors do not affect the final value conclusion. He may also supplement the appraisal file where the following factual data have been omitted:

a. Owner's and/or tenants' names.

b. Parties to transactions, date of purchase and deed book reference on sale of subject property and comparables.

c. Statement that there were no sales of subject property in past five (5) years.

d. Location, zoning or present use of subject property or comparables.

(5) The reviewing appraiser will initial and date his corrections and/or factual data supplements to an appraisal report.

(6) The reviewing appraiser will submit a signed and dated statement setting forth:

a. His estimate of just compensation including, where appropriate, his allocation of compensation for the real property acquired and for damages to remaining real property, and an identification or listing of the buildings, structures, and other improvements on the land as well as the fixtures which he considered to be a part of the real property to be acquired, if such allocation or listing differs from that of the appraisal(s).

b. That as a part of the appraisal review there was a field inspection of the parcel to be acquired and the comparable sales applicable thereto.

c. That he has not direct or indirect present or contemplated future personal interest in such property or in any monetary benefit from its acquisition.

d. That his estimate has been reached independently, without collaboration or direction, and is based on appraisals and other factual data.

(7) In the event that the review appraiser determines the value to be the same or greater than the value determined by the independent property appraisal (IPA) the county shall bear the cost of the review appraisal.

Section 12. Environmental Lands impact fee district created.

There is hereby established one (1) Environmental Lands impact fee district which shall be identical to the boundaries of St. Lucie County and shall encompass the incorporated and unincorporated areas.

Section 13. Environmental Lands impact fee trust fund established.

(a) There is hereby established an Environmental Lands impact fee trust fund, for the Environmental Lands impact fee district established by section 12 of this article.

(b) Funds withdrawn from this accounts must be used in accordance with section 14 of this article.

Section 14. Use of funds.

(a) The collecting governmental unit shall be entitled to up to but not more than four (4) percent of the funds collected to compensate them for the administrative expense of collecting and administering the Environmental Lands impact fee ordinance. All remaining funds collected from Environmental Lands impact fee shall be used solely for the purpose of capital expenditures for the protection and preservation of environmental lands. The funds shall be used to accomplish one or both of the following objectives: (1) The preservation of natural areas for the benefit of the environment and the natural inhabitants of those areas and (2) The preservation of natural areas as places of public passive recreation. The environmental lands for which impact fee funds can be spent are identified in a study entitled "An Environmental Lands Acquisition Impact Fee," by Dr. James Nicholas dated January 8, 2007, which is incorporated by reference and adopted as part of this ordinance, or with prior approval of the county commission those Environmental Lands, under the jurisdiction of the City of Ft. Pierce, Port St. Lucie, St. Lucie Village or the State of Florida and not for maintenance or operations. Land acquisition and improvements shall be of the type made necessary by the county's growth and development.

(b) Except for the up to four (4) percent retainage authorized above, all remaining funds collected from the Environmental Lands impact fee shall be used exclusively for the protection and preservation of Environmental Lands.

(c) Each January the county administrator shall present to the board of county commissioners a proposed capital improvement program for Environmental Lands, assigning funds, including any accrued interest, from the Environmental Lands impact fee trust fund to specific projects and related expenses. Monies, including any accrued interest, not assigned in any fiscal period shall be retained in the Environmental Lands impact fee trust fund until the next fiscal period except as provided by the refund provisions of this article. Funds shall be deemed expended in the order received.

(d) The Board of County Commissioners of St. Lucie County may enter into interlocal agreements with the governing bodies of the municipalities in St. Lucie County to ensure proper use of the funds collected pursuant to this article.

Section 15. Refund of fees paid.

(a) If a building permit or an electrical permit for a mobile home park or recreational vehicle park expires and no construction has been commenced, then the feepayer, his heirs, successors or assigns, shall be entitled to a refund of the impact fee paid as a condition for its issuance except that the county, and the collecting government entity, if not the county, shall retain four (4) percent of the funds as an administrative fee to offset the costs of refunding.

(b) Any funds not expended or encumbered by the end of the fiscal year immediately following ten (10) years from the date the Environmental Lands impact fee payment was received shall, upon application of the current owner within one hundred eighty (180) days of the expiration of the ten (10) year period, be returned to the current owner with interest at the rate of six (6) percent per annum.

Section 16. Exemptions.

The following shall be exempted wholly or in part from payment of the Environmental Lands impact fee:

(1) Alteration or expansion of an existing building where no additional units are created, the use is not changed, and where no additional need for Environmental Lands will be produced over and above that produced by the existing use.

(2) The construction of accessory buildings or structures which will not produce additional need for Environmental Lands over and above that produced by the principal building or use of the land.

(3) The replacement of a destroyed or partially destroyed building or structure in existence on or after January 1, 1996, with a new building or structure of the same or a different use provided that no additional need for Environmental Lands will be produced over and above those produced by the original use of the land.

(4) Any claim of exemption must be made no later than the time of application for a building permit or electrical permit for a mobile home. Any claim not so made shall be deemed waived.

Section 17. Appeals.

(a) Any decision made by the county administrator in the course of administering the provisions of this chapter may be appealed to the board of county commissioners by filing a petition of appeal within thirty (30) calendar days of the date of the rendition of the decision.

(b) The board of county commissioners shall review the petition at a public meeting within thirty (30) calendar days from the date of appeal of said decision. The petitioner shall be provided reasonable notice of the time, date, and place of the public meeting by certified mail, return receipt requested, and invited to attend. Testimony at the public meeting shall be limited to ten (10) minutes per side, unless an extension of time is granted by the board. The board's decision shall be final for the purpose of administrative appeals.

The board of county commissioners shall revoke the decision of the county administrator only if there is competent, substantial evidence in the record that the decision fails to comply with this article.

Section 18. Review and automatic adjustment of fees.

(a) The Environmental Lands impact fee shall be adjusted by the county administrator in April of each calendar year. Unless otherwise directed by the county commission, any adjustments to the Environmental Lands impact fee, made pursuant to this section shall be noticed no later than June 30 and shall become effective the first Monday in October of each calendar year. All adjustments to the Environmental Lands impact fee shall be based on the methodology described in subsection (b) of this section.

(b) The base for computing any adjustment is the January Consumer Price Index-All Urban Consumers for the United States, published by the United States Department of Labor, Bureau of Labor Statistics. For the purpose of this section the initial index to be referenced is January 2007. The Environmental Lands impact fee shall be adjusted by the percentage change in the index.

(c) If the index is changed so that the base year is different, the index shall be converted in accordance with the conversion factor published by the United States Department of Labor, Bureau of Labor Statistics. If the index is discontinued or revised, such other government index or computation with which it is replaced shall be used in order to obtain substantially the same result as would be obtained if the index had not been discontinued or revised.

(d) The board of county commissioners shall review the Environmental Lands impact fee at least once every five (5) years from the effective date of this article.

Section 19. Penalty Provision.

A violation of this ordinance shall be prosecuted in the same manner as misdemeanors are prosecuted and upon conviction the violator shall be punishable according to law; however, in addition to or in lieu of any criminal prosecution St. Lucie County shall have the power to sue in civil court to enforce the provisions of this ordinance.

Section 20. Severability.

If any section, phrase, sentence or portion of this ordinance is for any reason held invalid or unconstitutional by any court of competent jurisdiction, such portion shall be deemed a separate, distinct and independent provision, and such holding shall not affect the validity of the remaining portions thereof.

Section 21. Effective Date.

This Ordinance shall take effect from and after the ______ day of ______________

PASSED AND DULY ADOPTED THIS __________ DAY OF__________,

13

Proportionate-Share Fees for Operations and Maintenance

INTRODUCTION

New development impacts on facilities in more ways than requiring new or expanded facilities to serve it. It may create more demands for O & M than it generates in new revenues to cover. This chapter explores four ways to handle this problem using proportionate-share fee approaches. Three are in the context of transportation and a fourth is in the context of stormwater maintenance.

All approaches may be adaptable to other applications. The first is an impact fee directly for the purpose of generating revenues to finance O & M—the transit impact development fee (TIDF)—used for a generation in San Francisco. The second is a transportation utility fee (TUF), which is based on a proportionate-share calculation applied to all land uses to generate funds annually to cover transportation O & M costs, akin to an enterprise fund for water and wastewater facilities. The third is the stormwater utility fee (SUF), which also acts like an enterprise fund.

The chapter concludes with a case study composed of a technical report for a transportation facility O & M mitigation fee designed consistent with the impact fee methodology. An approach to implementing this program through an ordinance is included as Appendix 13A.

TRANSIT IMPACT DEVELOPMENT FEE

In 1981, the San Francisco Board of Supervisors enacted the transit fee to recover the capital and operating costs of increased peak-period transit service resulting from new office construction in downtown San Francisco. The TIDF applies to all projects increasing office space in the downtown area, akin to a service area. The fee is paid at a fixed rate of $5 per square foot. The fee generates from about $1 million to several million dollars annually.

Authority for the fee is based essentially on home rule (as opposed to explicit state enabling legislation) and is found in Chapter 38 of the San Francisco Administrative Code. The relevant code section provides:

> The demand for public transit service from downtown area office uses imposes a unique burden on the Municipal Railway, qualitatively different than the burden imposed by other uses of property in San Francisco. The need for that level of service provided by the Municipal Railway during peak-periods can be attributed in substantial part to office uses of property in the downtown area.

The fee is intended to capture "all costs incurred by the Municipal Railway in meeting peak-period public transit service demands created by office uses in each new development subject to the fee, including the expansion of service capacity through the purchase of new rolling stock, the installation of new lines, the addition of existing lines and the long term operation, maintenance, repair and replacement of those expanded facilities."[1] The overall fee thus includes capital in addition to O & M.

The O & M element of the fee itself is calculated based on a proportionate share of the impact that new downtown development has on transit facilities in relation to new O & M revenue it generates, plus reasonable consideration of nonlocal revenues (such as from federal and state agencies). In its original form, the O & M element of the fee was calculated (as shown in Table 13-1).

The analysis was extended over 40 years, or roughly the useful life of transit facilities. The net present values were estimated using long-term assumptions of inflation (about 2.6 percent) as were long-term revenues. The analytic approach may be applied to all facilities.

The TIDF was challenged in California courts,[2] which upheld the fee, and the U.S. Supreme Court denied review indicating at least that the concept was not ripe for review from a Constitutional perspective. As of this writing, San Francisco's TIDF may be the only U.S. example of this application of proportionate-share development fees.

TRANSPORTATION UTILITY FEES

Another approach to addressing long-term facility O & M concerns is offered by accounting systems akin to enterprise funds. Such funds are customarily used for water, wastewater, and drainage systems. A key feature is that they internalize all costs and revenues into a dedicated account, which is separate from the general fund. The example reviewed here is the TUF. The fee itself is based substantially on proportionate-share principles.

Table 13-1
Original San Francisco Transit
Operations Linkage Fee

Net present value O & M costs per square foot of office	$12.97
Net present value of O & M revenue per square foot of office	$9.46
Net present value of difference in O & M costs and revenues	$3.54

O & M = operations and maintenance

The analytic framework is posed below with examples that follow.

Conceptually, there is a mismatch between the revenues generated by all development (not just new) and the realistic needs to properly operate and maintain transportation facilities. The result in transportation manifests in such things as potholes, improperly operative signals, and outdated or destroyed signage. One solution is an enterprise-fund approach to operating and maintaining facilities. All development, not just new development, would be assessed on an annual basis.

TUFs are calculated similarly to impact fees except they are applied to all land uses. A standard approach—one considered by Orlando, Florida, in the 1990s—uses the following formula:

$$\text{TRANSPORTATION UTILITY FEE} =$$
$$\text{UNIT DEMAND} \times \text{TRIP GENERATION}$$
$$\text{FACTOR} \times \text{BASE RATE}$$

Where:

UNIT DEMAND = the number of dwelling units, square feet, or hotel rooms on a particular parcel

TRIP GENERATION FACTOR = the total average daily trips

BASE RATE = the average yearly costs based on total average daily trips

For example, in the 1990s, the Orlando TUF would have resulted in the following annual fees by land use:

$$\frac{\text{Average yearly costs @ \$6,465,000}}{\text{Total average daily trips @ 2,108,443}} = \$3.07/\text{annual trip}$$

The annual statement per unit of development that would be sent to property owners is shown in Table 13-2.

Oregon, because of special enabling legislation, offers important lessons. In Oregon, a TUF, like water or wastewater, is a monthly fee collected on development based on its estimated use of the transportation system. (The fees are also known by other names such as "road utility fee" and "road maintenance fee.") The fee is based on the estimated number of trips a particular use generates. In Oregon, the TUF used in a handful of communities is included in the regular water and wastewater bill. At this writing, those communities were Ashland, Eagle Point, Gresham, La Grande, Lake Oswego, Medford, Tigard, Tualatin,

Table 13-2
Orlando Transportation Utility Fee Proposal

Land Use	Daily Trips	Cost @ $3.07 Per Trip
Single family	10.44	$32.06
Multifamily	6.33	$19.44
Hotel room	9.03	$27.72
1,000 sq. ft. office	12.87	$39.52
1,000 sq. ft. commercial	69.15	$212.30
1,000 sq. ft. industrial	5.62	$17.24

Source: Marie York, Center for Urban and Environmental Problems, Florida Atlantic University.

and Wilsonville, among a growing list. Their population ranges from under 10,000 to more than 100,000.

The "street maintenance fee" in Lake Oswego, Oregon, is instructive.[3] The fee is a monthly fee based on use of the transportation system that is collected from residences and businesses within the city. It is based on the number of trips a particular land use generates, and is collected through the city's regular water, wastewater, and drainage utility bill. It is dedicated to the maintenance and repair of the city's transportation system.

In the mid-2000s, the city had about 172 miles of paved streets. Much of the system was old and not designed for the type and volume of traffic now seen. Historically, the largest source of funds for maintenance was the state gas tax, which has not changed in more than a decade and is not likely to, at least by much. In real dollar terms, gas tax revenue was declining relative to need. The city determined that the gas tax needed to be supplemented by new funds to keep the street system functioning adequately.

As an initial step, an inventory of all the existing uses parcels in the city was conducted. ITE trip generation rates were used to determine trip generation values for each use. Residential and nonresidential groups were established to help generate a maintenance fee rate to be applied to each group. Adjustments were made to the trip generation rates to account for pass-by trips, which are intermediate stops on the way from an origin to a primary trip destination. The groupings take into account the net trip generation rates after factoring in pass-by trip information. The groups include the following:

- Single family (detached)
- Multifamily
- Group 1 (land uses with less than 29 vehicle trip-miles per day per 1,000 square feet of building space)
- Group 2 (land uses with more than 29, but less than 90, vehicle trip-miles per day per 1,000 square feet of building space)
- Group 3 (land uses with more than 90 vehicle trip-miles per day per 1,000 square feet of building space)

The fee itself is based on the following formula:

$$\text{STREET MAINTENANCE FEE} = \frac{\text{STREET MAINTENANCE COST} - \text{REVENUES}}{\text{ESTIMATED DAILY TRIPS}} \times \text{ITE DAILY TRIPS/GROUP}$$

Where:

STREET MAINTENANCE COST = the budget for maintaining streets but not capital expansion (that is paid in part through a road "system development charge," which is a road impact fee). The cost is calculated as the full cost necessary to maintain the street system properly and avoid deferred maintenance for lack of funds.

REVENUES = projected revenues from state, regional, and local sources

ESTIMATED DAILY TRIPS = for the year of analysis using the city's inventory of land uses, multiplied by ITE's trip generation rates applicable to each group

ITE DAILY TRIPS/GROUP = the number of trips for each unit of land use (one dwelling for residential and 1,000 square feet for nonresidential)

Lake Oswego's fee for each land-use group is shown in shown in Table 13-3.

TUFs may become increasingly popular as transportation system O & M revenues become more stressed. The methods used for them, however, are very simple and reminiscent of the early days of impact fees. Analysis by the authors of all the TUF systems available to them indicates they all conform to the basic structure used by Lake Oswego, which is similar to the proposal considered by Orlando in the 1990s. While the residential fees are differentiated between single- and multifamily types, they are not refined to consider size and associated impact on the street system. Thus, a home of about 5,000 square feet may generate 50 percent more trips than a home of 1,500 square

Table 13-3
Street Maintenance Fee, Lake Oswego, Oregon

Land Use	Fee
Single-family detached residential (per unit)	$3.75 per month per unit
Multifamily residential (per unit)	$2.68 per month per unit
Nonresidential Group 1	$2.30 per month per 1,000 sq. ft.
Nonresidential Group 2	$5.17 per month per 1,000 sq. ft.
Nonresidential Group 3	$19.31 per month per 1,000 sq. ft.

feet, and residential units in urbanized areas of more than 6,000 units per square mile generate roughly half the trips of the same units in exurban areas with fewer than 250 units per square mile. On the other hand, like the impact fee methodology, it may be a relatively simple analytic step to incorporate these refinements in future fee structures.

STORMWATER UTILITY FEES

Much more common than TUFs are SUFs. They are structured quite similarly, however.

Communities manage stormwater through a system of swales, drainage inlets, pipes, storage, and related infrastructure. Managing stormwater is a fairly recent advancement in infrastructure. Many communities used to collect stormwater and run it through the sewer system, which was called the "combined sewer" approach. Because this overloads sewer treatment plants, major storm events often resulted in untreated sewerage entering water bodies. Building and maintaining separate stormwater systems has been one solution. This usually requires identifying and then connecting all stormwater drainage facilities into a unified network, but this has proven difficult because many communities simply do not have inventory of publicly and privately provided stormwater facilities, nor do they often have adequate easements to maintain especially private facilities.

A growing national trend has been to create stormwater utilities. Many of these utilities charge new development a stormwater system development connection fee (like a water and wastewater connection fee) to help finance capital costs. In some states with impact fee enabling legislation, the stormwater fee is separately authorized if it is not included in the act itself. Most, if not all, also charge a regular periodic fee to operate and maintain the stormwater system.

The general formula for setting these charges is as follows:

$$\text{STORMWATER UTILITY FEE} = \frac{\text{STORMWATER UTILITY O \& M COST}}{\text{IMPERVIOUS LAND AREA}} \times \text{IMPERVIOUS LAND AREA/USER}$$

Where:

STORMWATER UTILITY O & M COST = the budget for operating and maintaining the stormwater system but not capital expansion (which is often paid in part through stormwater impact fees, system development charges, or similar). The cost is calculated as the full cost necessary to maintain the system properly and avoid deferred maintenance for lack of funds.

IMPERVIOUS LAND AREA = the volume of impervious surface in the community

IMPERVIOUS LAND AREA/USER = the impervious area of a customer times the utility cost per unit of impervious surface

Stormwater runoff is complicated by differences in soils absorption capacity and differences in developed surfaces to absorb water. Fort Collins, Colorado, offers a conventional approach to setting its stormwater utility rates.

In Fort Collins, the SUF is based on the area of each lot or parcel of land and its "runoff coefficient." The purpose of the fee is to recover O & M costs and a portion of capital improvements needing rehabilitation or replacement. (The city has a separate system of funds to install new or expand existing stormwater facilities.) The utility fee starts with identifying the runoff coefficient applicable to the parcel. There are five runoff coefficient categories (as shown in Table 13-4).

The base rate for the stormwater utility as of the mid-2000s was set at $0.0041454 per square foot of land per month for all areas of the city. (This includes open space and common areas assigned to development.) The actual fee formula is thus:

$$\text{MONTHLY FEE} = (\text{LOT OR PARCEL AREA}) \times (\text{RATE FACTOR}) \times (\text{BASE RATE})$$

Table 13-4
Fort Collins, Colorado, Stormwater Runoff
Coefficient Categories

Development Category	Runoff Coefficient
Very light	0.25
Light	0.40
Moderate	0.60
Heavy	0.80
Very heavy	0.95

Conceptually, a 100,000-square-foot parcel in an area having a moderate runoff coefficient would pay:

$$\text{MONTHLY FEE} =$$
$$(100{,}000) \times (0.60) \times (\$0.0041454) =$$
$$\$248.72 \text{ PER MONTH}$$

This is the formula used for all developments that are not detached homes on residential lots. For single-family residential lots larger than 12,000 square feet but less than one-half acre, the fee is assessed at a base of 12,000 square feet plus, for the area above 12,000 square feet, the following increment:

$$\text{REMAINDER OF AREA} =$$
$$(\text{REMAINING AREA}) \times (\text{RATE FACTOR}) \times$$
$$(\text{BASE RATE}) \times (0.25)$$

Like many other stormwater utilities, Fort Collins has alternative fee structures available to encourage development—both existing and new—to reduce stormwater runoff. Yet, like all other such utilities, there is a base charge for detached residential, which inherently does not encourage more compact development that would result in less stormwater runoff per unit. Only if appealed can more efficient development be rewarded through lower monthly fees.

CASE STUDY: AVENTURA, FLORIDA TRANSPORTATION OPERATIONS AND MAINTENANCE MITIGATION FEE

We apply the foregoing principles to an in-depth case study. As background, in the late 2000s, the City of Aventura, Florida, considered the option to support its Transportation Concurrency Exception Area (TCEA), which is part of the Aventura Comprehensive Plan. The City of Aventura is largely built out with few if any opportunities to construct new roads or to expand existing roads. While the opportunities to construct expanded roadways is

limited, there is a continuing need for additional mobility within Aventura to meet the needs of residential and business developments in this city.

The City of Aventura had developed and provides a system of transit known as the Aventura Express, which is a system of bus routes provided to residents and nonresidents alike without charge. The objective of the Aventura Express is to provide mobility by means of buses and thus avoid the need to expand roadways or to suffer increased traffic congestion in the absence of such roadway expansion.

Florida law requires that new developments achieve and maintain adequate levels of transportation service as a prerequisite to development, commonly referred to as "transportation concurrency" (also known as "adequate public facilities" in other states). When this law was passed, it was recognized that such a policy would not be sensible in all situations. Aventura is one of those situations. Accordingly, the entire the City of Aventura has been designated a TCEA.

The law requires local governments with TCEAs to develop the means to support the TCEAs in order to promote public transit. The net effect is to allow developers to contribute to public transit, and thus proceed with development, when achieving transportation concurrency by traditional means is not possible or is impractical. Such a program is presented herein. This analysis shows how Aventura may accommodate the mobility needs of new developments by the expansion of the Aventura Express with the payment of a transportation mitigation fee. The amounts of the fees for various land uses are shown in Table 13-5.

These mitigation fees were found to represent a proportionate share of the city's costs to extend additional mobility to new development by means of the Aventura Express. The following section illustrates how the mitigation fee was designed and describes its relationship to impact fee calculation principles.

PLANNING RELATIONSHIP

Like most other states, the State of Florida recognizes the integral role that the ability to move goods and people plays in the economic success of the state and places within the state. Accordingly, the Florida Legislature enacted "transportation concurrency" into law:

> It is the intent of the Legislature that public facilities and services needed to support development shall be

Table 13-5
Transportation Mitigation Per Unit, City of Aventura, Florida

Land Use and Unit	Persons Per Unit	Cost Per Unit	Recommended Fee
Residence per dwelling	0.972	$944.76	$803.05
Office per 1,000 sq. ft.	1.557	$1,513.63	$1,286.59
Retail per 1,000 sq. ft.	2.175	$2,114.50	$1,797.33
Tourist accommodation per 1,000 sq. ft.	2.720	$2,643.79	$2,247.22
Industrial per 1,000 sq. ft.	1.319	$1,281.59	$1,089.35
Institutional per 1,000 sq. ft.	2.312	$2,247.17	$1,910.09

Source: James C. Nicholas for the City of Aventura, Florida (March 13, 2008).

available concurrent with the impacts of such development …

There are five public services subject to mandatory concurrency:

1. Water and sewer service;
2. Solid waste collection and disposal;
3. Parks and recreation;
4. Public schools[5]; and
5. Transportation.

These facilities must be adequately provided if development is to be allowed to proceed. In many instances, the attainment of transportation concurrency is achieved through the construction or expansion of streets and highways. However, there are frequent instances where the construction of new or expanded roadways is not possible or is impractical. The Florida Legislature foresaw such instances:

(5) (a) The Legislature finds that under limited circumstances dealing with transportation facilities, countervailing planning and public policy goals may come into conflict with the requirement that adequate public facilities and services be available concurrent with the impacts of such development. The Legislature further finds that often the unintended result of the concurrency requirement for transportation facilities is the discouragement of urban infill development and redevelopment. Such unintended results directly conflict with the goals and policies of the state comprehensive plan and the intent of this part. Therefore, exceptions from the concurrency requirement for transportation facilities may be granted as provided by this subsection.

(b) A local government may grant an exception from the concurrency requirement for transportation facilities if the proposed development is otherwise consistent with the adopted local government comprehensive plan and is a project that promotes

public transportation or is located within an area designated in the comprehensive plan for:

1. Urban infill development …[6]

Aventura is one of the places where an alternative means of providing movement is needed. There are few if any economically feasible street and highway options that will accommodate additional vehicles on Aventura's streets. In 1998, the city was designated a TCEA, thus new developments within Aventura are exempt from the concurrency provisions of the statute.[7] However, the statute established the promotion of public transportation as a prerequisite for such a concurrency exemption. In response to this requirement, the city has proposed the following policies to support the TCEA designation:

Policy 1.8. The City of Aventura shall continue to identify projects to support and fund mobility, enhance alternative modes of transportation, and ensure connectivity in its Capital Improvement Program …[8]

Policy 1.9 The City of Aventura … shall evaluate the impact of proposed development and redevelopment on its transportation system, Strategic Intermodal System facilities, and the adopted level of service standards of transportation facilities, and identify strategies to alleviate or mitigate such impacts in coordination with the developer and other agencies as appropriate.[9]

Policy 1.11 The City of Aventura shall, by ordinance, include proportionate fair share mitigation options in its concurrency management program … The intent of these options is to provide for the mitigation of transportation impacts through mechanisms that might include, but are not limited to, private funds, public funds, contributions of land, and the contribution of facilities.[10]

Policy 1.12 By 2007, or at the earliest feasible date, the City of Aventura will develop impact fees and other methods by which developers can mitigate impacts to the transportation system by contributing funds for alternative modes of transportation, particularly the expansion, operation and maintenance of the Circulator System.[11]

The purpose of these policies is to permit new development to proceed while still maintaining an appropriate level of transportation service by having developers mitigate their impacts on traffic circulation within Aventura. This mitigation would be in the form of contributing toward the Circulator System. The result would be that the increased demand for mobility resulting from new development or redevelopment within Aventura would be satisfied by the Circulator System rather than by expansion of Aventura's streets and highways. Thus, Aventura proposes to support its policy of transportation concurrency exception, exempting new developments from transportation concurrency if those new developments promote public transportation by payment of the mitigation fee.

The only means of public transportation known that can constitute an alternative mode of transportation within Aventura is the Circulator System. Section 163.180(5) provides a means for Aventura to structure a program of transportation mitigation that will allow developments to proceed while also advancing the mobility of the community. This section provides that:

(d) A local government shall establish guidelines in the comprehensive plan for granting the exceptions … which must be consistent with and support a comprehensive strategy adopted in the plan to promote the purpose of the exceptions.

(e) The local government shall adopt into the plan and implement strategies to support and fund mobility within the designated exception area, including alternative modes of transportation. The plan amendment shall also demonstrate how strategies will support the purpose of the exception and how mobility within the designated exception area will be provided.

The proposed changes to the Aventura Comprehensive Plan noted above would implement strategies necessary for the city to receive transportation concurrency exceptions. The next section reviews how the program would work.

TRANSPORTATION MITIGATION PROGRAM

The objective of an Aventura Transportation Mitigation Program is to support and fund the city's Circulator System so that the Circulator System can satisfy the need for enhanced mobility over time as the city continues to grow.

New residential and nonresidential developments within Aventura will contribute to the need for increased mobility. New residences will bring additional people that will live, shop, recreate, and work in or around the city. Each of these activities will require mobility. Additionally, new nonresidential developments will attract additional shoppers, employees, customers, and recreators to and within Aventura. Both types of developments will cause a need for enhanced mobility.

A mitigation program will involve the payment of a fee that offsets the costs of accommodating the mobility impacts of new residential and nonresidential developments with the Circulator System of the City of Aventura. The first step in developing a mitigation fee is to quantitatively define the Circulator Service. Table 13-6 provides the first part of this definition. At present, the Circulator System is 360,360 passenger seats per year. These seats are provided within five routes running 10 times per day on weekdays and 13 times on weekends.

The Circulator System serves the residents of and visitors to Aventura. Our convention in the United States is to define a population of a place, such as Aventura, as the number of people who reside within the borders of that place. This definition is fine for purposes of voting, but it is not acceptable for purposes of defining a population of people served by services such as police and fire protection, or Aventura's Circulator System. The population served by the Circulator System is the number of people within Aventura no matter if they are permanent residents, seasonal residents, employees of businesses, or patrons of those businesses within Aventura. The population served is the functional population. These people are served by the Circulator System even if they don't ride it. They are served by diverting those that do ride the buses out of their cars and away from the streets, thereby creating capacity for those that prefer driving to bus riding. Additionally, businesses are served even if the owners of the businesses do not ride the buses because the buses bring their employees and customers to and from those places of business.

Table 13-6
Circulator Service, City of Aventura

Day of Week	Routes	Runs	Seats	Seats Per Day	Seats Per Year
Weekday	5	10	22	1,100	286,000
Weekend	5	13	22	1,430	74,360
Total				1,155	360,360

Source: City of Aventura (February 2007).

The function population of an area is the number of people that can be expected to be present at businesses, residences, schools, parks, churches, or the many other places that people go or congregate. The number of people within Aventura's functional population is shown in Table 13-7. These are the people served by the City of Aventura.

Table 13-8 shows the derivation of the function population. These calculations use Miami-Dade County as the base for the calculations. Counties are used because employment data are not reported for geographic areas smaller than counties. Vehicular trip generation rates[12] are used to identify the total number of people present at a site. Employment data are used to identify how many of those persons present are employees, with the remainder being visitors. The ratios of persons per 1,000 feet of floor area for Miami-Dade County are applied to nonresidential floor area within Aventura to estimate Aventura's functional population at nonresidential areas. Because many of the people present at and assigned to nonresidential areas of Aventura are the occupants of residences within Aventura, it is necessary to adjust the population assigned to residences to avoid double counting those persons. This is done on a time-allocation basis. Table 13-8 shows the Miami-Dade County and Aventura

Table 13-7
Service Area Population, City of Aventura

Calculation Step	Resident	Functional
Residential population	28,207	14,104
Peak population	40,336	7,277
Visitors to:		
Offices		2,892
Retail		16,577
Industrial		1,987
Institutional		2,155
Total		47,963

Source: 2000 Census of the Population, Table 3.

allocations, resulting in a function population of 47,963 for Aventura.

Table 13-9 shows the functional population of Aventura in terms of persons per unit of land use, 1,000 square feet of floor area for nonresidential developments and the dwelling unit for residential development. Recall that many of the residents of Aventura are also the employees and patrons of the businesses within Aventura, thus the relatively low functional population assigned to residences.

The annual cost per seat for Circulator Service is shown in Table 13-10. The cost from Table 13-10 is used to calculate a per capita cost, using functional population, of the Circulator System for the present year and as a present value of future costs.

The LOS provided or expected to be provided in the future is 0.0206 seats per capita per year. The costs shown in Table 13-11 are the costs of continuing this LOS as the city continues to develop.

The basic annual cost of $6,552 per seat is reduced by 51 percent to reflect the allocation of funds to Aventura's Circulator System from Miami-Dade County's Transit System Surtax. The net cost to the city is $3,231 per seat. At an LOS of 0.0206 seats per capita, the cost per capita is $66.50 per year. This is a recurring cost to be borne by the city. The essence of a mitigation payment is that the developer would pay to the city an amount that reflects the future costs to the city of providing the Circulator System service. This future cost is expressed as a present value of $66.50 per capita per year for the next 25 years with a discount rate of 4.64 percent. The present value is $972 (as shown in Table 13-12).

The Circulator System mitigation cost per unit of development is shown in Table 13-13. These costs, assessed as an alternative to transportation concurrency, should recoup the City of Aventura's costs of meeting the need for mobility with the city's Circulator System. The total costs to the city have been adjusted for the availability of other funds to pay this cost. As such, the amounts shown represent a proportionate share of the City of Aventura's costs of meeting the needs of additional

Table 13-8
Functional Population City of Aventura

Land Use	Aventura		Miami/Dade	
	Floor Area	**Persons at Site**	**Floor Area**	**Persons at Site**
Nonresidential				
Office	1,857,080	2,892	91,889,361	143,096
Retail	7,620,218	16,577	185,691,556	403,964
Tourist accommodation	1,092,239	2,971	29,041,062	78,992
Industrial	1,506,918	1,987	182,695,376	240,890
Institutional and other	932,189	2,155	124,193,781	287,129
Total nonresidential	13,008,644	26,582	613,511,136	1,154,070
Residential				
Permanent residences	21,638,081	14,104	998,552,685	2,379,818
Seasonal residences	11,165,250	7,277	149,683,987	310,233
Grand total	45,811,976	47,963	1,761,747,808	2,690,051

Sources: Office of Demographic & Economic Research, Miami/Dade County Property Appraiser and Florida Agency for Workforce Innovation, Labor Market Statistics, "Quarterly Census of Employment and Earnings, Miami-Dade County" (2004).

Table 13-9
Functional Population Per Unit, City of Aventura

Land Use	Persons at Site	Units	Population Per Unit
Office per 1,000 sq. ft.	2,892	1,857,080	1.557
Retail per 1,000 sq. ft.	16,577	7,620,218	2.175
Tourist accommodation per 1,000 sq. ft.	2,971	1,092,239	2.720
Storage/industrial per 1,000 sq. ft.	1,987	1,506,918	1.319
Institutional and other per 1,000 sq. ft.	2,155	932,189	2.312
Residences per dwelling unit	21,381	20,782	0.972
Total	47,963		

Source: James C. Nicholas, City of Aventura, Florida (March 13, 2008).

Table 13-10
Circulator Cost Per Seat, City of Aventura

Calculation	Day	Year
Bus hours provided per …	53	16,380
Cost per hour	$44	$44
Circulator cost per …	$2,310	$720,720

Source: City of Aventura, Budget for FY 2006-07.

Table 13-11
Circulator Level of Service, City of Aventura

Calculation Step	Figure
Population served	47,963
Circulator seats per day *	987
Seats per capita per year	0.0206

* Average of weekdays and weekends

Source: James C. Nicholas, City of Aventura, Florida (March 13, 2008).

residential and nonresidential development by means of the city's Circulator System.

IMPLEMENTATION

In review, it should be recognized that the city is requiring developers to make a present payment to cover future costs of providing the Circulator System service. The preferred way of implementing such a program would be for the city to deposit all mitigation fees collected into a trust fund and then annually appropriate the earnings from this fund to the Circulator System. In this way, there is consistency between the assumptions of the fee calculations and the use of the funds. Appendix 13A presents an approach to implement this program through an ordinance. While crafted for specific

Table 13-12
Circulator Cost Per Capita, City of Aventura

Calculation Step	Figure
Cost per route	$144,144
Seats per route	22
Cost per seat	$6,552
Paid by County Transit System Surtax	50.7%
Net cost to city per seat	$3,231
Level of service	0.0206
Cost per capita	$66.50
Years	25.00
Discount rate	4.64%
Present value	$972

Source: James C. Nicholas, City of Aventura, Florida (March 13, 2008).

application to Aventura, the general features of the ordinance may be broadly applicable.

SUMMARY OBSERVATIONS

Proportionate-share concepts can be applied broadly and perhaps outside specific impact fee enabling legislation where home rule and related powers provide discretion or opportunities and where rational nexus relationships can be established. It is possible to imagine a future where most general services offered by local government would be financed through utility structures based on proportionate-share principles. While current applications of proportionate-share principles for transportation and stormwater utilities do not inherently recognize efficiencies associated with different development patterns—something impact fees increasingly do—there is every reason to expect that such utility rate structures will mature.

NOTES

1. San Francisco Planning–Urban Research Association, "Planning for Growth: A Proposal to Expand San Francisco's Transit Impact Development Fee Recommendations of the Spur Transportation Committee" accessed October 1, 2008 from www.spur.org/documents/010801_article_01.shtm.
2. 199 Cal.App. 3d 1496; 246 Cal.Rptr. 21.
3. This information is adapted from www.ci.oswego.or.us/engineer/street%20fee/questions.htm.
4. Chapter 163.3177(10)(h), Florida Statutes.
5. Not effective until July 208.
6. 163.3180, Florida Statutes.
7. While new developments in Aventura are exempted from transportation concurrency, developers are required to make safety improvements, such as acceleration or deceleration lanes, or intersection improvements when the staff review of site plans shows that such improvements are need to protect public health, safety, or welfare.
8. City of Aventura, Ordinance No. 2007–01, page 20.
9. *Ibid.*
10. *Ibid.*
11. *Ibid.*, at 21.
12. As reported by the Institute for Transportation Engineers (ITE), *Trip Generation*, 7th ed. (Washington, D.C.: ITE, 2003).

Table 13-13
Transportation Mitigation Fee Per Unit, City of Aventura

Land Use and Unit	Persons Per Unit	Cost Per Unit	Recommended Fee
Residence per dwelling	0.972	$944.76	$803.05
Office per 1,000 sq. ft.	1.557	$1,513.63	$1,286.59
Retail per 1,000 sq. ft.	2.175	$2,114.50	$1,797.33
Tourist accommodation per 1,000 sq. ft.	2.720	$2,643.79	$2,247.22
Industrial per 1,000 sq. ft.	1.319	$1,281.59	$1,089.35
Institutional per 1,000 sq. ft.	2.312	$2,247.17	$1,910.09

Source: James C. Nicholas for the City of Aventura, Florida (March 13, 2008).

APPENDIX 13A

SAMPLE ORDINANCE IMPLEMENTING OPERATIONS AND MAINTENANCE PROPORTIONATE SHARE FEES

ORDINANCE NO. 2008-

AN ORDINANCE OF THE CITY OF AVENTURA, FLORIDA, AMENDING CHAPTER 2, "ADMINIS-TRATION," ARTICLE IV "FINANCE," DIVISION 5 "IMPACT FEES," TO CREATE SECTION 2-302 "TRANSPORTATION MITIGATION IMPACT FEE"; ESTABLISHING A TRANSPORTATION MITIGATION IMPACT FEE AND SCHEDULE FOR MITIGATION OF TRANSPORTATION IMPACTS BY NEW DEVEL-OPMENT; PROVIDING FOR TRANSPORTATION MITIGATION IMPACT FEE COMPUTATION FOR-MULA; PROVIDING FOR EXEMPTIONS; PROVID-ING FOR IMPACT FEE EXPENDITURES; PROVIDING FOR ESTABLISHMENT OF A TRANSPORTATION MITIGATION IMPACT FEE FUND; PROVIDING FOR INCLUSION IN THE CODE; PROVIDING FOR SEV-ERABILITY; AND PROVIDING FOR AN EFFECTIVE DATE.

WHEREAS, pursuant to Section 163.31801, Florida Statutes, entitled the "Florida Impact Fee Act," the Florida Legislature found that impact fees are an important source of revenue for a local government to use in funding the infrastructure necessitated by new growth; and

WHEREAS, pursuant to Section 163.3177, Florida Statutes, the Legislature enacted a transportation concurrency law which provides that public transportation facilities and services needed to support development shall be available concurrent with the impacts of development; and

WHEREAS, the Legislature recognized that there are areas where construction of new or expanded roadways is not possible; and

WHEREAS, pursuant to Section 163.3180, Florida Statutes, local governments may exempt an area from transportation concurrency (a "Transportation Concurrency Exception Area") if the proposed development is 1) otherwise consistent with the local Comprehensive Plan, 2) a project that promotes public transportation or is within an area designated for urban infill development; and 3) the local government has adopted into its Comprehensive Plan strategies to support and fund mobility within the designated exception area; and

WHEREAS, the City of Aventura (the "City") was designated as a Transportation Concurrency Exception Area when it adopted the City of Aventura Comprehensive Plan in December of 1998; and

WHEREAS, the City of Aventura is in the unique position of a compact, high density, regional destination community nearing buildout that lacks parallel roadway facilities to provide relief to heavily congested and constrained corridors; and

WHEREAS, the City adopted strategies in the City of Aventura Comprehensive Plan to support and fund mobility within the designated exception area, including impact fees and other methods which developers can use to mitigate impacts to the transportation system by contributing funds for alternative modes of transportation that promote mobility, particularly, the expansion, operation and maintenance of the City's Circulator System, also known as the "Aventura Express" or as it may be renamed in the future or any similar future transit system operated by the City (the "Circulator System"), as further described in a study entitled "A Program of Transportation Mitigation" prepared for the City of Aventura by James C. Nicholas, PhD, dated August 15, 2007, and revised March 13, 2008 (the "Transportation Mitigation Study"); and

WHEREAS, the City included an impact fee analysis in the Transportation Mitigation Study to determine if an impact fee could be used to fund the expansion, operation and maintenance of the City's Circulator System; and

WHEREAS, the Transportation Mitigation Study finds that the City of Aventura can accommodate the mobility needs of new development by expansion of the Circulator System with the payment of a transportation mitigation impact fee, and recommends that the City adopt such a fee to support mobility through the use of mass transit within the City and the City's policy of transportation concurrency exception; and

WHEREAS, the City Commission has been designated as the Local Planning Agency for the City pursuant to Section 163.3174, Florida Statutes; and

WHEREAS, the City Commission, acting in its capacity as the Local Planning Agency has reviewed this ordinance to adopt a transportation mitigation impact fee during a required public hearing and has recommended approval to the City Commission; and

WHEREAS, the City Commission has held duly noticed public hearings on this transportation mitigation impact fee ordinance recommended by the City Commission, acting in its capacity as the Local Planning Agency; and

WHEREAS, the City Commission has reviewed this Ordinance and has determined that such action is consistent with the Comprehensive Plan.

NOW, THEREFORE, BE IT ORDAINED BY THE CITY COMMISSION OF THE CITY OF AVENTURA, FLORIDA, AS FOLLOWS:

Section 1. Recitals. That the above recitals are true and correct and are incorporated herein by this reference.

Section 2. City Code Amended. That the City Code of the City of Aventura is hereby amended by amending Chapter 2 "Administration," Article IV "Finance"; Division 5 "Impact Fees"; by creating Section 2-302 "Transportation Mitigation Impact Fee" to read as follows:

"Sec. 2-302. Transportation Mitigation Impact Fee.

(a) Impact Fee; In General.

1. This Section is intended to support and fund mobility within the City's Transportation Concurrency Exception Area by collecting a transportation mitigation impact fee (the "Transportation Mitigation Impact Fee") to allow the expansion, operation and maintenance of the City's Circulator System, also known as the Aventura Express, or as it may be renamed in the future or any similar future transit system (the "Circulator System").

2. In construing the provisions of Section 2-302, the pertinent definitions contained in Section 2-301(b) shall apply unless otherwise provided.

3. Any application for a Building Permit for Development Activity, as defined in Section 2-301(b),

within the corporate limits of the City shall be subject to the assessment of a Transportation Mitigation Impact Fee in the manner and amount set forth in this Section. No Building Permit shall be issued by the City until the applicant has paid the assessed Transportation Mitigation Impact Fee as calculated pursuant to this Section.

4. Notwithstanding payment of the Transportation Mitigation Impact Fees pursuant to this Section, other state and local regulations may limit the issuance of a Building Permit.

5. In the event Transportation Mitigation Impact Fees are paid prior to or concurrent with the issuance of a Building Permit and subsequently, the Building Permit is amended, the applicant shall pay the Transportation Mitigation Impact Fee in effect at the time the amended Building Permit is issued with credit being given for the previous fee paid.

6. In the case of Development Activity involving a change of use, redevelopment or expansion or modification of an existing use on site which requires issuance of a Building Permit, the Transportation Mitigation Impact Fee shall be based on the net increase in the Transportation Mitigation Impact Fee for the new use as compared with the use in effect on the effective date of this Section.

7. If a Building Permit is cancelled without development commencing, then the applicant who paid the Transportation Mitigation Impact Fee shall be entitled to a refund, without interest, of the Transportation Mitigation Impact Fee paid except that the City shall retain three percent (3%) of the fee to offset a portion of the costs of collection and refund. The applicant who paid the Transportation Mitigation Impact Fee shall submit an application for such a refund to the City Manager or his designee within thirty (30) days of the expiration of the order or permit, or thereafter be deemed to waive any right to a refund.

8. In the event the Circulator System is discontinued by action of the City Commission, or if the City fails to use or encumber any existing funds by the end of the calendar quarter immediately following ten (10) years from the effective date of this Section, upon application of the then current fee simple title holder, funds may be returned to such title holder, without interest, provided that the title holder submits an application for a refund to the City Manager or his designee within one hundred and eighty (180) days of the expiration of the ten (10) year period. However, this section shall not apply to Development of Regional Impact or any development with phased or long term buildout. Any claim not so timely made shall be deemed waived.

9. Funds shall be deemed expended for the purposes of this Section when a contract, agreement or purchase order encumbering all or a portion of the payment of said funds shall be approved by final City action.

(b) Impact Fee Computation Formula.

1. The applicant shall pay a Transportation Mitigation Impact Fee amount based on the formula set forth in the table below or as it may be amended by Ordinance of the City Commission. The fee shall be collected by the Community Development Department prior to issuance of a Building Permit for Development Activity. Such fee will be based on the cost required to serve the increased demand for use of the Circulator System resulting from the proposed new Development Activity. The formula to be used to calculate the Transportation Mitigation Impact Fee is established as follows for each property use:

2. The fee per Residential Dwelling Unit or fee per thousand nonresidential square feet shall be multiplied by the applicant's total number of dwelling units for residential property or total number of thousands of square feet for nonresidential property. The total will then be multiplied by 1.03 for a general administrative charge of three (3%) percent. The resulting total is the Transportation Mitigation Impact Fee and administrative charge, which amount shall be paid by the applicant.

3. An applicant may choose to prepare a study to identify a more precise calculation of the impact of his or her proposed Development Activity on the City's Circulator System. If the applicant chooses this option, the applicant shall prepare and submit to the City Manager an Alternative Transportation Mitigation Impact Fee Calculation Study (the "Alternative Fee Study"), containing professionally accepted methodologies and formats as well as traffic, engineering, occupancy and other documentation in support of the basis upon which the alternative calculation was determined. The Alternative Fee Study shall be prepared and presented by professionals qualified in their respective fields and employ methods recognized within those respective fields. The City Manager shall consider the Alternative Fee Study submitted by the applicant, but is not required to accept such documentation if he believes the information to be inaccurate or not reliable. In this case, the City Manager may require the applicant to submit additional or a different Alternative Fee Study for consideration. If an acceptable Alternative Fee Study is not presented, the applicant shall pay the Transportation Mitigation Impact Fee based upon the schedules shown in paragraph 1 of this section. If the City Manager approves a Transportation Mitigation Impact Fee in an amount other than that determined by the Alternative Fee Study, the applicant may appeal the City Manager's decision to the City Commission by filing a written request with the City Clerk within ten (10) days of the date of the City Manager's decision.

4. In the case of Development Activity involving a change of use or magnitude of use for which a Building Permit is required, the proposed development shall be required to

Land Use (Unit of Measure)	Persons Per Unit of Measure	Fee Per Unit of Measure
Residence per Dwelling	0.972	$803.05
Office per 1,000 FT²	1.557	$1,286.59
Retail per 1,000 FT²	2.175	$1,797.33
Tourist Accommodation per 1,000 FT²	2.720	$2,247.22
Industrial per 1,000 FT²	1.319	$1,089.35
Institutional per 1,000 FT²	2.312	$1,910.09

pay a Transportation Mitigation Impact Fee only for the increase in use of the Circulator System resulting from new Development Activity. The Transportation Mitigation Impact Fee shall be the difference between the computed Transportation Mitigation Impact Fee for the proposed Development Activity and the computed Transportation Mitigation Impact Fee for the existing Development Activity. Any Building Permit which expires or is revoked after the effective date of this Section and for which a fee has not previously been paid under this Section shall be required to comply with the provisions herein. No refunds will be given for proposed development activity resulting in a negative fee calculation.

5. If the type of activity within a proposed or current development is not specified, the City Manager or his designee shall use the activity most nearly comparable that will result in payment of a fair and equitable Transportation Mitigation Impact Fee.

6. In determining existing Development Activity and the units or thousands of square feet of proposed or existing development, the Community Development Department shall use the Building Permit and the Certificate of Use information contained in the building or zoning records of Miami-Dade County or the City.

(c) Impact Fee Exemptions.

1. Alteration, expansion or replacement of an existing building or residential dwelling unit where the use is not changed and the number of residential dwelling units or square footage is not increased shall not be subject to the Transportation Mitigation Impact Fee.

2. The burden of demonstrating the previous use or previous payment of a Transportation Mitigation Impact Fee shall be upon the applicant. In cases where there is an existing use, any additional fees shall be based upon the alteration and/or addition to the existing use.

3. Government or public facilities used for governmental purposes are exempt from the Transportation Mitigation Impact Fee, including those parcels, grounds, buildings or structures owned by the federal government, State of Florida, Miami-Dade County, the City, the Miami-Dade County Public Schools or the South Florida Water Management District, including, but not limited to, governmental offices, police and fire stations, airports, seaports, parking facilities, equipment yards, sanitation facilities, water control structures, schools, parks and similar facilities in or through which general government operations are conducted. It is provided, however, that the following shall not be considered governmental or public facilities and shall be subject to the provision of this Section: (1) privately owned properties or facilities leased for governmental operations or activities and privately owned charter schools; (2) public properties or facilities used for private residential, commercial or industrial activities.

4. The construction of accessory buildings or structures is exempt where 1) the use is not changed, 2) any additional impact on the Circulator System is negligible; and 3) the number of residential dwelling units or square footage is not increased.

5. A building replacement meeting the requirements of the Florida Building Code (where such replacement is necessitated by partial destruction), and meeting the requirements of the City's Land Development Regulations, is exempt.

6. Parking garages are exempt from the Transportation Mitigation Impact Fee when the structure is accessory to a primary use.

7. An exemption must be claimed by the applicant prior to paying the Transportation Mitigation Impact Fee. Any exemption not so claimed prior to payment shall be deemed to have been waived by the applicant.

(d) Impact Fee Expenditures.

1. Expenditures from the Impact Fee shall include, but not be limited to:

a) All costs related to expansion of the Circulator System;

b) All costs related to operation of the Circulator System; and

c) All costs related to maintenance of the Circulator System.

2. The three (3%) percent general administrative cost portion of the Transportation Mitigation Impact Fee, as provided for herein, shall be deposited into the General Fund and shall be used to offset the costs of administering the Transportation Mitigation Impact Fee.

(e) Establishment of Fund. Transportation Mitigation Impact Fees collected pursuant to this Section shall be accounted for in the Transportation and Street Maintenance Fund established by the City.

(f) Review and Assessment of Fee. The City Manager shall review the contents of this section at least every three (3) years and, if appropriate, make recommendations to the City Commission to revise it. The first such review shall be no later than January 1, 2011. The City Commission shall consider the City Manager's recommended revision(s) to this section and decide whether to adopt them."

Section 3. Inclusion in the Code. That it is the intention of the City Commission and it is hereby ordained that the provisions of this Ordinance shall become and made a part of the City of Aventura Code of Ordinances; that the sections of this Ordinance may be renumbered or relettered to accomplish such intentions; and that the word "Ordinance" shall be changed to "Section" or other appropriate word as needed.

Section 4. Severability. That the provisions of this Ordinance are declared to be severable and if any section, sentence, clause or phrase of this Ordinance shall for any reason be held to be invalid or unconstitutional, such decision shall not affect the validity of the remaining sections, sentences, clauses, and phrases of this Ordinance but they shall remain in effect, it being the legislative intent that this Ordinance shall stand notwithstanding the invalidity of any part.

Section 5. Special Notice. That, pursuant to Section 163.31801(3)(d), Florida Statutes, notice of the adoption of this Ordinance shall be published by the City Clerk no fewer than ninety (90) days before the effective date of this Ordinance imposing new impact fees.

Section 6. Effective Date. That following adoption on second reading, the provisions of Section 5 of this Ordinance shall be effective immediately, and the remaining provisions of this Ordinance shall be effective from and after the first day of January, 2009.

The foregoing Ordinance was offered by Commissioner _________________, who moved its adoption on first reading. This motion was seconded by Commissioner ______________ and upon being put to a vote, the vote was as follows:

Commissioner Zev Auerbach   _____
Commissioner Billy Joel   _____
Commissioner Michael Stern   _____
Commissioner Teri Holzberg   _____
Commissioner Luz Urbaez Weinberg   _____
Vice Mayor Bob Diamond   _____
Mayor Susan Gottlieb   _____

The foregoing Ordinance was offered by Commissioner _________________, who moved its adoption on second reading. This motion was seconded by Commissioner ________________ and upon being put to a vote, the vote was as follows:

Commissioner   _____
Commissioner   _____
Commissioner   _____
Commissioner   _____
Commissioner   _____
Vice Mayor   _____
Mayor   _____

PASSED on first reading on this 8th day of January, 2008.
PASSED AND ADOPTED on this 8th day of April, 2008.

____

Mayor

ATTEST:

____

CITY CLERK

APPROVED AS TO LEGAL SUFFICIENCY:

____

CITY ATTORNEY

4

Implementation

Critical in effecting proportionate-share development fee programs is an administrative structure that implements them. **Part 4** is devoted to **Implementation**. *Chapter 14* offers guidance in this respect by reviewing essential elements in administrative design, posing a model ordinance devised through a process managed by the State of Florida, and presenting a model ordinance based on the authors' experience over the past 30+ years. *Chapter 15* fills in many of the administrative details outlined in ordinances through a model administrative procedure code.

14

Model Proportionate-Share Development Fee Ordinance

This chapter has three parts. Principles of proportionate-share development fee design are reviewed in the first part. In the second, a model ordinance is presented (Appendix 14A), which is adapted from several developed for use in the State of Florida where there is no comprehensive impact fee statute. The third part is an impact fee ordinance (Appendix 14B) adopted by the City of Canton, Georgia. It is instructive in comparison with the Florida model because Georgia does have a comprehensive impact fee enabling act and because Canton was the first city (outside California) to adopt impact fees that vary by size of the structure (including residential) for all fees assessed.

PRINCIPLES OF ORDINANCE DESIGN AND DRAFTING

ADOPTION

Impact fee programs change the rules of the game for developers and communities. There are usually important considerations to make, including timing of the effective date and the transition period.

Most impact fee ordinances do not become fully effective on the day they are adopted. Those programs that become effective immediately usually require unanimous approval of the governing body under provisions of state emergency declaration statutes. Where an impact fee program results in lifting of moratoria (initially imposed because there was no money available to build facilities to support new development), there may indeed be a justifiable emergency declaration.

In general, the effective dates of new impact fee ordinances range from about 30 days to three months from the date of enactment, with some effective dates ranging more than a year in advance. Communities may delay effective dates of impact fees for several reasons.

First, there is the practical consideration of gearing up local government agencies to handle the new program. Impact fees are usually assessed at the time of building permit issuance, so it is usually the building agency that handles the fee determination and collection. However, coordination is usually required between planning to assure that building permit applications are consistent with land use and other plans; with revenue or budget agencies to assure that impact fee collection is properly recorded and allocated; and with the various agencies that will use impact fees including police, fire, libraries, public works, and parks and recreation. The shear magnitude of setting up a new, complex administrative system takes time. Public officials who do not give their agencies enough time to fully implement the system face the choice of delaying the effective date at the last minute, which does not look good politically, or risking mismanagement and possible court action.

Second, there is the practical political consideration of giving the development community enough time to adequately respond to a new assessment program. Developers thinking about projects must be forewarned about the magnitude of fees they will likely be assessed. This allows them time to change project dimensions and negotiate posture to press for lower land prices.

Third, there is the question of how to deal with projects that have already been approved. For those that have had building permits issued, it is usually impractical to assess fees retroactively. If fees are to be collected upon issuance of occupancy permits, then technically those projects for which fees were not assessed at the building permit stage may still be assessed under the new impact fee program. However, pragmatism usually requires that projects for which building permits have already been issued would be exempt from impact fees.

For those projects that have been approved but for which building permits have not been issued, impact fee programs usually can collect fees upon issuance of building permits. Here again, however, developers are likely to argue that initial project approval was based on a set of financial assumptions, one of which included government fees. If that assumption is to change dramatically, then the project may be less financially viable. Communities usually grant exemption to those projects that have been approved prior to the adoption date of the program. Projects approved after the adoption date and issued building permits before the effective date are also usually exempted. Projects approved after adoption date and issued building permits on or after the effective date are usually assessed impact fees.

ASSESSMENT

Impact fees should be assessed according to clear schedules or formulae. Ideally, a developer should be able to accurately predict the impact fee so that development dimensions and financing can take full account of the fees. However, clear direction must be given to the assessing agency on how to deal with unconventional cases. Among the most common of the unconventional cases are the demolition of a structure and replacement with a like structure, demolition and replacement with an unlike structure, building additions or expansions, additional buildings added to the same site, and construction of facilities whose impact dimensions (e.g., trips, park demand, and water and sewer demand) are difficult to determine.

In the case of demolition and replacement with a like structure, no impact fee is usually required. In the case where the structure is larger but of the same use, the impact fee is usually assessed on the incremental change in size. Where the structure is for a different use, either the entire impact fee may be assessed or the fee would be assessed on the incremental change in impact dimensions. Some agencies assess the lower of the two fee calculations.

Building additions, expansions, or new buildings should be assessed an impact fee on the incremental change in impact dimensions. Unfortunately, this sounds easier than it often is. Some building additions, expansions, or new buildings on the same site result in higher site activity than the sum of the existing and additional space suggests. Nonetheless, as most impact fee formulae are based solely on units (e.g., square feet or bedrooms), it should be a simple matter to determine the incremental change in demand dimensions resulting from such additions to the site.

The more problematic situation arises when a proposed use is not clearly anticipated by impact fee schedules. Road trip generation estimated for land uses, for example, usually do not cover all land uses. Sometimes the proposed use is like other uses on the schedule and so reasonable approximations can be made. Other times, officials may allow the developer to pay for an independent, professional determination of demand dimensions associated with that land use. Alternatively, officials may estimate a high fee, evaluate the observed demand for facilities generated by the development at the end of a year, and then either refund the difference between the initial fee paid and the actual amount necessary, or assess the additional amount necessary. As the latter situation may be problematic if the developer refuses to pay, communities should try to avoid having to assess fees after a development is built.

COLLECTION

Who will collect the fees? Since the objective of assessing impact fees is to provide the community and its various agencies with needed revenues, close collaboration is needed between the assessing agency and the expending agencies. Collection of impact fees should be handled by one agency—usually the building agency. Sometimes it is the planning agency or a centralized accounting office. In any event, all agencies need to know from the assessing agency is: (1) what the fee schedule is; (2) how many fees are collected from which developments; and (3) when the building permit was issued and the expected date of development completion. For example, Broward County uses a five-copy receipt that is distributed to the person who pays, the planning office, the accounting office, the public works staff, and the parks staff. In one county that assesses fees for schools, senior centers, child care, and housing, in addition to more traditional uses, copies of receipts are also sent to those agencies.

ACCOUNTING

Accounting procedures are needed to assure that impact fees collected are deposited into earmarked accounts, expenditures from which will benefit contributing development (i.e., impact fees collected for schools, parks, and roads must be earmarked for school, park, and road accounts). Furthermore, if the impact fee ordinance requires segregation of revenues geographically (by service area or district), the accounting system should incorporate such a segregation scheme. The accounting system should also be designed to make available to anyone information on where impact fees from individual contributing developments were spent. This allows public officials and developers to be assured that impact fees benefit contributing development.

DISBURSEMENT

Impact fees must be spent, but the manner of expenditure can be complex. Issues are raised relating to earmarking, timeliness of disbursement, location of disbursement, and effect on community capital financing policies.

Earmarking

While impact fees should be earmarked to accounts in the manner suggested above, care must be taken not to accumulate so many separate accounts that are too small to be useful, or restrict the use of money in accounts in a manner that jeopardizes specific capital improvements. Broward County, Florida, faced this very problem with its road impact fees. Impact fees were deposited into hundreds of accounts, each earmarked for a specific road improvement. Few accounts were large enough to pay for the intended improvement. Eventually, the county reduced the number of accounts and changed administrative procedures to allow pooling of revenue under certain conditions.

San Diego County, California, collects impact fees for specific projects but puts all money into a single, master account. That money is used to construct facilities based on a 20-year CIP. Technically, impact fees collected for one improvement but not scheduled for construction until several years later are loaned to another project scheduled for improvement in an earlier year. Impact fees collected for improvements that are already constructed repay funds borrowed from other accounts.

Timing

Impact fees must be expended within a reasonable amount of time. Most communities attempt to expend them within a five- or six-year CIP. There are exceptions, however. In San Diego County, some improvements are not built until nearly two decades after fees are collected. The program includes a master CIP that explicitly shows when those facilities would be built. The county further demonstrated that there would be no need for those facilities until future years. Contributing development is not deprived of benefits since facilities will be built benefiting development as the need arises.

When facilities financed by impact fees are scheduled for construction but must be delayed, impact fees need not be refunded. Among the conditions needed to extend the expenditure of impact fees is undercollection of impact fees due to reduced growth rates and discovery of extraordinary costs that affect prudent construction of facilities at the time originally planned.

Location

Various schemes are used to assure that contributing development benefits from the facilities it helps to finance. In Loveland, Colorado, it is presumed that all facilities financed in part by impact fees benefit all new development. This is an easy presumption since the town is rather small, and it is reasonable to expect that all new development benefits from construction of all new facilities.

Where impact fees are collected on a countywide basis or on larger cities, however, it is usually customary to devise benefit districts or zones for each facility to be financed by impact fees. For example, the City of Raleigh, North Carolina, divides its city into three road benefit zones. Road improvements within each zone are estimated and impact fees for each zone are determined. New development within each zone pays a different road impact fee.

Unlike the zonal system used by Raleigh, Broward County, Florida, expends impact fees for local parks within 2.5 miles of contributing development. It spends fees for regional parks within 15 miles of contributing development. However, some counties finance some facilities with impact fees that benefit all new development everywhere, and there is no need to devise benefit districts or zones. For example, Manatee County, Florida, applies the same solid waste disposal impact fee on all development.

Matching the location of contributing development with the location of facilities financed by impact fees depends on the facility. Each facility has its own unique service area: local parks may serve areas of a 2.5-mile radius; regional parks may serve areas of a 15-mile radius. Expressways may serve an entire county, but certain collector streets serve limited areas. Solid waste sites serve large regions, but compacting and transfer stations may serve smaller areas. In general, impact fees must be tailored to the service area of the facility being financed with those fees.

Effect on Capital Improvements Policy

Impact fees can, however, influence existing capital improvements policy. For example, suppose that impact fees are assessed for a regional park scheduled for construction in five years. Impact fees pile up and substantial revenue is on deposit. After five years, it is discovered that park construction prices have risen faster than impact fee collections and account yields. The local public officials face the choice of deferring construction of the park, at risk of political pressure or opposition by developers who contributed money to the park, or taking money from other projects and diverting it to the park.

The availability of impact fees that are dedicated to certain facilities may thus place them on higher priority than other projects. This will happen in those communities that must contribute general funds to projects because credits had to be given to new development for other payments new development made to existing facilities benefiting existing development. The effect, however, is to place at higher priority facilities that may solely benefit new development, and place at lower priority facilities that are long overdue but solely benefit existing development or that benefit the entire community.

ENFORCEMENT

Two factors dominate consideration of impact fee program enforcement: timely payment of impact fees and consistency of development with permitted activity.

Timely payment is an issue easily resolved when only one community is involved in collecting impact fees. It becomes a more complex issue when one jurisdiction—a county perhaps—must collect fees from developments located in separate jurisdictions, perhaps cities. Such was the case in Broward County, Florida. Several cities in Broward County issue their own building permits, but the county collected impact fees to finance facilities benefiting new development inside and outside of cities. Developers received building permits from cities and were required to pay impact fees to the county, but many developers "forgot" to do so. Broward County implemented a system to check the building permits of cities and notify cities when developers failed to pay impact fees. Average monthly impact fee revenue jumped from $409,000 to $800,000.

Another problem is assuring that developments use the land consistent with that which was approved. The most serious situation occurs when a development is approved for and is occupied by one kind of activity—perhaps low employee density activities—and is eventually replaced by higher employee density activities. Roads are more greatly impacted by the development than initial projections and impact fees estimated. Communities thus need to monitor the actual use of developments to assure consistency with initial permitted uses or initial fee payments. This may be accomplished by monitoring business license changes. When a license indicates a different or more intensive use, there may be a land-use violation. The remedy may include additional impact fees.

This element of impact fee programs is perhaps the least well developed and potentially the most problematic.

CREDITS

Chapter 6 spelled out several situations in which developers would be granted credit against impact fees. Those credits include recoupment of past and future payments the development will make toward the financing of existing facilities benefiting existing development, the time-price differential inherent in the expenditure of money at different times, and installation of facilities of general public benefit.

Communities must clearly describe the nature of these credits. Developers will naturally attempt to claim as many credits as possible. Administrative provisions can clearly specify the conditions under which credit is allowed, credit formulae, credit parameters (e.g., number of past and future years to consider, and interest or discount rates), and limitations of credit (i.e., the particular impact fees that can be reduced).

Communities can limit credit to only the impact fee; to allow more credit than the impact fee is to have communities pay for new development. Communities can also limit credit to like contributions (e.g., a credit for past and future property tax payments for parks would be applied only to the park impact fee and to no others).

Where a developer installs facilities for which credit will be given, there might be a question on the amount of credit due (i.e., a developer may claim more expenses than actually incurred to install the improvements). This is resolved by having public works officials estimate the value of the work to be undertaken by the developer, and then certify satisfactory completion of the work before the credit is given. Perhaps the developer can install the improvement at less than the public estimate but, as long as the improvement is installed satisfactorily, there should be no issue.

WAIVERS

Impact fees can have undesirable effects on the provision of low- or moderate-income housing, and on desirable economic development. At issue is the extent to which impact fees raise the price of housing or raise the price of rent to economic activities. These effects may be offset in two ways.

First, a community could waive the impact fee for qualifying low- and moderate-income housing, but there are problems with this approach. Waiving fees will result in lower revenue, and there is no explicit recoupment mechanism to make up for the loss of impact fees. A more difficult problem is that there is a risk of invalidation of ordinances that includes any waivers of impact fees for "desirable" developments that have impacts. There is no apparent way to show equal application or equal protection if the fees will vary while impact does not. These charges are fees and not taxes. As such, they must be applied equally and fairly. Any community feeling the need to incorporate waivers should seek legislative authority for such waivers. The better approach, however, would be to follow the following second option.

The second way entails the community paying the impact fee or a portion of it out of the general fund. Loveland, Colorado, for example, cuts the impact fee on low-income housing by half, but contributes the difference out of the general fund. Loveland also reduces the impact fee on new industrial activities after one year (i.e., the new industrial development pays the fee but, after one year, the city rebates the fee out of the general fund in proportion to the number of new jobs created after the first year). Hillsborough County, Florida, will pay the impact fee for developments that attain a public purpose from "other sources," which may include intergovernmental transfers or the general fund.

VARIANCES

Impact fee programs must include provisions for variance. At issue is the impossibility of knowing exactly the impact fee due for every project. Developers, for example, may claim lower road impact fees for a particular project than indicated or implied on the formal road impact fee schedule. Variance provisions would allow developers to perform their own impact fee analysis and present it to either administrators or the governing body (or its designee, such as the planning commission). Administrative hearings may be conducted where the fee proposed by the developer is up to approximately 25 percent less than the schedule would assess. Differences of more than that amount would be heard before the governing body. Differences of less than 10 percent may not be subject to hearing, however, as the estimated impact of the community would be close to that estimated by the developer.

The decision to allow all or part of the developer's variance request would probably depend on the community's independent analysis. One hedge is to require full deposit of the fee with an evaluation of the project's impact after approximately one year. The difference between the actual impact and the impact fees paid based on the community's estimate would be refunded with interest.

In any event, to protect against development delays, the impact fee would be paid in advance of the hearing, but the portion of the impact fee in dispute would be held in a special interest-bearing account. Refund of all or part of the disputed portion would be paid from this account.

REFUNDS

Sometimes impact fees collected may not be used as intended. Unlike tax revenue, they cannot be diverted to other purposes. Unspent impact fees may need to be refunded if the facilities they were to finance are cancelled or unreasonably delayed. The questions involved here focus on notice and the parties who should be paid.

Impact fees paid by a developer are recouped by the developer through lower land prices or higher development prices, or a combination of the two. Developers may also take a smaller profit. It is impossible for a community, however, to decide which party in the complex development process paid how much of the impact fee. Instead, communities may simply opt to entitle only current owners of the contributing development, under the theory that it is ultimately the owners who absorb most of the impact fee in higher priced, lower quality, and higher density development.

Notice may then be given to all owners of contributing development as shown on the local property tax records. Notice should be by registered mail. Owners should be given a reasonable period of time (perhaps three months to one year) to claim the refund. Refund claims should be relatively simple, involving only certification of ownership.

For its part, determining the appropriate impact fee to be refunded involves using the very formulae or schedules used to determine the impact fee when first paid. Refunds should also include interest, probably at the local government borrowing rate.

DATA MAINTENANCE

The impact fee program must be continually updated to reflect data such as assumptions, facility cost estimates, growth patterns and rates, and demographic changes. Impact fee assessments will therefore be kept current and less subject to adverse court review. Three considerations are posed.

First, the community should establish the frequency at which it updates each impact fee schedule or formula. Specific staff should be explicitly assigned this responsibility. Data updating may require establishing formal links among agencies. Perhaps an impact fee updating task force comprised of representatives of all affected agencies would meet annually to review changes. It is common practice to base impact fees on current cost estimates of new facilities. Those estimates should be made annually.

Second, the governing body or its designee should establish a formal process by which changes are effected. This may include a formal public hearing during which the changes are proposed and adopted. Citizens and developers would also be allowed to propose changes at that hearing. Changes that are adopted should be supported by findings. Such a process should remove the taint of arbitrariness whenever the changes result in higher fees.

Third, the community might decide the conditions under which unscheduled re-evaluation would occur. Changes may include substantially higher- or lower-than-projected growth rates, large formerly unplanned annexations, and major changes in the construction standards of new facilities (e.g., federal requirements for vastly improved and more expensive water and wastewater plants).

ADMINISTRATIVE EXPENSE

Impact fee programs carry initially high implementation costs (including the costs associated with analysis, planning, and programming), but they can be administered at relatively low cost. Figures vary, and figures reported here are informally gathered, but the cost of administering impact fee programs range from about 2 to 5 percent of impact fee collections.

If the cost of administration can be determined, it may be recovered by impact fees themselves. This is an acceptable practice throughout Florida, for example. The procedure involves reasonably documenting the cost of administering impact fee programs as a percentage of total impact fee receipts (sometimes divided into each impact fee assessed). This cost is then added to impact fees as a proportionate increase covering administrative costs.

APPENDIX 14A
MODEL ORDINANCE

1. Legislative Findings. The ordinance should include legislative findings in which the governing body of the local government determines that the impact fee meets the dual rational nexus test. As to the first part of the test, the governing body should determine that there is a reasonable connection between the need for new capital facilities and the new development charged the impact fee. As to the second part, the governing body should determine that there is a reasonable connection between the expenditure of the impact fees collected and the benefits to the new development.

Section One: Legislative Findings.

The Board of County Commissioners of ** County finds, determines and declares that:

A. ** County must expand its road system in order to maintain current levels of service if new development is to be accommodated without decreasing current levels of service. This must be done in order to promote and protect the public health, safety and welfare;

B. The ** Legislature through the enactment of ** Statutes has sought to encourage ** County to enact impact fees;

C. The imposition of impact fees is one of the preferred methods of ensuring that development bears a proportionate share of the cost of capital facilities necessary to accommodate such development. This must be done in order to promote and protect the public health, safety and welfare;

D. Each of the types of land development described in Section Seven hereof, will generate traffic necessitating the acquisition of rights-of-way, road construction and road improvements.

E. The fees established by Section Seven are derived from, are based upon, and do not exceed the costs of providing additional rights-of-way, road construction and road improvements necessitated by the new land developments for which the fees are levied.

F. The report entitled "** County, **, Impact Fee Methodology," dated ___________, sets forth a reasonable methodology and analysis for the determination of the impact of new development on the need for and costs for additional rights-of-way, road construction and road improvements in ** County.

2. Short Title, Authority and Applicability. It is generally recognized as good practice for an ordinance to include a recitation as to the authority upon which it is based. In the case of impact fees, the clause may cite to the home rule power of counties, the land use and regulatory powers of counties and the lengthy case law history of impact fees.

Section Two: Short Title, Authority and Applicability.

A. This ordinance shall be known and may be cited as the "** County Road Impact Fee Ordinance."

B. The Board of County Commissioners of ** County has the authority to adopt this ordinance pursuant to Article ______ of the Constitution of the State of **, and Chapter______ of the ** Statutes.

C. This ordinance shall apply in the unincorporated area of ** County and in the incorporated areas of ** County to the extent permitted by Article _________ of the Constitution of the State of **.

3. Intent and Purposes. This provision should identify the type of development subject to the fee. For example, an ordinance imposing an educational facilities impact fee will limit the fee to residential development, and a transportation impact fee characteristically applies to all types of development: residential, commercial and industrial development. The ordinance should indicate the scope of its effect, such as whether it applies to development throughout the entire county or only the unincorporated area or only in a municipality.

Section Three: Intents and Purposes.

A. This ordinance is intended to assist in the implementation of the ** County Comprehensive Plan.

B. The purpose of this ordinance is to regulate the use and development of land so as to assure that new development bears a proportionate share of the cost of capital expenditures necessary to provide roads in ** County.

4. Rules of Construction. Many ordinances contain rules of construction which facilitate the drafting and understanding of the ordinance.

Section Four: Rules of Construction.

A. The provisions of this ordinance shall be liberally construed so as to effectively carry out its purpose in the interest of the public health, safety and welfare.

B. For the purposes of administration and enforcement of this ordinance, unless otherwise stated in this ordinance, the following rules of construction shall apply to the text of this ordinance:

(1) In case of any difference of meaning or implication between the text of this ordinance and any caption, illustration, summary table, or illustrative table, the text shall control.

(2) The word "shall" is always mandatory and not discretionary; the word "may" is permissive.

(3) Words used in the present tense shall include the future; and words used in the singular number shall include the plural, and the plural the singular, unless the context clearly indicates the contrary.

(4) The phrase "used for" includes "arranged for," "designed for," "maintained for," or "occupied for."

(5) The word "person" includes an individual, a corporation, a partnership, an incorporated association, or any other similar entity.

(6) Unless the context clearly indicates the contrary, where a regulation involves two (2) or more items, conditions, provisions, or events connected by the conjunction "and," "or," or "either … or," the conjunction shall be interpreted as follows:

(a) "And" indicates that all the connected terms, conditions, provisions or events shall apply.

(b) "Or" indicates that the connected items, conditions, provisions or events may apply singly or in any combination.

(c) "Either … or" indicates that the connected items, conditions, provisions or events shall apply singly but not in combination.

(7) The word "includes" shall not limit a term to the specific example but is intended to extend its meaning to all other instances or circumstances of like kind or character.

(8) "County Administrator" means the County Administrator or the county or municipal officials he/she may designate to carry out the administration of this ordinance. Any municipal official so designated shall be approved by the appropriate municipality before exercising duties hereunder.

(9) A road right-of-way used to define road impact fee district boundaries may be considered within any district it bounds.

5. Definitions. Complex and lengthy ordinances typically include a definitional section for words and phrases used precisely and frequently through out the ordinance to lessen the complexity of the ordinance and facilitate its understanding.

Section Five: Definitions.

A. A "feepayer" is a person commencing a land development activity which generates traffic and which requires the issuance of a building permit or permit for mobile home installation.

B. A "capital improvement" includes transportation planning, preliminary engineering, engineering design studies, land surveys, right-of-way acquisition, engineering, permitting and construction of all the necessary features for any road construction project including, but not limited to:

(1) construction of new through lanes,

(2) construction of new turn lanes,

(3) construction of new bridges,

(4) construction of new drainage facilities in conjunction with new roadway construction,

(5) purchase and installation of traffic signalization (including new and upgraded signalization),

(6) construction of curbs, medians, and shoulders, and

(7) relocating utilities to accommodate new roadway construction.

C. "Expansion" of the capacity of a road applies to all road and intersection capacity enhancements and includes but is not limited to extensions, widening, intersection improvements, upgrading signalization, and expansion of bridges.

D. "Land Development Activity Generating Traffic" means any change in land use or any construction of buildings or structures or any change in the use of any structure that attracts or produces vehicular trips.

E. "Road" shall have the same meaning as set forth in Section ___________ of the ** Statutes.

F. "Arterial Road" shall have the same meaning as set forth in Section ___________ of the ** Statutes.

G. "Collector Road" shall have the same meaning as set forth in Section ___________ of the ** Statutes.

H. "Site-related Improvements" are capital improvements and right-of-way dedications for direct access improvements to and/or within the development in question. Direct access improvements include but are not limited to the following:

(1) access roads leading to the development;

(2) driveways and roads within the development;

(3) acceleration and deceleration lanes, and right and left turn lanes leading to those roads and driveways; and

(4) traffic control measures for those roads and driveways.

I. "Independent Fee Calculation Study" means the traffic engineering and/or economic documentation prepared by a feepayer to allow the determination of the impact fee other than by the use of the table in Section Seven (A) of this ordinance.

J. "Level of Service" shall have the same meaning as set forth in the Highway Research Board's Highway Capacity Manual (1965).

K. "Development Order" means a regulatory approval by ** County or a municipality therein.

L. "Mandatory or Required right-of-way dedications and/ or roadway improvements" means such non-compensated dedications and/or roadway improvements required by the County or by a municipality within ** County which has not opted out from the effect of this ordinance.

6. Imposition of Fee. An impact fee ordinance will impose the impact fee and identify at what point in the development process the impact fee will be due, such as the issuance of a building permit, the platting of the land, the issuance of a certificate of occupancy or some other point.

Section Six: Imposition of Road Impact Fee.

A. Any person who, after the effective date of this Ordinance, seeks to develop land within ** County, **, by applying for: a building permit; an extension of a building permit issued prior to that date; a permit for mobile home installation; or an extension of a permit for mobile home installation issued prior to that date, to make an improvement to land which will generate additional traffic is hereby required to pay a road impact fee in the manner and amount set forth in this ordinance. The impact fees established by this ordinance shall not be effective within the boundaries of any municipality which issues building permits until such municipality has executed an interlocal agreement with the county to collect such fees. The impact fees established by this ordinance shall not be effective within a municipality which has by municipal ordinance repealed the effect of this ordinance within its boundaries.

B. No new building permit or new permit for mobile home installation for any activity requiring payment of an impact fee pursuant to Section Seven of this ordinance shall be issued unless and until the road impact fee hereby required has been paid.

C. No extension of a building permit or permit for mobile home installation issued prior to the effective date of this ordinance, for any activity requiring payment of an impact fee pursuant to Section Seven of this ordinance shall be granted unless and until the road impact fee hereby required has been paid.

*7. Computation of the Amount of Impact Fee. Impact fee ordinances frequently incorporate and adopt the impact fee study which provides a factual and legal basis for the fees. The methodology may be actually placed in the ordinance. Fee schedules may be incorporated into the ordinance. **It is not unusual for an impact fee ordinance to authorize a developer to submit its own calculation of impact fees and to provide for a determination by staff as to the accuracy and adequacy of the developer impact fee**. An appeal process may be specified.*

Section Seven: Computation of the Amount of Road Impact Fee.

A. At the option of the feepayer, the amount of the road impact fee may be determined by the following fee schedule. The fee schedule includes a credit for future motor fuel tax payments and reflects a discount of __% from net cost to encourage use of this schedule in order to avoid the expenditure of administrative time on the processing of independent fee calculation studies.

FEE SCHEDULE

LAND USE TYPE (UNIT)

RESIDENTIAL PER LIVING UNIT:

SINGLE FAMILY DETACHED [Insert $ value of fee]

SINGLE FAMILY ATTACHED [Insert $ value of fee]

MULTI-FAMILY [Insert $ value of fee]

MOBILE HOME EACH UNIT [Insert $ value of fee]

HOTEL/MOTEL ROOM PER ROOM [Insert $ value of fee]
OTHER RESIDENTIAL EACH UNIT [Insert $ value of fee]

INDUSTRIAL AND WAREHOUSE PER 1,000 SQ. FT.:
INDUSTRIAL BUILDINGS [Insert $ value of fee]
WAREHOUSE BUILDINGS [Insert $ value of fee]
STORAGE BUILDINGS [Insert $ value of fee]

OFFICE AND FINANCIAL PER 1,000 SQ. FT.:
FINANCIAL OFFICES [Insert $ value of fee]
GENERAL OFFICES [Insert $ value of fee]
RETAIL PER 1,000 SQ. FT. [Insert $ value of fee]

(1) If a building permit is requested for mixed uses, then the fee shall be determined through using the applicable schedule by apportioning the space committed to uses specified on the applicable schedule.

(2) For applications for an extension of a building permit or an extension of a permit for mobile home installation, the amount of the fee is the difference between that fee then applicable and any amount already paid pursuant to this ordinance.

(3) If the type of development activity that a building permit is applied for is not specified on the applicable fee schedule, the County Administrator shall use the fee applicable to the most nearly comparable type of land use on the fee schedule. The County Administrator shall be guided in the selection of a comparable type by the report titled Trip Generation: An Information Report (_____ Edition) prepared by Institute of Transportation Engineers. If the County Administrator determines that there is no comparable type of land use on the applicable fee schedule then the County Administrator shall determine the fee by:

(a) using traffic generation statistics provided by the ** Department of Transportation or contained in a report titled Trip Generation: An Information Report (_____ Edition) prepared by Institute of Transportation Engineers and;

(b) applying the formula set forth in Section Seven (B) hereof; and

(c) reducing the fee so determined by the appropriate percentage as indicated in Section 7(A) above.

(4) In the case of change of use, redevelopment, or expansion or modification of an existing use which requires the issuance of a building permit or permit for mobile home installation, the impact fee shall be based upon the net positive increase in the impact fee for the new use as compared to the previous use. The County Administrator shall be guided in this determination by traffic generation statistics provided by the ** Department of Transportation or contained in a report titled Trip Generation: An Information Report (_____ Edition) prepared by Institute of Transportation Engineers.

B. If a feepayer opts not to have the impact fee determined according to paragraph (A) of this section, then the feepayer shall prepare and submit to the County Administrator an independent fee calculation study for the land development activity for which a building permit or permit for mobile home installation is sought. The independent fee calculation study shall follow the prescribed methodologies and formats for the study established by the Guidelines and Procedures Manual adopted by motion of the Board of County Commissioners of ** County. The traffic engineering

and/or economic documentation submitted shall show the basis upon which the independent fee calculation was made, including but not limited to the following:

(1) Traffic Engineering Studies:

(a) Documentation of trip generation rates appropriate for the proposed land development activity.

(b) Documentation of trip length appropriate for the proposed land development activity.

(c) Documentation of any other trip data appropriate for the proposed land development activity.

(2) Economic Documentation Studies:

(a) Documentation of the cost per lane per mile for roadway construction appropriate for proposed land development activity.

(b) Documentation of credits attributable to the proposed land development activity which can be expected to be available to replace the portion of the service volume used by the traffic generated by the proposed land development activity.

Independent fee calculation studies shall be prepared and presented by professionals qualified in their respective fields. The County Administrator shall consider the documentation submitted by the feepayer but is not required to accept such documentation as he/she shall reasonably deem to be inaccurate or not reliable and may, in the alternative, require the feepayer to submit additional or different documentation for consideration. If an acceptable independent fee calculation study is not presented, the feepayer shall pay road impact fees based upon the schedules shown in paragraph (A) of this section. Determinations made by the County Administrator pursuant to this paragraph may be appealed to the Board of County Commissioners by filing a written request with the County Administrator within ten (10) days of the County Administrator's determination.

Upon acceptance of an independent fee calculation study, the following formula shall be used by the County Administrator to determine the impact fee per unit of development:

[Insert formula used to calculate fees here]

8. Payment of Impact Fee. The collection method of impact fees may be provided by ordinance. The ordinance may make the fees payable in a lump sum or it may provide for the payment of the fee on an annual or monthly basis over a period of years. If a county-imposed impact fee is charged to development on a county-wide basis, **the impact fee ordinance may provide for an interlocal agreement with a municipality to address the administration of the impact fee within the incorporated area, including an administrative fee** *to the municipality for the cost of collection.*

Section Eight: Payment of Fee.

A. The feepayer shall pay the road impact fee required by this ordinance to the County Administrator or his designee prior to the issuance of a building permit or a permit for mobile home installation.

B. All funds collected shall be properly identified by road impact fee district and promptly transferred for deposit in the appropriate Road Impact Fee Trust Fund to be held in separate accounts as determined in Section Ten of this ordinance and used solely for the purposes specified in this ordinance.

9. Impact Fee Districts. Impact fee districts may be described to draw a tighter nexus between the fee and the benefit to the property.

Section Nine: Road Impact Fee Districts.

There are hereby established ______(_) road impact fee districts as shown in Appendix I attached hereto and incorporated herein by reference. No district shall include any area within a municipality that issues building permits and that has not entered into an interlocal agreement with the county to collect road impact fees or that has by ordinance repealed the effect of this ordinance within its boundaries

10. Impact Fee Trust Funds Established. The ordinance should establish a separate account so that there is assurance that the impact fees are properly expended in a manner that provides the requisite benefit to development charged the impact fee.

Section Ten: Road Impact Fee Trust Funds Established.

A. There are hereby established ______(_) separate Road Impact Fee Trust Funds, one for each road impact fee district established by Section Nine of this Ordinance.

B. Funds withdrawn from these accounts must be used in accordance with the provisions of Section Eleven of this ordinance.

11. Use of Funds. A delineation of the type of capacity-adding capital facilities that will be funded with the revenues from the impact fees should be included. Impact fees may be bonded.

Section Eleven: Use of Funds.

A. Funds collected from road impact fees shall be used for the purpose of capital improvements to and expansion of transportation facilities associated with the Arterial and Collector road network as designated by ** County and under the jurisdiction of ** County, any municipality within ** County which has not opted out from the effect of the ordinance, or the State of **.

B. No funds shall be used for periodic or routine maintenance.

C. Funds shall be used exclusively for capital improvements or expansion within the road impact fee district, including district boundary roads, as identified in Appendix I, hereof, from which the funds were collected or for projects in other road impact districts which are of benefit to the road impact district from which the funds were collected. Funds shall be expended in the order in which they are collected.

D. In the event that bonds or similar debt instruments are issued for advanced provision of capital facilities for which road impact fees may be expended, impact fees may be used to pay debt service on such bonds or similar debt instruments to the extent that the facilities provided are of the type described in paragraph A of this section and are located within the appropriate impact fee districts created by Section Nine of this ordinance or as provided in paragraph C of this section.

E. At least once each fiscal period the County Administrator shall present to the Board of County Commissioners a proposed capital improvement program for roads, assigning funds, including any accrued interest, from the several Road Impact Fee Trust Funds to specific road improvement projects and related expenses. Monies, including any accrued interest, not assigned in any fiscal period shall be retained in the same Road Impact Fee Trust Funds until the next fiscal period except as provided by the refund provisions of this ordinance.

F. Funds may be used to provide refunds as described in Section Twelve.

G. The collecting governmental entity shall be entitled to retain not more than _____ per cent (__%) of the funds collected as compensation for the expense of collecting the fee and administering this ordinance.

12. Refund of Fees Paid. Typically, an impact fee ordinance will provide for refunds to the owner of the property at the time of a refund in the event the impact fees are not expended within a reasonable period of time after collection.

Section Twelve: Refund of Fees Paid.

A. If a building permit or permit for mobile home installation expires without commencement of construction, then the feepayer shall be entitled to a refund, without interest, of the impact fee paid as a condition for its issuance except that the County shall retain _____ percent (__%) of the fee to offset a portion of the costs of collection and refund. The feepayer must submit an application for such a refund to __________ within 30 days of the expiration of the permit.

B. Any funds not expended or encumbered by the end of the calendar quarter immediately following six (6) years from the date the road impact fee was paid shall, upon application of the then current landowner, be returned to such landowner with interest at the rate of _____ percent (__%) per annum, provided that the landowner submits an application for a refund to ____________ within 180 days of the expiration of the six year period.

*13. Exemptions and Credits. An impact fee ordinance **may provide for an exemption from the fees for housing deemed affordable at specified income levels**. The exemption may be a credit against the fee or a refund for fees paid by low income owners. Credits may be given for the donation of property or improvements to a governmental entity which reduces that development's impact on the infrastructure served by the impact fee. Credits must be incorporated under two conditions. First, taxes or revenues paid by the newly constructed development must be legally available to fund the same infrastructure for which the impact fee is collected. Second, the taxes or revenues must have been applied toward reducing the cost of those infrastructure requirements for the newly constructed development which pays the impact fee.*

Section Thirteen: Exemptions and Credits.

A. The following shall be exempted from payment of the impact fee:

(1) Alterations or expansion of an existing building where no additional units are created, where the use is not changed, and where no additional vehicular trips will be produced over and above those produced by the existing use.

(2) The construction of accessory buildings or structures which will not produce additional vehicular trips over and above those produced by the principal building or use of the land.

(3) The replacement of a destroyed or partially destroyed building or structure with a new building or structure of the same size and use provided that no additional trips will be produced over and above those produced by the original use of the land.

(4) The installation of a replacement mobile home on a lot or other such site when a road impact fee for such mobile home site has previously been paid pursuant to this ordinance or where a mobile home legally existed on such site on or prior to the effective date of this ordinance.

Any claim of exemption must be made no later than the time of application for a building permit or permit for mobile home installation. Any claim not so made shall be deemed waived.

B. Credits:

(1) No credit shall be given for Site-related Improvements or right-of-way dedications.

(2) All Mandatory or Required right-of-way dedications and/or roadway improvements made by a feepayer, subsequent to the effective date of this ordinance, except for Site-related Improvements, shall be credited on a pro rata basis against road impact fees otherwise due or to become due for the development that prompted the County or the municipality to require such dedications or roadway improvements. Such credits shall be determined and provided as set forth in Section Thirteen B. (3) (a), (b), (c), and (d).

(3) A feepayer may obtain credit against all or a portion of road impact fees otherwise due or to become due by offering to dedicate non-Site-Related right-of-way and/or construct non-Site Related roadway improvements. This offer must specifically request or provide for a road impact fee credit. Such construction must be in accordance with County, Municipal, or State design standards, whichever is applicable. If the County Administrator accepts such an offer, whether the acceptance is before or after the effective date of this ordinance, the credit shall be determined and provided in the following manner:

(a) Credit for the dedication of non-Site-Related right-of-way shall be valued at (i) 115% of the most recent assessed value by the ** County Property Appraiser, or (ii) by such other appropriate method as the Board of County Commissioners may have accepted prior to the effective date of this ordinance for particular right-of-way dedications and/or roadway improvements, or (iii) at the option of the feepayer, by fair market value established by private appraisers acceptable to the County. Credit for the dedication of right-of-way shall be provided when the property has been conveyed at no charge to, and accepted by, the County in a manner satisfactory to the Board of County Commissioners.

(b) Applicants for credit for construction of nonsite-related road improvements shall submit acceptable engineering drawings and specifications, and construction cost estimates to the County Administrator. The County Administrator shall determine credit for roadway construction based upon either these cost estimates or upon alternative engineering criteria and construction cost estimates if the County Administrator determines that such estimates submitted by the applicant are either unreliable or inaccurate. The County Administrator shall provide the applicant with a letter or certificate setting forth the dollar amount of the credit, the reason for the credit, and the legal description or other adequate description of the project or development to which the credit may be applied. The applicant must sign and date a duplicate copy of such letter or certificate indicating his agreement to the terms of the letter or certificate and return such signed document to the County Administrator before credit will be given. The failure of the applicant to sign, date, and return such document within 60 days shall nullify the credit.

(c) Except as provided in subparagraph (d), credit against impact fees otherwise due will not be provided until:

(1) the construction is completed and accepted by the County, a municipality within the county which has not opted out from the effect of this ordinance, or the State, whichever is applicable;

(2) a suitable maintenance and warranty bond is received and approved by the Clerk of Courts of ** County, when applicable; and

(3) all design, construction, inspection, testing, bonding, and acceptance procedures are in strict compliance with the then current County Paving and Drainage ordinance, when applicable.

(d) Credit may be provided before completion of specified roadway improvements if adequate assurances are given by the applicant that the standards set out in Subparagraph (c) will be met and if the feepayer posts security as provided below for the costs of such construction. Security in the form of a performance bond, irrevocable letter of credit or escrow agreement shall be posted with and approved by the Clerk of Courts of ** County in an amount determined by the County Administrator consistent with the then current County Paving and Drainage Ordinance. If the road construction project will not be constructed within one (1) year of the acceptance of the offer by the County Administrator, the amount of the security shall be increased by ten percent (10%) compounded, for each year of the life of the security. The security shall be reviewed and approved by the Clerk of the Board of County Commissioners prior to acceptance of the security by the Clerk. If the road construction project is not to be completed within 5 years of the date of the feepayer's offer, the Board of County Commissioners must approve the road construction project and its scheduled completion date prior to the acceptance of the offer by the County Administrator.

(4) Any claim for credit must be made no later than the time of application for a building permit or permit for mobile home installation. Any claim not so made shall be deemed waived.

(5) Credits shall not be transferable from one project or development to another without the approval of the Board of County Commissioners and may only be transferred to a development in a different impact fee district upon a finding by the Board of County Commissioners that the dedication of right of way or road construction for which the credit was given benefits such different impact fee district.

(6) In the event that a municipality within ** County shall pass an ordinance or law that prevents the application of this ordinance within that municipality, there shall be no credit given for right-of-way dedications or roadway construction ordered by that municipality against fees due hereunder because of improvements constructed outside of the boundaries of the municipality.

(7) In the event fee schedules are subsequently changed to reflect increases or decreases in construction costs or other relevant factors, then a feepayer may request a recalculation of credits to fairly reflect such changed circumstances.

(8) Determinations made by the County Administrator pursuant to the credit provisions of this section may be appealed to the Board of County Commissioners by filing a written request with the County Administrator with ten (10) days of the County Administrator's determination.

14. Review. To assure the continued relevancy of the impact fee charges, the ordinance should provide for a periodic review of the impact fees. The ordinance should provide for the future review and update of the underlying construction costs and demographic data *upon which the impact fees are based. **An impact fee ordinance may provide for the appointment of an impact fee review task force prior to the periodic review and update of the impact fee as provided for in the ordinance.** Some local governments establish such a task force prior to the imposition of a new impact fee.*

Section Fourteen: Review.

The fees specified in Section Seven (A) shall be reviewed by the Board of County Commissioners at least once each fiscal biennium.

*15. Penalty Provision. An impact fee ordinance may include a provision that an uncollected impact fee operates **as a lien** against the property until the impact fee is paid.*

Section Fifteen: Penalty Provision.

A violation of this ordinance shall be prosecuted in the same manner as misdemeanors are prosecuted and upon conviction the violator shall be punishable according to law; however, in addition to or in lieu of any criminal prosecution ** County shall have the power to sue in civil court to enforce the provisions of this ordinance.

16. Severability. Lengthy ordinances with numerous distinct provisions may provide that in the event a portion of the ordinance is found unlawful, the remainder of it is to be considered valid, and the unlawful portion is to be deemed severed.

Section Sixteen: Severability.

If any section, phrase, sentence or portion of this ordinance is for any reason held invalid or unconstitutional by any court of competent jurisdiction, such portion shall be deemed a separate, distinct and independent provision, and such holding shall not affect the validity of the remaining portions thereof.

1. **Effective Date**. An impact fee ordinance typically provides an effective date for the imposition of the fees so that the fees apply to new development at a date certain in the future.

2. **Notice Requirements**. Notice requirements are imbedded in state laws governing ordinance promulgation for local governments.

Section Seventeen: Effective Date.

This ordinance shall become effective on .

APPENDIX 14B
CITY OF CANTON, GEORGIA, ROAD IMPACT FEE ORDINANCE

City of Canton, Georgia, Road Impact Fee Ordinance
ROAD DEVELOPMENT
IMPACT FEE ORDINANCE
**AMENDMENT TO THE CITY OF
CANTON CODE OF ORDINANCES
ORDINANCE NO. _____**

AN AMENDMENT TO THE CITY OF CANTON CODE OF ORDINANCES REGARDING ROAD DEVELOP-MENT IMPACT FEES; TO REPEAL CONFLICTING ORDINANCES, AND FOR OTHER PURPOSES.

AN ORDINANCE RELATING TO THE REGULATION OF THE USE AND DEVELOPMENT OF LAND IN THE CITY OF CANTON, GEORGIA; IMPOSING A DEVELOPMENT IMPACT FEE ON LAND DEVELOPMENT IN THE CITY OF CANTON FOR PROVIDING ROAD AND RELATED FACILITIES NECESSITATED BY SUCH NEW DEVELOP-MENT; STATING THE AUTHORITY FOR ADOPTION OF THE ORDINANCE; MAKING LEGISLATIVE FINDINGS; PROVIDING DEFINITIONS; PROVIDING A SHORT TITLE AND APPLICABILITY; PROVIDING INTENTS AND PURPOSES; PROVIDING RULES OF CONSTRUC-TION; PROVIDING DEFINITIONS; PROVIDING FOR THE COMPUTATION OF THE AMOUNT OF THE ROAD DEVELOPMENT IMPACT FEE; PROVIDING FOR THE PAYMENT OF A ROAD DEVELOPMENT IMPACT FEE; PROVIDING FOR ROAD DEVELOPMENT IMPACT FEE SERVICE AREAS; PROVIDING FOR THE ESTABLISH-MENT OF ROAD DEVELOPMENT IMPACT FEE TRUST FUNDS; PROVIDING FOR THE USE OF FUNDS; PRO-VIDING FOR THE REFUND OF FEES PAID; PROVID-ING FOR EXEMPTIONS AND CREDITS; PROVIDING FOR REVIEW OF THE FEE SCHEDULE; PROVIDING FOR APPEALS; PROVIDING A PENALTY PROVISION; PROVIDING FOR SEVERABILITY; PROVIDING A REPEALER; PROVIDING AN EFFECTIVE DATE.

Pursuant to the authority conferred by the Constitution of the State of Georgia, Article 9, Section 2, Paragraph III, and pursuant to Section 1-1-9 of the Code of Ordinances of the City of Canton, the City of Canton hereby amends the following Article for the purpose of promoting the health, safety, morals, convenience, order, prosperity, and the general welfare of the City of Canton, Georgia.

That Article _____ of the City of Canton Code of Ordinances, regarding _________________, is hereby amended to add Sections ___________________, to read as follows:

Section One: Legislative Findings

The City Council of the City of Canton has considered the feasibility of imposing development impact fees and finds, determines and declares that:

A. The Georgia Legislature, through the enactment of the Georgia Development Impact Fee Act, Georgia Code Title 36-71-1 through 36-71-13, has authorized the City of Canton to enact development impact fees;

B. The City of Canton established a Development Impact Fee Advisory Committee pursuant to the Georgia Development Impact Fee Act, Georgia Code Title 36-71-5, and that Committee has served in an advisory capacity and assisted and advised the City of Canton with regard to the development and adoption of this development impact fee ordinance.

C. The City of Canton Comprehensive Plan contains within it Land Use Assumptions, a Road Capital Improvement Element, and the establishment of a level of Service for Road Capital Facilities for the planning horizon to 2015; and the City of Canton Comprehensive Plan has been submitted to the Atlanta Regional Commission and certified by that Commission so as to qualify the City of Canton as a "Qualified Local Government" pursuant to the State of Georgia Planning Act of 1989.

D. The City of Canton must expand its Road system in order to maintain current Road standards if new development is to be accommodated without decreasing current standards. This must be done in order to promote and protect the health, safety, morals, convenience, order, prosperity, and the general welfare of the City of Canton, Georgia;

E. The imposition of development impact fees is a preferred method of ensuring the availability of capital facilities necessary to accommodate new development;

F. Each of the types of land development described in Section Seven hereof, will create demand for the acquisition or expansion of Roads and the construction of Road improvements.

G. The fees established by Section Seven are derived from, are based upon, and do not exceed a proportionate share of the costs of providing additional Roads and Road improvements necessitated by the new land developments on which the fees are levied.

H. The report entitled "The City of Canton, Georgia, Road Impact Fees," dated _________, sets forth a reasonable methodology and analysis for the determination of the development impact of new development on the need for and costs for additional Roads and Road improvements in the City of Canton.

I. The report entitled "The City of Canton, Georgia, Impact Fee Service Areas," dated _______ sets forth a reasonable basis for the establishment of service areas for Road facilities for the City of Canton.

Section Two: Short Title, Authority and Applicability

A. This ordinance shall be known and may be cited as the "The City of Canton Road Development Impact Fee Ordinance."

B. This ordinance shall apply throughout the incorporated area of the City of Canton.

Section Three: Intents and Purposes

A. This ordinance is intended to assist in the implementation of the City of Canton Comprehensive Plan.

B. The purpose of this ordinance is to regulate the use and development of land so as to assure that new development bears a proportionate share of the cost of capital expenditures necessary to provide Roads and Road improvements in the City of Canton.

C. This Ordinance is intended to comply fully with each and every relevant provision of the Georgia Development

Impact Fee Act, Georgia Code Title 36-71-1 through 36-71-13, and shall be interpreted and implemented to so comply.

Section Four: Rules of Construction

A. The provisions of this ordinance shall be liberally construed so as to effectively carry out its purpose to promote and protect the health, safety, morals, convenience, order, prosperity, and the general welfare of the City of Canton, Georgia;

B. For the purposes of administration and enforcement of this ordinance, unless otherwise stated in this ordinance, the following rules of construction shall apply to the text of this ordinance:

1. In case of any difference of meaning or implication between the text of this ordinance and any caption, illustration, summary table, or illustrative table, the text shall control.

2. The word "shall" is always mandatory and not discretionary; the word "may" is permissive.

Table 14B-1
City of Canton, Georgia Development
Impact Fee Schedule

LAND USE TYPE (UNIT)	Fee per FT²
RESIDENTIAL:	
Residential Unit	$0.86
NON-RESIDENTIAL:	
Walk-in Bank per 1,000 FT²	$3.70
Drive-Thru Bank per Lane	$4.86
Mini-Warehouse per 1,000 FT²	$0.27
Hotel/Motel per Room	$0.78
Movie Theatre per 1,000 FT²	$1.86
Church/Synagogue per 1,000 FT²	$0.82
Day Care Center per 1,000 FT²	$1.18
Car Sales 1,000 FT²	$3.55
Quality Restaurant per 1,000 FT²	$3.21
High-Turnover Sit-Down Restaurant per 1,000 FT	$3.79
Offices per 1,000 FT² :	$0.94
Medical Buildings:	
Medical Offices per 1,000 FT²	$2.31
Hospitals per 1,000 FT²	$1.12
Nursing Homes per 1,000 FT²	$0.39
Industrial Buildings:	
Gen. Industrial per 1,000 FT²	$0.13
Warehouse/Storage per 1,000 FT²	$0.09
Commercial/Retail per 1,000 FT²:	$2.13
Pharmacy with Drive-Thru	$2.63
Fast Food Restaurant	$3.69
Service Station per Fueling Station	$0.75
Convenience Retail	$3.30

3. Words used in the present tense shall include the future; and words used in the singular number shall include the plural, and the plural the singular, unless the context clearly indicates the contrary.

4. The phrase "used for" includes "arranged for," "designed for," "maintained for," or "occupied for."

5. The word "person" includes an individual, a corporation, a partnership, an incorporated association, or any other similar entity.

6. Unless the context clearly indicates the contrary, where a regulation involves two (2) or more items, conditions, provisions, or events connected by the conjunction "and," "or" or "either … or," the conjunction shall be interpreted as follows:

a. "And" indicates that all the connected terms, conditions, provisions or events shall apply.

b. "Or" indicates that the connected items, conditions, provisions or events may apply singly or in any combination.

c. "Either … or" indicates that the connected items, conditions, provisions or events shall apply singly but not in combination.

7. The word "includes" shall not limit a term to the specific example but is intended to extend its meaning to all other instances or circumstances of like kind or character.

8. "Impact Fee Administrator" means the municipal official designated by the Mayor to carry out the administration of this ordinance.

Section Five: Definitions

A. "Applicant" is a person applying for the issuance of a building permit.

B. "Building permit" is the approval issued by the City of Canton that authorizes the construction or permanent placement of a building, dwelling or other structure on a site.

C. "Capital Equipment" is buildings and other improvements which increase the service capacity of a public facility all with an expected use life of ten years or more.

D. "Capital improvement" includes planning, land acquisition, site improvements, and capital equipment, but excludes maintenance and operation.

E. "Developer" means any person or legal entity undertaking development.

F. "Development" means any construction or expansion of a building, structure, or use, any change in use of a building or structure, or any change in the use of land, any of which creates additional demand and need for roads and road facilities.

G. "Development approval" means any written authorization from the City of Canton which authorizes the commencement of construction.

H. "Development impact fee" means a payment of money imposed upon development as a condition of development approval to pay for a proportionate share of the cost of Road system improvements needed to serve new growth and development.

I. "Encumber" means to legally obligate by contract or otherwise commit to use by appropriation or other official act of the City of Canton.

J. "Feepayor" means that person who pays a development impact fee or his/her successor in interest. In the absence of any express transfer or assignment of the right or entitlement to any refund of previously paid development impact fees, the right or entitlement shall be deemed "not to run with the land."

K. "Floor area" shall have the same meaning as in the Building Code of the City of Canton.

L. "Living area" shall have the same meaning as in the Building Code of the City of Canton.

M. "Present value" means the current value of past, present, or future payments, contributions or dedications of goods, services, materials, construction, or money.

N. "Project" means a particular development on an identified parcel of land.

O. "Project improvements" means site improvements and facilities that are planned and designed to provide service for a particular development project and that are necessary for the use and convenience of the occupants or users of the project and are not system improvements. The character of the improvement shall control a determination of whether an improvement is a project improvement or system improvement and the physical location of the improvement on site or off site shall not be considered determinative of whether an improvement is a project improvement or a system improvement. If an improvement or facility provides or will provide more than incidental service or facilities capacity to persons other than users or occupants of a particular project, the improvement or facility is a system improvement and shall not be considered a project improvement. No improvement or facility included in a plan for public facilities approved by the governing body of the municipality or county shall be considered a project improvement.

P. "Proportionate share" means that portion of the cost of system improvements which is reasonably related to the service demands and needs of the project.

Q. "Roads and road facilities" may include roads, streets, and bridges, including rights of way, traffic signals, landscaping, and any local components of state or federal highways; as provided in Georgia Development Impact Fee Act, Georgia Code Title 36-71-2(16)(C).

R. "Service area" means a geographic area defined by the City of Canton in which a defined set of public facilities provide service to development within the area. Service areas shall be designated on the basis of sound planning or engineering principles or both.

S. "System improvement costs" means cost incurred to provide additional public facilities capacity needed to serve growth and development for planning, design and construction, land acquisition, land improvement, design and engineering related thereto, including the cost of constructing or reconstructing system improvements or facility expansions, including but not limited to the construction contract price, surveying and engineering fees, related land acquisition costs (including land purchases, court awards and costs, attorneys' fees, and expert witness fees), and expenses incurred for qualified staff or any qualified engineer, planner, architect, landscape architect, or financial consultant for preparing or updating the capital improvement element, and administrative costs, provided that such administrative costs shall not exceed 3 percent of the total amount of development impact fee receipts. Projected interest charges and other finance costs may be included if the development impact fees are to be used for the payment of principal and interest on bonds, notes, or other financial obligations issued by or

on behalf of the municipality or county to finance the capital improvements element but such costs do not include routine and periodic maintenance expenditures, personnel training, and other operating costs.

T. "System improvements" means capital improvements that are public facilities and are designed to provide service to the community at large, in contrast to "project improvements."

Section Six: Imposition of Road Development Impact Fee

A. Any person who, after the effective date of this Ordinance, seeks to develop land within the City of Canton, Georgia, by applying for a building permit is hereby required to pay a Road development impact fee in the manner and amount set forth in this ordinance.

B. No building permit for any activity requiring payment of a development impact fee pursuant to Section Seven of this ordinance shall be issued unless and until the Road development impact fee hereby required has been paid.

Section Seven: Computation of the Amount of Road Development Impact Fee

A. At the option of the applicant, the amount of the Road development impact fee may be determined by the following fee schedule.

The fees set forth above include a 3% charge for administrative expenses.

1. If a building permit is requested for mixed uses, then the fee shall be determined through using the above schedule by apportioning the space committed to uses specified on the schedule.

2. If the type of development activity that a building permit is applied for is not specified on the above fee schedule, the Impact Fee Administrator shall use the fee applicable to the most nearly comparable type of land use on the above fee schedules. The Impact Fee Administrator shall be guided in the selection of a comparable type by the City of Canton Comprehensive Plan, supporting documents of the City of Canton Comprehensive Plan, and the City of Canton Zoning Ordinance. If the Impact Fee Administrator determines that there is no comparable type of land use on the above fee schedule then the Impact Fee Administrator shall determine the appropriate fee by considering demographic or other documentation which is available from State, local and regional authorities.

3. In the case of change of use, redevelopment, or expansion or modification of an existing use which requires the issuance of a building permit, the development impact fee shall be based upon the net positive increase in the development impact fee for the new use as compared to the previous use. The Impact Fee Administrator shall be guided in this determination by the sources listed in (2) above.

B. If an applicant opts not to have the development impact fee determined according to paragraph (A) of this section, then the applicant shall prepare and submit to the Impact Fee Administrator an independent fee calculation study for the land development activity for which a building permit is sought. The documentation submitted shall show the basis upon which the independent fee calculation was made. The Impact Fee Administrator shall consider the documentation submitted by the applicant but is not required to accept such documentation as he/she shall reasonably deem to be inaccurate or not reliable and may, in the alternative, require the applicant to submit additional or different documentation for consideration. If an acceptable independent fee calculation study is not presented, the applicant shall pay Road development impact fees based upon the schedule shown in paragraph (A) of this section. If an acceptable independent fee calculation study is presented, the Impact Fee Administrator may adjust the fee to that appropriate to the particular development. Determinations made by the Impact Fee Administrator pursuant to this paragraph may be appealed to the City Council by filing a written request with the City Manager within ten (10) days of the Impact Fee Administrator's determination.

C. On the request of an applicant, the Impact Fee Administrator shall certify the Road development impact fee schedule or Road development impact fees resulting from an individual assessment, whichever is applicable, and said certification shall establish the applicable development impact fee for a period of 180 days from the date thereof.

Section Eight: Payment of Fee

A. The applicant shall pay the Road development impact fee required by this ordinance to the Impact Fee Administrator or his/her designee prior to the issuance of a building permit.

B. All funds collected shall be properly identified by Road development impact fee service area and promptly transferred for deposit in the appropriate Road Development Impact Fee Trust Fund to be held in separate accounts as determined in Section Ten of this ordinance and used solely for the purposes specified in this ordinance.

Section Nine: Road Development Impact Fee Service Areas

There are hereby established one (1) Road Development Impact Fee Service Areas; which shall cover the entire incorporated area of the City of Canton.

Section Ten: Road Development Impact Fee Trust Funds Established

A. There is hereby established one (1) Road Development Impact Fee Trust Fund, for the Road Development Impact Fee Service Area established by Section Nine of this Ordinance.

B. Development Impacts fees placed in this fund shall be maintained in an interest bearing account.

C. All Road development impact fees collected shall be promptly deposited in the Road Development Impact Fee Trust Fund and maintained there, including interest thereon, until withdrawn pursuant to this ordinance.

D. Funds withdrawn from these accounts must be used in accordance with the provisions of Section Eleven of this ordinance.

Section Eleven: Use of Funds

A. Funds collected from Road development impact fees shall be used solely for the purpose of acquiring and/or making capital improvements to Roads under the jurisdiction of the City of Canton, Cherokee County, or the State of Georgia, and shall not be used for maintenance or operations.

B. Funds shall be used exclusively for acquisitions, expansions, or capital improvements within the Road Development Impact Fee Service Area from which the funds were collected.

C. In the event that bonds or similar debt instruments are issued for advanced provision of capital facilities for which Road development impact fees may be expended, development impact fees may be used to pay debt service on such bonds or similar debt instruments to the extent that the

facilities provided are of the type described in paragraphs A and B.

D. In the event a developer enters into an agreement with the City to construct, fund or contribute system improvements such that the amount of the credit created by such construction, funding or contribution is in excess of the development impact fee otherwise due, the developer shall be reimbursed for such excess construction funding or contribution from development impact fees paid by other development located in the service area which is benefited by such improvements.

E. At least once each fiscal period the Impact Fee Administrator shall present to the City Council a report describing the amount of development impact fees collected, encumbered and used, and a proposed capital improvement program for Roads, assigning funds, including any accrued interest, from the several Road Development Impact Fee Trust Funds to specific Road improvement projects and related expenses. Monies, including any accrued interest, not assigned in any fiscal period shall be retained in the same Road Development Impact Fee Trust Funds until the next fiscal period except as provided by the refund provisions of this ordinance.

F. Funds may be used to provide refunds as described in Section Twelve.

G. Funds shall be considered expended on a first in, first out basis.

Section Twelve: Refund of Fees Paid

A. If a building permit expires without commencement of construction, and then the feepayor shall be entitled to a refund, without interest, of the development impact fee paid as a condition for its issuance except that the City shall retain three percent (3%) of the fee to offset a portion of the costs of collection and refund. The feepayor must submit an application for such a refund to the Impact Fee Administrator within 30 days of the expiration of the permit.

B. In the event that development impact fees have not been not expended or encumbered by the end of the calendar quarter immediately following six (6) years from the date the development impact fee was paid, the Impact Fee Administrator shall provide written notice of entitlement to a refund to feepayors or their successors in interest.

Funds not expended or encumbered by the end of the calendar quarter immediately following six (6) years from the date road development impact fee was paid shall, upon application of the then current landowner, they must returned to such feepayor with interest that is a pro rata share of the interest earned by the fund, provided that the feepayor submits an application for the refund to the Impact Fee Administrator within one year of the expiration of the six year period or the publication of the notice of entitlement, whichever is later. Refunds shall be made to the feepayor within 60 days after it is determined that a sufficient proof of claim for as refund has been made.

Section Thirteen: Exemptions and Credits

A. The following shall be exempted from payment of the development impact fee:

1. Alterations or expansion of an existing building where the use and size are not changed.

2. The construction of accessory buildings or structures.

3. The replacement of a building or structure with a new building or structure of the same size and use.

Any claim of exemption must be made no later than the time of application for a building permit. Any claim not so made shall be deemed waived.

B. Credits:

1. Road land and/or capital improvements may be offered by the applicant as total or partial payment of the required development impact fee. The applicant must request a Road development impact fee credit. If the Impact Fee Administrator accepts such an offer the credit shall be determined and provided in the following manner:

a. Credit for the dedication of land shall be valued at:

i. 115% of the most recent assessed value by the Property Appraiser, or

ii. By fair market value established by private appraisers acceptable to the City. Credit for the dedication of Road land shall be provided when the property has been conveyed at no charge to, and accepted by, the City in a manner satisfactory to the Impact Fee Administrator.

b. Applicants for credit for construction of Road improvements shall submit acceptable engineering drawings and specifications, and construction cost estimates to the Impact Fee Administrator. The Impact Fee Administrator shall determine credit for construction based upon either these cost estimates or upon alternative engineering criteria and construction cost estimates if the Impact Fee Administrator determines that such estimates submitted by the applicant are either unreliable or inaccurate. The Impact Fee Administrator shall provide the applicant with a letter or certificate setting forth the dollar amount of the credit, the reason for the credit, and the legal description or other adequate description of the project or development to which the credit may be applied. The applicant must sign and date a duplicate copy of such letter or certificate indicating his/her agreement to the terms of the letter or certificate and return such signed document to the Impact Fee Administrator before credit will be given. The failure of the applicant to sign, date, and return such document within 60 days shall nullify the credit.

c. Except as provided in subparagraph (d), Credit against development impact fees otherwise due will not be provided until:

i. The construction is completed and accepted by the City, the County, or the State, whichever is applicable; and

ii. A suitable maintenance and warranty bond is received and approved by the Impact Fee Administrator, when applicable.

d. Credit may be provided before completion of specified Road improvements if adequate assurances are given by the applicant that the standards set out above will be met and if the applicant posts security as provided below for the costs of such construction. Security in the form of a performance bond, irrevocable letter of credit or escrow agreement shall be posted with and approved by the Impact Fee Administrator in an amount determined by the Impact Fee Administrator. If the road construction project will not be completed within one (1) year of the acceptance of the offer by the Impact Fee Administrator, the amount of the security shall be increased by ten percent (10%) compounded, for each year of the life of the security.

e. The road facility for which credit is sought is consistent with the Road Element of the City of Canton's Comprehensive Plan, and

f. The request complies with the security provisions set forth in (B)(1)(c) of this Section.

2. Any claim for credit must be made no later than the time of application for a building permit. Any claim not so made shall be deemed waived.

3. Credits shall not be transferable from one project or development to another unless so provided in a development impact fee credit agreement.

Section Fourteen: Appeals

A. Any Applicant or Feepayor aggrieved by a decision of the Impact Fee Administrator made pursuant to this Ordinance shall have the right to appeal to the Mayor and City Council. Prior to any such appeal the aggrieved Applicant or Feepayor shall file a request for reconsideration with the Impact Fee Administrator who shall act upon such request within fifteen (15) days.

B. All appeals shall be taken within fifteen (15) days of the Impact Fee Administrator's decision on the request for reconsideration by filing with the Impact Fee Administrator a notice of appeal specifying the grounds therefore. The Impact Fee Administrator shall forthwith transmit to the Mayor and City Council all papers constituting the record upon which the action appealed from is taken. The Mayor and City Council shall thereafter establish a reasonable date and time for a hearing on the appeal, give due notice thereof, and decide the same within a reasonable period of time following the hearing. Any Applicant or Feepayor taking an appeal shall have the right to appear at the hearing, to present evident and may be represented by counsel.

C. An Applicant may pay a Road Development Impact Fee under protest to obtain a building permit and by making such payment shall not be estopped from;

1. Exercising the right of appeal provided for in this Section or

2. Receiving a refund of any amount deemed to have been illegally collected.

Section Fifteen: Review and Automatic Update of Fee Schedule

A. The fee schedule contained in Section Seven (A) shall be reviewed by the City Council at least once each fiscal biennium.

B. Unless otherwise directed by the City Council, the impact fee schedules shown in Section Seven A above shall be adjusted by the Impact Fee Administrator in May of each calendar year based on the methodology described in paragraph C of this section. Any adjustments to the impact fee schedules, made pursuant to this section, shall be effective the following first day of October.

C. The base for computing any adjustment is the January Highway and Street Construction Cost Index published by the United States Department of Commerce, Bureau of Labor Statistics, Series Identification # PCVBHWY. The percentage change in the impact fee shall be equal to the percentage change in the Highway and Street Construction Cost Index from the base year to the current year. For the purpose of this Section the initial index to be referenced is January of the last year when the impact fees were updated with cost or demographic data.

D. If the index is changed so that the base year is different, the index shall be converted in accordance with the conversion factor published by the United States Department of Labor, Bureau of Labor Statistics.

If the Highway and Street Construction Cost Index is discontinued or revised, the Construction Cost Index published by McGraw-Hill or such other index or computation with which it is replaced shall be used in order to obtain substantially the same result as would be obtained if the Highway and Street Construction Cost Index had not been discontinued or revised.

Section Sixteen: Penalty Provision

A violation of this ordinance shall be prosecuted in the same manner as misdemeanors are prosecuted and upon conviction the violator shall be punishable according to law; however, in addition to or in lieu of any criminal prosecution the City of Canton shall have the power to sue in civil court to enforce the provisions of this ordinance.

Section Seventeen: Severability

If any section, phrase, sentence or portion of this ordinance is for any reason held invalid or unconstitutional by any court of competent jurisdiction, such portion shall be deemed a separate, distinct and independent provision, and such holding shall not affect the validity of the remaining portions thereof.

Section Eighteen: Repealer

Any ordinances covering the subject matter contained in this Ordinance are hereby repealed and all ordinances or parts of ordinances inconsistent with the provisions of this Ordinance are hereby repealed.

Section Nineteen: Effective Date

This Ordinance shall take effect from and after the ______ day of ________________, 2008.

15

Development Impact Fee Administrative Code

Many local governments that adopt proportionate-share development impact fee programs find it helpful to also adopt administrative rules in regard to the administration of their programs. From the standpoint of the local government, comprehensive development fee administrative codes are particularly helpful as guides for their impact fee administrators and other staff members charged with implementation of their fee programs.

When a jurisdiction first adopts an impact fee program, the guidelines are almost essential. The same can be said for when there are newly appointed staff and administrators, even after the local government has had considerable experience with collecting and spending impact fees. Administrative codes are also valuable for members of the development community who will be paying impact fees. Having the "rules" available in advance helps them with planning and efficiency. It also helps guarantee equal treatment vis-a-vis other developers in regard to the local government's implementation of its impact fee programs.

The content of impact fee administrative codes varies widely but should focus on the procedures contained in the relevant ordinances and state statutory provisions (if any). Codes should include at least most of the following:

- The procedures for collecting impact fees and the payment schedule;
- The procedures for determining what development activities are required to pay impact fees;
- The formulae used to determine the amount of the fees through both fee schedules and independent fee determinations;
- Expenditure of impact fee funds;
- Credits;
- Refunds;
- Exemptions; and
- Appeals.

It is also helpful to include or attach forms that the feepayor will need to submit per the ordinance.

Although local government law and practice on point differ considerably from jurisdiction to jurisdiction, local governments may want to consider whether they should adopt an administrative code for impact fees as an ordinance or simply by resolution. In some states, there may be strict notice and hearing requirements for the adoption of an ordinance but considerably fewer formalities required for the adoption of a resolution. In addition, administrative codes adopted by ordinance may have more binding legal effect than resolution-adopted codes, but the trade-off can be that the latter are easier to revise and amend than the former.

The code in Appendix 15A may be considered a model since it is the product of the authors' experience in drafting such codes since the 1970s. It is the pending revised administrative code for the City of Canton, Georgia. The authors consider it one of the more easily adapted and comprehensive codes for most jurisdictions and most impact fee programs. Of course, careful attention should be paid to variations in state statutes and local ordinances.

APPENDIX 15A
SAMPLE IMPACT FEE ADMINISTRATIVE CODE

I. INTENT

The following guidelines and procedures shall guide staff in the administration of City of Canton Code of Ordinances, Chapter 100, Article IV, Section 110-101 through 129, City of Canton Park, Recreation and Open Space Development Impact Fee Ordinance (hereinafter referred to as Park, Recreation and Open Space Impact Fee Ordinance), Article V, Section 110-130 through 145, City of Canton Police Protection Development Impact Fee Impact Fee Ordinance (hereinafter referred to as Police Protection Impact Fee Ordinance) and Chapter 110, Article VII, Section 110 through 300, City of Canton Fire Protection Impact Fee Ordinance (hereinafter Fire Impact Fee Ordinance), Chapter 110, Article VI, Section 175 through 190, City of Canton Road Impact Fee Ordinance (hereinafter Road Impact Fee Ordinance). This Administrative Code elaborates upon the administrative directions contained in the impact fee ordinances and is intended to be used in tandem with those ordinances in their implementation and administration.

Tables and forms are provided for use in determining the amount of the impact fees for each land development activity. Terminology used herein corresponds to the definitions of words or phrases in the Georgia Development Impact Fee Act and in the City of Canton Park, Recreation and Open Space Impact Fee Ordinance, the Police Protection Impact Fee Ordinance, the Fire Protection Impact Fee Ordinance, and the Road Impact Fee Ordinance.

II. ADMINISTRATIVE ORGANIZATION & RESPONSIBILITY

A. Impact Fee Administrator

The Impact Fee Administrator, as identified in the Official City Organizational Chart, is designated to carry out the general administration of all impact fees enacted by the City of Canton. The Impact Fee Administrator shall have the responsibility to carry out the following:

1. When no equivalent type of land use is present in either the fee schedules or in Attachment A, or is a previously determined miscellaneous land use, the Impact Fee Administrator shall establish a fee applicable to the most nearly equivalent type of land use on the fee schedule.

2. When requested, the Impact Fee Administrator shall interpret the impact fee schedules as they may apply to a particular development using the procedures described in the appropriate impact fee ordinance and in this Administrative Code.

3. When requested, the Impact Fee Administrator shall certify the impact fees applicable to a particular development using the procedures described in the appropriate impact fee ordinance and in this Administrative Code.

4. With respect to an individual fee calculation, the Impact Fee Administrator shall:

a) Conduct a pre-application meeting with the applicant and representatives of appropriate departments of the city,

b) Review the individual fee calculation study for sufficiency, methodology, technical accuracy and findings, and

c) Establish the amount of the impact fee as a result of the independent study based on the procedures described in the Ordinance and in this Administrative Code.

5. The Impact Fee Administrator shall determine exemptions, as delineated in Section X of this Code, from a requirement to pay an impact fee.

6. The Impact Fee Administrator shall determine the availability of and the amount of any refund of impact fees as delineated in Section IX of this Code.

7. The Impact Fee Administrator shall calculate additional impact fees due in the event of change of use, redevelopment, or modifications of an existing use.

B. Other Departments

Other departments and offices of the City of Canton shall provide advice, information, or other such services upon the request of the Impact Fee Administrator.

III. IMPOSITION OF IMPACT FEES

A. Feepayer

Any person who, after the effective date of the appropriate impact fee ordinance, seeks to develop land by applying to the City of Canton for any of the following permits shall be required to pay an impact fee in the manner and amount set forth in the relevant Ordinance and in this Administrative Code:

1. The issuance or extension of a building permit.

2. The issuance or extension of a permit that would allow the construction or installation of a structure, including a mobile home.

3. The issuance or extension of a permit that would allow the installation or placement of a recreational vehicle.

Person shall include individuals, corporations, partnerships, proprietorships, legal entities, public authorities, units of government, non-profit organizations, and religious organizations.

[See Chapters V and X of this Administrative Code for exceptions and exemptions to the imposition of impact fees.]

B. Payment Due

1. **General**. Impact fees shall be paid prior to the issuance of a building permit for any activity requiring payment of an impact fee. All payments shall be made in the following manner:

a) Payment by personal or business check, cashier's check, or money order made payable to the City of Canton.

b) All payments are to be made at offices of the City of Canton.

2. **Invalid Payment**. In the event the payment of impact fees subsequently proves to be invalid due to insufficient funds, improper execution, or for any other reason, then the following actions shall be taken:

a) Any building permit issued based upon an invalid payment shall be void.

b) No further building permits, construction permits, inspections or Certificate of Use and Occupancy (C.O.) shall be issued by the City of Canton until the required impact fee is paid.

c) The Impact Fee Administrator shall, within 30 days of detection of such a deficiency, notify the feepayer, the contractor, and the property owner by certified mail, return receipt requested, that:

(1) An impact fee amount is due by valid payment immediately upon receipt of said notice;

(2) Permits, inspections or certificates shall not be issued until the amount is paid and, if not paid within 30 days, the Impact Fee Administrator shall have authority to instruct the Canton Building Department to stop all construction on the site of said building or construction until the payment is received;

d) The amount due shall be the amount of the impact fees plus the amount charged by the bank for the dishonored payment plus a service charge as established by the City of Canton.

3. Non-Payment at Time of Issuance of Building Permit. The issuance of a building permit without the collection of impact fees due shall not relieve the feepayer from the obligation to pay the fees and the City shall be entitled to collect the impact fees that should have been paid. A certificate of occupancy shall not be issued until the impact fees are paid.

4. Performance Bonds, Letters of Credit, etc. In the event the feepayer has received approval from the Impact Fee Administrator for credits for construction and the credits are provided before completion of the improvements, the following requirements shall be met:

a) The feepayer shall submit to the Impact Fee Administrator on appropriate forms a Surety Performance Bond or an automatically renewable, irrevocable Letter of Credit (Cash Performance Bond) (both hereinafter referred to as Bond) issued by a company registered in or licensed to do business in the State of Georgia, for an amount equal to 115% of the full amount of the impact fees otherwise due, and payable to the City of Canton;

b) The bond shall be reviewed and approved by the City Attorney prior to acceptance of the bond by the Impact Fee Administrator.

c) A Bond or Letter of Credit, pursuant to paragraph a. above, shall be automatically renewable unless notice of intent to cancel or not to renew is given to the Impact Fee Administrator not later than 90 days prior to the renewal date. In the event of a notice to cancel or of intent not to renew, the Impact Fee Administrator shall be entitled to declare a default and collect the full amount of the Bond. In the event the City has assigned its rights in such security to some other entity, then that entity shall be responsible for this action.

C. Determination of Fee

1. General. The amount of the impact fee shall be determined by the Impact Fee Administrator, who shall receive assistance from other departments when necessary and appropriate. The Impact Fee Administrator shall determine the amount of the fees due, whether the method of determination is based on the fee schedule contained in the appropriate impact fee ordinance or by independent fee calculation study. The calculation of exemptions, refunds, and credits, and the determination of the net impact fees due shall also be the responsibility of the Impact Fee Administrator with the assistance of appropriate City of Canton departments.

2. Credits. In lieu of monetary payment, up to 100% of impact fees due may be paid by the use of credits (see Chapter XI-Credits). However, park credits may be used only for the payment of park impact fees, police protection credits may be used only for the payment of police protection impact fees, fire protection credits may only be used for the payment of fire protection impact fees, and road credits may only be used for the payment of road impact fees.

D. Prepayment of Impact Fees

The Impact Fee Administrator may accept the prepayment of impact fees prior to the application for a building permit. If the building for which a building permit is requested is of a different size from that on which impact fees were prepaid, the Impact Fee Administrator shall refund any overpayment based on the fee schedules in effect at the time of the prepayment or collect any underpayment attributable to the difference in size, using the impact fee schedules in effect at the time of the prepayment. If the building for which a building permit is requested is of a different use, the impact fee administrator shall refund or collect any difference between the impact fees due using the impact fee schedules in effect at the time of the application for the building permit less the amount of the prepayment.

E. Expiration of Building Permits

1. If a permit expires, is revoked, or is voluntarily surrendered and is, therefore, voided and no construction or improvement of land has commenced, then the feepayer shall be entitled to a refund, without interest, of 95% of the impact fees which were paid as a condition for its issuance. The City shall retain 5% of the fees to offset the costs of collection and refund. The feepayer must submit an application for such a refund to the Impact Fee Administrator within 30 days of the expiration of the permit. In the case of an expired permit which was obtained in whole or in part by the use of credits, only that portion not paid by credits may be refunded, and it is from this part that the 5% administrative fee shall be deducted.

2. If a refund has been received by the feepayer, the feepayer must pay the appropriate impact fee if he/she reapplies for a permit. Conversely, if a permit expires and no refund has been issued, a feepayer will not have to pay the fee again if he/she reapplies for the permit on the same lot, parcel or tract unless the use or size of the structure has changed and then the amount due would be the change in the amount of the fee based upon the new structure as contrasted with the original.

3. A credit for previous payment of an impact fee must be requested by the feepayer. Any exemption or credit not so requested at the time of reapplication shall be deemed waived by the feepayer.

4. A refund of the impact fee shall not be granted if the permit expires and construction has commenced. In this case, the feepayer will not have to pay an impact fee if he/she reapplies for a permit. In any case of reapplication, the provisions of part IV.G-Change of Use shall apply.

5. The feepayer shall be responsible for requesting any credits or refunds.

F. Park, Recreational and Open Space Improvements Constructed for Private Use

It is common for developments to contain components of park, recreational or open spaces within a development and for the private use of the residents or occupants of that development. If these private improvements meet a public park, recreational or open space need, that provision of private park, recreational or open spaces may be accorded credit against impact fees otherwise due. See Chapter XI – Credits.

G. Private Security

No credit will be given against police protection impact fees for the provision of private security services or facilities. See Chapter XI – Credits.

H. Private Fire Protection or Rescue

No credit will be given against fire protection impact fees for the provision of private fire protection or rescue services or facilities. See Chapter XI – Credits.

IV. DETERMINATION OF FEES BASED ON FEE SCHEDULES

A. Payment from Schedule

At the option of the feepayer, the amount of the fees can be determined from the schedules set forth in the relevant ordinances as adjusted pursuant to the ordinance provisions for indexing.

If the type of development activity is not specified in the fee schedules the Impact Fee Administrator shall apply the fee of the most nearly equivalent type of land use on the fee schedules as described in the next paragraph.

The Impact Fee Administrator shall be guided in the selection of a comparable type by the City of Canton Comprehensive Plan and the land development regulations of the City of Canton, including but not limited to the zoning ordinance and subdivision regulations, and by the most recent edition of the publication entitled *Trip Generation*, published by the Institute of Transportation Engineers and other related publications by that entity.

If a feepayer shall opt not to have the impact fee determined according to the fee schedule or determined administratively, then the feepayer shall prepare and submit an individual fee calculation study in accordance with the appropriate impact fee ordinances (see Chapter XIV).

In the event that the sub-classification of a particular use of land into the classification established by the Ordinance is unclear, the Standard Industrial Classification Manual, as published by the Superintendent of Documents, US Government Printing Office, latest edition, shall be used as the final authority.

B. Residential Living Area

The amount of the impact fee for residential structures shall be based on the floor area of the structure that is designed to be provided with heat and/or air-conditioning and not on the gross floor area of the structure.

C. Non-Residential Gross Floor Area

The amount of the impact fee for non-residential structures shall be based on the gross floor area of a building. Gross floor area refers to the total area of all floors of a building as measured to the exterior walls and including halls, stairways, elevator shafts, attached garages, porches and balconies.

D. Mixed Use Development

If a development includes both residential and non-residential uses, the impact fees are to be assessed for each use based on the fee schedule and the results added together

E. Mixed Use Structures

If a structure includes both residential and non-residential uses, the impact fees are to be assessed for each use individually based on the relevant fee schedule and the results added together

F. Shell Permit

Builders will often apply for a building permit to construct the "shell" of a building. Remodeling permits would be issued later to finish construction of the interior of the structure. The impact fee shall be paid prior to the issuance of the building permit for construction of the shell. The amount of the fee should be based on the intended land use as described by the builder. If a builder applies for a "shell" permit and the intended land use is not known, the impact fees shall be assessed based on that land use which generates the greatest impact and is allowed under the existing zoning for the lot or parcel. If it is found during review of the application for a remodeling permit that the actual land use differs from the intended land use as described by the builder, a determination shall be made as to whether or not an additional impact fee is due based on the procedures for Change of Use. If so, the additional impact fee shall be paid prior to the issuance of a new building permit for the completion of the shell. If it is determined that there has been an over-payment of impact fees, a refund would become available pursuant to Chapter IX.F of this Administrative Code.

If a shell permit was issued prior to the effective date of the appropriate impact fee ordinance and left unfinished, no impact fee shall be assessed for permits issued to finish the structure. Subsequent change of use, redevelopment, or modification of the structure may be subject to an impact fee based on the procedures for Change of Use.

G. Change of Use

In the case of a change of use, redevelopment, or modification of an existing use which requires the issuance of a building permit, the impact fee shall be based upon the net increase in the impact fees for the new use as compared to the previous use. The amount of the impact fees that is due as a result of the change in land use shall be determined at the time the feepayer applies for a building permit. The impact fees shall be paid prior to the issuance of a building permit for construction or remodeling.

Previous land use shall be the lawful land use physically existing on the effective date of the Ordinance or the current lawful land use. The feepayer shall furnish all documentation required by the Impact Fee Administrator to determine the previous use.

Should the change of use, redevelopment, or modification result in a net decrease in the impact, no refunds or credits for impact fees previously paid shall be made.

If the change of land use does not require the issuance of a building permit, then there shall be no requirement to pay an impact fee.

H. Accessory Uses

Generally, no fee shall be assessed for accessory land uses, such as a clubhouse or tennis court in an apartment complex, unless it can be established by the Impact Fee Administrator that the land use serves as an individual attraction. However, structures that meet the definition of a "dwelling" in the Canton Building Code are not exempted as accessory uses.

I. Mobile Homes

When a person applies for a permit that would authorize the installation of a mobile home, the feepayer may request a determination by the Impact Fee Administrator as to whether or not a mobile home (or other dwelling unit) was legally in place on that lot, parcel, or space prior to the effective date of the Ordinance. If so, no impact fee shall be assessed for installation of the mobile home.

An exemption will be granted if it can be documented that an impact fee has been paid previously for a mobile home on that same lot, parcel, or space. Documentation to be used by the Impact Fee Administrator may include utility bills for the period of time in question or tax records.

J. House Moves and Mobile Home Moves

Impact fees shall be assessed for structures or mobile homes moved from one location to another unless the structure or unit being moved is a replacement of an equivalent use at the new location (for further discussion of equivalent uses see Chapter IX-Exemptions). If the structure or mobile home so moved is replaced by an equivalent use at the old location, no impact fee shall be due for the replacement use. In every case, the burden of proving past payment of impact fees, exemption, or equivalency of use rests with the feepayer.

K. Recreational Vehicles (RV's)

Reference to "recreational vehicles" refers to the recreational vehicle site which has been permitted by an applicable development approval. The development of an RV site, not the issuance of a permit, is the relevant regulatory issue for this Administrative Code and the administration of the impact fee. Recreational vehicle development approval should contain a condition of approval providing for payment of the impact fee. The impact fee shall be paid according to this condition of approval and the following provisions:

1. No impact fees shall be assessed for "move in" of a recreational vehicle in an RV park developed prior to the effective date of the Ordinance or that has paid an impact fee.

2. RV's located outside of RV parks shall be treated as mobile homes. RV owners who apply for a permit, etcetera, shall pay the impact fees at the same rate as a mobile home and are entitled to the same exemptions as mobile home owners.

L. Model Homes

Model homes on residentially zoned land shall be charged residential impact fees. Model homes on non-residentially zoned land shall be charged non-residential impact fees.

M. Replacement of Existing Buildings

See Chapter X-Exemptions.

N. Facilities for Private Recreational Use

1. Certain structures limited exclusively to private recreational use and which are internal to a particular development and, therefore, have no park, recreational or open space impact, e.g., a private clubhouse, may be exempt from the requirement to pay a park, recreation and open space impact fee. Feepayers wishing to claim this exemption must file for the exemption pursuant to Chapter IX of this Administrative Code.

2. Structures limited exclusively to private recreational use are not exempt from payment of the police protection, fire protection, and road impact fees unless exempt as provided in Section IX of this Administrative Code.

O. Interpretation of Fee Schedules

Individuals may request an interpretation of the impact fee schedules as they may apply to their developments. The Impact Fee Administrator shall determine the fee as follows (see Attachment B, Impact Fee Calculation Form):

Park, Recreation and Open Space Impact Fees. Using the park, recreation and open space statistics from the City's Comprehensive Plan and supporting documents, the impact fees from the impact fee schedules and applying the following formula:

RESIDENTIAL PARKS, RECREATION AND OPEN SPACE IMPACT FEE = SQUARE FEET OF LIVING AREA x RESIDENTIAL PARKS, RECREATION AND OPEN SPACE NET COST PER FOOT

NON-RESIDENTIAL PARKS, RECREATION AND OPEN SPACE IMPACT = SQUARE FEET OF GROSS AREA x PARKS, RECREATION AND OPEN SPACE NON-RESIDENTIAL NET COST PER FOOT

Police Protection Impact Fees. Using the police protection statistics from the City's Comprehensive Plan and supporting documents and applying the formula:

RESIDENTIAL POLICE PROTECTION IMPACT FEE = SQUARE FEET OF LIVING AREA x POLICE PROTECTION RESIDENTIAL NET COST PER FOOT

NON-RESIDENTIAL POLICE PROTECTION IMPACT FEE = SQUARE FEET OF GROSS AREA x POLICE PROTECTION NON-RESIDENTIAL NET COST PER FOOT

Fire Protection Impact Fees. Using the fire protection and rescue statistics from the City's Comprehensive Plan and supporting documents and applying the formula:

RESIDENTIAL FIRE PROTECTION IMPACT FEE = SQUARE FEET OF LIVING AREA x FIRE PROTECTION RESIDENTIAL NET COST PER FOOT

NON-RESIDENTIAL FIRE PROTECTION IMPACT FEE = SQUARE FEET OF GROSS AREA x FIRE PROTECTION NON-RESIDENTIAL NET COST PER FOOT

Road Impact Fees. Using the road statistics from the City's Comprehensive Plan and supporting documents and applying the formula:

RESIDENTIAL ROAD FEE = SQUARE FEET OF LIVING AREA x RESIDENTIAL ROAD NET COST PER FOOT

NON-RESIDENTIAL ROAD FEE = SQUARE FEET OF GROSS AREA x NON-RESIDENTIAL ROAD NET COST PER FOOT

If the feepayer disagrees with the interpretation of the impact fee schedules, the feepayer may prepare an individual fee calculation study in accordance with this Administrative Code and the relevant impact fee ordinance.

P. Miscellaneous Land Use Types

The Impact Fee Administrator shall maintain a list of the fees determined administratively for miscellaneous land use types.

V. AUTOMATIC INDEXING OF IMPACT FEE SCHEDULES

Unless the City Council directs that the several impact fee schedules not be increased, the impact fee schedules shown in Section Seven A above shall be adjusted by the Impact Fee Administrator in July each calendar year based on the methodology described below. Any adjustments to the impact fee schedules, made pursuant to this section, shall be effective the following the first business day of October. The Impact Fee Administrator shall post notice of a change to impact fee schedules on or before the first business day of September.

The base for computing any adjustment to an impact fee schedule is the May index for the prior calendar year and the May index for the current calendar year. The percentage change in the impact fee shall be equal to the percentage change in the appropriate index from the prior year to the current year. The formulae are:

ADJUSTED IMPACT FEES = EXISTING IMPACT FEE x (MAY INDEX CURRENT YEAR / MAY INDEX PRIOR YEAR)

A. Park, Police and Fire Impact Fee Schedules

The automatic indexing of the Parks, Recreation and Open Space Impact Fee Schedule, the Police Protection Impact Fee Schedule, and the Fire Protection Impact Fee Schedule shall employ the Construction Cost Index published by McGraw-Hill. If the Construction Cost Index published by McGraw-Hill is discontinued or revised so that it is no longer applicable, the Consumers Price Index or such other index or computation with which it is replaced shall be used in order to obtain substantially the same result as would be obtained if the Construction Cost Index had not been discontinued or revised.

B. Road Impact Fee Schedule

The automatic indexing of the Road Impact Fee Schedule shall employ the Highway and Street Construction Cost Index published by the United States Department of Commerce, Bureau of Labor Statistics, Series Identification # PCVBHWY. If the Highway and Streets Construction Cost Index is discontinued or revised so that it is no longer applicable, the Consumers Price Index or such other index or computation with which it is replaced shall be used in order to obtain substantially the same result as would be obtained if the Highway and Street Construction Cost Index had not been discontinued or revised.

VI. INDIVIDUAL FEE CALCULATION

A. Option of the Feepayer

If a feepayer shall opt not to have impact fees determined according to the fee schedule in Chapter IV, then the feepayer shall prepare and submit an individual fee calculation in accordance with this Administrative Code and the appropriate impact fee ordinance.

The utilization of this option by the feepayer shall not exempt him/her from paying the impact fee prior to the issuance of a permit.

B. Notice of Intent by Feepayer

The feepayer shall inform the Impact Fee Administrator of his/her intent to utilize an individual fee calculation. The Impact Fee Administrator shall then schedule a pre-application meeting with the applicant.

C. Pre-Application Meeting

Before beginning the individual fee calculation study, the feepayer or his/her representative shall be given the opportunity to attend a pre-application meeting with the Impact Fee Administrator. The purpose of the pre-application meeting is to discuss the procedures of the individual fee calculation study, the methodology to be employed, and the standards to be met.

Results, conclusions, and agreements reached at the pre-application meeting regarding methodology, required forms or documentation, or procedures, which may not constitute a waiver of ordinance provisions, shall be placed in writing by the Impact Fee Administrator. A copy of this memorandum shall be sent to the applicant. The agreements set out in the letter will expire in 30 days unless the applicant acknowledges receipt and acceptance of the agreements in writing, to the Impact Fee Administrator, within those 30 days.

The applicant may waive the pre-application meeting. Any applicant who waives this pre-application meeting has waived his/her right to administratively raise methodological or procedural issues at a subsequent time.

D. Guidelines

1. The purpose of the individual calculation study is to measure the impact of the development in question on the park, recreation and open space system, the police protection system, or the fire protection system of the City of Canton.

2. An individual calculation study must address the expected impact of the development over the projected life of the structures within the development. Any claim that the use or occupancy of the structures within the development will be different from normal use or occupancy must be supported by deed restrictions, recorded restrictive covenants or other appropriate documentation that will support the claim.

3. The individual fee calculation study shall follow the methodologies and formats which are agreed upon during the pre-application meeting and be in accord with any documentation or methodology required by this Administrative Code and the appropriate impact fee ordinance. These standards and requirements are discussed in this Chapter and in Chapter XIV - Individual Fee Calculation Guidelines.

4. The individual fee calculation study shall be prepared and presented by professionals qualified in their respective fields and accepted by the City of Canton. The methodology shall be consistent with best professional practice and support the central claim of the study. The study shall provide all necessary supporting documentation and information. Failure to adhere to best professional standards is a basis for rejection of the study. The applicant's submission must certify that the study complies with best professional practices and this attestation shall be sealed where and when applicable.

5. The applicant shall submit the study to the Impact Fee Administrator. This submission shall begin the 30 day clock referred to below.

E. Sufficiency Determination

1. The Impact Fee Administrator will review the individual fee calculation study for sufficiency, methodology, technical accuracy and findings. The Impact Fee Administrator shall have 30 days to inform the applicant, in writing, of any deficiencies or defects in the study, or to find the study complete and competent. The notice of sufficiency or lack thereof shall be posted certified mail, return receipt requested. In the event that this notice is not given within 30 days, the study shall be considered complete and competent.

2. The 30 day sufficiency review referred to in 1 above shall begin again when a resubmission is received and date stamped by the Impact Fee Administrator. If the study is again found to be deficient, the 30 day clock shall begin once again with the further resubmission of a new or modified study.

3. If the applicant does not respond to the Impact Fee Administrator regarding the finding of deficiency within 30 days of the receipt thereof, the Impact Fee Administrator will consider the individual fee calculation study to be inactive thus requiring a new submission.

F. Determination of Fee

1. The determination of the amount of the applicable impact fee shall be made by the Impact Fee Administrator based on his/her review of a competent and sufficient independent study.

2. If an applicant requests, the Impact Fee Administrator shall certify, as provided in the Georgia Development Impact Fee Statute, Section 36-71-2(h), the impact fees due for a development and said certification shall establish the applicable impact fees for such development for a period of 180 days from the date thereof.

G. Effective Date

The date at which the individual fee calculation study is found to be sufficient, or 30 days after submission if there is no finding, shall be the effective date for any fees established pursuant to an individual fee calculation.

H. Notification of Feepayer and Appeal

Within 30 days of the determination that the study is competent and complete, the Impact Fee Administrator shall notify the feepayer in writing of the acceptance, conditional acceptance, or rejection of the request. If the feepayer disagrees with the findings of the Impact Fee Administrator, the feepayer may appeal the decision pursuant to the provisions of Chapter XII.

I. Application for Permit

It shall be the responsibility of the feepayer, at the time of application for a building permit, to submit a claim for modified impact fees resulting from an approved individual fee calculation study. The feepayer shall present documentation enabling the Impact Fee Administrator to verify this claim.

VII. COLLECTION AND DISPOSITION OF IMPACT FEE

A. Park, Recreation and Open Space Impact Fees.

1. Service Areas. As indicated in Attachment F, there are two (2) Park, Recreation and Open Space Development Impact Fee Service Areas;

a) Service Area 1 (one) which shall be the area west and north of Georgia Highway 5 and

b) Service Area 2 (two) which shall be the area east and south of Georgia Highway 5.

2. Deposit into trust funds. All park, recreation and open space impact fees collected shall be properly identified by park, recreation and open space development impact fee service area and promptly transferred for deposit in the appropriate Park, Recreation and Open Space Development Impact Fee Trust Fund to be held in separate accounts until expended or encumbered in accord with this code and the Park, Recreation and Open Space Development Impact Fee Ordinance.

B. Police Protection Impact Fees.

1. Service Area. There is one (1) Police Protection Impact Fee Service Area, which is the entirety of the incorporated area of Canton.

2. Deposit of into trust funds. All police protection impact fees collected shall be properly identified and promptly transferred for deposit in the appropriate Police Protection Impact Fee Trust Fund to be held in a separate account until expended or encumbered in accord with this code and the Police Protection Impact Fee Ordinance.

C. Fire Protection Impact Fees.

1. Service Area. There are two (2) Fire Protection Impact Fee Service Areas, North and South, as shown in Attachment E to the Administrative Code.

2. Deposit of into trust funds. All fire protection impact fees collected shall be properly identified and promptly transferred for deposit in the appropriate Fire Protection Impact Fee Trust Fund to be held in a separate account until expended or encumbered in accord with this code and the Fire Protection Impact Fee Ordinance.

D. Road Impact Fees.

1. Service Area. There is one (1) Road Impact Fee Service Area, which is the entirety of the incorporated area of Canton.

2. Deposit of into trust funds. All road impact fees collected shall be properly identified and promptly transferred for deposit in the appropriate Road Impact Fee Trust Fund to be held in a separate account until expended or encumbered in accord with this code and the Road Impact Fee Ordinance.

VIII. USE OF IMPACT FEE FUNDS

A. Park, Recreation and Open Space Impact Fees.

1. Funds collected from park, recreation and open space development impact fees shall be used solely for the purpose of acquiring and/or making capital improvements to park, recreation and open spaces under the jurisdiction of the City of Canton, Cherokee County, or the State of Georgia, and shall not be used for maintenance or operations.

2. Funds shall be used exclusively for acquisitions, expansions, or capital improvements within the Park, Recreation and Open Space Development Impact Fee Service Area from which the funds were collected except funds collected from any and all service areas may be expended for acquisitions, expansion or capital improvements relating to the Etowah River Greenway and the Community Center because of the citywide nature of the benefit provided by these facilities.

3. In the event that bonds or similar debt instruments are issued for advanced provision of capital facilities for which park, recreation and open space development impact fees may be expended, park, recreation and open space development impact fees may be used to pay debt service on such bonds or similar debt instruments to the extent that the facilities provided are of the type described in sub-paragraphs 1 and 2 above.

4. In the event a developer enters into an agreement with the City to construct, fund or contribute system improvements so that the amount of the credit created by such construction, funding or contribution is in excess of the development impact fee otherwise due, the developer shall be reimbursed for such excess construction funding or contribution from development impact fees paid by other developments located in the service area which are benefited by such improvements.

5. At least once each fiscal period the Impact Fee Administrator shall present to the City Council a report describing the amount of development impact fees collected, encumbered and used, and a proposed capital improvement program for park, recreation and open spaces, assigning funds, including any accrued interest, from the several Park, Recreation and Open Space Development Impact Fee Trust Funds to specific park, recreation and open space improvement projects and related expenses. Monies, including any accrued interest, not assigned in any fiscal period shall be retained in the same Park, Recreation and Open Space Development Impact Fee Trust Funds until the next fiscal period except as provided by the refund provisions of the Park, Recreation and Open Space Impact Fee Ordinance.

6. Funds may be used to provide refunds.

7. Funds shall be considered expended on a first in, first out basis

B. Police Protection Impact Fees.

1. Funds collected from police protection impact fees shall be used solely for the purpose of acquiring and/or making capital improvements to police protection facilities and equipment under the jurisdiction of the City of Canton, Cherokee County, or the State of Georgia, and shall not be used for maintenance or operations.

2. Funds shall be used exclusively for acquisitions, expansions, or capital improvements within the Police Protection Development Impact Fee Service Area from which the funds were collected.

3. In the event that bonds or similar debt instruments are issued for advanced provision of capital facilities for which police protection development impact fees may be expended, police protection development impact fees may be used to pay debt service on such bonds or similar debt instruments to the extent that the facilities provided are of the type described in sub-paragraphs 1 and 2 above.

4. In the event a developer enters into an agreement with the City to construct, fund or contribute system improvements such that the amount of the credit created by such construction, funding or contribution is in excess of the development impact fee otherwise due, the developer shall be reimbursed for such excess construction funding or contribution from development impact fees paid by other developments located in the service area which are benefited by such improvements.

5. At least once each fiscal period the Impact Fee Administrator shall present to the City Council a report describing the amount of development impact fees collected, encumbered and used, and a proposed capital improvement program for police protection assigning funds, including any accrued interest, from the Police Protection Development Impact Fee Trust Fund to specific police protection improvement projects and related expenses. Monies, including any accrued interest, not assigned in any fiscal period shall be retained in Police Protection Development Impact Fee Trust Fund until the next fiscal period except as provided by the refund provisions of Police Protection Impact Fee Ordinance.

6. Funds may be used to provide refunds.

7. Funds shall be considered expended on a first in, first out basis

C. Fire Protection Impact Fees.

1. Funds collected from fire protection impact fees shall be used solely for the purpose of acquiring and/or making capital improvements to fire protection facilities and equipment under the jurisdiction of the City of Canton, Cherokee County, or the State of Georgia, and shall not be used for maintenance or operations.

2. Funds shall be used exclusively for acquisitions, expansions, or capital improvements within the Fire Protection Development Impact Fee Service Area from which the funds were collected.

3. In the event that bonds or similar debt instruments are issued for advanced provision of capital facilities for which fire protection development impact fees may be expended,

fire protection development impact fees may be used to pay debt service on such bonds or similar debt instruments to the extent that the facilities provided are of the type described in sub-paragraphs 1 and 2 above.

4. In the event a developer enters into an agreement with the City to construct, fund or contribute system improvements such that the amount of the credit created by such construction, funding or contribution is in excess of the development impact fee otherwise due, the developer shall be reimbursed for such excess construction funding or contribution from development impact fees paid by other developments located in the service area which are benefited by such improvements.

5. At least once each fiscal period the Impact Fee Administrator shall present to the City Council a report describing the amount of development impact fees collected, encumbered and used, and a proposed capital improvement program for fire facilities, assigning funds, including any accrued interest, from the Fire Protection Development Impact Fee Trust Fund to specific fire protection improvement projects and related expenses. Monies, including any accrued interest, not assigned in any fiscal period shall be retained in Fire Protection Development Impact Fee Trust Fund until the next fiscal period except as provided by the refund provisions of Fire Protection Impact Fee Ordinance.

6. Funds may be used to provide refunds.

7. Funds shall be considered expended on a first in, first out basis

D. Roads Impact Fees.

1. Funds collected from road impact fees shall be used solely for the purpose of acquiring and/or making capital improvements to roads under the jurisdiction of the City of Canton, Cherokee County, or the State of Georgia, and as listed in the City of Canton Capital Improvement Plan, and shall not be used for maintenance or operations.

2. In the event that bonds or similar debt instruments are issued for advanced provision of capital facilities for which road development impact fees may be expended, road development impact fees may be used to pay debt service on such bonds or similar debt instruments to the extent that the facilities provided are of the type described in sub-paragraph 1 above.

3. In the event a developer enters into an agreement with the City to construct, fund or contribute road system improvements such that the amount of the credit created by such construction, funding or contribution is in excess of the development impact fee otherwise due, the developer shall be reimbursed for such excess construction funding or contribution from development impact fees paid by other developments which are benefited by such improvements.

4. At least once each fiscal period the Impact Fee Administrator shall present to the City Council a report describing the amount of road development impact fees collected, encumbered and used, and a proposed capital improvement program for roads, assigning funds, including any accrued interest, from the Road Development Impact Fee Trust Fund to specific road protection improvement projects listed in the Capital Improvement Program and related expenses. Monies, including any accrued interest, not assigned in any fiscal period shall be retained in the Road Development Impact Fee Trust Fund until the next fiscal period except as provided by the refund provisions of Road Impact Fee Ordinance.

5. Funds may be used to provide refunds.

6. Funds shall be considered expended on a first in, first out basis

IX. REFUNDS

A. Expiration, Revocation, Surrender of Permit

1. Park, Recreation and Open Space Impact Fees. Under the conditions defined in part III.D-Expiration of Permit, and subject to the limitations in part VIII.B below, a feepayer shall be entitled to a refund equal to 95% of the park, recreation and open space impact fee paid. Five percent of the fee shall be retained by the City to offset the administrative costs of collection and refund.

2. Police Protection Impact Fees. Under the conditions defined in part III.D-Expiration of Permit, and subject to the limitations in part VIII.B below, a feepayer shall be entitled to a refund equal to 95% of the police protection impact fee paid. Five percent of the fee shall be retained by the City to offset the administrative costs of collection and refund.

3. Fire Protection Impact Fees. Under the conditions defined in part III.D-Expiration of Permit, and subject to the limitations in part VIII.B below, a feepayer shall be entitled to a refund equal to 95% of the fire protection impact fee paid. Five percent of the fee shall be retained by the City to offset the administrative costs of collection and refund.

4. Road Impact Fees. Under the conditions defined in part III.D-Expiration of Permit, and subject to the limitations in part VIII.B below, a feepayer shall be entitled to a refund equal to 95% of the road impact fee paid. Five percent of the fee shall be retained by the City to offset the administrative costs of collection and refund.

B. Refunds and Credits

In the case of an expired permit or development approval which was obtained in whole or in part by the use of credits, only the portion not obtained by credit may be refunded, and it is from this portion that the 5% administrative fee shall be deducted.

C. Denial of Service

1. Parks, Recreation and Open Space. In the event that park or recreational service or access to public parks, recreation and open space under the jurisdiction of the City of Canton is denied after a park, recreation and open space impact fee has been paid, the feepayer shall be entitled to a refund.

a) Before issuance of the refund can be authorized, the feepayer shall submit a written request for refund to the Impact Fee Administrator. This request must be submitted within 180 days of the date of the denial of service or access.

b) In applying for the refund, it shall be the applicant's responsibility to furnish, as required by the Impact Fee Administrator, all materials and information necessary to validate proof of payment by the feepayer or his/her successor in interest, the date and amount paid, and the permit issued as a result of that payment. The Impact Fee Administrator shall verify whether the park, recreation and open space impact fee is refundable and if so, process the feepayer's request.

2. Police Protection. In the event that police protection services under the jurisdiction of the City of Canton are denied after a police protection impact fee has been paid, the feepayer shall be entitled to a refund.

a) Before issuance of the refund can be authorized, the feepayer shall submit a written request for refund to the Impact Fee Administrator. This request must be submitted within 180 days of the date of the denial of service.

b) In applying for the refund, it shall be the applicant's responsibility to furnish, as required by the Impact Fee Administrator, all materials and information necessary to validate proof of payment by the feepayer or his/her successor in interest, the date and amount paid, and the permit issued as a result of that payment. The Impact Fee Administrator shall verify whether the police protection impact fee is refundable and if so, process the feepayer's request.

3. Fire Protection. In the event that fire protection service or access to fire protection service under the jurisdiction of the City of Canton is denied after a fire protection impact fee has been paid, the feepayer shall be entitled to a refund.

a) Before issuance of the refund can be authorized, the feepayer shall submit a written request for refund to the Impact Fee Administrator. This request must be submitted within 180 days of the date of the denial of service.

b) In applying for the refund, it shall be the applicant's responsibility to furnish, as required by the Impact Fee Administrator, all materials and information necessary to validate proof of payment by the feepayer or his/her successor in interest, the date and amount paid, and the permit issued as a result of that payment. The Impact Fee Administrator shall verify whether the fire protection impact fee is refundable and if so, process the feepayer's request.

4. Roads. In the event that road service or access to service under the jurisdiction of the City of Canton is denied after a road impact fee has been paid, the feepayer shall be entitled to a refund.

a) Before issuance of the refund can be authorized, the feepayer shall submit a written request for refund to the Impact Fee Administrator. This request must be submitted within 180 days of the date of the denial of service.

b) In applying for the refund, it shall be the applicant's responsibility to furnish, as required by the Impact Fee Administrator, all materials and information necessary to validate proof of payment by the feepayer or his/her successor in interest, the date and amount paid, and the permit issued as a result of that payment. The Impact Fee Administrator shall verify whether the fire protection impact fee is refundable and if so, process the feepayer's request.

D. Trust Accounts Not Expended

1. Unexpended Within 6 Years. Any funds within impact fee trust accounts not expended or encumbered by the end of the calendar quarter immediately following 6 years from the date the relevant impact fee was paid shall be considered refundable upon application of the feepayer or his/her successor in interest. No refunds of impact fees will be provided for in the event that there is no proper request for such a refund. Funds shall be deemed expended or encumbered when a contract or agreement obligating those funds is approved by the City of Canton.

Before issuance of the refund can be authorized, the feepayer or his/her successor in interest shall submit a written request for refund to the Impact Fee Administrator. This request must be submitted within 180 days of the date the funds are considered refundable.

In applying for the refund, it shall be the applicant's responsibility to furnish, as required by the Impact Fee Administrator, all materials and information necessary to validate proof of payment by the feepayer or his/her successor in interest, the date and amount paid, and the permit issued as a result of that payment. The Impact Fee Administrator shall verify whether the impact fee is refundable and if so, process the feepayer's request.

2. Termination. In the event that the imposition of an impact fee is terminated in a portion or in the whole of the City of Canton, the Trust Account balance(s) for that area shall be considered refundable upon application of the feepayer or his/her successor in interest. No refunds of fees will be provided for in the event the fees collected have been expended or encumbered or if a feepayer or his/her successor in interest does not request such a refund.

Within 30 days following the effective date of this termination, the City of Canton shall notify feepayers that they may be eligible for a refund upon application of the feepayer or his/her successor in interest. The notification shall meet the same requirements as that of notification of a Comprehensive Plan Amendment and shall specify how feepayers may submit a refund application. The refund application must be submitted by the feepayer or his/her successor in interest within 180 days following the publication of the first notice.

Fees available for refund shall be prorated over those eligible feepayers submitting proper application for refund. In no case shall the feepayer receive a refund greater than the amount originally paid plus interest. Any Trust Fund balance not so refunded shall be returned to the General Fund of City of Canton.

Holders of impact fee credits shall be considered feepayers for purposes of refund under this termination procedure.

E. Improper Fee Amount

See part III.B.2-Invalid Payment of Fee.

F. Overpayment

A refund will be made if it is determined by the Impact Fee Administrator that an overpayment of impact fees has occurred.

G. Interest on Refunds

Pursuant to Georgia Code 36-71-9 (4), all refunds shall include a pro rata share of interest actually earned on the unused or excess development impact fees collected.

X. EXEMPTIONS

A. Must Be Claimed by Feepayers

An exemption must be claimed by the feepayer at the time of application for a building permit. Any exemption not so claimed shall be deemed waived by the feepayer.

B. Exemptions

1. The following shall be exempted from payment of all Impact Fees:

a) Alteration of an existing building or use of land where the existing use of the property is not changed and there is no additional living area in residential structures or gross floor area in non-residential structures.

b) The construction of accessory buildings or structures which will not be occupied by residents, employees or customers will be exempt from the requirement to pay park, recreation and open space impact fees.

c) The replacement of a lawfully permitted building, mobile home, recreational vehicle, trailer or structure with a new unit, building or structure of the same type, use and size. If the existing unit, building, or structure is torn down, destroyed by fire or other natural disaster, or otherwise

eliminated or moved off the site, or if the original structure is converted to a utility building, garage, or other non-residential or non-commercial use the replacement structure will be exempt from the payment of impact fees. The permit applicant shall document such replacement.

d) An amendment to a development approval, provided that the amended development approval does not increase the impact of the development.

e) A permit for which the impact has been or will be paid or otherwise provided for pursuant to a written agreement, zoning approval or development approval which, by the written terms, clearly and unequivocally provides for the full mitigation of such impact by enforcement of the agreement, zoning approval or development approval, and not by the application of this ordinance.

f) A permit which does not result in any additional residents, visitors, building occupants, customers or employees within the City of Canton.

g) Land uses devoted entirely or partially to exclusive private use, which are internal to a particular development (for example a Club House) and which, therefore, have no off-site parks, recreation and open space impact may be exempt from the requirement to pay a park, recreation and open space impact fee. (See III.F of this Administrative Code.)

2. In applying for the above mentioned exemptions, it shall be the applicant's responsibility to furnish, as required by the Impact Fee Administrator, all materials and information necessary to validate the exemption including, but not limited to, the following:

a) Current Opinion of Title or Title Insurance,

b) Old and new construction plans,

c) Official Certificate of Occupancy and use records,

d) Statements from owner stating past and proposed land use,

e) Utility bills or receipts and

f) Tax records.

C. Exemption Based on Error or Misrepresentation

Exemptions from payment of an impact fee based on error or misrepresentation shall be subject to the provisions found in part III.B.2 of this code.

D. Exemptions for Vested Permit Applications

Applicants for permits must meet the following requirements in order to obtain and maintain an exemption from the payment of impact fees:

1. Complete Application For Building Permit, Permit For Mobile Home Installation or Permit for Recreational Vehicle Installation. The applicant must submit to the Impact Fee Administrator a completed application form with all necessary attachments, forms, and plans to meet the following requirements:

a) Applications for Residential Building Permits must meet all of the requirements of the items listed on the "Impact Fee Calculation Form," Attachment B.

b) Applications for Permit for Mobile Home Installation must meet all of the requirements of the items identified on the "Impact Fee Calculation Form," Attachment B.

c) Applications for Permit for Recreational Vehicle Installation must meet all of the requirements of the items identified on the "Impact Fee Calculation Form," Attachment B.

d) Applications for Non-Residential building permits must meet all of the items identified on the "Impact Fee Calculation Form," Attachment B.

The application form must have been reviewed and assigned an application number by the building permit clerk. In addition, the date and time stamped by the clerk on the application form must be prior to the effective date of the ordinance.

2. The Applicant must pick-up the permit within 30 days of the date stamped on the application by the Impact Fee Administrator.

3. Zoning Issues. In order for the applicant to pick-up a permit within the required 30 days, the Impact Fee Administrator will need to sign off on the application. If the Impact Fee Administrator determines that a variance may be necessary and applying for one could cause the applicant to lose an impact fee exemption, the Impact Fee Administrator may toll the relevant time period for a time reasonably sufficient for the applicant to pursue a variance procedure

4. Applicants whose requests for exemptions from impact fees are rejected may appeal the decision pursuant to Section XII of this Administrative Code.

E. Exemptions Provided by State Statute

Pursuant to O.C.G.A. 20-2-261(d) a local Board of Education shall be exempt from impact fees.

XI. CREDITS

A. General Conditions

Generally, an applicant may obtain credit for up to 100% of impact fees otherwise due or to become due by offering to dedicate land and/or construct improvements for City approved projects. Applicants should file an "Impact Fee Credit Application," Attachment C. Any claim for credit must be made no later than the time of application for a permit. Any claim not so made shall be deemed waived.

1. No credit shall be given for:

(a) Private recreational facilities except as provided in XI C below,

(b) Private police protection or security services,

(c) Private fire protection or rescue services

(d) Improvements which do not meet City, County, or state design standards, whichever is applicable;

(e) Improvements or land dedications that are not in the adopted Capital Improvement Element of the City of Canton's Comprehensive Plan;

(f) Improvements deemed to be project improvements pursuant to a City development or zoning approval;

(g) Improvements or land dedications for which compensation has previously been given by a governmental body.

2. Credits may be available for:

a) **Voluntary and Project Improvements**. No credit shall be given for project improvements or land dedications that do not service a public park, recreation or open space, public police protection or fire protection and rescue need. If a voluntary and/or project improvement meets a City of Canton identified public park, recreation or open space, police protection or fire protection need, then credit will be given pursuant to Chapter X of this Administrative Code.

b) **System Improvements**. All mandatory or required land dedications for park, recreation or open space, police protection, fire protection improvements, or road improvements made by a feepayer, subsequent to the effective date of the

appropriate impact fee ordinance shall be credited on a pro rata basis against impact fees otherwise due or to become due for the development that prompted the City to require such dedications or improvements. No credits shall be given for project improvements except for project improvements and improvements not in the Capital Improvement Element of the City of Canton's Comprehensive Plan, and system improvements not included in the Capital Improvement Element of the City of Canton's Comprehensive Plan.

3. The authority to determine credit lies exclusively with the City of Canton. In every case impact fee credits shall be calculated so as to be consistent with Title 36-71-1 through 36-71-13, Georgia Statutes.

B. General Documentation and Procedures

The offer to make capital improvements or dedicate land in lieu of paying impact fees shall be made in an application with the Impact Fee Administrator identifying the capital improvements and/or land dedications for which credits are requested. If the City of Canton accepted such an offer, whether the acceptance is before or after the effective date of the appropriate impact fee ordinance, the credit shall be determined and provided in the following manner:

1. Amount of credit requested. The applicant shall specify the dollar amount of the credit requested. The costs claimed by the applicant as the basis for the credit requested shall be no more than if the facility had been constructed by or purchased by the City of Canton.

2. Documentation. It is the obligation of the applicant to submit written determination, to the satisfaction of the Impact Fee Administrator, that supports the amount of the credit requested and indicates the basis on which the amount requested was calculated. This documentation shall include:

a) Invoices or other appropriate documents delineating costs claimed as a basis for the requested credit.

b) The method of attribution of any general costs to the improvement for which credit is requested.

c) Credit shall not be granted for the cost for design, engineering, contingencies, and overhead.

3. An applicant claiming credit for eligible capital improvements and/or land dedication shall provide the following information to the Impact Fee Administrator during development review or prior to application for the issuance of building permits:

a) **Construction of Capital Improvements**. The credit applicant shall submit a project description in sufficient detail and with cost estimates prepared by qualified professionals, to allow the Impact Fee Administrator to verify these cost estimates.

b) **Land Dedication**. When a person requests credit for land dedication for approved improvements, he/she shall present:

(1) A specimen of the deed which he/she proposes to use to convey title to the appropriate governmental body;

(2) A title opinion written by a licensed State of Georgia attorney and rendered within sixty (60) days of submission thereof, the content of which is satisfactory to the City Attorney and verifying that the proffered deed will convey unencumbered title to the appropriate entity;

(3) A certified copy of the most recent assessment of the property for tax purposes;

(4) Applicants may submit property appraisals if they are prepared by qualified professionals. In preparing their

reports, appraisers shall value the land in the following manner:

(a) If the dedication is made pursuant to a condition of zoning approval, is not a project improvement and the zoning condition does not specifically prescribe otherwise, the land shall be valued based upon the zoning of the land as it existed prior to the zoning approval which contains the condition of dedication;

(b) Otherwise, appraisers shall value the land at its then current zoning and without any enhanced value which could be attributed to improvements on adjacent lands.

4. Determination of Credit. The Impact Fee Administrator shall determine the credit for facility construction or land dedication. This determination shall be based upon either the cost estimates provided by the applicant or upon alternative engineering criteria, construction cost estimates, or property appraisals through the use of the methodology described in the relevant ordinance, if the Impact Fee Administrator determines that such estimates submitted by the applicant are either unreliable or inaccurate.

Credit for the dedication of land shall be valued at:

a) 115% of the most recent assessed value by the City of Canton for purposes of property taxation, or

b) At the option of the applicant, by fair market value established by appraisers acceptable to the City.

The written determination shall include the following:

a) Whether the credit may be used to pay park, recreation and open space impact fees, police protection impact fees or fire protection impact fees.

b) The dollar amount of the credit,

c) The reason for the credit, and

d) The legal description or other adequate description of the project or development to which the credit may be applied.

The applicant must sign and date a duplicate copy of such letter or certificate indicating his/her agreement to the terms of the letter or certificate and return such signed document to the Impact Fee Administrator before credit will be given. If the applicant fails to sign, date, and return such document within 30 days, the Impact Fee Administrator will consider the credit application to be inactive.

No increase in the amount of approved credit will be authorized unless it is determined during actual construction of the agreed-to improvements that change orders are to be made incurring additional expense for items that are necessary and are not shown on the approved plans and estimates previously furnished to the Impact Fee Administrator. It shall be the applicant's responsibility to obtain prior approval from the Impact Fee Administrator before all such change orders are made. All requests for an increase of the approved credit shall include all documentation required by the Impact Fee Administrator.

5. Credit for Construction. Except as provided in 6.c below, credit against impact fees otherwise due will not be provided until:

a) The construction is completed and accepted by the City, the County, or the State, whichever is applicable.

b) A suitable maintenance and warranty bond as may be required by the Impact Fee Administrator is submitted to and approved by the City of Canton.

c) In the case of 6.e below, upon completion of the agreed-to construction improvements and upon acceptance by the appropriate governmental authority pursuant to 6.a

above, the Bond may be reduced to an amount and a time period as provided for by the City to cover a maintenance period for the improvements.

d) All design, construction, inspection, testing, bonding and acceptance procedures are in strict compliance with the then current City ordinances, as they may be applicable.

e) Credit may be provided before completion of specified improvements if the feepayer posts security as provided below for the costs of such construction. Security in the form of a performance bond, irrevocable letter of credit or escrow agreement (hereinafter referred to as the Bond) shall be posted with the City in an amount determined by the Impact Fee Administrator equal to 150% of the full cost of construction. The Bond shall be automatically renewable. In the event of cancellation of the Bond, notice of intent to cancel or not to renew must be given to the Impact Fee Administrator not later than 60 days prior to the renewal date. In such event of a notice to cancel or of intent not to renew, the Impact Fee Administrator shall be entitled to declare a default and collect the full amount of the Bond.

If the construction project will not be completed within one (1) year of the acceptance by the Impact Fee Administrator of the offer to construct improvements, the amount of the security shall be increased by 10% compounded, for each year of the life of the security. The security shall be reviewed and approved by the City Attorney's office prior to acceptance of the security by the City. If the improvement is to be owned by some other entity, the City may assign its rights in such security to that entity if the entity requests it and the law permits it.

In the event that: (1) the City receives notification from the principal (guarantor) that the bond is being canceled before all agreed-to improvements have been completed and accepted by the appropriate governmental body; or (2) the City determines that terms of the agreement for construction as set forth in the Bond agreement are not being complied with, then the City shall, in accordance with the Bond agreement, default the Bond and collect the full amount of the Bond to be used for completion of the agreed-to improvements and other expenses. If the cost incurred by the City to complete the said improvements exceeds the amount received from the defaulted Bond, the City shall seek to recover their loss under the provisions of part III.B.3 of this Administrative Code.

6. Credit for Land Dedication. Credits for land dedication shall be created when the following procedures have been completed and the title to said land has been accepted by the appropriate governmental body and recorded in the Official Records of the City of Canton:

a) The delivery to the appropriate governmental body of a deed, with sufficient funds to pay all costs of transfer of title including recording.

b) The escrow of taxes for the current year, or the payment of said taxes for the year.

c) The issuance of a title insurance policy subsequent to recording of the deed and escrow of taxes.

7. Transferability of Credits. Impact fee credits shall not be transferable from one project or development to another.

8. Withdrawal of offer by Applicant. Any person who offers land and/or improvements in exchange for credits may withdraw the offer of dedication at any time prior to the transfer of legal title to the land or improvements in question and pay the full impact fees required by the appropriate impact fee ordinance.

9. Credits Claimed. Persons claiming credits shall submit sufficient documentation to permit the Impact Fee Administrator to determine whether such credits claimed are due and in what amount.

10. Cancellation of Credit. Once used, credits shall be canceled and shall not be re-established even if the permit for which they were used expires without commencing construction. Impact fees paid by credit shall run with the land.

C. Credit for Private Park, Recreation or Open Space Facilities.

An applicant may apply for credit against park, recreation and open space impact fees otherwise due for private park, recreation or open space improvements by filing a "Parks, Recreation and Open Space Application for Impact Fee Credit for Private Recreation Facilities," Attachment D. In no circumstance shall credit for private park, recreation or open space improvement exceed 50% of the park, recreation and open space impact fees otherwise due. Furthermore, any credit granted may not be used to pay more than 50% of the impact fee due. Credits may be applied to the impact fee due: however, the credit amount applied shall not exceed 50% of the amount due.

1. The private park, recreation or open space facilities for which credit is sought must serve a public recreational need; and

2. The private park, recreation or open space facilities for which credit is sought must be consistent with the Park, Recreation and Open Space Element of City of Canton's Comprehensive Plan.

3. An applicant wishing to receive credit for private recreational facilities shall submit a request to the Impact Fee Administrator – Attachment D. This request must contain:

(a) An inventory of the private park, recreation and open space facilities for which credit is sought, including:

(1) The nature or use of the park, recreation or open space,

(2) The size of the facilities and the equipment or apparatus available to the users,

(3) The availability of the spaces or facilities to development residents or occupants and the availability of the spaces or facilities to the general public,

(4) The public park, recreation or open space purpose that is served by the private facility, and

(5) The provisions of the Park, Recreation and Open Space Element of the Canton Comprehensive Plan that are furthered by the private facilities.

4. The Impact Fee Administrator shall consult with the City Community Development Director and the City Director of Parks and Recreation on the application for credit. After review, the Impact Fee Administrator shall, with 30 days, notify the applicant of the results of the review. If the request for credit is granted, the Impact Fee Administrator shall notify the applicant and provide a letter stating the amount of the credit which has been granted and how much can be applied against each impact fee due. The applicant must sign and date a duplicate copy of such letter or certificate indicating his/her agreement to the terms of the letter or certificate and return such signed document to the Impact Fee Administrator before credit will be given. If the applicant fails to sign, date, and return such document within 30 days of receipt, the Impact Fee Administrator will consider the credit application to be inactive.

5. The Impact Fee Administrator may enter into a development agreement with the applicant setting forth the terms for which credits will be used, the time frame for their use, and the percentage that can be applied to fees due.

6. Decisions of the Impact Fee Administrator may be appealed as set out in Chapter XI of this Administrative Code.

XII. APPEALS.

A. Procedure

1. Request for Reconsideration. If the applicant or feepayer is dissatisfied with a decision from the Impact Fee Administrator he/she may, within 15 days of that decision, ask for reconsideration by the Impact Fee Administrator by submitting a letter which explains the nature of the feepayer's disagreement with the decision of the Impact Fee Administrator. On the basis of the feepayer's letter and the recommendation of the other departments, the Impact Fee Administrator shall, within 15 days of the receipt for the request for reconsideration, provide a written determination with respect to the request for reconsideration to the applicant or feepayer.

2. Appeal to the Mayor and City Council. All appeals from the Impact Fee Administrator's determination shall be taken within fifteen (15) days of the Impact Fee Administrator's decision on the request for reconsideration by filing with the Impact Fee Administrator a notice of appeal specifying the grounds therefore. The Impact Fee Administrator shall forthwith transmit to the Mayor and City Council all papers constituting the record upon which the action appealed from is taken. The Mayor and City Council shall thereafter establish a reasonable date and time for a hearing on the appeal, give due notice thereof, and decide the same within a reasonable period of time following the hearing. Any applicant or feepayor taking an appeal shall have the right to appear at the hearing, to present evidence and may be represented by counsel.

3. Nothing in this Administrative Code or in the impact fees ordinances is intended to preclude any applicant who is dissatisfied with the determination of the City Council from seeking a judicial remedy.

B. Payment of Impact Fees Pending Appeal

1. The permit applied for will not be issued unless the impact fee as determined by the Impact Fee Administrator is paid in full, regardless of an appeal by an applicant.

2. Any reduction of impact fees resulting from a successful appeal shall be by refund of any excess amount paid at the time of the issuance of the permit. No interest will be paid on a refund of any such overpayment.

XIII. ENFORCEMENT

A. Misdemeanor

1. Knowingly furnishing false information on any matter relating to the administration of the impact fees ordinances to the Impact Fee Administrator, or any designee, shall constitute a violation thereof.

2. A violation of the impact fee ordinances shall be a misdemeanor punishable according to law. Staff of the City of Canton who are aware of such violations shall present their evidence to the office of the City Attorney for appropriate legal action.

B. Code Enforcement

In addition to the enforcement provision in part A above, those authorized to enforce City of Canton codes and ordinances may be requested by the Impact Fee

Administrator to enforce specified provisions of the impact fee ordinances.

XIV. INDIVIDUAL FEE CALCULATION GUIDELINES

A. Introduction

If a feepayer shall opt not to have the impact fee determined according to the fee schedule (Chapter IV of this Administrative Code), then the feepayer shall prepare and submit an individual fee calculation study in accordance with provisions of the appropriate impact fee ordinance and Chapter V of this Administrative Code. The purpose of this chapter is twofold:

1. To provide an explanation of the impact fee calculation found in the City of Canton impact fee ordinances, and

2. To present guidelines for conducting individual studies to re-calculate the impact fee for a specific unit of development. While the individual calculation of the impact fee by an individual is provided for in the Ordinances, the specific methodology and procedures for undertaking the individual study are elaborated upon in this Administrative Code.

B. Recoupment of Cost

1. The Impact Fee Administrator shall require applicants pursuing an individual fee calculation to reimburse the City for reasonable non-staff personnel and associated expenses it incurs in order to adequately review and evaluate independent fee calculation.

2. Subsequent to notification, the Impact Fee Administrator shall provide good faith estimates of the costs to be borne by the applicant.

C. General Methodology

The impact fee calculation is based on the size of residential and non-residential structures within the City of Canton. This fee represents an equitable proportion of facility and land costs, less credits for payments made by new development toward those costs.

D. Individual Fee Calculation

The impact fee schedules identified in the City of Canton Impact Fee Ordinances were established based on park usage, police patrol and fire protection, and major thoroughfare plan characteristics for land uses within the City of Canton. While those characteristics and resultant impact fees were based on the best available data and sound planning practices, it is recognized that individuals may desire to conduct individual studies of their project's impact and recalculate their particular impact fee per unit of development.

1. Park, Recreational and Open Space Usage Studies. The park, recreational and open space usage characteristics used in the City of Canton Park, Recreation and Open Space Impact Fee Ordinance were based on recommendation by the City's Impact Fee Advisory Committee and consulting planners together with the City's staff and are to be found within the technical materials on record with the City of Canton. However, individuals may desire and are permitted to conduct local, individual surveys of park, recreation and open space usage to confirm or contradict the usage data used in the Schedule or to establish rates for land uses which are not identified in the Schedule. The methodology to be followed is summarized below:

a) A minimum of three sites for the land use in question shall be selected. The selected sites should be single use sites and shall be located in the City of Canton.

b) The site inventory and sites proposed for the survey shall be reviewed by the Impact Fee Administrator. The Impact Fee Administrator must approve the sites to be surveyed prior to initiation of any survey.

2. Police Protection Studies. The police patrol data used in the City of Canton Police Protection Impact Fee Ordinance were based on recommendation by the City's Impact Fee Advisory Committee and consulting planners together with the City's staff and are to be found within the technical materials on record with the City of Canton. However, individuals may desire and are permitted to conduct local, individual surveys of police protection and patrol to confirm or contradict the data used in the Schedule or to establish rates for land uses which are not identified in the Schedule. The methodology to be followed is summarized below:

a) A minimum of three sites for the land use in question should be selected. The selected sites shall be single use sites and shall be located in the City of Canton.

b) The site inventory and sites proposed for the survey shall be reviewed by the Impact Fee Administrator. The Impact Fee Administrator must approve the sites to be surveyed prior to initiation of the survey.

3. Fire Protection Studies. The fire protection and rescue characteristics used in the City of Canton Fire Protection Impact Fee Ordinance were based on recommendation by the City's Impact Fee Advisory Committee and consulting planners together with the City's staff and are to be found within the technical materials on record with the City of Canton. However, individuals may desire and are permitted to conduct local, individual surveys of fire protection and rescue to confirm or contradict the data used in the Schedule or to establish rates for land uses which are not identified in the Schedule. The methodology to be followed is summarized below:

a) A minimum of three sites for the land use in question shall be selected. The selected sites should be single use sites and should, whenever possible, be located in the City of Canton.

b) The site inventory and sites proposed for the survey shall be reviewed by the Impact Fee Administrator. The Impact Fee Administrator must approve the sites to be surveyed prior to initiation of the survey.

4. Road Usage Studies. The road usage characteristics used in the City of Canton Road Impact Fee Ordinance were based on recommendation by the City's Impact Fee Advisory Committee and consulting planners together with the City's staff and are to be found within the technical materials on record with the City of Canton. However, individuals may desire and are permitted to conduct local, individual surveys of road usage to confirm or contradict the usage data used in the Schedule or to establish rates for land uses which are not identified in the Schedule. The methodology to be followed is summarized below:

a) A minimum of three sites for the land use in question should be selected. The selected sites should be single use sites and should, whenever possible, be located in the City of Canton.

b) The site inventory and sites proposed for the survey should be reviewed by the Impact Fee Administrator. The Impact Fee Administrator must approve the sites to be surveyed prior to initiation of any survey.

5. Other Studies. Alternative data or studies submitted by an applicant shall be based on studies, as appropriate, conducted in the City of Canton or at sites that are comparable to the proposed land development activity.

E. Cost/Revenues Studies

The impact fee structures identified in the City of Canton Impact Fee Ordinances were established based on the estimated park, recreation and open space costs, police facilities costs and fire protection and rescue facility costs and estimated land acquisition cost, road construction costs, and anticipated revenue sources.

While those factors and resultant impact fees are based on the best available data and sound planning practices, it is recognized that individuals may desire to conduct individual calculations of the improvement and land acquisition costs and the other revenue sources and to use those items in an individual calculation of impact fees per unit of development.

Those individuals who desire to calculate individually the construction and/or land cost figures should base such calculation on a review of recent new construction and land acquisition costs within the area of the City of Canton. The ordinances require that these calculations shall be appropriate for the proposed land development activity. The following information should be provided to the Impact Fee Administrator:

1. Facility type and name.
2. Type of improvement and number of acres.
3. Construction costs (including but not limited to survey, field administration, engineering, testing, design and the like) in current year dollars (exclusive of land).
4. Land acquisition costs (including but not limited to engineering, drainage, environmental mitigation, survey, appraisal and real estate fee costs) in current year dollars.
5. Calculated total cost for construction and for land.

F. Other Revenues.

1. Other revenues have been included as a reduction to the amount needed to be raised from impact fees in the City of Canton Capital Improvement Plan.
2. Individuals may submit alternate estimates of other revenues. Such alternate estimates should provide sufficient detail and documentation so that the Impact Fee Administrator can evaluate the reasonableness of those estimates. Upon submission of acceptable alternate revenue estimates, the Impact Fee Administrator shall adjust the impact fees of the individual project.
3. Other revenues have been calculated on a citywide basis and are not applicable to individual developments or types of development. Costs and revenues are assigned on an average basis. The City of Canton will not consider an independent study that cites unique revenue characteristics of individual developments unless that same study also inquires into the unique costs associated with that development.

G. Other Considerations

It is the wish of the City of Canton to reasonably and proportionately distribute the cost of growth accommodating improvements. To this end, all individuals are encouraged to present any and all studies, data and information as part of an individual fee calculation study that may be relevant to the issue of individual or collective proportionality. Such other data, studies, information or considerations should be prepared by individuals professionally qualified in their respective fields and must follow best professional practices.

XV. AMENDMENTS

All additions or changes to this Administrative Code shall be subject to review and approval by the Mayor and City Council as agended items during the regular meetings of the Council. Copies of this Administrative Code as revised and approved by the Mayor and City Council, and any subsequent amendments approved by the Mayor and City Council, shall be made available to all City Staff who administer impact fees and shall be made available to members of the general public, upon request, at designated locations in the City of Canton.

XVI. EFFECTIVE DATE

This Administrative Code shall take effect upon adoption by Mayor and Council.

Approved this ____ day _____, 2007
CITY OF CANTON, GEORGIA
By: ______________________
Mayor, City of Canton
ATTEST:

____
City Clerk
Approved as to form:

____
City Attorney

ATTACHMENTS

Attachment A, Land Use Categories

The types of structures in the Canton impact fee program are a simple division between residential and non-residential developments. Residential developments are structures designed for human habitation. Non-residential developments are all other structures requiring the issuance of a building permit or other appropriate permit from the City of Canton.

RESIDENTIAL LAND USES INCLUDE THE FOLLOWING

A. Single Family Units
1. Single Family Detached
2. Manufactured Homes
B. Multi-Family Units
1. Townhouses
2. Villas
3. Duplexes
4. Apartments
5. Condominiums
6. Triplexes
7. Fourplexes
8. Retirement Communities (condominiums, apartments, etc.)
9. Group Quarters (congregate living quarters, dormitories, rooming house)
C. Mobile Home
1. Mobile Homes in mobile home parks, subdivisions, etc.
2. Recreational Vehicles in new, phased or seasonal RV Parks
3. Recreational Vehicles in developed RV parks which are required to get a building permit
4. Recreation Vehicles which require building permit for electrical hook-up, etcetera as well as land- use permit.

NON-RESIDENTIAL LAND USES INCLUDE THE FOLLOWING

A. Hotel/Motels
1. Hotel
2. Resort hotel
3. Motel
B. Industrial
1. Light industrial

2. Manufacturing
3. Mining
4. Assembly plants
5. Printing plants
6. Industrial park
7. Heavy industrial
C Warehouse
1. Warehouses
2. Wholesale
3. Distribution centers
D. Storage
1. Mini-warehouses and climate control storage
2. Storage yards
3. Lumber yards
4. Storage warehouses

OFFICE
A. General
1. Medical offices
2. Dental offices
3. Ophthalmologists
4. Optometrists
5. Opticians
6. Chiropractors
7. Veterinarian offices (except large animal, agricultural services)
8. Clinics
9. General office buildings
10. Attorneys
11. Accountants
12. Real estate
13. Insurance
14. Engineering
15. Government offices
16. Corporate offices
17. Office park
18. Research center
19. Financial institutions
20. Banks (walk-in and drive-in)
21. Savings and loan (walk-in and drive-in)
22. Schools, both public and private.

RETAIL
1. Convenience food stores
2. Gas station/Service station
3. Neighborhood shopping centers (25,000-100,000 sq ft)
4. Specialty retail centers
5. Freestanding retail
6. Supermarkets
7. Drug stores
8. Department stores
9. Discount stores
10. Hardware/Paint stores
11. Furniture stores
12. Clothing/Apparel/Fabric stores
13. Jewelry/Watch stores
14. Barber shops
15. Beauty salons
16. Shoe repair shops
17. Dry cleaners
18. New/Used Car sales
19. Community shopping center (100,000-300,000 sq ft)
20. Regional shopping center (300,000 sq ft and over)

21. Fast food restaurants (with drive-through windows)
22. Restaurants
23. Bars/Night Clubs

Attachment B, Impact Fee Calculation Form

City of Canton
IMPACT FEE CALCULATION FORM

SECTION 1:

Property Owner	Contractor
Permit Reference Number	Permit Type
Property ID Number	Job Address

The impact fees calculated herein have been determined based on the fee schedules adopted in the City of Canton Code of Ordinances, Chapter 100, Article IV, Section 110-101 through 129, City of Canton Park, Recreation and Open Space Development Impact Fee Ordinance (hereinafter referred to as Park, Recreation and Open Space Impact Fee Ordinance), Article V, Section 110-130 through 145, City of Canton Police Protection Development Impact Fee Impact Fee Ordinance (hereinafter referred to as Police Protection Impact Fee Ordinance) and Chapter 110, Article VII, Section 110 through 300, City of Canton Fire Protection Impact Fee Ordinance (hereinafter Fire Impact Fee Ordinance), and Chapter 110, Article VI, Section 175 through 190, City of Canton Road Impact Fee Ordinance (hereinafter Road Impact Fee Ordinance).

This form is authorized only for those building projects expressly identified above. Changes or modifications to the building referred to above or amendments to the impact fee schedules contained in City of Canton development impact fee ordinances shall render this calculation form null and void.

ANY CLAIM FOR CREDIT OR EXEMPTION MUST BE MADE NO LATER THAN THE TIME OF APPLICATION FOR A BUILDING PERMIT OR PERMIT FOR MOBILE HOME INSTALLATION. ANY CLAIM NOT SO MADE SHALL BE DEEMED WAIVED.

____

Signature Date

LAND USE CATEGORY _________

FROM __________ TO _______

NUMBER OF UNITS _________

SQUARE FEET OF RESIDENTIAL LIVING AREA

____

GROSS SQUARE FEET ON NON-RESIDENTIAL FLOOR AREA ___________

CHANGE IN LAND USE CATEGORY? ( ) YES ( ) NO

SHELL PERMIT? ( ) YES ( ) NO

CREDIT REQUESTED ( ) YES* ( ) NO

CATEGORY REVIEW REQUESTED ( ) YES* ( ) NO

INDIVIDUAL FEE APPLICATION ( ) YES* ( ) NO

*IF YES IS CHECKED, DETERMINATION MUST BE MADE PRIOR TO RELEASE

PLANNING AND ZONING RELEASE _______________

DATE: ___________

PARKS, RECREATION AND OPEN SPACE IMPACT FEE

Residential

Square feet of living area _________ at $.__ per square foot

____

Non-Residential

Gross Square Feet of Floor Area _________ at $.__ per square foot ___________

Park, Recreation and Open Space Impact Fee ___________

Park, Recreation and Open Space Credits Applied _________

Net Park, Recreation and Open Space Impact Fees _________

Service Area ___________

POLICE PROTECTION IMPACT FEE

Residential

Square feet of living area _________ at $.__ per square foot

Non-Residential

Gross Square Feet of Floor Area _________ at $__ per square foot

Police Protection Impact Fee   ___________

Police Protection Credits Applied   ___________

Net Police Protection Impact Fees   ___________

FIRE PROTECTION IMPACT FEES

Residential

North Area   _________ at $.___ per foot of living area

South Area   _________ at $.___ per foot of living area

NON-RESIDENTIAL STRUCTURES

North Area   _________ at $___ per foot of gross floor area

South Area   _________ at $___ per foot of gross floor area

Fire Protection Credits Applied   ___________

Net Fire Protection Impact Fees   ___________

Service Area   ___________

ROADS IMPACT FEE

Residential

Square feet of living area _________ at $.__ per square foot

Non-Residential

Gross Square Feet of Floor Area _________ at $__ per square foot ___________

(By land use type according to ordinance)

Road Impact Fee ___________

Road Credits Applied ___________

Net Road Impact Fees

TOTAL IMPACT FEES DUE   ___________

SECTION 2. IMPACT FEES COLLECTION

To be filled out by building division CASHIER:

The total Impact Fees calculated in Section 1 of this form and shown here in Section 2 have been paid in full:

$

____

  (Amount)   (Date)   Cashier Signature

Check Number _________________

Attachment C, Impact Fee Credit Application

City of Canton
IMPACT FEE CREDIT APPLICATION

CREDIT REQUEST

The City of Canton development impact fee ordinances provide for the donation of property or the construction of facilities in lieu of impact fee payments for development projects within the City. Accordingly, you are hereby requested to review the submitted documentation to determine the applicable credit, if any.

Type of Credit Requested:

Park, recreation and Open Space   ____

Police Protection ____

Fire Protection   ____

Roads   ____

____

Name

____

Address

____

City   State   Zip   Telephone

____

Development Project

____

Development Number   Development Approval Date

CREDIT TRANSFER

Applicants for transfer of impact fee credits must attach a copy of the impact fee agreement approving the transferability of impact fee credits.

____________   ____________   ____________

  Account Number   Service Area   Amount

The above impact fee credit account has previously been established for the undersigned to be used to offset impact fee assessments in the City of Canton, Georgia. Accordingly, you are hereby directed to transfer these credits as identified above to:

Name

____

Address

____

City　　　State　　　Zip　　　Telephone

Thank you for your prompt attention to the above direction.

____

Name　　　　Signature　　　　Date

APPLY CREDIT

____

Account Number　　Service Area　　Amount

The above impact fee credit account has previously been established for the undersigned to be used to offset impact fee assessments in City of Canton, Georgia. Accordingly, you are hereby directed to apply these credits as identified above to:

____

Permit Reference Number Property ID

____

Sub-division/Project

Thank you for your prompt attention to the above direction.

____

Name　　　　Signature　　　　Date

DEPARTMENTAL USE ONLY

—Approved Amount—

__________________　__________________

__________________　__________________

__________________　__________________

__________________　__________________

____

Name　　　　Title　　　　Date

Attachment D, Application for Parks, Recreation and Open Space Credit for Private Facilities

City of Canton
APPLICATION FOR PARKS, RECREATION AND OPEN SPACE IMPACT FEE CREDIT FOR PRIVATE FACILITIES

The City of Canton Park, Recreation and Open Space Development Impact Fee Ordinance establishes that park, recreation and open space impact fees otherwise due may be reduced in recognition of the public benefit resulting from certain private park, recreational and open space facilities. The Impact Fee Administrator will review the following to determine the amount of reduction, if any, to be approved.

DEVELOPMENT _______________________________

Please provide the name and location of the development and name of the agent.

PRIVATE FACILITIES: The private facilities provided are:

____

Name　　　　Location　　　Use　　　Size

____

Name　　　　Location　　　Use　　　Size

____

Name　　　　Location　　　Use　　　Size

Are these facilities:

　Open to the public?　　　( ) Yes　　( ) No

　Open to all residents/Occupants?　( ) Yes ( ) No

PUBLIC PURPOSE

What public purpose is met by the provision of these private facilities? Please refer to the Canton Comprehensive Plan, Parks, Recreation and Open Space Element in responding.

Attachment E, Fire Protection Service Areas Map

Attachment F, Parks Service Areas Map

Epilogue

This book has addressed the theory, law, methods, and practice of development impact fees in the United States. The modern impact fee arose in the 1970s when constituents demanded that ever-increasing property taxes stop. Lower taxes—especially lower property taxes—have been the rallying cry of every election since that time. The property tax has long been a primary source of revenue for local governments, and property tax limitations and reforms have fallen particularly heavily on local governments. There has been no fall-off in the demand for or the cost of roads, utilities, parks, or the other items of public infrastructure that must be provided. In fact, the quantity of needed infrastructure has skyrocketed in recent years, and the quality of infrastructure that is acceptable to most citizens has also spiraled upward. For example, most parents expect public schools today to have computers, swimming pools, chemistry labs, and lighted athletic fields with modern locker rooms, which were considered "luxuries" in most areas of the country a short time ago.

If expansion of public infrastructure is not going to be funded by local taxes, then it must be funded by some other means. Development impact fees are one of those other means. The desirability of impact fees within the broader context of public finance is no longer an issue. Today the issues are about developing impact fee programs that are as consistent as possible with society's goals while at the same time achieving meaningful investment in public infrastructure.

Development impact fees have become institutionalized into modern public finance. They are part land development relations and part a means of raising revenue. The stress between these two roles presents some of the more vexing problems with impact fees themselves and with the ongoing administration of a system of impact fees.

However, despite their shortcomings, development impact fees are here to stay. In reviewing a constitutional challenge to impact fees, the Florida Supreme Court observed:

> [T]he use of impact fees has become an accepted method of paying for public improvements that must be constructed to serve new growth.[1]

While development impact fees are here to stay, they can be implemented in a number of different ways, each with its own set of consequences. The law demands proportionality in impact fees, but proportionality can be achieved in a variety of different ways. One of our goals was to show some of those ways so that communities can gain from the experiences of others as they design or redesign impact fee programs that meet their individual needs. Some of the principles of impact fees are absolute; the amounts imposed as impact fees must be proportional to the impact of the development, and the payment of impact fees must result in an expansion of infrastructure that benefits the development. Other principles of impact fees are relative; impact fees should be fairly and equitably applied.

The cry of "unfair" was coincident with the evolution of required dedications, "exactions," payments in lieu, and impact fees. Developers and their customers were being required to incur costs that had previously been public costs. Things had changed, and change—especially involving money—creates conflict. The state and federal courts and many state legislatures have examined the question, and have largely concluded that development impact fee programs were an important component of local government finance if proportionality of burden is achieved.

Today, fairness is defined in terms of proportionality. Simply put, if development fees are proportional, they are fair. However, communities must live with the development impact fees that they adopt. Living with the resulting fees goes far beyond the proportionality of the amounts of the fees, although amounts usually claim most of the energy in the public debate. Effective impact fee programs must be proportional, but they also must be perceived as reasonable.

The perception of reasonableness will require sound impact fee methodology, but it will require more. Today, the popular term is "transparency," where stakeholders not only can see what is happening but participate in the process. The result should be a perception of reasonableness that will aid immeasurably in the implementation of a program of development impact fees. The goal of impact fees should be to facilitate investment in public infrastructure and thereby accommodate new development. If that goal is achieved within a context of proportionality, then a program of development impact fees will benefit both the existing residents as well as new development, yielding the economic benefits of growth while not degrading existing facilities.

The authors are practitioners as well as academicians. As such, they have attempted to share some of the experience gained and the lessons learned. The most important lessons learned are:

- *Regarding the amount of the impact fee, be a bull or a bear, but don't be a pig.* Include only those costs that are clearly assignable to new developments. No one ever lost a lawsuit for not including a questionable cost. If credits are due, include them. After all, it's only fair.
- *Watch out for the impact of impact fees.* The goal is to get infrastructure built, not stop development or alter the nature of development.
- *Be transparent.* The people who will have to pay the impact fees will have a very different attitude about the program if they have had a role in designing it—and they might even have some good ideas.

IMPACT FEES IN THE FUTURE

While the principal goal of the authors has been to describe the current state of impact fee principles and practice, we will end by hazarding some predictions in regard to the future evolution of impact fee law and practice. To call them predictions is perhaps self-serving since they are also what the authors advocate happening.

UNIFICATION OF DEVELOPER FUNDING REQUIREMENTS

Currently, there are various approaches to a local government requiring developer funding of infrastructure, including required dedication, in-lieu fees, user fees, impact fees, and rezoning conditions. The legal frameworks for these various approaches have developed in different time periods and in different contexts and are therefore often subjected to different standards and legal requirements. While treating them differently and in a parallel manner has probably been helpful in obtaining their legal and political acceptability, the time has come to "unify" them for several reasons.

First, from a developer perspective, there is a possibility that, by treating them differently, the developer may be required to make overlapping "contributions," which, unless proper credit for one against the other is given, the developer could end up paying more than once for the same impact. This is usually avoided through credit provisions of impact fee programs, which require previously made dedications or payment be deducted from the impact fees otherwise due. Nonetheless, the coordination is not always clear or totally effective.

Second, in some jurisdictions, the funding required of the development may vary based on the stage in the development process that it is "collected" or required. This is not fair to either the developer (vis-a-vis other developers) or to the local government since, if they are mutually exclusive, the local government may not be able to collect for the total impact the development has on infrastructure needs.

Third, treating them separately may limit the "options" of both the developer and the local government in making the contributions as palatable as possible to the developer and as economically effective as possible for the local government.

Finally, from a legal perspective, coordination and assimilation of the various methods should result in clearer and more consistent standards for the various approaches that will increase fairness and efficiency for developers and local governments.

A new approach based on coordinating the various "methods" of developer funding requirements is beginning to emerge in Florida and elsewhere in regard to affordable and workforce housing programs. An interesting model is found in the recently adopted workforce housing ordinance by the City of Islamorada, Florida, and in a similar program that would be established by the adoption of a recently proposed workforce housing program ordinance for the City of Destin, Florida.

Under the Destin ordinance, the workforce housing obligation of a developer may be satisfied in the following possible ways:

- On-site construction of workforce housing;
- Off-site construction of workforce housing;
- Conversion of market rate housing to workforce housing;
- Payment of an in-lieu fee determined on the basis of the cost of construction; or
- Payment of money by the developer to a nonprofit organization, such as Habitat for Humanity, which is then obligated to provide the workforce housing units required of the developer.

Since the determination of which approach will be used involves negotiation between the city and the developer, the optimum flexibility and adaptation to the particular site and circumstances of the proposed development can be achieved.

Perhaps synthesizing the legal and planning principles and frameworks for the various developer funding approaches should aid and be aided by the development of a statute, similar to various impact fee enabling acts that now exist in many states, which would provide consistent standards, consistent procedures, and greater integration through clear crediting requirements of all developer funding approaches.

EXPANDING THE BASE AND SCOPE OF INFRASTRUCTURE FUNDING REQUIREMENTS

Two expansions of current developer funding of infrastructure requirements need to occur. First, social and green infrastructure needs to be added to traditional (sometimes referred to as "physical") infrastructure. In the long run, the quality of life that Americans seek requires much more than that because new development also usually creates the need for new or expanded "social" and "green" infrastructure. Roads, parks, and schools may be more obvious needs created by new development, but child care facilities, health care facilities, and workforce housing are also essential. The preservation and protection of green infrastructure (e.g., beaches, aquifer recharge areas, and open space) and environmentally sensitive lands are also key to the quality of life.

Not only must the scope of infrastructure be expanded in order to correctly assess the true costs and impacts of growth, but the types of development that cause impact and therefore should share in its provision must be expanded. For example, it is often the practice to confine developer funding requirements for parks and schools to residential development. This practice places an inequitable burden on residential developers because commercial and industrial developments also "use" school facilities (e.g., hurricane shelters, adult education, recreational facilities, and libraries) and parks (e.g., corporate athletic teams, office picnics, and sports competitions).

INNOVATIVE FUNDING PROGRAMS

Thus far, the land-use control power has been largely used to require developers to fund infrastructure either by paying money in the form of impact fees, user fees, or in-lieu fees, or to dedicate or convey land to the local government, which is obligated to use the money or land to provide infrastructure. Often, the developer is permitted or even encouraged to build infrastructure instead of making payments or dedications.

In the future, many more varied and sophisticated approaches should and will be used. In many states, there is already increased usage of a variant form of infrastructure provision by the development community through tax increment financing (TIF) or, as they are called in some jurisdictions, tax assessment districts. In this approach, the developer, or development authority, retains or receives for a specified period of time the taxes attributable to the developmentally caused increased value of the property to repay the costs of providing infrastructure for the new development. The justification is that the local government is relieved of the need to provide infrastructure to support the new development and, after the TIF period is over, the local government will receive increased revenues based on the new and increased value of the property. TIFs give the developer an incentive to make speedy, efficient, and adequate provision of the infrastructure needed by the new development.

Several states have statutory provisions for the creation of community development districts (CDDs), which somewhat parallel the TIF approach. Private developers are authorized to organize CDDs, which become "mini" local governments for many purposes with the power to tax property within the district to pay for construction and maintenance of infrastructure and provision of other governmental services. The act thereby provides an alternative streamlined method for financing the construction of infrastructure needed by the new development.

Still another approach, which is currently in its infancy, is for developers and the local governments to enter into private/public partnerships in which the local government provides all or a portion of the infrastructure needed by the new development in return for an equity or profit-sharing interest in the development. The basics of this concept are already being partially used in some transit-oriented developments (TODs) in which the public transit authority "furnishes" the land for the development and the mass transit infrastructure in return for lease payments from the developer, which can be keyed to the development's financial successes.

Further development of the "profit-sharing" approach seems both equitable and inevitable. The developer is relieved of providing through equity or loans a significant portion of the capital that would otherwise be needed for the development (land costs and transportation infrastructure) and has the local government as a "partner" financially interested in the economic well-being of the project. The local government or transit authority gets the advantage of a stream of future revenue with fewer strings attached than if it collected impact, user, or in-lieu fees from the developer. The developer is also freed from the need and expense to borrow the money to pay the fees up front, as well as to purchase outright the land needed for the project.

Adapting this approach to non-TODs presents challenges since the "beauty" of the TOD is that the contribution from the local government is clear (land and transit facilities) while in non-TODs, the local government may not own land or have existing transportation or other infrastructure to provide to the development. Nonetheless, if the local government is willing and able to supply a large range of infrastructure (e.g., roads, parks, schools, and libraries), which it could otherwise require the developer to pay for (through an impact fee, for example), then the local government's "investment" is as valuable to the developer as the cash it would receive from a private equity investor. Once again, the possible advantages to the local government are many: It has an income flow that it may receive indefinitely, and it may be less restrained in how that revenue can be spent than if it came as exactions from the development.

STATE AND REGIONAL IMPACT FEES

This book, like most others that discuss infrastructure finance, has emphasized local governments as the source of developer funding requirements. Unfortunately, this accurately corresponds to current practices. Leaving infrastructure provision to local governments ignores current realities and encourages—or even mandates—inequitable imposition of the burden on new growth based on its jurisdictional location. In the long run, local governments cannot be given the responsibility for infrastructure that needs to be provided on a regional and even statewide basis. Many metropolitan areas face an infrastructure disaster, which is created by myriad units of local government, many of which refuse to assume or even recognize regional infrastructure needs. With no regional or state authority to enact or require developer funding requirements on a regionwide basis, a hodgepodge of largely inadequate infrastructure is inevitable.

In the famous decision of the Supreme Court of New Jersey in the *Mt. Laurel* case,[2] the court recognized the concept of regional welfare and required the Village of Mt. Laurel to bear its fair share of the need of the region in which it is located for affordable housing. If expanding urban concentrations are not to suffer more infrastructure inequities, courts and state legislatures must recognize the regional or statewide need for infrastructure and require the adoption of developer funding programs, which ensure that each government entity will bear its fair share of the infrastructure burden of the region in which it is located.

STATE AND FEDERAL FUNDING TO CURE INFRASTRUCTURE DEFICIENCIES

As pointed out in this book, infrastructure funding by the private and public sectors is often viewed as the province and responsibility of local governments. In the future, there must be a greater state role. In fact, in most areas of the country, increased state funding of infrastructure is absolutely essential. Even if local governments use developer funding approaches to fund 100 percent of the cost of providing infrastructure adequate to finance the construction of the infrastructure required by new development—a very unlikely scenario!—local governments have no adequate revenue source to pay for remedying existing deficiencies or what, in impact fee terminology, is often called the "unfunded deficit."

It is unlikely that states alone will be able and willing to pay a major portion of the bill from a political and revenue standpoint. It therefore seems inevitable and necessary that the federal government must also return to its past practice of providing funding for local government infrastructure.

Proposals for federal funding in this area are not new. One of the first and most interesting was proposed by Senator Gary Hart of Colorado, and others, in 1985. Known as S.849, it was "A bill to establish a National Infrastructure Fund to provide funds for interest-free loans to State and local governments for construction and improvement of highways, bridges, water supply and distribution systems, mass transportation facilities and equipment, and wastewater treatment facilities...." Given this nation's current, pressing infrastructure needs, combined with unprecedented growth (America's population will grow by at least 100 million in the next generation), it may only be a matter of time before Congress acts to accomplish goals similar to the Hart proposal.

CONCLUSION

At the beginning of this book, we expressed the wish that this would be the last book on impact fees, and the first on proportionate-share development fees

that include physical, social, and environmental (green) facilities. Proportionate-share development fees would also include O & M costs applied to all development.

In this light, let us ponder that, whatever the future may hold for the evolution of impact fees and related impact-based developer funding requirements, we believe that the next generation of impact fees will become increasingly important ways of funding public infrastructure and its maintenance. Winston Churchill's frequently quoted statement about democracy is an excellent vehicle to describe the role of impact fees today and for many decades to come:

> Many forms of public finance have been tried, and will be tried in this world of sin and woe. No one pretends that impact fees are perfect or all-wise. Indeed, it has been said that impact fees are the worst form of finance except all those other forms that are presently available.

Let us now move on from impact fees to proportionate-share development fees.

NOTES

1. *St. Johns County v. Northeast Florida Builders Association, Inc.*, 583 So.2d 635.
2. 336 A.2d 713, appeal dismissed, cert. denied 423 U.S. 808, 96 S. Ct. 18 (1975).

References and Selected Bibliography

Aaron, Henry. 1975. *Who Pays the Property Tax?* Washington, D.C.: The Brookings Institution.

Abbott, William W. et al. 2001. *Exactions and Impact Fees in California*. Point Arena, Calif.: Solano Press.

Ackerman, Bruce A. and Richard B. Stewart. 1985. "Reforming Environmental Law." 37 *Stan. L. Rev.* 1333, 1335–38.

Alterman, Rachelle, ed. 1988. *Private Supply of Public Services: Evaluation of Real Estate Exactions, Linkage, and Alternative Land Policies*. New York: New York University Press.

Altshuler, Alan and Jose Gomez-Ibanez. 1993. "Regulation for Revenue: The Political Economy of Land Use Exactions." Washington, D.C.: Brookings; Cambridge, Mass.: Lincoln Institute of Land Policy.

Amborski, David P., Jane H. Lillydahl, Arthur C. Nelson, Timothy V. Ramis, Antero Rivasplata, and Steven R. Schell. April 1987. "State and Provincial Approaches to Development Impact Fees: California, Florida, Oregon, Colorado, and Ontario." Paper read at the American Planning Association Conference, New York.

American Association of State Highway and Transportation Officials. November 1986.

American Society of Civil Engineers. 2001. *Report Card for America's Infrastructure*. Accessed April 27, 2003, at www.asce.org/reportcard/index.cfm?reaction=full.

Andrews, Christine and Dwight Merriam. 1988. "Defensible Linkage." In *Development Impact Fees*. Ed. Arthur C. Nelson. Chicago: American Planning Association.

Auerhahn, Elliot. 1988. "Implementing Impact Fee Systems." In *Development Impact Fees*. Ed. Arthur C. Nelson. Chicago: American Planning Association.

Babcock, Richard F. 1987. "Impact Exactions: A Controversial New Way of Financing Development." *Law and Contemporary Problems* 50, 1: 1–04.

Baden, Brett M. and Don L. Coursey. "An Examination of the Effects of Impact Fees on Chicago Suburbs." Unpublished version of *Harris School working paper 99.20* (revised in January 2002). University of Chicago: Harris Graduate School of Public Policy Studies.

Barnebey, Mark P., Tom MacRostie, Gary J. Schoennauer, George T. Simpson, and Jan Winters. 1988. "Paying for Growth: Community Approaches to Developing Impact Fees." *Journal of the American Planning Association* 54, no. 1: 18–28.

Bauman, Gus and William H. Ether. 1987. "Development Exactions and Impact Fees: A Survey of American Practices." *Law and Contemporary Problems* 50, 1: 51–68.

Beatley, Timothy. 1988. "Ethical Issues in the Use of Impact Fees to Finance Community Growth." In *Development Impact Fees*. Ed. Arthur C. Nelson. Chicago: American Planning Association.

Been, Vicky. 2005. "Impact Fees and Housing Affordability." *Cityscape* 8(1): 135–89.

Bendavid-Val, Avron. 1983. *Regional and Local Economic Analysis for Practitioners*. Westport: Conn.: Abbey Publishing.

Blaesser, Brian and Christene M. Kentopp. 1990. "Impact Fees: The Second Generation." *Washington University Journal of Urban and Contemporary Law* 38: 55.

Blair, John and Robert Premus. 1987. "Major Factors in Industrial Location: A Review." *Economic Development Quarterly* 1(1): 72–85.

Blewett, Robert. A. 1983. "Fiscal Externalities and Residential Growth Controls: A Theory-of-Clubs Perspective." *Public Finance Quarterly* 11: 3–20.

Blewett, Robert A. and Arthur C. Nelson. 1988. "A Public Choice and Efficiency Argument for Impact Fees." In *Development Impact Fees*. Ed. Arthur C. Nelson. Chicago: American Planning Association.

Bosselman, Fred and David Callies. 1972. *The Quiet Revolution in Land Use Control*. Washington, D.C.: Council for Environmental Quality.

Bosselman, Fred and Nancy Stroud. 1985. "Pariah to Paragon: Developer Exactions in Florida 1975–85." 3 *Stetson Law Review* 14.

Braun, Mark. 2003. "Suburban Sprawl in Southeastern Wisconsin: Planning, Politics, and the Lack of Affordable Housing." In *Suburban Sprawl: Culture, Theory, and Politics*. Ed. Matthew Lindstrom and Hugh Bartling. Lanham, Md.: Rowman & Littlefield Publishers.

Bringardner, Bruce W. 2000. "Exactions, Impact Fees, and Dedications: National and Texas Law After *Dolan And Del Monte Dunes*." *Urban Lawyer* 32: 561.

Brueckner, Jan K. 1989. "Pricing Implications of Development Exactions on Existing Housing Stock." *Growth and Change* 20, 1–12.

———. 1997. "Infrastructure Financing and Urban Development: The Economics of Impact Fees." *Journal of Public Economics* 66, 383–407.

———. 1998. "Testing for Strategic Interaction Among Local Governments: The Case of Growth Controls." *Journal of Urban Economics* 44, 438–467.

Brueckner, Jan K. and Luz A. Saavedra. 2001. "Do Local Governments Engage in Strategic Property-Tax Competition?" *National Tax Journal* 54, 2, 203–30.

Brumbaugh, Robert W. (nd). "Wetland Mitigation Banking: Entering a New Era?" Available at www.wes.army.mil/el/wrtc/wrp/bulletins/v5n3/brum.html.

Burchell, Robert W. and David Listokin. 1978. *Fiscal Impact Handbook*. New Brunswick, N.J.: Center for Urban Policy Research.

———. 1995. *Land, Infrastructure, Housing Costs and Fiscal Impacts Associated With Growth: The Literature on the Impacts of Sprawl Versus Managed Growth*. Cambridge, Mass.: Lincoln Institute of Land Policy.

Burchell, Robert W. et al. 1994. *Development Impact Assessment Handbook*. Washington, D.C.: Urban Land Institute.

———. 2000. *The Costs of Sprawl—Revisited*. Washington: National Academy Press.

Burge, Gregory S. and Keith R. Ihlanfeldt. 2006. "Impact Fees and Single-Family Home Construction." *Journal of Urban Economics* 60: 284–306.

———. 2006. "The Effects of Impact Fees on Multifamily Housing Construction." *Journal of Regional Science* 46: 5–23.

California Office of Planning and Development. 1982. *Paying the Piper*. Sacramento: State of California.

Callies, David L. and Robert H. Freilich. 1986. *Cases and Materials on Land Use*. 5th ed., St. Paul: West, 2008.

Callies, David L., Daniel J. Curtin Jr., and Julie A. Tappendorf. 2003. *Bargaining for Development: A Handbook on Development Agreements, Annexation Agreements, Land Development Conditions, Vested Rights, and the Provision of Public Facilities*. Washington, D.C.: Environmental Law Institute.

Campbell, Douglas. 2004. "The Incidence of Development Impact Fees." Unpublished dissertation. Georgia State University.

Carrión, Carmen and Lawrence W. Libby. 2001. "Development Impact Fees: A Primer." Working Paper: AEDE-WP-0022-01. Ohio State University Extension, Department of Agricultural, Environmental and Development Economics.

Cervero, Robert. 1986. *Suburban Gridlock*. New Brunswick, N.J.: Center for Urban Policy Research, Rutgers University.

Cervero, Robert and John Greitzer. 1987. "Money For Mobility: Lessons from California on Off Site Road Financing." *Urban Land* 48, no. 8: 2–6.

Choat, P. and S. Walter. 1981. *America in Ruins*. Washington: Council of State Planning Agencies.

Clarke, Wes and Jennifer Evans. 1999. "Development Impact Fees and the Acquisition of Infrastructure." *Journal of Urban Affairs* 21: 281.

Connerly, Charles E. 1988. "Impact Fees as Social Policy: What Should be Done?" In *Development Impact Fees*. Ed. Arthur C. Nelson. Chicago: American Planning Association.

Connors, Donald and Michael High. 1987. "The Expanding Circle of Exactions: From Dedications to Linkage," 50 *Law & Contemp. Probs*. 51.

Crawford, James A. 1987. "Paying for Transportation Improvements: Public vs. Private Costs." *The Real Estate Finance Journal* 45–51.

DeHaven Smith, Lance. 1985. "Special Districts: A Structural Approach to Infrastructure Finance and Management." In *The Changing Structure of Infrastructure Finance*. Ed. James Nicholas. Cambridge, Mass.: Lincoln Institute of Land Policy.

Delaney, Charles J. and Marc Smith. 1989. "Impact Fees and the Price of New Housing: An Empirical Study." *AREUA Journal* 17: 41–54.

Denbo, Susan M. 1994. "Development Exactions: A New Way to Fund State and Local Government Infrastructure Improvements and Affordable Housing?" 23 *Real Est. L.J.* 7, 11 (Summer).

Dennison, Mark S. 1997. Wetland Mitigation 1–3.

Dennison, Mark S. and James F. Berry. 1993. "Wetlands: Guide to Science, Law, and Technology." Park Ridge, N.J.: Noyes Publications, 268.

Dowall, David E. 1980. "An Examination of Population Growth-Managing Communities." *Policy Studies Journal* 9: 414–27.

———. 1984. *The Suburban Squeeze*. Berkeley: University of California Press.

Downing, Paul and James Frank. 1982. *Recreational Impact Fees: A Discussion of the Issues and a Survey of Current Practice in the United States, with Guidelines For Florida Application*. Tallahassee: Policy Sciences Program, Florida State University.

Dreisen, David M. 1998. "Is Emissions Trading an Economic Incentive Program?: Replacing the Command and Control Economic Incentive Dichotomy." 55 *Wash & Lee L. Rev.* 289, 323.

Dresch, Marla and Steven M. Sheffrin. 1997. *Who Pays for Development Impact Fees and Exactions?* San Francisco: Public Policy Institute of California.

Duffy, Kevin. 2003. "Restoring Nature." *Atlanta Journal Constitution*, p. C1 (Monday, March 31).

Dunec, JoAnne L. 1998. "Economic Incentives: Alternatives for the Next Millenium." 12 *SPG Nat. Resources & Env't* 292.

Duncan, James B., Terry D. Morgan, and Norman R. Standerfer. 1986. *Simplifying and Understanding the Art and Science of Impact Fees*. Austin, Tex.: City of Austin Planning Department.

Elliott, Michael. 1981. "The Impact of Growth Control Regulations on Housing Prices in California." *AREUEA Journal* 9, no. 2: 115–33.

Ellickson, Robert C. 1977. "Suburban Growth Controls: An Economic and Legal Analysis." 86 *Yale Law Journal* 385.

Evans-Cowley, Jennifer S. and Larry L. Lawhon. 2003. "The Effects of Impact Fees on the Price of Housing and Land: A Literature Review." *Journal of Planning Literature* 17: 351.

Fischel, William. 1987. "The Economic of Land Use Exactions: A Property Rights Analysis." *Law and Contemporary Problems* 50, 1: 101–14.

Fischel, William A. 2001. *The Home Voter Hypothesis: How Home Values Influence Local Government Taxation, School Finance, and Land-Use Policies*. Cambridge, Mass.: Harvard University Press.

Florida Advisory Committee on Intergovernmental Relations. 1986. *Impact Fees in Florida*. Tallahassee: State of Florida.

Florida State Comprehensive Plan Committee. 1987. *The Keys to Florida's Future: Winning in a Competitive World*. Tallahassee.

Frank, James E. and Paul B. Downing. 1988. "Patterns of Impact Fee Use." In *Development Impact Fees*. Ed. Arthur C. Nelson. Chicago: American Planning Association.

———. 1988. "Determinants of Community Adoption of Fiscal Impact Fees." Paper presented to the American Planning Association, San Antonio. Tallahassee: Department of Urban and Regional Planning.

Frank, James E., Elizabeth R. Lines, and Paul B. Downing. 1985. *Community Experience with Sewer Impact Fees: A National Survey*. Tallahassee: Florida State University.

Frank, James E. and Robert Rhodes. 1987. *Development Exactions*. Chicago: American Planning Association.

Freilich, Robert. 2002. "Time, Space, and Value in Inverse Condemnation: A Unified Theory For Partial Takings Analysis." 24 *U. Haw. L.R.* 589, 616.

Freilich, Robert H. and Peter S. Levi. 1975. *Model Subdivision Regulations: Text and Commentary*. Chicago: APA.

Freilich, Robert H. and Brenda L. Nichols. 1986. "Public Private Partnerships in Joint Development: The Legal and Financial Anatomy of Large Scale Urban Development Projects." *Municipal Finance Journal* 71.

Freilich, Robert H. and David W. Bushek, eds. 1995. *Exactions, Impact Fees and Dedications: Shaping Land-Use Development and Funding Infrastructure in the Dolan Era*. Chicago: American Bar Association, State and Local Government Law Section.

Freilich, Robert H., S. Mark White, and Kate F. Murray. 2008. *21st Century Land Development Code*. Chicago: APA Planners Press, 2008.

Frieden, Bernard. 1979. *The Environmental Protection Hustle*. Cambridge, Mass.: MIT Press.

Gafney, Mason. 1973. "Tax Reform to Release Land." In *Modernizing Urban Land Policy*. Ed. Marion Clawson. Baltimore: Johns Hopkins University Press.

Gómez-Ibánez, Jose A. 1996. *The Debate Over Impact Fees*. Illinois Real Estate Letter.

Guorkyo, Joseph. 1991. "Impact Fees, Exclusionary Zoning, and the Density of New Development." *Journal of Urban Economics* 30: 242–56.

Haar, Charles. 1955. "In Accordance With A Comprehensive Plan." 68 *Harv. L.R.* 1154.

Hagman, Donald. 1982. "Landowner Developer Provision of Commercial Goods Through Benefit Based and Harm Avoidance 'Payments' (BHAPS)." 52 *Zoning & Planning L. Rev.*

Hagman, Donald and Julian C. Juergensmeyer. 1986. *Urban Planning and Land Development Control Law*, 2d ed. St. Paul: West.

Hahn, Robert W. and Robert N. Stavins. 1991. "Incentive-Based Environmental Regulation: A New Era From an Old Idea?" 18 *Ecology L.Q.* 1, 5.

Heyman, Ira M. and Thomas K. Gilhool. 1964. "The Constitutionality of Imposing Increased Community Costs on New Suburban Residents Through Subdivision Exactions." 73 *Yale Law Journal*, 1118.

Huffman, Forrest E., Arthur C. Nelson, Marc T. Smith, and Michael Stegman. 1988. "Who Bears the Burden of Development Impact Fees?" In *Development Impact Fees*. Ed. Arthur C. Nelson. Chicago: American Planning Association.

Ihlanfeldt, Keith R. 2004. "Exclusionary Land-use Regulations within Suburban Communities: A Review of the Evidence and Policy Prescriptions." *Urban Studies* 41: 261–83.

Ihlanfeldt, Keith R. and Timothy M. Shaughnessy. 2002. *An Empirical Investigation of the Effects of Impact Fees on Housing and Land Markets*. Cambridge, Mass.: Lincoln Institute of Land Policy.

———. 2004. "An Empirical Investigation of the Effects of Impact Fees on Housing and Land Markets." *Regional Science and Urban Economics* 34: 639–61.

Institute of Transportation Engineers (ITE). 2003. *Trip Generation: An Informational Report*, 7th ed. Washington, D.C.: ITE.

Jacobsen, Frederick A. and Jeffrey Redding. 1977. "Impact Taxes: Making Development Pay Its Way." 55 *N.C. L. Rev.* 407.

James B. Duncan & Associates, Arthur C. Nelson, et al. 1993. *Impact Fee Study: City of Atlanta, Georgia*. Atlanta: Commissioner of Planning.

Janis, Jay. 1975. "Impact Taxes: Unfair (Good Intentions Aside)." *Florida Environmental and Urban Issues* 2. Reprinted in R. Scott, *Management & Control of Growth*, vol. 1, 290–95. Washington, D.C.: Urban Land Institute.

Jeong, Moon-Gi and Richard C. Feiock. 2006. "Impact Fees, Growth Management, and Development: A Contractual Approach to Local Policy Governance." *Urban Affairs Review* 41(6): 749–68.

Johnson, Scott Lee and David M. Pekelney. 1996. "Economic Assessment of the Regional Clean Air Incentives Market: A New Emission Trading Program for Los Angeles." 72 *Land Econ.* 277, 279.

Journal of the American Planning Association, 54, no. 1 (1988). A series of articles on impact fee issues.

Juergensmeyer, Julian C. 1975. "Impact Fees." Ch. 17 of *Florida Land Use Restrictions* (looseleaf). Ed. Julian Juergensmeyer and James Wadley. Kennesaw, Ga.: D&S Publishers.

———. 1980. "Drafting Impact Fees to Alleviate Florida's Preplatted Lands Dilemma." 7 *Fla. Env'l & Urban Issues* 7 (April).

———. 1985. "Funding Infrastructure: Paying the Costs of Growth Through Impact Fees and Other Land Regulation Charges." In *The Changing Structure of Infrastructure Finance*. Ed. James Nicholas. Cambridge, Mass.: Lincoln Institute of Land Policy.

———. 1986. "Implementing Agricultural Preservation Programs: A Time to Consider a Novel Approach." *Gonzaga Law Review* 20: 701.

———. 1986. "Impact Fees after the Growth Management Act of 1985." In *Perspectives on Florida's Growth Management Act of 1985.* Ed. John M. DeGrove and Julian Conrad Juergensmeyer. Cambridge, Mass.: Lincoln Institute of Land Policy.

———. 1988a. "The Development of Regulatory Impact Fees: The Legal Issues." In *Development Impact Fees: Policy Rationale, Practice, Theory, and Issues.* Ed. Arthur C. Nelson. Chicago: American Planning Association.

———. 1988b. "The Legal Issues of Capital Facilities Planning." In *Private Supply of Public Services: Evaluation of Real Estate Exactions, Linkage, and Alternative Land Policies.* Ed. Rachelle Alterman. New York: New York University Press.

Juergensmeyer, Julian C. and Robert Blake. 1981. "Impact Fees: An Answer to Local Governments' Capital Funding Dilemma." 9 *Florida State University Law Review* 3: 415–45.

Juergensmeyer, J. and J. Nicholas. 2002. "Impact Fees Should Not Be Subject to Takings Analysis." In Chapter 15 of *Taking Sides on Takings Issues: Public and Private Perspectives.* Ed. Thomas E. Roberts. Chicago: American Bar Association.

Juergensmeyer, Julian Conrad. 2008. "Infrastructure and the Law: Florida's Past, Present and Future." 23 *Jr. Ld Use & Env'tl Law* 441.

Juergensmeyer, Julian Conrad and Thomas E. Roberts. 2007. *Land Use Planning and Development Regulation Law,* 2d ed. Practitioner Treatise Series. St. Paul: Thomson West.

Kaiser, Edward J. and Raymond J. Burby. 1988. "Exactions in Managing Growth: The Land Use Perspective." In *Private Supply of Public Services.* Ed. Rachelle Alterman. New York: New York University Press.

Kaiser, Edward J., Raymond J. Burby, and David H. Moreau. 1988. "Local Governments' Use of Water and Sewer Impact Fees and Related Policies." In *Development Impact Fees.* Ed. Arthur C. Nelson. Chicago: American Planning Association.

Kayden, Jerold and Robert Pollard. 1987. "Linkage Ordinances and Traditional Exactions Analysis: The Connection Between Office Development and Housing," 50 *Law & Contemp. Probs.* 1.

Kolo, Jerry and Todd Dicker. 1993. "Practical Issues in Adopting Local Impact Fees." *State and Local Government Review* 253: 197–206.

Kurtz, Johannes W. 1987. "Developer Contributions to Public Road Improvements." *ITE Journal* 29–32.

Ladd, Helen. 1998. *Local Government Tax and Land Use Policies in the United States: Understanding the Links.* Cambridge, Mass.: Lincoln Institute of Land Policy.

Landis, John D. 1986. "Land Regulation, Market Structure, and Housing Price Inflation: Lessons from Three California Cities." *Journal of the American Planning Association* 52, 1: 9–21.

Landis, John et al. 2001. *Pay to Play: Residential Development Fees in California Cities and Counties.* Sacramento: State of California Department of Housing and Community Development.

Ledman, Thomas W. 1993. "Local Government Environmental Mitigation Fees: Development Exactions, the Next Generation." 45 *Fla. L. Rev.* 835, 865.

Lee, Douglass B. 1988. "Evaluation of Impact Fees Against Public Finance Criteria." In *Development Impact Fees.* Ed. Arthur C. Nelson. Chicago: American Planning Association.

Leithe, Joni L. with Matthew Montavon. 1990. *Impact Fee Programs: A Survey of Design and Administrative Issues.* Washington, D.C.: Government Finance Research Center.

Leitner, Martin L. and Eric J. Strauss. 1988. "A Municipal Impact Fee Ordinance Based on the Standard Development Impact Fee Enabling Statute, with Commentary." In *Development Impact Fees.* Ed. Arthur C. Nelson. Chicago: American Planning Association.

Levine, Jonathan C. 1994. "Equity in Infrastructure Finance: When Are Impact Fees Justified?" *Land Economics* 70(2): 210–22.

Leyden, Pat. 1998. "The Price of Change: The Market Incentive Revolution." 12-WTR *Nat. Resources & Env't* 160, 161.

Lillydahl, Jane H., Arthur C. Nelson, Timothy V. Ramis, Antero Rivasplata, and Steven R. Schell. 1988. "The Need for a Standard State Impact Fee Enabling Act." In *Development Impact Fees.* Ed. Arthur C. Nelson. Chicago: American Planning Association.

Malizia, Emil, Richard Norton, and Craig Richardson. 1997. "Reading, Writing, and Impact Fees." *Planning* 63(9): 17–20.

Mayer, Christopher J. and C. Tsuriel Somerville. 2000. "Land Use Regulation and New Construction." *Regional Science & Urban Economics* 30: 639.

"Mandatory Dedication of Land by Land Developers." 1973. Note, 26 *U. Fla. L. Rev.* 41.

Mathur, S., H. Blanco, and P. Waddell. 2004. "The Effect of Impact Fees on the Price of New Single Family Housing." *Urban Studies* 41: 1303–12.

Mathur, Shishir. 2007. "Do Impact Fees Raise the Price of Existing Housing?" *Housing Policy Debate* 18(4): 635–59.

McFarlane, Alastair. 1999. "Taxes, Fees, and Urban Development." *Journal of Urban Economics* 46: 416.

McGee, Robert W. and Walter E. Block. 1994. "Pollution Trading Permits as a Form of Market Socialism and the Search for a Real Market Solution to Environmental Pollution." 6 *Fordham Envtl. L. J.* 51, 53.

McMillen, Daniel P. 1990. "The Timing and Duration of Development Tax Rate Increases." *Journal of Urban Economics* 28: 1–18.

Meck, Stuart, ed. 2002. *Growing Smart Legislative Guidebook.* Chicago: American Planning Association.

Merriam, Dwight. 1999. *The Takings Issue: Constitutional Limits on Land Use Control and Environmental Regulation.* Washington, D.C.: Island Press, 517.

———. 2001. "Reengineering Regulation to Avoid Takings." 33 *Urb. Law* 1, 16.

Mieszkowski, Peter. 1972. "The Property Tax: An Excise Tax or a Profit Tax?" *Journal of Public Economics* 1, 2: 73–96.

Morgan, Terry D. 1988. "Shortcomings of Impact Fee Law and Future Trends." In *Development Impact Fees.* Ed. Arthur C. Nelson. Chicago: American Planning Association.

Morgan, Terry D., James Duncan, and Bruce McClendon. 1986. "Drafting Impact Fee Ordinances." *Planners Advisory Service Memorandum*. Chicago: American Planning Association.

Musgrave, Richard A. and Peggy B. Musgrave. 1989. *Public Finance in Theory and Practice*, 5th ed. New York: McGraw-Hill.

Muth, Richard F. 1960. "The Demand for Non-Farm Housing." In *The Demand for Durable Goods*. Ed. Arnold C. Harberger. Chicago: University of Chicago Press.

National Association of Home Builders. 1984. *Impact Fees: A Developer's Manual*. Washington: National Association of Home Builders.

———. 1988. *Impact Fee Manual*. Washington: National Association of Home Builders.

Nelson, Arthur C. 1986. "Impact Fees as an Emerging Method of Infrastructure Finance." *Florida Policy Review* 2(1): 22–6.

———. 1988a. "Introduction: Development Impact Fee Symposium." *Journal of the American Planning Association* 54(1): 3–6

———. 1988b. "Preface." In *Development Impact Fees*. Ed. Arthur C. Nelson. Chicago: American Planning Association.

———. 1992. "Impact Fees As a Positive Factor in Urban Planning and Development." *Journal of Urban Planning and Development* 118(2): 59–64.

———. 1994. "Development impact fees: The next generation." *The Urban Lawyer* 26, 3: 541–62.

———. 1995. *System development charges for water, wastewater, and stormwater facilities*. Boca Raton, Fla.: CRC Press.

Nelson, Arthur C. and James B. Duncan. 1995. *Growth Management: Principles and Practices*. Chicago: American Planning Association.

Nelson, Arthur C. et al. 1991. "Price Effects of Road and Other Impact Fees." *Transportation Research Record* 1305: 36–41.

———. 2002. *The Link Between Growth Management and Housing Affordability: The Academic Evidence*. Discussion Paper. Washington, D.C.: The Brookings Institution Center on Urban and Metropolitan Policy.

Nelson, Arthur C. and Mitch Moody. 2003. *Paying for Prosperity: Impact Fees and Job Growth*. Working paper. Washington, D.C.: The Brookings Institution Center on Urban and Metropolitan Policy.

Nelson, Arthur C., James C. Nicholas, and Lindell L. Marsh. 1992. "Environmental Linkage Fees are Coming." 58 *Planning* 1, 2.

Netzer, Dick. 1988. "Exactions in the Public Finance Context." In *Private Supply of Public Services: Evaluation of Real Estate Exactions, Linkage, and Alternative Land Policies*. Ed. R. Alterman. New York: New York University Press.

Netzer, Dick, Michael Schill, and Scott Susin. 2001. "Changing Water and Sewer Finance: Distributional Impacts and Effects on the Viability of Affordable Housing." *Journal of the American Planning Association* 67: 420.

Nicholas, James C., ed. 1985. *The Changing Structure of Infrastructure Finance*. Cambridge, Mass.: Lincoln Institute of Land Policy.

———. 1987. "Impact Exactions: Economic Theory, Practice, and Incidence." *Law and Contemporary Problems* 50, 1: 85–100.

———. 1987. "The Use of Benefit Fees and Assessments in Financing Transportation Improvements." In *Understanding The Highway Finance Evolution/Revolution*. Washington D.C.: American Association of State Highway and Transportation Officials.

———. 1988a. *Calculating Impact Fees Under the Rational Nexus Test*. Chicago: American Planning Association.

———. 1988b. *Calculating Proportionate Share Impact Fees*. Chicago: American Planning Association.

———. 1988c. "Designing Proportionate Share Impact Fees." In *The Private Supply of Public Services*. Ed. Rachelle Alterman. New York: New York University Press.

———. 1992. "On the Progression of Impact Fees." *Journal of the American Planning Association*, vol. 58, no. 4.

Nicholas, James C. and Julian Conrad Juergensmeyer. 2003. "Market Based Approaches to Environmental Preservation: To Environmental Mitigation Fees and Beyond." *Natural Resources Journal* 43: 837.

Nicholas, James C. and Arthur C. Nelson. 1988. "Determining the Appropriate Development Impact Fee Using the Rational Nexus Test." *Journal of the American Planning Association* 54, no. 1: 54–66.

Nicholas, J., J. Juergensmeyer, and E. Basse. 1999. "Perspectives Concerning the Use of Environmental Mitigation Fees as Incentives in Environmental Protection." Part I, 7 *Env. Liab.* 27; Part II, 7 *Env. Liab.* 71.

Nicholas, James C., Arthur C. Nelson, and Julian C. Juergensmeyer. 1991. *A Practitioner's Guide to Development Impact Fees*. Chicago: American Planning Association.

Opinion No. 86 018, 71 Opin. of Atty. Gen'l. 87 (March 24, 1986).

Peiser, Richard B. 1988. "Calculating Equity Neutral Water and Sewer Impact Fees." *Journal of the American Planning Association* 54, no. 1: 38–48.

Pendall, Rolf. 2000. "Local Land Use Regulation and the Chain of Exclusion." *Journal of the American Planning Association* 66: 125.

Polesetsky, Matthew. 1995. "Will a Market in Air Pollution Clean the Nation's Dirty Air?: A Study of the South Coast Air Quality Management District's Regional Clean Air Incentives Market." 22 *Ecology L.Q.* 359, 369.

Porter, Douglas R. 1986. "The Rights and Wrongs of Impact Fees." *Urban Land* 45, 7: 16–19.

———. 1988. "Will Developers Pay to Play?" In *Development Impact Fees*. Ed. Arthur C. Nelson. Chicago: American Planning Association.

Porter, Douglas R., Ben C. Lin, and Richard B. Peiser. 1987. *Special Districts: A Useful Techniques for Financing Infrastructure*. Washington, D.C.: Urban Land Institute.

Porter, Douglas R. and Richard B. Peiser. 1984. *Financing Infrastructure to Support Community Growth*. Washington, D.C.: Urban Land Institute.

Powers, Ann. 1998. "Reducing Nitrogen Pollution on Long Island Sound: Is There a Place for Pollutant Trading?" 23 *Colum. J. Envtl. L.* 137, 161.

Recht, J. Richard. 1988. "Rose Bushes Have Thorns." In *Development Impact Fees*. Ed. Arthur C. Nelson. Chicago: American Planning Association.

Roberts, Thomas H. 1985. "Funding Public Capital Facilities: How Community Planning Can Help." In *The Changing Structure of Infrastructure Finance*. Ed. James Nicholas. Cambridge, Mass.: Lincoln Institute of Land Policy.

Rosenberg, Nick. 2003. "Development Impact Fees: Is Limited Cost Internalization Actually Smart Growth?" *Boston College Environmental Affairs Law Review* 30: 641.

Roth, Joy. 1998. *Mitigation Banking and the Clean Water Act*, Professional Geologist, October.

Sandler, Ralph D. and Edward T. Denham. 1986. "Transportation Impact Fees: The Florida Experience." Paper presented to the 1986 meeting of the Transportation Research Board, Washington, D.C., January.

Schechter, Barry. 1976. "Taxes on Land Development: An Economic Analysis." In *Economic Issues in Metropolitan Growth*. Ed. Paul R. Portney. Baltimore: Johns Hopkins University Press.

Schell, Steven R. and Timothy V. Ramis. 1987. "Systems Development Charges in Oregon." *Journal of the American Planning Association Development Impact Fee Symposium*, 1987 Conference of the American Planning Association.

Schnidman, Frank and R. Lisle Baker. 1983. "Planning for Platted Lands: Land Use Remedies for Lot Sales Subdivisions." 11 *Fla. Stat. Univ. L. Rev.* 505.

Schust, Sunny Mays. 1986. "States Explore Highway Funding Methods." Washington D.C.: American Association of State Highway and Transportation Officials, October.

Schuyler, Nina. 1995. "Clean Air Inc.: Do Market-Based Emissions Controls Mean the Poor Breathe the Dirtiest Air?" 15 *Cal. Law.* 39.

Scott, Randall with David J. Brower and Dallas Miner. 1975. *Management and Control of Growth*. Three volumes. Washington, D.C.: Urban Land Institute.

Selmi, Daniel P. 1998. "Impacts of Air Quality Regulation on Economic Development." 13 *Nat. Resources & the Env't* 382, 386.

Siemon, Charles, Wendy Larsen, and John D. Purdy. 1988. "Fiscal Impact Report for Citrus County, Florida." Chicago: Siemon, Larson & Purdy, February.

Singell, Larry D. and Jane H. Lillydahl. 1990. "An Empirical Examination of the Effect of Impact Fees on the Housing Market." *Land Economics* 66(1): 82–92.

Skaburskis, Andrejs and M. Qadeer. 1992. "An Empirical Estimation of the Price Effects of Development Impact Fees." *Urban Studies* 29(5): 653–67.

Skidmore, Mark and Michael Peddle. 1998. "Do Development Impact Fees Reduce the Rate of Residential Development?" *Growth and Change* 29(4): 383–400.

Slack, Enid and Richard Bird. 1991. "Financing Urban Growth Through Development Charges." *Canadian Tax Journal* 39: 1288.

Smith, Adam. 1999. "The Wealth of Nations." As quoted in R. Heilbroner, *The Worldly Philosophers*, Seventh Edition. New York: Touchstone, 50.

Smith, Tyson and Julian Conrad Juergensmeyer. 2007. "Development Impact Fees 2006: A Year in Review." 59 *Planning & Envt'l L.* 3 (February).

Snyder, Thomas P. and Michael A. Stegman. 1986. *Financing the Public Costs of Growth*. Washington, D.C.: Urban Land Institute.

———. 1987. *Paying for Growth: Using Development Fees to Finance Infrastructure*. Washington, D.C.: Urban Land Institute.

Somerville, C. Tsuriel and Christopher J. Mayer. 2002. *Government Regulation and Changes in the Affordable Housing Stock, Centre for Urban Economics and Real Estate*. University of British Columbia Working Paper 02-02.

Stewart, Harry A. 1988. "Impact Fees: The Mettle Public Officials Need to Meddle with the Market." In *Development Impact Fees*. Ed. Arthur C. Nelson. Chicago: American Planning Association.

Stroud, Nancy. 1988. "Legal Considerations of Development Impact Fees." In *Development Impact Fees*. Ed. Arthur C. Nelson. Chicago: American Planning Association.

Susskind, Lawrence. 1983. *Proposition 2½: Its Impact on Massachusetts*. Cambridge, Mass.: Oelgeschlager, Gunn & Hain Publishers.

Toombs, W. Scott. 1987. "The Linkage of Infrastructure Costs to Private Development." *The Real Estate Finance Journal* 40–43.

Townsend, Bradford. 1996. "Development Impact Fees: A Fair Share Formula for Success." *Public Management* 78(4): 10–16.

Turnbull, Geoffrey. 2004. "Urban Growth Controls: Transitional Dynamics of Development Fees and Growth Boundaries." *Journal of Urban Economics* 55: 215–37.

Turner, Marjut H. and Richard Gannon. 1999. "Mitigation Banking." In *Watersheds: Water, Soil, and Hydro-Environmental Decision Support System*, 1. Available at www.agiweb.org/legis105/tpgjoy.html.

U.S. Department of Transportation. 1985. *National Personal Transportation Study: Survey Tabulations 1983-84*. Washington, D.C.: Government Printing Office.

U.S. Environmental Protection Agency (US EPA). 2002. *Region 9 Air Problems: EPA's Evaluation of the RECLAIM Program in the South Coast Air Quality Management District*. Washington, D.C.: U.S. EPA (November).

Watkins, A. 1999. "Impacts of Land Development Charges." *Land Economics* 75(3): 415–24.

Weitz, Stevenson. 1984. "Funding Infrastructure for Growth.: In *Impact Fees: A Developer's Manual*. Washington, D.C.: National Association of Home Builders.

———. 1985. "Who Pays Infrastructure Benefit Charges?" In *The Changing Structure of Infrastructure Finance*. Ed. James C. Nicholas. Cambridge, Mass.: Lincoln Institute of Land Policy.

White House Council of Environmental Quality. 1993. "Protecting America's Wetlands: A Fair, Flexible, and Effective Approach" (August 24).

Whitsitt, Shirley J. 1997. "Wetlands Mitigation Banking." 3 *Envtl. Law.* 441, 454 (February).

Yinger, John. 1998. "The Incidence of Impact Fees and Special Assessments." *National Tax Journal* 51(1): 23–41.

York, Marie L. 1991. "The Orlando affordable housing demonstration project." *Journal of the American Planning Association* 57, 4: 490–93.

Index

A

Act, 114. *See also* enabling act, *as well as*
entries under individual states
203 (Wisconsin), 123–24
477 (Wisconsin), 123
1719 (Arkansas), 118, 124
California Mitigation Fee, 101, 110n69
Clean Air, 322n15
Comprehensive Planning and Land
Development Regulation, 291.
See also Destin (FL)
County Powers Relief (Tennessee), 123
Environmental Land and Water
Management (Florida), 324
Florida Impact Fee, 116, 123, 125, 343
Georgia Development Impact Fee, 98–99,
116, 129–39, 165, 349, 361–63, 369
Local Government Comprehensive
Planning and Land
Development Regulation
(Florida), 324
NEPA, 312, 322n15
New Mexico's Development Fees, 219
Quimby, 16. *See also* "Quimby fees"
Water Pollution Control (Clean Water),
101n6, 312, 322nn2, 15, 323n24.
See also Clean Water Act (CWA)
adequate facilities and infrastructure,
xviii, 4, 103, 155, 217, 335–38,
389–91. *See also* infrastructure, social
housing, affordable, 291. *See also*
affordable housing
LOS, 160, 166
maintenance, 8
tax, 123
administrative codes, 367–95. *See also*
impact fees
advisory committee, 122, 129, 132, 139,
361, 381
affordability
of new homes, 257
of workforce housing, 284–85
affordable
housing, xvii, xix, 106–8, 132–33, 156,
257, 258, 260, 261–62, 268–69,
272, 284–85, 309, 390. *See also*
infrastructure, social
fees or exactions for, 107, 158, 215,
217, 222

impact fee waivers for, 122, 129–30,
137–38, 158, 194, 358
public services, 3
workforce housing, 207, 263, 274–80,
283, 284–85, 291–92, 295, 388
new approach to in Florida, 388–89.
See also Destin (FL)
Agins, 102, 111n80
Agins formula, 102
air pollution, 311–12. *See also* pollution
Albuquerque (NM)
annual growth rate, 252
costs of roads, 251–52
credits, 143, 252
differences in capacity among the
service areas, 252, 255
drainage impact fee case study, 238–43
fire facilities impact fee case study,
214–15
"growth tier" impact fee system, 125
new development, 221, 243, 252, 255
parks impact fee case study, 143,
215–22
transportation impact fee case study,
245–56
Albuquerque Metropolitan Arroyo Flood
Control Agency (AMAFCA),
241–43
alternative
collection mechanism, 326–27
funding, xvii, 209, 390
impact fee
calculation approaches, 129–30
structure, 337
mitigation, 291, 293, 297, 299–300, 314
production techniques, 305–6
regulatory, 112n130
source of revenue, 6
transportation, 133–34, 136, 338–40,
343–44. *See also* Circulator
System
to transportation concurrency, 340–41
AMAFCA. *See* Albuquerque Metropolitan
Arroyo Flood Control Agency
Anne Arundel County (MD), 142–43, 164.
See also Montgomery County (MD)
appeals, 137, 324, 330, 337, 344, 357, 359,
361, 364, 365, 374, 378, 380. *See also*
state courts of appeal

applicability
of impact fees, 106, 130, 133
of *Nollan/Dolan* to, 100–101
of ordinance, 292, 299, 324, 342, 355,
359, 361, 379
of standards-based and plan-based
methods, 183
applicable
fee schedules, 136–37, 369, 374
generally
fees, 101
law, 102, 327
standards, 103
applicable
land uses, 137, 144
law, 142
LOSs, to existing and new growth and
development, 115, 133
approval
credits for, 138
of development, 4, 7, 16, 94, 96, 99–101,
106, 110n69, 137, 152, 155, 157,
292, 294–300, 309, 350, 352
planning, 6
voter, 7
Arizona
and California courts, 100
Court of Appeals, 100
enabling act, 115
and Florida, 16
statute regulating impact fees, 103, 137
Arkansas
Act 1719, 124
Act requires a "capital plan," 117–18
enabling act, 124
Army Corps of Engineers (Army Corps), 312
Atlanta (GA), 129, 130–34, 137
first to use functional population, 222
first to use recoupment-based fees,
222–27
functional population of, 172
impact fee case study, 215, 222–27
road impact fees and, 104
attributable
to adding capacity, percentage of cost, 162
cost, 221, 308
to employment, 173
future revenue credits, to new
development, 149–50

attributable (*continued*)
  needs, concept of benefits received
    clearly distinct from, 98
  to new development, 184, 243, 292, 298,
    309, 357, 389
  reasonably, 115–16, 308. *See also*
    necessitated by and attributable
    to; proportionate share;
    "reasonable relationship"
    standard or test; reasonably
    related
  "specifically and uniquely," 96–97,
    100, 308. See also *Pioneer Trust &*
    Savings Bank v. Village of Mount
    Prospect
  sufficiently, 97
  travel, 105, 112n110, 309
attribution of benefits and burdens
  environmental mitigation fees and, 305
  functional population approach and,
    222
authority to impose impact acts, 124
Aventura (FL)
  Circulator System, 339–41
  Comprehensive Plan, 337–46
  Express, 337–38
  Florida, case study of transportation
    operations, 337
  mitigation fee, 337
  policy of transportation concurrency
    exception, 339
  requires new means for movement, 338
  Transportation Mitigation Program,
    339–41
average
  cost method, 187
  fees
    by facility type, 17
    by land use, 17
    by state, 17
  impact fee, 16
  resident occupies residential space, 172
  single-family impact fees, 17
  total fee for states, 19
avoid current existing facility deficiencies,
  132

B

Banberry Development Corp. v. South Jordan
  City, 98, 105, 143, 145, 150
BART. *See* Bay Area Rapid Transit
base rate, 334
  total impact fees, 16
basin-based and basin-grouped approaches
  to drainage, 239–41
basis
  for attributing a portion of the cost of
    protection of new development,
    305–16
  for determining employees per unit of
    land use, 280
  for impact fees, 139
  of impact fees and the police power,
    7, 308

Bay Area Rapid Transit (BART), 148
benefit
  to advance mitigation, 314
  assessment, xvii, 165. *See also* impact fees
  districts, 165–70
Billings Properties, Inc., v. Yellowstone
  County, 100
Boulder (CO), 16
Bozeman (MT), 152
Branhaven Plaza v. Inland Wetlands Comm'n
  of Branford, 316
Broward County (FL), 307
  citizens attacked the land-use fee, 315
  land-use fee for road improvement,
    94
Broward County v. Janis Development Corp.,
  10
building permit, 293
  abandoned, 138
  expires, 138
  impact fee collection and, 95, 96, 106,
    121, 123, 138, 295, 326, 344–45,
    349–50, 352, 370–71
  issuance, 96, 99, 106, 109n20, 123, 138,
    295, 299, 325–26, 352, 356–57,
    371, 378, 382
burden
  borne by developers, 94, 95, 98–99, 105,
    106, 312
  of capital costs, 5, 93, 95, 108n6, 115,
    158, 222
  of growth, 97, 306
  legal, 96, 102, 110n69, 322n2
  of rapid population growth, 306
Bush, President George H. W.
  about wetlands loss, 312
"buy-in"
  fees, 134
  method, 183, 215, 217, 239, 242

C

calculating. *See also* revenue credits
  fees in Georgia, 116
  functional population, in Collier
    County (FL), 233–34
  future revenue credits, 148
  government buildings impact fee
    case study of, 232–34
    Collier County (FL), 232
  impact fees, 103, 105, 116, 120–22, 127,
    130, 138, 181, 209–13, 256, 308
    credits and, 141, 143, 145, 146,
      148–50, 152, 153
    for drainage systems, 242
    rational nexus and proportionate-
      share concepts, 256
    transportation for streets in Martin
      County (FL), 243–50
  local impact cost per land use, 245
  physical quantity of roads, 245, 309
  service areas for drainage in
    Albuquerque (NM), 239
  SDC, 184–85
calculations for housing linkage, 260

California. *See also* "Quimby fees"
  CIE, internal consistency required,
    158–59
  Court of Appeal, 101
  impact fee upheld, 98
  Mitigation Fee Act, 101, 110n69
  "reasonable relations" of, 307–8
  RECLAIM, 310–12
  school impact fees, widespread but
    capped, 91n1, 114, 118
  Supreme Court, 101–2
calls-for-service approach, 173–74
Canton (GA), 227–31, 349–66
  Comprehensive Plan, 361–66
  fees charged only on residential
    development, 227
  model ordinance, 349
  road impact fee ordinance, 361–66
capacity
  fees, 15
  LOS provided by roadways, 246–51
capital
  cost, 115, 131, 142–43, 144, 148
    project improvement, 162
  costs to the development, 95
  demand estimates general formula, 232
  facilities and service levels, xvii–xviii,
    16, 95, 103, 104, 115, 134, 136,
    142, 158–59, 161
  improvements, 15–16, 124, 131,
    138–39, 156. *See also* capital
    improvements element (CIE);
    capital improvements plan/
    program (CIP)
  costs and expenses, 7–8, 13, 94, 95,
    96–98, 103, 107, 130, 144, 158
  determining impact fees, 118
  element. *See* capital improvements
    element (CIE)
  facility needs, 103, 129, 155, 160
  financing, 5, 10, 15, 16, 93, 96, 104–5,
    139, 145, 146, 148, 152
  include major infrastructure
    investments, 105, 108, 161
  list, 152, 156
  and new development, 5
  projects proposed for each service
    area, 161, 162
  plan. *See* capital improvements plan/
    program (CIP)
  recovery fees, 15. *See also* impact fees
  spending, 5
capital improvements element (CIE),
  138–39, 155, 157, 158–59, 160–63,
  165–70, 181–82, 232, 247
capital improvements plan/program
  (CIP), 104, 118, 121, 123, 155–59,
  164, 239
  for Albuquerque (NM), 219, 221,
    242–43, 247
  calculation approaches and, 181–88
  capital improvements projects
    included in, 163
  "construction credits" and, 137–38

for DeKalb County, Canton (GA), parks and recreation system, 159, 165–70, 227
five- to 10-year, 104, 157, 158, 161, 219, 351
impact fee Magna Carta and, 155
"latecomer fee" and, 152
for Martin County (FL), 231, 243–45
transportation infrastructure and, 182
capitalization
period, 146
rate, 146. *See also* discount, factor
"captured" or "diverted" trips, 105, 309
"cash proffers." *See* proffer system
CDD. *See* community development district
Census Bureau, 3
changes in service area boundaries, 161
changing CIPs, 152. *See also* capital improvements plan/program (CIP), "latecomer fee"
Cherokee County (GA), 98–99, 364, 374–75
Cherokee County v. Greater Atlanta Home Builders Ass'n, 98–99
CIE. *See* capital improvements element
CIP. *See* capital improvements plan/ program
Circulator System, 339–42. *See also* Aventura (FL)
City of Arvada v. City and County of Denver, 98
City of Fayetteville decision (*City of Fayetteville v. IBI, Inc.*), 104
City of Olympia v. Drebick, 101, 104
Clean Water Act (CWA), 108n6, 312, 322n15, 323n24
CMSA. *See* combined metropolitan statistical area
collection of fees, 97, 138
Collier County (FL), 232–38
calculation of workforce housing needs, 283
case study of affordable housing, 263–79
comprehensive planning estimates, 234
critical employee's earnings, 275–76
earnings and employment data by land use, 280
government buildings, 234–39
historic employment by industry, 280–83
household earnings, 271
O & M activities, 274–76
outside help is found, 275
persons per square feet, 238
RRC survey of employers, 280
sales prices of housing, 264–65
housing affordability problem, 268
Colorado
enabling act, 115
federal funding in, 391. *See also* S.849
impact fees in, xvii, 16, 17, 115
Supreme Court, 98
combined metropolitan statistical area (CMSA), 189

Commercial Builders of Northern California v. City of Sacramento, 106, 309
communities
efficient provision of facilities, 163–64
Community Development Department, 344, 345, 380
community development district (CDD), 389
comprehensive
development fee administrative codes, 367–68, 369–95
drainage master plan, 17, 241–42
Growth Management Plan of Martin County (FL), 244
comprehensive
impact fee statute
formulated, in Georgia, 349
lack of, in Florida, 349
land-use plan, 156, 157
Comprehensive Growth Management Plan, 231, 244. *See also* growth; Martin County (FL)
comprehensive plan, 181, 182, 209, 291, 293, 296, 297, 361–66, 369–95. *See also* Comprehensive Growth Management Plan; and also *under individual state, county, and local municipalities*
CIE and, 158–59, 165–70
Destin (FL), 291–303
development impact and, 157
development performance standards and, 316
environment and
impact assessed in, 315
preservation or pollution control established by, 315–16
impact fees and, 102–3, 114, 115, 129, 130, 133, 155–56, 209–14
exemptions to, 137
methodologies used to formulate, 181, 182
"recoupment," 163
infrastructure needs and, 160–61
land-use element, 159–60, 163
land-use regulations, 103
Local Government Comprehensive Planning and Land Development Regulation Act, 191
LOSs and, 133–34, 159
mitigation banking or fees and, 313, 316
program as part of a, 316
service areas and, 160
system improvement and, 161
transportation infrastructure element, 181–82
concept of the environment, in mitigation and tradable emissions, 315–16
condition of approval, 152
Connecticut
Supreme Court, 316. See also *Branhaven Plaza v. Inland Wetlands Comm'n of Branford*

connection charges, 15–16. *See also* impact fees
consideration, need to provide, 98, 100–101, 103, 105, 115, 127, 131, 135, 142, 144, 145, 150–51
constant sample, 19–20
constitutionality
challenge to impact fees, 387
of impact fees, 95–96
in-lieu fees for educational and recreational purposes, 97
"land-use fee" determined to be unconstitutional, 94
required test, 100
standards for developer funding of infrastructure, 99
construction
cost component, 16, 24
credit, 115, 130, 137–38, 142
Consumer Price Index (CPI), 13n11, 13n13, 311
Contractors and Builders Assn. of Pinellas County v. City of Dunedin, 10, 13n11, 98, 104
content of impact fee administrative codes, 367. *See also* sample, impact fee administrative code
cost
capital facilities, 103
new infrastructure, 95
per functional resident, 234
per VMC, 182
subdivision improvements, 158
cost attribution method
systemwide and growth-related, 184
total, 187–88
county
authority to require development approval, 98–99
collection of impact fees, 118
gasoline tax, 245, 252
local governance, 7
Powers Relief Act, 123
school facilities act, 123
County Comprehensive Plan, 355–60. *See also* comprehensive plan
court, 148. *See also state and U.S. supreme courts and courts of appeal*
standard for impact fees, 99
trends, 107–8
courts
assess the validity of impact fees, 308
challenged the San Francisco (CA) transit fee, 334
and credits, 140
and fees, 94
fees as a police power, 96
the taking test, 99
tests for "reasonable" fees, 307
CPI. *See* Consumer Price Index
credit, 140–54, 148, 183
based on the gasoline tax equivalent, 256
different forms of, 143
for future payments, 237

credit (*continued*)
for lapsed approvals, 138
for less than the cost, a, 153
to offset impact fees, 308
provisions, 138
of impact fee programs, 108
for tax payments, 124
criteria
for delineating service areas, 135–36
employers, 274–75
CWA. *See* Clean Water Act

D

debt service on GO bond issues, 151. *See also* general obligation (GO) (bond)
decision charts, 209
decline of the environment, 305–6
dedicated
funding sources, 145
property tax, 151
requirement, 100, 107
revenues, 151
deficiency, 115, 132, 162, 183, 220–21, 227, 231, 242
DeKalb County (GA), 159
capital improvement plan, 167
comprehensive plan, 164–66
historic fund patterns, 167
recommended facility prototypes, 167
delineation of service areas, 159–60
demand, 141, 183
for certain facilities can be estimated, 172–73
for constituents, 93
for investment in public infrastructure, 306
schedule, 130
for travel, 246
description of employment activities related to land uses, 280
desired LOS standard, 105
Destin (FL)
comprehensive plan, 291–303
determining
how existing facilities were financed, 145–50
how much new development has already paid, 150
the quantity of roads, 105
reasonableness of fees, 105
developer, the
exactions, 95
funding fees
in Arizona and California courts, 100
and local government, 107
of public capital facilities, 95
developers
and street, water, sewer, and drainage facilities, 4
development
approval, 16
process and rezoning and subdivision exactions, 157
and capital facilities, 103
credits, 145, 151–52

excise tax, 16
fees
Act, New Mexico's, 219
administrative code, 367
affordable housing, 107
ordinance, sample, 349–66
proportionate-share, xix, 1, 127, 143, 150, 151–52, 207, 257, 283, 334, 347, 349, 387–88, 391
Fee Impact Act of 1990, 129, 165
further out and closer in, 164
Impact Fee Advisory Committee, 139
impact fees, xvii, 4, 23
impacts not covered by impact fees, 157
of the profit-sharing approach, 390
taxes, 16
dilemma: increase services not taxes, 307
"direct benefit" test. *See* Gulest, "direct benefit" test
discount
factor, 146
period, 146–48
rate, 146, 230, 328, 340
distribution of enabling acts. *See* enabling act
division of public services, 94
documents for the justification of impact fees, 155
Dolan v. City of Tigard (*Dolan*), 99–102, 110n61, 110n69, 111n75, 111n102, 322n11
Chief Justice Rehnquist and, 102
land regulation and, 101
Nollan and, 100–101
test, 100
double charging, 98
drafting impact fees to pass judicial scrutiny, 103–6
new capacity portion of the costs separate from total cost, 242
drainage
in Albuquerque (NM), 239
fully served area, 241
impact fees, 21
analysis within city limits of Albuquerque (NM), 241
master fees, 17
to pass judicial scruntiny, 103
reimbursement portion of impact fee, 242
bond repayment, 242
dual rational nexus test, 97–98, 99, 100, 102–4, 107, 109n24, 110n72, 111n78, 129–30, 133, 136, 139, 156, 181, 183, 185, 187–88, 239, 260, 308, 316, 322n10, 342, 355. *See also* Jordan, *Jordan v. Village of Menomonee Falls*
Duncan Associates, 16, 173, 215

E

economic
analysis
base, 176
in calculation of impact fees, 105, 242

of connection between development and linkage program, 99
in formulation and implementation of impact fees, 104–5, 308
burden of regulations, 99
development, 122, 129, 132, 137, 158, 161, 185, 258, 353
strategies, 159
literature, 177
waivers, 137
downturns, affect on acceptance of impact fees, 125
efficiencies, 6
foundation of environmental lands impact fees, 305–6
growth, 97, 137, 337, 388
impact, 176
incentives, 306, 314
recession or downturn, 268, 284, 322n18
economically active households, 258, 269, 271–72
EDU. *See* equivalent dwelling unit
Ehrlich, 101
decision approach, 102
Ehrlich v. City of Culver City, 100–101
eligible facilities, 116–18
emergency medical service (EMS), 6
emissions of nitrogen oxide, 310–11. *See also* pollution, air
EMS. *See* emergency medical service
enabling act
amendments, 124–25
of Canton (GA), 349
legislation and statutes, 16, 93, 96, 103, 125, 155–57, 189, 283, 312, 333, 334, 336, 342
limit impact fees, 209
state, 3, 4, 113–25, 141–42, 144, 155, 218, 389. *See also* Act, *as well entries under individual states*
distribution of, 113–16
planning and analysis requirements of, 118–20
procedural requirements of, 122–23
Senate Bill 185 (Montana), 124
Senate Bill 620 (Arkansas), 124
substantive requirements of, 120–22
encumber, 138–39, 330, 344, 358, 362, 364, 374–78
enterprise fund, 134, 333–34
environmental
impact, by new development on, 316–17
mitigation fees, 107, 305
goal of, 315
implementing the program, 316–17
legal ramifications, 316
preservation/degradation, 305
programs versus programs already in place, 315
use of, 314
Environmental Protection Agency (EPA), 311, 312, 323n24
EPA. *See* Environmental Protection Agency

Equal
    Protection
        Clause of the Fourteenth
            Amendment, 100
        issues, 98–99
        treatment in administration of impact
            fees, 367
equivalent dwelling unit (EDU), 174–75
equivalent residential unit (ERU), 184
ERU. *See* equivalent residential unit
establishing
    LOS standards, 171–72
    the need for new facilities, 164
estimated daily trips/groups, 335–36
evening peak hour, 246
exactions or extractions, 4, 15, 99,
        101–2. *See also* impact fees; physical,
        exactions
    of the development, 100
    and housing affordability, 158
    and planning, 156
    and takings, 102
exemptions. *See also* waivers
    for affordable housing and economic
        development, 132
    from the payment of impact fees,
        122, 137, 293–94, 330, 345, 350,
        358–59, 364–65, 377–78
    and waivers, 137
existing deficiency. *See* deficiency
expansion, facilities and infrastructure. *See*
        facilities; system, improvements
expenditure
    and accounting requirements, 138–39
    concepts, 129
    of funds, 103
export base to nonbasic multiplier, 176–77
expression of planning principles under
        impact fees, 103
external credit, 143–44
extradevelopmental
    capital
        expenditures, 95
        funding, 96
    fees, 97
    or system infrastructure, 95

F
facilities
    to benefit assessed subdivision, 97
    cost of, factor in proportionate-share
        calculation, 130–31
    eligible, on which impact fees may be
        imposed, 116–18
    for new development, 124, 129, 145
    new versus existing, 96–98, 103, 119,
        130, 132–34
    outside the boundaries of
        development, 4–5
    public or capital, xvii–xix, 3–5, 7, 16,
        93, 95, 98, 103–7, 108n6, 115,
        120, 132–35. *See also* system,
        improvements
    standards and expectations, 5
    tax, 16, 123

facility
    costs, xviii, 7
    fees, 15
    financing needs, 209
    type, 16–17, 21–22, 116, 130
fairness, 153
    of impact fee programs, 387–88
federal
    agencies exempt, 137
    funding, 391
    government, xviii
    mandates, 6
    and state funding, 93
    support, xviii
federal government fiscal retrenchment,
        93, 306. *See also* fiscal, retrenchment
        of federal government
fee, a, 93
    calculation
        methodology, 129–30
        process, 127
    cost of improvement and, 103
    incidence by state, 17
    increases, 2004 to 2008, 19–20, 22–23
    phase-in, 122
    schedule, 136
fees
    accepted by the courts, 106
    discriminatory, 95
    housing and employment needs and,
        106
    inflation and, 122
    land-use regulations and, 95
    maintain facilities to keep up with
        growth, 106
    offset by credits, 105
    for park acquisition or park facilities
        construction, 104
    as part of infrastructure finance, 106
    for recreational facilities, 123
    as takings without just compensation, 95
    as taxes, 96
    for transportation, 105
    updated, 122
    versus tax dispute, 94–96
    as a violation
        of equal protection principles, 95
        of property rights, 95
financial exaction, 106–7
financing public facilities, 5
fire
    emergency medical service and E9/11
        communications, 190
    facilities in Albuquerque (NM), 214
    police and, 171–72
        impact fees, 173–76
fiscal
    decision-making, 10
    impact fees as tool, 105
    impact of LOS, 205
    problems, 132, 134
    responsibility, xviii
    retrenchment of federal government,
        93, 306

revolt of the 1970s, 5. *See also* general
        obligation (GO) (bond)
    stress and burden, 5–6, 231
fixed-based taxes, 6, 146, 306
fixed source of revenue for facilities,
        143–44
flat rate fees, 11. *See also* impact fees
Florida
    average per single-family fee, 21
    CIE, internal consistency required, 158–59
    enabling act, 125
    functional population formula and,
        175–76
    Impact Fee Act, 123
    impact fees, 103
        role of, 8–9
        school, significant and extensive,
            91n1, 114, 118
    impact fee survey findings, 194
    law. *See also* Aventura (FL); Circulator
        System
        requires adequate transportation
            service, 337–42
    Legislative Committee on
        Intergovernmental Relations
        (LCIR), 8–9
    Legislature
        enacted transportation concurrency
            into law, 337
        new or old roadways, 338
        public areas subject to mandatory
            concurrency, 338
    new act, 123
    new developments and, 95
    planning legislation in, 103
    State Comprehensive Plan, xvii, 317
    statute governing impact fees, 103, 155,
        338, 349
    Supreme Court, 98–99, 307
        struck down road improvement
            fee, 307
form of the reasonable relationship
        test, 100. *See also* "reasonable
        relationship" standard or test
forms of credit and their application,
        143–45
formula for the charges set to operate and
        maintain a stormwater system, 336
formulation of impact fees and
        ordinances, 104
Fort Collins (CO)
    SUF, 336–37
Fort Lauderdale-Hollywood metropolitan
        area. *See* Broward County (FL)
foundations of proportionate share
    development fees on commercial
        developments, 257
    environmental mitigation fees, 306
functional population, 127, 130, 148,
        172–78, 214, 232, 233–34, 339–40
    of Albuquerque (NM), 214–15
    approach, first used by Atlanta (GA), 222
    of Aventura (FL), 340
    calculating, 233
    extensions of, 176

functional population (*continued*)
    impact cost per, 237
    two ways of measuring, 214–15
    used for, 176
functional resident. *See* functional
        population
funding
    to offset development, 107
    required of the development, 107
future
    direction of fees and fee methodology,
        153
    expansions of current developmental
        funding of infrastructure
        requirements, 389
    greater state role in, 390
    property taxes, 115
    rate of increase of sales tax receipts, 146
    revenue credit, 144, 151, 244
    service levels, 158

G

general
    government fees, 17
    taxes, 151
general obligation (GO) (bond), 5, 131, 148
    bond issue, 227–28, 230
    bonds, 242, 252
    debt service, 151
    funding source, 145, 221, 227
    retire debt, 141
Georgia
    2007, 104
    Act, the, 132–34, 135–39
    CIE, internal consistency required,
        158–59
    CIEs and CIPs related to, 157
    Department of Community Affairs, 156
    Development Impact Fee Act, 98–99,
        129
    enabling act, 115
    House Bill 232, 104
    and Nevada in 2007, 104
    procedural issues (and the Georgia
        Act), 136–39
    statute, 115–16, 127, 130, 137, 155, 374
GO. *See* general obligation (bond)
government
    bears its share, 390
    buildings and public facilities and
        combined public infrastructure,
        192
    capital financing, 5
governmental services, 94
    defined, 307
grants, 148
"green," xvii
    infrastructure needs, 309. *See also* social
        infrastructure
    social infrastructure, 106
growth, 3, 15, 95, 106, 156, 160
    allowed, 106
    calculating the cost of, 147
    community planning and, 156, 163, 227
    costs, 230–31, 321, 382

counties, 123
    credit defined by, 141, 183
    demands of, 125, 132, 156
    detrimental aspects of, 7, 94
    and development, 7, 155, 252
    and drainage, 239, 242, 243
    economic, 97, 388
    employment, 137, 156, 255, 264, 280
    ethic, the, 5
    fees 1992 through 2006 and, 123
    future, 132, 162, 182
growth
    high, 107, 108, 124, 125, 169, 170
    and impact fees, 182, 246, 309, 343, 362,
        387
    of impact fees, 8–9, 10, 20, 22, 24, 101
    impact on facilities, 156, 160, 163, 260,
        309, 363
    infrastructure and, 182, 389–91
    land acquisition and, 321, 330
    in local governments, 7
    management, 107, 136, 143, 159, 231, 244
    metropolitan, 3
    new, 115–16, 132–34, 166, 185, 252
    and new development, 5, 166, 237
    patterns, 3, 125, 182, 354
    population, 5, 9, 93, 166–67, 214, 218,
        306
    projections, 119, 131, 161
    quality of life, 7
    rapid, 161, 317
    rates, 127, 162, 181, 252, 351, 354
    requires changed facilities, 172
    revenues generated by, 252, 255
    slow, 161
    suburban, 97–98, 165
    "tier" impact fee system, 125
    urban, 163, 164, 307
growth-related
    CIPs, 15, 185, 186, 187. *See also* capital
        improvements plan/program
        (CIP)
    cost allocation method, 183, 184, 185
    facilities
        asset value of, 186, 187, 188
        total cost attribution method and,
            187
    fixed asset value, 185, 186
    marginal costs, 186
    replacement cost, 184, 188
Gulest
    "direct benefit" test
        requirement, 96–97
        test, 96–97
    *Gulest Associates, Inc. v. Town of
        Newburgh*, 96–97

H

habitat, fees to purchase, 315
harm, xviii, 314
Harris, Governor Joe Frank, 129
Hart, Senator Gary, 391. *See also* S.849
highest
    facility fee per single-family unit, 18
    fees, 23–24

highway system expansion and repairs,
        93. *See also* road; transportation
*Holmdel Builders' Ass'n v. Township of
        Holmdel*, 107, 322n6
home
    ownership and equity, 10
    rule, 342
        authority, 123, 125
        basis for transit fee in San Francisco
            (CA), 333
        powers, 93
*Home Builders Ass'n of Central Arizona v.
        City of Scottsdale*, 100–101
Homestead Option Sales Tax (HOST), 167
HOST. *See* Homestead Option Sales Tax
hostility to the taxation of real property,
        306
household size, 174–76, 217, 238
housing. *See also* Collier County (FL), case
        study of affordable housing
    affordable, xix, 106–7, 122, 129–33,
        137–38, 156, 158, 194, 207, 215,
        222, 257, 280, 284–85, 309, 353,
        390
    calculations for linkage, 260
    costs, 10
    demand for, 257
    effects of downturn on, 23–24
    profits and, 285
    slump of 2007, 284
    workforce, 207, 257–80, 283–84, 286–90,
        291–303, 388–89

I

Idaho
    enabling act, 124
identify the "service area," 117
Illinois
    "specifically and uniquely
        attributable" test, 308
    Supreme Court, 96
impact fees, 107, 171–72. *See also* benefit
        assessment; connection charges;
        development, fees; proportinate
        share
    accounts for, 104
    administrative code, 367–95
    administrative determinations of, 137
    adoption procedures, 139
    Advisory Committee, 132
    appeals of administrative
        determination of the, 137
    applicability of, 106
    applicability of *Nollan/Dolan* to, 101
    assessing, 10
    basic premise of, 257–58
    calculation
        methods, 184–88
        principles, 129
    case studies, 256
    CIPs in Texas and New Mexico, 156
    comprehensive plan consistency, 103
    as conditions on development, 307
    credits, 153, 157
    current issues related to, 387–88

dangers of, 124
defined, 129, 306
enabling legislation, 93
evaluation and uses, 115, 309
exactions, 157
examples of programs, 214
exist in all 50 states, 306
formula, 141
    implimentation considerations, 183
future of, 125
infrastructure of new development, 104
linkage and environmental mitigation
    fees, 314
Magna Carta, 155
monies, 104–5
most common use of, 209
needed, 209
not a tax, 307
ordinance, an, 16, 103, 349–54
process of adopting, 129
programs
    developing and implementing, 183
    selected nationally, 188–89
principles, 116
program, an, 107
proportionate-share, local
    government's cost, 153
public safety facilities, and, 209, 306
reasonable, 154
reason for, 153, 163–64
related ordinances, 103–4
revenue collections, 9–10
role of today, 391
seen as funding programs, 309
sensitive to affordable housing and
    other societal needs, 106
Task Force, 132
those tenets of, 176
transparency in, 388
unaffordable, 258
uses of, 105, 308–9
validity "tests" for, 103
versus linkage programs, 108
ways of implementing, 387
which do not cause physical invasions,
    102
impervious land area/surface/user, 172,
    173, 239, 243, 335–36
improvement, 152
    costs, 129–30
    "improvements-driven" methodology,
        119–20
inapplicability of subdivision regulations, 95
incomes and expectations, 6
income, sources of, 3
increased judicial acceptance of impact
    fees, 107–8
increase in fees 2004 to 2008, 21
increases
    in nonutility fees, 19–20
    population and housing impact new
        jobs, 259
individual assessments, 137
inflation, 5–6, 306
    of the 1970s, 93

infrastructure
    costs built before ordinance adopted, 168
    expansion of public, 387
    funding requirements, 389–90
    investments, 6
    provision leaving it to local
        governments, 390
    social, xix, 207
in-lieu
    fee, 4, 5, 16, 96, 99, 101, 108, 157, 291,
        292, 294, 295, 296, 298–300,
        388–90
        and impact fees, 95
        for recreational purposes, 97
    law, 5
    payment, 107
innovative funding programs, 389
"input-output" analysis, 177
Institute of Transportation Engineers (ITE)
    daily trips/group, 335
    trip generation rates, 111n108, 174, 233,
        335, 357, 371
Integrated Utilities Group, Inc. (IUG),
    238–41
interest, 150
interjurisdictional impact fees, 129
investment, 306
issuance of build permits, 96
ITE. *See* Institute of Transportation
    Engineers
IUG. *See* Integrated Utilities Group, Inc.
Ivy Steel and Wire Co. v. City of Jacksonville, 98

J

James Duncan and Associates, 215
Jenad, Inc. v. Scarsdale, 100
jobs, 176–77
Jordan
    court, 97
    Jordan v. Village of Menomonee Falls,
        97–98, 100
    test, 100. *See also* dual rational nexus test
jurisdiction adopts an impact fee program,
    367

L

labeling fees as "taxes," 96
Lafferty v. Payson City, 104–5
Lake Oswego (OR), 334–35
land
    component, 16
    dedication in-lieu fees, 16
    development
        and capital facilities, 103
        means to regulate, 103
    market value of, 99
land dedications, 157
land use
    assumptions, 155, 159, 252. *See also*
        comprehensive plan
    for Canton (GA), 227, 361
    by drainage area, 239, 243
    in New Mexico code, 155, 218–19
    in Texas code, 155

CIE and, 158
classification of, 137, 160, 280, 283, 382–83
controls, 3–4, 103
and demand schedule, 131
deny proposed, xviii
discretionary approval, 283
employee household incomes by, 280,
    283
employment activities related to, 280
estimating the functional population
    per, 173
and functional population, 174, 176,
    178, 215, 222, 233
impact fees, 3, 17, 94, 337
    basis, 136, 144, 173, 182, 194, 245
    in Broward County (FL), 307, 315
    as regulation device, 104, 155
level of impact, 127, 171, 172
local impact cost per, 244
net impact cost and, 232, 245
nonresidential, 17, 146, 222, 233
patterns, 159
plan, comprehensive or long-range,
    156, 157, 160, 163, 164, 164n1
projections, 119, 160
and provision of public facilities, 3
land use
    regulation, 4. *See also* comprehensive
        plan
        consistent with comprehensive
            plan, 103
        control power, 389
        defines impact fees, 104, 155
        under *Dolan*, 110n61
        ethic, 5
        forms, 4
        lack of, 4
        or taxation, 95–97, 99
    regulatory step, 157
    residential, 17, 146, 222, 233, 245, 326
    as service demand multiplier, 173–74
    TUF and, 333–34
    urban versus rural, 244
    violation, 352
lane-mile, 111n107
latecomer
    assessment, 158
    fee, 152
law enforcement
    facilities, 148
    impact fee, 148
LCIR. *See* Florida, Legislative Committee
    on Intergovernmental Relations
Lee County (FL), 153
    Roads Impact Fee Ordinance, 104
legislative
    versus adjudicative acts, 102
    adjudicatory question, 102
less-than-market-role units, 285
level of cost recovery, 134–35
level of service (LOS), 104, 105, 115, 120,
    130, 132–36, 148, 157, 158–59, 160,
    215, 217, 231, 239, 244, 318–19, 340
    Canton (GA), 227
    demand based on, 141, 144, 183

level of service (LOS) (*continued*)
  facilities deficiencies and, 132
  and functional population approach,
    174, 176
  measure units, 190–94
  Mesa del Sol, 219–20
  plan-based, 171–72, 182
  present and projected, 234
  set to recoup past investments, 132
  standards, 133–34, 166
    for each impact fee program area,
      184
    for a particular facility, 308
  standards-based, 171, 244, 246, 308
  time horizon and, 219
libraries, 192, 231
  Martin County (FL), 231–32
Lingle v. Chevron, USA, Inc., 102
linkage
  cases, 107. See also *Holmdel Builders'
    Ass'n v. Township of Holmdel; San
    Telmo Assoc. v. City of Seattle*
  developer funding requirements for
    "soft," "social," and "green"
    infrastructure, 106
  between development and benefit, 99
  fee
    calculations for, 260
    defined, 106
    local governments, 314
    low-income housing, 107
    relationship to other fees
      environmental mitigation fees,
        314–15
      impact fees, 107, 108, 257, 258,
        309, 314–15
    San Francisco Transit Operations,
      334
    validity of, 107
    "workforce housing," 257, 260–63,
      286–303
  housing, 260–63, 286–303
  premise of, 257–58
  program
    linked to social need, 106–7, 310
    primary goal, problem mitigation
      or abatement, 107
    rational nexus test, and, 107, 285
    susceptible to challenge, 99, 107,
      309
  requirement, 106
  specific approach, 244
listing of impact-fee-related capital
  improvements, 161
local
  governance being restructured, 7
  government, 151–53
    finance and the role of impact fees,
      8–10
    impact fee ordinances, 104
  governments, xvii
    and benefits districts, 104
    charged for proprietary services,
      307
    enablement, 93
    financing of capital costs, 13
    growth and development and, 7
    and impact fees
      use of, 155
      waiving of, 122
    jurisdiction, 4
    officials, 152
    powers, 94
    rent, 143
    responsibility for physical
      infrastructure, 306
      breakdown of the traditional
        approach, 98, 306
long-term
  debt, 148
  facility O & M concerns, 334
    addressed by TUFs, 334
Loretto doctrine (*Loretto v. Teleprompter
    Manhatten CATV Corp.*), 102
LOS. *See* level of service
Los Angeles (CA)
  pollution, 310–11
loss of wetlands, 312
Loveland (CO), 351, 353
lowering impact fees, 135
lowest fees 2004 to 2008, 21

M

maintain adequate transportation, service,
  337
maintenance of existing infrastructure, xvii
mandatory
  dedication, 5, 99
    of land, 102
    for school sites, 157
  set-asides, 5, 107,132
marginal cost, 130
  method, 186–87
market-based approach to environmental
    regulation, 310
  evaluation of mitigation wetlands
    banks, 314
  evaluation of tradable emission
    programs, 311
  federal wetlands regulation, 312
  goal of, 310
  mitigation programs for prevention of
    loss of wetlands, 312
  refers to, 310
  state wetlands regulation, 312
  tradable emissions, 310–11
  wetlands mitigation banking, 312–13
market value of land, 99
Martin County (FL). *See also* county,
    gasoline tax
  Comprehensive Growth Management
    Plan, 231–32, 244
  federal gasoline tax and, 245
  LOS, 244
  roads, 243
  rural/urban residents, 244
Maryland
  Anne Arundel County, 142–43, 164
  attorney general, 98
  lacks enabling act, 114
  Montgomery County, 104, 164
  school impact fees, significant and
    extensive, 91n1, 114, 118
Mass Transportation Administration
  grants, 148
master planned developments, 7
maximum fees, 117
measure of police power, 97
median household income and median
  housing prices, 258–59
Mesa del Sol, 219–21. *See also* Albuquerque
  (NM)
methodologies and credits, 142
metropolitan
  areas, 3
  growth, 3
metropolitan statistical area (MSA), 189
Miami-Dade County (FL). *See also*
  Aventura (FL)
  functional pupulation in, 340
  Transit System Surtax, 340
Micron property tax credit claim, 124
Mid-Region Council of Governments,
  242–43
Mississippi
  court decisions, 125
mitigation, 310, 312
Mitigation Fee Act, 101, 110n69. *See also*
  California
model
  acts, 4
  ordinance with as comprehensive
    impact fee statute, 349
  planning and zoning enabling acts of
    the 1920s, 3
modern
  impact fee began its existence, 387
  land-use regulation, 4
modification of officially adopted service
  levels, 161
money
  for capital expenditures, 104
  payment
    and dedication of land, 95
    requirement, 97
Montana
  enabling act, 124
  Senate Bill 185, 124
  statute, 115
Montgomery County (MD), 104, 164. *See
    also* Anne Arundel County (MD)
motor fuel tax, 93, 146
MSA. *See* metropolitan statistical area
Mt. Laurel (NJ)
  Mt. Laurel case, 390
  Mt. Laurel doctrine, 107

N

NAA. *See* National Apartment Association
National Apartment Association (NAA),
  194n1
National Environmental Policy Act
  (NEPA), 312, 322n15
National Infrastructure Fund, 391

National Pollution Discharge Elimination
    System compliance, 241
necessitated by and attributable to,
    115–16. *See also* attributable;
    proportionate share; "reasonable
    relationship" standard or test;
    reasonably attributable; reasonably
    related
need
    assessment, 160
    -based methodology, 182
    to preserve and protect green
        infrastructure in development, 305
negative
    aspects of urban growth, 94, 307
    impacts on affordable housing and
        economic development, 132
negotiated payments, 15
NEPA. *See* National Environmental Policy
    Act
net impact cost, 143, 244
Nevada
    in 2007, 104
    amendment to its enabling act, 124
    Assembly Bill 104, 253
new
    and existing home prices, outpaced
        median income, 258
    or expanded infrastructure, 5–6
    government building space cost to
        construct, 234–39
    growth and housing affordability, 259
    projects, 152
    roads, 150
newcomers, xvii
new development, xvii, xviii, 3, 144, 150.
    See also credit, for future payments
    Canton (GA), 227–31
    cost of new facilities, 151
    creates demands, 257
    impact fees and, 15
    impacts on facilities, 333
        approach to implementation of a
            program, 339
        case study, 333
        proportionate-share fee approaches,
            333
    need for service and improvements, 103
    new service area, 243
    shares of capital costs, 95
    should not be charged twice for the
        same facilities, 115
    tax, 16
    and zoning, 164
New Jersey
    linkage case, 107. See also *Holmdel*
        Builders' Ass'n v. Township of
        Holmdel
    Supreme Court of, *Mt. Laurel* case, 107,
        390
New Mexico. *See also* Albuquerque (NM)
    CIE, internal consistency required, 158–59
    land-use assumptions, 155
    statue governing planning horizon, 215
New Orleans (LA), 164

nexus test for impact fees. *See* dual
    rational nexus test
Ninth Circuit, 106, 309. *See also* court
Nollan/Dolan
    legislative adjudicatory question, 102
    test for taking, 101, 102
Nollan v. California Coastal Commission,
    99–102, 106, 110n69, 112n122, 308,
    309. See also *Nollan/Dolan*
nonimpact
    impact sources, 150
    system to recoup the value of
        infrastructure, 158
nonlocal
    funding sources, 130
    share, 244
        of total impact cost, 231–32
nonresidential
    development, 280–83
    land uses, 17
nonutility impact fees, 10, 16, 19–22, 24
North Carolina
    court decisions, 125
    lacks enabling act, 114
    lacks impact fee authority, 114

O

O & M. *See* operations and maintenance
objective of credits, 140
object of development regulations, 4
off-site facility impacts, 157
on-site
    improvements, 157
    infrastructure exactions, 157–58
open legislative process, 102
operations and maintenance (O & M)
    cost of development and infrastructure,
        8, 164, 207, 333, 391
    employees
        earnings, 275
        critical employees and, 276, 280
        number required per residence, 275
    and impact fees, 209, 333
    performing on residences, activities, 274
    proportionate-share principles for, xix,
        333–46, 391
    SUFs and, 336–37. *See also* stormwater
        utility fee (SUF)
    TIDFs and, 333–34. *See also* transit
        impact development fee (TIDF)
    TUFs and, 334–36. *See also*
        transportation utility fee (TUF)
ordinance
    adopt by, 159
    implementing O & M proportionate-
        share fees, 343–46
Oregon, xvii
    CIE, internal consistency required,
        158–59
    impact fees in, 17, 122–23
    lessons of enabling legislation, 334–35
    street maintenance fee, 335
    Supreme Court, 99, 110n69. See also
        Dolan v. City of Tigard (*Dolan*)
    TUFs in certain communities, 334–35

Orlando (FL)
    TUF and, 334–35
        annual fees by land-use, 334
        formula for, 334
outcomes of SDCs, 184
owners or developers of raw land, 150

P

pace of urban development, 93
Palm Beach County (FL), 153
park facility impact fee,123, 132
    for Canton (GA), 227–31
parks, 157, 215
    public safety impact fees and, 132
    park facilities, 103–4
    and recreation, open space, trails, 190
    and recreational facilities
        in Albuquerque (NM), 215–22
    and recreation program, 159
    and recreation section of the element of
        a comprehensive plan, 165
    and schools, 4, 16, 106
past
    payment credit due, 151
    revenue credit, 144, 244
        defined, 231
pay-as-you-go financing, 148
paying
    general taxes, 151
    a social cost, 107
payment
    for capital facilities, 95
    in lieu, 5
    requirements, 97
        for system infrastructure capital
            funding, 98
    requirement under the police power, 97
    of taxes to be credited, 142
percentage reduction, 153
PGS. *See* Planned Growth Strategy
physical
    exactions, 99
    infrastructure of American
        communities, 93
    invasion. *See* threatened physical
        invasion
        triggers *Loretto*, 102
Pioneer Trust & Savings Bank v. Village of
    Mount Prospect, 96, 100
plan amendment, 161
plan-based
    Albuquerque's impact fee, 214
    approach, 244
    impact fees, 182
    LOS standards, 171, 172
    Martin County's impact fee, 231, 244
    method of calculating impact fees,
        119–20. *See also* improvement,
        "improvements-driven"
        methodology
    versus standards-based calculations,
        129–31, 181–83
Planned Growth Strategy (PGS), 217, 238–
    39, 243, 245. *See also* Albuquerque
    (NM)

planned improvements forming the basis
for impact fee calculation, 244
Planners Estimating Guide, 233
planning
periods to analyze credits, 143
principles upon which impact fees are
granted, 103
standard of LOS, 120
zoning enabling acts of the 1920s and, 4
plat-approach process, 96
police
call data, 175–76
and criminal justice or combined
public safety, 191
fire, and library fees, 17, 173
power, xviii, 7, 94–99, 102, 105, 107,
124, 156, 308
issues, 102–3
local governmental discretion to
regulate and exercise, 307, 316
required dedications, 96
system benefits under, 98
the "taking" test (exaction), 99
valid exercise of the, 97
powers
function of local government, 7
in home rule charters, 156
protection fee, 372–76, 381
polluter, 310
pollution
abatement, 310
air, 305, 310, 311, 315, 322n18
compensation for impact of, 306
control programs, market-based, 310,
315, 316
costs associated with, 310, 311
credits, 310–12
growth causes, 5
levels, 311–12
National Pollution Discharge
Elimination System compliance,
241
prevention, 315
reducing, 310, 311, 312, 322n16
water, 305
control. *See also* Clean Water Act
(CWA)
charge, 98
facilities, 6, 93, 108n6, 306–7, 322n2
population. *See also* growth; weighted
population
growth, 5, 93, 148
of larger and smaller houses, 238
portable water and sanitary sewer
facilities, 105
*Practitioners' Guide to Development Fees,
A.*, 125
preordinance credits, 138
present value language, 138
principles
for estimating credit with applications,
145
of ordinance design and drafting
accounting, 351
adoption, 349–50

assessment, 350
collection, 350
disbursement, 351
private
funding of public infrastructure, 95
mitigation company, a, 316
of proportionate-share development
fee design, 349
privilege
tax, 16
theory, 95, 97
procedural issues (and the Georgia Act),
136–39
proffer system, 109n17, 114–15. *See also*
Virginia, "cash proffers"
programmed capital improvements, 130
project
costs and growth projections, 161
versus system improvements, 129
projection of needs, 160–61, 166–67
proper cost appoitionment in an impact
fee rate determination, 98
property
rights, 102
taxes, 6, 148, 150, 387
values, 6
proportionality, 11, 153
of burden in impact fees, 387
proportionate
equity, 11
fair share, 115, 129
concepts, 342
intent of the Georgia Act, 133
methodology, 136
proportionate share, 115–16. *See also*
attributable; necessitated by
and attributable to; "reasonable
relationship" standard or test;
reasonably attributable; reasonably
related
basis for assessing nonresidential
development, 127
concepts for stormwater and utilities,
342
development fees, xix, 1, 143, 150,
151–52, 207, 257, 283, 334, 347,
349, 387–88, 391
environmental mitigation fees, 306–8
fiscal impact accountability, iii
language, 124
principles applied to workforce
housing, 139, 257, 263–80
standard, 117
Proposition
13 (California), 5, 6
2 ½ (Massachusetts), 5, 6
proprietary and governmental services,
94, 307
protecting
health, safety, and welfare, 94
the public, 5
public
facilities, xvii
for which interest is payable, 150
facility extension policies, 4

financing programs, 3
hearing, 122
infrastructure, 93
investments, 6, 93
safety impact fees, 10
service funding lost, 94
services and taxes, 94
support for taxes, xvii
purpose in establishing LOSs, 133. *See also*
level of service (LOS)

Q
quality
in the demand for public
infrastructure, 387
of life, xvii, 5, 94, 177, 307
the key to, 389
"Quimby fees," 16

R
raise
dollars/funds/money/revenue, xvii,
xviii, xix, 96, 106, 109n14, 125,
164, 309, 322n6, 382, 387
fees, 20
existing, 21
impact fees, 125, 152, 153, 255
issues, 99, 102, 107, 112n126, 152, 351,
373
legal defense, 102
operational LOS standard for parks,
133
price of housing or rent, 353
service levels, 161
taxes, xvii, xix, 153
local property, 94, 307
rapid population growth, 93
rate of inflation, 6
rational nexus test, 129. *See also* dual
rational nexus test
a two-prong test of impact fees, 308
real estate, 6
reasonable
access, 227
affordability of housing, 291
benefit, 136, 139
"connection" between need and
growth, 97
credit, 137–38
estimates of system improvement
costs, 130, 139, 144
impact fee, 98, 105, 107, 130, 150, 153–54,
186, 309, 327, 382, 388
test for, 307–8
method of apportionment, 178, 243–44,
329, 355, 358, 382, 388
period of time, 104, 134, 148, 150, 183,
351, 354, 358, 365, 380
proximity, 136
quality of public facilities, xix, 4
regulations, 5
representation of public safety
demands for service, 176
system payment requirements, 98, 153

"reasonable relationship" standard or test, 97, 99–100, 110n69, 115–16, 136, 159, 307–8, 322n6, 355, 363. *See also* attributable; *Dolan v. City of Tigard (Dolan)*; dual rational nexus test; Jordan, *Jordan v. Village of Menomonee Falls*; necessitated by and attributable to; *Nollan v. California Coastal Commission*; reasonably attributable; necessitated by and attributable to; proportionate share; reasonably attributable; reasonably related
reasonably attributable, 115–16, 308. *See also* attributable; necessitated by and attributable to; proportionate share; "reasonable relationship" standard or test; reasonably related
reasonably related, 115–16. *See also* attributable; necessitated by and attributable to; proportionate share; "reasonable relationship" standard or test; reasonably attributable
recalculation requirement, 121
RECLAIM. *See* Regional Clean Air Incentives Market
recoup
    costs, 121, 163, 340
    impact fees, 354
    past investments, 98, 132, 313
    value of infrastructure, 158, 215
recoupment, 98, 163
    -based fees, 133, 137, 163, 222
    of cost, 381
    revenues, 129
    value method, 183, 185–87
refund
    of the contributions, 103–4
    for expired permits, 300
    of impact fees, 138, 354, 364, 376–77
    period, 104
Regional Clean Air Incentives Market (RECLAIM), 310–12. *See also* California
regressive effect, 11
regulation, 307
    of land development, 155
    and police power, 99
    violates due process, 102
regulatory
    agencies, 5
    impact fees, 156
    leveraging, 101
Rehnquist, Chief Justice, 99–100
    ruling on *Dolan*, 102
relation of impact fees. *See also* impact fees
    to community comprehensive land-use planning goals, 163
    to community planning goals, 163
    to comprehensive plan, 102–3
relevance of *Nollan/Dolan*, to exactions, dedications, and fees, 102
replacement cost method, 186
required
    credits, 116
    dedication, 94–95, 99–100, 106
        relevance of *Nollan/Dolan* to, 102

degree of connection between exactions and development's projected
impact, 99
improvements. *See* exactions or extractions
payments for capital expenditures, 97
residential
    costs divided with nonresidential development, 231
    demand unit cost unit, 190
    development
        and school fees, 23
    dwelling unit, xvii
    fees
        single- and multifamily types, 335
    units in urbanized areas, with TUF, 335
responsibility of local government, xviii
restrictions on taxation of real property, 5
restructuring of the public finance system, 7–8
revenue, xvii, xviii
    enhancing sources, 6
    generating capability, xvii
    from impact fees, 8–10
    in interest-bearing accounts, 139
    new development will generate per lane-mile, 245
    sources, 6, 157
    for street maintenance fee, 335
revenue credits, 115, 119, 124, 131, 137–38, 141
    future, 124, 144–45, 148–50, 151, 231–32, 244, 353
    past, 124, 144–45, 151, 231–32, 244, 353
rezoning
    application for, 114
    process, 157
Rhode Island
    state enabling act, 121
road
    capacity, 244
    cost of construction, xviii, 105, 146, 150–51, 252, 309
    county, 243–44
    expansion project, 162
    and highway systems, 105
    impact, 146
    impact fee, xix, 10, 16, 17, 21, 24, 104, 124, 146, 255, 351–52
        calculation of, 105, 112n109, 309
        also called TUF, 334
        "construction" credits for, 141, 152
        different schedules among service areas, 136
        dominant portion of, 17, 23
        earmarking, 351
        and Georgia House Bill 232, 104
        increase driven oil prices, 24
        Lee County's Roads Impact Fee Ordinance, 104
        lower, 150, 353
        in Martin County (FL), 243
        ordinances, 137, 355–60, 361–66, 369–85
        and school fees, 21

service area and, 243
"system development charge," 335
trust funds for revenues, 104
uses, 105, 307
and utility fees, 17
improvements, 16–17, 94, 145, 152, 181–82, 307, 351–52, 355
"maintenance fee," 334
maintenance of, government service, 94, 307
new, 112n109, 150
paid for, 252
    by fuel taxes, 112n110
quantity of, 105
traffic signals, and transit, 191
trip generation, 350
"utility fee," 334
role
    of impact fees, 10, 13, 108
        as a regulatory device, 158
    of linkage fees, 257
rough proportionality requirement of the Fifth Amendment, 100
RRC, Incorporated, survey, 275

S

S.849, 391
sale of transferable credits, 153
sales tax revenues, 115
sample
    impact fee administrative code, 369–85
    workforce housing mitigation impact fee ordinance, 291–304
San Diego (CA), 164
San Francisco (CA)
    cost
        of commercial office building construction, 262
        of new housing in 1984, 262
    downtown office development and new housing, 261
    housing linkage, 260
        fees in California, 262
        fees in early 2000s, 262
        programs, 262
    linkage fees, 258, 262
    O & M element, 334
    objective of the housing linkage impact fee, 261
    Residential Hotel Unit Conversion and Demolition Ordinance, 101
    subsidy to provide new house holds with affordable homes, 262
    TIDF, 333–34, 342
        authority for the fee, 333
San Remo Hotel v. City and County of San Francisco, 101
San Telmo Assoc. v. City of Seattle, 107
Scalia, Justice, in *Nollan*, 308
SCAQMD. *See* South Coast Air Quality Management District
schedule of improvements, 161–62
school, 193–94
    and benefits, 177
    and credits, 143

school (*continued*)
   districts, 9
   facilities, 98
   fees, 17
      in Florida, 24
   impact fees, 17–18, 23, 114, 117, 177
      in Florida and California, 21
Scottsdale (AZ)
   case, 101
SDC. *See* systems development charge
Seattle (WA) preservation housing
   ordinance, 107
Senate
   Bill 185, 124
   Bill 620, 124
   Bill 849. *See* S.849
service areas, 104, 129, 135, 158, 165
   applied in Atlanta (GA), 136
   as assessment districts, 136
   as benefit districts, 136
service level policies
   drive the capital facility planning
      process, 159
sewer and water facilities, 95
SFE. *See* single-family equivalent
single-family equivalent (SFE), 190
single-family unit
   calculations of fee credit, 146
   connection fee, 15, 18
   demand for service, 174–75
   impact fee, 10–11, 13n10, 17, 19, 20, 23,
      124, 337
   price, 13n2, 268
   shopping-center impact on, 105, 308
   water and wastewater usage, 171
social infrastructure. *See also*
      infrastructure, social
   needs, 106, 309–10
   proportionate-share fees for, 257, 389
South Carolina
   statute, 115
South Coast Air Quality Management
   District (SCAQMD), 311, 322n18
special
   service districts, 7–8
   trusts funds, 104
"specifically and unequally attributable"
   test, 96–97, 100, 308
speculators, 4
standardized fees
   as impact fees, 15
standards-based
   impact
      cost analysis, 246
      fees, 181–82
         an advantage to, 182
   measures, 176
standards for calculating impact fees, 116
state
   acts, 116, 120–21
   authorizing legislation, 103
   court decisions, 100
   enabling acts, 4, 115. *See also* state, acts
   enabling impact fees, 103, 114

federal funding to cure infrastructure
      deficiencies and, 390–91
fee statututes, 104
of Florida model ordinance, 349
with the highest fees, 17–18
and local governments' responsibility,
   93
and regional impact fees, 390
statute. *See also entries under individual*
     states
   land-use projections, 118
   regulating impact fees, 23, 95–97, 99,
      100, 104, 108n2, 113–25, 389
   requires replacement revenues be
      identified, 137
   silent on exemptions or waivers, 137
statutory
   authority, 103
   provisions for impact fees, 103–4
St. Lucie County (FL)
   case study of, 317–23
   comprehensive plan, 324–31
   environmental lands impact fee
      draft ordinance, 324–31
      program, 305
   environmentally significant lands in,
      318
   growth cost of environmental land
      acquisition, 318
   implementation through an ordinance,
      305
   LOS, 318
stormwater
   drainage impact fees, 17, 194
   management, 336
   runoff, 335–37
   San Francisco (CA), 333
   utility O & M cost, 336
stormwater utility fee (SUF), 336–37
   formula, 336–37
   Fort Collins (CO), 336
street
   drainage and lot drainage, 239
   maintenance
      cost, 335
      fee based on a formula, 335
      fee in Lake Oswego (OR), 335
subdividing, 4
subdivision regulations, 4, 94, 157
substantially advances test, 102
SUF. *See* stormwater utility fee
sum of the average fees, 16
Supreme Court. *See also* court, and *entries*
     for individual states
   Arizona, 100
   Arkansas, 103–4
   California, 101–2
   Colorado, 98
   New Jersey, 390
   Oregon, 99
   U.S., 99, 101–2
      on exactions, 101
      and refusal to review transit fee, 334
      remand, 100

Utah, 98, 104–5
Washington, 101, 107
survey
   2004 to 2008, 19
   2007 and 2008, 24
   of impact fees, 15–24
system
   capacity, 184
   improvements, xvii, 5–6, 93–94, 103,
      106, 107, 124, 125, 129, 132–33,
      134, 141, 143, 148, 155–58,
      162–64, 172, 183–84, 207, 231,
      246, 306–7, 309, 333–36, 387,
      388–89
systems development charge (SDC),
   184–85

T
taking, a, 106–7
   challenge, 99, 106
   issue, 99–102
   principles applied to impact fees, 102
   of property, 99
   test, 100, 101, 112n122
   unconstitutional, 96–97, 111n104, 308,
      316
takings
   analysis, 102
   clause, 102
      of the Fifth Amendment, 101
      and the payment of money, 102
   exactions are not, which meet dual
      rational nexus test, 102
   per se takings rule, *Loretto* doctrine, 102
   regulatory, 95, 322n10
target nonresidential development, 132
tax, 5
   assessment districts, 144, 389
   revolt, xvii, 6, 94, 307
taxation of real property, 93
tax increment financing (TIF), 389. *See also*
      community development district
      (CDD); tax, assessment districts
"taxpayer's revolt." *See* tax, revolt
TCEA. *See* Transportation Concurrency
      Exception Area
Tennessee
   and authority to impose impact fees,
      114
   lacks enabling act, 114, 123
tests
   for impact fee validity, 95–96, 103
   objective of all of these, 308
Texas
   act
      limits service areas, 118
      provisions of, 121–22
   CIE, internal consistency required,
      158–59
   determine impact fees, 118–19
   first enabling act, 113
   Georgia, and New Mexico impact fees,
      103
theory of the police power, 105

threatened physical invasion, 102, 322n10
TIDF. *See* transit impact development fee
TIF. *See* tax increment financing
time
    to be expanded, 139
    to collect fees, 95
    impact fees versus in-lieu fees, 95
    of platting
Tindale-Oliver & Associates, 232, 243, 256, 277, 278
TOD. *See* transit-oriented development
total
    cost
        attribution method, 187–88
        and fees for residential land-uses, 17
        per unit of development, 130
    impact cost, 244
        defined, 231
    impact fees in California, 23
    nonutility fee per single-family unit, 20
    projects costs local governments define, 162–63
track ownership and worth credits, 153
tradable emissions
    credits, 310
    program, 310
traditional regulation of the environment, 310
transferable credits, 153
transit impact development fee (TIDF), 333–34, 342. *See also* San Francisco (CA)
    challenges in California courts, 334
transit-oriented development (TOD), 390
transperancy in impact fees, 388
transportation
    fee, 10
    impact, 145
        fees, 138, 334
    improvements, 144
    network fees, 105
    streets, impact fees
        for Martin County (FL), 243
Transportation Concurrency Exception Area (TCEA), 337, 338–39
    Aventura (FL) exempt, 338
    features of the ordinance, 342n7, 343
    five subject to mandatory concurrency, 338
transportation utility fee (TUF)
    example, 334–36
    growing popularity, 335–36
    in San Francisco (CA), 333–34
trip generation
    factor, 334
    rates, 105, 111n108, 335
        of restructure, 181–82

TUF. *See* transportation utility fee
two-part "rational nexus" test. *See* dual rational nexus test
type of development that cause impact, 106

U

unauthorized tax, an, 107
unconstitutional
    taking, 97, 308
    tax, 94, 307
underestimating funding sources, 151
underfunding, 151
undeveloped land, 150
unfunded deficit, 391
unification of developer funding requirements, 388
unit
    cost, 140, 183
    demand, 334
United States (U.S.)
    environmental mitigation principles, 314
    evolution of 1900 to 2006, 3
    population of 1960s, 3
    Supreme Court. *See* Supreme Court
urban infill, 164
urbanization, 6
user fees, 94, 307
uses of impact fees, 308–9
Utah
    amendments to its enabling act, 124
    courts ruled about fees, 96
    defines "proportionate share," 115
    statute, 115
    Supreme Court, 98, 104–5. See also *Banberry Development Corp. v. South Jordan City*
    view impact fees as charges for services rendered, 96
utility
    connection fees, 15–16
    fees and inflation, 24
utility connection fees. *See* wastewater; water

V

vacant land paid toward parks, 150
validity
    of extradevelopmental impact and in-lieu fees, 97–98
    of impact fee, 102–5, 107
    of inclusionary zoning devices, 107
    of linkage fees, 107
variance procedure, 103
varying LOS by service areas, 134–35
vehicle-mile of capacity (VMC), 182, 255
vehicle-mile traveled (VMT), 105, 141, 255, 309

Virginia
    "cash proffers," 109n17, 114–15
VMC. *See* vehicle-mile of capacity
VMT. *See* vehicle-mile traveled

W

waivers
    or exemptions in the enabling acts, 122
    of impact fees, 129
Washington
    CIE, internal consistency required, 158–59
    Court of Appeals, 101
Washington
    impact fees common in, 17
    school impact fees, significant and extensive, 91n1, 114, 118
    Supreme Court, 101, 107. See also *City of Olympia v. Drebick; San Telmo Assoc. v. City of Seattle*
wastewater, 193
    treatment, 5
water, 5
    fees, 16–17
    impact fees, 116, 181–85
        applications of variations to, 183–84
        infrastructure and water resources, 192
    pollution control, 93, 98
    sewer, drainage roads, 5
    wastewater, 124, 130. *See also* utility connection fees
        bill, includes TUF, 334–35
        bill in Orlando (FL), 334
        connection fees, 132
        facilities, 171
        utility fees, 17
Water Pollution Control Act. *See* Clean Water Act (CWA)
weighted population, 234–38
wetlands mitigation programs, 312–14
    banking for, 312–13
Wisconsin
    Act 477, 123
    decision, 100
    Legislature, 123
    retrenchment of impact fee authority, 125
    Supreme Court, 97
workforce
    is defined, 258
    housing impact fee effected through an ordinance, 283
    housing linkage fees, 257
        programs in California, 286
written analysis, 118

Z

zoning, 97
    and other land-use regulations, 155

About the Authors

Arthur C. (Christian "Chris") Nelson, PhD, FAICP, is Presidential Professor of City & Metropolitan Planning at the University of Utah where he is also Director of the Metropolitan Research Center. He was formerly the founding Director of the Urban Affairs and Planning Program at Virginia Tech's Alexandria Center and served as Co-director of the Metropolitan Institute at Virginia Tech. Prior to his Virginia Tech appointment, Dr. Nelson was Professor of City and Regional Planning and Professor of Public Policy at the Georgia Institute of Technology, as well as Adjunct Professor of Law at Georgia State University. Dr. Nelson has helped write some of the leading works in impact fees including, for the American Planning Association, editing two issues of the *Journal of the American Planning Association*, focusing on the subject; editing *Development Impact Fees: Policy Rationale, Practice, Theory, and Issues*; and coauthoring *A Practitioners Guide to Development Impact Fees*. His work is cited in several courts including the U.S. Supreme Court.

James C. Nicholas, PhD, is Emeritus Professor of Urban and Regional Planning and Emeritus Professor of Law at the University of Florida where he also served as Co-director of Growth Management Studies. Dr. Nicholas was previously Professor of Economics at Florida Atlantic University and Acting Director of the Joint Center for Urban and Environmental Problems. Through research, professional practice, and service as an expert witness principally on behalf of local governments, Dr. Nicholas pioneered development of the economic and planning rationale for the rational nexus test that is now commonly accepted impact fee practice nationally.

He has pioneered the development and application of proportionate-share exaction principles to many other areas of planning and public policy as well. For the American Planning Association, Dr. Nicholas is author of *The Calculation of Proportionate-Share Impact Fees* and coauthor of *A Practitioners Guide to Development Impact Fees*. His work is cited routinely in state and federal courts, and by the U.S. Supreme Court.

Julian Conrad Juergensmeyer is Professor and Ben F. Johnson Jr. Chair in Law at the Georgia State University College of Law where he is also Co-director of the Center for the Comparative Study of Metropolitan Growth. He serves additionally as Adjunct Professor of City and Regional Planning at the Georgia Institute of Technology. Professor Juergensmeyer is Emeritus Professor of Law, Emeritus Gerald A. Sohn Research Scholar, and Emeritus Affiliate Professor of Urban and Regional Planning at the University of Florida. At the University of Florida, Professor Juergensmeyer at various times was Director or Co-director of the Cambridge Warsaw International Trade Law Program, the Center for Agricultural Law, Growth Management Studies, and the LL.M. Program in Comparative Law. Professor Juergensmeyer pioneered the legal foundations of the rational nexus test that now guide the legal framework for impact fees nationally. His work has been used in and cited by state and federal courts throughout the nation, including the U.S. Supreme Court. For the American Planning Association, Professor Juergensmeyer is a coauthor of *A Practitioners' Guide to Development Impact Fees* (Nicholas, Nelson, and Juergensmeyer (1991)).